Martial Arts
of the World

Martial Arts of the World

An Encyclopedia

Volume One: A–Q

Edited by Thomas A. Green

A B C ⬤ C L I O

Santa Barbara, California   Denver, Colorado   Oxford, England

Copyright © 2001 by Thomas A. Green

Library of Congress Cataloging-in-Publication Data

Martial arts of the world: an encyclopedia / [edited] by Thomas A. Green.
    p. cm.
Includes bibliographical references and index.
ISBN 1-57607-150-2 (hardcover: alk. paper); 1-57607-556-7 (ebook)
1. Martial arts—Encyclopedias. I. Green, Thomas A., 1944–

GV1101.M29 2001
796.8'03—dc21   2001002823

06 05 04 03 02 01   10 9 8 7 6 5 4 3 2 1

This book is also available on the World Wide Web as an e-book. Visit abc-clio.com
for details.

ABC-CLIO, Inc.
130 Cremona Drive, P.O. Box 1911
Santa Barbara, California 93116-1911

This book is printed on acid-free paper ∞.

Manufactured in the United States of America

Contents

Editorial Board, ix
Contributor List, xi
Introduction, xv
A Note on Romanization, xix

Martial Arts of the World:
An Encyclopedia

Editorial Board

Contributor List

Bill Adams
Director, Bill Adams Fitness
    and Martial Arts Center
Buffalo, New York

Mikael Adolphson
Harvard University
Cambridge, Massachusetts

Joseph S. Alter
University of Pittsburgh
Pittsburgh, Pennsylvania

Ellis Amdur
Edgework
Seattle, Washington

Jeff Archer
Independent Scholar
La Mesa, California

David Bachrach
University of Notre Dame
Notre Dame, Indiana

C. Jerome Barber
Erie Community College/South
Orchard Park, New York

William M. Bodiford
University of California
Los Angeles, California

D'Arcy Jonathan Dacre Boulton
University of Notre Dame
Notre Dame, Indiana

Dakin R. Burdick
Indiana University
Bloomington, Indiana

John Clements
Director, Historical Armed Combat
    Association
Houston, Texas

Phil Dunlap
Advanced Fighting Systems
Mahwah, New Jersey

Aaron Fields
Independent Scholar
Seattle, Washington

Karl Friday
University of Georgia
Athens, Georgia

Tommy Gong
Bruce Lee Educational Foundation
Clovis, California

Loren Goodman
State University of New York
    at Buffalo
Buffalo, New York

Ronald A. Harris
Director of Research, Evaluation
  and Information Technology
Louisiana Office for Addictive
  Disorders
Baton Rouge, Louisiana

Stanley E. Henning
Asia-Pacific Center for Security
  Studies
Honolulu, Hawaii

Ronald Holt
Weber State University
Ogden, Utah

G. Cameron Hurst III
University of Pennsylvania
Philadelphia, Pennsylvania

William J. Long
University of South Carolina
Columbia, South Carolina

Carl L. McClafferty
United States Renmei
Sekiguichi Ryû Batto Jutsu
Del Rio, Texas

Kevin P. Menard
University of North Texas
Denton, Texas

Richard M. Mooney
Dragon Society International Tai Chi
  Kung Fu Club
Wichita Falls, Texas

Glenn J. Morris
McNeese State University
Lake Charles, Louisiana

Ron Mottern
Independent Scholar
Elgin, Texas

Keith F. Otterbein
State University of New York
  at Buffalo
Buffalo, New York

Michael Pederson
St. John's College
Santa Fe, New Mexico

Sohini Ray
Harvard University
Cambridge, Massachusetts

Roy Ron
University of Hawaii
Honolulu, Hawaii
Historiographical Institute
University of Tokyo
Tokyo, Japan

Anthony Schmieg
Independent Scholar
Lexington, Virginia

Bruce Sims
Midwest Hapkidô
Chicago, Illinois

John Starr
State University of New York,
  Medical School
Buffalo, New York

Gene Tausk
Independent Scholar
Houston, Texas

Kimberley Taylor
University of Guelph
Guelph, Ontario, Canada

Michael Tran
Mount Sinai Hospital of Queens
New York, New York

Noah Tuleja
Independent Scholar
Kensington, California

T. V. Tuleja
Saint Peter's College
Saint Peter's College, New Jersey

Tad Tuleja
Harvard University
Cambridge, Massachusetts

Chi-hsiu D. Weng
United States Shuai Chiao Association
Cupertino, California

Phillip Zarrilli
University of Exeter
Exeter, England

Introduction

As many gallons of ink have been spilled in trying to define "martial arts" as have gallons of blood in the genuine practice of martial activities. In this place I will not spill more ink. On the other hand, I do not contend that the efforts of those who try to develop such definitions waste their time. My only contention is that these definitions are inevitably focused by time, place, philosophy, politics, worldview, popular culture, and other cross-cultural variables. So focused, they are destined to be less than universal. The same is true, however, of any attempt to categorize phenomena that, while universally human, are inevitably tied to worldview, to mindset, and to historical experience.

Many of the attempts to determine the boundaries of the martial arts draw on the model of the Japanese "cognate arts" by distinguishing between *bujutsu* (from *bu,* "warrior," and *jutsu,* also romanized as *jitsu,* "technique" or "skill") and *budô* (from "warrior" and *dô,* "way"). Those forms that are considered bujutsus are conceived to be combative ancestors of those that are considered part of budô, and the latter are characterized as disciplines derived from the earlier combat forms in order to be used as means of self-enhancement, physically, mentally, and spiritually. *Bugei* ("martial methods," used to refer collectively to the combat skills), itself, is commonly compartmentalized into various *jutsu,* yielding, for example, *kenjutsu* (technique or art of the sword), just as each way has its own name, in this case, *kendô* (way of the sword).

Such compartmentalization was a product of Japanese historical experience in the wake of *Pax Tokugawa* (the enforced peace of the Tokugawa shogunate—A.D. 1600–1868), and it gained widespread acceptance with the modernization of Japan in the late nineteenth century. Even in the twenty-first century, however, such segregation is not universal, as demonstrated by the incorporation of various martial skills (striking, grappling, and an arsenal of weapons) in the traditional *ryûha* (schools or systems) of contemporary Japan (see Friday 1997).

Outside the contemporary Western popular context and the influence of the Japanese model, it is clear that a vast number of the world's martial systems do not compartmentalize themselves as armed as distinct from unarmed, as throwing and grappling styles rather than striking arts. Grappling and wrestling "at the sword" in European tradition; the use of knives, trips, and tackles in the "weaponless kicking art" of *capoeira;* the spears and swords (and kicks) of Chinese "boxing" *(wushu);* and the no–holds (or weapons)– barred nature of Burmese *thaing* compel a reformulation of the distinctions among martial arts that have informed our popular conceptions of them.

In this context, even the notion of "art" is problematic. First, the term may be used simply as a means of noting excellence, as a reference to quality rather than attributes. A more serious issue, however, arises from the fact that, in Western European culture, we commonly draw distinctions between art and life, the aesthetic and the utilitarian, work and sport, and art and science. These Eurocentric distinctions break down in the face of Thai *ram dab,* Indonesian *pentjak silat,* and Brazilian *capoeira,* which are at once dance and martial exercise, and have been categorized as both, depending on the interests of commentators who, with a few notable exceptions, have been outsiders to the traditions.

In addition, attempts to comprehend the nature of "martial art" have been further obscured by distinctions between self-defense/combat and sport (itself a culture-bound concept). George Godia characterizes the lack of fit between the contemporary category of sport and the physical culture of traditional societies well. "To kill a lion with a spear needs a different technique and different training than to throw a standardized javelin as far as possible. Spearing a lion was a duty to the young *moran* [Masai warrior], and different from a throw for leisure, enjoyment or an abstract result in terms of meters, a championship, or a certificate" (1989, 268). Perhaps for the same reasons, both our mechanisms for converting combatives (i.e., combat systems) to sports and for categorizing them cross-culturally frequently have fallen short of the mark.

The present volume does maintain some working parameters, however. Martial arts are considered to be systems that blend the physical components of combat with strategy, philosophy, tradition, or other features that distinguish them from pure physical reaction (in other words, a technique, armed or unarmed, employed randomly or idiosyncratically would not be considered a martial art). While some martial arts have spawned sports, and some of these sports are considered in this volume, the martial cores of such activities rather than the sports per se are emphasized. Also, entries focus on those martial systems that exist outside contemporary military technology. Thus, topics include Japanese samurai (despite their part in the Japanese armies in earlier centuries), American frontier gunslingers, and nineteenth-century European duelists (despite their use of firearms), as well as the sociocultural influences that have led to changing fashions in modern military hand-to-hand combat.

Moreover, this volume is not instructional. Rather, it strives to present clear, concise descriptions of martial topics based on sound research principles. In an effort to ensure this, the overwhelming majority of authors are both academics and active martial practitioners.

Obviously, a single work cannot hope to cover such a wide-ranging field as the martial arts of the world comprehensively. Although every attempt has been made to include major topics from a broad spectrum of traditions—insofar as material exists to document such traditions and qualified authors could be found to clarify them—any overview cannot be exhaustive within this format. The richness and diversity of the world's martial traditions make it inevitable that there is much that has been summarized or omitted entirely. The entries, however, do provide an introduction to the growing scholarship in the subject, and, to facilitate the pursuit of more specialized topics, each entry concludes with a bibliography of relevant works. Readers are urged to explore their relevant interests by means of these references. *Martial Arts of the World* attempts to range as widely as possible in its regional coverage and its subject matter. In general, longer, more comprehensive essay formats for entries (e.g., "India," "Religion and Spiritual Development: Japan") have been favored over shorter entries (e.g., "Zen Buddhism").

I am indebted to Texas A&M University for a Faculty Development Leave from the College of Liberal Arts in 1999–2000 that allowed me to devote extra time to the project at a crucial stage in its development. Courtney Livingston provided invaluable research on the historical backgrounds of a number of Asian traditions. My colleague Bruce Dickson lent his considerable knowledge of anthropological theory and African cultures on more than one occasion. The nonmartial Roger D. Abrahams, Dan Ben-Amos, and Bruce Jackson all provided significant research leads during the formative stages of this project—as they have on so many other occasions. Many martial artists whose names do not appear in the list of authors made valuable contributions of time, information, introductions, e-mail addresses, and encouragement: David Chan, Vincent Giordano, Hwong Chen Mou, Leung Yee Lap, Nguyen Van Ahn, Peng Kuang Yao, Guy Power, Mark Wong, and especially Jerry McGlade. I am grateful for the labors of Karl Friday, Gregory Smits, and Jessica Anderson Turner in creating consistency in the romanization of Japanese, Okinawan, and Chinese languages respectively. Their attention to linguistic and cultural detail went far beyond reasonable expectations. Todd Hallman and Gary Kuris at ABC-CLIO took the process—from beginning to end—seriously, but in stride.

My family maintained inconceivable tolerance for my behavior and clutter when I was in the throes of research. Alexandra was born into the family with only minor turmoil. Colin provided computer expertise, library assistance, and camaraderie during field research. My wife, Valerie, as always served as advisor, translator, and second opinion while keeping us all intact.

My deepest gratitude goes out to you all.

Thomas A. Green

References

Friday, Karl, with Seki Humitake. 1997. *Legacies of the Sword: The Kashima-Shinryu and Samurai Martial Culture*. Honolulu: University of Hawai'i Press.

Godia, George. 1989. "Sport in Kenya." In *Sport in Asia and Africa: A Comparative Handbook*. Edited by Eric A. Wagner. New York: Greenwood, 267–281.

A Note on Romanization

In 1979, the People's Republic of China (PRC) decided to employ the pinyin system of romanization for foreign publications. The pinyin system is now recognized internationally. As a result, the pinyin system is the preferred method in the present volume. Prior to this decision by the PRC, the Wade-Giles system had gained wide international acceptance. Certain terms, therefore, may appear under spellings unfamiliar to the reader. For example, Wade-Giles *Hsing I Ch'uan* or *Hsing I Chuan* appears as pinyin *Xingyiquan,* and *Wing Chun* is romanized as *Yongchun.* Pinyin spellings will be used in most cases. Old spellings, often unsystematic, are given in parentheses, for example *Li Cunyi* (*Li Tsun-I*). For those terms that are well established in another spelling, pinyin is noted in parentheses for consistency; for example, *Pangai Noon* (pinyin *banyingruan*). For Chinese names and terms that are not associated with the PRC, we have chosen to follow locally preferred romanizations.

Africa and African America

Although many of the societies of Africa developed in close proximity to Egyptian civilization, with its highly developed fighting arts and rivalry with other "superpowers" such as the Hittites, their martial systems developed in relative isolation from Middle Eastern combat disciplines. Rather, the martial arts, particularly those of the sub-Saharan Africans, belong to a world where (until the arrival of Europeans) the greatest martial threats came from the other sub-Saharan groups, rather than from another continent. Some of the African peoples did have contact with the Arabs, who brought Islam to the region and threatened the indigenous populations with enslavement. To the best of current knowledge, however, the technology and martial development of cultures relying on the same subsistence bases (for example, hunting and gathering and agriculture) were roughly the same for most of the civilizations of Africa, and they continued to be so until the arrival of the Europeans in the beginning of the fifteenth century. Even at this point, some groups resisted advanced weaponry when it became available because of cultural biases. For example, the Masai and Kikuyu viewed firearms as the weapons of cowards.

When one discusses the traditional African martial arts, it is important to note the wide variety and diversity of weapons that were available. Some groups had mastered the art of iron smithing. Although this knowledge probably crossed the Sahara in the fourth to fifth centuries B.C., the spread of iron occurred much later, and, in fact, the distribution patterns were irregular. For example, when the Portuguese entered southern Africa ca. 1500, the Khoisan pastoralists ("Hottentots") and hunter-gatherers ("Bushmen") did not have access to iron.

Those groups who did obtain iron were able to develop the usual variety of weapons that came from the art of iron smithing, such as swords, daggers, and metal spear points. For example, in Benin, Portuguese merchants encountered soldiers armed with iron swords and iron-tipped spears. Their shields, however, were wooden, and their anteater skin armor

A picture of a Zulu warrior holding a large shield and a short spear (assagai) characteristic of their armed combat system. This illustration appeared in a British publication during the war between British settlers and the native population in Africa, 1851. (Corbis)

was of greater significance as magical than as practical protection. In fact, magical powers were attributed to most West African weapons and defenses. Even without metallurgy, other groups produced lethal clubs, staves, and spears with stone points. African societies, some of them small states with standing armies, were militarily formidable even without the trappings of their European and Middle Eastern contemporaries.

Among the armed combat systems that developed were the ones that were used by the Zulu peoples of South Africa. The Zulu were proficient in combat with club, spear, and shield. Because they lacked body armor, the shield became the protective device used by the Zulu warriors. They initiated combat by either throwing a spear at the opponent or using it for a charge. When spear combat became impractical because of the range, the club was used for close-quarters combat. The club-and-shield combination could be used in ways similar to the sword-and-shield combination of warriors in Europe.

This type of fighting gave the Zulu an advantage in combat, as they had all of their ranges covered. The spear could either be used as a pole-arm weapon that allowed the warrior to fight from a distance or as a short-range stabbing weapon. In fact, Shaka Zulu revolutionized indigenous warfare by the use of massed formations and of the *assagai* (a stabbing spear with a shortened shaft) in conjunction with a redesigned shield. Modern use of the spear in traditional Zulu ceremonies has demonstrated that they continue to be able to use the spear in conjunction with the shield effectively. If the spear was lost, then clubs were used for effective close-range combat.

Perhaps no weapon signifies African martial arts more than the throwing iron. These instruments had many names from the different peoples that used them. They have been known as *mongwanga* and *hungamunga*. Many cultures have developed throwing weapons, from sticks to the famous *shuriken* of the Japanese Ninja. Similarly, many African societies placed a premium on these types of weapons. The throwing irons were multibladed instruments that, when thrown, would land with one of the blade points impaling its target. These weapons were reported effective at a range of up to 80 meters. The wounds inflicted at such a long range were not likely to be deadly. At distances of 20 to 30 meters the weapons could connect with lethal impact.

In addition, these bladed weapons were also effective for hand-to-hand combat. Most of them had a handle, and so the blade projections also served as parrying devices if needed. The iron from which the instruments were created was durable enough to stand the rigors of combat, even when one was struck against another throwing iron. Thus, the African warriors who wielded these weapons had not only a reliable projectile device that could be used for long-range combat, but also a handheld weapon for closing with the enemy. Therefore, it was not uncommon for a warrior to carry three or four of these implements, always being certain to keep one in reserve.

These throwing implements were also able to serve as the backbone of a system of armed combat. Given the absence of advanced forms of armor, African warriors were able to use these throwing irons to maximum effect. Once a practitioner was able to penetrate the shield defenses of an opponent, a lethal or incapacitating wound was likely to occur, unless the recipient was able to avoid the strike. The effectiveness of these weapons against an armored opponent is unknown.

Another unique weapon is found among the Nilotic peoples of the southern Sahara region. These groups fought with wrist bracelets that incorporated a sharpened edge. Known by some groups as *bagussa* (Shangun; things that cause fear), the bracelets were said to be used for defense against slavers. They were also used in ceremonial wrestling matches associated with agricultural festivals. These distinctive weapons continue to be utilized by the East African Nilotic groups of Kenya, Somalia, and Ethiopia. For example, contemporary Turkana women of Nigeria still utilize the bracelets in self-defense. The weapons are brought into play by holding the arms in a horizontal guard position in front of the body until the opportunity arises to attack in a sweeping arc across the same plane using the razor-sharp bracelets to slash an opponent.

Combat training was as essential to African martial arts as practice is for martial arts of other cultures. One of the more interesting features of African combat systems was the reliance in many systems on the rehearsal of combat movements through dances. Prearranged combat sequences are well known in various martial arts around the world, the most famous examples being the kata of Japanese and Okinawan karate. Such sequences were also practiced in ancient Greece, through the Pyrrhic war dances. The African systems used drums and stringed instruments to create a rhythmic beat for fighting. Warriors, either individually or in groups, practiced using weapons, both for attacking and defensive movements, in conjunction with the rhythm from the percussion instruments. The armies of the Angolan queen Nzinga Mbande, for example, trained in their combat techniques through dance accompanied by traditional percussion instruments.

From the evidence that survives, which, unfortunately, is scarce, many scholars now believe that this type of training was central to the development of African martial arts systems. The enforcement of learning martial arts through the rhythm created by percussion instruments developed an innate sense of timing and effective movement for the practitioner. In addition, these movements developed effective footwork for the warriors. Although these training patterns have been dismissed as "war dances," expressive movement rather than martial drills, they actually played a central role in the training of African warriors. In a nonliterate culture, this type of direct transmission through music allowed for consistent and uniform training without the need for written communication. This type of training is replicated today in the most popular of the African/African American martial arts, *capoeira* (see below).

Among the weapons that were used extensively by the Africans, one of the most important was the stick. Stickfighting, which is practiced in many cultures the world over, has especially been practiced in sub-Saharan Africa. A variety of sticks continue to be used. For example, in addition to a knife and a spear, contemporary Nilotic men carry two sticks: a *rungu* (Swahili; a potentially deadly knobbed club) and a four-foot stick that is used for, among other things, fighting kin without causing serious injury.

Stickfighting has existed in Africa as both a fighting sport and a martial art. In the sporting variant, competitors met for matches, and a match concluded when a certain number of blows were registered against one of the combatants. The number ranged from one to three, and the match would be halted to avoid serious injury. Blows against vital points of the body or against the head were forbidden in most cases. For the Zulu, as well as the Mpondo, who staged intergroup as well as intravillage stick fights, matches with neighboring polities often took on a deadly earnest quality. The head is reported to have been the preferred target.

Thus, this type of martial arts activity fulfilled two functions for the African practitioners. First, this practice allowed participants to directly experience combat at a realistic level with weapons. Although the target areas were limited, the possibility of injury was very real. Participants had to have a high level of skill just to survive such a bout without injury. For this reason, this type of stickfighting was an excellent preparation for direct military combat.

In addition, stickfighting provided a sporting (although "sport" does not translate well in many non-Western contexts) outlet for the competitors and the societies involved. The contests were a test not only of the competitors' ability, but also of the training mechanisms that were imparted to the competitors. In this respect, these matches were a point of pride for the villages themselves. The warriors were representatives of the village or society, and when intersociety or intervillage competitions were held, each competitor fought for the society's as well as for his own honor. This type of nonlethal outlet for warrior instincts allowed for a cathartic release of energy that helped to avoid all-out warfare.

Stickfighting also gave warriors a foundation for armed combat. Learning how to strike, block, thrust, and move with the weapon is critical for any aspect of armed combat. Learning how to perform these basic moves with a stick can be a foundation for building the movements needed for different weapons. In the case of the Zulu, for example, two sticks were used. One was grasped in the middle and used to block and parry the opponent's blows, while the other stick was used to deliver offensive blows. This practice served to develop skills similar to those needed for the combination of shield and offensive weapon typical of their warfare. For African military societies, this practice provided a method for training warriors that was both nonlethal and inexpensive, and the latter is a relevant consideration. Iron weapons in most cases were expensive and hard to produce. Moreover, in Africa iron weapons, like the smiths who produced them, were often thought to have supernatural properties. Therefore, their use entailed supernatural as well as practical sanctions.

African societies developed systems of unarmed combat as well. Perhaps the best-known type of unarmed combat was wrestling. From the oral accounts that survive, from Egyptian etchings and paintings of Sudanese Nuba wrestlers, and from the few remaining native wrestling traditions still practiced, African wrestling systems, beyond serving as a means of combat, fulfilled both a ceremonial and a sporting function. In most recorded cases, primarily from the Sudan and Nigeria, wrestling was associated with the agricultural cycle (e.g., harvest, yam-growing season) or the individual life cycle, as with the southern Nigerian Ibo, among whom wrestling was associated with male initiation.

Many African wrestling systems seem to have resembled modern freestyle methods, which is to say that the competitors were allowed to throw and to seize any part of the body, including the legs. The well-understood, though unwritten, rules of Nigerian traditional wrestling may be taken as representative: (1) opponents are matched by age; (2) contestants cannot use charms or drugs; (3) the genitals cannot be seized; (4) striking is prohibited; (5) attacks cannot take place before a signal to begin; (6) the match ends when one contestant is prone on the ground (Ojeme 1989, 251).

There are exceptions, however; the Senegalese style called *laamb* more closely resembles Greco-Roman than modern freestyle wrestling. Nevertheless, in sporting and ceremonial wrestling, as in modern amateur wrestling, the object was to pin the opponent. This meant forcing the opponent's shoulders to touch the ground, thus placing the antagonist in a "danger" position. Once this was accomplished, the match was completed.

This way of ending the match was not always the case, however. A wide variety of cultural and regional styles existed. In southeast Africa, a tradition of wrestling from a kneeling (in the case of adult men) or seated (in the case of boys) position employing a single arm developed. As an adjunct to grappling skills, the Nilotic cultures just south of the Sahara (the Bambara of Mali among others) wore bagussa (mentioned above) during their ritual wrestling matches. In these sanguinary contests, one attempted to attack the opponent's head and in the process shed as much of his blood as possible. The blood that was shed in this fashion was believed not only to make the crops grow, but also to heal the sick. The Khoikhoi of southwest Africa, although fighting unarmed, engaged in a type of no-holds-barred wrestling, which came closer to the Greek *pankration* than to the catch-as-catch-can amateur style. Nor was wrestling a uniformly male pursuit. There are traditions of women wrestling in various groups scattered throughout the continent: Nigeria (Ibo), Sudan (Nuba), Senegal, Cameroon, Benin (Fon), Gabon, Gambia. The reasons for doing so vary, of course. In some cases, as with the men, the grappling is connected with the annual round of agricultural ceremonies; in others, it is an aspect of the courtship process.

As with stickfighting, intervillage and even interstate competitions existed. The Bachama, for example, staged tournaments in conjunction with their agricultural festivals, which included their Nigerian neighbors. On these ceremonial occasions the Bata, Bwaza, Jen, and Mbula were invited to field teams of their best wrestlers. This martial tradition continues into the contemporary period, as evidenced by the 1990 Nigerian national wrestling championship of Julius Donald Ngbarato, a man of Bachama heritage. Similarly, the Luo of Kenya held competitions in which villages or districts were pitted against each other. Although the tournaments were organized, the actual matches seemed less so, for wrestling—like Luo stickfighting—is reported as "having no rules at all" (Godia 1989, 68).

Given the fact that African wrestling champions have been regarded not only as superior athletes but also as superior warriors, it can be assumed that combat wrestling systems also existed. The matches reported among the Khoikhoi certainly sound combat effective. Therefore it is likely that, beyond the sporting repertoire reported in the literature, wrestlers learned the techniques of choking and joint locking (in which a joint is forced beyond its maximum range of mobility) appropriate to the battlefield. These systems were probably auxiliary training for warriors, to assist them if they lost their weapons in combat. Much of this must be left to speculation, however, given the paucity of written descriptions of these arts.

Beginning in 1415, after the Portuguese established their foothold in North Africa, Europeans introduced firearms in West Africa in exchange for slaves. Therefore, with the beginning of the slave trade, the nature of war in West Africa became Europeanized, although wrestling and stick-fighting persisted in local festivals.

European influence was not, however, the only threat to the traditional martial arts in Africa. Prior to the European incursions, most of sub-Saharan Africa had been infiltrated by Islam, which spread along trade routes both inland and on the coast. In exchange for gold, ivory, and slaves, the African kingdoms received goods from North Africa, many of whose rulers accepted Islam in order to improve trade relations with Muslim merchants. At first Islam's influence on sub-Saharan Africa was limited. The nineteenth century, however, brought a wave of Islamic revitalization to non-Arab Africa. Calling for reform, the establishment of Islamic states, and the crushing of pagan practices through the agency of jihad (holy war against heretics and unbelievers), these revitalization movements sought to crush traditional martial arts such as wrestling and stickfighting, which were elements of the ceremonies of those religions the jihadists so vigorously opposed. These arts survived the movements that sought to crush them.

Ironically, the European colonialist policies that proved destructive to many African peoples provided an agency for preserving and spreading at least modified elements of African culture. During much of the sixteenth century (1530–1600) the Portuguese, who were the major European slave power at that time, transported over a thousand slaves from West Africa to the Americas monthly. Captured Africans brought many of their native traditions with them as they were forcibly relocated to the New World. Some of these traditions included martial arts, which were sometimes transported in a disguised or hidden version. Because of this dispersion, some of the martial traditions of Africa (particularly of sub-Saharan Africa, from which many of the slaves were drawn) still survive and live in altered form.

Given the Portuguese role in the transport of Africans to the New World, it should not be surprising that the Portuguese colony of Brazil became a focal point of African fighting arts (as well as for many other Africanisms, such as the religion of Candomblé) in the Americas.

Brazilian capoeira is undoubtedly the most well known and widely disseminated of a complex of New World martial arts that rely primarily on kicks and head-butts as weapons and that are usually practiced to musical accompaniment. The origins of capoeira are recorded only in the traditional legends of the art, which invariably focus on African influence. Considerable debate exists among practitioners and historians as to whether capoeira is the New World development of an African martial art or a system originating in the New World with African influences ranging from terminology to the *berimbau,* the primary musical instrument used to provide accompaniment for the *jôgo* ("match" or "game").

Scholar and practitioner J. Lowell Lewis maintains that capoeira manifests an "undeniably African esthetic" by virtue of body mechanics and music among other features (Lewis 1992, 18). The customary label for the earliest form of the art, *Capoeira Angola,* pays homage to its legendary African origins, usually in dances whose movements were converted to martial applications. One candidate for the ancestor of capoeira is the *ngolo* (zebra dance) performed by young Mucupe men of southern Angola in conjunction with girls' puberty rites. Robert Farris Thompson, perhaps the strongest advocate of the theory of African origins, notes the similarities between capoeira's *cabeçada* (head-butt) and the *ngwíndulu mu-tu* (striking with the head) of African *Ki-Kongo.* At any rate, some scholars argue that the similarity among the various New World arts is due to common origin, generally somewhere in Bantu Africa.

Capoeiristas practice to a beat that is set through various percussion instruments, the most important of which is a musical bow with a gourd resonator known as a berimbau. The rhythm that is developed by these instruments determines the cadence in the fight. There is a school of thought among capoeira practitioners that the use of these musical instruments developed to hide the martial function of the physical movements from the Portuguese overlords in Brazil. However, the historical foundations of African arts noted above seem to argue that the use of musical accompaniment for martial arts practice is a strong tradition. This would make the music used with capoeira part of a much older tradition.

Songs involving a leader and a response pattern are sung during play. The words of these songs embody, for example, comments on capoeira in general, insults directed toward various types of styles of play or types of players, or biographical allusions to famous capoeiristas. The sense of capoeira as a dance is established by this musical frame for the action and completed by the movements taking place within the *roda* (Portuguese; "wheel"—the circle of capoeira play). The basic stance of capoeira places one foot forward in a lunging move with the corresponding hand forward and the other back. There is, however, considerable variety in the execution of the stance (both between individual players and between the Regional and the Angola traditions), and stances rapidly shift, with feet alternating in time to the tempo of the musical accompaniment in a dancelike action called a *ginga.* The techniques of capoeira rely heavily on kicks, many of them embodied in spectacular cartwheels, somersaults, and handstands. Players move from aerial techniques to low squatting postures accompanied by sweeps or tripping moves. Evasion rather than blocking is used for defense. Head-butts and hand strikes (using the open hand) complete the

Many African combat systems relied heavily on the rehearsal of combat movements through dances. Here, game preserve guards in Ndumu, South Africa, practice a martial dance using rungu *(knobbed sticks) in conjunction with the rhythm from percussion instruments, 1980. (Jonathan Blair/Corbis)*

unarmed arsenal of the capoeirista. Again, there is a distinction between Angola and Regional, with the former relying more on low kicks, sweeps, and trips "played" to a slower rhythm.

As an armed fighting art, capoeira has incorporated techniques for the use of paired short sticks and bladed weapons (particularly straight razors, knives, and machetes). Even in those cases in which the art has moved from the streets to the training hall, training in weapons remains in the curriculum in forms such as *maculêlê*, which entails a rhythmic clash of short sticks while performing a dancelike action. Stickfighting persists on the streets of Trinidad during Carnival as *kalinda*.

Though not as well known as capoeira, other similar martial arts have been noted throughout the African Americas.

In Martinique a particularly well-documented form exists, which is called *ladjia* in the south, *damié* in the north, and also *ronpoin* and *kokoyé*. Like capoeira, ladjia is played to the accompaniment of percussion instruments (primarily drums, but also sticks that are clashed together) and leader-and-response songs, and it is characterized by vigorous acrobatic movements. The music controls the pace and character of the fight and therefore is of major importance to the event. Practitioners echo the sentiments of capoeiristas in claiming that without song there is no ladjia. With movements guided by the tempo of the music, the combatants maneuver in ways that are reminiscent of the *ginga* (Portuguese; from *gingar,* "to sway, to waddle"). When an opportunity develops, they kick, punch, and eye-gouge. When one lifts the other and throws him on his back, the winner is proclaimed. There are regional variants of the play, the most striking being the bloody ferocity of combative ladjia in the south versus the dancelike performance of damié in the north. The various regional forms of Martinique have been successfully compared to the *kadjia* of Benin, a similar ritualistic form of activity practiced in conjunction with agricultural ceremony, but one that emphasizes grappling and throwing actions rather than the striking, kicking, and gouging of the New World form. A combat form of kadjia, designed for use when a warrior loses his weapons, incorporates a wider range of techniques.

In Venezuela, *broma* (literally, "just joking") is played among Venezuelans of African descent, particularly in the coastal city of Curiepe. Contemporary broma does not maintain a structured curriculum, accepting a variety of new influences at the whim of practitioners. The traditional essence of the style, however, consists of kicks, head-butts, and sweeps.

Other African Caribbean and South American fighting arts such as *maní* (Cuba), *chat'ou* (Guadeloupe), and *susa* (Surinam) may already be extinct. The same may be true of the last vestiges of a similar African American art that had at least one surviving master in the 1980s.

The art of "knocking and kicking" developed in the southern United States. According to Jackson Jordan Jr. of North Carolina, a master of the style, it was widely practiced by African Americans, particularly in the Carolinas and the Georgia Sea Islands, during his youth at the turn of the twentieth century. One hundred and fifty years earlier, Henry Bibb, a runaway slave from Kentucky, reported that slaves were forced by their masters to fight. In these contests, "The blows are made by kicking, knocking, and butting with their heads; they grab each other by their ears, and jam their heads together like sheep" (1969, 68). Bibb may well be describing the core repertoire of knocking and kicking. His description also may be the best surviving description of this martial art.

Just as little is known regarding susa, an activity reported from Saramakan Maroon groups in Suriname (Dutch Guyana) by Dutch sources in the late seventeenth century. The obviously martial activity was accompanied by percussive music (drumming and hand-clapping). The goal of the "game" was to knock down one's opponent. The folk history of this group, whose members claim African and African Indian descent, remembers susa as a dance derived from an African martial art called *nsunsa*.

The African martial arts in the Americas obviously share a common set of characteristics. It has been suggested that similar features developed as a result of similar circumstances. There are equally strong arguments, however, that martial arts, like many other cultural traditions, survived the Middle Passage (the transport of Africans to slavery in the Americas) to be adapted to the changed cultural context of the Americas. Under less constrained circumstances, the process continues, as contemporary Senegalese immigrants compete in their traditional wrestling art of laamb in parks in Washington, D.C., on the Muslim holiday of Tabaski.

Thomas A. Green
Gene Tausk

See also Capoeira; Middle East; Performing Arts

References
Almeida, Bira. 1986. *Capoeira: A Brazilian Art Form.* Berkeley: North Atlantic Books.
Balent, Matthew. 1993. *The Compendium of Weapons, Armour, and Castles.* Taylor, MI: Palladium Books.
Bibb, Henry. 1969 [1850]. *Narrative of the Life and Adventures of Henry Bibb, an American Slave, Written by Himself.* Introduction by Lucius C. Matlack. Miami, FL: Mnemosyne Publishing.
Boahen, A. Adu. 1962. "The Caravan Trade in the Nineteenth Century." *Journal of African History* 3: 2.
Bryant, A. T. 1949. *The Zulu People: As They Were before the White Man Came.* Pietermaritzburg, South Africa: Shuter and Shooter.
Capoeira, Nestor. 1995. *The Little Capoeira Book.* Berkeley: North Atlantic Books.
Davidson, Basil. 1969. *Africa in History: Themes and Outlines.* New York: Macmillan.
Fage, J. D. 1978. *A History of Africa.* London: Hutchinson.
Godia, George. 1989. "Sport in Kenya." In *Sport in Asia and Africa: A Comparative Handbook.* Edited by Eric A. Wagner. New York: Greenwood.
Gwaltney, John. 1981. *Drylongso: A Self-Portrait of Black Americans.* New York: Random House.
Hill, Erroll. 1972. *Trinidad Carnival: Mandate for a National Carnival.* Austin: University of Texas Press.
Katz, William Loren. 1986. *Black Indians: A Hidden Heritage.* New York: Atheneum.
Lewis, J. Lowell. 1992. *Ring of Liberation: Deceptive Discourse in Brazilian Capoeira.* Chicago: University of Chicago Press.
Michelon, Josy. 1987. *Le Ladjia: Origin et Pratiques* (Ladjia: Origin and Practice). Paris: Editions Caribéennes.
Mutti, Maria. 1978. *Maculéle.* Salvador, Brazil: Prefectura da Cidade do Salvador.
Ojeme, E. O. 1989. "Sport in Nigeria." In *Sport in Asia and Africa: A Comparative Handbook.* Edited by Eric A. Wagner. New York: Greenwood.
Oliver, Roland Anthony, and Brian M. Fagan. 1975. *Africa in the Iron Age, c. 500 B.C. to A.D. 1400.* Cambridge: Cambridge University Press.
Ortiz, Fernando. 1985 [1951]. *Los Bailes y el Teátro de los Negros en el Folklore de Cuba* (Dances and Theatre of the Blacks in Cuban Folklore). Havana: Editorial Letras Cubanas.

Paul, Sigrid. 1987. "The Wrestling Traditions and Its Social Functions." In *Sport in Africa: Essays in Social History.* Edited by William J. Baker and James A. Mangan. New York: Africana.

Poliakoff, Michael. 1995. *Combat Sports in the Ancient World: Competition, Violence, and Culture.* New Haven: Yale University Press.

Shinnie, Margaret. 1970. *Ancient African Kingdoms.* New York: New American Library.

Stevens, Phillips, Jr. 1993. "Traditional Sport in Africa: Wrestling among the Bachama of Nigeria." Paper presented at the International Conference on the Preservation and Advancement of Traditional Sport, Waseda University, Shinjoku, Japan (March).

Svinth, Joseph R. 2000. *Kronos: A Chronological History of the Martial Arts and Combative Sports.* http://www.ejmas.com/kronos/.

Thompson, Robert Farris. 1993. *Face of the Gods: Art and Altars of Africa and the African Americans.* New York: Museum for African Art.

———. 1992. Introduction to *Ring of Liberation: Deceptive Discourse in Brazilian Capoeira,* by J. Lowell Lewis. Chicago: University of Chicago Press.

Aikidô

Aikidô is a modern martial system of Japanese derivation, developed by founder Ueshiba Morihei (1883–1969) over the course of his lifetime. Aikidô employs the redirection of an attacker's energy (or *ki*) into a variety of holds, locks, and projections, and is probably best known for an exclusive focus on defensive maneuvers and for its unique martial philosophy.

The principle of *aiki*, a method of defeating an attack through harmonizing with rather than directly opposing the aggressive motion, predates aikidô, and it found expression in many of feudal Japan's sophisticated martial systems. Aikidô's most direct predecessor art, *Daitô-ryû jûjutsu,* laid particular emphasis on this strategy and on the techniques that employed it most efficiently (many of which would be seen in some form in Ueshiba's modern *budô* ["martial way"]). Indeed, Ueshiba was first known as a high-quality Daitô-ryû instructor, and he used the terms *jûjutsu* and *aikibudô* for his art through his early decades of teaching.

Among the schools derived from Ueshiba's pioneering efforts, patterns in technique and philosophy correlate closely with teachers' historical associations with Ueshiba and, later, with Tôhei. Prewar students of aikibudô retained an emphasis on *atemi* (striking) and generally expressed indifference (at best) about the well-being of an attacker as a result of the defense, resulting in a flavor closer to aiki-jûjutsu than to the peaceful art developed by Ueshiba in his later years.

The philosophy of aikidô correlates closely to the art's techniques, and though even the orthodox branches of aikidô are not in complete agreement on either, some generalizations can be made. In aikidô an attack is not responded to with a counterattack, in the classic rhythm of strike, block, return strike; rather, the practitioner seeks to allow a committed attack to pass by, and then to exploit the attacker's resulting imbalance. Thus both the initial attack and forceful opposition to such an attack are characterized as futile and maladjusted endeavors, out of harmony with the universe; an aikidô approach to conflict (physical or otherwise) begins with searching for a way to "blend with" rather than oppose aggressive action. From this point a physical application normally proceeds to projection or control of the attacker, usually with an emphasis on preventing any (or at least any serious) injury to the attacker. The curricula of many aikidô schools lack or de-emphasize hand strikes, and most lack kicking techniques, although defenses against both are practiced.

Manipulation of the *ki* energy of both the attacker and defender is implied even in the art's name, but interpretation of the nature of ki, and its proper manipulation, vary. Aikidô is often classed among the "soft" or "internal" martial arts, like the Chinese *taijiquan* (tai chi ch'uan), *xingyiquan* (hsing i ch'uan), and *baguazhang* (pa kua ch'uan), and an emphasis on breathing exercises and ki exercises (meant to improve a practitioner's control of his own energy) is common. Aikidô schools descending from Tôhei Kôichi's tradition even maintain separate ki rankings (related but not identical to the student's aikidô *kyû* or *dan* rank, discussed below) based on the student's mastery of ki concepts and applications, including *kiatsu*, a healing method practiced by Tôhei Kôichi. Interpretations of ki in aikidô range from the mystical (complete with tales of miraculous feats by Ueshiba Morihei) to the utilitarian and prosaic.

Uses of the *bokken* (a wooden representation of the Japanese sword) and *jô* (a four-foot staff) are common auxiliary training methods in aikidô, reflecting the elements of timing, distance, and initiative that aikidô and its predecessor arts took from the armed disciplines of the samurai. In general, the use of these weapons in aikidô training is undertaken for the illustration and practice of aikidô principles, rather than for the sake of combat-oriented proficiency with the weapons themselves, although weapon-handling methods taught in various aikidô schools are widely divergent. Disarming and weapon-retention techniques are often included in this practice and related to similar unarmed procedures in other arts.

The *tantô,* a wooden replica of a Japanese dagger, is also maintained as a training tool, although unlike the other wooden weapons it is rarely considered from the wielder's perspective. Instead, the tantô is used exclusively for the practice of disarming techniques. (An exception to this occurs in Tomiki Aikidô dôjô, which engage in a competitive sport revolving around tantô offense and defense. In their matches, a rubber tantô may be used by the offensive player to score, while successful defense yields the defender both points and the tantô.)

Aikidô training is usually centered on partner practice, in which students alternate practicing the roles of *uke* (the attacker and the one who ordinarily takes a fall) and *nage* (the defender). Other aikidô training methods may include *aiki taisô* (specialized calisthenics for the application of energy in the aikidô manner), weapon forms, sword and staff disarms and sword and staff retention techniques, *kokyu hô* ("breath power exercise") breath and balance training, and a multiple-attacker exercise called *randori*.

In aikidô's randori, a single nage uses aikidô protective strategy and techniques against a number of attackers, who may or may not be limited in the methods that they are allowed to employ against nage. Randori encourages versatile, decisive movement on nage's part and rewards swift and efficient unbalancing techniques rather than involved control holds or throws. It is often a prominent feature of aikidô rank tests.

Ranking in most aikidô dôjô is based on a belt system derived from the one originated for sport jûdô. A variety of kyû ranks lead up to certification as *shôdan* (first dan, usually translated as first-degree black belt), usually designated by a black belt. Dan ranks proceed from this important step, and upper ranks may vary according to the particular affiliation of the dôjô.

The *hakama,* a traditional divided-skirt garment, is seen in many aikidô dôjô, often as a rank designator similar to the black belt. Ueshiba considered the wearing of this garment to be a matter of basic courtesy for students of all ranks, but modern dôjô traditions vary widely, and the wearing of the hakama may be required for all students or restricted to particular students according to local custom.

With its lack of tournaments and its unusual philosophical emphasis, aikidô has spread through different venues than other popular martial arts. Seen from its inception as an art with broad philosophical implications and many applications outside the realm of physical conflict, aikidô has attracted more academic interest than most martial arts and has been advocated in adapted forms as a paradigm in psychology, business, and conflict management. The physical effectiveness of aikidô, along with its humane priorities, has held considerable appeal for law enforcement applications as well, and Shioda Gôzô's Yoshinkan Aikidô (a style heavily influenced by prewar aikibudô) was chosen for the training of the elite Tokyo police. However, the art has generally had a low media profile, with the exception of the film career of senior aikidô practitioner Steven Seagal. (His movies have featured a great deal of aikidô-influenced fight choreography.)

Training in aikidô is today readily available in much of the world, thanks in part to deliberate efforts by Ueshiba to establish his art worldwide as a way of promoting his ideals.

William J. Long

See also Jûdô; Ki/Qi; Religion and Spiritual Development: Japan; Wrestling and Grappling: Japan

References

Dobson, Terry. 1993. *Aikido in Everyday Life: Giving in to Get Your Way.* Berkeley: North Atlantic Books.

Higashi, Nobuyoshi. 1989. *Aikido: Tradition and New Tomiki Free Fighting Method.* Burbank, CA: Unique Publications.

Pranin, Stanley. 1991. *Aiki News Encyclopedia of Aikido.* Rolling Hills Estates, CA: Aiki News.

Shioda, Gôzô. 1997. *Total Aikido: The Master Course.* Tokyo: Kodansha International.

Sosa, Bill. 1997. *The Secrets of Police Aikido: Controlling Tactics Used by Law Enforcement Professionals.* Burbank, CA: Citadel Press.

Stevens, John. 1987. *Abundant Peace: The Biography of Morihei Ueshiba, Founder of Aikido.* Boston: Shambhala Publications.

Tôhei, Koichi. 1978. *Ki in Daily Life.* San Francisco: Japan Publications.
Ueshiba, Kisshomaru, and Ueshiba Morihei. 1986. *Aikido.* San Francisco: Japan Publications.
Westbrook, Adele, and Oscar Ratti. 1994. *Aikido and the Dynamic Sphere: An Illustrated Introduction.* Rutland, VT: Charles E. Tuttle.

Animal and Imitative Systems in Chinese Martial Arts

Very early, the Chinese observed the characteristics of their natural environment, including the wildlife and, as early as 300 B.C., there is evidence in the writings of Zhuangzi (Chuang-tzu) that they were imitating animal movements (birds and bears) as a form of exercise. The doctor Hua Tuo is said to have developed the Five Animal exercises (tiger, deer, bear, ape, and bird) around A.D. 100, and it is very easy to imagine how animal characteristics were adapted to fighting techniques. Another view is that at least some animal forms may hark back to a distant totemic past that still occupies a place in the Chinese psyche. This totemic influence is difficult if not impossible to trace in majority Han Chinese boxing styles; however, it can be seen in the combination of martial arts and dance practiced by some of China's many national minorities. Cheng Dali, in his *Chinese Martial Arts: History and Culture,* points to Frog Boxing, practiced by the Zhuang Nationality of the Guangxi Zhuang Autonomous Region, as an example, the frog being considered their protector against both natural and man-made disasters.

The monkey or ape, with its combination of human characteristics and superhuman physical skills, has long been associated with martial arts. The most notable early reference is to the ape in the story of the Maiden of Yue (ca. 465 B.C.). In this story, an old man transforms himself into an ape who tests the swordsmanship of the Maiden of Yue before she is selected by the king of Yue to train his troops. Perhaps better known are the exploits of the monkey with the magic staff in the Ming novel *Journey to the West* (sixteenth century). He fights his way through a host of demons to protect the monk, Xuan Zang, during his pilgrimage to India and return to China with Buddhist scriptures.

Monkey Boxing was among the prominent styles listed by General Qi Jiguang in his *New Book of Effective Discipline* (ca. 1561), and Wang Shixing (1547–1598) was impressed with a Monkey Boxer he observed practicing at Shaolin Monastery (Tang 1930). General Qi also mentions the Eagle Claw Style.

During the Qing period (1644–1911), the Praying Mantis Style appeared in Shandong province, and numerous other animal routines became associated with major styles of boxing, such as the five animals of Hong-

The magic monkey Songoku from a Chinese fable creates an army by plucking out his fur and blowing it into the air—each hair becomes a monkey-warrior. Illustration created by Yoshitoshi Taiso in 1882. (Asian Art & Archaeology, Inc./Corbis)

quan (dragon, tiger, leopard, snake, crane), sometimes seen as synonymous with Shaolin Boxing; the twelve animals (tiger, horse, eagle, snake, dragon, hawk, swallow, cock, monkey, Komodo dragon–like lizard, tai, and bear) of Shanxi-style xingyi boxing; and the ten animals of Henan-style xingyi boxing (tiger, horse, eagle, snake, dragon, hawk, swallow, cock, monkey, and cat). These styles and forms represent a human attempt to mimic specific practical animal fighting and maneuvering techniques. Of course, the dragon is a mythical beast, so this form is based on the Chinese vision of the dragon's undulating movement and the way it seizes with its claws—a pull-down technique. The tai is an apparently extinct bird whose circular wing movements suggest a deflecting/defensive form. Some of the so-called animal forms could be categorized in other ways. For instance, some of the animal techniques in xingyi boxing could be subsumed under the basic Five Element forms (crushing, splitting, drilling, pounding, and crossing). In addition to the actual animal forms, many Chinese boxing forms have flowery titles such as "Jade Maiden Thrusts the Shuttle," "Step Back and Straddle the Tiger," and "White Ape Offers Fruit." These are merely traditional images, familiar to most Chinese, used as mnemonic devices to assist when practicing routines.

The pure animal styles of boxing exude a certain amount of individual showmanship in the same way as does the Drunken Style, which is said to have evolved from an ancient dance, and some other particularly acrobatic styles. These are all basically popular folk styles as opposed to no-frills, military hand-to-hand combat styles, whose techniques can be seen subsumed in some existing styles, but whose separate identity has essentially been lost in modern times.

Stanley E. Henning

See also Baguazhang (Pa Kua Ch'uan); Boxing, Chinese; Boxing, Chinese Shaolin Styles; Xingyiquan (Hsing I Ch'uan)

References
Cheng Dali. 1995. *Zhongguo Wushu: Lishi yu Wenhua* (Chinese Martial Arts: History and Culture). Chengdu: Sichuan University Press.
Qi Jiguang. 1988 [1561]. *Jixiao Xinshu* (New Book of Effective Discipline). Ma Mingda, ed. Beijing: People's Physical Culture Press.
Tang Hao. 1930. *Shaolin Wudang Kao* (Shaolin Wudang Research). 1968. Reprint, Hong Kong: Unicorn Press.
Wu Dianke et al., ed. 2000. *Xingyi Quanshu Daquan* (Complete Book of Xingyi Boxing). Taiyuan: Shanxi People's Press.
Xi Yuntai. 1985. *Zhongguo Wushu Shi* (Chinese Martial Arts History). Beijing: People's Physical Culture Press.
Xu Cai et al., ed. 1993. *Zhongguo Wushu Quanxie Lu* (Record of Chinese Boxing and Weapons Styles). Beijing: People's Physical Culture Press.
Yu, Anthony C., ed. and trans. 1984. *The Journey to the West*. 4 vols. Chicago: University of Chicago Press.

Archery, Japanese

The practice of kyûdô or Japanese Archery is traced to two roots: ceremonial archery associated with Shintô and combative archery developing from warfare and hunting. Kyûdô has been called the earliest martial sport of Japan, as the warrior and noble classes used it for recreational hunting. Kyûdô was also considered to be one of the primary arts of a warrior, and the Japanese attachment to it and swordsmanship was so great that Japan rejected the use of firearms in the seventeenth century in favor of traditional arms.

The history of kyûdô is claimed to go back to the possibly mythical Emperor Jimmu (660 B.C.), who is always portrayed holding a longbow. Certain court rituals, probably imported from China, involved archery, and skill in ceremonial archery was considered a requirement of a refined man. During the ancient period, mentions of a *Taishi-ryû* of archery are found about A.D. 600. About 500 years later, Henmi Kiyomitsi founded what is generally accepted as the first kyûdô *ryûha* (style), the *Henmi-ryû*. His descendants later founded the *Takeda-* and *Ogasawara-ryû*. The Genpei War (1180–1185) led to an increased demand for warriors to develop archery

A young woman aims at a barrel of straw to practice the style of her archery, at the Tsurugaoka Hachiman Grand Shrine in Kamakura, Japan, 1986. (Robert Downing/Corbis)

skills. Unlike in Western Europe, in Japan the aristocratic warrior class considered the bow a warrior's weapon.

This emphasis increased in the feudal period, especially when Minamoto no Yoritomo gained the title of shôgun. He standardized the training of his warriors and had the founder of the Ogasawara-ryû, Ogasawara Nagakiyo, teach *yabusame* (mounted archery). During the fifteenth and sixteenth centuries, civil wars raged throughout Japan, and the techniques of shooting were refined. Heki Danjô developed a new devastatingly accurate approach to archery he called hi, kan, chû (fly, pierce, center), which was quickly adopted. His school, the Heki-ryû, spread into many branches, and these "new schools" continue to this day. Use of the bow peaked in the sixteenth century, just before the Portuguese introduced the gun into Japan. By 1575, Oda Nobunaga used firearms to win a major battle, beginning the bow's decline.

This decline was temporarily halted by Japan's self-imposed period of isolation, and during this period as well as the following Meiji period and the modern period, the art of kyûdô has developed as a mental and physical discipline. Today, kyûdô is taught as a mental, physical, and spiritual discipline under the *Zen Nihon Kyûdô Renmei* (All Japan Archery Federation) rather than as a competitive sport. It is now taught in the high schools and universities as well as extensively practiced in private *kyûdôjo* (archery halls).

The Japanese bow, or *yumi*, is about seven feet long and constructed of laminated bamboo. The grip is placed one-third of the way up from the bottom, unlike the grip on Western and Chinese bows. This placement of the grip allows the bow to be used on horseback while retaining the advantages of a longbow. The arrows, or *ya*, are also longer than Western arrows, due to the Japanese method of drawing the bow to the right shoulder instead of the chin or cheek. Because the bow is drawn with the thumb as in other styles of Eastern archery, the glove, or *yugake*, is different, with a reinforced inner thumb. No thumb ring is used, as was the case in Korea and China. Only after the Ônin Wars, when an archer no longer had to use his sword, did the modern kind of glove with a hardened thumb and wrist develop. The uniform worn is normally the obi (sash) and *hakama* (split skirt) with either a *kyûdô-gi* (jacket) or a kimono (for the higher ranks). White *tabi* (socks constructed with the big toe separated from the other toes) are also worn.

Training begins with learning to draw the bow and shooting blunt and unfletched (featherless) arrows into a *mato* (target). The beginner practices the eight stages of shooting until his teacher is satisfied that he is ready to move to regular practice. The eight stages are (1) *ashibumi* (positioning), (2) *dôzukuri* (correcting the posture), (3) *yugamae* (readying the bow), (4) *uchiokoshi* (raising the bow), (5) *hikiwake* (drawing the bow), (6) *kai* (completing and holding the draw), (7) *hanare* (releasing the arrow, which also includes a step called *yugaeri,* or the turning of the bow in the hand), and (8) *yudaoshi* (lowering the bow). Each step is practiced until it is as perfect as possible. In this way, the beginner learns proper technique without the distraction of an actual target. Unlike Western longbows, the bow is not drawn in a push-pull movement but in a spreading movement as the bow is lowered. Since kyûdô is practiced as a means of personal development, mere accuracy is not prized. The proper approach and a sense of *zanshin* (the quiet period after the release of the arrow) are more important. Three levels of skill are described: *tôteki,* or arrow hits target, *kanteki,* or arrow pierces target, and *zaiteki,* or arrow exists in target. The first is also called "rifle shooting" and is concerned only with hitting the center. In the second, the archer pierces the target as if it were an enemy. An intensity is seen that is absent in the first level. The final level, zaiteki, is where the archer has unified his mind, body, and bow into one, and shooting becomes natural and instinctive. This is the true goal of kyûdô.

Kevin Menard

See also Kendô; Religion and Spiritual Development: Japan

References

Acker, William. 1998. *Kyûdô: The Japanese Arts of Archery.* Rutland, VT: Charles E. Tuttle.

Draeger, Donn, and Robert Smith. 1981. *Comprehensive Asian Fighting Arts.* Tokyo: Kodansha International.

Herrigel, Eugen. 1989. *Zen in the Art of Archery.* New York: Random House.

Hurst, G. Cameron, III. 1998. *Armed Martial Arts of Japan.* New Haven: Yale University Press.

Onuma, Hideharu. 1993. *Kyûdô: The Essence and Practice of Japanese Archery.* Tokyo: Kodansha International.

Ratti, Oscar, and Adele Westbrook. 1973. *Secrets of the Samurai: The Martial Arts of Feudal Japan.* Rutland, VT: Charles E. Tuttle.

Archery, Mongolian

See Mongolia

Arnis

See Philippines

B

Baguazhang (Pa Kua Ch'uan)

Of the four internal martial arts of China, the most distinctive appearing is baguazhang. The name means "eight-trigram palm," in reference to the bagua (eight-trigram) pattern used in Chinese philosophy, magic, and fortune telling. Part of the training in baguazhang is walking a circle while practicing certain moves, and this walking a circle gives the art its distinctive appearance. The bagua practitioner walks a circle of various sizes, reversing his movement, twisting and turning through eight sets of movements (called palms for the hand position used). Between the sets of movements, he walks the circle with his hands in one of the eight positions.

While a few claims of baguazhang's origins go back to the fifteenth century, most experts believe the art originated with Dong Haichuan (1789–1879), who claimed to have learned the method of divine boxing from a Daoist, who is sometimes given the name of Dong Menglin. Dong Haichuan used no name, claiming only that he learned from an old man in the mountains. He became a servant or possibly a eunuch in the Imperial Palace and, because of his graceful movements, was one day asked to demonstrate his skill at martial arts. The twisting, turning beauty of baguazhang impressed the emperor, and Dong Haichuan became a bodyguard and instructor to the court. Of his many students, five learned the art fully and formed the schools of baguazhang taught today: Cheng Tinghua, Li Cunyi (Li Tsun-I), Yin Fu, Zhang Zhaodong, and Liang Zhenpu. Many variations of baguazhang are practiced today and, depending on who is counting, there are five to fourteen substyles. The most popular today appear to be Emei, Wudang, Cheng family, Yin family, and Yin Yang.

Many stories are told about Dong Haichuan. The most famous tells how Dong fought Guo Yunshen for three days, with neither being able to win. Impressed with each other's techniques, they began cross-training their students in the two arts. More probable is the story that many masters of both systems lived in this province, and many of them became friends, especially bagua's Cheng Tinghua and xingyiquan's Li Cunyi (Li

Baguazhang is closely associated with Daoist yoga or inner alchemy and other Chinese esoteric traditions. Cultivation of inner energy (qi) and breathing practices are taught along with the fighting techniques. A student of baguazhang practices these moves at the Shen Wu Academy of Martial Arts in Garden Grove, California. (Courtesy of Tim Cartmell)

Tsun-I). The linear drills practiced in some styles of baguazhang are believed to descend from the interaction with xingyi. The style taught by Zhang Junfeng, a student of Cheng Tinghua, for example, teaches eighteen exercises that are fairly linear in nature.

Baguazhang is closely associated with Daoist yoga or inner alchemy and other Chinese esoteric traditions. Cultivation of inner energy (*qi*) and breathing practices are taught along with the fighting techniques. It has been suggested that baguazhang is a descendant of certain Daoist schools that practice moving meditations while walking in a circle. Baguazhang is still practiced as a form of *qigong* (exercise that develops psychophysiological energy) and Daoist yoga as well as a fighting art.

The student in baguazhang begins by learning to walk the circle. In the beginning, the circle is six to twelve feet in diameter. As mastery of the art is obtained, the circle can be as small or large as needed. Initially, the student walks the circle while concentrating on moving correctly and breathing. In the old days, this could continue for as long as three years. When the student is able to move correctly, he is introduced to the single and then double palm changes. After this foundation is learned, the student learns the eight mother palms. This is a long form that consists of eight sets of movements done to both sides, separated by periods of walking the circle in different positions. When observed, the bagua player is seen to go through patterns of fluid movement, fluidly twisting and turning in both high and low stances. Between these periods of activity, he tranquilly circles.

After he attains a certain degree of proficiency, the student is introduced to two-person drills, pole training, and weighted training. Two-person training teaches him how the movements of the form conceal striking, grappling, and throwing techniques and also how to respond to an opponent. Pole training and weighted training teach power transfer and condition the body. Other techniques are used to train the development and release of applied internal power (*jing*). As the training continues, the student may learn other forms, such as swimming-body baguazhang, as well as weapon techniques. The range of baguazhang forms is great: Thirteen empty-handed forms, five two-person forms, and sets for the standard Chinese weapons exist.

When fighting, the baguazhang practitioner twists and weaves about his opponents, entrapping limbs and striking to vital points. Drills exist to train for multiple enemies that are similar to Hebei xingyi's Nine Palace Boxing, and it is claimed baguazhang allows one to fight eight opponents simultaneously. The elusive and entrapping nature of this style has given rise to the analogy that baguazhang is like a wire ball, where attacks are trapped and twisted around.

While baguazhang uses the standard Chinese arsenal of *jian* (two-edged sword), *dao* (broadsword or cutlass), *qiang* (spear), *gun* (staff), *dao* (long saber), *gou* (hook sword), double knives, and *guai* (crutch), it also has two specialized weapons: a metal ring like a hoop and the lu jiao dao (deer hook sword). This latter weapon, unique to baguazhang styles, looks like two crescents interlocked to create a weapon with points. Used in pairs, the swords are close-quarter weapons designed to trap and destroy the enemy.

Kevin Menard

When fighting, baguazhang practitioners twist and weave about their opponents, emphasizing the use of the open hand in preference to the closed fist. Two men demonstrate a throw using this distinctive technique at the Shen Wu Academy of Martial Arts in Garden Grove, California. (Courtesy of Tim Cartmell)

See also Xingyiquan (Hsing I Ch'uan)

References

Bracy, John, and Xing-Han Liu. 1998. *Ba Gua: Hidden Knowledge in the Taoist Internal Martial Art*. Berkeley, CA: North Atlantic Books.

Crandall, Joseph. 1994–1996. *Classical Ba Qua Zhang*. 6 vols. Pinole, CA: Smiling Tiger Martial Arts.

Hsieh, Douglas H. 1983. *Pa Kua Chuan for Self Defense*. Honolulu, HI: McLisa Publications.

Johnson, Jerry. 1994. *The Essence of Internal Martial Arts*. 2 vols. Pacific Grove, CA: Ching Lung Martial Arts Association.

———. 1984. *The Master's Manual of Pa Kua Chang.* Pacific Grove, CA: Ching Lung Martial Arts Association.

Johnson, Jerry, and Joseph Crandall. 1986. *Classical Pa Kua Chang Fighting Systems and Weapons.* Pinole, CA: Smiling Tiger Martial Arts.

Liang, Shou-Yu, Yang Jwing-Ming, and Wu Wen-ching. 1994. *Emei Baguazhang: Theory and Applications.* Jamaica Plains, MA: Yang Martial Arts Association.

Smith, Robert W. 1967. *Pa Kua: Chinese Boxing for Fitness and Defense.* Tokyo: Kodansha International.

Sugarwara, Tetsutaka, and Xing Lujian. 1996. *Aikido and Chinese Martial Arts.* 2 vols. Tokyo: Kodansha International.

Bandô

See Thaing

Banshay

See Thaing

Bersilat

See Silat

Boxing, Chinese

Chinese boxing is a versatile form of bare-handed fighting, variously combining strikes with the hands, kicks and other leg maneuvers, grappling, holds, and throws. Piecing together the scattered passages in ancient writings, one can reasonably conclude that the origins of Chinese boxing go back as far as the Xia dynasty (twenty-first to sixteenth centuries B.C.), making it one of the oldest elements of Chinese culture still practiced.

Originally called *bo* (striking), it was a skill practiced among China's early ruling classes, when strength and bravery were characteristics admired in leaders. There are even references to some of these leaders grappling with wild beasts. There are also descriptions of individuals skilled in empty-handed techniques against edged weapons. Thus, boxing appears generally to have been considered a life-and-death combat skill that supplemented weapons, although there are indications that it was treated as a sport in some circumstances.

However, about 209 B.C., the first emperor of Qin designated wrestling as the official ceremonial military sport. Then, for the first time, commentaries in the *Han History Bibliographies* (ca. A.D. 90) clearly distinguish between boxing and wrestling. This work lists six chapters (no longer extant) on boxing, *shoubo* (hand striking) as it was then called. Boxing is described under the subcategory "military skills," alongside archery, fencing, and even a form of football, for "practice in using the hands and feet, facilitating the use of weapons, and organizing to ensure victory in both attack and defense" (Gu 1987, 205). So by the Warring States period (475–221 B.C.), boxing had become a basic military skill to develop strength and agility for use of weapons in hand-to-hand combat by the mass infantry forces of that time.

After the Southern Song capital was established at Hangzhou in 1135, the modern term *quan* (fist) appears and replaces shoubo as the common term for boxing. This seemingly abrupt change may have been based on common usage in the dialect spoken in the new capital. Some support for this view can be found in a later work by Zhu Guozhen (ca. 1621), who notes that boxing was more commonly known as *daquan* in his day (the term introduced during the Song period and still used today), but was called *dashou* (hitting hands) around Suzhou.

One contemporary Song author describes *shiquan* (employing the fists) as different from wrestling but similar to the skills used in the military. He thus infers that there was a popular form of boxing, similar to but not quite the same as that practiced in the military. This statement was probably based on the fact that military boxing was limited to practical, no-frills techniques employed in military formations, primarily to supplement the use of weapons, while the popular forms were likely to have been more individualistic and performance oriented, in the manner Ming general Qi Jiguang (1528–1587) condemned as "flowery."

During the short, oppressive Mongol rule (1206–1368) that followed the Song, Chinese (called *Hanren*) were prohibited from practicing martial arts, but opera scores from the period reveal that boxing was included in military scenes of the operatic repertoire. This dramatic use of boxing undoubtedly encouraged the "flowery" phenomenon General Qi noted.

The Ming period (1368–1644) opens the first window in China's long history through which to get an illustrated glimpse of Chinese boxing. The Ming experienced a chronic rash of large-scale Japanese and indigenous marauding and piracy in the southern coastal provinces during the mid-sixteenth century—an environment conducive to the application of traditional military martial arts. The ultimate solution came in the form of a well-led, disciplined volunteer peasant force trained in hand-to-hand combat by General Qi Jiguang and others. The existence of such a force in turn demanded a bottom-up training program supported by standardized, illustrated, easy-to-understand manuals that set an example and contributed greatly to what we now know about the martial arts in general and boxing in particular. General Qi Jiguang's "Boxing Classic," a chapter in his *New Book of Effective Discipline* (ca. 1561), not only provides illustrations of the thirty-two forms Qi selected from the most well-known styles of the

Chinese children in a martial arts class in Beijing, November 1997. (Karen Su/Corbis)

day, but also records the names of sixteen of these styles for posterity. Prior to Ming times, boxing had only been mentioned in generic terms. Writings by several other Ming-period authors further raise the number of known styles to about thirty-six. These writings also offer insights into boxing techniques such as *changquan* (long fist) and *duanda* (short hitting), and they reveal a number of related boxing skills, including *pofa* (breaking), *jiefa* (escaping), *nafa* (seizing), and *diefa* (falling), some of which could be categorized as independent fighting systems, which show a striking similarity to Japanese jûjutsu.

According to the *Ming History* (Zhang 1936), boxing was even included in the official military examinations toward the end of the Wanli era (1573–1620), possibly in recognition of General Qi Jiguang's successes. Qi realized that boxing, in itself, was not particularly useful in battle, but that it was a confidence builder and provided the necessary foundation for effective use of the traditional weapons with which most of his troops were armed.

During this same period, some monks from Shaolin Monastery volunteered individually and in groups to help fight pirates. They were known to have practiced boxing, but no specific style of boxing was named for the monastery. Their main claim to fame lay in their skill with iron staves, and

A martial artist in Beijing practices Chinese boxing, one of the oldest elements of Chinese culture still practiced. (Karen Su/Corbis)

on one occasion their heroic exploits earned them the everlasting reputation of Shaolin Monk Soldiers.

With the Manchu conquest of China in 1644, Chinese boxing became politicized, perhaps to a greater degree than it had ever been before. Among his writings, the pro-Ming historian, Huang Zongxi, included comments on an epitaph dated 1669 (1936, 5a–6b) that appear to have been misinterpreted ever since. In the context of the times, his description of an External School of boxing originating in Buddhist (foreign religion) Shaolin Monastery meeting its match in an Internal School originating on Daoist (indigenous religion) Mount Wudang can be seen as symbolizing Chinese opposition to the Manchus. However, less critical individuals took this piece literally as a serious discourse on Chinese boxing theory, an interpretation that has encouraged a degree of divisiveness in the Chinese martial arts community to this day.

Other anti-Manchu intellectuals and teachers such as Yan Yuan (1635–1704) practiced boxing and other martial arts as part of what they considered to be a well-rounded education. Heterodox religious groups such as the Eight Trigrams and White Lotus sects used martial arts for self-defense and included them in their religious practices. The Heaven and Earth Society, otherwise known as the Triads or Hong League, practiced martial arts, including *Hongquan* (Hong Boxing), and attempted to identify their organization with the fame of Shaolin Monastery. Professional martial artists ran protection agencies and escort bureaus to protect commercial enterprises and the homes of the wealthy, and to ensure the safe transport of valuable items. Finally, there were various protest groups such as the Boxers United in Righteousness, whose antiforeign movement in

1900 brought the retaliation of an eight-nation expeditionary force comprising British, French, Italian, Russian, German, Japanese, Austro-Hungarian, and American troops.

The boxer's fists and talismans proved no match for bullets as China entered the twentieth century. Under the Manchu Qing dynasty they were a symbol of China's backwardness, but after the Revolution of 1911, the traditional martial arts became a symbol of nationalism when they were introduced into the public school system as a uniquely Chinese form of physical fitness.

One survey conducted in 1919 identified 110 different boxing styles being practiced throughout the country (73 in the Yellow River region of north China, 30 in the Yangze River region, and 7 in the Pearl River area). Many professional martial artists opened their own *guoshuguan* (training schools), and some became associated with a government-sponsored Central Martial Arts Institute that was established in the Nationalist capital of Nanjing in 1927. The institute was originally organized into Wudang (internal—including only taijiquan, baguazhang, and xingyiquan) and Shaolin (external—comprising all other styles) branches according to the Chinese view of their two major boxing schools. Using boxing as its foundation, the institute produced martial arts instructors for public service. Prior to the anti-Japanese War of Resistance (1937–1945), nationwide form and contact competitions were held, with mixed results.

The Nationalists abandoned the program when they retreated to Taiwan in 1949, but the Communists built upon its foundation. Under the Physical Culture and Sports Commission, they integrated traditional martial arts into their physical education programs and developed standardized routines of *changquan* (long boxing), *nanquan* (southern boxing), taijiquan, and weapons routines for nationwide practice and competition.

During the Great Proletarian Cultural Revolution (1966–1976), aspects of the traditional martial arts, such as teacher-disciple relationships, were severely criticized, and many old, valuable documents were destroyed in what could be termed a decade of blind ignorance. Since the Cultural Revolution, especially after 1979, there has been a revival of the program, although interest in state-sponsored activities has dwindled.

Meanwhile, there has been recognition of the fact that the earlier emphasis on standardized routines has resulted in neglect and loss of some as-

A modern picture of a Buddhist monastery on Mount Wudang. (Courtesy of Paul Brians)

pects of the traditional arts, particularly in the practical application of fighting techniques. But Chinese boxing and the martial arts in general have already begun to take on a new life outside China.

The world is beginning to realize that the term *kung fu* or *gongfu* really means "skill" in Chinese, not "boxing," and that Chinese boxing has a long and colorful history, deeply rooted in Chinese society and culture for many centuries before the founding of Shaolin Monastery (ca. A.D. 425).

Stanley E. Henning

See also Animal and Imitative Systems in Chinese Martial Arts; Baguazhang (Pa Kua Ch'uan); Boxing, Chinese Shaolin Styles; Taijiquan (Tai Chi Ch'uan); Xingyiquan (Hsing I Ch'uan)

References

Ban Gu. 1936. *Qianhanshu* (Former Han History). Shanghai: Zhonghua Shuju.

Chen Menglei. 1977. *Gujin Tushu Jicheng* (Encyclopedia of Ancient and Modern Literature). Taibei: Dingwen Shuju.

Cui Hong. 1886. *Shiliuguo Chunqiu* (Sixteen State Spring and Autumn Annals). Hebei: Guanshu Chu.

Esherick, Joseph W. 1987. *The Origins of the Boxer Uprising.* Berkeley: University of California Press.

Fang Xuanling. 1936. *Jin Shu* (Jin History). Shanghai: Zhonghua Shuju.

Giles, Herbert A. 1906. "The Home of Jiu Jitsu." *Adversaria Sinica* 5: 132–138.

Gongyang Gao. 1936. *Gongyang Zhuan* (The Gongyang Commentaries). Shanghai: Zhonghua Shuju.

Gu Shi. 1987. *Hanshu Yiwenzhi Jiangshu* (Explanation of the Han History Bibliographies). Shanghai: Guji Chubanshe.

Guliang Yi. 1936. *Guliang Zhuan* (The Guliang Commentaries). Shanghai: Zhonghua Shuju.

Guo Xifen. 1970 [1919]. *Zhongguo Tiyushi* (Chinese Physical Culture History). Taibei: Taiwan Commercial Press.

Hao Yixing. 1934. *Erya Yishu* (Meaning of and Commentary on the Erya). Shanghai: Shangwu Yinshuguan.

Henning, Stanley E. 1981. "The Chinese Martial Arts in Historical Perspective." *Military Affairs* [now *Journal of Military History*] 45, no. 4: 173–178.

———. 1995. "General Qi Jiguang's Approach to Martial Arts Training." *The Chenstyle Journal* 3, no. 2: 1–3.

———. 1998. "Guojia Tiwei Wushu Yanjiu Yuan, bianzuan (National Physical Culture and Sports Commission Martial Arts Research Institute, editors and compilers). Zhongguo Wushu Shi (Chinese Martial Arts History)." *China Review International* 5, no. 2: 417–424.

———. 1999. "Review of Zhongguo Wushushi (Chinese Martial Arts History) by Xi Yuntai," Beijing: People's Physical Culture Publishers, 1985. In *Journal of Asian Martial Arts* 8, no. 1: 103–105.

Huang Zongxi. 1936. *Nanlei Wending* (Nanlei's Definitive Writings). Shanghai: Zhonghua Shuju.

Kang Gewu. 1995. *The Spring and Autumn of Chinese Martial Arts: 5000 Years.* Santa Cruz, CA: Plum Publishing.

Liu Xi. 1985. *Shiming* (Elucidation of Names). Vol. 78, *Sikuquanshu Huiyao* (Major Works from the Complete Collection of Books in the Four Repositories). Taibei: Taiwan Shijie Shuju.

Meng Yuanlao, et al. 1962. *Dongjing Menghualu Waisizhong* (Record of Reminiscences of the Eastern Capital and Four Other Works). Shanghai: Zhonghua Shuju.

Murray, Dian H., and Qin Baoqi. 1994. *The Origins of the Tiandihui: The Chinese Triads in Legend and History.* Stanford: Stanford University Press.

Naquin, Susan. 1976. *Millenarian Rebellion in China.* New Haven: Yale University Press.

———. 1981. *Shantung Rebellion: The Wang Lun Uprising of 1774.* New Haven: Yale University Press.

———. 1985. "The Transmission of White Lotus Sectarianism in Late Imperial China." In *Popular Culture in Late Imperial China.* Edited by David Johnson, Andrew J. Nathan, and Evlyn S. Rawski. Berkeley: University of California Press.

Qi Jiguang. 1988 [1561]. *Jixiao Xinshu* (New Book of Effective Discipline). Edited by Ma Mingda. Beijing: Renmin Tiyu Chubanshe.

Sima Qian. 1972. *Shiji* (Historical Records). Edited by Takigawa Kintaro. Shiji Huizhu Kaozheng. Reprint, Taibei: Hongwen Shuju.

Wu Wenzhong. 1967. *Zhongguo Jinbainian Tiyushi* (History of Physical Education in China over the Last Hundred Years). Taibei: Taiwan Commercial Press.

Yates, Robin. 1988. "New Light on Ancient Chinese Military Texts: Notes on Their Nature and Evolution, and the Development of Military Specialization in Warring States China." *T'oung Pao* 74: 211–248.

Zhang Bo, ed. 1892. *Han Wei Liu Chao Baisan Mingjia Jishu* (Collected Writings of 103 Famous Authors of the Han, Wei, and Six Dynasties). Vols. 18–19, *Wei Wendi Ji* (Writings of Emperor Wen of Wei).

Zhang Tingyu. 1936. *Ming Shi* (Ming History). Shanghai: Zhonghua Shuju.

Zhu Guozhen. 1959 [1621]. *Yongchuang Xiaopin* (Yongchuang Essays). Beijing: Zhonghua Shuju.

Zuo Qiuming. 1966. *Zuo Zhuan* (Zuo Commentaries). Translated by James Legge. Vol. 5, *The Chinese Classics.* Taibei: Wenxing Shudian.

Boxing, Chinese Shaolin Styles

Chinese boxing systems have commonly been understood in terms of dichotomies: hard versus soft, external versus internal, northern versus southern, Wudang versus Shaolin. Using these folk categories, the "Shaolin tradition" has been understood as covering those systems that are hard and external as distinct from soft and internal. The Shaolin arts may be further subdivided into northern and southern styles.

The distinction between northern and southern boxing reflects traditional beliefs in China that the martial systems that developed in the north (using the Chang River [also known as the Yangtze] as a point of demarcation) emphasize kicks and long-distance attacks, while southern systems rely on hand techniques and short-range combat. The source of both styles of fighting was believed to be the Buddhist Shaolin Temple. Although these traditional assumptions have been questioned recently, the power of this tradition and the related tradition of a dichotomy between internal (Daoist) and external (Buddhist) arts is demonstrated by the adoption of a variation of the traditional categories of *Wudang* (internal, *taijiquan, baguazhang,* and *xingyiquan*) and *Shaolin* (external, all other styles) for the two major branches of their Chinese boxing schools by the Nationalist government–sponsored Central Martial Arts Institute in 1927. In the 1950s, following the Nationalists' lead, the Communists' Physical Culture and Sports Commission integrated traditional martial arts into their physical education programs and developed standardized practice and competitive routines for boxing labeled as *changquan* ("long boxing"), *nanquan* ("southern boxing"), and *taijiquan* (the only one of the internal systems so enfranchised). The distinction of northern (legs) versus southern (hands) that is used as a traditional designation between the "external" (or Shaolin) arts is actually derived from a very ancient aphorism that alludes to what have been regarded as the main practices of each specific method. These differences are attributed to geographic conditions that were believed to play a role in the development of both northern fist arts, or *beiquan shu,* and southern fist arts, or *nanquan shu.*

According to this traditional theory, the people who lived in the north occupied an environment that was physically and socially different from southern China. The area in which they lived was characterized by wide-open expanses. Land transportation required skilled horsemanship. Moreover, since the cultural centers of China from approximately 2200 B.C. were located in the north, the population had greater access to education than did inhabitants of southern China. To a degree at least, the quality of a man's education was to be seen in the quality of his calligraphy. These facts provide the raw material for the traditional theory of the north-south distinction.

The martial arts popularized in the north were called by many names, among them *changquan* (long fist) and Northern Shaolin. "Long fist" is a double entendre: The forms themselves were quite long, but more than that, the movements were elongated, with many acrobatic movements, particularly kicks, in them. These characteristics are believed to be due in part to the geographic area in which practitioners lived. The living conditions made their legs quite strong, and they capitalized on that through the development and use of all manner of punishing kicks. Combat on an open, stable surface encouraged the development of wide stances and high leaps and kicks. The desire to protect the hands also influenced the fighting styles. An injured hand impairs the ability to write well.

In contrast, the people south of the Chang River were relegated to very cramped living conditions. In this area of rice paddies, coastal shallows, and urbanized settings, many worked the waters in trade, commerce, and fishing. In fact, a portion of the inhabitants spent most of their lives on the boats that sailed the coasts and inland waterways. The primary demands for physical labor were placed on the muscle groups of the upper body. As another contrast, the distance from the cultural centers of the north meant in many cases that a southerner's education was gained at home, and the vast majority of them were functional illiterates who relied on professional readers to read official decrees and personal letters and to write for them when the need arose. The factors of relatively greater upper body strength and the decreased need for fine-motor skill utilizing finger dexterity led to a reliance on punching as opposed to kicking techniques.

The "short-hitting" styles of the south were marked by constricted, inclose movements, ones that could be employed in tight alleyways, on the decks of boats, and in other cramped quarters. The southern fighting styles

A 74-year-old Buddhist monk practices boxing exercises at a Shaolin monastery near Zengzhou, Henan, China, 1981. (Lowell Georgia/Corbis)

also developed, for the most part, shorter forms, although a given southern system (e.g., *Hung Gar* [pinyin *hongjiaquan*] and *Choy Lay Fut* [pinyin *cailifoquan*]) could contain a greater number of forms in its curriculum than some northern systems.

One might also surmise that the restrictions placed upon people due to the restrictions of various articles of clothing would play a role in defensive techniques as well. The cold climate of the north and the clothing adapted to such an environment would no doubt hinder the use of hand techniques, but to a lesser extent the use of the legs. The south was more subtropical, and the clothing appropriate for that environment allowed the unencumbered development of the upper-body techniques suitable for the social conditions previously described. Various weapons also saw their use dictated by their geographic location. In the north one would have the luxury of being able to use a long pole arm, such as a spear or long sword, and so those skills were more deeply researched and trained. In the south, where it was much more crowded and urbanized, the weapons that would find the most use were shorter. These included cleavers and similar chopping weapons, knives, short rods, and short swords.

The credit for the origin of both types of boxing is attributed to the Shaolin Temples and to necessity. Law enforcement during the formative period of Chinese boxing was often the province of important people with hired police forces and private standing armies. Commonly, villages were responsible for their own defenses against marauding bands of thieves, slavers, and other brigands who survived on what they could steal, whom they could sell off, and the services gained from those whom they could enslave. Other social services, particularly educational, were absent as well.

In this regard, similarities exist between European and Chinese feudal societies. In Europe during the Middle Ages, one of the only ways a person of low birth could gain an education was through the Roman Catholic Church. In medieval Europe, it was possible for a community to send the brightest of their progeny to one of the monasteries that dotted the landscape to learn Latin (the lingua franca of the era), mathematics, and rudimentary medical skills. After completing this education, the student returned home and used the knowledge to benefit the town from which he came. Also, a percentage of the monks who lived in the monasteries of that time were not merely men who had a calling from their God, but who were fugitives from the law, as well. In some cases, sanctuary from prosecution was their primary motivation. For example, those who had gained the disfavor of the nobility or had been in the ranks of a losing army might find a refuge by joining an order. Therefore, among the members of an order were former fighting men who had renounced their family ties and taken on different names. Records of thirteenth-century German monks practicing sword and buckler (small, round shield) combat as a martial sport, along with claims that knights were intimidated by the wrestling skills of medieval monks, demonstrate the availability and efficacy of fighting skills within monastery walls.

Similarly, in China Buddhist temples not only concerned themselves with the promulgation and study of Buddhism, but also served as sources of education in literacy, mathematics, and martial skills. The medical profession was also intertwined with the martial traditions. Soldiers had wounds that needed tending, training practices resulted in various injuries from blunt trauma and from weapons practice, and the monks had only themselves to rely on. Tradition maintains that the birth of acupuncture stemmed from soldiers who, upon receiving arrow wounds that were not fatal, found themselves cured or relieved of certain non-combat-related illnesses, pains, or other injuries.

Grand Master Rich Mooney demonstrates various defensive moves from Southern Shaolin Tiger Crane Fist, 2001. (Courtesy of Rich Mooney, Dragon Society International)

The temples were impromptu banks as well as storehouses for harvested grains. Because of this, the temples were also targets of brigands; therefore, they had to have a standing army of their own to defend themselves from outside attacks.

When novitiates entered monastic life, they not only gave up their allegiance to their natural family; they also gave up their life on the outside and their allegiance to secular rulers. Those who became monks out of desperation found a new life, and those who became monks because of outside necessity kept their heads firmly attached to their shoulders. Over a period of centuries they collected various techniques that had helped the former soldiers stay alive on the battlefield, and this accumulation of knowledge gave rise to introspective researching aimed at finding the best fighting methods. These methods were then codified, and this codification, in turn, gave rise to many systems of self-defense and martial science.

The monasteries in the West did not maintain the study of the arts of war in the same fashion as those in the East, although religious military orders such as the Knights Templar attest to the strong links between the martial and the religious, at least in the European medieval period. Some attribute the eventual neglect of the martial arts in European monastic tradition to the development of military technology, namely the development of firearms and artillery. Social factors were of course major factors, as well. In the East, however, warfare continued to be associated with the monastic life. In China, the most famous and well known of these temples came to be known as "Shaolin." Tradition maintains that there were actually five of these tem-

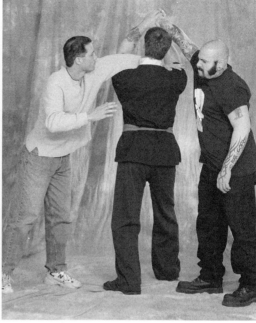

Grand Master Rich Mooney demonstrates various defensive moves from Southern Shaolin Tiger Crane Fist, 2001. (Courtesy of Rich Mooney, Dragon Society International)

ples over a period of many hundreds of years. One of these temples, located in Henan province, in northern China, has been restored.

According to tradition, in the Henan temple there was a cadre of religious monks and also a cadre of fighting monks. The sole duty of the fighting monks was to train and to ensure the safety of the temple in the event of attack. The wealth of martial arts skills became systematized, and various curricula were developed under the guidance of the warrior monks. Moreover, many of the religious monks also gained an interest in personal self-defense. When their duties took them outside the temple walls, they were easy targets because of a prohibition against carrying weapons. Therefore, they had to rely on the various skills that they could develop within the monastery. Tradition states that in time these monks became known for their fighting prowess, and also for the marks that were branded into their arms, the famed Dragon and Tiger of Shaolin.

The mere exposure of these marks to an attacker was reputed to end confrontations on the spot. It has been surmised that in the villages they visited, not only did they expound the path of the Buddha to those who had an interest, but they also instructed locals in boxing and the use of weapons.

Written history notes the prowess of the monks in an antipirate campaign in the sixteenth century, and the written record agrees with the legends of Shaolin staff techniques. Thus, it is correct to assume that the Shaolin Temple was a repository of fighting knowledge. It is incorrect, however, to assume that the development of martial arts was a primary function of the Shaolin Temple, and that all fighting arts of China may be traced back to the Shaolin arts. In fact, at this time, the People's Republic of China recognizes only two forms as being authentic Shaolin fist methods: the *Xiao Hing Quan* (little red fist) and the *Da Hong Quan* (big red fist). In contemporary usage, the appellation "Shaolin" functions primarily to establish credibility for the lineage and therefore the efficacy of a given style.

Other arts that did not claim to originate in the temple were no less effective or devastating. In fact, other arts, especially the "internal arts," such as *xingyiquan, baguazhang, liu ho ba fa,* and *taijiquan,* are regarded as being diametrically opposed to the Shaolin arts. These arts make up the "internal" martial arts, while the arts of Shaolin are thought of as "external" martial disciplines. The internal methods primarily seek to cultivate the esoteric inner strength known as qi. The external methods have traditionally been seen as relying mostly on building up muscle and bone strength. On the other hand, the famous five animals of Shaolin—the Dragon, Tiger, Crane, Snake, and Leopard—were said to develop not only physical but mental attributes. The Dragon forms were practiced to develop an indomitable spirit, the Tiger to develop bone strength, the Crane to develop the tendons, or sinews, the Snake to develop the qi, and the Leopard to develop speed. The origins of both the internal and external styles are similarly the subject of traditional narrative, which is subject to distortion. In fact, Stanley Henning claims that both the origin legends (of the external styles in Shaolin and the internal arts at a site on Wudang Mountain) are derived from a single political allegory.

In time, and based upon the geographic location of the various temples, tradition maintains the styles were modified to suit their respective environments. As noted earlier, the stylists of the north became extremely skilled in kicking techniques, and those in the south devoted themselves to striking techniques. The major feature of northern styles of Chinese boxing is that the techniques avail themselves of greater acrobatic methods and a wider variety of kicking techniques. These types of movements can be found in styles such as *Mi Zhong Lo Han* (Lost Track Lohan [Buddhist disciple]), *Tanglangquan* (Praying Mantis Boxing), and *Bei Ying Jow Pai* (Northern Eagle Claw; pinyin *Bei Yingzhaoquan*). The major features of the southern methods are the lower stances and a greater emphasis on punching techniques and close-range methods, including *qinna* (grasp and seize) and *dianxue* (spot hitting), in Cantonese called *dim mak* (death touch). This emphasis can be seen in such arts as *Nan Shaolin Hu Hao Quan* (Southern Shaolin Tiger Crane Fist); *yongchun,* better known by the Cantonese term w*ing chun* (Eternal Spring); various *Hequan* (Crane Boxing) styles; and Choy Lay Fut Boxing (pinyin Cailifoquan). The Southern

Shaolin arts have quite a diversity of short-range weapons, but also train in long-pole weapons, though not to a greater extent.

The Northern Shaolin Temple is now a tourist attraction in Henan province, China. The Southern Shaolin Temple was located in what is now Putian County in the Fujian province, and went by the name Lingquanyuan Temple. The other temples that called themselves Shaolin were in Wudang, Guangdong, and Er Mei (also spelled Emei), each with its own unique brand and flavor of martial art culture and discipline. Yang Jwing-Ming and Jeffery Bolt in their traditionally based brief history of the Shaolin systems set the number at ten.

At certain times in the history of China, various emperors called upon the monks to defend the state against foreign incursion. One spectacular event is a well-chronicled one, in which a group of monks went to the aid of the Tang emperor Li Shimin (A.D. 600–649), also known as Emperor Taizong. Although the narratives of Li Shimin have been submitted to the distortions of oral tradition and popular vernacular literature (telling of intervention by celestial dragons, for example), the traditions surrounding his reign chronicle events in which thirteen monks helped to save his life. He tried to reward them with official court posts, probably in an effort to keep them under his surveillance and control. They decided to refuse the honor, but the emperor authorized them to build a force of warrior monks in case their services were needed again.

According to the legends of the Hong League (better known as the Triad Society) summarized by Fei-ling Davis in *Primitive Revolutionaries of China,* in the late seventeenth century (around 1674) the Shaolin monks of Fujian Monastery were called upon by the Qing emperor Kangxi (1664–1722) to defend against invading tribes of Eleuths. According to some sources, a former Ming patriot named Cheng Wan Tat led the monks. They were successful in their mission, and again they were offered high court postings, which they politely refused. This was a major mistake, for the emperor's ears were filled with the idea that such a group, so small yet so powerful, must pose a threat to national security. As a result, the emperor ordered the Shaolin Temples razed and all in them slaughtered.

Luckily efforts to exterminate the monks were unsuccessful. According to legend, five survived, which hardly seems a large enough number to have perpetuated the Shaolin arts, but this aspect of the story is far more credible than the magical yellow clouds, grass sandals turning into boats, and wooden swords sprouting from the ground that permitted the successful flight (Davis 1977, 62–64).

The vested interest of the anti-Qing/pro-Ming secret societies in Shaolin traditions becomes apparent in the narrative of the subsequent exploits of the Five Ancestors (as the fugitives came to be called). Many of the monks went underground and formed patriotic societies determined to overthrow the unjust regime that had almost wiped them out. In support of this tradition, many commentators (e.g., Yang and Bolt) argue that the traditional Shaolin salute, the right fist covered by the left palm, originated as a secret society symbol. The Chinese character for the Ming dynasty is composed of the symbols for sun and moon, which together mean "bright." The positions of the hands in that salute formation fairly closely resemble that pictograph. By the use of that salute, people came to know each other as supporters of the same cause, to restore the Ming and overthrow the Qing. Many of the refugee monks went to work at a variety of occupations, such as opera, which always featured martial scenes. Many opera companies would ply the waters and travel in their trademark red boats.

In time, tradition maintains, these boats played two important roles in the history of the external Shaolin arts. They served as crucibles for blending the combat arts of north and south, and the plays that were acted out came to embody subtle messages for resistance members about meeting places and anti-Qing activities. The oral traditions of many external systems, which look to Shaolin as their point of origin, maintain a link between Shaolin anti-Qing sentiments, martial arts, and elements of popular culture. The Lion Dance, for example, is performed at auspicious events, such as the openings of new businesses, and New Year festivals. At the end of a Lion Dance the lion goes up a pole to catch a head of lettuce to eat. The expression used to describe this feat is "cai qing" (Cantonese "choi qing"), which literally means "Get the green." It also derides the Qing dynasty, since the term "qing" is a homonym for the word "green" but could also be taken to mean "Get the Qing dynasty." Lucky money in a red envelope was given to the lion dancers, and it may be surmised that these funds were used to support various rebel causes that were popular at the time.

The transmission of fighting arts also took place along trade routes that crisscrossed China, including the Silk Road, which led all the way to the outer reaches of the Roman Empire. There is no doubt that practitioners of both northern and southern styles, internal and external systems, met as members of caravan guards assigned to take loads of merchandise to their destinations. Exchanges of information for both armed and unarmed techniques ensued, for the length of one's life often came down to the combat skills developed in as many areas as possible. A good northern stylist learned to use fists as effectively as feet. A good southern stylist learned that one had to be an effective kicker as well as excelling at close-quarter conflict. The same held true for the use of weapons, and in this context all manner of them flourished, including maces, clubs, whips of leather and chain, darts, dirks, daggers, swords, and pole arms.

Time went on, but the Ming dynasty was never restored. However, there continued to be an association between secret societies, radical religion, and the martial arts. The results of this materialized in the activities of the "Righteous and Harmonious Fists" at the turn of the twentieth century, which culminated in the Boxer Rebellion (1900). In 1911, the Triads played a role in the overthrow of the Qing in the Republican Revolution. Afterwards, however, the once patriotic groups became less and less beneficent, and became more concerned with criminal activity, slavery, drug running, and other socially detrimental activities. Throughout the history of these groups, martial arts had had a greater ritual than practical significance in their activities. As with the boxing systems mentioned earlier, a Shaolin association served a need for validating and legitimizing and was not necessarily a genuine point of origin.

The Shaolin hard-fist styles played an influential role in the development of martial arts outside China as well. Trade and diplomacy allowed for the dissemination of the Shaolin external tradition throughout East and Southeast Asia. Okinawan and Japanese martial arts can serve as examples. After the Battle of Sekigahara (A.D. 1600), the Shimazu clan, despite opposition to shôgun Tokugawa Ieyasu (1542–1616), was allowed to remain in charge of Satsuma on the island of Kyushu. Further, in 1609 the Shimazu were given the shogunate's permission to launch an invasion of Okinawa. Some have suggested that the invasion was allowed in order to dissipate Shimazu energies in directions other than the Tokugawa shogunate. Ruling the islands from their base on Satsuma and through the Ryûkyûan monarchy, the Shimazu forbade the practice of native martial arts. Also, most weapons were confiscated under a weapons edict, originally passed by Okinawan ruler Shô Shin (who was in power from 1477 to 1526), forbidding the wearing of the swords and the stockpiling of arms, and eventually banning the import of bladed weapons in 1699.

The Okinawans, however, had developed a long-term relationship with the Chinese, particularly with the Fujian province, and tradition holds that during this period some of their best fighters traveled to China to learn martial arts and thus build upon an exchange initiated in 1393 with the settlement of the "thirty-six families" who emigrated from China to Kuninda (Kume village) in the district of Naha. One art in particular, *Sukunai Hayashi Tomari Te* (Shaolin Small Pine Tomari [a village in Okinawa] Hand), manifests the influence of Chinese Crane styles. Contemporary systems maintain the Chinese influence. For example, *Uechi-ryû*, the *ryûha* (style) founded by Uechi Kanbun, was based on the Pangai Noon (pinyin banyingruan, hard-soft) of Zhou Zihe (Chu Chi Wo; Okinawan Shu Shi Wa), a Fujianese teacher suspected of having ties to the Ming secret societies that are alleged to have played a central role in the history of the external Shaolin styles.

Also, during the Ming dynasty, a monk by the name of Chen Yuanpin

(Gempin in Japanese) was sent to the court of the Japanese emperor, ostensibly to teach pottery. It was also surmised that the monk fled to Japan after arousing the ire of an official at the Chinese court. After a time, Chen befriended a few samurai who lived in the area where he was staying. He taught these three samurai "methods of catching a man." Those methods are also known as qinna (or ch'in na in the Wade-Giles method of romanization). Qinna means "to grasp and seize," and elements of the art of grasping and seizing are a facet of many Chinese martial arts. The methods Chen taught to these samurai were to later take on a life of their own and were collectively christened Kito-ryû, a form of jûjutsu.

Other similarities are also to be seen in Okinawan kenpô in the practice of methods called *kyûsho* and *tuite*. Kyûsho is essentially the striking of vital points, much in the same way as it is practiced as dianxue, better known by the Cantonese name dim mak. Tuite is virtually the same art as qinna. Qinna and dianxue are usually performed together. When applying a joint lock, one also attacks pressure points, with the goal of weakening an opponent's ability to fight, controlling movement through limiting the range of motion, and sapping the will to fight through inflicting pain in sensitive areas. Kyûsho and tuite methods were popularized in the 1990s through the efforts of men like Grand Masters Rick Moneymaker and Tom Muncy of the Dragon Society International. Therefore, although an art may utilize Japanese *gi* (uniforms) and Japanese terms, the history of the method may well reveal a Chinese connection.

The role of Shaolin Boxing was reoriented when the Communists came to power in 1949. The government of the People's Republic undertook many reforms. One area toward which reform was directed concerned plans for improving the health of the citizens. Famine, plagues, and war had sapped the vitality of many of the people who had survived from the first Japanese incursion in the 1930s to the time when Chiang Kai Shek (pinyin Jiang Jieshi) and thousands of others fled to Taiwan. A group of martial artists and government officials came upon the idea of popularizing the practice of taijiquan.

The goal was to create a healthy populace without encouraging sophisticated martial abilities. The relationships between the Triads, martial arts, and antigovernment activity remained in the memory of the bureaucrats as well. Mao Zedong's first writings were replete with exhortations to empower the mind and make savage the body, but efforts were made to make the practice of martial arts benefit the party in its quest for total domination of the people. Later, the Red Guard took this to heart during the ten years of the Cultural Revolution, from 1966 through 1976, when the practice of the ancient ways was forbidden as being antiquated and superstitious.

In order to accomplish the goals of a healthy populace and to create a new orientation for martial arts suitable to the new Communist China, a two-faceted program came into being: a standardized form of taijiquan and the concept of *wushu*. Taiji was promoted as a few simple and standardized routines, the Yang twenty-four-section form, and the five-section form. All instruction was geared toward improving and maintaining health, and practical application was discouraged. *Wushu* originally meant "martial," or "military," arts, and as such this is the proper term for those systems designated kung fu in contemporary popular culture. In the postmodern sense of the Communist Party, however, the term designated acrobatic martial gymnastics.

This program gave the people what they wanted, but only in a form modified by the Communist Party. Many of the wushu forms seen today are replete with high leaping kicks and fast and furious punches. There are also flips, somersaults, and other acrobatic maneuvers best performed by the young. Weapons forms have been developed as well, but only using what are called thunder blades, very light and very thin blades that fold and bend and make a loud noise, but that are far easier to handle than real combat-quality weapons. Wushu has its merits as a sport and art form, but the current system is not a traditional combat art.

There was a push in the last few years of the 1990s to promote what is called *san da* (loose hit) or *san shou* (loose hand). These are martial sports reminiscent of kickboxing, which allow various throws, locks, and sweeping techniques. The bouts have been compared to the earlier *Lei Tai* form of contest in which combatants, sans protective gear, would fight on a raised platform to see who had the better skills. A contestant tossed off the platform would be declared the loser. The no-holds-barred spectacles popularized in North and South America, Europe, and Japan during the 1990s undoubtedly gave impetus to san shou.

The state-sanctioned forms of boxing developed within the People's Republic of China may have eclipsed the traditional fighting arts, but they did not eradicate them. Even outside the mainland, practice of the traditional external (and internal) arts survives with refugees who fled after the Communist victory of 1949 to Hong Kong, Southeast Asia, the United States, Canada, Europe, and particularly Taiwan. Many external arts, in fact, have enjoyed a renaissance in new settings. Yongchun (more commonly known as wing chun), for example, can easily be found in most big cities in Europe and America, due probably to popularization by the late Hong Kong film actor Bruce Lee. The motion pictures of Jackie Chan (trained in Hong Kong opera), wushu great Pan Qingfu, wushu-trained actor Jet Li, and others from the 1990s through the turn of the twenty-first century have continued to popularize hard-style boxing and perpetuate the legendary connection of the Shaolin Temple to these styles.

Richard M. Mooney

See also Animal and Imitative Systems in Chinese Martial Arts; Baguazhang (Pa Kua Ch'uan); Boxing, Chinese; External vs. Internal Chinese Martial Arts; Karate, Okinawan; Kung Fu/Gung Fu/Gongfu; Political Conflict and the Martial Arts; Taijiquan (Tai Chi Ch'uan); Xingyiquan (Hsing I Ch'uan); Yongchun/Wing Chun

References

Bishop, Mark. 1989. *Okinawan Karate: Teachers, Styles and Secret Techniques.* London: A. C. Black.

Davis, Fei-ling. 1977. *Primitive Revolutionaries of China: A Study of Secret Societies in the Late Nineteenth Century.* Honolulu: University Press of Hawai'i.

Draeger, Donn, and Robert Smith. 1986. *Comprehensive Asian Fighting Arts.* Palo Alto, CA: Kodansha International.

Hegel, Robert E. 1985. "Distinguishing Levels of Audiences for Ming-Ch'ing Vernacular Literature." In *Popular Culture in Late Imperial China.* Edited by David Johnson, Andrew J. Nathan, and Evelyn S. Rawski. Berkeley and Los Angeles: University of California Press.

Henning, Stanley E. 1997. "Chinese Boxing: The Internal versus External Schools in the Light of History and Theory." *Journal of Asian Martial Arts* 6, no. 3: 10–19.

———. 1998. "Reflections on a Visit to the Shaolin Monastery." *Journal of Asian Martial Arts* 7, no. 1: 90–101.

———. 1998. "Southern Fists and Northern Legs: The Geography of Chinese Boxing." *Journal of Asian Martial Arts* 7, no. 3: 24–31.

Naquin, Susan. 1985. "The Transmission of White Lotus Sectarianism in Late Imperial China." In *Popular Culture in Late Imperial China.* Edited by David Johnson, Andrew J. Nathan, and Evelyn S. Rawski. Berkeley and Los Angeles: University of California Press.

Ratti, Oscar, and Adele Westbrook. 1973. *Secrets of the Samurai: The Martial Arts of Feudal Japan.* Rutland, VT: Charles E. Tuttle.

Reid, Howard. *The Fighting Arts: The Great Masters of the Martial Arts.* New York: Simon and Schuster.

Reid, Howard, and Michael Croucher. 1995 [1983]. *The Way of the Warrior: The Paradox of the Martial Arts.* Woodstock, NY: Overlook Press.

Wang Hongjun. 1988. *Tales of the Shaolin Monastery.* Translated by C. J. Lonsdale. Hong Kong: JPC Publications.

Wong Kiew Kit. 1966. *The Art of Shaolin Kung Fu: The Secrets of Kung Fu for Self-Defence, Health and Enlightenment.* Rockport, MA: Element Books.

Yang Jwing-Ming and Jeffery A. Bolt. 1982. *Shaolin Long Fist Kung Fu.* Burbank, CA: Unique Publications.

Boxing, European

Boxing is an ancient martial art combining hand strikes, controlled aggression, evasiveness, and bone-crushing force. The term *boxing* derives from the box shape of the closed hand, or fist, which in Latin is *pugnus* (hence the alternative terms *pugilism* and *fisticuffs*). *Pungent,* sharing the Indo-European root, describes the art rightly executed: "sharply painful, having a stiff or sharp point; marked by sharp incisive quality; caustic; being sharp and to the point." *Pugnus* derives from the Greek *pugme*, meaning "fist." Though boxing is mentioned in the ancient Hindu epic the *Mahabharata*, the origins of the art traditionally have been traced to ancient Greece. Both Homer and Virgil poeticize the art in their epics, and designs on ancient Greek pottery feature boxers in action. In Greek mythology, the divine boxer Pollux (also called Polydeuces), twin of Castor (with whom he presided over public games such as the Olympics), was said to have sparred with Hercules.

Ancient Greek and Roman pugilists developed the art of using the fists to pummel their opponents while wearing leather thongs and binders, known as *himantes* and *sphairai,* wrapped around the hands and wrists. The Greeks also used the *amphotidus,* a protective helmet; Egyptian boxers are depicted wearing similar headgear. Originally used to protect the wrists and fragile bones in the hands, the leather thongs (also known as cesti) were twisted so as to inflict greater injury. By the fourth century B.C., the thongs were replaced with hardened leather gloves. The first famous Greek boxer, Theagenes of Thaos, champion of the 450 B.C. Olympics, is said to have won 1,406 battles with the cesti, killing most of his opponents. In Roman times, the cestus was studded with metal, and the art was reduced to a gladiatorial spectacle.

The art of boxing in combat disappeared with the advent of heavy armor. Upon the introduction of the firearm—and the resulting obsolescence of armor—the "noble science of self-defense" was reborn. James Figg, an eighteenth-century British cudgel-fighter, swordsman, and the first modern boxing champion, was the central figure in this renaissance. When he opened his boxing school in London in 1719, the art of boxing had been dormant for over a thousand years—since the fall of the Roman Empire. Figg taught young aristocrats the art of self-defense by applying the precepts of modern fencing—footwork, speed, and the straight lunge—to fisticuffs. Thus, Western fistfighters learned to throw straight punches, the basis of modern boxing, from fencers. To some extent boxing replaced the duel, allowing men of all social classes to defend themselves and their honor without severely maiming or killing each other.

Despite this connection with fencing, boxing encounters during this early modern era were largely unstructured and highly uncivilized. Boxers fought bare-knuckle (without gloves), and wrestling, choking, throwing, gouging, and purring (stomping on one's opponent with spiked boots) were commonplace. The art began to be refined when Figg's successor, Jack Broughton (the "Father of Boxing"), drafted the first set of rules in 1741 after killing an opponent in the ring. According to "Broughton's Rules," a square was established in the center of the fighting ring (a circular border of spectators) to which fighters were to return after a knockdown, which marked the end of a "round." The down man was given thirty seconds to get back up; it was illegal to hit a down man, and wrestling below the waist was not allowed. Broughton also advocated the use of gloves in training. As an innovator of technique, he is known for "milling on the retreat," or blocking while moving back in order to draw an attacker into one's punches, compounding their force. By the end of the century Daniel Mendoza, a British-Portuguese Jew, refined the art by incorporating footwork, choreographed combinations, lateral movement, and fighting from a crouch. At 5 feet, 7 inches, and scarcely over 160 pounds, Mendoza's unique strategies enabled him to defeat much larger men and lay claim to the championship of England.

"Broughton's Rules" remained in effect until the Pugilists Protective Association, in an attempt to make boxing safer, issued the "London Prize Ring Rules" in 1838 after another death in the ring. Further revisions of these rules in 1853 and 1866 (by which time boxing was actively outlawed) banned choking and head butting, but still did not limit the number or length of rounds. In the interest of safety and fairness, weight classes were first introduced in the 1850s: heavy (over 156 pounds), middle (134–156 pounds), and light (under 134 pounds).

In 1866, a new set of rules was issued that completely revolutionized the art of boxing and that serves as the basis for the governance of the sport today. The "Queensbury Rules," named for the marquis of Queensbury, consisted of twelve clauses, prohibiting wrestling altogether and mandating a 24-square-foot ring, three-minute rounds with a one-minute rest period after each round, and the use of gloves. Subsequent revisions limited the number of rounds to twenty, set the minimum glove weight at six ounces, and introduced a scoring system of points.

The manifestation of the art of boxing in sport and spectacle has become a significant source of revenue and a nexus for social commentary. The martial art of boxing reaches its highest level in the professional athletes who perform in the prize ring. Boxing continues to be a primary self-defense technique employed by several military institutions and by law enforcement agencies such as the FBI. Boxing instruction remains widely disseminated at urban youth centers run by the Police Athletic League and YMCA. Bruce Lee's Jeet Kune Do and Israeli krav maga borrow heavily from boxing's arsenal. Boxing is also the striking art of choice of many martial artists, such as shootfighters (modern, professional no-holds-barred competitors) and grapplers, determined to augment their primary nonstriking skills.

The philosophy of boxing is simple: "Hit and don't get hit." Despite the simplicity of this premise, over the centuries the art has been developed to such a degree that it is often referred to as a science—"the sweet science." Boxing is both an art and a science, as boxers learn strategic moves and techniques, undergo expert coaching and training (Broughton referred to his boxing lessons as "lectures"), practice in specialized facilities with special equipment, and follow a special diet. Boxing is often likened to a chess game because boxers think several steps ahead. Boxers employ feints and gambits, sometimes allowing themselves to be hit in order to deliver a knockout blow, as chess players sacrifice a piece in order to reach checkmate or gain a positional advantage.

Though physical conditioning is essential, the most important element of boxing is mental and psychological: the capacity to relax, think clearly, and control oneself during a fight. Boxers are aware that their fights are often under way before the occurrence of any physical contact, and they are studied in psychological warfare and body language. They attempt to gain advantages by forcing their opponents to break eye contact or by feigning fear. Many boxers train their faces to be blank while shadowboxing in the mirror so that they do not convey (or telegraph) their punches with their facial expression and eyes.

Initiate boxers spend as long as their first year learning to "work the floor" before engaging in their first sparring session. Learning to move—even to stand—properly as a boxer is learning to walk all over again. The boxer stands relaxed on his toes in a crouch, slightly bent forward at the waist, left side forward at an angle, hands held up to throw punches and protect the face, elbows close in to the ribs to protect the body. The chin is dropped to the chest so that the line of vision is directed out and slightly up from beneath the eyebrows with the shoulders rounded to protect the chin.

The boxer moves forward with small steps by pushing off the back leg, which he "sits" on. To move backward, he reverses the process. Boxers stand on their toes in order to move nimbly and maintain balance. Boxers are trained to move in a continual circle to the left (when facing a right-handed opponent) and to keep the left foot outside the opponent's right foot (so as to have more target area while giving up less). Boxers train for hours, moving from side to side and in circles, forward and back, learning to punch with leverage while moving in any direction. The boxer learns to use his body as a gravitational lever; the boxer's force comes from the ground. The boxer's feet are also his most important defensive tools, maneuvering him out of harm's way.

The boxer's hands are the projectiles, and the boxer's punches are the tools that launch them. Boxers land their punches with three knuckles simultaneously—those of the middle, ring, and little fingers. The knuckle of the ring finger—the middle of the three—is the "aiming" knuckle. The boxer's own nose is the "target finder" or "sight" through which the fists are fired. Punches in boxing are thrown from the shoulders. Power is derived not so much from the muscles as from the joints and ligaments.

If there is one punch that defines boxing, it is the jab, a straight punch thrown from the shoulder with a short step forward. This lunge makes it possible to fight from a distance beyond even the range of kicks. The jab snaps forward from a blocking position; upon striking, the fist snaps back in direct line, retracing its path. Beginners traditionally practice only the jab from four to six months before learning the other punches. This is intended to raise the level of the weaker side of the body to that of the stronger. Thus the jab is the boxer's first lesson in self-control, and the primary indicator or measuring device of skill level in the art. The jab is also an external measuring tool, in the sense that it has been called a range finder, or means of determining and establishing the distance between the boxer and the opponent. It is used to keep the opponent at bay, to spark combinations, and to set up the KO (knockout) punch (the classic instance of which is the "one-two punch," left jab, straight right).

The straight right is thrown from the chest with a forward step from the right leg, and counterclockwise rotation of the fist, with the full twisting force of the hips. The left hook, apocryphally said to be the last punch to be developed in boxing, has an aura of mystery. It is delivered from the side with a bent elbow, palm down. Boxers are often taught to end every combination with a left hook. In order to throw the uppercut, the boxer bends his knees and explodes from floor to ceiling, palm facing the puncher. The blow is designed to land under the chin, brow, nose, or ribs. The overhand right and roundhouse punches tend to be used more often in Western films, barrooms, back alleys, and hockey games than in boxing rings, because they travel in wide, long, swooping arcs and are thus easier for a trained boxer to see and avoid. When a boxer can "get off" these punches outside the opponent's line of vision, however, they are highly effective.

Since the boxer's goal is to "stop" his opponent, the vulnerable organs and bones are primary targets. When boxers aim for the solar plexus, liver, kidneys, and ribs, though the targets change, the punches do not; boxers simply bend at the knees and throw the jabs, hooks, straight rights, and uppercuts to the body. Straight rights and lefts to the body are also thrown with the elbow, hip, and fist moving together in a plane with the palm facing up.

The so-called illegal tactics of boxing are not only integral to the martial art, they have always been a part of the sport. In addition to low blows and holding and hitting, which are commonly practiced in the ring and occasionally penalized, many techniques other than hitting with the knuckles above the waist are used. Rabbit punches are short, chopping blows thumped to the back of an opponent's neck, usually while in a clinch. These punches are outlawed in the ring because the back of the neck, vertebrae, base of the brain, and the nerves located there are particularly vulnerable. Boxers routinely try to trip each other and throw each other to the ground.

Korean boxer Joe Teiken gets advice from his manager Frank Tabor during a fight in California, 1933. (Courtesy of Joe Svinth)

Wrestling, hip throws, armlocks (and arm breaking submission holds), chokes, and to some extent biting are all part of the arsenal. Elbow and forearm blows are often used in combination. Gouging is also prevalent; the boxer simply extends his thumb while jabbing to catch the opponent's eye. The boxer's "third fist" is the head. The upper part of the cranium is used offensively to butt as well as defensively to break a punching opponent's hand or wrist. Boxers also attack with the fleshy part of the fist (knife-hand edge) and palm-heel strike. Though boxing is officially an empty-handed art, boxers have been known to load their gloves with anything from plaster of Paris to lead dust (recall the studded cestus), or to clench their fists around a solid object, such as a roll of quarters, making their punches much more damaging.

Boxing may be distinguished from many other martial arts by the practicality and intensity with which training in the art is undertaken. Such training takes place outside the gym in the form of running and cross-training, and inside the gym in the form of sparring, floor work, and exercises.

Roadwork, or running, is essential for boxing. It develops mental toughness, aerobic and anaerobic capacity, and the lower body. Boxers typically run early in the morning before any other training. Even in the bare-knuckle era, boxers ran up to 150 miles a week.

Full-contact sparring is perhaps the element of boxing training that contributes most to its effectiveness as a martial art. Though boxers wear protective headgear and gloves with more padding while sparring, nothing more simulates the conditions and experiences of real combat. In sparring boxers learn what it is like to be hit—hard, repeatedly, and from unexpected angles—how to adjust and recover from it, how to feign injury and well-being. In sparring, boxers learn the unchangeable truths, or reflexes, of the human body when it is hit in different ways, and therefore, where the body will be after it is hit by a certain punch in a certain place. As hazardous as it sounds, sparring is a valuable process through which boxers learn what it feels like to be stunned and knocked down, and how to fight on with a bloody nose or swollen eye. In addition, as brutal as it may seem, sparring is the mechanism through which most boxers condition their bodies for punishment. This conditioning enables them to withstand greater punishment in real combat.

Shadowboxing is an element of boxing training comparable to the forms of Asian martial arts. In the ring or in front of a large mirror, the boxer visualizes his opponent and goes through all the motions of fighting, punching in combination, slipping and blocking punches, and moving forward, back, and from side to side.

Practitioners of various other martial arts who take the opportunity to spar with boxers often come away amazed at their ability to punch powerfully, rapidly, and continually. It makes sense when one takes into account the daily training regimen of up to thirty minutes (ten three-minute rounds) boxers spend hitting cylindrical sand-filled leather or canvas hanging bags weighing up to 150 pounds. With the exception of sparring, working the heavy bag most simulates the experience of punching another person, and it provides invaluable training in learning to put together skillful punches with maximum force.

Boxers jump rope to improve stamina and coordination. The speed-bag (teardrop-shaped bag hung from a swivel) is used to develop hand-eye coordination, timing, arm strength, endurance, and rhythm. Trainers use punch pads, or punch mitts (padded mitts similar to a baseball catcher's mitt), to diagnose and correct slight errors in form in the way their boxers throw punches and combinations, and to instill conditioned responses.

Trainers often use such tools, together with repetition, to teach boxers to defend themselves, "see" openings, and throw punches without thinking. Such "automatic" punches are all the more dangerous, because they are seldom telegraphed.

Training partners take turns throwing the heavy leather medicine ball into each other's stomachs in order to psychologically prepare themselves for body blows while developing the arms, legs, endurance, hand-eye co-ordination, and leverage.

Exercises, or calisthenics, are usually done to conclude training for the day. Several varieties of sit-ups, crunches, and leg lifts strengthen the stomach muscles and abdomen. Pull-ups, push-ups, and dips develop the arms, back, latisimus dorsi, and chest. Some fighters also undergo light weight training and massage.

There has always been a certain amount of curiosity as to how boxers would fare against other martial artists in combat (and vice versa). This accounts for the public "mixed contests" that have been arranged from the beginning of the modern boxing era to the present. In 1897, in Carson City, Nevada, the heavyweight challenger (and later champion) Bob Fitzsimmons knocked out Ernest Roeber (wrestling) with one punch to the head. On December 31, 1908, in Paris, France, heavyweight boxer Sam McVey knocked out Tano Matsuda (jûjutsu) in ten seconds. On January 12, 1928, in Yokohama, Japan, Packey O'Gatty, a bantamweight boxer, knocked out Shimakado (jûjutsu) with one punch in less than four seconds. On September 11, 1952, in New Jersey, Marvin Mercer (wrestling) defeated Cuban heavyweight Omelio Agramonte in five rounds. On July 27, 1957, in Bangkok, Lao Letrit (Muay Thai) knocked out Filipino boxer Leo Espinosa in three rounds. Perhaps the most famous of these mixed matches occurred on June 25, 1976, in Tokyo, when heavyweight champion Muhammad Ali faced Antonio Inoki (wrestling). The result was a fifteen-round draw, and both men were seriously injured.

Loren Goodman

See also Europe; Masters of Defence; Pankration

References

Anderson, Dave. 1991. *In the Corner: Great Boxing Trainers Talk about Their Art*. New York: William Morrow.

Beaumont, Ned. 1997. *Championship Streetfighting: Boxing as a Martial Art*. Boulder: Paladin Press.

Collins, Nigel. 1990. *Boxing Babylon*. New York: Citadel Press.

Dempsey, Jack. 1983. *Championship Fighting: Explosive Punching and Aggressive Defense*. Downey, CA: Centerline Press.

Early, Gerald. 1994. *The Culture of Bruising: Essays on Prizefighting, Literature, and Modern American Culture*. Hopewell, NJ: Ecco Press.

Fleischer, Nat. 1959. *The Ring Record Book and Boxing Encyclopedia*. New York: The Ring Book Shop.

Gilbey, John F. 1986. *Western Boxing and World Wrestling: Story and Practice.* Berkeley: North Atlantic Books.

Oates, Joyce Carol. 1994. *On Boxing.* New York: Ecco Press.

Odd, Gilbert. 1989. *The Encyclopedia of Boxing.* Secaucus, NJ: Chartwell Books.

O'Dell, Derek, and O. F. Snelling. 1995. *The Boxing Album: An Illustrated History.* New York: Smithmark Publishers.

Wills, Gary. 1999. "The Great Black Hope." *New York Review,* February 4, 1999.

Brazilian Jiu-Jitsu

Brazilian jiu-jitsu is a grappling system that maintains both sport and combat forms. The art was derived from Japanese antecedents in twentieth-century Brazil.

Brazilian jiu-jitsu is virtually synonymous with the Gracie family, through whose lineage the system was passed and whose members modified the original Japanese art into its present state. Currently, however, instructors are not necessarily members of the Gracie family. Therefore, a distinction exists between Brazilian jiu-jitsu in general and Gracie Jiu-jitsu (a registered trademark).

The parent system of Brazilian jiu-jitsu is *Kôdôkan Jûdô,* and although Mitsuyo Maeda was not the first *jûdôka* (jûdô practitioner) in Brazil (this was a 1908 immigrant named Miura), he was certainly the first to be influential. Therefore some background on Maeda is required.

Maeda was born in Aomori Prefecture, Japan, in November 1878. At age 17 he moved to Tokyo where, on June 6, 1897, he joined Japan's most famous jûdô school, the Kôdôkan. There he was a direct student of Kôdôkan director Sakujiro Yokoyama, a man famous for his participation in challenge matches and fights.

By 1903 Maeda was graded fourth *dan* (fourth-degree black belt) in jûdô. Since the highest rank in those days was seventh dan, this suggests enormous talent. As a result, in 1904 he was invited to go to the United States with Tsunejiro Tomita, jûdô founder Kanô Jigorô's original student; the idea was for Tomita to explain the theory of jûdô while Maeda demonstrated its application. After arriving in the United States, however, Tomita was publicly challenged and defeated. This embarrassed Maeda, who went off on his own to become a professional wrestler, which in turn embarrassed the Kôdôkan.

From 1906 to 1908, Maeda wrestled in the United States, Britain, Belgium, and Spain, and it was in the latter country that he adopted his stage name of *Conde Koma.* The name was a pun: Read one way, it meant "Count of Combat," while read another it meant "Count of [Economic] Troubles."

From 1909 to 1913, Maeda wrestled in Mexico, Cuba, Costa Rica,

Rorion Gracie stands in front of the Gracie Jiu-jitsu Academy in Torrance, California, 2001. (Courtesy of Mike Lano, wrealano@aol.com)

and the Canal Zone, and he is said to have had only 2 defeats in over 2,000 matches. Unlike contemporary Brazilian jiu-jitsu stylists, who often attack with strikes and then follow up with groundwork, Maeda concentrated almost solely on chokes and joint locks. In other words, he did orthodox Japanese *ne-waza* (groundwork).

As a wrestler, Maeda was known for issuing challenges, including one to Jack Johnson, the reigning heavyweight boxing champion. Maeda's student Carlos Gracie followed this example by advertising in Brazilian newspapers his willingness to take on all comers. In turn, Carlos's younger brother, Hélio, challenged Joe Louis, while decades later Hélio's son Royce challenged Mike Tyson. Of course nothing came of these challenges, as there simply was not enough money in such contests to interest the boxers.

Maeda's methods have been described as more rough-and-tumble than is normal in jûdô. However, some of this apparent roughness is owed to the venue—professional wrestling takes place in music halls, circus tents, and armories rather than high school gyms, and is performed for the amusement of a paying crowd rather than judged on points.

There are differences in the accounts of how Maeda met the Gracies. In the accounts generally given by the Gracie family, Carlos Gracie, one of five sons of Gastão Gracie, began his training with Maeda in 1914 (or 1915). Other sources maintain that in 1915 Maeda was a member of a Japanese wrestling troupe known as "the Four Kings" and that he did not start working for the Queirollo Brothers' American Circus until 1917. If so, then the circus was probably where he met the Gracie family, as in 1916 Gastão Gracie was reportedly managing an Italian boxer associated with the Queirollo circus. At any rate, during the mid to late 1910s Maeda began teaching the rudiments of jûdô to Carlos Gracie.

Around 1922 Maeda left the circus to begin promoting Japanese immigration into Brazil. Three years later Gracie opened a wrestling gym in Rio de Janeiro, and this latter event marks the official birth of the system known today as Gracie Jiu-jitsu.

After Gracie quit training with Maeda, the core art underwent a process of modification. Many articles state that Gracie Jiu-jitsu's emphasis on groundwork is due to Maeda and Carlos Gracie not having *tatami* (mats) on which to practice falls. However, inasmuch as Japanese aikidô and Scandinavian *Glima* practitioners sometimes practice falls on wooden floors, it is likely that Gracie Jiu-jitsu's emphasis on groundwork owes more to the innovations of Hélio Gracie than to any desire to avoid injury on the part of Carlos Gracie or Maeda.

As a boy Hélio Gracie was the youngest and least robust of five brothers. Because of this, he soon learned to rely on technique rather than strength, and legs rather than arms. As an adult, he became a fairground wrestler, and when faced with larger opponents, he found it useful to go to the ground, where his greater skill at ground submission fighting served him well. So when the Japanese professional wrestler Masahiko Kimura wrestled Hélio Gracie in October 1951, "What he [Kimura] saw reminded him of the earlier jûdô methods that were rough and tumble. Prewar [prior to World War II] jûdô had body locks, leg locks, unusual choking techniques that were discarded because they were not legal in contest jûdô, which had evolved slowly over the years" (Wang).

During the 1980s, Hélio Gracie's sons took the family art to California, and during the 1990s the victories of Rorion and Royce Gracie in pay-per-view Ultimate Fighting Championship™ (UFC) events made Gracie Jiu-jitsu famous. In 1994, the U.S. Army also introduced Gracie Jiu-jitsu into its Ranger training programs at Fort Benning, though here the idea was more to teach self-confidence than to improve individual lethality in combat.

Punches, kicks, and fighting from the standing position were added to the Brazilian jiu-jitsu curriculum during the 1990s. The reason was to keep its practitioners competitive during UFC matches. Nevertheless, the Gracies continued to emphasize maneuvering for opportunities in which to apply joint locks and chokes. The reason, they insisted, was that most one-on-one fights end up as grappling contests on the ground, and one might as well get there as quickly as possible.

Toward this end, particular attention is paid to the ground positions labeled the "mount" and the "guard." In the mounted position, the combatant straddles an opponent lying on his back, essentially sitting on the opponent's abdomen. The goal is to set up a choke or a joint lock or to deliver strikes. A variation is the "side mount," in which the practitioner is on top of an opponent, chest to chest at a 90-degree angle. Meanwhile, the "guard" refers to the opposite position, in which the opponent is attempting to get on top of the practitioner. The standard Brazilian jiu-jitsu guard places the opponent between one's legs, which encircle the attacker just above the hips. If the encircling legs' ankles are crossed, then it is a "closed guard"; if the legs are not crossed, then it is an "open guard." An alternative is the "half-guard," in which the defender uses the legs to trap one of the legs of the opponent attempting to mount.

Although Rorion Gracie maintains that one can learn the techniques of Brazilian jiu-jitsu after just forty lessons, learning to apply these techniques against uncooperative opponents in combative contexts requires years of practice. So, toward showing relative standing, Brazilian jiu-jitsu utilizes a ranking system similar to that of Kôdôkan Jûdô. Rank is designated by a colored belt wrapped and tied at the waist of the uniform (which is also similar to the loose cotton trousers and jacket of jûdô). Belt ranks for children run from white (for beginners) to yellow, orange, green, brown, and black and for adults, white, blue, purple, brown, and black. As in the dan system of contemporary Japanese martial arts, the black belt progresses through various grades of ascending numbers (i.e., first degree, second degree, etc.).

During the 1990s, various organizations arose both in Brazil and abroad espousing variations of the core teachings of Maeda as modified by Carlos and Hélio Gracie. Thus Gracie Jiu-jitsu has become a trademark used by various members of the Gracie family of Brazil whose schools are autonomous, while other instructors, such as the Machado brothers (nephews and students of Carlos Gracie), refer to their systems as Brazilian, as distinct from Gracie, jiu-jitsu.

Thomas A. Green
Joseph Svinth

See also Jûdô; Wrestling and Grappling: Japan
References
Barbosa de Medeiros, Rildo Heros, "The History of Judo: The Arrival to Brazil: Count Koma." http://www.Judobrasil.com.br/komtr.htm.
Gorsuch, Mark, "Mitsuyo Maeda (Count Koma) Biography" http://bjj.org/interviews/maeda.html.
Harrison, E. J. 1982. *The Fighting Spirit of Japan*. Woodstock, NY: Overlook Press.
Kimura, Masahiko. *My Judo*. http://www.judoinfo.com/kimura2.htm
Lima, Andre Alex. 1999. "Who's Who in the Gracie Family." In *Martial Arts Masters*. Burbank, CA: C.F.W. Enterprises, 102–109.
Marushima, Takao. 1997. *Maeda Mitsuyo: Conde Koma*. Tokyo: Shimazu Shobo.
Smith, Robert W. 1999. "Kimura." In *Martial Musings: A Portrayal of Martial Arts in the 20th Century*. Erie, PA: Via Media Publishing Co.
Wang, George. "History of Gracie Jiu-Jitsu." http://www.geocities.com/Colosseum/5389/maeda.html.
Williams, James, and Stanley A. Pranin. "Interview with Rorion Gracie." *Aikido Journal* 105 (Fall 1995). http://www.aikidojournal.com/articles/ajInterviews/RorionGracie.asp.

Budô, Bujutsu, and Bugei

Editorial note: Bracketed number codes in this entry refer to the list of ideograms that follows.

The meaning and usage of the terms *budô*, *bujutsu*, and *bugei* as appellations for the martial arts of Japan are subjects of considerable confusion and misinformation among practitioners and aficionados of these arts—Japanese as well as Western. Among modern authorities in Japan the terms have acquired a more or less conventional usage adopted mainly to facilitate discussion of the multiple goals and purposes of combative training: Bujutsu (warrior skills [1]) describes the various Japanese martial disciplines in their original function as arts of war; budô (the warrior's way [2]) denotes the process by which the study of bujutsu becomes a means to self-development and self-realization; and bugei (warrior arts [3]) is a catchall term for the traditional Japanese military sciences, embracing both bujutsu and budô.

It must be stressed, however, that such precise usage is modern—adopted for analytical purposes—not traditional. Projecting it backward into earlier times, as much literature on Japanese martial art does, is anachronous.

Western texts on Japanese fighting arts often assert that during the Tokugawa period (A.D. 1600–1868) martial art masters began replacing the suffix jutsu [4], meaning "art" or "skill," with dô [5], meaning "way" or "path," in the names of their disciplines, to distinguish the sublime from the purely technical applications and purposes of martial art. Thus *kenjutsu,* "the art of swordsmanship," became kendô, "the way of the sword"; bujutsu, "the martial skills," became budô, "the martial way"; and so on. The historical record, however, does not support this conclusion. Some

Meiji-period (1868–1912) educators did differentiate -jutsu and -dô in precisely this fashion, but their forebears did not.

Historically the samurai employed a cornucopia of terms for their fighting arts, some still in common use today, others not (swordsmanship, for example, was called kenjutsu [6], kendô [7], *kenpô* [8], *hyôhô* [9], *tôjutsu* [10], *gekken* [11], *shigeki no jutsu* [12], and various other appellations, without distinction of form or content). The meaning and popularity of each term varied from age to age. Two of the oldest words for martial art are *bugei* and *hyôhô* (more commonly pronounced *heihô* in modern usage). Both are Chinese borrowings, and both appear in Japanese texts as far back as the turn of the eighth century. The early meanings of the two words overlapped to a substantial extent, but by the Tokugawa period, hyôhô had narrowed considerably, from a general term to one of several alternative names for swordsmanship. *Bugei,* in the meantime, had become a generic appellation for the fighting arts. Today, *heihô* simply means "strategy" in general usage, while scholars and practitioners of swordsmanship and related arts often apply it in more restricted fashion to designate the principles around which a particular school's approach to combat is constructed.

Budô and bujutsu came into fashion during the medieval and early modern periods. Budô, which appeared in print at least as early as the thirteenth century, seems to have been rather ambiguous in meaning until the Tokugawa period, when it sometimes carried special connotations. Nineteenth-century scholar and philosopher Aizawa Yasushi differentiated budô from bugei in the following manner: "The arts of the sword, spear, bow and saddle are the bugei; to know etiquette and honor, to preserve the way of the gentleman, to strive for frugality, and thus become a bulwark of the state, is budô" (Tominaga 1971, 1). For at least some Tokugawa-period writers, in other words, budô had far broader implications than it does today, designating what modern authors often anachronistically call bushidô [13]—that is, the code of conduct, rather than the military arts, of the warrior class. Nevertheless, pre-Meiji nomenclature for the martial disciplines betrayed no discernible systematization. The sources use *bujutsu* interchangeably with *bugei,* and use both in ways that clearly imply a construct with moral, spiritual, or social components, as well as technical ones.

Karl Friday

See also Japan; Koryû Bugei, Japan; Samurai; Swordsmanship, Japanese
References

Friday, Karl. 1997. *Legacies of the Sword: the Kashima-Shinryû and Samurai Martial Culture.* Honolulu: University of Hawai'i Press.
Hurst, G. Cameron, III. 1998. *The Armed Martial Arts of Japan: Swordsmanship and Archery.* New Haven: Yale University Press.
Rogers, John M. 1990. "Arts of War in Times of Peace: Archery in the Honchô Bugei Shôden." *Monumenta Nipponica* 45, no. 3: 253–284, 3.

———. 1990. "Arts of War in Times of Peace: Swordsmanship in the Honchô Bugei Shôden, Chapter 5." *Monumenta Nipponica* 45, no. 4: 413–447, 4.

———. 1990. "Arts of War in Times of Peace: Swordsmanship in the Honchô Bugei Shôden, Chapter 6." *Monumenta Nipponica* 46, no. 2: 173–202, 2.

Tominaga Kengo. 1971. *Kendô gohya Kunen-shi.* Tokyo: Hyakusen Shobo.

List of Ideograms

1	warrior skills	武術
2	the warrior's way	武道
3	warrior arts	武芸
4	jutsu	術
5	dô	道
6	kenjutsu	剣術
7	kendô	剣道
8	*kenpô*	剣法
9	*hyôhô*	兵法
10	*tôjutsu*	刀術
11	*gekken*	撃剣
12	*shigeki no jutsu*	刺撃の術
13	bushidô	武士道

C

Capoeira

Capoeira is a Brazilian martial art that relies primarily on striking techniques, although some grappling maneuvers, especially takedowns utilizing
the legs in either tripping or scissoring motions, and weapon techniques
complete the repertoire of the *capoeirista* (practitioner or "player" of
capoeira). Various etymologies of the name *capoeira* are offered in the
scholarly literature. The root *ca* or *caá* from Native Brazilian languages
refers to forests or woods. This linguistic stem is often used to connect the
origins of the term and the art to which it refers to African slave originators
who, the oral traditions of the art maintain, escaped to or practiced in the
bush from the sixteenth through the nineteenth centuries. Alternatively, the
Portuguese words *capão* (cock) and *capoeira* (cage for cocks) have been
used to link the word to a poultry market area in Rio de Janeiro where
slaves held capoeira *rodas* (roda [wheel], the playing area formed by
capoeiristas standing in a circle; also the contest or game played within such
a circle) and to cockfighting. Neither these nor any of a multitude of other
explanations for the origin of the term have been universally accepted.

The origins of capoeira are recorded only in the traditional legends of
the art and invariably focus on African influence. Considerable debate exists among practitioners and historians as to whether capoeira is the New
World development of an African martial art or a system originating in the
New World with African influences ranging from terminology to the
berimbau, the primary musical instrument used to provide accompaniment
for the *jôgo* ("match" or "game"). There are even suggestions that some of
the kicking techniques are derived from French *savate* via European sea-
men who manned the cargo vessels that docked in Brazilian ports.

Regardless of the genealogy, the legends invariably associate capoeira
with the slave experience, which in Brazil lasted from the beginnings of the
sixteenth century until 1888. The vehicle of dance that characterizes the
practice of capoeira, oral traditions argue, allowed the practice of martial
techniques but concealed their intent from the overseers. Blows struck with

Theatrical reproduction of the maculelé dance associated with capoeira. (Julie Lemberger/Corbis)

the feet and head-butts, some argue, could be delivered by men in chains. Moreover, many oral traditions claim that the practice of capoeira allowed those slaves who escaped and survived to establish communities in the bush to defend themselves from the groups of armed men who sought to apprehend and return them to captivity.

Written records alluding to the art date only to around the last century of the slave experience (beginning in 1770), and in them capoeira was identified, not with African Brazilians, but with a Portuguese bodyguard of the viceroy. Throughout the nineteenth century, references to capoeira identify it not with the rural settings of the folk histories but with urban centers such as Recife, Salvador, and Rio de Janeiro. The art was generally associated with the street, petty crime, and social disorder into the early decades of the twentieth century. Contemporary traditions echo this earlier disreputability. For example, it has been traditional to receive a nickname at one's *batizada* ("christening," or acceptance into the art). This harks back to the necessity of a street name among earlier capoeiristas. As one might expect with an art of the street, the traditional way to learn capoeira was by observing play, by playing, or by using it in street defense. Any instruction was extremely informal. Brazilian author Jorge Amado in his novel *Jubiabá* gives several accounts of capoeira as it existed on the streets of his native Bahia. These vignettes reflect both the unstructured way of acquiring knowledge of capoeira and the vicious quality of its use as a street-fighting system. The customary label for this art, Capoeira Angola, pays homage to its legendary African origins.

In the late 1920s to early 1930s, however, a new way to study capoeira became available. During that period, Manoel dos Reis Machado—Mestre (Master) Bimba—opened his school and began attempts both to legitimize the art and to systematize its transmission. The difficulties he faced are suggested by the fact that it was not until 1937 that his school, Centro de Cultura Física e Capoeira Regional, was granted official state recognition. Mestre Bimba's system came to be known as Capoeira Regional (after his school's name) in order to distinguish it from the traditional style still played on the streets and taught by conservative mestres—Capoeira Angola. In contrast to the earlier trial-and-error learning acquired by entering the roda, Machado developed a structured curriculum in a training hall setting. He has been accused of appropriating elements of Asian arts, particularly karate and jûjutsu, into his style of capoeira. The best evidence suggests, however, that his system grew from traditional street capoeira with some influences from *batuque* (a rough game of kicking and tripping with obvious martial qualities) via his father. Nevertheless, the structure Machado set up is imbued with elements familiar to students of many Asian martial arts, such as formalized exercises containing series of basic movements (*sequencias*), uniforms consisting of white trousers and T-shirts, and colored belts indicating rank (*cordãos*). The cordão system is not uniform—different local clubs (*grupos*) use different colors to indicate rank or level of experience—nor has it been universally adopted—those organizations following the Angola tradition do not use belts, or white uniforms, at all.

Capoeira is said to be "played"; therefore, a match is labeled a jôgo (a game). The jôgo takes place in a ring called a roda (wheel) formed by participants waiting their turns to play. Roda is also the label used for an occasion for capoeira play, for example, "next Sunday's roda." The jôgo is played to the musical accompaniment of percussion instruments derived in the New World from African archetypes: the berimbau (a large musical bow utilizing a gourd resonator that is played by striking its metal bowstring with a stick), the *pandeiro* (tambourine), the *agogô* (a pair of clapperless bells struck with a metal stick), the *reco-reco* (a notched scraper), and the *atabaque* (conga drum). The berimbau is the primary instrument and is venerated by players. For example, its placement provides spatial orientation for play, in that its location is called *pé do berimbau* (foot of the berimbau), and players enter the roda after kneeling facing one another and performing a private ritual (e.g., making the sign of the cross) in front of the berimbau. Thus, the instrument creates a "sacred space" in the roda.

An acrobatic kick from a one-handed handstand, a signature move of capoeira, November 14, 1996. (Julie Lemberger/Corbis)

Songs involving a leader-and-response pattern are sung during play. The words of these songs embody, to take a few examples, comments on capoeira in general, insults directed toward various types of styles of play or types of players, and biographical allusions to famous capoeiristas. The sense of capoeira as a dance is established by this musical frame for the action and completed by the movements taking place within the roda. The basic stance of capoeira places one foot forward in a lunging move with the corresponding hand forward and the other hand back. There is, however, considerable variety in the execution of the stance (both between individual players and between the Regional and the Angola traditions), and stances rapidly shift, with feet alternating in time to the tempo of the musical accompaniment in a dance-like action called a *ginga*. The techniques of capoeira rely heavily on kicks, many of them embodied in spectacular cartwheels, somersaults, and handstands. Players move from aerial techniques to low squatting postures accompanied by sweeps or tripping moves. Evasion rather than blocking is used for defense. Head-butts and hand strikes (using the open hand) complete the unarmed arsenal of the capoeirista. Again, there is a distinction between Angola and Regional, with the former relying more on low kicks, sweeps, and trips, played to a slower rhythm.

As an armed fighting art, capoeira has incorporated techniques for the use of paired short sticks and bladed weapons (particularly straight razors, knives, and machetes). Even in those cases in which the art has moved from the streets to the training hall, training in weapons remains in the curriculum in forms such as *maculêlê*, which entails a rhythmic clash of short sticks while performing a dancelike action.

In the 1970s capoeira spread to the United States. Mestres Jelon Viera and Loremil Machado brought the art to New York in 1975, and by 1979 Bira Almeida began teaching in California. Other mestres from both major traditions followed suit—for example Mestre Cobra Mansa (Cinezio Feliciano Pecanha) of the International Capoeira Angola Foundation in Washington, D.C., who visited and eventually moved to the United States in the early 1990s. By the late 1990s capoeira had developed an international following. The popularity of the art has been fostered by its inclusion in Hollywood films such as *The Quest, Mortal Kombat II,* and especially *Only the Strong,* with its capoeira mestre protagonist. Capoeira has even appeared recently in video game formats, played, for example, by the character of Eddie Gordo in "Tekken III."

Thomas A. Green

See also Africa and African America; Political Conflict and the Martial Arts
References
Almeida, Bira. 1986. *Capoeira: A Brazilian Art Form.* Berkeley, CA: North Atlantic Books.
Capoeira Angola. n.d. Washington, DC: International Capoeira Angola Foundation.
Capoeira, Nestor. 1995. *The Little Capoeira Book.* Berkeley, CA: North Atlantic Books.
Lewis, J. Lowell. 1992. *Ring of Liberation: Deceptive Discourse in Brazilian Capoeira.* Chicago: University of Chicago Press.
Thompson, Robert Farris. 1988. "Tough Guys Do Dance." *Rolling Stone,* March 24, 135–140.

Chi

See Ki/Qi

China

In early times, a number of terms were used to describe Chinese martial arts, which are now known as *wushu.* The term *jiangwu* (teach military matters) was a comprehensive concept comprising training in general and martial arts in particular. In the state of Zhou (475–221 B.C.), jiangwu took place during the winter, while farming occupied the other three seasons. The term *jiji* (attack, skilled striking) was used in reference to the troops of the state of Qi (a state that occupied much of the present province of Shandong between 480 and 221 B.C.). Some have claimed that this term refers to boxing, but it more likely refers to individual hand-to-hand combat, both bare-handed and with weapons. The *Han History Bibliographies* of ca. A.D. 90 (Gu 1987, 205) use the term *bing jiqiao* (military skills).

For at least the last seven centuries, the Chinese martial arts have been primarily called *wuyi,* which translates directly into "martial arts" in English, and reflects skills associated with the profession of arms in Chinese. An exception is the term *gongci zhi shu* (attack and stabbing skills), used to describe the martial arts practices prohibited under Mongol rule. During the Qing period (1644–1911), the term *quanbang* (boxing and staff) was also commonly used by the Manchu regime to describe popular Han Chinese martial arts practices (group practice outside the military, primarily among the Han Chinese majority, as opposed to Manchu practices of wrestling and archery on horseback), especially those of heterodox religious groups and secret societies. In traditional Chinese society, martial arts practice was not so much spiritual as it was the equivalent of keeping firearms. These groups were often considered subversive by the authorities and, indeed, some were. For example, the Taipings, a quasi-Christian cult, grew into a major threat to the regime, occupying a large portion of southeast China between 1850 and 1863.

The term *wushu* as it is used today in the People's Republic of China is only rarely seen in ancient texts. This term also translates into "martial arts" in English. The term *wushu* had become commonplace early in the twentieth century (possibly following the Japanese use of *shu* or *jutsu,* as in *jûjutsu* [pliant skill]). Even the young Mao Zedong referred favorably to the Japanese practice of jûjutsu (*roushu* in Chinese), which he carefully noted had evolved from Chinese skills.

The Nationalist government (controlled by the Nationalist Party, known as the *Guomindang*) adopted the term *guoshu* (national arts) in 1927 to associate them with modern Chinese nationalism. As a result, the term *guoshuguan* (national arts hall) has carried over to the present in some overseas Chinese communities.

The term *kung fu* (*gongfu*) merely means "skill" or "effort" in Chinese. In the eighteenth century, a French Jesuit missionary in China used the term to describe Chinese yogalike exercises. It was accepted for English usage in the United States during the 1960s to describe Chinese self-defense practices seen outside Mainland China as being similar to karate. It was widely popularized by the *Kung Fu* television series in the 1970s and is now a household word around the world. However, this term evokes a fanciful, exaggerated association of the Chinese martial arts with Shaolin Monastery and Buddhism—a distorted image of these arts, whose origins go back much further than either Buddhism in China or Shaolin Monastery.

From early times, the martial arts emphasized weapons skills. The *Conversations of the States* (Conversations of Qi) mentions five edged weapons: broad sword, straight sword, spear, halberd, and arrow. The Rites of Zhou also lists five weapons: halberd, lance, pike, and long and short spears. The Book of Rites includes archery, charioteering, and wrestling in the seasonal martial training regimen. In the section on music, it further describes martial dances with shield and axe and choreographed halberd and spear movements—early examples of combining ritual with martial techniques into routines commonly known in modern karate parlance as kata. The ancient Chinese aristocracy doubled as priests. Religion and governance converged; therefore, there were rites to support military as well as peacetime activities.

The entries on archery, straight sword, boxing, and even football (more like soccer, which required considerable agility as well as endurance) in the *Han History Bibliographies* reveal that manuals were written on important martial arts and related skills, although those extant date back no earlier than the Ming dynasty (ca. sixteenth century). Boxing was the basic skill that supplemented weapons, and certain boxing-related techniques were used on horseback as well as on foot, especially weapons-seizing techniques. For example, General Deng Zhan of Wei (ca. A.D. 220–226) was known for his skill with the "five weapons" and for his ability to take on armed opponents empty-handed. During a campaign in A.D. 582, Sui troops, outnumbered and their "five weapons" depleted, successfully fought off a Tujue (Turkic tribe) force with their bare fists, with such ferocity that "the bones in their hands were visible" (Wang 1960, 395, 4694). General Weichi Jingde of Tang (ca. A.D. 627–649) could ride into an opposing army, dodge the enemy's lance thrusts, seize an enemy lance, and use it against the attackers.

When the military examination system was established in 702, the martial arts emphasized for leaders were lance and spear from horseback, and archery from horseback and on foot. There was a test of strength, as well, that consisted of lifting a large city gate log bolt ten times (based on a story that Confucius had displayed great strength by lifting and placing just such a bolt) and carrying approximately five bushels of rice for a distance of twenty paces. Common soldiers were categorized based on their skills with archery, spear, halberd, pike, and sword, and their daring in hand-to-hand combat. A premium was placed on strength and endurance.

By the Song dynasty there was a saying: "There are thirty-six types of weapons, and the bow is the foremost; there are eighteen types of martial

Young children in Beijing going through basic martial arts training, November 1997. (Karen Su/Corbis)

arts, and the bow [archery] is the first." From this time on, exceptional martial artists were commonly described as "skilled in the eighteen martial arts." One can find essentially two versions of the eighteen weapons in various sources. The matchlock is included in the eighteen weapons listed in the early Ming novel *Water Margin* (also known as *All Men Are Brothers* and *Outlaws of the Marsh* in English). Later Ming versions drop the matchlock and include boxing at the end of the list, perhaps influenced by General Qi Jiguang's chapter on boxing, which is also the oldest extant illustrated Chinese boxing manual. The most common listing of the eighteen weapons includes the composite bow, crossbow, spear, broad sword, straight sword, pike, shield, arrow axe, broad axe, halberd, flail, iron rod or bar (a tapered, smooth or segmented, solid iron rod [also called "iron whip"] with a sword grip, often used in pairs), claw (metal talons attached to a cord thrown to seize and unhorse a rider), lance, trident, rake (similar to an agricultural tool), dart and cord, and boxing. This selection seems a bit arbitrary, and at least one Chinese author has noted that some of these weapons appear more suited for use in interclan feuding than in large-scale military combat. Thus, the phrase "eighteen martial arts" appears to reflect a convergence of military and popular forms. The "Song Period Essentials" from the *Military Classics* (Wujing Zongyao) (ca. 1044) includes illustrations of the variety of weapons used by the military.

Contemporary literature provides a peek at martial arts activities in and around the Southern Song capital, Hangzhou (1127–1279). The military forces scheduled training exercises every spring and autumn at designated locations, where, amid the crash of cymbals and beating of drums, they practiced combat formations and held archery competitions, polo matches, and numerous other martial arts demonstrations, such as spear and sword fighting.

Associations were organized among the citizenry by those interested in wrestling, archery, staff fighting, football, polo, and many nonmartial activities. Also, outdoor entertainment at certain locations in the city included wrestling matches (both men's and women's), martial arts demonstrations, acrobatics, and other physical displays.

Some of these activities (considered secular folk entertainment, not religious activities) could still be seen at the temple festivals (which were combination county fairs and swap meets) and other festive occasions well into the twentieth century.

Japanese swords were popular during the Ming, and both General Qi Jiguang's *New Book of Effective Discipline* (*Jixiao Xinshu*) (ca. 1561) and Mr. Cheng's *Three Kinds of Insightful Techniques* (*Chengshi Xinfa Sanzhong*) (ca. 1621) include illustrated Japanese sword routines to emulate. Japanese swords had begun to enter China during the Song period, when their fine quality was even described in a poem by the famed literary figure Ouyang Xiu (1007–1072). Records show that Japanese swords and poled weapons (*naginata,* weapons similar to the European halberd) were presented as tribute to a number of Ming-period rulers. Ming military leaders were able to observe firsthand the effectiveness of Japanese weapons and fighting techniques during the large-scale Japanese pirate activities in the Chinese coastal provinces during the mid-sixteenth century. The Chinese were suitably impressed, and the experience resulted in Chinese use of Japanese weapons as well as indigenous production of Japanese-style swords and the adoption of Japanese sword techniques.

By the Qing period (1644–1911), the *Comprehensive Study of Documents* (*Wenxian Tongkao*) reveals that, among the types of individual weapons officially produced for military use in 1756, special emphasis was placed on as many as nineteen varieties of broad swords and sixteen types of poled weapons categorized as spears—a bewildering mix facing military martial arts drill instructors.

When the Nationalist government–sponsored Central Martial Arts Institute was established in Nanjing in 1927, its founders were faced with the daunting task of attempting to satisfy the sensitivities of numerous martial arts factions within a single national program. They got off to a troublesome start by dividing the institute into Shaolin and Wudang

A crowd watches as
a couple stages a
martial arts
demonstration on
a sidewalk in
Shanghai, October
1983. (KellyMooney
Photography/Corbis)

branches. The Wudang branch included only instruction in taijiquan, xingyiquan, and baguazhang, while the Shaolin branch arbitrarily comprised all other martial arts styles. This arrangement was based on the popular belief that Chinese boxing consisted of an External or Shaolin School (Buddhist), which emphasized strength and speed, versus an Internal or Wudang School (Daoist), which emphasized use of an opponent's strength and speed against him. This simplistic view originated with a 1669 piece titled *Epitaph for Wang Zhengnan*, written by the Ming patriot and historian Huang Zongxi. At the time, however, it was probably meant as a veiled political jab at the foreign Manchu regime rather than as a serious discussion of boxing theory. In any case, division of the institute into these two branches resulted in infighting, so the branches were quietly phased out.

After 1949, traditional sports, including the martial arts, were placed under a government Physical Culture and Sports Commission. Martial arts for nationwide competition were standardized into three major categories of boxing (*changquan, nanquan,* and *taijiquan*), while weapons were limited to four basic types with standardized routines (broad sword, straight sword, staff, and spear). Changquan (long boxing) routines have combined techniques from the more acrobatic so-called northern styles of boxing, while nanquan, or "southern boxing," has combined the "short hitting" emphasis on arm movements prominent in most styles of boxing found in South China (especially in Fujian and Guangdong provinces).

Standardized taijiquan, including a shortened routine of twenty-four forms, was based on the widely practiced Yang style of taijiquan. Many of the traditional styles continued to be practiced individually, and more liberal policies in recent years have resulted in the resurgence of some, such as the original Chen style of taijiquan.

Stanley E. Henning

See also Animal and Imitative Systems in Chinese Martial Arts; Baguazhang (Pa Kua Ch'uan); Boxing, Chinese; Boxing, Chinese Shaolin Styles; Kung Fu/Gung Fu/Gongfu; Medicine, Traditional Chinese; Religion and Spiritual Development: China; Taijiquan (Tai Chi Ch'uan); Women in the Martial Arts: China; Wrestling and Grappling: China; Written Texts: China; Xingyiquan (Hsing I Ch'uan); Yongchun (Wing Chun)

References

Chen Tingjing. 1709. *Dushu Jishu Lue* (Reader's Guide to Numeric Listings).

Cheng Dali. 1995. *Zhongguo Wushu: Lishi yu Wenhua* (Chinese Martial Arts: History and Culture). Chengdu: Sichuan University Press.

Cheng Dong and Zhong Shaoyi. 1990. *Zhongguo Gudai Bingqi Tuji* (Collected Illustrations of Ancient Chinese Weapons). Beijing: People's Liberation Army Press.

Gu Shi. 1987. *Hanshu Yiwenzhi Jiangshu* (Commentaries on the Han History Bibliographies). Shanghai: Shanghai Guji Chubanshe.

Guo Zisheng. 1997. *Shijing Fengqing: Jingcheng Miaohui yu Changdian* (City Customs: Capital City Temple Festivals and Fairgrounds). Shenyang: Liaohai Chubanshe.

Guojia Tiwei Wushu Yanjiuyuan, bianzuan (National Physical Culture and Sports Commission Martial Arts Research Institute, editors and compilers). 1997. *Zhongguo Wushushi* (Chinese Martial Arts History). Beijing: People's Physical Culture Publishers.

Henning, Stanley E. 1999. "Academia Encounters the Chinese Martial Arts." *China Review International* 6, no. 2: 307–320.

———. 1997. "Chinese Boxing: The Internal versus External Schools in the Light of History and Theory." *Journal of Asian Martial Arts* 6, no. 3: 10–19.

———. 1998. "Observations on a Visit to Shaolin Monastery." *Journal of Asian Martial Arts* 7, no. 1: 90–101.

———. 1998. "Southern Fists and Northern Legs: The Geography of Chinese Boxing." *Journal of Asian Martial Arts* 7, no. 3: 24–31.

Hua Yue. 1972. *Cuiwei Xiansheng Beizheng Lu: Cuiwei Xiansheng Nanzheng Lu* (Mr. Cuiwei's Records of Campaigns in the North and South). Taibei: Guangwen Press.

Huang Zongxi. 1936. *Nan Lei Wen Ding* (Nan Lei's Definitive Writings). Shanghai: Zhonghua Shuju.

Kuang Wennan. 1990. *Zhongguo Wushu Wenhua Gailun* (A General Discussion of Chinese Martial Arts Culture). Chengdu: Sichuan Jiaoyu Chubanshe.

Li Quan. 1921. *Taibo Yinjing* (Dark Classic of the Planet of War). Wenyou Shuju.

Liu Xiang. 1927. *Li Ji* (Book of Rites). Shanghai: Zhonghua Shuju.

Meng Yuanlao et al. 1962. *Dongjing Menghualu Waisizhong* (Record of Reminiscences of the Eastern Capital and Four Other Works). Shanghai: Zhonghua Shuju.

Wang Qinnuo. 1960. *Ce Fu Yuan Gui* (Grand Tortoise Library). Hong Kong: Zhonghua Shuju.

Xie Zhaozhe. 1935. *Wuzazu* (Five Mixed Categories). Zhongyang Shudian.

Yang Hong. 1982. "China's Ancient Weapons." *China Reconstructs* 1: 57–62.

Zhang Bo, ed. 1892. *Han Wei Liu Chao Baisan Mingjia Jishu* (Collected Writings of 103 Famous Authors of the Han, Wei, and Six Dynasties). Vols. 18–19, *Wei Wendi Ji* (Writings of Emperor Wen of Wei).

Zhong Fangbai. 1869. *Jianben Liji Tizhu Quanwen Yaoquan* (Imperial Academy Edition Commentary, Complete Annotated Book of Rites). Jujing Tang.

Zhou Jiannan. 1979. "Wushu Zhong Shaolin Pai Zhi Yanjiu" (Research in the Shaolin School of Martial Arts). Collection of Chinese Martial Arts Historical Materials. Taibei: Ministry of Education, Physical Education Department, 4: 125–157.

Zhou Li (Rites of Zhou). 1936. Shanghai: Zhonghua Shuju.

Zhou Wei. 1957. *Zhongguo Bingqi Shigao* (A Draft History of Chinese Weapons). Sanlian Shudian.

Zhu Guozhen. 1959. *Yongchuang Xiaopin* (Yongchuang Essays). Beijing: Zhonghua Shuju.

Zuo Quiming. 1936. *Guoyu* (Conversations of the States). *Qiyu* (Conversations of Qi). Shanghai: Zhonghua Shuju.

Chivalry

The age of chivalry flourished between A.D. 1100 and the opening of the sixteenth century. It was a time when the mounted nobility of Western Europe lived out their lives in obedience to the code of chivalry, which charged each knight with the defense of the Church, his sovereign king, and the weak and the poor. He was to be just and brave and highly skilled in warfare. As a soldier of God, he must be sinless, pious, and charitable. In time a knight's duties would include the safeguarding of women, which brought an aura of romance to chivalry. By the time of the early crusades, knighthood and chivalry were inseparably bonded.

Chivalry sprang up almost simultaneously throughout Western Europe without an inspirational founder. It spread as a contagious dedication of the armed nobility to the Christian faith, to audacity on the field of battle, and to gallantry in the presence of noble ladies. The source of this phenomenon, with all of its pageantry and heroism, must be traced to evolving events of an earlier time.

When the western part of the Roman Empire collapsed in A.D. 476, German tribes that had menaced the empire's northern borders for centuries moved south to settle among the more numerous Romanized inhabitants. In those chaotic times, the new invaders were often quartered on both state lands and the holdings of private landowners. Of the several Germanic tribes that tramped across the tumbled bastions of Rome's old provinces, the Salian Franks were most closely related to the later development of medieval chivalry and knighthood.

Clovis, one of the earliest Frankish leaders, established in 481 a Germanic kingdom on the discarded civilization of Roman Gaul, where an evangelizing church had already impressed its influence. Clovis, for piously political reasons, became a Christian without learning to turn the other cheek. He first extended his rule over the Ripuarian Franks. Before his death in 511 he had, through treachery, murder, and brutal conquest, enforced his rule on surrounding Teutonic peoples—Alemanni, Burgundians, and Visigoths. His military campaigns, because they won converts for Christianity, went forward with the blessings of the Church.

Clovis's Frankish state was an unstable predecessor of Charlemagne's resplendent realm, which flourished three centuries later as the Carolingian Empire. Between the times of these two Frankish rulers, the embryo of medieval knighthood and chivalry began slowly to evolve. But there would have been neither knighthood nor chivalry had not the system of feudalism emerged from the Frankish historical experience.

A typical early German institution was the *Gefolgschaft,* or *comitatus* in its Latin form, in which a distinguished war leader gathered about him a select group of young men from his tribe to engage in warfare for glory and booty. We learn from the *Germania* of the Roman historian Tacitus that young German warriors, already invested with the shield and spear according to custom, swore a sacred oath that they would protect their chief in battle and try to emulate his bravest deeds but never exceed them, for it would have been a violation of their oath ever to outshine their veteran leader. This was as much a practical matter as one of loyalty: it was from the leader that the warriors would receive a share of the war booty, which might include a horse, weapons, and other gifts looted from the enemy as plunder. If their leader should die in battle and they returned home unscathed, or if they abandoned their weapons and fled the field, they became outcasts and faced a life of scorn. Some ended their shame by their own hand.

The strong bond that existed between a war chief and his loyal followers became a fixed element in the military structure of the Merovingian dynasty that began with Clovis and ended in the mid-eighth century. During this time, the military leaders and their young warriors became the lords and vassals of a feudal system in which the war booty of old became grants of conquered lands divided into fiefs, for which the endowed warrior pledged his loyalty and his military service.

To visualize this precursor of knighthood and chivalry, one should know that a medieval vassal was not a menial or serf, as modern usage sometimes implies. The word *vassal* is Celtic in origin and in time came to mean a loyal soldier or knight. Nor did the nobility, including lords and vassals, make up a substantial part of medieval society. The privileged class comprised no more than 10 percent of the entire population, often much less. Within this very small assemblage of landed gentry rested the wealth, the political power, and the military strength of the domain, thus enabling the noble class to become an hereditary aristocracy. The numerous remainder of society was made up mostly of toiling peasants who tilled the soil they did not own and performed other servile duties that fell to their lot. Their relationship to the lord whose lands they worked was called manorialism and had little to do with the feudal hierarchy.

During the decentralization of political power that for centuries followed the fall of Rome, many displaced warriors sought domestic security in an inconstant age. Their hope was to find a propertied magnate willing to accept them as military vassals in return for land. The process created an integrated feudal hierarchy of lords and vassals that rested like a small pyramid upon the vast populace of peasants. At the apex of this martial consortium was the king, who held his realm from God. Below him were the royal vassals, such as viscount and barons, whose fiefs were generally expansive. These they parceled out among the higher-ranking members of the noble class, who then became vassals. They, in turn, were able to continue the practice of subinfeudation, going down the broadening levels of the pyramid to the bottom, where one would find a few humble knights holding modest fiefs, whose income was barely enough to support them and their families. When a lord sponsored every knight and every tract of feudal land became hereditary, European feudalism became complete, with the fief serving as the basic bond of lord/vassal dependency.

A collection of feudal estates, little more than a disparate cluster of landholdings, soon weakened the power of the king. Most fiefs had been created essentially for military purposes, and the men who received them had been trained for warfare and became the soldiers who controlled the military strength of the kingdom. If war threatened, the king was obliged to call upon his royal vassals to provide arms for the coming encounter. They, in turn, called upon their own vassals to answer the call to arms. Because there was so much intermittent fighting in the Middle Ages, warfare became an oppressive burden for the knightly class, and an agreement was reached that limited a knight's obligated military duties to forty days a year.

At the heart of the feudal fabric was the armored knight, whose ideal role in life was to uphold the code of chivalry to which he had dedicated himself. The term *chivalry*, defining the code of western knights, appears in Middle English as *chivalrie* and is related to the French *chevalier* (knight). In late Latin, we find the word *caballarius*, meaning horseman or cavalier. The medieval knight, therefore, was an armored horseman, bearing shield, sword, and lance, the weaponry of his day. Soon chivalry and cavalry become synonymous.

A candidate for knighthood, after serving as a page, often began his apprenticeship at the age of 12 under a veteran knight, who instructed him in both military and worldly matters. When his term as squire was over, he followed his sponsor into battle as his bearer of arms; and when he was judged to be ready for knighthood he was dubbed by his sponsor, who tapped him on the shoulder with the flat of his sword. The initiation ceremony for knighthood varied in its formalities from place to place, but the code of chivalry was firmly fixed in its ethos, if not always in its fulfillment.

The earlier pagan practice in which elder warriors bestowed arms upon younger initiates, without benefit of prayer and benedictions, was sanctified when the Church took part in the ceremony, adding religious symbolism and solemnity. Eventually, the secular nobility and the clergy shared the investiture ceremony of knighthood.

At an earlier time, the knightly ceremony, when performed on the battlefield, was sudden and brief. A young arms-bearer, having distinguished himself in combat, might be recognized by an older knight, who would simply strike him with his fist or the flat of his sword and call out: "Sir knight!" It is not likely that many of the noble demands of chivalry were transmitted in such a nimble encounter, but they would be learned later.

The ceremony of knighthood was greatly changed by the end of the eleventh century. Now, the knight-to-be took a ritual bath to cleanse him of his sins. He then spent a night alone at the altar of his local church in quiet prayer, with his arms beside him. At dawn he went to mass, received communion, and listened to the celebrant affirming his obligations to knighthood and chivalry, the role of the knight being often likened to the role of a priest in a perilous society.

We learn of a more elaborate knightly ceremony from the writings of a thirteenth-century bishop, Guillaume Durand. He tells us in his *Pontifical* that the sword of the knightly candidate was placed on the altar by the officiating bishop, who called upon God to bless the weapon so that the wielder might defend churches, widows, and orphans against the cruelty of heretics and infidels. The initiate was admonished that he must be a good soldier, faithful and courageous; and with words from the Old Testament, he was reminded that the Lord God had formed his hands for battle and his fingers for war.

The bishop then girded the sword on the new knight, who unsheathed it, brandished it three times, and returned it to its scabbard. Finally, the bishop gave the knight a slight blow on the cheek and exhorted him to "awake from evil dreams and keep watch, faithful in Christ and praiseworthy of fame" (Barber 1995, 27).

The consecration of a warrior and his arms gave moral strength to chivalry and knighthood, as well as support for the feudal system in which they flourished. Chivalric behavior became an ideal of civilized fellowship among the privileged class, and although much easier to achieve in contemporary ballads than in real life, became a code of conduct that served society as a model of knightly aspiration.

During periods of peace, knights engaged their energies in the tournament, an armed sport that allowed them to flaunt their military skills and personal courage before an assembly of their peers. Contenders came from far and wide to the domain of some renowned prince, where many pavilions and platforms were raised around a mock battlefield. Here the challenging knights would rest their heraldic shields, affirming that they were of noble birth and pure character and truly sons of chivalry's elite. The encounter of two knights, called jousting or tilting, took place on horseback, with each knight trying to unhorse the other with lance and sword. Although the weapons were blunted, the martial passion of the combatants led to some brutish duels. The tournament remained a display center for knightly courage and prowess until the Renaissance.

When warfare came to feudal Europe, whether from land disputes, breaches of contract, or other contentious causes, it was often a brief local affair. The ones who suffered most from these internecine clashes were the defenseless peasants and the Church, whose lands were often bound up in the network of feudal dependencies. It was the Church that tried to subdue the violence of an unruly society when it proclaimed the *Pax Dei* (Latin; Peace of God) in 989, and a half century later, the *Truga Dei* (Truce of God). The first banned warfare against the weak and so sought to save women, children, and priests from the brutalities of the age. The second, more ambitious, decree attempted to mark out whole religious seasons of the year when fighting would be prohibited. Neither decree was entirely successful, but each lessened to some degree the incessant warfare of the armed nobility.

Toward the end of the eleventh century, European knighthood was to receive a challenge from the Near East that would extend knighthood's conventions and its belligerency as far as the Holy Land and even beyond. The Seljuk Turks, a menacing military force arising out of Asia made up of warriors who embraced Islam fervently, overran the exposed eastern borders of the Byzantine Empire. The Greek emperor, Alexius Comnenus, appealed to Pope Urban II to send military aid for the Christian cause; the events that followed revealed the quixotic essence of medieval knighthood.

The pope, himself a man of France, gathered about him an assembly of Frankish leaders at Clermont in 1095. He first reminded them that they were of the Frankish race "chosen and loved by God" and that the deeds of their ancestors should inspire them to take the road to the Holy Land and wrest it from the accursed Turks who had mutilated their Christian brethren and desecrated the holy places. Urban, sorely mindful of the intermittent warfare that was despoiling Europe, severely reproached the gathering of French nobility: "You, girt about with the badge of knighthood, are arrogant . . . you rage against your brothers. You, the oppressors of children, plunderers of widows . . . vultures who sense battles from afar and rush to them eagerly. If you wish to be mindful of your souls, either lay down the girdle of such knighthood or advance boldly as a knight of Christ" (Krey 1921, 30).

The papal speech created a mild hysteria that aroused Western chivalry to advance upon Jerusalem as a great crusading army, shouting its battle cry: "God wills it!" Urban did not know that he had set into motion a prolonged war between the cross and the crescent that would continue well into the thirteenth century.

There were eight crusades between 1096 and 1270. Except for the rowdy mobs of ravaging peasants who were later massacred by the Turks, the First Crusade began in high spirits, with a righteous purpose and banners flying. The response to the call came mostly from the knighthood of France, which left an enduring French stamp on the movement. The crusading army fought its way through Asia Minor and Syria, taking Jerusalem from Muslim control in 1099 and setting up a Latin Kingdom of Jerusalem.

Turkish attacks on the new Frankish protectorate, followed by the fall of Edessa in 1144, inspired a new crusade. The second effort achieved little against a revival of Muslim military aggression, but the capture of Jerusalem by the famed Saladin in 1187 quickened a new papal call. The Third Crusade attracted the support of the Holy Roman Emperor, Frederick I, Philip II of France, and Richard I, called the Lion-Hearted, of England. Known as the King's Crusade, it did little more than capture a few cities along the Mediterranean coast. In the chronicles of chivalry, the romanticized King Richard must remain unhonored: Saladin released his Christian captives; Richard massacred 2,700 of his own prisoners of war.

The Fourth Crusade of 1204 debased the chivalric ideal of crusading knighthood. Its forces overwhelmed the Christian world of Byzantium, partitioned much of its territory, and impressed upon the land a Frankish imprisonment that, fortunately for the Greeks, did not last longer than 1261.

In 1212, the response to the religious call was answered by bands of adolescents from France and Germany. Called the Children's Crusade, it was not a crusade at all but a calamitous outpouring of innocent faith that displaced countless numbers of children from their homes and led many into the slave markets of the Levant. The Fifth Crusade accomplished nothing, and its successor, under Frederick II, managed to negotiate some treaties favorable to the Christian side.

The earlier high purpose of the crusading movement was regained during the last two fated crusades led by the sainted Louis IX of France. His first expedition was an assault on Damietta in Egypt, where he surpassed his knights in valor by leaping into the surf on landing and wading ashore with shield and lance. It was an act of daring that might have earned him an honored place in the heroic lines of the chansons de geste (French; songs of heroic deeds), but his effort was of no avail in Egypt. He tried to redeem himself in 1270, an enfeebled old warrior, but he failed again, giving up his life on an alien Tunisian shore.

In the fourteenth century, the crusading movement was briefly revived, and French chivalry was again represented at Nicopolis in 1396, when the king of Hungary led a campaign against the advancing Turks. Early battle successes were reversed when the French knights, spurning wise counsel, attacked the Turkish front in a spirited charge but were massacred by a vengeful sultan, except for twenty-five of the wealthiest nobles, who were held for exorbitant ransoms. In 1444 the last medieval crusade, undertaken by knights from Poland and Hungary with the support of a Burgundian naval force, reached Varna on the shores of the Black Sea, where it was scattered in defeat.

Nevertheless, the spirit of the crusades endured through a unique blending of monasticism and chivalry in the military orders of the Templars and the Hospitallers. The first of these, taking their name from their quarters near the Temple of Solomon, were the Knights Templars. Like Western monks, they took the monastic vows of poverty, chastity, and obedience, but they also pledged themselves to the code of chivalry and dedicated themselves to fighting in the defense of pilgrims. Eventually, their knightly zeal succumbed to ventures in trade and banking, which made the order enviably wealthy. In 1312, the French king Philip IV (called the Fair), in order to seize the Templars' riches, collaborated with Pope Clement V to destroy the order on grounds of sacrilege and Satanism.

The Hospitallers, whose full title was The Sovereign Military Order of the Hospital of Saint John of Jerusalem, also took the three monastic vows, but they carried out their chivalric duties in caring for sick pilgrims and crusaders. They fared better than the Templars. At the failure of the earlier crusades, the order went to the island of Rhodes where, in 1312, they received the confiscated property of the disbanded Templars. They came to be called the Knights of Rhodes, and with their naval force, they kept the eastern Mediterranean free of Muslim corsairs until, in 1522, they were driven out by the Ottoman Turks; they later found a home on Malta. In 1961, Pope John XXIII recognized the Knights of Malta as both a religious community and an order of chivalry.

The chivalric age also left many enduring monuments. During the crusading movement, the eastern Mediterranean coast became studded with defiant stone castles that French knights had built to safeguard the Holy Land against Islam. The massive walls and towers left on the Levant a lasting imprint of medieval France.

The age of chivalry was one of contrasts and contradictions. Jakob Burckhardt, the renowned scholar of the Italian Renaissance, visualized medieval consciousness as something that "lay half dreaming or half awake beneath a common veil . . . woven of faith, illusion, and childish prepossession, through which the world and history were seen clad in strange hues" (Burckhardt 1944, 81). His perception somewhat clarifies how the carnage of knightly battle could be so oddly tempered by the romantic respite of courtly love. Born of chivalric ideals, it evolved into a body of rules defining the proper conduct of noble lovers.

Most aristocratic marriages in the Middle Ages were made chiefly for the dowry of feudal lands the wife would bring to the union. Often a knight simply married a fief, and his wife came as an encumbrance. She entered into his life as a household helper and childbearer, rarely as a romantic lover. Medieval poets wrote that the true love of a knight must not be his wife, or even a damsel he might have wedded for love. Such marriages were incompatible with true chivalric love. A knight's chosen lady could be another noblewoman, married or not. When a knight had chosen his lover-to-be, he wrote her amorous letters and promised to prove his constant devotion by performing valorous deeds. Once they had given their hearts to each other, they pledged that their love would forever remain secret, and he swore that he would serve her for all his days, no matter what her commands might be. He was expected to compose songs and poems to extol her virtues, and it was fitting for him to sigh for his lady and suffer the pain of love's melancholy heartache.

Chivalry's demand that the suitor remain gallant in all things sometimes unfairly challenged a knight when his frivolous lady commanded him to perform extravagant feats to prove his love for her. According to the poets, Queen Guinevere, faithless wife of King Arthur, ordered Lancelot to undergo a round of ordeals before she surrendered to him in their adulterous love affair. Yet, the central theme of such unchaste love remained firm—a knight must perform heroic deeds for his lady.

The theme of chivalric love emerged in the poetry of the troubadours of southern France, who sang their voluptuous verses in the Provençal tongue. Then came the romantic minstrels of northern France, the trouvères, and the minnesingers of Germany, whose balladry carried on the same harmonious motif. The love theme that wanders through the tales of medieval knighthood and its chivalric code was enriched by the grande dame, Eleanor of Aquitaine. Married first to Louis VII of France, then to Henry II of England, she brought the songs of the troubadours into the royal court. Later, at Poitiers, she organized the first love court, where the code of courtly romance was woven into the military discipline of knightly chivalry and where an assembly of noblewoman settled quarrels between lovers and judged which gallant knight had loved the best. The proceedings of such courts were frivolous and artificial. Ideally, the knightly lover was expected to keep some distance from his lady, knowing that his love must remain hopeless. In truth, the lover's muted yearnings were not always unheard or unrewarded, and adultery often became an emotional release for many noblewomen hopelessly caught in a loveless marriage of convenience.

The rules for lovemaking among the nobility were set down in an irreverent manual by Andreas Capellanus, *De Arte Honeste Amandi* (Latin; On the Art of Loving Honestly). It became a guide for knightly romance and elevated courtly love to a form of religion. Although that religion came into conflict with the Church's stand against adultery, it provided a clear mirror reflecting the romantic idealism of medieval nobility.

From the abundance of melodic poetry and heroic literature that served the cause of chivalry, there emerged several enduring narratives, such as *Lancelot,* by Chrétien de Troyes; Gottfried von Strassburg's *Tristan and Isolde; Le Roman de la Rose* of Guillaume de Lorris; and the legends of the Holy Grail, the cup used by Jesus at the Last Supper and searched for devotedly by King Arthur's knights.

From the time of the Norman Conquest, French literature exerted a strong influence on English literary forms, and until the fourteenth century the French language replaced English in general composition. Jean Froissart, the itinerant historian from Valenciennes, became prominent among the literati of the fourteenth century. His major work, *Chronique de France, d'Angleterre, d'Ecosse et d'Espagne* (simply called the Chronicle), carries his account of the Hundred Years' War between France and England. Not a history in the modern sense, because Froissart was preoccupied with knightly deeds and "the fine feat of arms," it is rather a saga of chivalric display in the midst of battle.

The diverse documents of the later Middle Ages give us an ambivalent image of a chivalrous knight. One side shows us a young noble hero in bright armor, astride a magnificent white charger, lance poised, ready to defend his monarch, his ladylove, the Church, the poor and oppressed, and all good Christians who sought shelter under his protective shield.

The other side shows that knightly warfare was direct and savage. The crusader, heavily protected, first with chain mail, later with plate armor, was equipped with battle-ax and double-edged sword, forged in fire to slay the enemy swiftly. The Black Prince, Edward of England, who was prince of Wales during the Hundred Years' War, was, in spite of his violence in battle, compassionate to his war prisoners. In contrast, as was mentioned above, Richard the Lion-Hearted slaughtered his Muslim prisoners during the Third Crusade. As much as the code of chivalry was obeyed, it was also ignored. In any case, knightly comportment was reserved for the gentry. A knight extended his chivalrous courtesies only to a member of his class; and his ethereal devotion to his lady did not bridle his predatory advances toward women of the lower class.

The vast number of enthralled peasants who tilled the soil and reaped the crops on the feudal estates were part of another world, dominated by the small but powerful aristocracy. Revolts of the peasantry were inevitable. In 1358, the French peasants rose up in a jacquerie (peasants' revolt), demanding relief from their economic and judicial oppression; and in 1381, the Wat Tyler Rebellion, just across the English Channel, convulsed

England's gentry. In Luther's time, German peasants vented their rage against their noble masters. These risings were put down with vindictive slaughter, showing that the gentle knight of legend was also a ruthless killing machine.

And yet, chivalry as an exemplary way of life left rules of gentlemanly conduct for Europe's future society. After gunpowder made castles and armored knights obsolete, the ideals of chivalry were preserved in Baldassare Castiglione's *Book of the Courtier,* which set standards of chivalric courtesy in the urban courts of Renaissance Italy, and the faded image of medieval knighthood emerged again in modern times as the Knights of the Golden Fleece, the Order of the Knights of the Garter, and the French Order of the Star. European monarchs continue to confer the title of chevalier or knight on distinguished public figures.

The ghost of the armored knight as a bloodied savage fighter lies with his bones under the sod of countless battlefields. As a virtuous warrior of ballad and song, he lives on in popular legend.

T. V. Tuleja

See also Europe; Heralds; Knights; Orders of Knighthood, Religious; Orders of Knighthood, Secular; Religion and Spiritual Development: Ancient Mediterranean and Medieval West; Swordsmanship, European Medieval

References

Atiya, Aziz S. 1938. *The Crusade in the Later Middle Ages.* London: Methuen.

Barber, Richard. 1995. *The Knight and Chivalry.* London: Boydell Press.

Bornstein, Diane. 1975. *Mirrors of Courtesy.* Hamden, CT: Archon Books.

Bridge, Antony. 1982. *The Crusades.* New York: Franklin Watts.

Burckhardt, Jacob. 1944. *The Civilization of the Renaissance in Italy.* London: Oxford.

Evans, Joan. 1969. *Life in Medieval France.* London: Phaedon Press.

Gautier, Léon. 1965. *Chivalry.* London: Phoenix House.

Grousset, René. 1936. *Histoire des Croisades et du Royaume Franc de Jerusalem.* Paris: Plon.

Krey, August C. 1921. *The First Crusade.* Princeton, NJ: Princeton University Press.

La Monte, John L. 1932. *Feudal Monarchy in the Latin Kingdom of Jerusalem, 1106–1291.* Cambridge, MA: Medieval Academy of America.

Oman, Charles W. C. 1953. *The Art of War in the Middle Ages, 375–1515.* Reprint, revised and edited by John H. Beeler. Ithaca, NY: Cornell University Press.

Runciman, Steven. 1978. *A History of the Crusades.* New York: Penguin Books.

Wood, Charles T. 1970. *The Age of Chivalry: Manners and Morals, 1000–1450.* New York: Universe Books.

Wright, Sylvia. 1988. *The Age of Chivalry: English Society, 1200–1400.* New York: Warwick Press.

Combatives: Military and Police Martial Art Training

Combatives is the collective term used to describe military or paramilitary training in hand-to-hand fighting. For police, the emphasis is usually on restraining the opponent, while for armies the emphasis is usually on increasing soldiers' self-confidence and physical aggressiveness. During such training, the virtues of "national" martial arts frequently are extolled, often at the expense of actual tactical advantage.

Police and militaries also have displayed considerable interest in *nonlethal combatives*. This term refers to methods and techniques (manual, mechanical, or chemical) that are designed and used to physically control or restrain people but, unless used with deliberate malicious intent, are unlikely to cause crippling injury or death to healthy teens or adults. Most unarmed martial art techniques fall into this category.

Perhaps the first systematic attempt to use Asian martial art techniques by a modern military came in 1561, when the Ming general Qi Jiguang included moves from a Northern Shaolin sword form in his text called *Ji Xiao Xin Shu* (New Text of Practical Tactics). Shaolin Boxing also was mentioned, apparently because Qi believed that recruits handled their weapons more confidently if first taught to wrestle and box.

During the 1590s, peasant infantry of southern Japan's Satsuma clan were observed practicing firearm kata (forms), and in 1609 the Satsuma conquest of Okinawa owed much to the Japanese bringing 700 muskets and 30,000 bullets to what the Ryûkyûans, the native inhabitants of the island, expected to be a battle of arrows and pikes. Meanwhile in Europe the Republican Dutch began developing military musket drills. Mostly a form of industrial safety (accidental discharges pose a serious risk in closed ranks), the Dutch taught their methods using rote patterns like the Japanese kata (forms).

To counter the Dutch, the French and Spanish began developing bayonets. Firearms were slow to reload in those days, and not accurate much past fifty meters. So if one could close quickly enough, then one could be inside the enemy ranks before they could reload. Originally companies of pikemen made the charge, but with the development of socket bayonets in 1678, European infantrymen became musketeers.

Throughout the eighteenth century, European professional soldiers concentrated mostly on developing close-order drills designed to move troops en masse, and bayonet practice consisted of little more than troops sticking straw dummies. Following the Napoleonic Wars, however, interest developed in using sword and bayonet drills as a form of physical exercise.

The first such proposals came from amateurs. In 1817, for instance, the English fencing master Henry Angelo published a book that showed cavalry fencing side by side on horseback; his inspirations included the Continental equestrian techniques performed at Philip Astley's London circus. Real cavalrymen were of course dismayed. "I, myself, as an ex-cavalryman who participated in cavalry charges during the First World War," sputtered Vladimir Littauer, "can assure you that the success of an attack does not depend on refinements of equitation but rather on the moment being rightly chosen" (Littauer 1991, 100–101).

Of more interest to military professionals was the program that Pehr Ling developed in Sweden. A graduate of Franz Nachtigal's academy, Ling believed that schoolchildren and soldiers needed to do exercises that made them respond quickly to their superiors. Furthermore, they needed to be graded in everything they did, and performances needed to show measurable improvement over time. Finally, physical training was something that both children and soldiers did for the nation, not for fun. So, with the support of the French general who was the Swedish crown prince, Ling established a Royal Central Institute of Gymnastics in Stockholm in 1813. Swedish military officers were required to attend this school, and in 1836 Ling, a noted fencer, published a manual on bayonet fencing for the Swedish Army.

For Ling, sticking the target with the point of the bayonet was especially important. If the opponent also has no bullets and the fighting is one-on-one, then his reasoning is sound, as thrusting provides the soldier with a better defensive posture and also protects the firearm's mechanism. However, in practice, the soldiers most likely to use bayonets were infantrymen suddenly ambushed by horsemen. Here, Richard Francis Burton explained in his 1853 *Complete System of Bayonet Exercise,* the bayonet was not used by one man working alone or even by a mass of men in a charge, but instead by four men working together in what was called a rallying square. Furthermore, the bayonet was not rammed deep, but instead used to slash. First, the victim was inconvenienced similarly either way, and more importantly, the slashing motion did not cause the bayonet to become stuck in the target. But this approach assumed that the bayonet was being used for combat rather than to teach aggressiveness, which was not always the case.

Of equal (and more enduring) interest to nineteenth-century military reformers were Ling's "Swedish gymnastics." Essentially modern calisthenics, Swedish gymnastics differed from German gymnastics mainly because they did not require bars, rings, and other equipment. Thus they were cheaper and easier to organize. Plus they had the advantage, at least to the Lutheran mind, that they were not much fun to do. Fun, after all, was the work of the devil. Hardship, on the other hand, built character.

Similar exercises became part of Swiss military training during the 1840s (a Swiss physical culturalist coined the word *calisthenics*) and British and German military training during the 1850s. The French followed suit during the 1870s, as did the Japanese during the 1880s and the Americans during the 1890s. In all cases, the reforms coincided with the establishment of centralized training depots. Perhaps more than physical fitness, a key learning objective was conditioning recruits to respond instantly and appropriately to shouted commands.

Although nationalism played a part in choosing the exercises used (thus Germans and Japanese wrestled while Americans and British boxed), other arguments were also given. One was the nineteenth-century belief that physical training in boxing and similar sports built character, which in those days typically translated into reduced male sexual desire. (Sexually transmitted diseases were a serious problem in nineteenth-century militaries, causing 37 percent of hospital admissions in the British Army in India in 1888 [Hayton-Keeva 1987, 76–80].) Another was that such sports provided commanders with a tool with which they could demonstrate superiority over other commanders. And as always victories could be orchestrated for political purposes; as early as 1929 the Nazis staged a boxing tournament between French Algerians and German "Aryans" for the express purpose of inciting race hatred.

During the late nineteenth century, swords and bayonets fell into disfavor with most professional soldiers. The reason was that cavalrymen came to prefer revolvers and shotguns and infantry came to prefer breech-loaded firearms. Unfortunately, Japanese successes during the Russo-Japanese War of 1904–1905 convinced some politicians that the spirit of the bayonet was a key to victory. So when ammunition stocks fell low at the beginning of World War I, Allied conscripts were trained to attack with bayonets rather than shoot. Ammunition expenditure was reduced, but casualties were enormous.

As early as 1908 Colonel Sir Malcolm Fox of the British military gymnastics department claimed to see correlation between boxing and bayonet fighting, so throughout the 1910s the British, Canadians, and Americans recruited professional boxers as combatives instructors. Privately, the boxers were appalled, as most had enough experience in rough parts of town to know that anyone who brought a bayonet to a gunfight was going to end up dead. Still, the methods were easily taught to huge numbers of men, and the bayonets were effectively used by Allied military police to quell the British, French, and Italian mutinies of 1917.

For their part, the Germans and Austrians never devoted much effort to teaching bayonet fighting; as a German officer named Erwin Rommel put it, "The winner in a bayonet fight is he who has one more bullet in his magazine" (Rommel 1979, 59–60). Instead, at mass levels the focus was on squad and team development, while at the individual level the focus was on teaching picked sharpshooters to use cover, concealment, and bolt-action

Sven J. Jorgensen teaches Seattle police officers jûjutsu disarming tricks, November 23, 1927. (Seattle Post-Intelligencer Collection, Museum of History & Industry)

rifles mounted with telescopic sights. The pedagogy seems to have been sound, too, as, unlike the Allies, the German and Austrian armies did not suffer mutinies until the collapse of the Western Front in 1918.

Following the Armistice in 1918, training budgets shrank. Of course that didn't stop professionals from conducting quiet experiments during colonial and civil wars, and as early as the Spanish Civil War the Germans had begun replacing bayonets with light machine guns supported by tanks, artillery, and dive-bombers. In other words, they replaced banzai with blitzkrieg, a method that the U.S. Marines perfected against the Japanese in the Pacific and the Chinese in Korea.

In China, budgets were also slim. So in 1912, Feng Yuxiang, "the Christian general," ordered his officers and men to run obstacle courses, lift weights, do forced marches with packs, and practice *quanfa* (Chinese boxing). In 1917, a Communist student leader named Mao Zedong also encouraged his followers to practice *taijiquan*. But in both cases, this was because they viewed the boxing as a gymnastic that took little space and no special equipment rather than as a practical battlefield combative. (As recently as 1976, Red Army generals asked about the value of *quanfa* said, "Amidst heavy gunfire, who would want to enjoy the dance posture of swordplay?" [P'an 1976, 2].)

But outside military academies, fantasy ruled. Thus, during the 1920s and 1930s, comic books and movies featured lantern-jawed heroes knocking out hordes of enemies using weapons no more powerful than a single right cross to the jaw. Heavyweight champion Jack Dempsey literally made a million dollars starring in a series of forgettable Hollywood films featuring exactly this technique.

Around the same time, police departments began providing officers with professional instruction. In New York City, Theodore Roosevelt authorized firearm instruction for police officers as early as 1895, and in Berlin, Erich Rahn began teaching *jûjutsu* to detectives in 1910. During the 1930s the Gestapo became interested in Japanese close-quarter methods; in 1938 a German policeman named Helmut Lehmann was sent to Japan specifically to learn *jûdô*, and upon his return to the Reich the following year, he was ranked fourth *dan* (fourth-degree black belt).

In Britain and Canada, policemen boxed or wrestled. (During the 1930s, a surprising number of Canadian amateur wrestling champions were police officers.) During the 1920s several London Metropolitan policemen also took *jûdô* instruction at the Budôkai, and in Vancouver, British Columbia, eleven Royal Canadian Mounted Police constables achieved *shôdan* (jûdô first-degree black belt ranking) by 1934.

In the United States, officer S. J. Jorgensen started a *jûjutsu* program for the Seattle Police Department in 1927. Police in Minnesota, Michigan, New Jersey, and California also started jûjutsu programs, and by 1940 such programs were nationwide. A British show wrestler named Leopold MacLaglan was often involved in establishing these programs, and the quality of instruction was not always the best.

J. Edgar Hoover's G-men had their own system of applied mayhem. The Bureau of Investigation's primary close-combat instructor was Major Anthony J. Drexel Biddle, U.S. Marine Corps, Retired. Biddle had done some boxing and fencing, and he enjoyed telling old ladies and little children Bible stories illustrated by homilies about how turning a bayonet equipped rifle sideways would keep the bayonet from sticking to the opponent's ribs (McEvoy 1942, 538–539). During the late 1920s, Biddle taught some grip releases and disarming techniques to the Philadelphia police, and after Franklin Roosevelt made Biddle's cousin Francis the attorney general of the United States, the FBI hired him to teach close-combat techniques to agents. Since FBI training took place at a Marine base in Virginia, Biddle also got to show his tricks to Marine officers during summer encampments, and as a result the Marine Corps Association published Biddle's *Do or Die: Military Manual of Advanced Science in Individual Combat* in 1937. *Cold Steel*, a 1952 text written by a former student named John Styer, is an improved version of *Do or Die*.

The Soviet method of unarmed combat was called *sambo*, short for *samooborona bez oruzhiya* (Russian; self-defense without weapons). Sambo started life as Kôdôkan Jûdô. From Sakhalin Island, 14-year-old Vasilij Sergevich Oshchepkov was sent to Tokyo in 1906. Admitted to the Kôdôkan in 1911, he earned his jûdô shôdan ranking in about six months and his second-degree grade in about two years. In 1914 he moved to Vladivostok, where he taught jûdô and did translations. In 1921 he went to work for the Red Army, and in 1929 he introduced jûdô to Moscow. In 1936 the Leningrad Sport Committee prohibited a competition between the Moscow and Leningrad teams; Oshchepkov complained, was arrested on a charge of being a Japanese spy, and subsequently died from what the Soviet police termed a "fit of angina." His students took the hint, and in November 1938 Anatolij Arcadievich Kharlampiev announced the invention of "Soviet freestyle wrestling," which coincidentally looked a lot like Russian-rules jûdô.

Following World War II, Soviet leader Joseph Stalin decided that the Soviets would compete in the Olympics. The Olympics already had international freestyle wrestling, so in 1946 Soviet freestyle wrestling was renamed *sambo*. (The acronym itself was the creation of Vladimir Spiridonov, but as he had been an officer in the Tsarist army, of course the Soviets downplayed his contributions, too.) Over time sambo and jûdô diverged, with the biggest difference perhaps being that sambo's philosophy emphasizes competition and self-defense rather than mutual benefit and welfare.

Colonies were not exempt from these nationalistic tendencies. For example, during the 1910s British policemen introduced boxing into Southern Rhodesia and the Union of South Africa. The idea was partly to wean black Africans from fencing with sticks and Afrikaners from practicing big-bore rifle shooting, and mostly to have fun. The Rhodesian and South African whites were never happy about the black boxers, however. Put crudely, settlers feared that black boxers would get uppity, while district officers feared the development of pan-tribal networks of any kind, including the ones required to organize a boxing tournament. Therefore competitions were mostly all-white affairs.

Racist attitudes also applied in India. As the British extended their control into the Punjab during the 1840s and 1850s, British wrestlers began meeting Muslim and Sikh wrestlers. Wrote Richard Francis Burton, "Not a few natives in my Company had at first the advantage of me, and this induced a trial of Indian training" (Letter from Paul Nurse, August 28, 1996). As in Africa, Europeans were not happy about seeing white men lose, so the Indian government prohibited mixed-race matches in 1874. Deterring rajahs from wrestling with Europeans was harder, though. "My great-grandfather Shivaji Rao . . . was a keen wrestler who loved to call people off the streets to come into the old city palace to wrestle with him," Richard Shivaji Rao Holkar told Charles Allen during the 1980s. "In 1903 he beat up the British Resident. They said, 'This will never do, so out you go,' and he had to abdicate in favour of my grandfather Tukoji Rao III" (Allen and Dwivedi 1985, 248).

In 1910, the Bengali millionaire Sharat Kumar Mishra sent the Indian champions Great Gama, Ahmed Bux, Imam Bux, and Gulam Mohiuddin to Europe to prove that they could best Europeans, and after they did, the British Foreign Office prohibited them from having any further matches in London. And, following Japanese military successes in Burma in 1942, the British also prohibited all Indian professional wrestling, ostensibly to reduce the risk of factional violence between Hindus, Sikhs, and Muslims.

U.S. servicemen introduced boxing into the Philippines as early as 1899, but Filipinos did not appear in the ring until around 1914. The reason for the American support was that the YMCA and the Knights of Columbus hoped that boxers would lead clean lives (the VD admissions rate in the Philippines for U.S. soldiers averaged around 17 percent [Sturdevant and Stolzfus 1992, 312–313]). Meanwhile the Filipinos wanted a gambling game with which to replace the banned cockfighting. Filipino collegiate athletes took up boxing after it was legalized in 1921, and this led to several medals during Far Eastern Championship Games. During the 1930s, the Filipino Constabulary also started encouraging members to practice freestyle wrestling. Here, however, the idea was less the improvement of skill in close-quarter battle than the desire to collect more medals during Far Eastern Championship Games.

A partial exception to this rule of nationalism being the driving force in the spread and development of twentieth-century military combatives appeared in China during the 1920s. In 1909, Shanghai police began receiving instruction in quanfa for the usual combination of nationalist and practical purposes. But by the 1920s the Shanghai police had come under the control of Europeans, and at the insistence of the British police captain William E. Fairbairn, officers began learning a combination of Japanese throws, British punches, Chinese kicks, Sikh wrestling, and American quick-draw pistol drills. The result was easy to teach, reasonably practical, and impressive in demonstration. During World War II the U.S., British, and Canadian governments hired Fairbairn, Dermot O'Neill, and other former Shanghai policemen to teach close-combat skills to commandos. Once again the demonstrations were impressive—and influential, too, as James Bond's superhuman skills in applied mayhem apparently date to a demonstration put on outside Ottawa in 1943.

But Fairbairn's pragmatism was an aberration, and during the late 1930s and early 1940s the establishment of Home Guard and Hitler Youth organizations created quite a market for jingoistic books. Examples include *Unarmed Combat* by Britain's James Hipkiss, *Combat without Weapons* by Canada's E. Hartley Leather, and *How to Fight Tough* by America's Jack Dempsey and Frank G. Menke. Inuring readers to violence and dehumanizing the enemy were important leitmotifs in all these books. As for the methods shown, well, let's just say that they worked better on willing partners than armed SS Panzergrenadiers. For instance, consider the training in mayhem illustrated in *Life Magazine* on February 9, 1942, pages 70–75. Two of the men shown in the pictures are Frank Shibukawa and Robert Mestemaker. Private Shibukawa had learned his *jûdô* in Japan and was a prewar Pacific Northwest *jûdô* champion. Corporal Mestemaker, meanwhile, had started studying *jûjutsu* while in high school and had kept at it during the years he worked as a corrections officer at the Michigan state penitentiary. So both men entered the army already possessing a considerable base of knowledge. Furthermore, what they showed was not something taught everyone, but instead rehearsed tricks specially developed to impress Groucho Marx and other visiting dignitaries (Svinth, forthcoming) So too much should not be made of their expertise.

In Japan, sports, calisthenics, and military drill were widely used to prepare the adolescent male population for military service. This was not because the Japanese generals really expected soldiers to wrestle or box on the battlefield, but because they believed that such training instilled *Yamato damashii* (the Japanese spirit) into shopkeepers' sons. So, under pressure from Diet, in 1911 Japan's Ministry of Education decided to require schoolboys to learn *jûjutsu* and *shinai kyôgi* (flexible stick competition), as *jûdô* and *kendô* were known until 1926. The idea, said the ministry, was to ensure that male students should be trained to be soldiers with patriotic conformity, martial spirit, obedience, and toughness of mind and body. During the 1920s, Japanese high school girls also began to be required to study halberd fencing (*naginata-dô*). In 1945, the girls were told to drive their halberds into the groins of descending American paratroops, but of course the atomic bomb put an end to that plan.

Following Hiroshima and Nagasaki, most Americans believed that the bomb had rendered hand-to-hand combat obsolete. Therefore the U.S. military quickly abandoned all training in close-quarter battle, which is unfortunate, since the U.S. Navy's wartime V-5 program of hand-to-hand fighting was practical. Freedom fighters and terrorists, on the other hand, lapped it up. For example, Indonesian Muslims attributed nearly magical power to *silat*, Israelis developed *krav maga* for use by commandos, and the Koreans developed a version of karate called *taekwondo*. ("Through *Taekwondo*, the soldiers' moral armament is strengthened, gallantry to protect the weak enhanced, courage against injustice fostered, and patriotism firmly planted," boasted the Korean general Chae Myung Shin in 1969 [Letters to the Editor, *Black Belt,* May 1969, 4–5].)

And, with decolonization on the horizon, imperial masters began encouraging "native" soldiers to box and wrestle. In Uganda, for example, Idi Amin became a boxing champion in the King's African Rifles, while in Malaya, silat was taught to Malaysians opposing Chinese Communist insurgency.

The fear of Communism also inspired the Americans to rethink their attitudes toward combatives training. For example, labor unrest in Japan caused the Americans to reintroduce *kendô* and jûdô into Japanese police training programs as early as 1947, and in 1949 fear of Communist saboteurs encouraged General Curtis LeMay to introduce jûdô into U.S. Air Force physical fitness programs. The U.S. Air Force program also had a profound effect on the modern Japanese martial arts. Said future Japan Karate Association leader Nakayama Masatoshi: "The Americans simply were not satisfied with following blindly like the Japanese. So, under Master Funakoshi [Gichin]'s guidance, I began an intense study of kinetics, physiology, anatomy, and hygienics" (Singleton 1989, 83–84). Equally importantly, discharged servicemen returned home to open jûdô and karate schools, which in turn introduced Asian martial arts to Middle America.

During the Vietnam War, military psychologists decided that the best way to create killers was to replace time spent sticking bayonets into straw bales with time spent chanting phrases such as "Blood makes the grass grow; kill, kill." Although these methods reportedly increased firing rates (U.S. Army studies of debatable reliability report firing rates of 25 percent in 1944, 55 percent in 1951, and 90 percent in 1971), they also increased individual soldiers' risk of post-traumatic stress disorders such as alcoholism, drug abuse, and suicide (Grossman 1995, 35, 181, 249–261). The new methods didn't do much for accuracy, either—another Vietnam-era study found that while soldiers could put 300 rounds in the air per minute, at 50 meters they still only hit a paper target one time per minute (Davis 2000, 10).

So following Vietnam there was renewed interest, at least in the United States, in teaching hand-to-hand combatives to prospective combat infantry. The Marines experimented with various systems based on boxing and karate, while the army went New Age.

The base document for the army's program was a position paper called "First Earth Battalion," and among the latter document's recommendations was the suggestion that soldiers practice "battle tuning," which was described, in so many words, as a combination of yogic stretches, karate kata, paced primal rock, and Belgian waffles (Channon 1979). Although "battle tuning" was a bit esoteric for many old soldiers, in 1985 the army hired former Marines Jack Cirie and Richard Strozzi Heckler to provide a couple of dozen Special Forces soldiers with training in biofeedback, aikidô, and "mind-body psychology." After six months, the soldiers were not aikidô masters but were on average 75 percent fitter than when they started (Heckler 1992, 1–2, 77, 91–92, 153, 263–264). Navy SEALs received an abbreviated version of this course in 1988, as did a company of U.S. Marines in 2000. Army Rangers, on the other hand, adopted Gracie Jiu-jitsu in 1994. In all cases, the idea was not to create great hand-to-hand fighters, but instead to instill the warrior ethos.

During the 1980s the United States decided to allocate significant resources to developing nonlethal technologies for use in what were euphemistically termed "operations other than war." Developments included chemical sprays, electronic stun guns, sticky foam, net guns, rope sprays, blinding lasers, and acoustic weapons. As suggested by the list, most of the new developments were technological rather than physical in nature. Police forces also began training officers in the use of pepper sprays. However, whether these changes were substantive or cosmetic remains to be seen, as by the mid-1990s the U.S. military had announced the initiation of research into robotic devices designed to replace human infantry altogether.

Joseph R. Svinth

References

Abe, Ikuo, Yasuharu Kiyohara, and Ken Nakajima. 2000. "Sport and Physical Education under Fascistization in Japan." http://ejmas.com/jalt/jaltart_abe_0600.htm.

Allen, Charles, and Sharada Dwivedi. 1985. *Lives of the Indian Princes.* New York: Crown Publishers.

Alter, Joseph S. 1995. "Gama the World Champion: Wrestling and Physical Culture in Colonial India." *Iron Game History,* October, 3–7.

Applegate, Rex. 1976. *Kill or Get Killed: Riot Control Techniques, Manhandling and Close Combat, for Police and the Military.* Boulder, CO: Paladin Press.

Bennett, Bruce. 1990. "Physical Education and Sport at Its Best—The Naval Aviation V-5 Pre-Flight Program." *Canadian Journal of History of Sport* 21, no. 2: 254–258.

Biddle, Cordelia Drexel, as told to Kyle Crichton. 1955. *My Philadelphia Father.* Garden City, NY: Doubleday.

Burton, Richard Francis. 1853. *A Complete System of Bayonet Exercise.* London: William Clowes and Sons.

Butts, Edmund L. 1903/1904. "Soldierly Bearing, Health and Athletics." *Outing* 63: 707–711.

Cassidy, William L. 1979a. "The Art of Silent Killing, WWII British Commando Style." *Soldier of Fortune,* July, 35–39.

———. 1979b. "Fairbairn in Shanghai." *Soldier of Fortune,* September, 70.

Cammell, Charles Richard. 1936. "Early Books of the Sword, No. III—English and Scottish." *The Connoisseur* 97 (June): 329–330.

Channon, James B. 1979. *The First Earth Battalion: Ideas and Ideals for Soldiers Everywhere.* Fort Monroe, VA: U.S. Army Training and Doctrine Command. Reprinted at http://ejmas.com/jnc/jncart_channon_0200.htm.

Chartrand, René, and Francis Back. 1988. *Louis XIV's Army.* London: Osprey Publishing.

Coe, Michael D., Peter Connolly, Anthony Harding, Victor Harris, Donald J. Larocca, Thom Richardson, Anthony North, Christopher Spring, and Fredrick Wilkinson. 1989. *Swords and Hilt Weapons*. New York: Weidenfeld and Nicolson.

Coffey, Thomas M. 1986. *Iron Eagle: The Turbulent Life of General Curtis LeMay*. New York: Crown Publishers.

Crosland, Philip. 1915. "The Bayonet and the Boxing Glove." *Health & Strength*, January 16, 37.

Davis, Darryl. 2000. "Infantry Weapons Revisited." *Marine Corps Gazette* 84, no. 12: 10.

Donvito, Ronald S. 1995. "Close Combat: The LINE System." *Marine Corps Gazette* 79, no. 2: 23.

Geraghty, Tony. 1982. *Inside the S.A S.* New York: Ballantine Books.

Grossman, Dave. 1995. *On Killing: The Psychological Cost of Learning to Kill in War and Society*. Boston: Little, Brown, and Co.

Harries, Meirion, and Susie Harries. 1991. *Soldiers of the Sun: The Rise and Fall of the Imperial Japanese Army*. New York: Random House.

Hayton-Keeva, Sally. 1987. *Valiant Women in War and Exile*. San Francisco: City Lights Books.

Heckler, Richard Strozzi. 1992. *In Search of the Warrior Spirit*. 2d ed. Berkeley, CA: North Atlantic Press.

Huang, Ray. 1981. *1587: A Year of No Significance: The Ming Dynasty in Decline*. New Haven: Yale University Press.

Hutton, Alfred. 1995. *The Sword and the Centuries*. New York: Barnes and Noble, 1995.

Jacomb, William J. 1918. *Boxing for Beginners with Chapter Showing Its Relationship to Bayonet Fighting*. Philadelphia: Lea and Febiger.

Jacques, Brett, and Scott Anderson. 1999. "The Development of Sambo in Europe and America." *Journal of Asian Martial Arts* 8, no. 2: 20–41.

Jeffers, H. Paul. 1994. *Commissioner Roosevelt: The Story of Theodore Roosevelt and the New York City Police, 1895–1897*. New York: John Wiley and Sons, 1994.

Keegan, John. 1996. "Marching in Time through History." *Times Literary Supplement*, July 12. See also letters to the editor in *Times Literary Supplement* dated August 2, August 9, and August 16, 1996.

Kolatch, Jonathan. 1972. *Sports, Politics, and Ideology in China*. Middle Village, NY: Jonathan David Publishers.

Kopets, Keith, ed. 2000. "The Origins of the Fire Team: Excerpts from an Interview with Homer L. Litzenberg, 27–30 April 1951." *Marine Corps Gazette* 84, no. 12: 43–44.

Leyshon, Glynn A. 1984. *Of Mats and Men: The Story of Canadian Amateur and Olympic Wrestling from 1600 to 1984*. London, Ontario: Sports Dynamics.

Littauer, Vladimir S. 1991. *The Development of Modern Riding*. New York: Howell Book House.

Lukashev, Michail. 2000. "Creation of Sambo." http://cclib.nsu.ru/projects/satbi/satbi-e/statyi/sambo.html.

Macleod, David I. 1983. *Building Character in the American Boy: The Boy Scouts, YMCA, and Their Forerunners, 1870–1920*. Madison: University of Wisconsin Press.

Mandell, Richard. 1984. *Sport: A Cultural History*. New York: Columbia University Press.

Marshall, S. L. A. 1978. *Men against Fire.* Gloucester, MA: Peter Smith.

McEvoy, J. P. 1942. "Drexel Biddle: Gentleman Tough." *American Mercury* 54: 538–539.

McNeill, William H. 1995. *Keeping Together in Time: Dance and Drill in Human History.* Cambridge, MA: Harvard University Press.

Morris, Ivan I. 1960. *Nationalism and the Right Wing in Japan: A Study of Post-War Trends.* London: Oxford University Press.

Nawrocki, Selma, and Eleanor Raskovich. 1993. "Power Technology Demonstrators for the Future Land Warrior." *Army RD&A Bulletin,* PB 70-93-2, March-April, 26–29.

Noble, Graham. 1992. "Unarmed Combat and Its Literature." Unpublished manuscript.

P'an Shih. 1976. "Theatrical Swordplay and Actual Combat with Bayonet on the Battlefield." Beijing *Jen-Min Jih-Pao,* December 13, 2.

Parker, Geoffrey. 1996. "Parade-ground Practice." *Times Literary Supplement,* June 14, 26.

Peiser, Benny Josef. 2000. "Western Theories about the Origins of Sport in Ancient China." http://www.umist.ac.uk/UMIST_Sport/peiser2.html.

Perrin, Noel. 1979. *Giving Up the Gun: Japan's Reversion to the Sword, 1543–1879.* Boston: David R. Godine.

Power, Guy H. 1998. "*Budō* in Japanese and U.S. Policies." M.P.A. thesis, San Jose State University.

Ralston, David B. 1996. *Importing the European Army: The Introduction of European Military Techniques and Institutions into the Extra-European World, 1600–1914.* Chicago: University of Chicago Press.

Rheingold, Howard. 1991. *Virtual Reality.* New York: Summit Books.

Rommel, Erwin. 1979. *Attacks.* Provo, UT: Athena Press.

Romminger, Donald W., Jr. 1985. "From Playing Field to Battleground: The United States Navy V-5 Preflight Program in World War II." *Journal of Sport History* 12, no. 5: 254–258.

Sheppard, M. C. 1958. "Silat: The Malay Art of Self-Defence." *The Straits Times Annual,* 12–15.

Sheridan, James E. 1966. *Chinese Warlord: The Career of Feng Yü-hsiang.* Stanford, CA: Stanford University Press.

Singleton, Ken. 1989. *An Introduction to Karate.* London: McDonald Optima.

Smith, Robert W. 1999. *Martial Musings: A Portrayal of Martial Arts in the 20th Century.* Erie, PA: Via Media Publishing.

Sturdevant, Saundra Pollock, and Brenda Stolzfus. 1992. *Let the Good Times Roll: Prostitution and the U.S. Military in Asia.* New York: New Press.

Styers, John. 1974. *Cold Steel.* Boulder, CO: Paladin Press.

Suvorov, Viktor. 1990. *Spetsnaz: The Inside Story of the Soviet Special Forces.* New York: Pocket Books.

Svinth, Joseph R. Forthcoming. *Getting a Grip: Judo in the Nikkei Communities of the Pacific Northwest, 1900–1950.*

Trench, Charles Chenevix. 1972. *A History of Marksmanship.* Chicago: Follett Publishing.

United States Air Force. 1963. "Stead Air Force Base Student Study Guide 140004-3 (Academic), Combative Measures Instructor Training (Judo), February 1963." Reprinted at http://ejmas.com/jnc/jncart_aircrew_1100.htm.

United States Army. 1992. Field Manual 21-150. *Combatives.*

——. 1942. Field Manual 21-150. *Unarmed Defense for the American Soldier.* Portions reprinted at http://ejmas.com/jnc/jncart_FM21–150a_0800.htm.

United States Marine Corps. 1966. *Hand-to-Hand Combat.* Proposed Fleet Marine Force Manual 1-4.

Wakeman, Fred, Jr. 1995. *Policing Shanghai, 1927–37.* Berkeley: University of California Press.

Weir, L. H. 1937. *Europe at Play: A Study of Recreation and Leisure Time Activities.* New York: A. S. Barnes.

Williams, F. D. G. 1994. *SLAM: The Influence of S. L. A. Marshall on the United States Army.* Edited and introduced by Susan Canedy. Fort Monroe, VA: Office of the Command Historian, U.S. Army Training and Doctrine Command.

Dojang
See Training Area

Dôjô
See Training Area

Dueling

A typical definition of the duel holds that it is a "combat between two persons, fought with deadly weapons by agreement, usually under formal conditions and in the presence of witnesses (seconds) on each side" or "any contest between two antagonists" (*Webster's New Collegiate Dictionary*).

Discussions of dueling abound, but—except for Mr. Webster—precise definitions are missing. Characteristics of the duel, however, are in most discussions agreed upon:

1. Duelists fight with matched weapons, which are lethal
2. Duelists agree upon conditions, such as time, place, weapons, who should be present
3. Duelists are from the same social class
4. Motives range from preserving honor to revenge to the killing of a rival, with honor most frequently mentioned

Yet, a slight fuzziness remains as to what dueling is, making the classification of some encounters difficult. There is even fuzziness as to how *dueling* and *duelist* should be spelled. Webster gives the first spelling as a single *l*, the second as two *l*s. Webster's gives both *dueling* and *duelling*, both *duelist* and *duellist*, and considers both spellings equally acceptable.

The weapons used in duels are handheld personal weapons, the most common being bladed weapons (swords, sabers, rapiers, and knives) and firearms (generally single-shot pistols). Although the combatants may not intend to kill each other, the weapons used have that potential. Thus piano duels in late eighteenth-century Germany, or for that matter any musical contest, such as the Eskimo song duel, do not qualify as true duels. Differently equipped champions from different military forces, such as David and Goliath (First Book of Samuel, Old Testament), probably should also not be considered duelists, whereas similarly equipped Zulu warriors carrying shields and throwing spears who have stepped forward from their ranks to challenge each other can perhaps be considered duelists. It is harder, though, to decide whether military snipers with scoped rifles hunting each other in Vietnam or fighter pilots in that war or in earlier wars are duelists. Perhaps they should not be considered such because no rules are followed—ambushing whether in the jungle or from behind clouds being the primary tactic—rather than because of minor differences in weapons.

Duels are staged, not for the public, but before select witnesses, assistants (called in English seconds), and physicians. News of a duel, however, becomes public when word spreads of a wounding or fatality. Although duels are almost always between individuals, there is the possibility that they could be between teams. American popular literature and its movies abound with gunfights. Are these duels? When the Earp brothers met the Clanton and McLaury brothers for a gunfight at the OK Corral, was this a duel? Probably not, because witnesses and the other members of the typical duelist's entourage were not invited. Later, both Morgan and Virgil Earp were ambushed in separate encounters, with Morgan killed and Virgil crippled. Wyatt later killed the presumed assailants, probably in ambushes.

Although equal rank is not given as a defining attribute by Webster's, nearly all scholars who have studied the duel emphasize that duelists are from the same social class. If a lower-class person issues a challenge to an upper-class person, it is ignored and seen as presumptuous. The custom of dueling has died out in the English-speaking world, but when it was prevalent, it was considered bad form to challenge royalty, representatives of the Crown such as royal governors, and clergy. Indeed, it was treason to contemplate the death of the king or one of his family members. If the challenge came from a social equal, it might be hard to ignore. If the upper-class person chose not to ignore the lower-class person's challenge or insults, he might assault him with a cane or horsewhip.

The notion that gentlemen caned or horsewhipped men of lesser social status had symbolic significance. Any person hit with a cane or lashed with a whip was being told in a very rough and public way that he did not rank as high as his attacker; hence the importance of the choice of weapons by southern senator Preston Brooks for his merciless attack on New England senator Charles Sumner in Washington in 1856.

Sumner, in a speech, had used such words as "harlot," "pirate," "falsifier," "assassin," and "swindler" to describe elderly South Carolina sen-

A Code of Honor—A Duel in the Bois de Boulogne, Near Paris. *This illustration of a typical duel appeared in the January 8, 1875, edition of* Harper's Weekly *and clearly shows all the elements of a "duel." (Harper's Weekly)*

ator Andrew Pickens Butler. Preston Brooks, Butler's nephew, sought out Sumner and is reputed to have said: "Mr. Sumner, I have read your speech carefully, and with as much calmness as I could be expected to read such a speech. You have libeled my State, and slandered my relation, who is aged and absent, and I feel it to be my duty to punish you for it." The punishment followed, and Sumner was caned senseless (Williams 1980, 26).

General Andrew Jackson, future president of the United States, attempted in 1813 to horsewhip Thomas II. Benton, a future U.S. senator, but Benton reached for a pistol while Jackson dropped the whip and drew his own firearm. Benton's younger brother Jesse, who had the grudge against Jackson, was on the scene; he shot Jackson with a pistol loaded with a slug of lead and two bullets. Jackson's shoulder was shattered and his left arm pierced, but he refused amputation. Fifteen years later, when both Andrew and Thomas were U.S. senators, they became reconciled. During Jackson's presidency (1829–1837), Benton was a staunch supporter, and on Jackson's death in 1847 Benton eulogized him. Both Jackson and Benton killed men in duels.

Although motives for challenging and accepting a duel can vary, honor is most frequently mentioned. For members of an upper class, honor is directly linked to class membership. Dueling not only defines who is in the upper class, but it also projects the message that the upper class is composed of honorable men. To decline challenges from members of one's own class can result in diminished class standing. For members of a lower class to decline to fight can also place them in physical jeopardy; they may become the targets of bullies who would steal from them, take girlfriends or mates, or injure them for sport. Upper-class members can call upon the police authority of the state to protect them. When unimportant people request protection, they are often ignored (unless perhaps they are spies or informers for the state).

A survey of armed combat among peoples without centralized political systems (i.e., those who live in bands and tribes) reveals numerous encounters that resemble dueling but fail to meet all four characteristics. Weapons are not matched, there are no agreed-upon conditions (or at least there is no evidence for such), or the social position of the combatants differs (social stratification is not found in bands, but may occur in tribes). Since motives can vary, the characteristic four cannot be used to rule out an armed combat that meets the other three characteristics. Sometimes, however, the criteria are met. Several examples of armed combat will be examined. The purpose of the survey is not to create a taxonomy but to reveal the conditions under which dueling arises. Several conclusions may be drawn from the following examples.

Although armed combat occurs among bands (usually hunters and gatherers), dueling, if it occurs at all, is rare. Among more politically complex social units known as tribes, dueling sometimes occurs. When it does, it is usually between combatants from different political communities, which are sometimes even culturally different. The survey indicates that dueling has its origin in the military, particularly within those societies that develop elite warriors. While nearly all societies have military organizations, by no means all warring societies produce elite warriors and a warrior tradition. Put another way, in political systems that are not centralized, every able-bodied male becomes a warrior, but in some societies some men become specialists in the use of weapons. If this occurs, there emerges a military elite with a warrior tradition. (Militaries that stress subordination of soldiers to the military organization do not develop an elite, even though the society may be highly militaristic.) These elites provide the first duelists. The duels take place, as noted above, between different political communities, rather than within a single political community. The combatants stand in front of their respective military organizations and represent them. This pattern is also found among peoples with centralized political systems (chiefdoms and states). At this level of sociopolitical complexity, duels between military personnel may occur within the political community. However, in some societies another factor—feuding—comes into play, which strongly works against the development of internal dueling. Feuding societies do not have dueling. In societies without feuding, those no longer in the military and civilians imitating them may also engage in duels provided they are of the same social class, stratification being a characteristic of most centralized political systems. Middle and lower classes may imitate upper classes and/or adopt their own forms of dueling. Thus, dueling first arises in warfare and is then transferred to the civilian realm. The evidence suggests the following sequence of stages: (1) no duels, (2) duels between elite warriors from two political communities, (3) duels between military personnel within a political community, (4) duels between civilians within a political community.

For those societies at the first two stages, the following features are apparent. In nearly all uncentralized political systems every able-bodied man carries weapons for hunting—the spear, the bow and arrow, or the club. These weapons can also be used in warfare, assassinations, executions, self-defense, and dueling. A two-component warfare pattern consisting of ambushes and lines occurs in nearly all uncentralized political systems that engage in warfare. Ambushes combine surprise with a shoot-on-sight response, with better weapons than one's enemies if possible—no duel here. Line formations, however, may place opposing combatants a short distance from each other. Here is the place to start looking for duels. Paintings on rock walls provide the first evidence for armed encounters that could be duels. In Arnham Land, northern Australia, 10,000 years ago, Aborigines depicted warriors confronting each other with boomerangs, used as throwing and shock weapons, and barbed spears. Spears are shown plunged into fallen figures. Given the multiplicity of weapons both in flight and sometimes lodged in one figure, these scenes appear to illustrate line formations rather than duels. These native Australians, as well as !Kung Bushmen of South Africa, went armed most of the time. For egalitarian societies, James Woodburn has noted that "hunting weapons are lethal not just for game animals but also for people." He describes "the access which all males have to weapons among the !Kung [and other hunting and gathering peoples]. There are serious dangers in antagonizing someone. . . . [H]e could respond with violence. . . . Effective protection against ambush is impossible" (1982, 436). No duel here.

Tribes, the more developed of the two types of uncentralized political systems, provide examples of dueling. The line formations of the Dani of Highland New Guinea place enemy warriors in direct confrontation. The ethnographic movie *Dead Birds* by Robert Gardiner shows individual spear-throwers skirmishing. Although weapons are matched, this is not a duel. The confrontation arose during a battle, and there was no pre-arrangement for these warriors to meet. While the Zulu were still at the tribal level of sociopolitical complexity (ca. 1800) they engaged in "dueling battles":

> When conflict arose between tribes, a day and a place were arranged for settling the dispute by combat. On that day the rival tribes marched to battle, the warriors drawing up in lines at a distance of about 100 yards apart. Behind the lines stood the remaining members of each tribe, who during the battle cheered their kinsmen on to greater effort. The warriors carried five-foot tall, oval shields and two or three light javelins. These rawhide shields, when hardened by dipping in water, could not be penetrated by the missiles. Chosen warriors, who would advance to within 50 yards of each other and shout insults, opened the combat by hurling their spears. Eventually more and more warriors would be drawn into the battle until one side ceased fighting and fled. (Otterbein 1994, 30)

The criteria for dueling seem to be met. Prearranged, challenges by individual warriors, matched weapons, same culture and social class. However, when more warriors join in and a general battle ensues, the duel is over. Zulu "dueling battles" just make it to Stage Two.

Plains Indians of North America provide a better example of dueling. These Native Americans belonged to military societies and were deeply concerned with honor and personal status. The following duel between a Mandan and a Cheyenne warrior recounted by Andrew Sanders tells it all:

> Formal single combats between noted warriors or between champions of groups are reported from warrior societies around the world. They are frequently reported for nineteenth-century Plains Indians. Sometimes they involved behavior comparable to the medieval European idea of chivalry, at least under the proper set of circumstances. A classic example is the American artist George Catlin's account of a duel between the noted Mandan leader Mato-Topé ("Four Bears") and a Cheyenne war chief. When a party of Mandans met a much larger Cheyenne war party, Mato-Topé made towards them and thrust his lance into the ground. He hung his sash (the insignia of his position in his military association) upon it as a sign that he would not retreat. The Cheyenne chief then challenged Mato-Topé to single combat by thrusting his ornate lance (the symbol of his office in his military association) into the ground next to that of Mato-Topé. The two men fought from horseback with guns until Mato-Topé's powder horn was destroyed. The Cheyenne threw away his gun so that they remained evenly matched. They fought with bow and arrow until Mato-Topé's horse was killed, when the Cheyenne voluntarily dismounted and they fought on foot. When the Cheyenne's quiver was empty both men discarded bow and shield and closed to fight with knives. Mato-Topé discovered that he had left his knife at home, and a desperate struggle ensued for the Cheyenne's weapon. Although wounded badly in the hand and several times in the body, Mato-Topé succeeded in wresting the Cheyenne's knife from him, killing him, and taking his scalp. Consequently, among his war honors Mato-Topé wore a red wooden knife in his hair to symbolize the deed, and the duel was one of the eleven war exploits painted on his buffalo robe. (1999, 777)

This pattern of an elite warrior stepping forward to take on a challenger is found in centralized political systems but gives way under pressure of intensifying warfare. The next example, from a chiefdom-level society, took place in northeastern North America between the Iroquois and their enemies the Algonquins. Prior to 1609, these Native Americans wore body armor, carried shields, and fought with bows and arrows. The opposing sides formed two lines in the open; war chiefs would advance in front of their lines and challenge each other. Samuel de Champlain, the French explorer, was with the Algonquins; he recounts his reaction to the encounter: "Our Indians put me ahead some twenty yards, and I marched on until I was within thirty yards of the enemy, who as soon as they caught sight of me halted and gazed at me and I at them. When I saw them make a move to draw their bows upon us, I took aim with my arquebus and shot straight at one of the three chiefs, and with this shot two fell to the ground and one of their companions was wounded who died thereof a little later. I had put four bullets into my arquebus" (Otterbein 1994, 5). Iroquois dueling came, thus, to an abrupt end. Iroquois and Huron campaigns and battles in the next forty years provide no examples of dueling.

Zulu "dueling battles" also ceased as warfare intensified. As the Zulu evolved into a chiefdom and then a state, a remarkable elite warrior, Shaka, devised a new weapon and new tactics in approximately 1810. He replaced his javelins with a short, broad-bladed stabbing spear, retained his shield, but discarded his sandals in order to gain greater mobility. By rushing upon his opponent he was able to use his shield to hook away his enemy's shield, thus exposing the warrior's left side to a spear thrust. Shaka also changed military tactics by arranging the soldiers in his command—a company of about 100 men—into a close-order, shield-to-shield formation with two "horns" designed to encircle the enemy. Shaka's killing of an enemy warrior with a new weapon and a new tactic brought an end to Zulu duels.

In the ancient Middle East (Middle Bronze Age, 2100 to 1570 B.C.), Semitic tribes of Palestine and Syria had individual combat "between two warrior-heroes, as representatives of two contending forces. Its outcome, under prearranged agreement between both sides, determined the issue between the two forces" (Yadin 1963, 72). Although Yadin refers to these contests as duels, the combatants were not equipped the same. In the example given, the Egyptian man who was living with the Semites had a bow and arrow and a sword; he practiced with both before the "duel." The enemy warrior had a shield, battle-ax, and javelins. The javelins missed, but the arrows found their mark, the neck. The Egyptian killed his opponent with his own battle-ax. Duels of this nature continued to be fought as the tribes developed into centralized political systems. In the most famous duel of all—approximately 3,000 years ago—the First Book of Samuel tells us that Goliath, a Philistine, was equipped with a coat of mail, bronze helmet, bronze greaves to protect the legs, and a javelin. He was also accompanied by a shield bearer. David, later to become king of the Hebrews, armed with a sling, could "operate beyond the range of Goliath's weapons" (Yadin 1963, 265). Yadin insists that these contests are duels because they took "place in accordance with prior agreement of the two armies, both accepting the condition that their fate shall be decided by the outcome of the contest" (265). Yadin describes other duels where the soldiers are similarly equipped with swords (266–267). These are duels. Stage Two had been reached.

Duels between men of the same military organization, Stage Three, occur during more recent history in the West—that is, during the Middle Ages, and civilian duels, Stage Four, occur even more recently in Euro-American Dueling. Stage Three is not easily reached because a widespread practice, feuding, works against the development of dueling within polities. Approximately 50 percent of the world's peoples practice feuding (the practice of taking blood revenge following a homicide). In feuding societies honor focuses not upon the individual, as it does in dueling societies, but upon the kinship group. If someone is killed in a feuding society, his or her relatives seek revenge by killing the killer or a close relative of the killer, and three or more killings or acts of violence occur. In a feuding society, no one would dare to intentionally kill another in a duel. If a duel occurred in an area where feuding was an accepted practice, the resulting injuries and possible deaths would start a feud between the kinship groups of the participants. In other words, dueling neither develops in nor is accepted by feuding societies: Where feuds, no duels. Data from the British Isles support this conclusion. Feuding occurred over large areas of Scotland, and arranged battles between small groups of warriors (say thirty on a side) sometimes took place; dueling was rare in Scotland, and when it did occur it was likely to be in urban centers such as Edinburgh.

Stage Three dueling developed in Europe during the early Middle Ages, in areas where feuding had waned. Dueling within polities by elite military personnel is regarded by most scholars as a uniquely European custom, although they recognize that in feudal Japan samurai warriors behaved similarly. Monarchs at war, such as the Norman kings, banned feuding. (This is consistent with the cross-cultural finding of Otterbein and Otterbein that centralized political systems, if at war, do not have feuding even if patrilocal kinship groups are present.)

Several sources for the European duel have been proposed. Kevin McAleer suggests a Scandinavian origin: "The single combat for personal retribution had its beginnings as an ancient Germanic custom whose most ardent practitioners were pagan Scandinavians. They would stage their battles on lonely isles, the two nude combatants strapped together at the chest.

A knife would be pressed into each of their hands. A signal would be given—at which point they would stab each other like wild beasts. They would flail away until one of them either succumbed or begged for quarter" (1994, 13).

These "duels" are perhaps the origin of trial by combat or the judicial combat. The belief was that God would favor the just combatant and ensure his victory. Authorities would punish the loser, often hanging him. Judicial combats may have occurred as early as A.D. 500. Popes sanctioned them. Such trials largely disappeared by 1500. During the interval, the practice was "increasingly a prerogative of the upper classes, accustomed to the use of their weapons" (Kiernan 1988, 34).

Another possible source for the duel was the medieval tournament, which seems to have had its origin in small-scale battles between groups of rival knights. By the fourteenth century, the joust, or single combat, took the place of the melee, as the small-scale battle was called. Sometimes blunted weapons were used and sometimes they were not. Kiernan asserts that "all the diverse forms of single combat contributed to the 'duel of honour' that was coming to the front in the later Middle Ages, and was the direct ancestor of the modern duel. Like trial by combat or the joust, it required official sanction, and took place under regulation" (1988, 40).

Chivalry developed, and by the 1500s treatises on dueling were published. The duel in modern form became a privilege of the noble class. Stage Four was finally reached. For an individual, the ability to give and accept challenges defined him as not only a person of honor, but as a member of the aristocracy. As Europe became modern, the duel did not decline as might be expected, for the duel became attractive to members of the middle class who aspired to become members of the gentry. Outlawing of the duel by monarchs and governments did not prevent the duel's spread. The duel even spread to the lower classes, whose duels Pieter Spierenburg (1998) has referred to as "popular duels" in contrast to "elite duels." The practice even persisted into the twentieth century.

Perhaps because the duel persisted in Germany until World War II, creating a plethora of information, recent scholarly attention has focused on the German duel in the late nineteenth century. Three theories for its persistence have been offered: (1) Kiernan sees the duel, including the German duel, as a survival from a bygone era that was used by the aristocracy as a means of preserving their privileged position; (2) Ute Frevert argues that the German bourgeois adopted dueling as a means by which men could achieve and maintain honor by demonstrating personal bravery; (3) McAleer views the German duel as an attempt at recovery of an illusory past, a practice through which men of honor, by demonstrating courage, could link themselves to the ruling warrior class of the Middle Ages. The theories are different, yet they have similarities, and together they shed light on the nature of the German duel.

Dueling was brought to the United States by European army officers, French, German, and English, during the American Revolution. Fundamental to the formal duel, an aristocratic practice, is the principle that duels are fought by gentlemen to preserve their honor. Dueling thus became established only in those regions of the United States that had established aristocracies that did not subscribe to pacifist values, namely the lowland South, from Virginia through the low country of South Carolina to New Orleans. Two theories have been offered to explain the duel in America. The first asserts that the rise and fall of dueling went hand in hand with the rise and fall of the southern slave-owning aristocracy. As Jack K. Williams puts it, "The formal duel fitted easily and well into this concept of aristocracy. The duel, as a means of settling disputes, could be restricted to use by the upper class. Dueling would demonstrate uncompromising courage, stability, calmness under stress" (1980, 74). Lee Kennett and James LaVeme Anderson, on the other hand, point out, "Its most dedicated practitioners were army and navy officers, by profession followers of a quasi-chivalrous code, and southerners, who embraced it most enthusiastically and clung to it longest. Like most European institutions, dueling suffered something of a sea change in its transfer to the New World. In the Old World it had been a badge of gentility; in America it became an affirmation of manhood. . . . Dueling was a manifestation of a developing society and so it was natural that men resorted to it rather than the legal means of securing a redress of grievance" (1975, 141, 144).

Yet the duel occurred primarily in areas where there were courts. "The duel traveled with low-country Southerners into the hill country and beyond, but frontiersmen and mountain people were disinclined to accept the trappings of written codes of procedure for their personal affrays!" (Williams 1980, 7). Several reasons seem quite apparent. The people of Appalachia were not aristocrats, many could barely read or write, and feuding as a means of maintaining family honor was well established. As argued above, if a duel occurs in an area where feuding is an accepted practice, the resulting injuries and possible deaths will start a feud; dueling can enter a region only if the cultural practices do not include feuding. Thus feuding and dueling do not occur in the same regions.

American dueling, unlike its European counterpart in the nineteenth century, was deadly. In Europe the goal of the duelist was to achieve honor by showing courage in the face of death. Winning by wounding or killing the opponent was unnecessary. On the other hand, many American duelists tried to kill their opponents. This difference was noted by Alexis de Tocqueville in 1831 in his *Democracy in America:* "In Europe, one hardly ever fights a duel except in order to be able to say that one has done so; the offense is generally a sort of moral stain which one wants to wash away and which most often is washed away at little expense. In America one only fights to kill; one fights because one sees no hope of getting one's adversary condemned to death" (Hussey 1980, 8).

Dueling in the American South occurred from the time of the Revolution to the Civil War. Duels were frequent. Many of the duelists were prominent political figures, and the consequences were often fatal. Anyone doubting this statement should look at the first five denominations of U.S. paper money. One man whose head is shown died in a duel, while another killed a man in a duel: respectively, Alexander Hamilton and Andrew Jackson.

Political opponents Alexander Hamilton and Vice President Aaron Burr met on the dueling ground at Weehawken, New Jersey, on July 11, 1804, with their seconds. Hamilton's persistent libeling of Burr precipitated Burr's challenge. As the challenged party, Hamilton supplied the matched dueling pistols. The seconds measured the distance, ten full paces. The duelists loaded the pistols in each other's presence, after which the parties took their stations. On the command "Present," each raised his pistol and fired. Apparently, Burr fired first, with the ball hitting Hamilton in the right side; Hamilton swayed and the pistol fired, missing Burr. A surgeon friend of Hamilton attended to him. The surgeon's account says that Hamilton had not intended to fire, while Burr's second claimed Hamilton fired first. It was obvious to both Hamilton and the surgeon that he was fatally wounded.

Andrew Jackson's killing of Charles Dickinson in a duel in Logan County, Kentucky, on May 30, 1806, is less well known. The animosity between them grew out of a dispute about stakes in a horse race that did not take place. Jackson issued the challenge, which Dickinson eagerly accepted, although he did not have a set of dueling pistols. Yet Dickinson, a snapshooter who did not take deliberate aim, practiced en route to the dueling field. The agreed-upon distance was 24 feet. Jackson, a thin and ascetic man, dressed in large overgarments and twisted his body within his coat so that it was almost sidewise. Dickinson was a large, florid man. On the command to fire, Dickinson shot, and Jackson held his fire. Jackson was hit, his breastbone scored and several ribs fractured, but he stood his ground. Jackson's twist of body had saved his life. Jackson aimed and pulled the trigger, but the hammer stopped at half cock. He recocked it and took aim before firing. The bullet passed through Dickinson's body below the ribs. Dickinson took all day to bleed to death. Jackson was later criticized for recocking his pistol, something an honorable man would not have done. But each man wanted to kill the other.

Keith F. Otterbein

See also Gunfighters; Masters of Defence; Swordsmanship, European Medieval; Swordsmanship, European Renaissance; Swordsmanship, Japanese

References

Barra, Allen. 1994. "Who Was Wyatt Earp?" *American Heritage* 49, no. 8: 76–85.

Brown, Keith M. 1986. *Bloodfeud in Scotland, 1573–1625: Violence, Justice and Politics in an Early Modern Society.* Edinburgh: John Donald Publishers.

Catlin, George. [1903] 1926. *North American Indians: Being Letters and Notes on Their Manners, Customs, and Conditions, Written during Eight Years' Travel amongst the Wildest Tribes of Indians in North America, 1832–1839.* Edinburgh: John Grant.

Daly, Martin, and Margo Wilson. 1988. *Homicide.* New York: Aldine de Gruyter.

Frevert, Ute. 1995. *Men of Honour: A Social and Cultural History of the Duel.* Translated by Anthony Williams. Cambridge: Polity Press.

Hussey, Jeanette. 1980. *The Code Duello in America.* Washington, DC: Smithsonian Institution Press.

Kennett, Lee, and James LaVeme Anderson. 1975. *The Gun in America: The Origins of a National Dilemma.* Westport, CT: Greenwood Press.

Kiernan, V. G. 1988. *The Duel in European History: Honour and the Reign of Aristocracy.* Oxford: Oxford University Press.

McAleer, Kevin. 1994. *Dueling: The Cult of Honor in Fin-de-Siècle Germany.* Princeton: Princeton University Press.

Otterbein, Keith F. 1996. "Feuding." In *The Encyclopedia of Cultural Anthropology.* Edited by David Levinson and Melvin Ember. New York: Henry Holt.

———. 1994. *Feuding and Warfare: Selected Works of Keith F. Otterbein.* Langhorne: Gordon and Breach.

———. 1997. "The Origins of War." *Critical Review* 11: 251–277.

Otterbein, Keith F., and Charlotte Swanson Otterbein. 1965. "An Eye for an Eye, a Tooth for a Tooth: A Cross-Cultural Study of Feuding." *American Anthropologist* 67: 170–1482.

Sanders, Andrew. 1999. "Anthropology of Warriors." In *Encyclopedia of Violence, Peace and Conflict.* Edited by Lester R. Kurtz. San Diego: Academic Press.

Seitz, Don C. 1929. *Famous American Duels: With Some Account of the Causes That Led up to Them and the Men Engaged.* Freeport, NY: Books for Libraries Press.

Spierenburg, Pieter, ed. 1998. *Men and Violence: Gender, Honor, and Rituals in Modern Europe and America.* Columbus: Ohio State University Press.

Tacon, Paul S., and Christopher Chippendale. 1994. "Australia's Ancient Warriors: Changing Depictions of Fighting in the Rock Art of Arnhem Land, N.T." *Cambridge Archaeological Journal* 4: 211–248.

Williams, Jack K. 1980. *Dueling in the Old South: Vignettes of Social History.* College Station: Texas A & M Press.

Woodburn, James. 1982. "Egalitarian Societies." *Man* n.s. 17: 431–451.

Yadin, Yigael. 1963. *The Art of Warfare in Biblical Lands: In the Light of Archaeological Study.* New York: McGraw-Hill.

E

Escrima

See Philippines

Europe

The term *martial arts* today typically refers to high-level Asian fighting methods from China, Japan, Korea, the Philippines, and, to a lesser extent, Thailand, Burma, Indonesia, India, and Vietnam. This perspective is derived primarily from Western popular culture. The standard view holds that non-Asian contributions to the martial arts have been restricted to sport boxing, *savate*, Greco-Roman wrestling, and the modern fencing sports of foil, épée, and saber. Not only have substantial and highly sophisticated fighting systems, true martial arts, existed outside Asian contexts, but many survive and others are experiencing a renaissance. Like their Asian counterparts, Western martial arts offer their practitioners both self-defense and personal growth.

Proceeding from a concept of martial arts as formulated systems of fighting that teach the practitioners how to kill or injure an opponent while protecting themselves effectively, these combat systems may employ unarmed techniques or hand weapons (firearms excluded). The term *Western martial arts,* loosely used in this instance to encompass systems developing outside the greater Asian context, can refer to any martial art system that originated in Europe, the Americas, Russia, and even the Middle East or Central Asia. This entry will primarily focus on the martial arts of Europe, as its title suggests, but will also include arts from other areas that are usually ignored, although they are basically in the Western tradition. Sporting systems (such as boxing, wrestling, and modern fencing) that emphasize the use of safety equipment and intentionally limit the number and kind of techniques in order to be competitively scored are eliminated from consideration.

Although no claims can be made for an unbroken record, historical evidence suggests that Western martial arts have been in existence for at least 5,000 years. The first direct evidence of a high-level unarmed combat system dates to the Egyptian Middle Kingdom (2040–1785 B.C.), where techniques of throws, kicks, punches, and joint locks can be found painted on the walls of the tombs of Beni-Hassan. This is the oldest recorded "text" of unarmed fighting techniques in existence. From the variety of physical maneuvers that are demonstrated, it can be inferred that a high-level system of self-defense and unarmed combat existed in Egypt by this time. In addition, Egyptians clearly had extensive training in armed combat. They developed two-handed spears that could be wielded as lances, created shields to protect their warriors in an age when armor was scarce and expensive, and developed a unique sword, the *khopesh,* that could be used to disarm opponents. It is not difficult, in retrospect, to see that military and martial prowess was one of the reasons that this great civilization was able to endure for thousands of years.

If one moves forward 2,500 years to the Greek peninsula, martial arts are clearly documented, not only through material artifacts such as painted ceramics, but also by firsthand written accounts of practitioners and observers of these arts. In unarmed combat, the Greeks had boxing, wrestling, and the great ancestor of the "Ultimate Fighting Championship": the *pankration* (all powers). Boxing during this era was not limited to blows with the closed fists, but also involved the use of the edge of the hand, kicks, elbows, and knees. Wrestling was not the "Greco-Roman" variant of today, but was divided roughly into three main categories. The first type involved groundwork wherein the participants had to get opponents into a joint lock or hold. In the second variant, the participants had to throw each other to the ground, much as in jûdô or Chinese wrestling. The third type was a combination of the two. In the pankration, the purpose was to get the opponent to admit defeat by any means possible. The only forbidden techniques were eye-gouging and biting. This meant that practitioners could use punches, kicks, wrestling holds, joint locks and choke holds, and throws in any combination required to insure victory.

The ancient Greeks were famously well trained in the military use of weapons as well. The Greek hoplite warrior received extensive instruction in spear and short sword as well as shield work. History provides us with the results of soldiers well trained in these arts both for single combat and close-order drill. When the Hellenized Macedonian youth Alexander the Great set out in the third century B.C. to conquer the world using improved tactics and soldiers well trained in pankration and the use of sword, shield, and long spear, he very nearly succeeded. Only a revolt from his own soldiers and his final illness prevented him from moving deeper into India and beyond. It would be reasonable to assume that Alexander and his forces, which brought Greek civilization in the areas of warfare, mathematics, architecture, sculpture, music, and cuisine throughout the conquered territories of Asia, also would have spread their formidable martial culture.

Even more is known about the martial arts of the Roman Empire than about those of the Greeks. Indeed, it is from Latin that we even have our term *martial arts*—from the "arts of Mars," Roman god of war. From the disciplined training of the legionnaires to the brutal displays of professional gladiators, Romans displayed their martial prowess. In addition to adopting the skills and methods of the Greeks, they developed many of their own. Their use of logistics and applied engineering resulted in the most formidable war machine of the ancient world. Romans of all classes were also adept at knife fighting, both for personal safety and as a badge of honor. Intriguing hints of gladiator training with blunt or wooden weapons and of their battles between armed and unarmed opponents as well as the specialty of combat with animals suggest a complex repertoire of combat techniques. Speculation exists that some elements of such methods are reflected in the surviving manuals of medieval Italian Masters of Defence.

The decline of Roman civilization in the West and the rise of the feudal kingdoms of the Middle Ages did not halt the development of martial arts in Europe. In the period after the fall of the empire, powerful Germanic and Celtic warrior tribes prospered. These include many notorious for their martial spirits, such as the Gauls, Vandals, Goths, Picts, Angles, Jutes, Saxons, Franks, Lombards, Flems, Norse, Danes, Moors, and the Orthodox Christian warriors of the Byzantine Empire. The medieval warrior was a product of the cultural synthesis between the ordered might of the Roman war machine and the savage dynamism of Germano-Celtic tribes.

The feudal knight of the Middle Ages was to become the very embodiment of the highest martial skill in Western Europe. Medieval warrior cultures were highly trained in the use of a vast array of weaponry. They drilled in and innovated different combinations of arms and armor: assorted shields and bucklers, short-swords and great swords, axes, maces, staffs, daggers, the longbow and crossbow, as well as flails and war-hammers designed to smash the metal armor of opponents, and an array of deadly bladed pole weapons that assisted in the downfall of the armored knight.

The formidable use of the shield, a highly versatile and effective weapon in its own right, reached its pinnacle in Western Europe. Shield design was in constant refinement. A multitude of specialized shield designs, for use on foot and in mounted combat as well as joust, siege, and single duel, were developed during the Middle Ages.

During the medieval period, masters-at-arms were known at virtually every large village and keep, and knights were duty-bound to study arms for defense of church and realm. In addition, European warriors were in a constant struggle to improve military technology. Leather armor was re-

placed by mail (made of chain rings), which was eventually replaced by steel plate. Late medieval plate armor itself, although uncommon on most battlefields of the day, is famous for its defensive strength and ingenious design. All myths of lumbering, encumbered knights aside, what is seldom realized is plate's flexibility and balance as well as its superb craftsmanship and artistry. In fact, the armor used by warriors in the Middle Ages was developed to such quality that when NASA needed joint designs for its space suits, they actually studied European plate armor for hints.

Medieval knights and other warriors were also well trained in unarmed combat. Yet, there is also ample literary evidence that monks of the Middle Ages were deemed so adept at wrestling that knights were loath to contest them in

An armored ninth-century Franconian warrior, assuming a defensive position with sword and shield. This figure is based on a chess piece from a set by Karl des Grossen. (Christel Gerstenberg/Corbis)

any way other than armed. Unarmed techniques were included throughout the German *Kunst des Fechtens* (art of fighting), which included an array of bladed and staff weaponry along with unarmed skills. It taught the art of wrestling and ground fighting known as *Unterhalten* (holding down). The typical German *Fechtmeister* (fight-master) was well versed in close-quarters takedowns and grappling moves that made up what they called *Ringen am Schwert* (wrestling at the sword), as well as at disarming techniques called *Schwertnehmen* (sword taking). Practical yet sophisticated grappling techniques called collectively *Gioco Stretto* (usually translated as "body work") are described and illustrated in numerous Italian fighting manuals and are in many ways indistinguishable from those of certain Asian systems.

In the 1500s, Fabian von Auerswald produced a lengthy illustrated manual of self-defense that described throws, takedowns, joint locks, and numerous traditional holds of the German grappling and ground-fighting methods. In 1509, the *Collecteanea*, the first published work on wrestling, by the Spanish master-of-arms Pietro Monte, appeared. Monte also produced large volumes of material on the use of a wide range of weapons and on mounted fighting. He considered wrestling, however, to be the best foundation for all personal combat. His systematic curriculum of techniques and escapes was presented as a martial art, not as a sport, and he emphasized physical conditioning and fitness. Monte's style advocated counterfighting. Rather than direct aggressive attacks, he taught to strike the openings made by the opponent's attack, and he advised a calculating and even temperament on the part of the fighter. He also stressed the importance of being able to fall safely and to recover one's position in combat. Clearly, Monte's martial arts invite comparisons to the Asian arts.

The illustrated techniques of Johanne Georg Paschen, which appeared in 1659, give an insight into a sophisticated system of unarmed defense in that the work shows a variety of techniques, including boxing jabs, finger thrusts to the face, slapping deflects, low line kicks, and numerous wrist- and armlocks. Similarly, Nicolaes Petter's *fechtbuch* (fighting manual) of 1674 even includes high kicks, body throws and flips, and submission holds, as well as assorted counters against knife-wielding opponents.

Similar unarmed combat systems can be found, among other contexts, in Welsh traditions and in the modern wrestling arts of *Glima* in Iceland, *Schwingen* in Switzerland, and *Yagli* in Turkey. Investigation into the multitude of unarmed styles and techniques from surviving European written sources is still in its infancy.

Obviously, then, the advent of the Renaissance only accelerated the experimentation and creation of Western fighting arts. Swordsmanship continued to develop into highly complex personal fighting systems. The development of compound-hilt sword guards led to extreme point control with thrusting swords, which gave great advantage to those trained in such techniques. With warfare transformed by the widespread introduction of gunpowder, the nature and practice of individual combat changed significantly. Civilian schools of fencing and fighting proliferated in these times, replacing the older orders of warriors. Civilian "Masters of Defence" in Italy, Spain, and elsewhere were sought after for instruction, and members of professional fighting guilds taught in England and the German states.

The art of sword and buckler (small hand-shield) was also a popular one throughout Western Europe at this time. It was once even practiced as a martial sport by thirteenth-century German monks. This pastime served to develop fitness as well as to provide self-defense skills. Sword and buckler practice was especially popular in northern Italy, also. Later, among commoners in Elizabethan England, it became something of a national sport. Similar to the sword and shield of the medieval battlefield, the sword and buckler was a versatile and effective combination for war as well as civilian brawling and personal duels. Its nonmilitary application eventually contributed to the development of an entirely new civilian sword form, the vicious rapier.

The slender, surprisingly vicious rapier was an urban weapon for personal self-defense rather than a military sword intended for battlefield use,

An old German woodcut illustrating various methods of the "art of fighting," Kunst des Fechtens, which included an array of bladed and staff weaponry along with unarmed skills. (Courtesy of John Clements)

and indeed, was one of the first truly civilian weapons developed in any society. It rose from a practical street-fighting tool to the instrument of a "gentleman's" martial art in Western and Central Europe from roughly 1500 to 1700. No equivalent to this unique weapon form and its sophisticated manner of use is found in Asian societies, and no better example of a distinctly Western martial art can be seen. The rapier is a thrusting weapon with considerable range and a linear style well suited to exceedingly quick and penetrating attacks from difficult angles. Dueling and urban violence spurred the development of numerous fencing schools and rapier fighting styles. The practitioners of rapier fencing were innovative martialists at a time when European society was experiencing radical transformations. By the late 1600s, this environment led to the creation of the fencing salons and *salles* ("halls") of the upper classes for instruction in dueling with the small-sword. The small-sword was an elegant tool for defending gentlemanly honor and reputation with deadly precision. An extremely fast and deceptive thrusting tool, it has distant sporting descendants in the modern Olympic foil and épée. Both rapier and small-sword fencing incorporated the use of the dagger and an array of unarmed fighting techniques. Each was far more martial than the sporting versions of today and far more precise than the amusing swashbuckling nonsense of contemporary films.

Russia was also a land where martial arts were in constant development. During the eleventh and twelfth centuries, before the Mongol invasions, Russian warriors wore armor of high quality and wielded shields and long-swords in deadly combination. A Russian proverb confidently stated that a two-bladed sword from the *Rodina* (motherland) was more than a match for any one-bladed scimitar from the "pagans" (Muslims and Tartars). When Peter the Great assumed power in 1682, Russian peasants were so proficient at stickfighting that one of his first official acts was to put a stop to it. Peter was going to war against the Ottoman and Swedish empires, and he was going to need healthy troops for the army. In the stickfighting matches, a favorite village pastime, both combatants often were severely injured.

Russians also have a long history of indigenous wrestling traditions. Accounts from writers in the 1700s describe wrestling matches that lasted a great portion of the day, ending only when the victor had his opponent in a joint lock. We also know that as the Russian Empire expanded into Central Asia, the officers would write of native wrestling systems. Local wrestling champions from these conquered areas sometimes would be pitted against soldiers from the invading armies. Joint locks and choke holds were commonly mentioned as ways that such fights ended.

As they began the exploration and conquest of the globe, Western Europeans carried their martial systems with them. The Spanish, for example, maintained their own venerable method of fighting, *La Destreza* (literally, "dexterity," "skill," "ability," or "art"—more loosely used to mean "Philosophy of the Weapons" or "The Art and Science" of fighting). Spanish strategic military science and the personal skill of soldiers played a major role in the defeat of their opposing empires in the Americas and in the Philippines. It has been suggested in fact that the native fighting systems of these islands and Spanish techniques are blended in the modern Filipino martial arts.

Also during this time, new Western unarmed combat systems were being created and refined. Two examples that are still with us today are French *savate* and Brazilian *capoeira*. Since both systems developed as street combat styles rather than among the educated and literate classes, the origins of both are subjects of speculation and the oral traditions generated by such conjecture.

According to popular tradition, capoeira is a system of hand-to-hand combat developed by African slaves transplanted to work on the Portuguese plantations of Brazil. The style of fighting involves relatively little use of the hands for blocking or striking as compared to foot strikes, trips, and sweeps, and it often requires the practitioner to assume an inverted position through handstands and cartwheels. One of the most popular explanations for these unique characteristics is that with their hands chained, the African slaves took their native dances, which often involved the use of

This "art of fighting" also included the art of wrestling and ground fighting known as Unterhalten ("holding down") and close-quarters take-downs and grappling moves, shown here in this Albrecht Dürer illustration. (Courtesy of John Clements)

handsprings, cartwheels, and handstands, and created a system of self-defense that could be performed when manacled. Following emancipation in the nineteenth century, capoeira became associated with the urban criminal. This association kept the art in the streets and underground until well into the twentieth century. Currently, the art is practiced in what is regarded as the more traditional Angola form and the Regional form that shows the influence of other (perhaps even Asian) arts. In either form, however, capoeira is a martial art that developed in the New World.

The origins of savate are equally controversial, but it is known that by the end of the seventeenth century, French sailors fought with their feet as well as their hands. Although savate is the best known, various related foot-fighting arts existed throughout Europe. Like capoeira, savate began as a system associated with the lower and criminal classes but eventually found a following in salles similar to those European salons devoted to swordsmanship. Savate, in fact, incorporates forms using canes, bladed weapons, and wrestling techniques. A sporting form of savate—*Boxe Française*—survives into the contemporary period, as well as a more self-defense-oriented version—*Danse de rue Savate* (loosely, "Dance of the Street Savate"). Modern savate (especially Boxe Française) incorporates many of the hand strikes of boxing along with the foot techniques of the original art. Among the practitioners of this outstanding fighting art were Alexandre Dumas and Jules Verne. Indeed, the character of Passepartout in Jules Verne's *Around the World in Eighty Days* is a savate expert who is called upon to save his employer.

Despite gaps in the historical record, it is apparent that for better than two millennia unarmed combat was developed, refined, and practiced by cultures as empires rose and fell. Armed combat shifted and changed with the advent of new and improved military technology. Clearly, fighting systems that required sophisticated training and practice have been in use in the "Western" regions of the globe as long as many Asian martial arts.

The development of firearms, however, led to an unprecedented technological revolution in Western military science that radically changed ideas of warfare and personal safety in that sector of the world. By the late 1600s, the firearm was the principal tool of personal and battlefield combat, and all practical armor was useless against it. The availability of pistols discouraged the use of rapiers or small-swords for personal defense or as dueling weapons. At the time of the American Civil War, repeating revolvers and rifles, Gatling guns, and cannons loaded with grapeshot ensured that attempts to use swords and cavalry charges against soldiers armed with such weapons would end as massacres.

In the twentieth century the West "discovered," and in many cases redefined, Asian martial arts and recovered many of their own fighting tra-

Illustration published in 1958 of a victorious gladiator standing over his defeated opponent as the crowd gives the thumbs down, indicating death, at the Colosseum in Rome. (Library of Congress)

ditions. For example, the contemporary Russian martial art of *sambo* (an acronym in Russian for "self-defense without weapons") draws on both European and Asian systems for its repertoire of techniques. Sambo was developed in the 1920s by Anatolij Kharlampiev, who spent years traveling around the former Soviet Union analyzing and observing the native fighting systems. He duly recorded and freely borrowed techniques from Greco-Roman and freestyle wrestling (from the Baltic States), Georgian jacket wrestling, *Khokh* (the traditional fighting system of Armenia), traditional Russian wrestling, Turkish wrestling systems from Azerbaijan and Central Asia, and Kôdôkan Jûdô. The result was a fighting system that was so effective that when it was first introduced by European *jûdôka* (Japanese; jûdô practitioners) in the early 1960s, the Soviets won every match. The Soviets also were the first to best the Japanese at their own sport of jûdô in the 1972 Munich Olympics. The Soviet competitors were sambo practitioners cross-trained in jûdô rules.

An example of the redefinition of Asian martial arts can be found in the 1990s craze of Brazilian jiu-jitsu. Although accounts of the creation of the art vary, it is generally accepted that Hélio Gracie, the founder of Gracie Jiu-jitsu, studied briefly with a Japanese jûjutsu instructor and then began to formulate his own system. He was very successful; the Ultimate Fighting Championship, which has achieved worldwide fame, is a variation of the *Vale Tudo* (Portuguese; total combat) of Brazil where Gracie practitioners reign supreme. *Karateka* (Japanese; practitioners of karate) and other Asian martial artists have been far less successful.

A similar redefinition is found in the contemporary Israeli martial art of *krav maga* (Hebrew; contact combat), developed by Imi Lichtenfeld. It is the official fighting art of the Jewish State. Rather than relying on an Asian model, however, Lichtenfeld synthesized Western boxing and several styles of grappling to create a fighting art that is easy to learn and extremely effective.

These unarmed fighting arts demonstrate that Westerners are far from unlearned in hand-to-hand combat. Such traditions are part of Western history.

While it has been said that there are many universal principles common to all forms of fighting, it is misleading and simplistic to suggest that Eastern and Western systems are all fundamentally the same. There are significant technical and conceptual differences between Asian and European systems. If there were not, the military histories, the swords, and the arms and armor of each would not have been so different. Forcing too many similarities does a disservice to the qualities that make each unique.

As both military science and society in the West changed, most indigenous martial arts were relegated to the role of sports and obscure pastimes. Sport boxing, wrestling, and sport fencing are the very blunt and shallow tip of a deep history that, when explored and developed properly, provides a link to traditions that are as rich and complex as any to emerge from Asia.

Currently, however, efforts are under way to perpetuate and revive traditional martial arts of the Western world. For example, armed combat using the weapons of medieval and Renaissance Europe is being rediscovered by organizations whose members have drawn on the historical fighting texts of Masters of Defence for guidance. Today, as more and more students of historical European martial arts move away from mere sport, role-playing, and theatrics, a more realistic appreciation and representation of Western fighting skills and arms is emerging.

Gene Tausk
John Clements

See also Boxing, European; Dueling; Knights; Krav Maga; Masters of Defence; Pankration; Sambo; Savate; Stickfighting, Non-Asian; Swordsmanship, European Medieval; Swordsmanship, European Renaissance; Wrestling and Grappling: Europe

References

Anglo, Sydney. 1987. "How to Kill a Man at Your Ease: Chivalry in the Renaissance." *Antiquaries Journal* 67: 1–4.

———. 1988. "How to Win at Tournaments: The Techniques of Chivalric Combat." *Antiquaries Journal* 68: 248–264.

Aylward, J. D. 1956. *The English Master of Arms—From the Twelfth to the Twentieth Centuries.* London: Routledge and Kegan Paul.

Castle, Egerton. 1885. *Schools and Masters of Fence: From the Middle Ages to the Eighteenth Century.* London: Arms and Armour Press.

Clements, John. 1998. *Medieval Swordsmanship: Illustrated Techniques and Methods.* Boulder: Paladin Press.

———. 1997. *Renaissance Swordsmanship: The Illustrated Use of Rapiers and Cut and Thrust Swords.* Boulder: Paladin Press.

Corcoran, John, and Emil Farkas. 1983. *Martial Arts: Traditions, History, People.* New York: Gallery Books.

Delahyde, Michel. 1991. *Savate, Chausson, and Boxe Française.* Paris: Editions François Reder.

Edge, David, and John Miles. 1988. *Arms and Armor of the Medieval Knight.* London: Crescent Books.

Galas, S. Matthew. 1997. "Kindred Spirits: The Art of Sword in Germany and Japan." *Journal of Asian Martial Arts* 6: 20–47.

Gardiner, E. Norman. 1910. *Athletics of the Ancient World.* Oxford: Oxford University Press.

———. 1930. *Greek Athletic Sports and Festivals.* Oxford: Oxford University Press.

Hutton, Alfred. 1892. *Old Swordplay.* London: H. Grevel and Company.

———. 1901. *The Sword and the Centuries.* London: H. Grevel and Company.

Lewis, J. Lowell. 1992. *Ring of Liberation: Deceptive Discourse in Brazilian Capoeira.* Chicago: University of Chicago Press.

Lichtenfeld, Imi, and Eyal Yanilov. 1998. *Krav Maga: Self Defense and Fighting Tactics.* Tel Aviv: Dekel.

Oakeshott, R. Ewart. 1974. *Dark Age Warrior.* London: Lutterworth Press.

———. 1964. *A Knight and His Weapons.* Philadelphia: Dufour Edition.

Oakeshott, R. Ewart, and Henry Treece. 1963. *Fighting Men.* New York: G. Putnam's Sons.

Poliakoff, Michael. 1995. *Combat Sports in the Ancient World: Competition, Violence, and Culture.* New Haven: Yale University Press.

Wise, Arthur. 1971. *The Art and History of Personal Combat.* London: Hugh Evelyn.

External vs. Internal Chinese Martial Arts

In general, Chinese fighting arts have been classified as external or internal, hard or soft. This classification system depends on the source of the energy applied: In theory, an art may apply muscular and structural force (the external element) activated by forceful muscular contraction (the hard aspect), or it may depend on control of the circulation of an inner force called *qi* (*chi*) (the internal factor), which can be accumulated in the *dantian* (area below the navel) by physical and spiritual exercise and can flow only through a relaxed body (the soft aspect).

An alternative approach to these categories focuses on the mechanics of the application of force. A soft art is one in which the martial artist yields in the face of an opposing force, either evading the force entirely or redirecting it without directly clashing. These systems may couch explanations in terms of "borrowing" force from an opponent (which involves applying force in the direction in which an opponent moves while evading the attack itself). The movements are rounded or even circular in such systems, and great emphasis is put on relaxed, or even relatively slow, motions involving the body working as a whole, rather than on using the limbs divorced from the trunk. These systems employ throws, joint locks, kicks, and punches. Evasion and redirection are favored over blocking.

Hard styles call for a confrontation of force by force, with the defending force generally applied at angles to the oncoming force. The movements are categorized as linear and applied with maximum power and speed. The limbs are said to operate independently from the rest of the body. These martial arts tend to favor strikes over locks and throws and blocking over evasion.

The principal soft martial arts are *taijiquan* (tai chi ch'uan), *xingyiquan* (hsing i ch'uan), and *baguazhang* (pa kua ch'uan). As well as being fighting systems, these arts are regarded as physically and spiritually therapeutic, due to the stimulation of qi. Many traditional explanations of the beneficial effects of these martial exercises rely on Daoist alchemy. In fact, the internal arts in general have been associated with the boxing of the Daoist Zhang Sanfeng (Chang Sang-feng) of Wudang (Wu Tang) Mountain.

The most popular hard styles are those that are believed to be derived from Shaolin Temple boxing systems. Therefore, these arts are associated with Buddhism. Damo (Ta Mo; Bodhidharma), who, according to tradition, brought the doctrines of the Chan (Zen) sect from India to the Songshan Temple of Henan province, is looked to as the progenitor of the Shaolin arts. Many of the fighting arts familiar both in China and internationally are based on these systems. They are regarded as more easily and quickly learned than the soft arts.

Philosophically, then, the soft or internal arts have been associated with Daoism, while the hard or external arts have traditionally been connected to the Chan Buddhism practiced at Shaolin Temples, especially the one in Henan. Attempts to connect the respective styles to wandering monks, Daoist hermits, or temples are traditional in the martial arts. All these etymologies reflect shared understandings of the arts by practitioners but, given the oral traditions on which they rely, may be heavily laden with mythologizing.

Not only the origins of the respective styles, but the veracity of this classification system itself have been questioned. The presence of softness, circularity, and even postures similar to those of taiji and the other "internal" soft styles has been noted for Shaolin styles. For example, the popular Southern Shaolin art of yongchun (wing chun) embodies relaxation, yielding, and clinging energy in its *chi shou* (chi sao; sticking hands) techniques, along with linear punches. By the same token, Chen-style taiji utilizes forceful stamping and explosive movement as well as rhythmic, whole-body motion. Xingyi is linear and forceful, its internal classification notwithstanding.

In this vein, Stanley Henning has presented compelling historical arguments that the distinction between internal and external is spurious. Tracing the first reference to an Internal School (Wudang Boxing) as distinct from an External School (Shaolin Boxing) to the Qing dynasty (1644–1912) and to historian and Ming supporter Huang Zongxi (1610–1695), Henning puts forth the hypothesis that the split developed as a misinterpretation of work that was intended as an anti-Manchu parable alluding to the fall of the Ming to the Manchu Qin dynasty. He goes on to note that the principles of both soft/internal and hard/external are apparent in Chinese fighting arts in general, regardless of the labels imposed under the soft-hard dichotomy. Both the political motivations of the initial division of the arts during the Qing dynasty and the artificiality of an internal-external split are transmitted orally within Chinese Boxing, although a variety of hypotheses coexist.

Nevertheless, the popular opinion holds that there is a meaningful distinction between the internal and external schools. Robert Smith, Chinese martial arts master and author of the first books in English on the arts of baguazhang, taijiquan, and xingyiquan, in a body of work spanning three decades, steadfastly maintains profound differences between the two categories on all levels. At least through the end of the twentieth century, the internal-external taxonomy prevails.

Thomas A. Green

See also Baguazhang (Pa Kua Ch'uan); Boxing, Chinese; Boxing, Chinese Shaolin Styles; Ki/Qi; Taijiquan (Tai Chi Ch'uan); Xingyiquan (Hsing I Ch'uan)

References
Draeger, Donn F., and Robert W. Smith. 1981. *Comprehensive Asian Fighting Arts.* Tokyo: Kodansha International.
Henning, Stanley E. 1997. "Chinese Boxing: The Internal versus the External in the Light of History and Theory." *Journal of the Asian Martial Arts* 6: 10–19.
Reid, Howard, and Michael Croucher. 1983. *The Way of the Warrior: The Paradox of the Martial Arts.* London: Eddison Sadd Editions.

Smith, Robert W. 1974. *Chinese Boxing: Masters and Methods*. Tokyo: Kodansha International.

———. 1974. *Hsing-I: Chinese Mind-Body Boxing*. Tokyo: Kodansha International.

Smith, Robert W., and Allen Pittman. 1990. *Pa-Kua: Eight Trigram Boxing*. Rutland, VT: Charles E. Tuttle.

F

Folklore in the Martial Arts

The martial arts, like all areas of human endeavor, have developed folklore (materials that are learned as an element of the common experience in a special interest group, which could be based on ethnicity, avocation, gender, among other factors) as an integral element of their core knowledge. In fact, by virtue of the secrecy and exclusively oral transmission inherent in most traditions, martial arts communities provide especially favorable conditions for the development of folklore. The most highly developed folk genres in the martial arts fall into three principal categories: myth, legend, and folk belief. The first two genres often focus on origins and include tales ranging from those concerning the origins of war and weapons in general to the origins of specific styles of martial arts. The third type tends to focus on the qualities of particular arts and, in general, articulates relationships between fighting systems and larger belief systems (e.g., religion, medicine).

Myths are narratives set in an environment predating the present state of the cosmos. The world and its features remain malleable. The present order and laws of cause and effect have not yet been set into motion. The actors in such narratives tend to be gods, demons, or semidivine ancestors. Myth characteristically concerns itself with basic principles (the ordering of the seasons, the creation of moral codes).

Legends, on the other hand, are set in the historical reality of the group, are populated by human (though often exceptional) characters, and focus on more mundane issues. In many cases, these narratives are based to some degree on historically verifiable individuals. Although the events described may be extraordinary, they never cross the line into actions that are implausible to group members.

Folk belief may be cast in narrative form, may exist as a succinct statement of belief, or may survive simply as allusions to elements of the common knowledge of the group (i.e., as traditional axioms). Finally, the label "folk" should not serve as a prejudicial comment on the validity of the material so labeled. Such elements of expressive culture invariably reflect qualities of self-image and worldview, and thus merit attention.

These materials frequently exist apart from written media (although committing a narrative, for example, to print does not change the folk status of those versions of the tale that continue to circulate by oral or other traditional means). While orally transmitted narratives have the potential for maintaining thematic consistency, factual accuracy in the oral transmission of historical information over long periods of time is rare. Oral tradition tends to force events, figures, and actions into consistency with the worldview of the group and the group's conventional aesthetic formulas (seen, e.g., in plots, character types, or narrative episodes). Also, since the goal of these genres is rhetorical, not informative, history is manipulated or even constructed in an effort to legitimize the present order.

Moreover, in the martial arts information equates to a kind of power; the purveyor of information controls that power, and others will seek to benefit from it. Some martial arts myths seek to elicit patriotic sympathies or, at a minimum, to identify with familiar popular symbols. One should also keep in mind that some of these myths may be intentionally deceptive and may have a political agenda. Often, the possible motives behind the myths are more fascinating than the myths themselves.

Origin Narratives

Probably the earliest martial arts–related Chinese myth is the story of the origin of war and weapons. This narrative goes back to the legendary founder of Chinese culture, the Yellow Emperor, and one of his officials, Chi You, who rebelled against him. Chi You, China's ancient God of War, who is said to have invented weapons, is depicted as a semihuman creature with horns and jagged swordlike eyebrows. The story describes the suppression of Chi You's rebellion and the attaining of ultimate control over the means of force by the Yellow Emperor. Symbolically, it reflects the perpetual conflict between authority and its opponents.

Such mythic narratives substantiate the claims of smaller groups within larger cultures as well. The origin narrative orally perpetuated within *Shôrinjin-ryû Saitô Ninjitsu* is representative. Oppressed by raiders, a group of northern Japanese farmers sent a young man to find help. Reaching a sacred valley, he fasted and meditated for twenty-one days, until the Shôrinjin (the Immortal Man) appeared and granted him the art of "Ninjitsu Mastery, the 'Magical Art'" (Phelps 1996, 70). While returning home, he was swept up by *tengu* (Japanese; mountain demons) who took him to Dai Tengu (king of the Tengu), who bestowed upon him the art of double-spinning Tengu Swordsmanship. He then returned to his village to defeat their enemies by means of the system he had acquired, a

A nineteenth-century depiction of Minamoto no Yoshitsune, a famous and chivalrous warrior, being taught martial arts by the tengu *(mountain goblins) on Mount Kurama, outside Kyoto. (Asian Art & Archaeology, Inc./Corbis)*

system that has been passed down along the Saitô family line to the present (Phelps 1996).

Similar narratives of origin ascend the social strata. Although the previous narrative is preserved solely by means of oral tradition, historian Roy Ron notes similar mythic motifs in Japanese sword schools during the Tokugawa period. He observes that the historical documentation of a school's lineage, along with such information as "the founder's biography and some historical information relating to the style; often they included legends and myths of sacred secret transmission of knowledge from legendary warriors, supernatural beings, or from the divinities themselves to the founder's ancestors. Such divine connection provided the school with authority and 'proof' of superior skills in an increasingly competitive world of swordsmanship."

In contrast, legends occur in a more contemporary setting and are often more widely disseminated, as is the story of the Maiden of Yue, a legend that reveals the principles of Chinese martial arts, including yin-yang theory (complementary opposition). It is also part of a larger story of how Gou Jian, king of the state of Yue, sought to strengthen his state by employing the best assets available (including women in this case). As a result he overcame his old opponent, the king of Wu, and became the dominant hegemon at the close of the Spring and Autumn period (496–473 B.C.).

Legends Associated with Locales
Legends of the Shaolin Monastery represent this narrative category well, since the site literally swims in an ocean of greater and lesser myths and legends formed from a core of facts. The monastery is the home of Chinese Chan (Zen) Buddhism, which is said to have been introduced by the Indian monk Bodhidharma around A.D. 525. History further records that thirteen Shaolin monks helped Tang emperor Taizong (given name Li Shimin) overcome a key opponent in founding the Tang dynasty. In the mid-sixteenth century, a form of staff fighting was named for the monastery. Numerous references from this period also cite martial arts practices among the Shaolin monks, and the heroic exploits of some of the monks in campaigns against Japanese pirates during this period brought them lasting fame as the Shaolin Monk Soldiers. These basic shreds of fact provide the raw materials for constructing folk historical narrative.

In discussing the more prominent traditional narratives associated with Shaolin Monastery, it is instructive to address them in the chronological order of their appearance on the stage of history. The earliest of these is the story (recorded ca. 960) of the monk Seng Zhou (ca. 560) who, in his youth, is said to have prayed to a temple guardian figure to help him become strong enough to ward off his bullying fellow acolytes. The guardian figure offers him meat to build his strength. Ironically, while the story is exaggerated, it may reveal something about the actual nature of monastic living during Buddhism's early years in China, including loose adherence to the vegetarian dietary codes prescribed for Buddhists. Another much later legend (oral and of unknown origin) claims Tang emperor Taizong issued a decree exempting Shaolin monks from the strict Buddhist vegetarian diet because of their assistance in capturing one of the emperor's opponents (a mix of fact and fiction).

There is only one narrative directly associated with an identifiable Shaolin martial art; this is the story (related on a stone tablet dated ca. 1517) of a kitchen worker who, the tale relates, is said to have transformed himself into a fierce guardian spirit called King Jinnaluo. According to this text, the worker in spirit form scared off a band of marauding Red Turban rebels with his fire-stoking staff and saved the monastery during the turbulence at the end of the Yuan dynasty (ca. 1368). Actually, the monastery is known to have been largely destroyed and to have been abandoned by the monks around this time. Therefore, the story seems to have served a dual purpose: to warn later generations of monks to take their security duties seriously and (possibly) to reinforce the martial image of the place in order to ward off would-be transgressors. In any case, in the mid-sixteenth century, a form of staff fighting was named for the monastery.

The next Shaolin narrative, which appears in *Epitaph for Wang Zhengnan,* written by the Ming patriot and historian Huang Zongxi in 1669, is wrapped up in the politics of foreign Manchu rule over China. According to this story, the boxing practiced in Shaolin Monastery became known as the External School, in contrast to the Internal School, after the Daoist Zhang Sanfeng (ca. 1125) invented the latter. Here, Internal School opposition to the External School appears to symbolize Chinese resistance to Manchu rule. In the twentieth century, proponents of Yang-style *taijiquan* (tai chi ch'uan) adopted Zhang Sanfeng as their patriarch, giving this legend new life.

Migratory Legends

According to at least one of the origin legends circulating in the taijiquan repertoire, one day Zhang Sanfeng witnessed a battle between a crane and a snake, and from the experience he created taiji. It is probably not coincidental that this origin narrative is associated with more than one martial art. For example, Wu Mei (Ng Mui), reputed in legends of the Triad society (originally an anti-Qing, pro-Ming secret society, discussed below) to be one of the Five Elders who escaped following the burning of the Shaolin Monastery by the Qing, was said to have created *yongchun* (wing chun) boxing after witnessing a battle between a snake and a crane, or in some versions, a snake and a fox. From Sumatra comes the same tale of a fight between a snake and a bird, witnessed by a woman who was then inspired to create Indonesian *Silat.*

Folklorists label narratives of this sort migratory legends (believed by the folk, set in the historical past, frequently incorporating named legendary figures, yet attached to a variety of persons in different temporal and geographic settings). Among the three possible origins of the tale type—cross-cultural coincidence of events, cross-cultural creations of virtually identical fictions, and an original creation and subsequent borrowing—the latter is the most likely explanation.

The animal-modeling motif incorporated into the taiji, yongchun, and silat legends is common among the martial arts. This motif runs the gamut from specific incidents of copying the animal combat pattern, as described above, to the incorporation of general principles from long periods of observation to belief in possession by animal "spirits" in certain Southeast Asian martial arts.

Sometime after 1812, a legend arose with the spread of membership in the Heaven and Earth Society (also known as the Triads or Hong League), a secret society. Associating themselves with the heroic and patriotic image of the Ming-period Shaolin Monk Soldiers, Heaven and Earth Society branches began to trace their origins to a second Shaolin Monastery they claimed was located in Fujian province. According to the story, a group of Shaolin monks, said to have aided Emperor Kangxi to defeat a group of Mongols, became the object of court jealousies and were forced to flee south to Fujian. There, government forces supposedly located and attacked the monks' secret Southern Shaolin Monastery. Five monks escaped to become the Five Progenitors of the Heaven and Earth Society. Around 1893, a popular knights errant or martial arts novel, *Emperor Qianlong Visits the South* (also known as *Wannian Qing,* or Evergreen), further embellished and spread the story. Like such heterodox religious groups as the Eight Trigrams and White Lotus sects, and the Boxers of 1900, secret-society members practiced martial arts. The factors of their involvement in martial arts, the center of their activity being in southern China, and identification with the mythical Southern Shaolin Monastery resulted in a number of the styles they practiced being called Southern Shaolin styles.

The connection of sanctuaries, political resistance, and the clandestine practice of martial arts apparent in these nineteenth-century Chinese legends is a widespread traditional motif. The following two examples suggest its dissemination as well as suggesting that this dissemination is not due to the diffusion of an individual narrative. Korean tradition, Dakin Burdick reports, holds that attempts to ban martial arts practice by the conquering

Japanese led the practice of native arts (many of which were Chinese in origin) to move "to the Buddhist monasteries, a traditional place of refuge for out-of-favor warriors" (1997, 33). Similarly, in the African Brazilian martial culture of capoeira, the traditional oral history of the art ties it to the *quilombo* (Portuguese; runaway slave settlement) of Palmares. Under the protection of the legendary King Zumbi, capoeira was either created in the bush or retained from African unarmed combat forms (sources differ regarding the origin of the art). Preserved in the same place were major elements of the indigenous African religions, from which were synthesized modern Candomble (a syncretic blend of Roman Catholicism and African religions) and similar New World faiths. Thus, capoeira's legendary origins are associated with both ethnic conflict and religions of the disenfranchised in a manner reminiscent of the Shaolin traditions.

Traditional texts of this sort should be read as political rhetoric as much as—or perhaps more than—history. As James C. Scott argues, much folk culture amounts to "legitimation, or even celebration" of evasive and cunning forms of resistance (1985, 300). Trickster tales, tales of bandits, peasant heroes, and similar revolutionary items of expressive culture help create a climate of opinion.

Folk Hero Legends

One of the most recently invented and familiar of the Shaolin historical narratives is a story that claims that the Indian monk Bodhidharma, the supposed founder of Chinese Chan (Zen) Buddhism, introduced boxing into the monastery as a form of exercise around A.D. 525. This story first appeared in a popular novel, *The Travels of Lao T'san,* published as a series in a literary magazine in 1907. This story was quickly picked up by others and spread rapidly through publication in a popular contemporary boxing manual, *Secrets of Shaolin Boxing Methods,* and the first Chinese physical culture history published in 1919. As a result, it has enjoyed vast oral circulation and is one of the most "sacred" of the narratives shared within Chinese and Chinese-derived martial arts. That this story is clearly a twentieth-century invention is confirmed by writings going back at least 250 years earlier, which mention both Bodhidharma and martial arts but make no connection between the two.

Similarly, several styles of boxing are attributed to the Song-period patriot Yue Fei (1103–1142), who counseled armed opposition against, rather than appeasement of, encroaching Jin tribes and was murdered for his efforts. Yue Fei is known to have trained in archery and spear, two key weapons. Therefore, it is reasonable to assume that he also studied boxing, considered the basic foundation for weapons skills other than archery, but we have no proof of this. Not until the Qing, about six centuries later, and a time of opposition to foreign Manchu rule are boxing styles attributed to Yue Fei. The earliest reference is in a *xinyiquan* (now more commonly known as xingyiquan [hsing i ch'uan], form and mind boxing) manual dated 1751. The preface explains that Yue Fei developed *yiquan* (mind boxing) from his spear techniques. In fact, key xingyiquan forms do have an affinity to spear techniques, but this is not necessarily unusual, since boxing and weapons techniques were intimately related. Cheng Zongyou, in his *Elucidation of Shaolin Staff Methods* (ca. 1621), emphasizes this point by describing a number of interrelated boxing and weapons forms.

Local legends attempt to extend the legend to regional figures, thus providing a credible lineage for specific styles of xingyi. For example, narratives of the origin of the Hebei style (also known as the Shanxi-Hebei school) continue to circulate orally as well as in printed form. One narrative, the biography of Li Luoneng (Li Lao Nan), maintains that he originally brought xingyi back to Hebei. Subsequently, the Li Luoneng's xingyiquan was combined with *baguazhang* (pa kua ch'uan) to become the Hebei style. Kevin Menard observes that, within the Hebei system, two explanations of the synthesis exist. More probable is that "many masters of both systems lived in this province, and many became friends—especially bagua's Cheng Tinghua and xingyi's Li Cunyi. From these friendships, cross-training occurred, and the Hebei style developed." More dramatic yet less likely is the legend of an epic three-day battle between Dong Haichuan, who according to tradition founded baguazhang, and Li Luoneng's top student, Guo (Kuo) Yunshen. According to xingyi tradition the fight ended in a stalemate (Menard). Other versions (circulated primarily among bagua practitioners) end in a decisive victory by Dong on the third day. In either case, each was so impressed with the other's fighting skills that a pact of brotherhood was sworn between the two systems, which resulted in students of either art being required to learn the other.

During the Qing period, because of its potential anti-Manchu implications, the popular novel *Complete Biography of Yue Fei* was banned by Emperor Qianlong's (given name Hong Li) literary inquisition. When the Manchus came to power, they initially called their dynasty the Later Jin, after their ancestors, whom Yue Fei had opposed. Thus, here is another example of the relationship between martial arts practice, patriotism, and rebellion. However, it is not until after Qing rule collapsed in the early twentieth century that styles of boxing actually named after Yue Fei appear.

Another interesting possible allusion to Yue Fei can be found (ca. 1789) in the name of the enigmatic Wang Zongyue (potentially translated as "Wang who honors Yue"), to whom the famous *Taijiquan Theory* is attributed. Whether or not Wang Zongyue actually wrote this short treatise or whether Wang was the invention of Wu Yuxiang (1812–1880?), whose brother supposedly discovered the treatise in a salt store, remains one of the fascinating uncertainties of modern martial arts history. Suffice it to note here that the term "taijiquan" is only found in the title of the treatise, while the treatise itself is essentially a concise, articulate summary of basic Chinese martial arts theory, not necessarily the preserve of a single style of Chinese boxing.

As noted above, the traditional history of yongchun maintains that this southern Chinese boxing system was invented by a Buddhist nun named Wu Mei (Ng Mui) who had escaped from the Shaolin Temple in Hunan (or in some versions, Fujian) province when it was razed in the eighteenth century after an attack by the dominant forces of the Qing dynasty (1644–1911) that officially suppressed the martial arts, particularly among Ming (1368–1644) loyalists. After her escape and as the result of witnessing a fight between a fox (or snake, in some histories) and a crane, Wu Mei created a fighting system capable of defeating the existing martial arts practiced by the Manchu forces and Shaolin defectors. Moreover, owing to its simplicity, it could be learned in a relatively short period of time. The style was transmitted to Yan Yongchun, a young woman whom Wu Mei had protected from an unwanted suitor. The martial art took its name from its creator's student.

Traditional histories of yongchun (and of other systems that claim ties to it) portray a particularly close connection between yongchun practitioners and the traveling Chinese opera performers known as the "Red Junk" performers after the boats that served as both transportation and living quarters for the troupes. These troupes reportedly served as havens for Ming loyalists involved in the resistance against the Qing rulers and offered refuge to all manner of martial artists.

Incontrovertible historical evidence of the exploits of Bodhidharma, Yue Fei, and Wu Mei has been blurred, if not eradicated, by the passing centuries. Details from the biographies of such figures remain malleable and serve the ends of the groups that pass along their life histories. Recently, arguments have been presented, in fact, that suggest that Wu Mei and Yan Yongchun are fictions into whose biographies have been compressed the more mundane history of a martial art. Such may be the case for many of the folk heroes who predate the contemporary age. Even in the case of twentieth-century figures, traditional patterns emerge.

Japanese karate master Yamaguchi Gôgen exemplifies the contemporary martial arts folk hero—particularly within the karate community and especially among students of his own *Gôjû-ryû* system. Peter Urban, a leading United States Gôjû master, has compiled many of the orally circulated tales of Yamaguchi. Typical of these narratives is the tale of Yamaguchi's captivity in a Chinese prison camp in Manchuria. Urban recounts the oral traditions describing the failure of the captors' attempts to subdue Yamaguchi's spirit via conventional means. As a result, he became an inspiration for his comrades and an embarrassment to his guards. Ultimately, Yamaguchi was thrust into a cage with a hungry tiger. According to Urban, not only did Yamaguchi survive by killing the tiger, he did so in twenty seconds. This story (like similar stories of matches between martial artists and formidable beasts) has been hotly debated. Whether truth or fiction, however, such narratives serve not only to deify individuals (usually founders), but to argue for the superhuman abilities that can be attained by diligent practice of the martial arts. Consequently, these fighting systems are often touted as powerful tools for the salvation of the politically oppressed.

Within the oral traditions of Brazilian capoeira, legends circulate that Zumbi, king of the *quilombo* (runaway slave colony) of Palmares, successfully led resistance against conquest of his quilombo and recapture of his people by virtue of his skills as a *capoeirista*. J. Lowell Lewis, in his study of the history and practice of the martial art, notes, however, that these narratives did not appear in the oral tradition until the twentieth century. Thus, while the martial art itself may not have figured in the military resistance by Brazil's ex-slaves, the contemporary legends argue for ethnic pride within the African Brazilian capoeira community.

Folk Belief

The most prominent boxing styles practiced in southern China appear to emphasize "short hitting"—namely, arm and hand movements as opposed to high kicks and more expansive leg movements. This characteristic, as opposed to the more acrobatic movements of standardized "long boxing," which was developed from a few of the more spectacular "northern" styles, has resulted in southern styles (called *nanquan*) being placed in a separate category for nationwide martial arts competitions. The apparent difference is reflected in the popular martial arts aphorism, "Southern fists and Northern legs." The fictionalizing, in this case, lies in the reasons given for the difference: different north-south geographical characteristics and different body types of northern versus southern Chinese. The main problem with this argument is that it fails to account for the full spectrum of northern styles or the fact that a number of the southern styles are known to have been introduced from the north. It also fails to take into account other historical factors, such as the possibility that southern styles evolved from "short-hitting" techniques introduced for military training by General Qi Jiguang and others during their antipirate campaigns in the south.

Other beliefs focus not on the mechanics of martial arts, but on the internal powers acquired through practice. Within the Indonesian martial art of *pentjak silat* exists the magical tradition of *Kebatinan*. The esoteric techniques of the art, it is said, permit practitioners to kill at a distance by the use of magic and to render themselves invulnerable. In Java, it was believed that the supernormal powers conferred by silat (rather than world opinion and United Nations intervention) had forced the Dutch to abandon colonialism there in the aftermath of World War II. Lest it be believed that such traditional beliefs are disappearing under the impact of contemporary Southeast Asian society, however, James Scott reports that when an organization claiming thirty thousand members in Malaysia was banned, among the organization's offenses were teaching silat and encouraging un-Islamic supernatural practices by use of magical chants and trances.

The beliefs in invulnerability acquired by esoteric martial practice fostered by the Harmonious Fists (the Chinese "Boxers" of the late nineteenth to the early twentieth centuries) represent an immediate analogy to this Southeast Asian phenomenon, but belief in the magical invulnerability engendered by traditional martial arts is not limited to Asia. Brazilian capoeira, many of whose practitioners enhance their physical abilities by simultaneously practicing Candomble (an African-based religion syncretized in Brazil), maintains beliefs in the ability to develop supernormal powers. In addition to the creation of the *corpo fechado* (Portuguese; closed body) that is impervious to knives or bullets, oral tradition attests to the ability of some capoeiristas to transform into an animal or tree, or even to disappear at will.

Worth noting is the fact that not only are individual martial artists transformed into ethnic folk heroes in instances of political conflict, beliefs in the invulnerability developed by the practice of the martial arts are foregrounded in such contexts, as well. Capoeira, silat, and Chinese boxing have each been reputed to give oppressed people an advantage in colonial situations. Martial resistance and supernatural resistance are not invariably yoked, however. For example, in the late nineteenth century the Native American Ghost Dance led by the Paiute prophet Wovoka promised to cleanse the earth of the white man by ritual means, at least as it was practiced among the tribes of the Great Basin. A contemporary religiously fueled guerilla movement, God's Army, led by the twelve-year-old Htoo Brothers in Myanmar, manifests no martial arts component in the sense used here. Thus, utilizing magical beliefs embedded in martial arts is common in grassroots rebellions, but not inevitable.

On the other hand, folklore is an inevitable feature of the martial arts. Certainly, these traditions cannot be treated as, strictly speaking, historically or scientifically verifiable. Neither should they be discounted as nonsense, however. The sense they embody is an esoteric one of group identity, a metaphysical sense of the ways in which martial doctrines harmonize with the prevailing belief systems of a culture, and a sense of worldview consistent with the contemporary needs of practitioners.

Stanley E. Henning
Thomas A. Green

See also Boxing, Chinese Shaolin Styles; Capoeira; Ninjutsu; Political Conflict and the Martial Arts; Silat

References

Almeida, Bira. 1986. *Capoeira, a Brazilian Art Form: History, Philosophy, and Practice.* Berkeley: North Atlantic Books.

Burdick, Dakin. 1997. "Taekwondo's Formative Years." *Journal of Asian Martial Arts* 6, no. 1: 30–49.

Christie, Anthony. 1968. *Chinese Mythology.* Feltham, UK: The Hamlyn Publishing Group.

Green, Thomas A. 1997. "Historical Narrative in the Martial Arts: A Case Study." In *Usable Pasts: Traditions and Group Expressions in North America.* Edited by Tad Tuleja. Logan: Utah State University Press.

Henning, Stanley E. 1997. "Chinese Boxing: The Internal versus External Schools in the Light of History and Theory." *Journal of Asian Martial Arts* 6, no. 3: 10–19.

———. 1998. "Observations on a Visit to Shaolin Monastery." *Journal of Asian Martial Arts* 7, no. 1: 90–101.

———. 1998. "Southern Fists and Northern Legs: The Geography of Chinese Boxing." *Journal of Asian Martial Arts* 7, no. 3: 24–31.

Kang Gewu. 1995. *The Spring and Autumn of Chinese Martial Arts: 5000 Years.* Santa Cruz, CA: Plum Publishing.

Lewis, J. Lowell. 1992. *Ring of Liberation: Deceptive Discourse in Brazilian Capoeira.* Chicago: University of Chicago Press.

Liu T'ieh-yun. 1986. *The Travels of Lao T'san.* Translated by Harold Shadick. Westport, CT: Greenwood Press.

Menard, Kevin. 2001. "Xingyiquan." In *Martial Arts of the World: An Encyclopedia.* Edited by Thomas A. Green. Santa Barbara, CA: ABC-CLIO.

Phelps, Shannon Kawika. 1996. "Gift of the Shôrinji: The Art of Shôrinjin-Ryû Saitô Ninjitsu." *Journal of Asian Martial Arts* 5, no. 4: 69–91.

Ron, Roy. 2001. "Swordsmanship, Japanese." In *Martial Arts of the World: An Encyclopedia.* Edited by Thomas A. Green. Santa Barbara, CA: ABC-CLIO.

Scott, James C. 1985. *Weapons of the Weak: Everyday Forms of Peasant Resistance.* New Haven: Yale University Press.

Smith, Robert W., and Allen Pittman. 1989. *Pa-Kua: Eight-Trigram Boxing.* Rutland, VT: Charles E. Tuttle.

Spiessbach, Michael F. 1992. "Bodhidharma: Meditating Monk, Martial Arts Master or Make-Believe?" *Journal of Asian Martial Arts* 1, no. 4: 10–27.

Urban, Peter. 1967. *The Karate Dojo: Traditions and Tales of a Martial Art.* Rutland, VT: Charles E. Tuttle.

Wang Hongjun. 1988. *Tales of the Shaolin Monastery.* Translated by C. J. Lonsdale. Hong Kong: Joint Publishers.

Wilson, James. 1993. "Chasing the Magic: Mysticism and Martial Arts on the Island of Java." *Journal of Asian Martial Arts* 2, no. 2: 10–43.

Yang Hong and Li Li. 1991. *Wenwu zhi Tao* (The Way of Civil-Military Affairs). Hong Kong: Zhonghua Shuju.

Young, Robert W. 1994. "Bodhidharma and Shaolin Temple." *Karate/Kung Fu Illustrated.* (No. 10, October): 30.

———. 1994. "Bodhidharma and Shaolin Temple." *Karate/Kung Fu Illustrated,* December, 48.

Form/Xing/Kata/Pattern Practice

Editorial note: Bracketed number code in this entry refers to the ideogram that follows.

This pedagogical device, best known by its Japanese name, *kata* ([1]; pronounced *hyung* in Korean, *xing* in Mandarin), represents the central methodology for teaching and learning the body of knowledge that constitutes a traditional school or system of martial art throughout much of East Asia. The standard English translation for kata is "form" or "forms," but while this may be linguistically accurate, it is uninformative at best and misleading at worst. The nature and function of kata training are better conveyed by the phrase "pattern practice."

Students engaged in pattern practice rehearse combinations of techniques and countertechniques, or sequences of such combinations, arranged by their teachers. In Chinese, Korean, and Okinawan boxing schools, such training often takes the form of solo exercises, while in both traditional and modern Japanese fighting arts students nearly always work in pairs, with one partner designated as the attacker or opponent, and the other employing the techniques the exercise is designed to teach.

In many modern martial art schools and systems, pattern practice is only one of several more or less coequal training methods, but in the older schools it was and continues to be the pivotal method of instruction. Many schools teach only through pattern practice. Others employ adjunct learning devices, such as sparring, but only to augment kata training, never to supplant it.

The preeminence of pattern practice in traditional martial art training often confuses or bemuses modern observers, who characterize it as a kind of ritualized combat, a form of shadowboxing, a type of moving meditation, or a brand of calisthenic drill. But while pattern practice embraces elements of all these things, its essence is captured by none of them. For kata is a highly complex teaching device with no exact analogy in modern sports pedagogy. Its enduring appeal is a product of its multiple functions.

On one level, a school's kata form a living catalog of its curriculum and a syllabus for instruction. Both the essence and the sum of a school's teachings—the postures, techniques, strategies, and philosophy that comprise it—are contained in its kata, and the sequence in which students are taught the kata is usually fixed by tradition and/or by the headmaster of

Women at an annual martial arts festival in Seattle, Washington, perform kata *(forms) in unison. (Bohemian Nomad Picture-makers/Corbis)*

the school. In this way pattern practice is a means to systematize and regularize training and to provide continuity within the art or school from generation to generation, even in the absence of written instruments for transmission. In application, the kata practiced by a given school can and do change from generation to generation—or even within the lifetime of an individual teacher—but they are normally considered to have been handed down intact by the founder or some other important figure in the school's heritage. Changes, when they occur, are viewed as being superficial, adjustments to the outward form of the kata; the key elements—the marrow—of the kata do not change. By definition, more fundamental changes (when they are made intentionally and acknowledged as such) connote the branching off of a new system or art.

But the real function of pattern practice goes far beyond this. The importance of this learning device in traditional East Asian martial—and other—art training stems from the belief that it is the most efficient vehicle for passing knowledge from teacher to student, an idea that in turn derives from broader Chinese educational models.

Learning through pattern practice is a direct outgrowth of Confucian pedagogy and its infatuation with ritual and ritualized action. This infatuation is predicated on the conviction that man fashions the conceptual frameworks he uses to order—and thereby comprehend—the chaos of raw experience through action and practice. One might describe, explain, or even defend one's perspectives by means of analysis and rational argument, but one cannot acquire them in this way. Ritual is stylized action, sequentially structured experience that leads those who follow it to wisdom and understanding. Therefore, it follows that those who seek knowledge and truth must be carefully guided through the right kind of experience if they are to achieve the right kind of understanding. For the early Confucians, whose principal interest was the proper ordering of the state and society, this need meant habituating themselves to the codes of what they saw as the perfect political organization, the early Zhou dynasty. For martial art students, it means ritualized duplication of the actions of past masters.

Confucian models—particularly Zhu Xi's concept of investigating the abstract through the concrete and the general through the particular, but also Wang Yangming's emphasis on the necessity of unifying knowledge and action—dominated most aspects of traditional education in China, Korea, and Japan, not just martial art training. In Japan, belief in the efficacy of this approach to learning was further reinforced by the Zen Buddhist tradition of *ishin-denshin* (mind-to-mind transmission), which stresses the importance of a student's own immediate experience over explicit verbal or written explanation, engaging the deeper layers of a student's mind and bypassing the intellect.

Thus, attaining mastery of the martial or other traditional arts came to be seen as an osmosis-like, suprarational process, in which the most important lessons cannot be conveyed by overt explanation. The underlying principles of the art, it was believed, can never be wholly extrapolated; they must be experienced directly—intuited from examples in which they are put into practice.

The role of the teacher in this educational model is to serve as exemplar and guide, not as lecturer or conveyor of information. Traditional martial art teachers lead students along the path to mastery of their arts, they do not tutor them. Instruction is viewed as a gradual, developmental process in which teachers help students to internalize the key precepts of doctrine. The teacher presents the precepts and creates an environment in which the student can absorb and comprehend them, but understanding—mastery—of these precepts comes from within, the result of the student's own efforts. The overall process might be likened to teaching a child to ride a bicycle: Children do not innately know how to balance, pedal, and steer, nor will they be likely to discover how on their own. At the same time, no one can fully explain any of these skills either; one can only demonstrate them and help children practice them until they figure out for themselves which muscles are doing what at which times to make the actions possible.

Pattern practice in martial art also bears some resemblance to medieval (Western) methods of teaching painting and drawing, in which art students first spent years copying the works of old masters, learning to imitate them perfectly, before venturing on to original works of their own. Through this copying, they learned and absorbed the secrets and principles inherent in the masters' techniques, without consciously analyzing or extrapolating them. In like manner, kata are the "works" of a school's current and past masters, the living embodiment of the school's teachings. Through their practice, students make these teachings a part of themselves and later pass them on to students of their own.

Many contemporary students of Japanese, Chinese, and Korean martial art, particularly in the West, are highly critical of pattern practice, charging that it leads to stagnation, fossilization, and empty formalism. Pattern practice, they argue, cannot teach students how to read and respond to a real—and unpredictable—opponent. Nor can pattern practice alone develop the seriousness of purpose, the courage, decisiveness, aggressiveness, and forbearance vital to true mastery of combat. Such skills, it is argued, can be fostered only by contesting with an equally serious opponent, not by dancing through kata. Thus, in place of pattern practice many of these critics advocate a stronger emphasis on free sparring, often involving the use of protective gear to allow students to exchange blows with one another at full speed and power without injury.

Kata purists, on the other hand, retort that competitive sparring does not produce the same state of mind as real combat and is not, therefore, any more realistic a method of training than pattern practice. Sparring also inevitably requires rules and modifications of equipment that move trainees even further away from the conditions of duels and the battlefield. Moreover, sparring distracts students from the mastery of the kata and encourages them to develop their own moves and techniques before they have fully absorbed those of the system they are studying.

Moreover, they say, it is important not to lose sight of the fact that pattern practice is meant to be employed only as a tool for teaching and learning the principles that underlie the techniques that make up the kata. Once these principles have been absorbed, the tool is to be set aside. A student's training begins with pattern practice, but it is not supposed to end there. The eventual goal is for students to move beyond codified, technical applications to express the essential principles of the art in their own unique fashion, to transcend both the kata and the techniques from which they are composed, just as art students moved beyond imitation and copying to produce works of their own.

But while controversy concerning the relative merits of pattern practice, free sparring, and other training methods is often characterized as one of traditionalists versus reformers, it is actually anything but new. In Japan, for example, the conflict is in fact nearly 300 years old, and the "traditionalist" position only antedates the "reformist" one by a few decades.

The historical record indicates that pattern practice had become the principal means of transmission in Japanese martial art instruction by the late 1400s. It was not, however, the only way in which warriors of the period learned how to fight. Most samurai built on insights gleaned from pattern practice with experience in actual combat. This was, after all, the "Age of the Country at War," when participation in battles was both the goal and the motivation for martial training. But training conditions altered considerably in the seventeenth century. First, the era of warring domains came to an end, and Japan settled into a 250-year Pax Tokugawa. Second, the new Tokugawa shogunate placed severe restrictions on the freedom of samurai to travel outside their own domains. Third, the teaching of martial art began to emerge as a profession. And fourth, contests between practitioners from different schools came to be frowned upon by both the government and many of the schools themselves.

One result of these developments was a tendency for pattern practice to assume an enlarged role in the teaching and learning process. For new generations of first students and then teachers who had never known combat, kata became their only exposure to martial skills. In some schools, skill in pattern practice became an end in itself. Kata grew showier and more stylized, while trainees danced their way through them with little attempt to internalize anything but the outward form. By the late seventeenth century, self-styled experts on proper samurai behavior were already mourning the decline of martial training. In the early 1700s, several sword schools in what is now Tokyo began experimenting with equipment designed to permit free sparring at full or near-full speed and power, while at the same time maintaining a reasonable level of safety. This innovation touched off the debate that continues to this day.

In any event, one should probably not make too much of the quarrels surrounding pattern practice, for the disagreements are largely disputes of degree, not essence. For all the controversy, pattern practice remains a key component of traditional East Asian martial art. It is still seen as the core of transmission in the traditional schools, the fundamental means for teaching and learning that body of knowledge that constitutes the art.

Karl Friday

References

Armstrong, Hunter B. 1995. "The Koryû Bujutsu Experience." In *Koryû Bujutsu: Classical Warrior Traditions of Japan.* Edited by Diane Skoss. Berkeley Heights, NJ: Koryû Books.

Eno, Robert. 1990. *The Confucian Creation of Heaven: Philosophy and the Defense of Ritual Mastery.* Albany: State University of New York Press.

Friday, Karl. 1997. *Legacies of the Sword: The Kashima-Shinryû and Samurai Martial Culture.* Honolulu: University of Hawai'i Press.

Herrigel, Eugen. 1953. *Zen in the Art of Archery.* New York: Pantheon.

Hurst, G. Cameron, III. 1998. *The Armed Martial Arts of Japan: Swordsmanship and Archery.* New Haven: Yale University Press.

Keenan, John P. 1990. "The Mystique of Martial Arts: A Response to Professor McFarlane." *Japanese Journal of Religious Studies* 17, no. 4: 421–432.

———. 1989. "Spontaneity in Western Martial Arts: A Yogâcâra Critique of Mushin (No-Mind)." *Japanese Journal of Religious Studies* 16, no. 4: 285–298.

McFarlane, Stewart. 1990. "Mushin, Morals, and Martial Arts: A Discussion of Keenan's Yogâcâra Critique." *Japanese Journal of Religious Studies* 17, no. 4: 397–420.

Nishioka Tsuneo. 1995. "Uchidachi and Shidachi." In *Sword and Spirit: Classical Warrior Traditions of Japan.* Edited by Diane Skoss. Berkeley Heights, NJ: Koryû Books.

Slawson, David. 1987. *Secret Teachings in the Art of Japanese Gardens: Design Principles and Aesthetic Values.* New York: Kodansha International.

List of Ideograms

1   *kata*   型

G

Gladiators

Although Rome deserves credit for developing much of what we know as Western society, many aspects of Roman life were brutal and harsh, even by contemporary standards. The great gladiatorial games, where participants, the gladiators (Latin; "sword men"), fought to the death in hand-to-hand combat, are the primary example of this brutality.

The origin of the games (called circuses in Rome) is unknown. The Romans themselves believed that the concept of fighting to the death for spectators came from the Etruscans, the rulers of Italy before the Romans, who would allow slaves to fight for their freedom once their master died. The first recorded instance of gladiatorial games was in the third century B.C. By A.D. 100, however, the great Colosseum had been constructed, and the well-known principle of "bread and circuses" to keep the masses happy was a core feature of Roman life. Many public holidays featured gladiatorial contests. At such events, sometimes thousands of gladiators were paired against one another in grisly duels.

Unlike the combat arts of the Roman military, which emphasized group fighting and mass combat, gladiator training emphasized individual combat and fighting for a spectator audience. This focus did not diminish the fighting skills of the gladiators, but did give them a different experience from that of a soldier. The gladiators were excellent fighters, and during some of the revolts against the Romans, most notably the Spartacan Revolt of 70 B.C., they proved themselves well against the famous Roman legions. Unlike the Roman soldier, who might never see combat, a gladiator was sure of either killing or being killed in the arena.

Gladiators were usually slaves, sentenced to the arena by their masters, although there are many instances of Roman citizens and even noblemen pursuing this dangerous profession. There was even female gladiatorial combat until it was outlawed around A.D. 200. Once a person was forced into (or chose) the gladiator's life, training began in a professional school. It is estimated that a gladiator training school existed, at one point, in every province of the empire. Although gladiatorial games existed throughout the empire, the greatest, and by far the most prominent, were held at the Colosseum in Rome.

Roman sources, such as Livy and Cicero, report that the training standards for gladiators were high. These warriors were expected to become proficient in a variety of weapons as well as in unarmed combat. Gladiators were expected to be able to handle themselves well in an arena. Gladiator schools themselves often had intense rivalries with one another, and gladiators carried the reputation of a school with them whenever they stepped into an arena. Gladiators who fought poorly, besides being in danger of losing their lives, reflected badly on their schools. To make matters even more demanding for the fighters, wealthy Romans often placed high wagers on them. Those who fought poorly and lived often found that their reception on returning to their school was just as bloody as had been their time in the arena. Gladiators, therefore, had every incentive to learn how to fight well.

The swordplay learned by the gladiators was an exacting and advanced science. So intricate was the swordplay, for example, that a speech of the Roman educator Quintilian compared the speeches of council members with the fencing of gladiators: "The second stroke becomes the third, if the first be made to make the opponent thrust; or becomes the fourth, if there is a double feint, so that there are two bouts of parrying and riposte." This comparison suggests both the high level of swordsmanship that was expected of gladiators and the spectators' familiarity with the complexities of the art.

In the arena itself the real issue of life or death was decided. Upon entering, the gladiators faced the emperor and cried, "Ave Imperator! Morituri te salutant!" (Hail Emperor! Those who are about to die salute you!) The fight to the death then began. There existed many different types of gladiators, who were classed generally by two different criteria: the weapons used and the region of origin.

Probably the two most famous types of gladiators were the Thracian and the *retiarius* (net fighter). The Thracian carried a curved scimitar (*sica*) and a small square or round shield (*parma*), which looked and functioned a great deal like a buckler of later medieval and Renaissance times. The Romans used this name for a gladiator who carried these weapons because of a stereotype that Thracians used these weapons. The retiarius was armed with a harpoon or trident, a net, and a dagger, which was sometimes attached to the net. Many times these two types of gladiators faced each other in the arena.

The victor in these encounters was the gladiator who knew how best to use his own weapons effectively while cutting off the advantages of his

An incredible and fantastic display of massed gladiatorial combat, appearing in Hieronimy Mercurialis's Arte Gymnastica, *1573. (Courtesy of Gene Tausk)*

opponent. In these contests, armor played an important role, as well. The retiarius was the more lightly armored of the two, wearing only a leather or metal shoulder-piece on his left shoulder. The Thracian's upper body was protected by armor, either leather or studded leather, and greaves protected his legs; one arm was usually encased in chain armor. Luck was also a factor in these contests.

In such an encounter, one might assume that the retiarius had superior weaponry, while the Thracian had superior armor. However, such assumptions can be misleading, and certainly such a contest between two highly trained individuals would not be decided simply on these factors alone. There are some general observations that can be made about this type of combat.

First, the object of the Thracian fighter would be to get the trident or harpoon "off-line." This is to say that if the Thracian could get inside the effective range of the trident, he would be able to move in close enough to employ his sica. Then the Thracian would have the advantage in combat. The Thracian could not afford to stay in a position where the retiarius would have the advantage of reach.

To get the trident off-line, the Thracian would have a few advantages. First, his shield, although it was small and only offered a small portion of protection, was light and mobile. He could move it easily to deflect the trident. Second, the armor of the Thracian meant that he could afford to take a less powerful strike from the trident and emerge with only a bruise. In such combat, it was far better to get a bruise and close with the enemy to deliver a fatal blow than to be held at bay and suffer trident thrusts. Finally, the Thracian also was well trained with his short scimitar and knew well the effective range of the weapon. It was unlikely that he would be caught miscalculating its effective range.

The retiarius had the following factors in his favor. One good thrust with the trident could pierce the Thracian's armor. Although the retiarius was trained in using the trident with one hand, he could if necessary wrap the net in his off-hand and wield the trident with two hands. In this case, the retiarius would be like a traditional spearman or pole-arm user, and unless the Thracian could step inside the trident he would be at a disadvantage, possibly a fatal one.

Yet there is another factor in this whole equation: The retiarius was also equipped with a net. Evidence suggests that the net was employed one of three ways. The first way was for the retiarius to drag the net in front of him, which would force the Thracian to remain at a distance, since the Thracian could not afford to close in and have his feet swept out from under him. This forced the Thracian to stay at an extreme reach disadvantage. The second method was to use the net as a distraction, throwing it at the Thracian in the hope of entangling him. It should be noted here that the retiarius was an expert in throwing the net as well, so his first object would be to throw it effectively enough so that it would indeed entangle the limbs of the Thracian. The third method was to use the net as the primary weapon. By this method, the retiarius would attempt to first use the net to entangle his opponent and then use the trident to finish him off, keeping the trident in a secondary position.

The laquearius (from the Latin word for lasso) was a subclass of the retiarius who, as the name suggests, fought with a lasso instead of a net. The same considerations would apply to this type of fight as well. The laquearius would attempt to use the lasso to entangle or distract the Thracian long enough to employ the trident. As before, the Thracian would have to get the trident off-line and avoid the entanglements of the lasso to close in quickly to a distance where his weapons would have the advantage. The only tactic that the laquearius would not be able to employ would be to drag the lasso on the ground in the hope of tripping up an opponent. Otherwise, the retiarius and laquearius would employ many of the same tactics.

Two other types of gladiators that were popular in the arenas were the Samnite and the *secutor*. The Samnite was supposedly modeled on the warrior of a people who were defeated in 312 B.C. by Rome's Capuan allies.

The Samnites were indeed a civilization on the Italian peninsula that was hostile to Rome; the Romans encountered them in the fourth century B.C. Whether the historical Samnites actually used the type of armament worn by the gladiator of that name or the Romans were stereotyping again is unknown. The Samnite had a large oblong *scutum* (shield) and was armored with a metal or boiled leather greave (*ocrea*) on his left leg. Often he had an ocrea on his right arm as well. The Samnite protected his head with a visored helmet (*galea*) and was armed with a *gladius* (short thrusting sword). The secutor was an offspring of the Samnite; his name literally means "pursuer." Secutors fought virtually naked; they had no armor and wore only an ocrea on the left leg and carried a scutum for protection. Their arms were often protected by leather bands at the elbows and wrists (*manicae*). The secutor was armed with a gladius as well, although sometimes he fought with a *pugio* (dagger) only.

Secutors and Samnites were matched against each other, as well as against the retiarius and Thracian. Fighting against each other, the secutor and Samnite would be evenly matched, although the extra protection given to the Samnite through his ocrea on the arm could prove decisive. The reason for the ocrea was to armor the sword arm to allow for protection when the sword arm was exposed, that is, when the fighter was striking with the sword. With fighters who were so evenly matched, the contest would become more a matter of individual strategy than strategy with different weapons. Their weapons, the short-swords, were used mainly for thrusting attacks, although they could make cutting attacks when necessary. The greatest advantage for these two gladiators would be the large shields that they carried; these would protect them well when fighting the Thracian or retiarius.

Through reconstructions of Western medieval and Renaissance martial arts, there is enough evidence to demonstrate that large shields are extremely effective in protecting the body. A trained fighter using a shield does not have to sacrifice mobility or dexterity while using such a large device. The Samnite and secutor would have the same mobility as the Thracian and retiarius. Because of the awkward shape of the scutum, however, it would be difficult to use the vertical edge as a striking tool, although this could be done. It would be easier to use the horizontal edge for such striking. However, the shields could easily be used for attacking directly with the flat. These large objects, when force and momentum are placed behind them, can be formidable striking weapons. The scuti could at least unbalance an opponent when used as a striking weapon; used against an unarmored part of the opponent, they could disable. It would be a mistake to characterize these unique devices merely as defensive aids; they could easily be used for offensive maneuvers when needed.

The question, of course, arises about the issue of combat between the Samnite or secutor and the Thracian or retiarius. Much of the same analysis applies. The retiarius has the advantage of reach with his trident and can throw the net for entanglement or attempt to trip his opponent. However, his lack of armor can prove fatal. The large shields of the Samnite and secutor would have provided a great deal more protection against the reach of the trident than the small shield of the Thracian. However, this in no way makes the Samnite or secutor a clear winner over the retiarius.

When either was matched against the Thracian, once again the large shields of the Samnite and secutor could prove to be of decisive advantage. However, the Thracian had extreme mobility and his sword-arm was well protected by the ocrea. The Thracian would have been able to maneuver his small shield well against the thrusting attacks from the gladius of the Samnite or secutor. The Thracian would have been able to maneuver around the shield of the Samnite or secutor to find a way to stop these opponents.

There is also the issue of unarmed combat. The Greeks developed advanced martial art systems in boxing, wrestling, and most notably, the *pankration* (a kind of all-in fighting where all techniques were legal). Other Mediterranean societies in the ancient world, such as the Cretans, had advanced systems of unarmed combat. Curiously enough, however, the Romans are not credited with developing unarmed combat systems of their own. Some of this bias is due to the fact that Roman society did not appreciate athletic events in the same way the Greeks did. Gladiatorial games were the rule, rather than the exception, to Roman taste, and the accompanying cruelties that went with such contests meant that it has been assumed that Romans never used unarmed combat as the Greeks did.

However, if evidence from (unfortunately scant) surviving mosaics is any indication, it is obvious that Roman gladiators were well versed in boxing and wrestling techniques. These techniques were used to advance the training of the gladiators in much the same way that jûjutsu was used to supplement the training of Japanese *bushi* (warriors) and wrestling techniques were used to supplement the training of knights and men-at-arms of the Middle Ages in Western Europe. The Romans did not view unarmed combat as a discipline in and of itself, but as a supplementary one, especially for gladiators, that was needed for survival in the arena. Unarmed combat techniques were intended to work with weapons. If a gladiator lost his weapons in the arena, which was always a possibility, he had to have some skill to at least try to survive. Also, when an opponent had closed in, fists, choking, and joint locking were often appropriate weapons.

Therefore, it is likely that Roman gladiators were also taught the skills of entering, seizing, trapping, disarming, and tripping their opponents. Such actions are well known to Asian martial arts and, as demonstrated in the *fechtbuchs* (Dutch; fighting manual) of the European masters, to warriors of the Middle Ages and Renaissance as well. These skills were not practiced for "possible" use in the street; rather, they were taught as an expected method of combat.

Another point of "evidence" that is sometimes used to prove the Romans' supposed unfamiliarity with unarmed combat is the use of the cestus (a version of brass knuckles) by the gladiators. The argument goes that the Romans used the cestus because they did not take the time to study how to box correctly; the advantage went to the fighter who could land the first punch. Boxers armed with such a weapon would, of course, have a tremendous advantage over those who went bare-knuckled into the arena. However, this argument fails for two reasons. First, the cestus fighters had an even greater incentive to learn to fight correctly, since being hit with these early brass knuckles would have incapacitated most fighters immediately. Second, since often both parties were equipped with cesti, it was critical to know the possible moves of an opponent in order to know what to expect in the arena. Gladiator fights sometimes did consist of boxers squaring off against one another armed with cesti. There also were, in all likelihood, battles between cestus boxers and other weaponed gladiators. The boxer, with his arms protected by armor, would not be at as much of a disadvantage when matched against other weapons as one might expect.

In addition, the Romans were well aware of the details of human anatomy. This knowledge came, in part, from the Greeks and Egyptians, who were among the first physicians of the ancient world and who had centuries of experience in learning the parts of the human body, as well as the weaknesses. It is important to note here that the average life span of a Roman was longer than that of a Western European during the Middle Ages. This longevity was due, in no small part, to Roman medical knowledge. The Romans logically applied this knowledge to unarmed fighting. Learning how to break joints and bones at their weak points, punch and kick correctly, and choke off the air and blood supply to the brain was critical for gladiatorial combat.

Gladiators who entered the competitions as slaves but survived and fought well could often earn freedom. Gladiators who entered the profession willingly, survived, and fought well could become rich. Gladiators therefore did not take their training lightly, nor did they compartmentalize their training into unarmed and armed, sword, spear, or trident. For these warriors, all martial arts skills were a vital necessity for them to survive and prosper.

Because they created consummate fighters with a range of combat skills, gladiator training schools were also used to train bodyguards and those interested in self-protection skills. Also, gladiators who survived to earn freedom or retirement often found their fighting skills in demand.

Although providing martial training for use outside the arena was not the primary function of the *lanistae* (trainers of gladiators), it did serve as a secondary source of income. The techniques that worked so well in the bloody arenas were obviously also useful on the street.

Gladiatorial combat was an element of the paganism that ruled Roman society until the conversion of the emperor Constantine to Christianity in the fourth century. Rome was a polytheistic society, and the temples of the deities and demigods from dozens of nations all vied for attention in the capital city. Gladiatorial events were often part of pagan religious festivals. Also, despite the fact that Romans prided themselves on their society of law, the idea of the supremacy of the state, including the state-supported cults, was paramount. The individual, along with the value of individual life, was subordinated to the empire. For a person to die in front of adoring crowds was thought to be an honor, especially if the emperor, often thought to be a deity himself, was present in the arena.

After Constantine made Christianity the official state religion, the practice of paganism, in any form, was discouraged. The gladiatorial games, therefore, lost their official patronage. Also, the Judeo-Christian emphasis on the individual and the sanctity of life was at odds with the violence and casual disregard for humanity often found in the arena. As Christianity, with this ethos, spread throughout the empire, the spectacle of gladiatorial combat became a symbol less of bravery than of bloodlust. The Western Empire fell in A.D. 476, and while the Eastern (Byzantine) Empire lasted for a thousand more years, this date marked the end of the Roman world for what would later be known as Western Europe. The upheavals and barbarian incursions that accompanied the end of the Roman Empire sealed the end of the gladiators. Finally, the gladiators found themselves the victims of changing social conditions.

Gene Tausk

See also Europe; Pankration; Swordsmanship, European Medieval; Wrestling and Grappling: Europe

References

Burton, Richard F. 1987. *The Book of the Sword*. London: Dover.

Cary, M., and H. H. Scullard. 1975. *A History of Rome*. New York: St. Martin's Press.

Dudley, D. R. 1980. *Roman Society*. London: Pelican.

Grant, Michael. 1967. *Gladiators*. New York: Barnes & Noble.

Gongfu

See Kung Fu/Gung Fu/Gongfu

Gunfighters

Gunfighters, also known as gunslingers, shootists, pistoleers, or simply gunmen, were a fixture of the nineteenth-century American West. The term is applied generally to individuals who were celebrated for their proficiency with handguns and their willingness to use them in deadly confrontations. Because fights between men armed with "six-shooters" were common on the frontier, the gunfighter is often viewed as the prototypical westerner. Yet not all westerners used (or even carried) guns, and only a fraction used them to settle disagreements. The term is therefore best applied more narrowly to those who employed guns in a regular, professional capacity. This would exclude mere hotheads armed with pistols and would include lawmen, professional criminals, and quasi-legal figures like private-army "regulators" and bounty hunters.

The word *quasi-legal* suggests an important proviso. During the gunfighter's heyday—roughly the three decades following the Civil War—social order on the frontier was shaky at best. With centers of legal authority widely dispersed, a large vagrant population, and suspected crimes often punished by impromptu hangings, there was truth to the literary image of the Wild West. The cattle culture in particular precipitated violence, both on the range, where rustlers battled regulators, and at the railheads, where inebriated cowboys sometimes "shot up the town." In this milieu, a gunman's ability to keep order was often more respected than legal niceties; hence, some of the most famous gunfighters of western legend were ambiguous characters like the hired gun William (Billy the Kid) Bonney (1859–1881) and the gambling "civilizer" James Butler (Wild Bill) Hickock (1837–1876). The intermediary status of such historical characters is reflected in the movies' fascination with the "good bad man"—a central figure since the days of actor William S. Hart (1872–1946).

Hickock was the first gunfighter to attain legendary status, and his career illustrates the importance of a mythmaking machinery. Born James Butler Hickock in 1837, he acquired the nickname "Wild Bill" in the 1860s, after he allegedly made a lynch mob back down. After working as a Union Army scout, a wagon master, and a gambler, he rose to national prominence in 1867 on the strength of a *Harper's Magazine* story that depicted him as a superhuman "Scout of the Plains." Dime novel treatments fleshed out the formula, highlighting the shooting of this "Prince of Pistoleers." Although he served only two years as a frontier lawman, popular media made him a national icon, the swiftest and deadliest practitioner of his trade: Anecdotes about his, in Joseph Rosa's words, "almost hypnotic" marksmanship are firmly in the frontier "roarer" tradition (1969, 61–76). Later, thanks to Gary Cooper's portrayal in the 1937 film *The Plainsman*,

A late-nineteenth-century engraving of Billy the Kid, American outlaw, shooting down his foe, who had taken refuge behind a saloon bar. (Bettmann/Corbis)

Hickock acquired a mantle that he never wore in life, that of a defender of American civilization against gunrunning and savagery.

Because writers also romanticized other gunmen, the best known of these characters are not necessarily the deadliest, but those who caught the fancy of novelists and moviemakers. Bill O'Neal, who "rated" over 250 gunfighters based on the number of verified killings and the number of fights, ranked among the deadliest gunmen the celebrities Hickock, Billy the Kid, John Wesley Hardin, King Fisher, and Ben Thompson. But the most lethal of all shootists, "Deacon" Jim Miller, is obscure to the general public, while the famous trio of Wyatt Earp, Doc Holliday, and Bat Masterson long enjoyed reputations that, O'Neal notes, "greatly exceeded their accomplishments" (1979, 5). Earp's fame was made by a biography by Stuart Lake that provided the basis for John Ford's 1946 film *My Darling Clementine*. Holliday's fame soared largely on Earp's coattails, and Masterson, once he retired his guns, became his own best publicist. In his later career as a journalist, he wrote a series of sketches of "famous gunfighters" for *Human Life* magazine.

In addition to skewing individual reputations, the popular press and movies contributed heavily to the image of the gunfighter as a heroic loner who employs his skills in the defense of justice. The most famous fictional example, Shane, comes to the aid of embattled ranchers "out of the heart of the great glowing West" and, after killing his evil counterpart, disappears, like Cain, "alone and unfollowed . . . and no one knows where," Jack Schaefer writes (1983, 115). A similar mythic isolation defines other film gunfighters, including the heroes of *The Gunfighter* (1950), *Warlock* (1959), *The Magnificent Seven* (1960), and *The Shootist* (1976). While most actual gunfighters had more or less stable occupations—many in law enforcement—the Hollywood version is a more paradoxical figure, protecting helpless citizens with a lethal skill whose very possession brands him as a pariah. In one standard plotline the gunfighter is hired as a town tamer, then shunned by his respectable employers for doing his job. In another, the "good" gunslinger fights an evil twin who is the objectification of his own dark urges; this doubling is humorously parodied in *Cat Ballou* (1965), where the villain and the hero are both played by Lee Marvin.

The mechanics of the gunfighter's skill, including variable rules for carrying, drawing, and firing a gun, have been much debated, especially in response to the moviemakers' penchant for standardization. Among actual westerners, for example, some guns were worn with the butt end facing backward, some with the butt end facing forward to facilitate a reverse draw, others in shoulder holsters, and yet others tucked into waistbands or pockets. Yet virtually all Hollywood gunfighters wear side holsters with the butt ends of their guns facing backward. This has become the standard version of "fast draw" dress.

The fast draw itself (the nineteenth-century term was "quick draw") defines the normative gunfight, which the movies give the invariant etiquette of a formal duel. In the typical movie showdown, the hero, often forced to fight despite the apprehensions of his wife or sweetheart, faces down the villain in a western street. The villain draws his gun first, and when he does, the hero draws and kills him in a "fair fight"—sometimes by "fanning" the pistol's hammer for even greater speed. With the exception of the fanning trickery, all of the dramatic motifs of this convention were established in Owen Wister's 1902 novel *The Virginian*, successfully filmed by Victor Fleming in 1929.

As for the accuracy of this tableau, Texas gunman King Fisher is reputed to have said, "Fair play is a jewel, but I don't care for jewelry" (quoted in Horan 1976, 4). Many of his compatriots seem to have agreed. Sheriff Pat Garrett shot Billy the Kid from the protection of a darkened room. Fisher himself died in a vaudeville theater scuffle. The "unerring" Hickok accidentally killed his own deputy. And the canonical gunfight at the OK Corral, according to one version, started when Morgan Earp, Wyatt's brother, ignored Billy Clanton's protestation "I don't want to fight" and shot the teenage rustler at point-blank range (O'Neal 1979). Alert to such unromantic facts, filmmakers in the 1960s turned increasingly to more realistic treatments, including the "spaghetti Westerns" of director Sergio Leone and the *Unforgiven* (1992), by his protégé Clint Eastwood, which makes a point of debunking the heroic tradition. Yet in popular memory the fair fight remains de rigueur.

With regard to the fast draw, too, convention rules, with movies ritualizing the instant of "getting the drop" on the bad guy. Wyatt Earp, recalling the value of mental deliberation, said he never knew "a really proficient gun-fighter who had anything but contempt for the gun-fanner, or the man who literally shot from the hip. . . . [They] stood small chance to live against a man who . . . took his time and pulled the trigger once" (Lake 1931, 39). Ben Thompson, the famous city marshal of Austin, Texas, agreed. "I always make it a rule to let the other fellow fire first," he said. "I know that he is pretty certain in his hurry, to miss. I never do" (quoted in Horan 1976, 142). But deliberation is not emphasized by fictional gunmen. A rare exception is the Anthony Mann film *The Tin Star* (1957), in which veteran gunfighter Morgan Hickman (Henry Fonda) counsels the novice sheriff (Anthony Perkins), "Draw fast but don't snap shoot. Take that split second."

Mythology also surrounds the idea that gunfighters kept tallies of their victims by carving notches in the handles of their guns—one notch for each man killed. In fact, although the practice was not unknown, it was far from routine. Outlaw Emmett Dalton recalled that braggarts and "fake bad men" sometimes notched their guns, but that the custom's alleged ubiquity was "a fiction writer's elaboration." Wyatt Earp reflected that no man "who amounted to anything" ever observed it (Hendricks 1950, 45).

Not that gunfighters or their followers were oblivious to the numbers. Indeed, a gunman's reputation was fatefully linked to the number of men he was thought to have slain, and tallies of a dozen or more were not uncommon. Billy the Kid's reputation was linked to the belief that he had killed twenty-one men—one for each year of his life—and similar beliefs swelled the legends of other gunmen. Although even Hardin, the most lethal of the celebrated bad men, probably had no more than eleven victims (O'Neal 1979, 5), popular culture has enshrined western gunmen as profligate "man-killers" (Masterson 1957, 25). The aging Jimmy Ringo in Henry King's *The Gunfighter* kills an even dozen before he himself is gunned down, while in the Louis L'Amour novel *Heller with a Gun,* King Mabry is credited with fifteen—before he corrects the record by admitting to just eleven (1992, 19).

Mabry's tally, it should be noted, is "not counting Indians." L'Amour here alludes to a racial peculiarity that gunfighter legends often overlook. In the animosities evoked by the Mexican War, the Civil War, Reconstruction, and Indian removal, the phrases "not counting Indians," "not counting Negroes," and "not counting Mexicans" were common grotesque refrains in western tales. To the "rip-roarin', hell-raisin', fire-spittin' American bad man of probable Anglo-Saxon birth," nonwhites didn't count because "everybody shot them" (Hendricks 1950, 46, 92).

This racist disdain made the gunfighter less an anomaly than a paralegal extension of mainstream mores, and when the mores began to change, "socially conscious" western films reflected the shift. "Bad" gunmen, like the villain of *The Tin Star,* demanded the customary immunity for shooting Indians, while "good" gunmen, like the mercenary cavaliers of John Sturges's *The Magnificent Seven* (1960), could now defend a black man's right to a proper burial and admit a Mexican hothead as a member of their band.

Of all the legends built around the western gunfighter, none has been more resonant than the knight errant image, which sees the gunman as "a two-gun Galahad whose pistols are always at the service of those in trouble" (Rosa 1969, 4). The 1950s television series *Have Gun, Will Travel* featured a professional gunman called Paladin, and defense of the weak is a common attribute of the movies' "good bad man." Chivalry has also been applied to unlikely historical prototypes. Billy the Kid became a southwestern Robin Hood in Walter Noble Burns's *The Saga of Billy the Kid* (1926), a book that inspired countless "good Billy" westerns; a similar fate befell Frank and Jesse James. In Bob Dylan's song "The Ballad of John Wesley Harding," even Wes Hardin, who claimed his first victim at the age of fifteen, became "a friend to the poor" who was "never known to hurt an honest man." Ever since *The Virginian,* fictional gunmen have been similarly characterized, lending popularity to the notion that, next to quickness, the gunfighter's most valued quality was a sense of honor.

Questions of honor invite comparisons not only to European knights but also to Asian martial artists, and the parallel is not lost on students of the Western. It animates Terence Young's film *Red Sun* (1971), where a gunfighter comes to appreciate the importance of honor by watching a samurai bodyguard observe the code of bushidô (or budô). The 1970s television series *Kung Fu* pitted a wandering Shaolin monk against Wild West badmen, and one of the most successful of gunfighter vehicles, *The Magnificent Seven,* was a sagebrush remake of Akira Kurosawa's *Seven Samurai.*

The differences between East and West are, to be sure, profound. Despite jocular references to "triggernometry" and to "leather slapping as a fine art" (Cunningham 1947), gunfighting was too chaotic and personal a practice to ever be considered a martial system. Gunfighters formed no schools, passed on no fighting "styles," and respected no lineages or training hierarchies. Nor, beyond the quick draw and a few "eye-training, finger flexing exercises" like the finger roll (Cunningham 1947, 424), did they perfect marksmanship; even the few print and film references to shooting lessons suggest only perfunctory admonitions: Shane's "Your holster's too low" (Schaefer 1983, 53) and Morgan Hickman's "Take that split second." In addition, gunfighter culture was, to borrow Ruth Benedict's famous distinction, as Dionysian as samurai culture was Apollonian. A high percentage of gunmen were gamblers, highwaymen, saloonkeepers, rowdies, or drifters.

Nonetheless, they observed a certain wild decorum, memorialized in the often cited Code of the West: Play fair, stand by your word, and don't run. Again the locus classicus is found in Wister's *The Virginian,* when the hero, explaining to his fiancée why he must face the villain, says that a man who refuses to defend his name is "a poor sort of jay" (Wister 1956, 343). The gunman's bravery, Bat Masterson suggested, was made up largely of "self-respect, egotism, and an apprehension of the opinion of others" (Masterson 1957, 54); the critic Robert Warshow put it pointedly when he observed that the westerner in general (and the gunfighter in particular) defends at bottom "the purity of his own image—in fact his honor" (1974, 153). The dying gunfighter of Don Siegel's elegiac *The Shootist,* John Wayne's last film, puts it eloquently: "I won't be wronged, I won't be insulted, and I won't be laid a hand on. I don't do these things to other people, and I require the same from them."

The gunfighter dramatizes the contradiction of a society that must hire professional killers to ensure tranquillity, a society where a gun called the Peacemaker was an instrument of progress. He resolves the contradiction with a personal style that is as much about deportment as it is about courage. Warshow again gets to the heart of the matter. He asks us to observe a child playing with toy guns: "What interests him is not . . . the fantasy of hurting others, but to work out how a man might look when he shoots or is shot. A hero is one who looks like a hero" (1974, 153). In this the mythic gunfighter, no less than the samurai, pays an ironic allegiance not only to fairness, but also to a public, theatrical behavior that popular culture enshrines as a mythical dramatization of the paradox of violence.

Tad Tuleja

See also Dueling

References
Cunningham, Eugene. 1947. *Triggernometry: A Gallery of Gunfighters.* Caldwell, ID: Caxton Printers.
Hendricks, George D. 1950. *The Bad Man of the West.* San Antonio, TX: Naylor Company.
Horan, James D. 1976. *The Gunfighters.* New York: Crown Publishers.

Lake, Stuart. 1931. *Wyatt Earp, Frontier Marshal.* Boston: Houghton Mifflin.

L'Amour, Louis. 1992. *Heller with a Gun.* 1955. Reprint, New York: Bantam Books.

Masterson, W. B. 1957. *Famous Gunfighters of the Western Frontier.* 1907. Reprint, Houston: Frontier Press of Texas.

O'Neal, Bill. 1979. *Encyclopedia of Western Gunfighters.* Norman: University of Oklahoma Press.

Rosa, Joseph G. 1969. *The Gunfighter: Man or Myth?* Norman: University of Oklahoma Press.

———. 1996. *Wild Bill Hickock: The Man and His Myth.* Lawrence: University Press of Kansas.

Schaefer, Jack. 1983. *Shane.* 1949. Reprint, New York: Bantam Books.

Warshow, Robert. 1974. "Movie Chronicle: The Westerner." In *The Immediate Experience.* 1954. Reprint, New York: Atheneum.

Wister, Owen. 1956. *The Virginian.* 1902. Reprint, New York: Pocket Books.

Gung Fu

See Kung Fu/Gung Fu/Gongfu

Hankuk Haedong Kumdô

See Swordsmanship, Korean/Hankuk Haedong Kumdô

Hapkidô

Hapkidô (Way of Coordinated Power) is a Korean method of combat utilizing hand strikes, kicks, joint locks, throws, restraints, and chokes. In its most specific use the term *Hapkidô* identifies that art transmitted to Ji Han-Jae by Choi Yong-Shul. In a broader sense, the term *Hapkidô* has also come to identify Korean martial arts that incorporate both strikes and grappling according to the three guiding principles of Hapkidô, and derive from, or are heavily influenced by, the Japanese martial art *Daitô-ryû Aikijujitsu*. Into this category fall a wide range of organizations (*kwan*), including but not limited to *Mu Sul Kwan, Yon Mu Kwan, Hapki Yu Sool,* and *Jung Ki Kwan.* There are also various Hapkidô federations and associations, the most notable of which are the World Kidô Federation, the International Hapkidô Federation, and the Korean Hapkidô Association.

In its widest usage Hapkidô also may identify organizations and arts whose intent is a greater representation of the Korean martial tradition. These organizations' heritages may derive in some part from either the teachings of Choi Yong-Shul or his students. However, the biomechanics of these arts may be just as likely to reflect instead the strong Chinese and Buddhist heritage of Korean culture. This category may include the arts of *Kuk Sool Won, Han Mu Do, Hwarang-dô, Han Pul, Mu Yei 24 Ban,* as well as the martial training practices of the Sun Monasteries.

Modern Hapkidô is the product of more than 2,000 years of martial tradition. This heritage can be subdivided into five major cultural infusions and a myriad of lesser cultural influences.

The first of these major infusions are the ancient tribal techniques (*Sado Mu Sool*), which are thought to have incorporated those forms of combat best accomplished from horseback. These systems would have included archery, lance, stone sword, and knife, as well as the brand of wrestling common across most of Central Asia. Practiced by the migrating tribes of the steppes of northeastern Asia, these martial skills formed the foundation for Korean martial tradition.

The second and third infusions to Hapkidô were the introduction of Buddhist and Confucian belief systems, respectively, to Korean culture, as well as the attendant martial and administrative traditions, from China during the fourth and fifth centuries A.D. The introduction of Buddhist beliefs is reflected in the establishment of various codes that were established to guide the warrior's efforts in meeting his responsibilities to his community and country. Buddhist tradition pressed an accomplished warrior to submit to a code based on patriotism (*Chung*), filial piety (*Hyo*), fraternity (*Shin*), justice (*Yong*), and benevolence (*Im*). In this way the role of Buddhist thought for the Korean warrior was not unlike that played by the Christian Church in Western Europe in the development of chivalry.

The Confucian system, for its part, advocated a reverence for governmental authority and supported this through a hierarchy of levels, examinations, and offices. Such a strict hierarchical system readily lent itself to affirming the rigid Korean class system, composed of the aristocracy, bureaucracy, farmers, and slaves, a system that emphasized the supremacy of the king.

In addition to their respective religious and administrative influences, Buddhism and Confucianism were venues for the introduction of a variety of cultural and martial traditions from China. Among these contributions were various weapons and martial skills, strategies, tactics, history, science, medicine, and literature. These two belief systems (especially via Buddhist influences on governmental policy) inculcated and supported central elements of Korean martial tradition, particularly at the local and individual levels. The rise of the Confucian ethic, however, ultimately led to the degradation of Korean martial systems through the code's minimization of militarism and the consequent relegation of militarism to internal and defensive roles. As a result, Korean military tradition may be characterized as an informal patchwork quilt of cultural influences whipstitched together by immediate need. These forces remained in effect up to the occupation by the Japanese in 1910.

Initially relatively bureaucratic, the Japanese occupation forces faced steadily growing resistance by the Korean people until the Japanese instituted harsh repressive measures in the 1930s that outlawed nearly all expression of Korean culture and demanded the adoption of Japanese cultural counterparts. Japanese nationals were brought to Korea to dominate the agricultural and industrial base of that country, and they brought with them such martial art traditions as *jûdô*, *jûjutsu*, *karate*, *aikidô*, *kendô* (fencing), and *kyûdô* (Japanese Archery). Korean nationals were relocated to Japan to service the needs of Japanese industry, farming, and domestic service.

The fourth infusion to the Korean martial tradition that followed in the wake of Japanese occupation is best represented in the personal experiences of Choi Yong-Shul, whose teachings subsequently set the foundation for much of modern Hapkidô. At the age of 8, Choi was reportedly taken to Japan from Korea, later abandoned, and subsequently taken into the household of Takeda Sokaku, teacher of Daitô-ryû Aiki-jujitsu. Choi states that he remained in Takeda's employ for some thirty years, before being repatriated to Korea at the end of World War II. To date, no documentation has been found to support Choi's statements regarding either his residence with the Takeda family or his instruction in the art of Daitô-ryû. However, it remains clear that Choi, along with a very limited number of other Korean nationals such as Jang In Mok and General Choi Hong-Hi, returned to Korea to add the martial skills he had acquired in Japan to those arts of the Korean culture that had survived or those arts that had been introduced from Japan by the occupation.

In 1948 Choi began teaching his art, *Yu Sool,* to Suh Bok-sup, a *yudô* (*jûdô*) black belt and president of a brewery. The name Yu Sool (Korean; soft technique) itself suggests that the art's techniques included joint locks and throws. However, following an incident in 1954 in which Choi's student Suh used a side thrust kick in an altercation, the name was changed to Yu Kwon Sool (Korean; soft fist technique), indicating that the art utilized kicks and punches as well.

Ji Han-Jae began to train with Choi in 1953. Working with the head instructor of the school, Kim Moo-woong, Ji organized the kicking repertoire that came to be identified with Yu Kwon Sool. This introduction of various kicking techniques by Kim and Ji Han-Jae to the Yu Sool curriculum constitutes the fifth and latest infusion of techniques to Hapkidô. The sources for this kicking repertoire were the historic national pastimes of *t'aek'kyŏn* and *su bahk,* both kicking arts of long standing in the Korean culture. Similar indigenous influences have been suggested for the kicks incorporated into the martial sport of *taekwondo.*

On beginning his own school in 1957 as a third-degree black belt, Ji is credited with changing the name of the art to its present form, Hapkidô, from Hapki Yu Sool. In this way, Ji is thought to have emphasized Hapkidô as a *dô* (Japanese; way of living) rather than merely a *sool* (Korean; collection of techniques). In this way, whatever principles may be examined on a physical plane, such as motion, balance, leverage, timing, and focus, may also be regarded as principles existing on intellectual, emotional, and spiritual planes. The result is that the art of Hapkidô is as much a method of character development as a martial endeavor.

A preponderance of Hapkidô practitioners can trace their instruction back to Choi Yong-Shul, or to Choi through Ji. Among the most notable personalities who have trained with Choi directly, or with Choi through Ji, are Lee Joo Bang (*HwaRangDô*), Myung Jae-nam (International Hapkidô Federation), Myung Kwang-Shik (World Hapkidô Federation), and Bong-Soo Han (International Hapkidô Federation). These martial descendants from his line support Ji's reputation as the "father of modern Hapkidô." There are also large networks of contemporaries to Ji who have sought to introduce their own innovations to Hapkidô. These include Suh In Hyuk (*Kuk Sool Won*), Won Kwan-wha (*Moo Sool Kwan*), and Lim Hyun Su (*Jung Ki Kwan*).

If one compares Daitô-ryû, Hapkidô, and aikidô, another Daitô-ryû derivation, it is not surprising that one can identify a number of similarities. All three arts support practice in both unarmed and weapons techniques. Though curricula vary from organization to organization, all three arts hold to the position that techniques remain biomechanically the same whether a weapon is incorporated into the movements or not.

The weapons themselves continue to reflect a certain consistency in biomechanics, despite cultural variations. The Japanese iron fan or iron truncheon (*jutte*) is represented in Korean Hapkidô by the short stick, or *dan bong*. The Korean cane approximates the Japanese *jô* (stick). Sword, knife, and staff techniques are often comparable in either Japanese or Korean culture, though the Korean biomechanics more often attest to Chinese influence by using circular rather than linear motion. To a lesser degree, Hapkidô practitioners continue to incorporate rope or belt techniques, as well as the larger Chinese fans on occasion.

A second point of intersection among Daitô-ryû Aiki-jujitsu, Hapkidô, and aikidô is the fact that all apply the same three principles on the physical, intellectual, emotional, and spiritual planes. These are the Water Principle, Point and Circle Principle, and Economy of Energy Principle.

The Water Principle calls for adaptation to circumstances and a readiness to adjust an action or response with ease. Sometimes characterized as "tenacity" or "relentlessness" for the penetrating qualities of the liquid, the Water Principle is better represented by the manner in which water adapts to the shape of the container that holds it. In this way, the practitioner accepts whatever is given to work with and makes the most of it.

The Point and Circle Principle acknowledges that "all things are a cycle" and as such can be much easier to understand by means of cause and effect. A punch, thrown, does not remain extended, but is "recycled" to become perhaps a block, another strike, or a grab. The same can be said for a kick, or a throw, perhaps walking, eating—in fact any activity. Actions occur and are recycled to become other actions as thoughts recycle to become other thoughts. In combat application, the interception and management of an attack is open to a greater number of options along the track of an arc rather than a straight line. An appreciation of the cyclical nature of events also allows for anticipation according to a variety of options and an execution of a particular option in a tangential rather than confrontational manner.

The Economy of Energy Principle encourages the practitioner to identify the most efficient way of accomplishing goals and admonishes the student to avoid "working harder than one's opponent." In this way, whatever one learns, one is under constant pressure to perform it more accurately, efficiently, and effectively. In this way a practitioner learns to "work smarter, not harder" in dealing with conflicts.

A final significant overlap among Daitô-ryû, Hapkidô, and aikidô is their reliance on a subtle hierarchy of sophistication that guides the practitioner to identify ever increasing levels of efficiency and effectiveness in the arts. For the Japanese arts, the first level of expertise is identified as *jû jitsu* (gentle technique), which is expressed as *yu sool* in the Korean tradition. Essentially an art based on strength, leverage, and speed, this level of expertise often includes a degree of forcing compliance by means of causing pain for the successful execution of the technique. Though the least sophisticated of the three levels, this skill level is perhaps the most widely exhibited among Hapkidô practitioners and contributes to its reputation as a no-nonsense form of self-defense.

The second level of sophistication is identified in the Daitô-ryû tradition as *aiki-jujitsu* (coordinated mind/spirit technique); this is *hapki yu sool* (coordination of power in soft technique) in the Korean tradition. Aikidô, for its part, speaks of "blending" with one's partner. All three phrases indicate the ability to use the nature of attackers' own physical structures against them. Disrupting an attacker's foundation, balance, direction, timing, or focus allows defenders to optimize their assets in confrontations with individuals of greater size or ability. Well known among aikidô and Daitô-ryû practitioners, this level is less well-known in the Hapkidô community, with the exception perhaps of practitioners in Korea itself.

The highest level of expertise is designated *aiki-jitsu* (spirit techniques) and is the subject of much debate within both the aikidô and Daitô-ryû Aiki-jujitsu community. This level of training allows the practitioner to exploit the biomechanical responses of the attacker's own body, such as conditioned responses and reflexes. In such cases the defender, then, is able not only to engage enemies, unbalance them, and use their strength against them, but to incorporate the intent behind their actions in defeating the attack as well.

The organization of a typical Hapkidô school reflects many of the accepted organizational practices common to most martial arts in both Korea and Japan. A director (*kwang jang nin*) attends to the managing affairs of the school, while an instructor (*sabunim*) oversees regular instruction. Nearly all Hapkidô organizations have adopted a hierarchy of ascending student (*guep*) ranks numbering ten through one and usually assigned a belt color indicative of rank. Individuals committed to continued study, following completion of the student ranks, are assigned a rank of one through seven indicating various levels of competence and designated by a black belt. Ranks eight, nine, and ten are essentially administrative positions. Consistent with the use of a Confucian educational model, criteria for advancement, testing policies, certification, and licensing vary greatly from organization to organization and are regularly a source of negotiation and discussion in the Hapkidô community regarding significance and relative merit.

Bruce Sims

See also Aikidô; Korea; Taekwondo; T'aek'kyŏn
References
Kim Sang H. 2000. *The Comprehensive Illustrated Manual of Martial Arts of Ancient Korea*. Hartford, CT: Turtle Press.
Kimm He-Young. 1991. *Hapkidô*. Baton Rouge, LA: Andrew Jackson College Press.
Lee Joo Bang. 1979. *The Ancient Martial Art of HwaRangDo*. 3 vols. Burbank, CA: Ohara Publications.
Lee Ki-Baik. 1984. *A New History of Korea*. Cambridge: Harvard University Press.
Lee Peter H. 1993. *Sources of Korean Civilization*. 2 vols. New York: Columbia University Press.
Myung Kwang-Shik. 1982. *Hapkidô: Ancient Art of Masters*. Seoul: World Hapkidô Federation.
Omiya Shiro. 1992. *The Hidden Roots of Aikido*. Tokyo: Kodansha International.
Suh In Hyuk. 1987. *Kuk Sool*. Privately published.
Yang Jwing-ming. 1992. *Analysis of Shaolin Ch'in na*. Jamaica Plain, MA: YMAA Publication Center.

"Hard" Chinese Martial Arts

See External vs. Internal Chinese Martial Arts

Heralds

Like most other warrior orders known to history, the knightly nobility of Latin Christendom that flourished from the later twelfth to the early seventeenth centuries developed a distinctive ideology reflective of its peculiar nature and traditions, and largely embodied in the cycles of quasi-historical romances centered on the courts of Alexander, Caesar, Charlemagne, or (most commonly) Arthur of Britain. Contemporaries usually referred to this ideology by a word meaning "knightliness": in Old and Middle French, *chevalerie,* and in English, *chivalry.* Like some other comparable ideologies, chivalry came to be served by an order of ministers who grew up with it, became experts in all of its aspects, and converted it into a kind of secular religion in rivalry with the Catholic Christianity that was officially practiced by all of its votaries.

The most general name given to the ministers of chivalry was "herald," a title of unknown origin first attested in France ca. 1170 (in the form *heralt*) and soon adopted in most of the other languages of Latin Christendom. It was first applied to men who specialized in matters associated with the tournament, a type of knightly team sport invented in France ca. 1050, and slowly converted between about 1180 and 1220 from a wild and dangerous form of mock battle into a carefully regulated game that was set within festivities designed to celebrate and promote the new ideology of chivalry. In documents heralds were at first closely associated with minstrels, and *heraldie,* or heraldry (as their craft came to be called), may probably be seen as an offshoot of minstrelsy. During a tournament the heralds present (at first quite numerous) announced the combatants as they entered the field, heaped praise upon their past performances, and discussed their merits with fellow heralds and spectators while each combat was in progress. Like minstrels, they were at first hired for the occasion, and followed the tournament circuit along with the newly knighted "youths" and other, older knights who found they could make a profit from the sport. They were probably paid both by the organizers of the tournament and by the knights whose deeds they praised—often in the form of songs they composed, in the manner of minstrels.

By the early thirteenth century, the duties of heralds seem to have multiplied, and some, at least, had acquired a more steady form of employment in the households of the princes who alone could afford to hold the grandiose sort of tournament that had come to be fashionable. In any case princes had begun to use them as messengers in matters related to tournaments, and sent them forth with some regularity to proclaim tournaments at various courts, royal and baronial, throughout France, the Holy Roman Empire, and even the lands beyond these. Having delivered the challenge, they returned with the replies of those challenged, and accompanied their master to the place appointed for the combat. As tournaments were officially banned in England until 1194, it is unlikely that heralds were active there before that date. In fact there is no mention of heralds in English records before the accession of Edward I in 1272, but from at least that date, and probably from 1194, English heralds carried out the same range of functions as their Continental namesakes.

Heralds soon acquired several new areas of expertise. Their need to

A medieval trial by combat between two knights inside a fenced ring, ca. 1350. The victor would be deemed to have been vindicated by God. (Hulton Getty/Archive Photos)

be able to identify individual knights in tournaments gave them a special interest in the cognizances or "arms" whose use (on shields, pennons, and banners) was first adopted by princes in the 1130s and became general among ordinary knights in the period between ca. 1190 and ca. 1250. It is likely that heralds not only encouraged the use of such cognizances among those who took part in tournaments, but played an important role in designing them and in systematizing their use. In fact, there is reason to believe that "armory," as this aspect of heraldry came to be called, was largely the creation of heralds, who certainly provided it with its technical terminology. They also kept its records. Possibly from as early as 1250, and certainly from 1275, some English heralds prepared books or rolls of arms, collected from various sources, to assist them in remembering the hundreds of distinct but often similar arms they encountered in their work, and this practice soon spread to France and from there to other kingdoms of northern Europe.

From ca. 1390 a growing number of heralds also wrote treatises on armory and the other aspects of heraldry, and from about 1450 these were aimed not only at apprentice heralds but at all members of the nobility and those who had hopes of working for them. From about 1480, heralds also began to invent new rules to govern the use of the various additional emblems of identity and insignia of rank, office, and honor that had come since about 1300 to be added to the shield of arms in the complex iconic sign eventually known as an "armorial achievement" in all its various forms: the "crest" of carved wood or boiled leather borne atop the helm in Germany from ca. 1250 and the rest of Latin Europe from ca. 1300–1330 as a supplementary symbol of personal identity, especially in tournaments; the headgear of dignity (crowns, coronets, miters, and so forth) that sometimes replaced the helm and its crest over the shield from about the same period; and the collars and other insignia of the Orders of the Garter, Golden Fleece, St. John of Jerusalem, and other knightly orders and aristocratic societies, both lay and religious, into which noblemen were admitted, which were displayed in conjunction with the shield of arms from ca. 1400.

After about 1480, the heralds also brought within their expertise (and growing jurisdiction) most of the livery emblems that emerged in rivalry to armory in the later fourteenth century, and formed part of a still broader set of what are now called paraheraldic emblems. Most important of these were the livery colors, livery badge, livery device, and motto, used from the 1360s to as late as the 1550s to mark the household servants, soldiers, and political clients and allies of kings, princes, and great barons, and displayed both on livery uniforms and a variety of livery flags, all of which had a primarily military function. The livery banderoles, guidons, and standards, divided into bands of the livery colors and strewn with livery badges and mottoes, all supplemented, in the various nonfeudal companies, the more traditional armorial pennoncelles, pennons, and banners that were still used to indicate the presence of the lord or his chief deputy.

As the existence of these various forms of flags indicates, armorial and paraheraldic emblems generally were closely associated with the role of the knight as warrior. This was true not only in the increasingly sanitized combats of the tournament and joust (which themselves frequently took on the outward form of a scene in a romance), but in the combats *à l'outrance* (to the death) of real warfare (when armorial banners were alone displayed), and in certain *pas, emprinses,* or *imprese* (as enterprises of arms were variously called) undertaken by some eminent knights to demonstrate their prowess (in the manner of the knights-errant of the Arthurian romances). All three forms of combat were regarded as of value for establishing and defending reputations, and the various emblems displayed in them came to be seen as the embodiments of the (primarily military) honor not merely of the individual knight, but of his whole lineage. This notion was facilitated by the fact that, by about 1300, the basic form of each coat of arms and achievement was normally common to all members of a particular patrilineage descended from the first to adopt the arms, though each junior member had normally to add some sort of "difference," in keeping with rules developed by heralds. Thus, the interest of the herald in arms and the deeds and honor of individual knights led to an interest in the genealogies of all knightly houses and in their collective deeds and honor.

As admission to knightly status was by ca. 1250 generally (and by ca. 1300 universally) restricted to the descendants of knights, and the noble status even of the descendants of barons, princes, and kings was partially redefined so that nobility could be associated with the functional status of knight, the heralds came to be the principal keepers of the honor of the whole nobility, from emperors to simple gentlemen. A herald in the service of a prince might produce an armorially illustrated genealogy or even compose a chivalric biography of his lord, recording his deeds in the manner of the contemporary romances and inserting him into the quasi-historical mythology of chivalry. Heralds also came to play a leading role in the increasingly elaborate funerals of the greater members of the nobility and probably in the design of their increasingly elaborate tombs, both of which were marked by a display of all of the armorial emblems and insignia to which the deceased had any claim, including those of his immediate ancestors and those of his wife. The heralds' ceremonial functions—which continued unabated into the nineteenth century—naturally led to their playing a comparable role in other forms of procession, assembly, and ritual in which noblemen were arranged in order of rank and precedence, or displayed their arms on banners or other flags. These came to include coronations, investitures with dignities, and solemn knightings, as well as the array of an army preparing for battle.

In keeping with these more exalted forms of function, during the course of the later thirteenth and early fourteenth centuries heralds were converted into regular officers of the households of kings, princes, and major barons, and from the 1330s officers of arms were increasingly entrusted with more weighty diplomatic and military duties than those concerned with tournaments. In consequence the body of heralds throughout Latin

Christendom gradually acquired the character of an international professional corps comparable to the clergy, with distinct ranks and jurisdictions. By 1276, England (for example) had been divided at the Trent River into two territories or "marches of arms," one to the north and one to the south, each presided over by a "king of heralds" (or from ca. 1380 "king of arms") in the direct service of the ruler. A similar sort of division was probably made in France and several adjacent countries in the same period. Within his march, each king of heralds was given the task of overseeing all matters that touched not only on tournaments and armorial bearings, but eventually on knighthood, chivalry, and nobility. Apprentice heralds were from about the same period given the title "pursuivant (of arms)," so that the old generic designation "herald (of arms)" became the special title of master heralds who were not yet kings, and the generic title for all three grades became "officer of arms."

From about 1330, officers of all three grades came to be given special styles at the time of their appointment, and certain of these became the titles of regular offices. On the continent the styles of kings were normally taken from the name of their march, which usually corresponded to a kingdom or principality (Sicily, Guelders, Anjou, Guienne, and so forth), while in England they initially represented the location of the march (Norroy King of Arms north of the Trent, Surroy or later Clarenceux King of Arms south of the Trent). The principal king of arms, however, came to bear a special title, taken in France from the war cry of the real king (Montjoie), in Scotland from the royal arms (Lyon), and in other countries increasingly from the monarchical order of knighthood to which they were also attached (Garter, Golden Fleece, and so on). The styles of the lesser officers were commonly derived from the name of one of their master's possessions (Windsor Herald), dignities (Hastings Pursuivant), or badges (Blanche Sanglier Pursuivant, Crescent Pursuivant), but might be fanciful in the manner of the contemporary romances (Bonespoir Herald, Bien Alaunt Pursuivant).

The formal jurisdictions of the royal officers remained only very loosely defined and organized before the early fifteenth century. In 1406, however, Charles VI of France increased the dignity of the heralds of his kingdom by incorporating them in a "college" under the presidency of Montjoie King of Arms, and in 1415 his rival, Henry V of England, achieved a similar effect by creating the new office of Garter Principal King of Arms of Englishmen, attached to the knightly Order of the Garter, which since 1349 had been the institutional embodiment of the ideals of chivalry in his kingdom. Henry also increased the authority of his officers of arms in 1417 when he gave them the right to visit a number of counties, determine which of their inhabitants had the right to use armorial bearings, and record those that were legitimately borne. This gave rise by 1450 to the even more significant right to invent and grant new armorial achievements, both to individuals and to corporations, thus giving official recognition to the new nobility of the former.

The right to grant new armorial achievements was only rarely extended to heralds on the continent, where kings and princes retained the right to grant them only to those whom they themselves had formally ennobled. Nevertheless, heralds tended everywhere to remain at least the registrars of the knightly nobility, and their rolls of arms served to identify those whose ancestry and rank qualified them for participation in princely tournaments and other forms of activity restricted to the old military nobility. The French incorporation of the national corps of heralds into a college was imitated at later dates in some other countries, including England in 1484 (and again in 1555), while the English practice of attaching the chief herald of the realm to its monarchical order of knighthood was emulated in a number of other states, including Burgundy in 1430, peninsular Sicily in 1465, and France itself in 1469.

As a result of the military revolutions of the sixteenth century, the importance of the French and many other Continental heralds gradually declined after about 1520, and heraldry was everywhere removed from its practical relationship to warfare. Nevertheless, in most of the surviving European monarchies (and in Canada, where an heraldic authority was established in 1988), the royal heralds have continued to this day to preside over the design and use of the emblems of the armed forces, as well as those of the state in general, and still issue letters patent admitting people to a now essentially honorary membership in the old military nobility.

D'A. Jonathan D. Boulton

See also Chivalry; Europe; Knights; Orders of Knighthood, Religious;
    Orders of Knighthood, Secular

References

Dennys, Rodney. 1982. *Heraldry and the Heralds*. London: Jonathan Cape.
Galbreath, D. L., and L. Jéquier. 1977. *Manuel du Blason*. Lausanne: Spes.
Pastoureau, M. 1997. *Traité d'Héraldique*. 3d ed. Paris: Picard.
Wagner, A. 1956. *Heralds and Heraldry in the Middle Ages*. 2d ed. Oxford:
    Oxford University Press.
———. 1967. *Heralds of England*. London: Her Majesty's Stationery Office.
Woodcock, T., and J. M. Robinson. 1988. *The Oxford Guide to Heraldry*.
    Oxford: Oxford University Press.

I

Iaidô

Iaidô is the Japanese martial art of drawing and cutting in the same motion, or "attacking from the scabbard." It dates from the mid-sixteenth century, when warriors began to wear the sword through the belt with the edge upward. Iaidô is practiced solo with real blades, in set routines called kata. Some iaidô styles also practice kata with a partner, using wooden swords or training blades with rebated edges. Some styles incorporate test cutting. Others, however, regard cutting as peripheral to the art. Iaidô is considered a method of self-development but is also practiced as a sport, with two competitors performing kata side by side, and a panel of judges declaring a winner.

The idea of cutting from the draw may have originated as early as the eleventh century, but modern iaidô dates to about 1600. Most styles trace their origin to Hayashizaki Jinsuke Shigenobu (ca. 1546–1621). His students and those who followed developed hundreds of different styles, dozens of which are still practiced. Today the two most popular are the Musô Jikiden Eishin-ryû and the Musô Shinden-ryû.

In the mid-twentieth century two major governing bodies for iaidô were formed: the All Japan Iaidô Federation, and the iaidô section of the All Japan Kendô Federation. Both organizations developed common sets of kata to allow students of different styles to practice and compete together. Although not overly common even in its country of origin, iaidô has followed the Japanese martial arts around the world.

The art has had many names over the years, but iaidô was accepted about 1930. The "I" comes from the word *ite* (presence of mind) and the "ai" alternate pronunciation of the word *awasu* (harmonize) in the phrase *kyû ni awasu* (flexible response in an emergency).

The art is a Japanese *budô* and as such is intended mainly as a method of self-development. The concentration and focus needed to perfect the movements of drawing and sheathing a sharp sword while watching an (imaginary) enemy have a beneficial effect on the mind. The art also de-

A photo of Nakamura Taizaburo taken at the Noma Dôjô, which appeared in his book Nippon-to Tameshigiri no Shinzui *(The Essence of Japanese Sword Test Cutting). (Courtesy of Nakamura Taizaburo)*

mands excellent posture and the ability to generate power from many positions. The art appeals to those who are looking for something deeper than a set of fighting skills. For many years iaidô was considered esoteric, and it was often assumed one had to be Japanese to fully understand it. In the past decades that thinking has changed, and iaidô is now practiced around the world. Apart from its exotic look, iaidô does not generally appeal to spectators, being restrained and quiet in its performance.

The main practice is done alone, and iaidô kata contain four parts, the draw and initial cut (*nuki tsuke*), the finishing cut(s) (*kiri tsuke*), cleaning the blade (*chiburi*), and replacing the blade in the scabbard (*notô*). The swordsman learns many patterns of movement for dealing with enemies, who may attack alone or in groups from various angles.

One of the simplest of the kata is as follows: From a kneeling position the sword is drawn from the left side and a horizontal cut is made from left to right while stepping forward. The sword is raised overhead and a two-handed downward cut is made. The blade is then circled to the right and the imaginary blood is flicked off while standing up. The feet are switched while checking the opponent, and the blade placed back into the scabbard while kneeling.

Various styles of iaidô may practice with the long sword (over 60 centimeters [about 2 feet]), the short sword (30–60 centimeters [1–2 feet]), or the knife (under 30 centimeters [less than 1 foot]). Many styles also include partner practice in the form of stylized kata performed with wooden blades for safety.

No matter where or which style is practiced, iaidô remains rooted in Japan, in traditions that have been handed down for centuries. With the advent of film and video, scholars can see that the art does change over time, but as the natural consequence of physical skills that are passed from teacher to student, not from deliberate attempts to improve it.

Iaidô has grading systems administered by two governing bodies. The All Japan Kendô Federation (as well as the International Kendô Federation) bases its curriculum mainly on a common set of ten techniques, while the All Japan Iaidô Federation has a set of five. A test requires the swordsman to perform a number of techniques from these common sets. For the senior grades, techniques from an old style (*koryû*) must also be performed. A judging panel observes the performance and passes or fails the challenger. Both organizations use the *kyû-dan* system of ranking, with several student, or *kyû*, grades and ten senior, or *dan*, grades.

Some older styles of iaidô have never joined a major organization. They argue that an organization containing several styles and a common set of techniques will lead to a modification or dilution of the pure movements of the individual style, and that all styles will eventually come to look alike. In the case of the Kendô Federation, that argument is sometimes extended to speculation that the movements of kendô will eventually influence the movements of iaidô.

Iaidô competitions are becoming more common outside Japan. The usual format consists of two competitors performing several kata side by side, with a panel of judges deciding on the winner, who then moves on to the next round. The judging is done on a number of criteria and would be equivalent to that done in gymnastics or skating.

The major organizations hold a number of competitions each year, and the International Kendô Federation is considering a world championship for iaidô. The European Kendô Federation and its national bodies hold European and national championships. In North and South America, there are occasional meets but no organized competitive schedule as yet.

As in many martial arts, there is an ongoing discussion as to whether competition is a good thing in an activity that is supposed to improve the practitioner. Those in favor of competition will point out that all sports benefit the players. Their opponents will suggest that the benefits of martial arts are quite different and that they are incompatible with the benefits derived from competition.

Kim Taylor

See also Japan; Kendô; Sword, Japanese; Swordsmanship, Japanese
References
Budden, Paul. 1992. *Looking at a Far Mountain: A Study of Kendô Kata.* London: Ward Lock.
Craig, Darrell. 1988. *Iai: The Art of Drawing the Sword.* Tokyo: Charles E. Tuttle.
Draeger, Donn F. 1974. *The Martial Arts and Ways of Japan.* 3 vols. New York: Weatherhill.
Finn, Michael. 1982. *Iaido: The Way of the Sword.* London: Paul H. Compton.
———. 1984. *Jodô: The Way of the Stick.* Boulder, CO: Paladin Press.
———. 1985. *Kendô No Kata: Forms of Japanese Kendô.* Boulder, CO: Paladin Press.
Fujii, Okimitsu. 1987. *ZNKR Seitei Iai.* London: Kenseikai Publications.
Hoff, Feliks F. 1983. *Iai-Do: Blitzschnell die Waffe Ziehen und Treffen.* Berlin: Verlag Weinmann.
Krieger, Pascal. 1989. *Jodô: The Way of the Stick.* Gland, Switzerland: Sopha Diffusion SA.
Lowry, Dave. 1986. *Bokken: Art of the Japanese Sword.* Burbank, CA: Ohara Publications.
Masayoshi, Shigeru Nakajima. 1983. *Bugei Ju-Happan: The Spirit of Samurai.* Tokyo: G.O.
Maynard, Russell. 1986. *Tanto: Japanese Knives and Knife Fighting.* Burbank, CA: Unique Publications.
Mitani, Yoshiaki. 1986. *Muso Jikiden Eishin Ryû.* Tokyo: Kendô Nihon.
Nalda, Jose Santos. 1986. *Iaido—Todas las Bases y los Katas Exigidos para Cinto Negro.* Barcelona: Editorial APas.
Obata, Toshishiro. 1987. *Crimson Steel: The Sword Technique of the Samurai.* Westlake Village, CA: Dragon Enterprises.
———. 1986. *Naked Blade: A Manual of Samurai Swordsmanship.* Westlake Village, CA: Dragon Enterprises.
Otake, Ritsuke. 1978. *The Deity and the Sword.* Trans. by Donn F. Draeger, Terue Shinozuka, and Kyoichiro Nunokawa. 3 vols. Tokyo: Minato Research and Publishing.
Reilly, Robin L. 1989. *Japan's Complete Fighting System—Shin Kage Ryû.* Tokyo: Charles E. Tuttle.
Sasamori, Junzo, and G. Warner. 1964. *This Is Kendô.* Tokyo: Charles E. Tuttle.
Suino, Nicholas. 1994. *Eishin-Ryû Iaidô: Manual of Traditional, Japanese Swordsmanship.* New York: Weatherhill.
———. 1995. *Practice Drills for Japanese Swordsmanship.* New York: Weatherhill.
Taylor, Kim. 1987–1995. *The Iaido Newsletter.* Guelph, Ontario: Sei Do Kai.
———. 1992, 1994. *Kim's Big Book of Iaido.* 5 vols. Guelph, Ontario: Sei Do Kai.
Warner, Gordon, and Donn F. Draeger. 1982. *Japanese Swordsmanship.* New York: Weatherhill.

Watanabe, Tadashige. 1993. *Shinkage-ryû Sword Techniques, Traditional Japanese Martial Arts.* Trans. by Ronald Balsom. 2 vols. Tokyo: Sugawara Martial Arts Institute.

Yukawa, Yoshi. 1990. *Japanska Svard.* Stockholm: Berghs.

Zen Nippon Kendô Renmei. 1990. *Zen Nippon Kendô Renmei Iai.* Tokyo: Kendô Nihon.

India

Martial arts have existed on the South Asian subcontinent since antiquity. Two traditions have shaped the history, development, culture, and practice of extant South Asian martial arts—the Tamil (Dravidian) tradition and the Sanskrit Dhanur Veda tradition. The early Tamil Sangam "heroic" poetry informs us that between the fourth century B.C. and A.D. 600 a warlike, martial spirit predominated across southern India. Each warrior received "regular military training" in target practice and horse riding, and specialized in use of one or more weapons, such as lance or spear (*vel*), sword (*val*) and shield (*kedaham*), and bow (*vil*) and arrow (Subramanian 1966, 143–144). The heroic warriors assumed that power (*ananku*) was not transcendent, but immanent, capricious, and potentially malevolent (Hart 1975, 26, 81). War was considered a sacrifice of honor, and memorial stones were erected to fallen heroic kings and warriors whose manifest power could be permanently worshipped by their community and ancestors (Hart 1975, 137; Kailasapathy 1968, 235)—a tradition witnessed today in the propitiation of local medieval martial heroes in the popular *teyyam* cult of northern Kerala.

The Sanskrit Dhanur Vedic tradition was one of eighteen traditional branches of knowledge. Although the name "Dhanur Veda" (science/knowledge of archery) reflects the fact that the bow and arrow were considered the supreme weapons, the tradition included all fighting arts from empty-hand grappling techniques to use of many weapons. Knowledge of the Dhanur Vedic tradition is recorded in the two great Indian epics, the *Mahabharata* and the *Ramayana,* whose vivid scenes describe how princely heroes obtain and use their humanly or divinely acquired skills and powers to defeat their enemies. They train in martial techniques under the tutelage of great gurus like the Brahman master Drona, practice austerities and meditation giving one access to subtle powers, and may receive a gift or a boon of magical powers from a god. A variety of paradigms of martial practice and power are reflected in the epics, from the strong, brutish Bhima who depends on his physical strength to crush his foes with grappling techniques or his mighty mace, to the "unsurpassable" Arjuna who uses his subtle accomplishments in meditation to achieve superior powers to conquer his enemies with his bow and arrow.

The only extant Dhanur Vedic text—chapters 249 through 252 of the

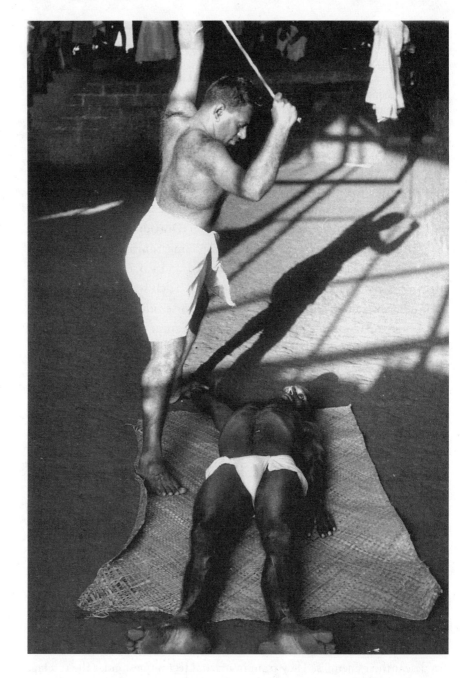

Demonstration of the power of Kalarippayattu (a southern Indian martial art) to withstand weapon strike during a Kalari Payat practice in Kerala, India, 1966. This ancient art of warfare is now performed as a sport in the province. (Hutton Getty/Archive)

encyclopedic collection of knowledge and practices, the *Agni Purana*—is very late, dating from no earlier than the eighth century A.D. These four chapters appear to be an edited version of one or more earlier manuals briefly covering a vast range of techniques and instructions for the king who needs to prepare for war and have his soldiers well trained in arms. Like the purana as a whole, the Dhanur Veda chapters provide both sacred knowledge and profane knowledge, in this case on the subject of martial training and techniques. They catalogue the subject, stating that there are five training divisions (for warriors on chariots, elephants, and horseback;

for infantry; and for wrestling), and five types of weapons to be learned (those projected by machine [arrows or missiles], those thrown by hands [spears], those cast by hands yet retained [nooses], those permanently held in the hands [swords], and the hands themselves). Either a Brahman (the purest high caste, serving priestly functions) or Kshatriya (the second purest caste, serving as princes or warriors to maintain law and social order) should teach the martial arts because it is their birthright, while lower castes can be called upon to learn and take up arms when necessary. Beginning with the noblest of weapons, the bow and arrow, the text discusses the specifics of training and practice, including descriptions of the ten basic lower-body poses to be assumed when practicing bow and arrow. Once the basic positions are described, there is technical instruction in how to string, draw, raise, aim, and release the bow and arrow, as well as a catalogue of types of bows and arrows. More advanced techniques are also described with bow and arrow and other weapons.

Encompassing everything from nutrition to socialization, the martial arts in Southeast Asia always include a spiritual dimension. Accordingly, just as important as the technical descriptions is the major leitmotif of the text— the intimation that the ideal state of the martial practitioner is achieved through attaining mental accomplishment via meditation and use of a mind-focusing mantra. "Having learned all these ways, one who knows the system of karma-yoga [associated with this practice] should perform this way of doing things with his mind, eyes, and inner vision since one who knows [this] yoga will conquer even the god of death [Yama]." To "conquer the god of death" is to have "conquered" the "self," namely, to have overcome all physical, mental, and emotional obstacles in the way of cultivating a self-possessed presence in the face of potential death in combat (Dasgupta 1966).

Practice of a martial art was a traditional way of life. Informed by assumptions about the body, mind, health, exercise, and diet implicit in indigenous Ayurvedic and Siddha systems of medicine, rules of diet and behavior circumscribed training and shaped the personality, demeanor, behavior, and attitude of the long-term student so that he ideally applied his knowledge of potentially deadly techniques only when appropriate. Expertise demanded knowledge of the most vulnerable "death" spots (*marman* in Sanskrit) of the body (Zarrilli 1992) for attack, defense, or for administration of health-giving massage therapies. Consequently, martial masters were also traditional healers, usually physical therapists and bonesetters.

Historically each region of the subcontinent had its own particular martial techniques, more or less informed by the Dhanur Vedic and Sangam traditions. Among those traditions still extant are Tamil Nadu's *varma ati* (Tamil; striking the vital spots) and *silambam* (Tamil; staff fighting), Kerala's *kalarippayattu* (exercises practiced in a special earthen pit,

Relief carving on the headstone of an Indian warrior outside Meherangarh Fort in Jodhpur, India. (Jeremy Horner/ Corbis)

called a *kalari*), North India's *mushti* (wrestling) and *dandi* (staff fighting), and Karnataka's *malkambh* (wrestler's post). Among these, Kerala's kalarippayattu is the most complete extant South Asian martial tradition today.

Kalarippayattu is unique to the southwestern coastal region known today as Kerala State. Dating from at least the twelfth century and still practiced by numerous masters today, kalarippayattu combines elements of both the Sangam Tamil arts and the Dhanur Vedic system. Like their puranic and epic martial counterparts, the kalarippayattu martial practitioners traditionally sought to attain practical power(s) to be used in combat—powers attained through training and daily practice of the art's basic psychophysiological exercises and weapons work, mental powers attained through meditation or actualization in mantra as well as ritual practices, and overt physical strength and power. Sharing a set of assumptions about the body and body-mind relationship with yoga, practice began with "the body" and moved inward through the practice of daily exercises from the early age of seven. Kalarippayattu was traditionally practiced primarily by Nayars, Kerala's martial caste, as well as by a special sub-caste among Kerala's Brahmans, the Yatra Brahmans; lower-caste practitioners known as *chekavar* drawn from among special families of Tiyyas (a relatively low-ranking caste); Muslims (especially Sufis in northern Kerala); and Christians. The art is practiced by both boys and girls for general health and well-being as well as the preparation of martial practitioners; the external body eventually should "flow like a river." The state of psychophysiological actualization was accomplished through practice of dietary and seasonal restraints, the receipt of a yearly full-body massage, development of the requisite personal devotional attitude, and practice of exercises. Kalarippayattu's body exercise sequences (*meippayattu*) link combinations of yoga asana-like poses (*vativu*), steps (*cuvat*), kicks (*kal etupp*), a variety of jumps and turns, and coordinated hand and arm movements performed in increasingly swift and difficult succession and combinations back and forth across the kalari floor. The poses usually number eight, and they are named after dynamic animals such as the horse, peacock, serpent, lion, and the like. Students eventually take up weapons, beginning with the long staff (*kettukari*) and then advancing to the short stick (*ceruvadi*), curved elephant tusk–like *otta* (which introduces empty-hand combat), dagger, sword and shield, flexible sword, mace, and spear.

Closely related to kalarippayattu in the southern Kerala region known as Travancore, which borders the present-day Tamil Nadu State, is the martial art known variously as *adi murai* (the law of hitting), varma ati (hitting the vital spots), or *chinna adi* (Chinese hitting). Some general features of the Tamil martial arts clearly distinguish them from kalarippayattu—they were traditionally practiced in the open air or in unroofed enclosures by Nadars, Kallars, and Thevars. These are three relatively "low-ranking" castes of Travancore District. Nadar was used as a title granted to some families by the ancient Travancore kings. During the last few centuries, a number of Nadars in the southern part of Travancore converted to Christianity, and, given their historical practice of fighting arts, some claim to be from the traditional princely class (Kshatriya). These forms begin with empty-hand combat rather than preliminary exercises. Students learn five main methods of self-defense, including *kuttacuvat* and *ottacuvat* (sequences of offensive and defensive moves in combinations), *kaipor* (empty-hand combat), *kuruvatippayattu* (stickfighting), *netuvatippayattu* (short-staff combat), and *kattivela* (knife against empty hand).

Beginning in 1958 with the founding of the Kerala Kalarippayattu Association as part of the Kerala State Sports Council, the Tamil forms become known as "southern-style kalarippayattu" in contrast to kalarippayattu per se, which became known as "northern" kalarippayattu, since it was extant primarily in the central and northern Kerala regions. The association began with seventeen kalari, as the groups that practice the art are called, with the goals of "encouraging, promoting, controlling, and popularizing" kalarippayattu, holding annual district and state championships, setting standards for practice and construction of kalari, accreditation and affiliation of member kalari, and the like. Today well over 200 kalari are either officially affiliated with the association or remain unaffiliated.

Students of northern and southern kalarippayattu practice a variety of form training, either solo or in pairs (with weapons), at the yearly district and statewide competitions and are judged by a panel of masters. The panel awards certificates and trophies in individual aspects of the art, as well as choosing overall champions in each of the two styles.

Phillip B. Zarrilli

See also Kalarippayattu; Religion and Spiritual Development: India; Thang-Ta; Varma Ati; Wrestling and Grappling: India; Written Texts: India

References

Alter, Joseph S. 1992. *The Wrestler's Body: Identity and Ideology in North India*. Berkeley: University of California Press.

Balakrishnan, P. 1995. *Kalarippayattu: The Ancient Martial Art of Kerala*. Trivandrum, India: Shri C. V. Govindankutty Nair Gu-rukkal, C. V. N. Kalari, Fort.

Dasgupta, Guatam, trans. 1966. Unpublished translation for the author of *Agnipurana of Haharsi Vedavyasa*. Chokhambra Sanskrit Series.

Freeman, J. Richardson. 1991. "Purity and Violence: Sacred Power in the Teyyam Worship of Malabar." Ph.D. dissertation, University of Pennsylvania.

Gangadharan, N., trans. 1985. *Agni Purana*. Delhi: Motilal Banarsidass.

Hart, George L. 1975. *The Poems of Ancient Tamil: Their Milieu and Their Sanskrit Counterparts*. Berkeley: University of California Press.

———. 1979. *Poets of the Tamil Anthologies: Ancient Poems of Love and War*. Princeton, NJ: Princeton University Press.

Kailasapathy, K. 1968. *Tamil Heroic Poetry*. Oxford: Clarendon Press.

Kurup, K. K. N. 1973. *The Cult of Teyyam and Hero Worship in Kerala*. Indian Folklore Series no. 21. Calcutta: Indian Publications.

Mujumdar, D. C. 1950. *Encyclopedia of Indian Physical Culture*. Baroda, India: Good Companions.

Raj, J. David Manuel. 1977. "The Origin and Historical Development of Silambam Fencing: Ancient Self-Defense Sport of India." Ph.D. dissertation, University of Oregon.

———. 1975. *Silambam Fencing from India*. Karaikudi, India.

———. 1971. *Silambam Technique and Evaluation*. Karaikudi, India.

Staal, Frits. 1993. "Indian Bodies." In *Self as Body in Asian Theory and Practice*. Edited by Thomas P. Kasulis et al. Albany: State University of New York Press.

Subramanian, N. 1966. *Sangam Polity*. Bombay: Asian Publishing House.

Zarrilli, Phillip B. 1994. "Actualizing Power(s)and Crafting a Self in Kalarippayattu, a South Indian Martial Art and the Yoga and Ayurvedic Paradigms." *Journal of Asian Martial Arts* 3, no. 3: 10–51.

———. 1986. "From Martial Art to Performance: Kalarippayattu and Performance in Kerala." *Sangeet Natak* 81–82: 5–41; 83: 14–45.

———. 1995. "The Kalarippayattu Martial Master as Healer: Traditional Kerala Massage Therapies." *Journal of Asian Martial Arts* 4, no. 1: 66–83.

———. 1989. "Three Bodies of Practice in a Traditional South Indian Martial Art." *Social Science and Medicine* 28: 1289–1309.

———. 1992. "To Heal and/or to Harm: The Vital Spots in Two South Indian Martial Arts." *Journal of Asian Martial Arts* 1, no. 1: 36–67; 1, no. 2: 1–15.

———. 1998. *"When the Body Becomes All Eyes": Paradigms and Discourses of Practice and Power in Kalarippayattu, a South Indian Martial Art*. New Delhi: Oxford University Press.

Internal Chinese Martial Arts

See External vs. Internal Chinese Martial Arts

J

Japan

The historical development and evolution of warfare in Japan are as old as Japanese civilization itself, over the centuries making warfare in Japan a distinct culture that significantly contributed to the shaping of Japanese society. The importance of martial traditions in Japan cannot be overstated, as warfare has always been an integral aspect of and deeply embedded in Japan's polity, society, and culture. Warfare was the practical method taken by powerful local magnates of ancient Japan to consolidate power, eventually leading to the emergence of a dominant lineage and the establishment of the imperial dynasty. Later, during the medieval period, warfare spread in many provinces, dividing Japan into autonomous domains, and in the early modern period it was used to unify Japan. Warfare also brought to an end seven hundred years of warrior dominance, toppling the Tokugawa *bakufu* (military government) and restoring military powers to the emperor. After Japan entered the modern period, the martial culture that had become so embedded in the Japanese mind contributed to the rise of militarism, which eventually developed into imperialism and military confrontations with other Asian nations and the West.

Centuries of warfare and warrior dominance also eventually produced well-systematized martial disciplines. In that respect, warfare in the form of cultivated martial traditions is still very much a part of Japanese culture, continuously influencing Japanese life. In this sense, warfare has never disappeared in present-day Japan; rather, it is contained within the larger context of Japan's cultural heritage.

Warfare and Geography

The development of Japan's martial culture and traditions is intricately intertwined with Japan's geographical setting and sociodemographic distribution. Being an island nation only a short distance from the Korean peninsula created a sense of isolation and at the same time allowed for continuous contacts with the continent. Indeed, the contact with Korea and

China since the ancient period has allowed the Japanese to borrow selected aspects of Chinese culture (including martial knowledge), which they successfully assimilated into their own native culture.

In addition to being an island nation, Japan has other geographical features that have had a strong influence. The geographic layout of the Japanese island of Honshu, which has always been the central island for Japanese society, produced a diversity of local subcultures, societies, and eventually, martial specializations. High mountains covering most of the island, with relatively few narrow passes crossing them, and many rivers flowing across open plains are the major reasons for this phenomenon. Isolated communities developed unique local dialects, cultural variations, food and craft specialties, and even distinct martial skills. For example, Takeda warriors in the *Kantô* area were highly skillful at mounted archery, while the Kuki family in western Japan was known for their naval capabilities. However, it is important to note a larger social division, that between courtiers and professional warriors, who were also separated geographically—courtiers in the western provinces and warriors in the eastern provinces.

Warriors who were located in and around the capital of Kyoto in western Japan and who served powerful court families acquired refined manners and courtly behavior. At the same time, warriors of imperial descent who were sent, beginning in the eighth century, to the eastern provinces to protect court interests there developed over the centuries a much more distinct warrior culture. They emphasized military prowess over refined courtly behavior and were much more pragmatic in their military training than were warriors in western Japan, eventually setting themselves up as a separate social group in the twelfth century with the establishment of a separate ruling apparatus for warriors commonly known as the bakufu. From that time on, the dual political ruling structure of court and bakufu set the direction in which warrior society was to evolve.

Perhaps the most noticeable effect of geographical separation as a factor in the occurrence of warfare and the development of martial traditions occurred during the fifteenth and sixteenth centuries, when local *daimyo* (warlords) aspired to create independent domains and were primarily concerned with controlling land. Since domain borders were clearly marked by a distinct topography and strategic locations were of great importance, mountain ranges, valleys, and rivers were selected as natural strategic borders. In fact, some of the fiercest battles were fought in these places. In any case, warriors who founded martial traditions often did so in the service of one of these daimyo, and therefore were limited to teaching in a certain region.

Warfare, Politics, and Society

Warfare in Japanese history has been inextricably related to changing politics and society. Knowledge of warfare in Japan prior to the appearance of written records (eighth century A.D.) is limited to archaeological evidence and evidence from Chinese records. While archaeology indicates the existence of warfare and the types of armor and weapons used by the early Japanese warriors, it provides limited information on the social structure and on the conflicts that brought about military confrontations. For this kind of information we must look at records written by Chinese who visited the Japanese islands.

The *Weizhi* (History of the Kingdom of Wei, A.D. 297) mentions more than one hundred peaceful communities on the Japanese islands. At that time the country had a male ruler, but for seventy or eighty years there were widespread disturbances. Then the people selected a female ruler, known as queen Himiko (or Pimiko), who was a shaman. After her death, a male ruler was selected, but disturbances and assassinations ensued. Once again, a female ruler was selected. From this record it seems that warfare was localized and that local chieftains who controlled territories were engaged in warfare, but that there was one strong family whose chieftains were becoming more dominant than others were. Some hundred and fifty years later, the *Hou Hanshu* (The History of the Latter Han, 445) confirms the rise of such a dominant chieftain. It states that each community had a ruler, but there was a supreme ruler, called the "King of the Great Wa," who resided in Yamatai. The records mention Himiko again, stating that there was great instability and constant warfare before she was appointed as queen. Queen Himiko, then, is mentioned as the ruler who was able to extend her authority over other local rulers, thus reducing the frequency of warfare.

According to the *Songshu* (The History of the Liu Song Dynasty, 513), Emperor Yûryaku requested the Chinese court to recognize him by the title "Generalissimo Who Maintains Peace in the East Commanding with Battle-Ax All Military Affairs in the Six Countries of Wa, Paekche, Silla, Imna, Chin-han and Mok-han." In his letter of request Yûryaku writes: "From of old our forebears have clad themselves in armor and helmet and gone across the hills and waters, sparing no time for rest. In the east, they conquered fifty-five countries of hairy men; and in the west, they brought to their knees sixty-six countries of various barbarians. Crossing the sea to the north, they subjugated ninety-five countries" (Tsunoda, de Bary, and Keene 1958, 8). Similarly, in the *Xin Tangshu* (New History of the Tang Dynasty, ca. eleventh century, compiled from earlier records of the Tang dynasty, 618–906) there is a clue to the existence of some sort of fortifications constructed by erecting high walls made of timber (all translations of Chinese records are taken from Tsunoda, de Bary, and Keene 1958).

A samurai in full battle armor brandishes a katana (longsword) in Japan, 1860. The armor is from a much earlier period. (Historical Picture Archive/Corbis)

Until the sixth century, Japan experienced a process of state formation and power consolidation through frequent warfare among local powerful chieftains. In addition, it was during this period (Kofun, 250–600) that mounted archery first appeared, under Emperor Ôjin's reign (ca. late fourth to early fifth centuries). Since it was expensive to acquire a horse, related equipment, and weapons, the mounted warriors were probably members of the elite. These warriors were the forerunners of the later professional warriors who emerged in the provinces from among the hereditary provincial elite—especially in the Kantô area, where some of the strongest families and most skillful warriors have appeared. At any rate, it was in the Yamato region (present-day Nara prefecture) where one dynasty was able to consolidate power, later claiming supreme rulership of the Japanese people and eventually establishing itself as the imperial family.

The imperial family founded its court with the support of a few powerful families, namely the Soga, in charge of finances; Mononobe, in charge of arms and warfare; and Nakatomi, in charge of religious affairs. However, the introduction of Buddhism (ca. 530) in Japan was followed by strong disputes concerning the acceptance of a system of belief that, the Soga argued, would pose a threat to the sanctity of the Japanese people and the imperial family. The court finally recognized Buddhism when Prince Shôtoku patronized the construction of a Buddhist temple, eventually leading to the popularization of Buddhism among elite court families. Prince Shôtoku's patronage of Buddhism, together with other reforms, set the stage for a series of political, land, and judicial reforms.

Rivalry at court among its elite families resulted in the rise to power of the Soga family at the expense of the Nakatomi and Mononobe. The Soga became influential in court matters to the degree of making decisions concerning imperial successions. Naturally, the other court families sought an opportunity to eliminate the Soga family. In 645, an imperial prince, Naka-no-ie, with the support of Nakatomi-no-Kamatari and others, rallied against the Soga family and was victorious. Following his success, Prince Naka-no-ie promulgated a series of reforms known as the Taika Reforms. He then became Emperor Tenji, while Nakatomi-no-Kamatari was given a new family name, Fujiwara. While Emperor Tenji's lineage ended rather quickly, the Fujiwara family became the most influential court family in the following centuries and survived in that position until the modern period. In any case, under the reign of Emperor Tenji, Japanese forces experienced a defeat on the Korean peninsula (Battle of Paekcheon River, 663); this affair prompted Tenji to adopt the Chinese model of state, which led to the promulgation of the Imi Codes (668).

Emperor Tenji's reign came to an abrupt end in the Jinshin War (672–673). The war was the result of a succession dispute between Tenji's son, who was named by Tenji as his successor, and Tenji's brother. Tenji's brother won the war and became Emperor Tenmu. Supported by Kantô warriors, Tenmu emphasized constructing a strong army to achieve a formidable position at court. His foot soldiers used crossbows, and his officers were mounted. He establishing a system of decentralized militia units (*gundan*) based on a conscription system. Each conscript had to provide himself with the necessities for war, including weapons and food. Naturally, such a system placed a heavy burden on impoverished peasants recruited as soldiers. Militarily, the gundan provided guards at court, participated in clashes, and helped settle disputes that took place in the capital.

Tenmu's conscript army eventually had to be restructured based on new guidelines provided by the Taihô Codes of 702.

The Taihô Codes defined government offices and a bureaucratic system based on the T'ang Chinese model. The codes provided legislation for military matters aiming at building an organized imperial army. The codes specified that the army was to be constructed based on a conscription system and that the fundamental unit of its organizational structure was the local militia. In addition to delineating the duties of the military in apprehending outlaws and fighting enemies of the court, and the obligations of its rank-and-file, it specified that soldiers were to practice martial skills (*bugei*). Unfortunately, neither the type of practice involved nor the method of warfare and weapons is clear. Nevertheless, the Taihô Codes clearly indicate a new era in warfare. Emperor Tenmu's military, strictly based on the Chinese model, proved to be impossible to support. However, the guidelines for the army as stipulated in the Taihô Codes made the earlier system more suitable for the Japanese. Yet, it took less than a century for court aristocrats to realize that they must abolish the conscription army in favor of a smaller army of professional warriors.

During the Nara period (711–794), the imperial army engaged in battles against Fujiwara no Hirotsugu (740), against whom it was victorious, and in the latter half of the Nara period the court attempted to assert control over the Emishi people in northern Honshu. A series of campaigns against the Emishi proved to be a total failure, since the Emishi were formidable warriors, making it impossible for the imperial army to subdue them. These repeated failures by an army of poorly trained and poorly motivated soldiers led by civilian courtiers (i.e., the Abe family) brought the final abolition in 792 of an army based on the Chinese model. Then, after Emperor Kanmu (737–806) moved the capital to Heian in 794, an army led by military aristocrats and well-trained soldiers under the leadership of Sakanoue-no-Tamuramaro, whom Kanmu selected as the first *sei-tai-shôgun* (barbarians-subduing generalissimo), resumed the campaign against the Emishi. Tamuramaro's successful campaigns not only strengthened the court and its economy, but also proved that military professionalism was far more beneficial in protecting court interests.

The growth of a professional class of warriors led by a military aristocracy was made possible by a process commonly known as imperial (or dynastic) shedding. As the size of court families grew significantly during the seventh to tenth centuries, they rid themselves of younger sons for whom there was no room at court by sending them out from the court, after providing them with a new family name. This process resulted in the formation of the two most important warrior families—Taira and Minamoto—from whom branched most of Japan's warrior families. The role of the Taira and the Minamoto as viewed by the court was to protect the interests of the imperial and other court families in the countryside where they held lands. However, Taira and Minamoto warriors soon became the military arm of individual court families, namely the Fujiwara and the imperial families, who were competing for power at court. Changing rivalries and shifting alliances eventually led to military conflicts and to a change in the characteristics of warfare.

The tenth century marked a transition in the Japanese military, as reflected in the revolts of Taira no Masakado in the Kantô region and Sumitomo in western Japan between the years 935 and 940, during which time economic difficulties and unstable politics had weakened the court. Masakado, whose initial reason for armed uprising was his uncle's refusal to marry his daughter to Masakado, also targeted the court. Though Masakado directed his attacks at the court, his revolt was primarily for the purpose of establishing his lineage within the Taira clan. Thus, a new era in Japanese society and warfare began with the use of military actions to resolve intrafamilial rivalries. Masakado's tactics relied on existing Chinese-influenced methods of fighting, but his superior organization, technology, and strategy allowed him to defeat his rivals. Similarly, Sumitomo, a pirate leader in western Japan, heard of Masakado's revolt and used the opportunity of a weakened court to expand his activity to such an extent that the Kyoto court felt seriously threatened. Instead of fighting both rebels simultaneously, the court first targeted Sumitomo by offering him a high court rank in return for his allegiance. After Sumitomo accepted the offer, the court sent Taira and Fujiwara forces to seek and destroy Masakado and his allies. In 940 Masakado forces in eastern Japan were destroyed, and Sumitomo in western Japan became a member of the court. Nevertheless, both men left their mark on the evolution of warfare, making it more sophisticated and professionalized.

Four major military conflicts occurred between 1056 and 1160 involving Taira and Minamoto warriors. The first war, known as The Former Nine Years War (lasting from 1056 to 1062, it was in fact only six years long), took place between Minamoto-led forces and the Abe family in the Tôhoku region. The second war, known as The Latter Three Years War (lasting from 1083 to 1087, it was actually four years long), was between the same Minamoto warriors and the Kiyowara family from the same region, who in The Former Nine Years War had been allied with the Minamoto. The purpose of these wars was to restore control of their lands in the Tôhoku region. Remaining records related to the wars show that warfare in Japan was further progressing toward smaller groups of professional warrior bands. Siege warfare and mounted combat replaced large armies of foot soldiers who fought in rigid formations, and war technology shifted toward a more extensive use of the bow and arrow (*yumiya*).

The third war was more accurately a one-night armed conflict known as the Hôgen Conflict (1156), usually characterized as a factional dispute at court. The emperor and one Fujiwara faction, backed by factions of the Taira and Minamoto, fought the retired emperor and another faction of the Fujiwara, backed by yet other factions of the Taira and Minamoto families. The fourth war, the Heiji Conflict (1159–1160), was, like the Hôgen Conflict, a matter of political rivalries within the court. However, the main difference was that Taira and Minamoto were clearly fighting each other. By the end of the conflict, Minamoto no Yoshitomo had lost to Taira no Kiyomori, who then became a dominant figure with unprecedented influence at court. At any rate, the most striking features of these armed conflicts are the small forces, numbering only a few hundred, and the use of a single mounted warrior as the basic fighting unit. In addition, night attacks and setting fires have become effective tactics, given the smaller number of warriors participating in fighting. These characteristics remained common until the next great conflict between the Minamoto and the Taira.

Between 1180 and 1185 Japan experienced its first countrywide civil war, the Genpei War, between Minamoto supporters led by Minamoto no Yoritomo, and Taira supporters led by Taira no Kiyomori and his successors. The war erupted as a result of a succession dispute at court. A disgruntled Prince Mochihito, who was passed over for the title of emperor, issued a call to arms to Minamoto warriors to rise against the Taira, who supported and protected the court. Although the two competing forces are usually identified as Taira (also Heike) and Minamoto (also Genji), there were Taira warriors in the Minamoto camp and vice versa. For Minamoto no Yoritomo, the war against the Taira was for the sake of reviving his lineage of the Minamoto and establishing an independent coalition of warriors in the eastern provinces led by him and his descendants. For warriors supporting Yoritomo, more than anything else it was a war for benefits that came in the form of land rewards. The Genpei War, therefore, could be labeled as a political and economic war, of which the originally unplanned result was the formation of a distinct self-governed society of professional warriors. Leading this society of warriors was the bakufu, its shôgun (military general), and regents.

Although a new political institution, the Kamakura bakufu did not introduce any major innovations in methods of warfare, even when threatened by foreign invaders. Japan's refusal to become a tributary state to the Chinese court and the decapitation of Chinese messengers who came to convince the Japanese to submit to the Chinese court led to two massive invasions by Mongol forces in 1274 and 1281. The Japanese forces were able to defeat the Mongols, who, according to Chinese sources, ran short on arrows and lacked effective coordination. The well-known tales of divine winds that blew the invading armada off the Japanese coast have taken much of the credit Japanese warriors deserve. Though Japanese warriors did not use any technological innovations in their defense of the landing site, consolidated war efforts contributed to their success. Nevertheless, despite the bakufu's military success, economic difficulties and social instability that followed the Mongol invasions contributed to the weakening of the Kamakura bakufu and its eventual downfall in 1333.

During the late Kamakura period, the court established a system of alternate imperial succession between two imperial lineages. In 1318 Godaigo became an emperor, but he later refused to relinquish the title to the successor from the main imperial line and as punishment was sent into exile. In 1333 Godaigo escaped from exile and returned to Kyoto to claim his right to the title of emperor. Two major warrior families became involved in this imperial dispute, Ashikaga and Nitta. Ashikaga Takauji was sent by the bakufu to counter Godaigo, who was supported by Nitta Yoshisada. Godaigo also recruited the renegade warrior Kusonoki Masashige and his band of warriors. During three years of confrontations between Godaigo and Ashikaga forces, the nature of warfare began to change. Kusonoki Masashige introduced unconventional warfare in defending or penetrating fortifications, while Ashikaga Takauji made an impressive tactical move when he combined land and sea forces to trap and destroy the Kusonoki forces. Eventually, in 1336, Godaigo was set in a newly established Southern Court, while the main imperial line was kept in what became the Northern Court. Similarly, Ashikaga Takauji used the Godaigo affair to topple the Kamakura bakufu and establish the Ashikaga shogunate.

The establishment of the Ashikaga shogunate in 1336 was the beginning of a new form of warrior rule, in which the lord-vassal/lord-vassal vertical structure replaced the direct rule of the Kamakura bakufu. The Ashikaga bakufu exercised direct control over its vassals, but did not control its vassals' retainers, thus relying on effective pyramidal distribution of authority from top to bottom. After the first three Ashikaga shôguns, the system eventually led to fragmentation of the warrior society and frequent disputes. After the death of Ashikaga Yoshimitsu in 1408, local conflicts erupted countrywide. The shôgunal deputy office was established and was filled alternately by three powerful families, Hatakeyama, Hosokawa, and Shiba, who were collateral vassals of the Ashikaga. By 1460, Ashikaga Yoshimasa, not having a successor, chose to name his brother, a priest, as his successor. The brother agreed, but then Yoshimasa's wife gave birth to a son. This led to a succession dispute between Yoshimasa's brother, backed by the Hosokawa, and Yoshimasa's son who was supported by the Yamana. Soon, Hatakeyama and Shiba took sides and joined the dispute. The dispute erupted in 1467 in an intense war in Kyoto commonly known as the Ônin War, and lasted until 1477, after which it spread to the provinces until the rise of dominant daimyo.

The gradual breakdown of central government and the rise of powerful warlords who controlled independent domains led to internal strife that climaxed in a period of intense warfare known as the Sengoku period (1477–1573). The period was characterized by the inability of the Ashikaga shogunate to assert control over daimyo who sought to establish their domains as independent states and who asserted direct control over individual villages. Between 1500 and 1568 new smaller domains were ruled effectively by local chieftains, called Sengoku daimyo, who were a new breed of territorial rulers. Some of them rose to power from the lower echelons, but the majority were local powerful warriors (*kokujin*). During that period there was an emphasis on true ability and much less emphasis on name or status; what concerned these daimyo most was the idea of *tôgoku kyôhei*— enrich the domain and strengthen the military. This principle prompted the daimyo to find various ways to improve their domain's economy by promoting trade and production. In addition, the Sengoku daimyo established a type of hierarchical relationship with their vassals, separating them into two groups, *fudai* and *tôzama*. The fudai were close to the daimyo and were expected to show more loyalty to him, while the tôzama vassals were less loyal to the daimyo and more concerned with practical benefits.

The primary concern for the Sengoku daimyo was control of land, which dictated both defensive and offensive strategies. To improve their military capability, many of the daimyo studied Sunzi's *Art of War* (Chinese book of military strategy) and frequently consulted the *Yijing* (*I Ching*, "The Book of Changes," a Confucian classic on divination). Their warriors, to whom the saying "call a warrior a dog, call a warrior a beast, but winning is his business" was directed, worked on improving their fencing skills, as well as their archery, among other weapons. In these chaotic times many vassals and warriors at various levels were primarily concerned with their own survival, rather than the well-being of their lord. More than in any other period in Japanese history, loyalty was a conditional situation, in which reciprocity dictated the nature of service and degree of loyalty.

Due to the unstable nature of the warriors' behavior, daimyo composed "house laws" (*kahô*) for their domains. An important aspect of the kahô was their emphasis on lawful behavior within the domain, as expressed in the *kenka ryô seibai* (mutual judgment of a quarrel). According to this principle, warriors who engaged in fighting had to be punished, regardless of who was the instigator or who was at fault. The Imagawa family's kahô even stated that the punishment would be death by execution. The Takeda house, though not specifying a punishment, proclaimed that whoever supported the fight, even without actually participating in it, would be punished. The kenka ryô seibai was also a way for the daimyo to deal with the problems caused by their vassal's desire for revenge when wronged and a tool to better control them. The purpose of having strict laws within the domain was to allow the daimyo an uninterrupted control over his domain, and ultimately, increase his efficiency during wartime. The need to control one's domain by any means was a result of the unforgiving nature of Sengoku confrontations and the appearance of many war-minded ambitious daimyo, who waited for a moment of weakness in neighboring domains to launch an attack.

Among the fiercest warriors of the period were Takeda Shingen and Uesugi Kenshin, whose armies confronted each other in some of the most well-known battles of the Sengoku period. They met five times in Kawanakajima, Shinano province, without resolution. Another celebrated battle is that between Oda Nobunaga, the first to begin a successful unification of Japan, and the Imagawa army at Okehazama (1560)—a battle that is widely regarded as a classic surprise attack. But Nobunaga is probably most remembered for his victory over Takeda forces led by Takeda Katsuyori at the battle of Nagashino (1575). Nobunaga, with the support of Tokugawa Ieyasu, won the battle with three thousand gunners, who were organized in small teams to achieve effective continuous firepower.

One of the most important results of Sengoku warfare, which significantly contributed to the spread of martial traditions, was the appearance of castles and castle towns. This trend began when Oda Nobunaga built his Azuchi Castle in 1576, followed by Toyotomi Hideyoshi's Momoyama Castle, and later followed by other daimyo. In war, the castle was not intended to hold out to the end. When the attacking army reached *ni-no-maru* (second line of defense) the lord of the castle would typically commit *seppuku* (ritual suicide).

Toyotomi Hideyoshi succeeded Nobunaga, the second of the three unifiers, who became known as a master of siege warfare by coalition. His supreme military strategy was complemented by unusual diplomacy; defeated daimyo were given the opportunity to join Toyotomi's camp after swearing allegiance. In addition, his effective policies—*heinô bunri* (separation of warriors and farmers) and *katana-gari* (sword hunt)—contributed greatly to his success in unifying Japan. Toyotomi successfully implemented a policy of moving samurai from the countryside to castle towns where they could be closely monitored.

Following Toyotomi's death (1592), his leading generals were divided into two camps, the western camp of Toyotomi allies and the eastern camp of Tokugawa forces. In 1600 the two camps met in what is perhaps the most famous battle in Japanese history, the Battle of Sekigahara. Relying on a last-minute betrayal within the Toyotomi coalition, Tokugawa forces led by Tokugawa Ieyasu won a decisive victory, and Toyotomi supporters retreated to Ôsaka Castle. The third of the three unifiers, Tokugawa Ieyasu, successfully ended a long period of warfare, and established his Tokugawa shogunate in Edo (present-day Tokyo). In 1614 Tokugawa Hidetada signed a peace treaty with Toyotomi Hideyori, according to which the moats and obstructions around Ôsaka Castle were to be removed. A year later, Tokugawa forces attacked Ôsaka Castle and set it on fire as Hideyori and his mother committed seppuku.

Under the Tokugawa regime Japan finally enjoyed a long period of internal peace that drastically changed the characteristics of the Japanese samurai. Samurai had been uprooted from the countryside, had lost their landed estates, and were placed in urban areas. It was during that time that the ideal image of the samurai based on Confucian thought was promoted, schools of martial discipline became popular, and the foundation of martial lineages by experienced able warriors became common. By the end of the Tokugawa shogunate there were hundreds of established martial lineages in the form of organized schools, some of which enjoyed official patronage by the bakufu and daimyo. Since the great social and political reforms of the Meiji Restoration (1868), some martial traditions have become extinct, others have been further divided into branches, and still other schools have made a successful transition to sport competition.

Weapons and Technology

The arsenal of the Japanese warrior included a wide variety of bladed weapons, bows, chain weapons, stick and staff, firearms, concealed weapons, tools, projectiles, explosives, poisons, and many specialized weapons for specific purposes. The appearance of these weapons coincided with technological developments such as the casting of iron and the use of wood-processing methods, while other weapons were developed as a result of contacts with foreign cultures. Other reasons for the appearance of certain weapons were social and political changes that resulted in the intensification of warfare, or political stability, which reduced warfare to police duties.

Perhaps the most well known among Japanese weapons is the curved single-edged sword (the main types of which include the tachi, the katana, the kodachi, and the wakizashi), which has always symbolized the soul and spirit of the Japanese warrior. It has been in use in warfare from the earliest Japanese civilization until the modern period. Iron-casting technology necessary for the production of swords was introduced to Japan from the continent in the Yayoi period, during which there was intensive social stratification and state formation. Knowledge of iron casting was crucial for those local chieftains competing for power, who at the same time sought to improve their arsenal of weapons using that technology. Consequently, even more important than swords, Japanese smiths forged other bladed weapons such as the *yari* (spear), *naginata* (halberd), and *bisentô* (great halberd), which were far more effective as battlefield weapons. Furthermore, blades for pole-arms were easier to manufacture, since they did not require the same cumbersome process as making a sword blade, the blades were usually smaller in size (thus requiring less iron), and the fittings that accompanied the blade were reduced to bare wood with minimal reinforcement parts. They thus took a shorter time to produce and allowed for mass production. Picture scrolls from the Heian period, such as the Former Nine Years War Picture Scroll and the Latter Three Years War Picture Scroll, depict warriors wielding naginata or yari, but portray a considerably smaller number of sword-wielding warriors.

The technology for producing blades is said to have reached its highest level during the thirteenth and fourteenth centuries, but since then not much has changed. In fact, contemporary sword makers proudly claim to have retained the knowledge of sword making that was used in the early medieval period. In that sense, blade making has become a matter of mastery of a technology that has been frozen in time. It is also perhaps one among very few unique examples of technology that has taken on a sacred, religious character, requiring the blade maker to follow a purification ritual that is meant to complement the mundane nature of technology in order to produce a superior blade. Nevertheless, some changes have occurred in the making of swords; during the sixteenth century when swords were in high demand for local use (due to internal countrywide strife) or for export to the continent, the number of blade makers grew while the quality dropped. The political stability and social changes that followed the end of a period of civil war in the early seventeenth century resulted in a significant reduction in the production of naginata and yari blades while promoting a new style of sword.

Somewhat similar to the development of blade technology was the production of bows as the primary weapon until the medieval period. It is impossible to examine bows that were produced prior to the Heian period simply because bamboo, the material used for making the bows, could not have survived the forces of nature. Yet, from sketches and drawings found in picture scrolls, as well as by examining bows from later periods, we can confirm that the design of the bow and the technology used for making it have changed very little if at all since they were first produced. In the Obusuma Saburô Picture Scroll from the Kamakura period, a depiction of warriors stringing a bow indicates that nothing much has changed since then in the manner of setting the bow and shooting arrows. Neither the relatively peaceful Kamakura period nor the chaotic Sengoku period had much influence on the production of the common bow. It is also surprising that the Japanese did not borrow the more advanced technology for producing the Mongolian bow and that there is no evidence of extensive use of any other type of bow, including the Great Bow (Ôyumi) and the crossbow, after the ninth century. Using the same materials for making the long common bow, the Japanese also produced the half-size bow (hankyû) that was designed for close-range encounters or narrow areas, and was to be used by foot soldiers. The use of the hankyû was most common among those involved in covert warfare during the sixteenth century.

Equal in importance to bladed weapons and bows were the importation and later the production of firearms. The governor of Tanegashima, Tanegashima Tokitaka, who was quite fascinated by the new technology, bought the first two rifles from the Portuguese in 1543. Yet, full recognition of the battlefield advantages of firearms occurred only thirty-two years later when Oda Nobunaga used well-armed and trained units to win the battle of Nagashino. In fact, it was Nobunaga who established the first method of firing in battle, even before the Europeans. The introduction of firearm technology proved to be a decisive factor in the direction Japanese society and politics were to take. It was arguably an important contribution to the successful pacification of Japan by Oda Nobunaga, Toyotomi Hideyoshi, and Tokugawa Ieyasu, who, although they did not desert the use of swords, made extensive use of firearms. Unfortunately for the Japanese warriors, three centuries later when the American commodore Perry arrived with an armada of battleships, the Japanese found out that their firearms were outdated and were no match for modern guns and cannons. This inferiority, which they unsuccessfully attempted to overcome in a hurry, eventually created political turmoil and the downfall of the Tokugawa shogunate, bringing to an end seven hundred years of military dominance.

In addition to the weapons mentioned above, it is important to point out that the arsenal of weapons and tools included much more. Before the Tokugawa period, Japanese warriors developed special weapons with some sort of a blade to which an iron ball or ring was attached by a chain. Special battlefield tools were designed to break down doors, others to climb walls, and still others to cross water barriers. Individual warriors used hidden weapons of many sorts, such as hidden blades, spikes, and projectiles. Among the weapons that were used since the ancient period and that gained popularity during the Tokugawa period were those designed to subdue an opponent. These usually consisted of a long pole, at the end of which there was attached some kind of a device for grabbing an attacker's helmet, armor, or clothes. Other such poles were designed to pin down a violent opponent by locking the neck or limbs. Tokugawa policemen whose main duty was to catch criminals made extensive use of such weapons. In fact, some of these weapons were converted to modern use and are currently part of standard equipment for riot police units.

Engaging in Battle

Engaging in battle has always been a distinct part of warfare in Japan. Historians identify two general types of engagements: predetermined battle and surprise attack. The predetermined battle theoretically included five stages, as follows: the setting of the time and place, exchange of envoys to declare each side's intention to engage in battle, exchange of humming arrows (*kaburaya*) to mark the beginning of battle, massive exchange of arrows between the armies while advancing toward each other, and close combat using swords and daggers while occasionally utilizing grappling techniques. However, most battles were probably conducted without formal exchanges. That is, the armies met on the battlefield and exchanged humming arrows as a marker to their own troops to begin shooting arrows. Then they closed distance until they engaged in close combat using bladed weapons. Military confrontations according to these stages continued even during the Sengoku period, with some variations resulting from changing attitudes and technology.

Surprise attacks, on the other hand, relied heavily on preliminary intelligence gathering concerning the exact location of the enemy's forces, number of warriors, terrain, and equipment. These attacks were commonly carried out at night or early dawn and were led by warriors who rushed to be first in battle, as such an initiative was highly regarded and well rewarded. Another characteristic of the surprise attack was the relatively small number of troops participating in it. Rarely were many troops involved in a surprise attack. Toyotomi Hideyoshi's midnight march, in which he led his army without letting them take a rest so that they could surprise their enemy, who expected to meet them in battle much later, is a good example of the surprise attack. Other confrontations, especially in the fifteenth and sixteenth centuries, relied on siege tactics, but the two important stages of engaging at a distance followed by close combat seem to have otherwise been the common practice.

Traits of the Warrior

Having been professional warriors whose livelihood depended on performing duties in the service of a lord and having their status and income determined by how well they performed these duties, Japanese warriors developed a culture in which loyalty to one's lord and parents and bravery in battle were highly esteemed ideals. Those warriors who followed their lord's command without hesitation or were first to rush and engage in battle (*senjin*) with the enemy were highly praised and sometimes well rewarded.

Stories of loyal warriors were often recorded in the various war tales, from the very early tales during the Heian and medieval periods to much later accounts, among which are the most well known and celebrated, *Chushingura,* and literary works such as the sixteenth-century *Budô shoshinshu* (The Code of the Samurai) and the twentieth-century *Bushidô* (Way of the Warrior). Among earlier records, perhaps the best known is the story of Kusonoki Masashige's exemplary display of loyalty to Emperor Godaigo in the final scene of the Battle of Minatogawa. Having his forces reduced to just a few tens of men, Masashige withdrew with his brother Masasue to a house where they planned to commit *seppuku* (suicide). Their retainers lined up in front of them and after reciting a prayer they cut open their bellies (*hara kiri*). Then, Masashige asked his brother into which of the nine existences (i.e., the nine possible levels of rebirth, according to Buddhist teaching) he wished to be reborn. Masasue laughed and answered that he wished to be reborn into this same existence for seven more times so that he could fight the enemies of Emperor Godaigo. Masashige affirmed a similar wish after which they pointed their swords at each other and fell on the swords simultaneously. Some six hundred years later, the Japanese kamikaze fighters of World War II wrote down the same resolution on their headbands before going out on their last mission.

Such behavior embodies the ideal for a samurai, but many famous warriors fell far short of that ideal. Loyalty and disloyalty were often complementary. Minamoto no Yoritomo hunted down his younger half brother Yoshitsune, forcing him to commit seppuku. Takeda Shingen forced his father into exile so that he could become the head of the Takeda clan. Akechi Mitsuhide, one of Oda Nobunaga's most trusted generals, betrayed Nobunaga and assassinated him while Nobunaga was camping at a temple. Toyotomi presented his rush to take revenge as an act of supreme loyalty toward his lord. In practical terms, the general who avenged the death of Nobunaga could claim to be his successor by virtue of loyalty. Toyotomi knew that this reasoning was not good enough to secure his position, so immediately after killing Akechi Mitsuhide he appointed himself as the guardian of Nobunaga's son, who was a young child at the time. Again, he claimed this role on the pretext of supreme loyalty to Nobunaga, but its practical implications were that Toyotomi now secured his position.

Nevertheless, Toyotomi's reliance on his display of loyalty as a way to support his claim to replace Nobunaga shows that appreciation for loyalty indeed existed, even if only superficially. Indeed, when Toyotomi was on his deathbed he made his generals sign a blood oath to maintain peaceful succession after his death. Although they all showed loyalty to Toyotomi and signed the oath, shortly after his death they fought each other in the Battle of Sekigahara.

The periodic emphasis on the ideal character and behavior of a samurai, especially during the samurai decline in the Tokugawa period, indicates the need for reminding samurai who and what they ought to be. The ideal traits of the warrior, then, were emphasized as a measure of persuasion to encourage warriors to adhere to the "right" way. Yamaga Sokô (1622–1685), a thinker and a Confucian scholar, first took on the task of systematically codifying the proper "way and creed of the warrior" (shidô bukyô). Sokô was concerned with the degeneration of warrior society following a prolonged period of peace during which they were gradually becoming idle and abusing their hereditary status. Sokô argued that since warriors do not produce or trade in anything, they in fact live off the work of others. Therefore, according to Confucian thought, being a ruling elite places them as the moral exemplars for all social classes, and their role was to protect moral principles. Sokô viewed the role of the samurai as shifting from a purely military function to that of an intellectual military aristocracy whose role is to provide the people with a righteous government. The "way of the warrior" was to be achieved by learning the Confucian classics, and in addition, diligently practicing military disciplines. Of course, the latter was in sharp contrast to Confucian thought, but nevertheless the combination of "military" and "letters" (bunbu) set the basis for what is now known as bushidô.

Another way to view the role of the concept of ideal warrior traits is to place it in its political context. Historically, top retainers and close relatives were potentially the most dangerous adversaries. Since the thirteenth century, warrior houses had promulgated their own house laws (kahô) and house regulations (kakun) as a way to eliminate any such danger, but there never existed a unified system of thought until the establishment of the Tokugawa shogunate. The shogunate emphasized samurai ideals because this code contributed to its own security and stable politics, reducing the probability of rising opposition. The bakufu made use of Confucian ideology and native beliefs to create a clear image of the ideal samurai, looking back at the age of the early samurai and romanticizing it to fit a certain desirable image, then using the image of early legendary warriors as a model. It is therefore important to emphasize that although samurai ideals had become part of the warrior heritage centuries earlier, the Tokugawa codification and promotion of these ideals was largely a method of securing loyalty and obedience to the bakufu, and on the other hand, dealing with economically exhausted and disgruntled samurai.

Sokô's thought no doubt contributed greatly to the increasing popularity of martial disciplines in the Tokugawa period. Training in these disciplines became a way for self-improvement for Tokugawa samurai. Yet, the most celebrated ideals of shidô, those of obligation and ultimate loyalty to one's parents and lord, moral principles, and frugality, were more often ignored than followed. The case of the forty-seven warriors of Akô who took revenge for injustice incurred by their lord has always been a subject of disagreement. Were they truly loyal retainers? As such, they were supposed to act immediately and not wait two years before taking revenge. Also, how is one to explain that out of hundreds of retainers only a small fraction remained to carry out the act of justified revenge? Such questions, together with the increasing number of samurai giving up their status to become merchants, show that the way of the warrior often remained a matter of theory rather than practice.

High Culture

Letters and arts have always been part of warrior culture, though reserved mostly for warriors of higher status. Since the early ancient period when leading warriors were military aristocrats, the study of Chinese classics and poetry, as well as writing Japanese poetry, has been a way for warriors to maintain their aristocratic identity. Similarly, acquisition of valuable ceramics or patronage of craftsmen and artisans has been a warrior's way of expressing his refined manners and taste. Attention to high culture among elite warriors reached its apex twice during the medieval period, a time when, for the most part, warriors were more involved in warfare than they were to be later. The third Ashikaga shôgun, Yoshimitsu (1358–1408), under whose rule order prevailed in most of Japan, was an enthusiastic patron of the arts. His personal fondness for refined culture, which stood in contrast to his character as a warrior, is perhaps the central reason for the beginning of a period of flourishing arts and culture, commonly known as the Kitayama epoch, named after the place in which Yoshimitsu built a Zen temple, the Golden Pavilion.

The Kitayama epoch not only brought new life into existing aristocratic culture, but also gave birth to new art forms such as Nô drama (a form of theater based on dance, which developed from native and foreign influence, sarugaku, and dengaku kyôgen theater) and Kyôgen theater ("mad words," comical or farcical skits that were first interluded with Nô, but were later performed independently), after Yoshimitsu attended a Sarugaku performance ("monkey music," whose characteristics are unknown, but the name suggests monkeylike comical performance) by Kanami and Zeami and became a generous patron of the performing arts. In the latter part of the Kitayama epoch, during the rule of Yoshimitsu's grandson, Yoshimasa (1436–1490), there was a further development, with Yoshimasa's patronage of linked verse poetry, the tea ceremony, and monochrome painting.

After Yoshimasa relinquished the shôgunal post to his son in the midst of the bloody Ônin War (1467–1477), he devoted himself to promotion and patronage of the arts more than Yoshimitsu had before him, thus bringing the arts to higher levels of achievement than ever before. He first constructed the Silver Pavilion at the outskirts of Kyoto in Higashiyama, from which the name Higashiyama epoch is derived. Cultural achievements during the Higashiyama epoch exceeded those of the Kitayama epoch, as it further brought together court and warrior cultures. Rigid rules in *waka* (court poetry adopted from China in the seventh and eighth centuries, which included long and short forms; the preferred short form was made of thirty-one syllables consisting of five lines of 5-7-5-7-7 syllables) were softened by a new approach, according to which one person was to link verses to those first expressed by another, resulting in a new form of poetry called *renga*. The increased popularity of renga, together with the Nô, Kyô-gen, Sarugaku, and Dengaku ("field music," performance based on the style developed by peasants singing and performing in the fields), contributed to increased interaction not only among warriors, as well as among peasants and townsmen, but also between warriors and other social groups. In contrast, other forms of arts and culture, such as the tea cere-mony, painting, and landscape gardening, remained elitist, reaching a larger audience only later in the Tokugawa period.

In the late medieval period, with the construction of Oda Nobunaga's Azuchi Castle and Toyotomi Hideyoshi's Momoyama Castle, there began a new era of cultural flourishing. The Azuchi and Momoyama Castles, from which the epoch's name (Momoyama) comes, marked the beginning of a new age of architectural design, which not only saw grandiose castles but also a greater number of warriors, namely the daimyo, involved in patron-age and collection of art; the emerging castles and castle towns were the most suitable grounds for such cultural activity. Nobunaga's interest in for-eign culture as presented to him by the Jesuits led to Japanese specializa-tion in Western painting and production of *nanban* (southern barbarians) screens depicting foreigners in Japan. However, it was Toyotomi's personal preference for court culture and his lavish display of wealth that gave a new boost to Japanese art forms and theater. His golden tea room is perhaps the best example of his combined taste for the tea ceremony and grandeur, but his great tea ceremony in Kitano Shrine in 1587 also brought this culture of the elite to people of lower social status. For this grand tea ceremony Toyotomi invited courtiers, daimyo, warriors, townsmen, and peasants, and he displayed his collection of tea utensils for everybody to see. With Toyotomi setting such an example, daimyo all over the country became pa-trons and collectors of art as a way of presenting themselves as cultured men in addition to being powerful warriors. In fact, patronage and collec-tion of art had become symbols of a daimyo's wealth and power.

Toyotomi's death and the eventual establishment of the Tokugawa shogunate ended a long period of warriors' patronage of the arts. Social changes that led to the economic decline of many warriors and to accumulation of wealth among townsmen and merchants produced new patterns of patronage. Warriors were now following the lower classes' tastes and interests, rather than their own.

Conclusion

Japanese martial disciplines and traditions developed and evolved within the larger context of Japanese society. Politics of the ruling elites, social changes, and cultural trends strongly influenced the birth of identifiable military schools in the medieval and early modern periods. Similarly, the contours and customs of what have become military traditions were often the result of religious influence, as well as influence from established cultural traditions such as the tea ceremony, or from prevailing modes of thought such as Confucianism. Just as these have evolved and changed their characteristics to accommodate changing preferences, so have the various martial traditions. Furthermore, a common characteristic that must be emphasized is the constant sense of rivalry among schools of similar discipline, whether schools of painting, tea ceremony, or military disciplines. Among schools of military disciplines, such rivalry has occasionally ended in violent encounters, but more often, especially in the modern period, has resulted in wars of words.

Consequently, the absence in the modern period of the cultural grounds in which martial disciplines flourished, the common view of martial disciplines as an anachronism in a world of modern warfare, and the international popularization of Japanese martial traditions have resulted in a profound misunderstanding of these traditions. Although many Japanese hold a misguided view of their own martial traditions, non-Japanese in particular, lacking knowledge of the language and history of Japan, and having been captured by a romantic view of an exotic culture, tend to misconstrue the true nature of Japan's long history of martial disciplines. Japan's military traditions remain a most important part of this nation's history and culture.

Roy Ron

See also Aikidô; Archery, Japanese; Budô, Bujutsu, and Bugei; Japanese Martial Arts, Chinese Influences on; Jûdô; Karate, Japanese; Kendô; Kenpô; Ki/Qi; Koryû Bugei, Japanese; Ninjutsu; Religion and Spiritual Development: Japan; Samurai; Sword, Japanese; Swordsmanship, Japanese; Warrior Monks, Japanese/Sôhei; Wrestling and Grappling: Japan; Written Texts: Japan

References
Adolphson, Mikael. 2000. *The Gates of Power: Monks, Courtiers, and Warriors in Premodern Japan.* Honolulu: University of Hawai'i Press.

Berry, Marry Elizabeth. 1994. *The Culture of Civil War in Kyoto*. Berkeley: University of California Press.

Farris, William Wayne. 1992. *Heavenly Warriors: The Evolution of Japan's Military, 500–1300*. Cambridge: Harvard University Press.

Friday, Karl F. 1992. *Hired Swords: The Rise of Private Warrior Power in Early Japan*. Stanford, CA: Stanford University Press.

Hall, John Whitney. 1991. *Japan: From Prehistory to Modern Times*. Ann Arbor: University of Michigan Press.

Hall, John Whitney, et al., eds. 1981. *Japan before Tokugawa: Political Consolidation and Economic Growth, 1500 to 1650*. Princeton: Princeton University Press.

Ikegami, Eiko. 1995. *The Taming of the Samurai: Honorific Individualism and the Making of Modern Japan*. Cambridge: Harvard University Press.

Ooms, Herman. 1985. *Tokugawa Ideology: Early Constructs, 1570–1680*. Princeton: Princeton University Press.

Piggott, Joan R. 1997. *The Emergence of Japanese Kingship*. Stanford, CA: Stanford University Press.

Tsunoda, Ryûsaku, William T. de Bary, and Donald Keene, eds. 1958. *Sources of Japanese Tradition*. New York: Columbia University Press.

Varley, Paul H. 1967. *The Ônin War*. New York: Columbia University Press.

———. 1970. *Samurai*. New York: Delacorte Press.

———. 1984. *Japanese Culture*. Honolulu: University of Hawai'i Press.

———. 1994. *Warriors of Japan: As Portrayed in the War Tales*. Honolulu: University of Hawai'i Press.

Japanese Martial Arts, Chinese Influences on

It is no surprise that Japan's feudal society, with its samurai-dominated martial culture, spawned an abiding interest in martial arts. Although weapons techniques, primarily archery and swordsmanship, were the main traditional Japanese martial arts, today the first things that normally come to mind are *jûdô* and *karate*. These, however, are not traditional Japanese martial arts in the purest sense. In fact, Japanese bare-handed martial arts, including *sumô* (grappling), which had a combat variation, have all been influenced to some degree by Chinese martial arts.

The earliest Japanese historical reference to sumô traces its origins to 23 B.C., but the reference itself was recorded in the first Japanese history, *Nihon Shoki*, in 720, using the Chinese term *jueli*. Another entry in the same work, dated 682, uses the current term for sumô (*xiangpu* in Chinese). While the Japanese, like the other peoples on China's periphery, probably practiced an indigenous form of wrestling, they adopted Chinese terminology for it during China's Tang dynasty (618–960), the height of Japanese cultural contact with China. They also seem to have adopted some of the Chinese ceremonial trappings of the period, which they combined with their own customs and transmitted to the present. Like Chinese wrestling, sumô contained hand-to-hand combat techniques, which were emphasized for military use from the late Heian through the Kamakura periods (ca. 1156–1392).

Kagamisato (left) and Yoshibayama (right), Japanese sumô wrestlers during a match in Tokyo, 1952. In addition to native elements, sumô shows evidence of Chinese influence. (Library of Congress)

Establishment of the Tokugawa shogunate (1603) included strict control over weapons and the activities of the samurai class, but encouraged their continued cultivation of a "martial spirit." In this environment, *jûjutsu* and ultimately *jûdô* developed. Meanwhile, in China, Zheng Ruozeng's *Strategic Situation in Jiangnan* had been published (ca. 1568). In addition to discussing the strategic situation in China's coastal provinces and mid-sixteenth-century campaigns against Japanese marauders, it lists martial arts styles, including escape and seizing techniques (*pofa, jiefa, na*), among boxing styles of the period. Also, the *Complete Book of Miscellany* (1612 and 1746 editions) contains illustrations of some of these techniques with a hint of jûjutsu in them. At the same time, some Chinese migrated to Japan in the wake of the Manchu conquest in 1644. One of these, Chen

Yuanyun (1587–1671, usually pronounced Chin Gempin in Japanese), was a Renaissance man of sorts, who wrote some books, made pottery, and was apparently an interesting conversationalist. He resided for a while in a Buddhist temple in Edo (now Tokyo), where he was said to have been visited by three rônin (masterless samurai), Fukuno, Isogai, and Miura, and with whom he supposedly discussed boxing (*quanfa* in Chinese, *kenpô* in Japanese). According to the Kito-ryû Kenpô Stele (1779), located in the precincts of modern Tokyo's Atago Shrine, "instruction in kempô began with the expatriate, Chen Yuanyun." Tracing this association to the 1880s, one can find a connection to Kanô Jigorô, who is credited with founding modern jûdô.

While the actual degree of Chen Yuanyun's contribution is unknown, the reference to him on the Kitoryû Kenpô Stele gives some credence to the contention that at least some Japanese jûjutsu and jûdô techniques may have evolved from Ming-period Chinese bare-handed fighting methods, including boxing. Perhaps jûjutsu (pliant skills) evolved more from grappling, escape, and throwing techniques, which were not necessarily clearly distinguished from boxing at the time. Also, the Chinese skills may have been an ingredient added to indigenous Japanese *atemi* (striking) and combat sumô techniques. In any case, there remains a plausible argument for this Chinese contribution to Japanese martial arts.

The Chinese origins of karate are more certain. By the middle of the nineteenth century, and possibly earlier, Chinese boxing appears to have entered Okinawa from Fujian, China. After being modified by the Okinawans, possibly with some of their own indigenous techniques, it was further introduced to the main Japanese islands by Funakoshi Gichin in 1922, and was developed into the modern sport of *karatedô*, "way of the empty hand," or, thanks to Japanese adaptations of Chinese characters (*kara* meaning both "empty" and "Tang"), even "way of Tang hands" in reference to the Chinese dynasty that so strongly influenced Japanese culture. In fact, as further evidence of karate's Chinese origins, the Okinawans originally even used the so-called Chinese or *on* pronunciation for the term *Tang hands*, that is, *Tôde* (long "o") rather than karate.

In 1917, the young Mao Zedong claimed that jûjutsu was a vestige of Chinese culture that was helping the Japanese maintain a "martial spirit" through physical culture in a manner similar to what he termed "the civilized countries of the world, with Germany in the lead." Mao's claim was not without justification.

Stanley E. Henning

See also Japan; Jûdô; Karate, Japanese; Karate, Okinawan; Kenpô; Okinawa; Wrestling and Grappling: China; Wrestling and Grappling: Japan

References

Cuyler, P. L. 1979. *Sumo: From Rite to Sport.* New York: John Weatherhill.

Draeger, Donn F., and Robert W. Smith. 1969. *Asian Fighting Arts.* Tokyo: Kodansha International.

Giles, Herbert A. 1906. "The Home of Jiu Jitsu." *Adversaria Sinica* 5: 132–138.

Hurst, G. Cameron, III. 1998. *Armed Martial Arts of Japan: Swordsmanship and Archery.* New Haven: Yale University Press.

Imamura, Yoshio. 1970. *Nihon Taikushi* (Japanese Physical Culture History). Tokyo: Fumido Shupanshe.

Kenrick, Doug. 1969. *The Book of Sumo: Sport, Spectacle, and Ritual.* New York: Weatherhill.

Kouichi, Kubodera. 1992. *Nihon Sumo Taikan* (Japanese Sumo Almanac). Tokyo: Jinbutsu Oraisha.

Lindsay, Rev. T., and J. Kanô. 1889. "Jiujutsu: The Old Samurai Art of Fighting without Weapons." *Transactions of the Asiatic Society of Japan* 16: 192–205.

Mao Zedong. 1917. "Tiyu Zhi Yanjiu" (Physical Education Research). *Xin Qingnian* (New Youth) 3 (March), no. 2.

Nagamine, Shôshin. 1976. *The Essence of Okinawan Karate-dô.* Rutland, VT: Charles E. Tuttle.

Wu Yu and Jiang An. 1986. "Chen Yuanyun, Shaolin Quanfa, Riben Roudao" (Chen Yuanyun, Shaolin Boxing, and Japanese Judo). *Wuhun* (Martial spirit) 3 (March), no. 86: 17–19.

Yokoyama, Kendô. 1991. *Nihon Budô Shi* (Japanese Martial Arts History). Tokyo: Doshin Shobo.

Jeet Kune Do

Jeet Kune Do (the way of the intercepting fist) was founded by Bruce Lee in 1967. The most recognized martial artist in the world, Lee had an approach to martial arts that was simple, direct, and nonclassical, a sophisticated fighting style stripped to its essentials. However, his primary emphasis in Jeet Kune Do (JKD) was to urge all martial artists to avoid having bias in combat, and in reaching toward the level of art, to honestly express themselves. Although Lee named his art Jeet Kune Do in 1967, the process of liberation from classical arts had been occurring throughout Lee's evolution in the martial arts.

The name Bruce Lee is well known in the martial arts, since his theatrical films helped gain worldwide acceptance for the martial arts during the 1970s. Lee called his approach in martial arts Jeet Kune Do, which translates as "the way of the intercepting fist," but JKD meant much more to Lee than simply intercepting an opponent's attack. Furthermore, defining JKD simply as Bruce Lee's style of fighting is to completely lose its message. Lee once said, "Actually, I never wanted to give a name to the kind of Chinese Gung Fu that I have invented, but for convenience sake, I still call it Jeet Kune Do. However, I want to emphasize that there is no clear line of distinction between Jeet Kune Do and any other kind of Gung Fu for I strongly object to formality, and to the idea of distinction of branches" (Little 1997a, 127). Bruce Lee was more interested in JKD's powerful liberating qualities, which allowed individuals to find their own path to excellence in the martial arts.

Origins and Evolution of Jeet Kune Do

Bruce Lee's personal history and dynamic personality provided the foundation for Jeet Kune Do. Lee began his formal martial arts training in Hong Kong as a teenager studying yongchun (wing chun) under the famous teacher Yip Man (Cantonese; Mandarin Ye Wen). However, Lee was already beginning to experiment with other forms of combat, such as Western boxing and other Chinese martial arts styles.

A turning point in the development of Jeet Kune Do occurred after Lee had moved to the United States and was involved in a challenge match with another Chinese martial artist. The challenge was to prevent Lee from teaching non-Chinese students, which was taboo during the early 1960s. Although Lee defeated his opponent, he was unhappy with how long the fight lasted and with how unusually winded he was afterwards. Up to that point, Lee had been content with improvising and expanding on his yongchun, but he realized that a strict adherence to it limited his performance. In addition, he saw that he needed to be in peak physical condition to fully actualize his potential. "This momentous event, then, was the impetus for the evolution of Jeet Kune Do and the birth of his new training regime" (Little 1998a, 12).

"By the time Lee came to Los Angeles, he had scrapped his modified Wing Chun and searched out the roots of combat, to find the universal principles and concepts fundamental to all styles and systems" (Wong and Cheung 1990, 9–10). In 1967, Bruce Lee named his approach Jeet Kune Do. However, Lee was perfectly clear in his article, "Liberate Yourself from Classical Karate," that he was not inventing a new style of martial arts with its own traditional moves, since styles were "merely parts dissected from a unitary whole" (1986, 65). He urged all practitioners to objectively seek the truth in combat when on their path to self-discovery. This article was controversial, since it advised martial artists to not uncritically accept prescribed formulas and to be free from the bondage of any style's doctrine, which he called "organized despair" (42).

On July 20, 1973, Bruce Lee passed away, leaving a huge legacy for the martial arts. Lee's films created a whole new genre, the martial arts action film. As a result, he became a cult figure like Elvis Presley, Marilyn Monroe, and James Dean. Furthermore, Lee's tremendous impact on the martial arts is still felt today. His personal writings have become best-sellers and have influenced many progressive martial artists and styles. In fact, many would

say that Bruce Lee is the "gold standard," the best role model for aspiring martial artists to emulate.

Stripped to Its Essentials

Although Bruce Lee hated to refer to Jeet Kune Do as a style or system, there was a distinct flavor or character to Lee's personal way of fighting. Lee stated, "It is basically a sophisticated fighting style stripped to its essentials" (Pollard 1986, 46). After carefully examining various forms of combat, Lee found that the simplest techniques were almost always the most effective. He also utilized direct lines of attack and offensive responses in his defense rather than wasting time and energy with passive blocking. Furthermore, Lee would not be limited by any style or system, so he researched and experimented with other forms of combat. As a result, the techniques typically performed in JKD are simple, direct, and nonclassical.

The primary sources for Lee's art are from three disciplines: "I'm having a gung fu system drawn up—this system is a combination of chiefly Wing Chun, fencing and boxing" (Little 1998b, 60). On the other hand, Jeet Kune Do was not simply a combination of all three. Bruce Lee did not fight like a typical boxer, fencer, or yongchun (wing chun) fighter. He transcended these foundations and made the fusion naturally fit his way of fighting. Furthermore, there are only a few techniques in the basic JKD arsenal. Since a large number of techniques only serve to confuse and clog up the mind, the JKD man learns to fully utilize a small, functional arsenal by adapting it to any situation.

Scientific street fighting is a term Lee informally used to describe his art. By applying sciences like physics, kinesiology, and psychology (to name a few), he was able to develop his legendary fighting skill. Bruce Lee said that Jeet Kune Do was a devastating combination of speed, power, and broken rhythm. Although one understands why speed and power are important to combat, broken rhythm is not as obvious. Instead of always performing techniques fluidly, the seasoned fighter uses broken rhythm to throw off his opponent. (In the same way, clumsy and uncoordinated students may beat those with more experience because of the inherent unpredictability of their awkward rhythm.) Thus JKD is geared to prepare the student for all-out combat.

Realistic Training

Bruce Lee emphasized hard physical training in Jeet Kune Do. He was one of the first martial artists to utilize training from various physical disciplines (cross-training, if you will) to enhance his skill. Since he found boxing to be practical, Lee used a lot of the training from it. And he trained like a professional prizefighter, working out from four to eight hours a day. In addition, his regime was prototypical for many of the best athletes today: running, weight training, calisthenics, isometrics, flexibility, and so on. He was always willing to try something new to improve himself.

More importantly, Bruce Lee advocated heavy doses of realism in his training. Since he wanted his students to cultivate their strikes and kick for function, they would not pull their punches and kicks or strike into the air (as in kata training). Instead, Lee had them actually hitting targets (heavy bag, focus mitts, kicking shield) with full power and speed when practicing. Lee believed that if one pulled his punches in practice, that was the way one would punch for real.

To further increase realism in sparring, Lee advocated the use of safety equipment (gloves, headgear, shin pads, chest protector) so his students could go all-out. This approach was to prepare them to hit and be hit, so that they would not be fazed in the heat of battle. Since combat is unpredictable, practicing with uncooperative opponents prepares the students physically, mentally, and emotionally. They soon discover their techniques will not always work without modifying or adapting them.

It is for this very reason that Bruce Lee did not advocate forms or kata training, which he used to call "idealistic dry land swimming," because one must get into the water to learn how to swim. Forms and kata were the primary means of training for many martial arts throughout the 1960s. Although they cultivate a fair degree of coordination and precision of movement, forms do not completely prepare one for live and changing opponents. In Lee's opinion, unrealistic stances and classical forms were too artificial and mechanical. For instance, forms hardly ever equip practitioners to deal with opponents of various sizes and/or talent levels. Lee argued, "There's no way a person is going to fight you in the street with a set pattern" (Uyehara 1986, 6). Furthermore, students who blindly follow their instructor develop a false sense of confidence that they can handle themselves in a fight. Bruce Lee was not to be bogged down by formalities or minor details because for him, "efficiency is anything that scores" (Lee 1975, 24). Elsewhere, he wrote, "When, in a split second, your life is threatened, do you say, 'Let me make sure my hand is on my hip, and my style is "the" style?' When your life is in danger do you argue about the method you will adhere to while saving yourself?" (Lee 1975, 22).

Philosophy of Jeet Kune Do

Jeet Kune Do meant much more to Bruce Lee than simply an efficient reality-based fighting art. Lee's philosophy toward martial arts and life, in general, was a fusion of Eastern and Western culture. While he studied philosophy at the University of Washington, Lee was exposed to a wide spectrum of philosophers such as Socrates, Plato, and Descartes, as well as to Daoism, Zen, and Krishnamurti. He also delved into the self-help books of the late 1960s and utilized self-affirmations. As a result, Lee's philosophy stressed the individual growth of a martial artist.

The symbol Lee used to represent his art was the yin-yang symbol, surrounded by two arrows, along with two phrases: "Using No Way as Way" and "Having No Limitation as Limitation." The yin-yang symbol surrounded by the two directional arrows represents the continuous dynamic interaction between opposites in the universe. When one is using no particular way (style or method), true adaptability can take place. One is to approach combat without any preconceived notions and respond to "what is," being like water. When one has no limitation one can transcend martial arts boundaries set by style or tradition. The JKD practitioner is given the freedom to research any source to reach full potential.

Bruce Lee said that Jeet Kune Do was the first Chinese nontraditional martial art. While he had respect for the traditional martial arts and past fighters, Lee challenged the status quo, believing that students often lose their own sense of self when rigidly adhering to tradition because that is the way it was done for hundreds of years. He writes, "If you follow the classical pattern, you are understanding the routine, the tradition, the shadow—you are not understanding yourself" (Lee 1975, 17). Furthermore, Lee felt that styles tend to restrict one to perform a certain way and therefore limit one's potential. While a style is a concluded, established, solidified entity, man is in a living, evolving, learning process. Lee said that "man, the living creature, the creating individual, is always more important than any established style or system" (Lee 1986, 64).

Lee put a miniature tombstone at the entrance of his school in Los Angeles Chinatown, inscribed with the message: "In memory of a once fluid man, crammed and distorted by the classical mess." This stone symbolized that the stifling traditions and formalities of the past, which have little or no relevance today, are contributing to the "death" of independent inquiry and the complete maturation of a martial artist. Lee argued, "How can one respond to the totality with partial, fragmentary pattern" (Lee 1975, 17).

Furthermore, Lee believed that one develops a totality of combat not by an accumulation of technique, but by simplification. True mastery is not daily increase, but daily decrease. Hacking away the nonessentials was the order of the day, so that students would respond naturally according to their own personal inclinations, without any artificial restrictions imposed on them. Lee felt that martial artists could function freely and totally if they were "beyond system" (Little 1997c, 329). By transcending styles and systems, they could approach combat objectively, without any biases, and respond fluidly to the particular situation at hand. "Unlike a 'classical' martial art, there is no series of rules or classifications of technique that constitute a distinct jeet kune do method of fighting. JKD is not a form of special conditioning with its own rigid philosophy. It looks at combat not from a single angle, but from all possible angles. While JKD utilizes all ways and means to serve its end, it is bound by none and is therefore free. In other words, JKD possesses everything but is in itself possessed by nothing" (Lee 1986, 66).

According to Lee, a true martial artist does not adapt to his opponent by adopting his opponent's style or techniques, but rather he adapts his own personal arsenal to "fit in" with his opponent to defeat him. He told his students to be like water, formless and shapeless, continually adapting to the opponent. Lee wrote, "Jeet Kune Do favors formlessness so that it can assume all forms and since Jeet Kune Do has no style, it can fit in with all styles" (Lee 1975, 12).

The main objective of martial arts, Lee discovered, is not necessarily learning how to fight better, but understanding yourself better so that you can express yourself. He argued, "To me, ultimately, martial arts means honestly expressing yourself" (Little 1999, 11). Lee wanted one to be self-sufficient, searching deep within one's self to find what works best for one. No longer need one be dependent on the teachings of various styles or teachers. By taking an honest assessment of one's strengths and weaknesses, one can improve one's skill as well as one's daily living. With this freedom to improve oneself in any way that one likes, one is able to honestly express one's self.

Jeet Kune Do: It's An Individual Experience

Since Lee is highly recognized for his martial arts, it would have been simple for his followers to blindly take his art as the ultimate truth. Because of his great success, martial artists are often encouraged to "be like Bruce." However, Lee said that if people were to differentiate JKD from other styles, then the name should be eliminated, since it serves only as a label. Bruce Lee felt that it was more important for martial artists to discover their own truths in combat, and subsequently discover themselves: "Remember that I seek neither your approval nor to influence you toward my way of thinking. I will be more than satisfied if you begin to investigate everything for yourself and cease to uncritically accept prescribed formulas that dictate 'this is this' or 'this is that'"(Lee 1986, 63).

Jun Fan Jeet Kune Do

Following Lee's death in 1973, his students began to pass on their knowledge in Jeet Kune Do in their own individual ways. Some operated commercial schools or taught seminars around the world, while others chose to teach a few students in the backyard. More importantly, the students taught their own interpretations of what Lee taught them. Typically, traditional martial arts teachers teach the same material or emphasize the same principles to all students, because styles are steeped in traditions and formalities. But the fluid nature of JKD, along with Lee's dynamic evolution in the martial arts, caused diverse and contrary viewpoints among Lee's students, since the individual is most important. While there were those who chose to teach Lee's art as it was taught to them, others chose to teach key principles and concepts Lee espoused, along with additional research into other martial arts in an attempt to further or advance the art. The first group was accused of turning Lee's art into a style, precisely what Lee was against. At the same time, the latter group was criticized for passing off an art as coming from Lee that bore little to no resemblance to Lee's movements and genius, thereby risking that Lee's martial arts contributions would be lost forever.

In 1996, Lee's widow, Linda Lee Cadwell, his daughter, Shannon Lee Keasler, and Lee's students and second-generation practitioners created the nonprofit Bruce Lee Educational Foundation to preserve and perpetuate his teachings. The organization was formed to maintain the integrity of Jeet Kune Do by giving a clear and accurate picture of Lee's evolution in the martial arts. In this way, the foundation would be able to distinguish the technical and philosophical knowledge studied and taught by Lee and act as a living repository for those seeking information on his body of work.

A greater challenge for the foundation is maintaining the accuracy in Bruce Lee's teachings while at the same time inspiring its followers to further their own personal growth. Indeed, Bruce Lee did not discourage those who found truths in combat contrary to his Jeet Kune Do, since he urged them to find their own paths. However, the problem arises when one is personally expressing himself, yet still calling it Jeet Kune Do, a term that is obviously linked to Bruce Lee. Linda Lee Cadwell responded to this issue: "The most fundamental principle of Bruce's art is that an individual should not be bound by a prescribed set of rules or techniques, and should be free to explore and expand—including expanding away from the core or root of Bruce's teachings. However, confusion arises when a martial artist deviates from the complete circle provided by Bruce's teachings and develops a personal way of martial art, but continues to call it 'Jeet Kune Do.' It is understandable that the definition of Jeet Kune Do can be taken to mean the concept of one's own freedom of expression, but once that step is taken, it needs to be labeled in a personal way, much as Bruce did when he created the name Jeet Kune Do to describe his way" (Cadwell and Kimura 1998, 2).

As a result, the foundation decided to establish the name *Jun Fan Jeet Kune Do*® to refer to Bruce Lee's body of work (art, philosophy, history, and so on). Lee Jun Fan was Bruce Lee's name in Chinese, and, in fact, he originally called his art Jun Fan Gung Fu before coming up with the term *Jeet Kune Do*. Hence, Jun Fan Jeet Kune Do identifies Bruce Lee's personal expression of Jeet Kune Do. This would distinguish the historical art Lee practiced during his life in addition to his inspirational message. Jun Fan Jeet Kune Do is the "launching pad" from which the individuals initiate their own exciting journey of self-discovery and self-expression.

Tommy Gong

See also Yongchun (Wing Chun)
References
Bruce Lee Educational Foundation. 1997. First Annual Jun Fan Jeet Kune Do Seminar Program Booklet.
Cadwell, Linda Lee, and Taky Kimura. 1998. "X Is Jeet Kune Do." *Knowing Is Not Enough: The Official Newsletter of the Bruce Lee Educational Foundation* 1, no. 4: 1–4.

Inosanto, Dan. 1980. *Jeet Kune Do: The Art and Philosophy of Bruce Lee.* Los Angeles: Know Now Publishing.

Lee, Bruce. 1986. "Liberate Yourself from Classical Karate." In *The Legendary Bruce Lee.* Edited by Jack Vaughn. Burbank, CA: Ohara Publications, Inc.

———. 1975. *Tao of Jeet Kune Do.* Burbank, CA: Ohara Publications.

Little, John, ed. 1997a. *Words of the Dragon.* Vol. 1 of *Bruce Lee Library.* Boston: Charles E. Tuttle.

———. 1997b. *The Tao of Gung Fu: A Study in the Way of Chinese Martial Art.* Vol. 2 of *Bruce Lee Library.* Boston: Charles E. Tuttle.

———. 1997c. *Jeet Kune Do: Bruce Lee's Commentaries on the Martial Way.* Vol. 3 of *Bruce Lee Library.* Boston: Charles E. Tuttle.

———. 1998a. *The Art of Expressing the Human Body.* Vol. 4 of *Bruce Lee Library.* Boston: Charles E. Tuttle.

———. 1998b. *Letters of the Dragon.* Vol. 5 of *Bruce Lee Library.* Boston, Mass: Charles E. Tuttle.

———. 1999. *Bruce Lee: Words from a Master.* Lincolnwood, IL: Contemporary Books.

Pollard, Maxwell. 1986. "In Kato's Kung Fu, Action Was Instant." In *The Legendary Bruce Lee.* Edited by Jack Vaughn. Burbank, CA: Ohara Publications.

Uyehara, Mito. 1986. "The Man, the Fighter, the Superstar." In *The Legendary Bruce Lee.* Edited by Jack Vaughn. Burbank, CA: Ohara Publications.

Wong, Ted, and William Cheung. 1990. *Wing Chun/Jeet Kune Do: A Comparison.* Vol. 1. Santa Clarita, CA: Ohara Publications.

Wong, Ted, and Tommy Gong. 1998. "Jun Fan Jeet Kune Do: Bruce Lee's Personal Expression and Evolution in the Martial Arts." *Bruce Lee Magazine,* February, 70–74.

Jûdô

Jûdô is a martial art of Japanese origin, now practiced worldwide. A highly evolved grappling art, it focuses on jûjutsu-derived techniques chosen for their efficiency and safety in sporting competition. Jûdô athletic competitions reward effective throws and groundwork that result in control of the opponent through a hold-down, a sport-legal joint lock, or a choking technique that results in either submission or unconsciousness. An Olympic sport since 1964, jûdô is a modern derivation of jûjutsu as interpreted by founder Dr. Kanô Jigorô (1860–1938).

Kanô, one of the most remarkable figures in the modern history of the martial arts, chose the term *jûdô* (sometimes rendered *jiudo* in his time) quite deliberately. "Jûjutsu" he interpreted as "an art or practice (jutsu) of first giving way (jû) in order to attain final victory" (Kanô 1989, 200); he intended his jûdô to be not a contrast, but an expansion of this stratagem. "Jûdô means the way or principle (dô) of the same," he wrote (Kanô 1989, 200). He further explained that jûjutsu, as he experienced it prior to the founding of his school, was the specific application to personal combat of the "all-pervading" jûdô principle (Kanô 1989, 200). Jûdô, then, as Kanô envisioned it, included the wide application of martial virtues outside a strictly combative context.

Kanô, an educator, favored the preservation of traditional jûjutsu partially through its development into a modern sport compatible with postfeudal Japanese society. Thus athletic competition in the Western sporting sense has been a distinguishing feature of jûdô since its inception, although the techniques that are legal and effective in jûdô matches actually comprise only part of the art's syllabus of instruction. Because of jûdô's comparatively recent development and the academic orientation of its founder, the art's history is very well documented.

The roots of jûdô are in the traditional jûjutsu *ryûha* (styles) of the late nineteenth century, particularly the Tenjin Shinyo-ryû and the Kito-ryû, which Kanô studied extensively, and in Yôshin-ryû, from which some of his senior students, including Yoshiaka Yamashita, were drawn. These schools of unarmed combat, while all referred to as jûjutsu, were distinct entities with separate courses of instruction on the feudal pattern. Tenjin Shinyo was particularly noted for its *atemi* (striking) techniques and its immobilizations and chokes; Kito-ryû, for projective throws, spiritual ideals, and strategy. Yôshin-ryû, attributed to an ancient doctor's application of resuscitation methods for combative purposes, took its name from the flexible (and thus enduring) willow tree, a manifestation of jû. The idea of selective yielding for tactical advantage was common to these schools of jûjutsu, though it varied in development and expression.

Kanô had acquired both a classical Japanese education and thorough instruction in the English language in his youth, but apparently his father (a Meiji reformer) did not encourage an early interest in the martial arts. Jigorô was 17 years old when he began his study of Tenjin Shinyo-ryû, but he threw himself relentlessly into his training and showed a remarkable facility for deriving and applying the essential principles behind techniques. He took every opportunity to expand his knowledge and prowess. In fact, he researched even Western wrestling at the Tokyo library, drawing from it an effective throwing technique later included in the jûdô syllabus as *kata guruma* (the shoulder wheel).

By 1882, it was clear that Kanô was a martial prodigy, and he had determined that his life's work lay in the martial arts. He founded his Kôdôkan (Institute for the Study of the Way) in that year and set about the imposing twofold task of preserving jûjutsu while adapting it to the changing times.

The new school soon attracted attention, both from students enthusiastic for the training and from skeptics wary of Kanô's new approaches to training. Perhaps the best of the former was Yoshiaka Yamashita, who

A photo of the women's section at the Kôdôkan dôjô, 1935. Kanô Jigorô is seated at the center and K. Fukuda is kneeling in the front row, third from the left. (Courtesy of Joe Svinth)

came from Yôshin-ryû and became Kanô's right-hand assistant. Certainly the most dramatic instance of the latter came with the "great tournament" of 1886, a jûjutsu competition in which Kanô's school (represented by Yamashita and some other highly skilled students) scored decisive victories over prominent and long-established jûjutsu styles.

After this tournament, Kôdôkan Jûdô enjoyed increasing levels of governmental support, and was eventually (in 1908) even made a required subject in Japanese schools. This was especially gratifying to Kanô, whose intended focus was on character development for the succeeding generations rather than simple martial prowess for a selected elite.

Even before the turn of the century, jûdô had also attracted attention overseas. Stories of the prowess of jûjutsu practitioners had circulated in the West since the opening of Japan in the mid-nineteenth century. Now a new form of this art had arisen, and it was not only shorn of the feudal secrecy that tended to shield jûjutsu from Western eyes, but was being developed and promoted by a fluent English speaker well versed in Western educational thought. Thus, jûdô was the first Oriental martial art to be truly accessible to the West, and it caused an immediate sensation upon reaching foreign shores.

Naturally, it was immediately compared and contrasted with the unarmed combative sports most common in the West, boxing and wrestling, and early jûdô manuals in English devote much space to instructions on countering these methods. "Challenge matches" were not uncommon in the early days of Western jûdô, and since these matches were not overwhelmingly decided for or against any of the sports, speculation (informed or otherwise) on the relative merits of the methods was even more common. Matters were complicated further by a certain confusion about the distinction between jûdô and jûjutsu, with practitioners of either using both terms freely.

Yoshiaka Yamashita, still Kanô's senior student at the turn of the century, was one of jûdô's pioneers in the West. No less a personage than the American president Theodore Roosevelt (a lifelong enthusiast of combative sports) requested a jûdô instructor in 1904, and this prestigious duty fell to Yamashita, who was already touring the United States. Roosevelt was a good student and an influential voice in support of the new sport, and his studies (coinciding with much American and British sympathy for Japan in the Russo-Japanese War) helped ignite the first Oriental martial arts boom in the English-speaking world. For many years jûdô remained the dominant Oriental martial art outside the East and was in fact often incorrectly used as a catchall term for unfamiliar forms of Asian fighting.

Jûdô was uniquely suited to dissemination across cultures, and in Japan Kanô was pioneering the dissemination of jûdô in another direction as well. *Joshi jûdô* (women's jûdô) began with his acceptance of his first female student in 1883. Over the following years, a Women's Section of the Kôdôkan, with its own separate syllabus and eventually with women's sport competitions, developed. Kanô is said to have commented that the Women's Section preserved more of his intentions for jûdô, with its lesser emphasis on competition.

The growing emphasis on sport jûdô probably occasioned this comment. The evolution of mainstream jûdô has progressed steadily in the direction of competitive sport in the manner of Western wrestling, much to the chagrin of many instructors. An Olympic event since 1964, jûdô is often coached today simply as an athletic activity, without regard to Kanô's principles of strategy or character development or to martial arts applications outside the set of techniques useful in competition.

However, Kôdôkan Jûdô retains its traditional elements, including all seven divisions of technique. These include, of course, the throws, immobilizations, and chokes (*nage-waza, osae-waza,* and *shime-waza*), but also dislocations and strikes (*kansetsu-waza* and *ate-waza*), formal exercises (kata), and resuscitation methods (*kappô*). Jûdô ranking (indicated by the color of belt worn with the traditional *dôgi* [training uniform]) is depen-

Top: Thomas R. Goudy attempting an armlock, 1962. Bottom: Toyoshige Tomita demonstrating the seoi otoshi throw, 1962. (Courtesy of Joe Svinth)

dent on demonstrated proficiency in these areas as well as points scored in competition.

The belt color ranking system, which originated with jûdô, has been adopted by a great many martial systems and has occasioned much debate. The *dan/kyû* system, in which the more advanced or dan ranks are usually designated by a black belt and the lesser kyû grades by a variety of colors, is one of the most widely recognized features of Japanese and some other Asian martial arts, and it is often assumed to be of great antiquity. In reality, it represented another facet of Kanô's innovation and modernization, since it presented a format for standardizing the development of the *jûdôka*

214 JŪDŌ

(jûdô practitioner). Older systems more commonly awarded diplomas or certificates, and historically seldom established any formal hierarchies among students prior to graduation from training. Recognition of various intermediate ranks among students became more common during Japan's peaceful Tokugawa era, but retained a feudal flavor of esoteric initiation. Rank among students was not signified in any uniform, visible manner. The emphasis instead was on access to, and eventual mastery of, a school's "inner" or "secret" teachings (*okuden*). The highest award in this methodology was the *menkyo kaiden,* which certified that the bearer had attained mastery of the system. By contrast, the "black belt" of the dan/kyû system is usually taken to indicate a "serious student" or "beginning teacher" of a style; the lack of secrecy in the jûdô tradition, and in most modern derivations of martial arts, changes the meaning of initiation. Progress in the pursuit of jûdô can include rites of passage and formal recognition of proficiency, but tends to reflect the Meiji values of Kanô rather than the feudal orientation of its root arts. As the American jûdôka Bruce Tegner wrote in response to assorted Western folklore about the black belt, "The earliest black belt holders were not deadly killers; they were skilled sportsmen" (1973). Indeed, belt rank and sport competition were both highly controversial Kanô innovations that continue to lend themselves to a wide range of interpretations, criticisms, and uses and abuses to this day.

The freestyle practice of jûdô techniques takes two forms, *shiai* (contest) and *randori,* which is an unchoreographed but not formally competitive exchange of throws and counters. *Kuzushi,* or unbalancing, is fundamental to both practice forms, and is carried out in accord with the jûdô proverb "When pulled, push; when pushed, pull!" It is also a jûdô cliché, first widely noted in the early years of Western jûdô, that size and strength are relatively unimportant in the employment of the art; this probably derived largely from the success of relatively diminutive Japanese experts against larger but unschooled antagonists. Unfortunately, this proved illusory in the case of jûdô players of comparable skill who were greatly mismatched in size, and designated weight classes are thus a feature of modern sport jûdô.

Today, the International Jûdô Federation is the governing body of Olympic jûdô, while the Kôdôkan in Japan remains the world headquarters. A variety of national and international federations for jûdô study and practice exist worldwide, and instruction is relatively easy to come by. Jûdô players have also ventured into interstyle grappling events, and jûdô remains a strong influence on grapplers of other styles (especially those, such as the Russian *sambo,* that include the wear and use of a jacket).

As the first Asian martial art to gain a worldwide following, jûdô had important formative influences on many other styles. In particular, those styles (such as the Israeli *krav maga*) that descend in part from military commando training, and sport grappling or "submission" styles, including Brazil's Gracie Jiu-jitsu, owe a considerable debt to jûdô. Worldwide, military and police trainers have seen the advantages of jûdô for unarmed hand-to-hand combat and have integrated it into their programs of instruction almost from the beginning of the twentieth century. Jûdô movements are not as inhibited by typical battle dress as are the techniques of many other martial arts, while the presentation of the art in a physical-education format has made it easier for military instructors to adopt (and adapt to their own ends) than the more esoteric curricula of other styles might have been. Wrestling or submission styles, meanwhile, profited both from direct instruction by jûdôka and by interaction with the new jûdô techniques and strategies they encountered. Kanô student Mitsuyo Maeda, one of the jûdôka assigned to bring the new art to the West in the first decade of the twentieth century, accepted both jûdô challenges and matches as a professional wrestler, and was the original instructor of the formidable Gracie family of Brazil (where Maeda was known as Conte Comte [also Conde Koma], the "Count of Combat"). Renowned wrestler George Hackenschmidt, meanwhile, declined to accept challenges from jûdôka (probably because, as world heavyweight champion, he had nothing to win and everything to lose in a bout with the much smaller Japanese who challenged him) but recommended training in jûdô, as well as Greco-Roman and freestyle wrestling, for any serious grappler. He saw the development of excellent balance, as well as the unique "idea" of the style (by which he probably meant the jû principle), as invaluable benefits of training.

Jûdô advocates commonly add that jûdô includes the benefits of most traditional Asian martial arts and adds to them those of a modern, competitive, full-contact (but safe) sport.

Dr. Kanô's jûdô continues to enjoy a prominent place among the world's martial arts, and while it may not always manifest his original ideals in practice, it remains the most successful fusion to date of Oriental martial art with Western principles of physical education.

William J. Long

See also Japanese Martial Arts, Chinese Influences on; Wrestling and
   Grappling: Japan
References
Cunningham, Steven. 1996. "A Brief Look at the Root Arts of Judo."
   Available at http://judo1.net/ju01001.htm.
Inokuma, Isao, and Nobuyuki Sato. 1987. *Best Judo*. Reprint, New York:
   Kodansha International.
Kanô Jigorô. 1989. "The Contribution of Jiudo to Education." In *The
   Overlook Martial Arts Reader*. Edited by Randy Nelson. New York:
   Overlook Press.

———. 1994. *Kôdôkan Judo*. 1986. Reprint, New York: Kodansha International.

Otaki, Tadao, Donn F. Draeger, Tabeo Orako, Tabao Otako. 1991. *Judo Formal Techniques: A Complete Guide to Kôdôkan Randori No Kata*. Reprint, Rutland, VT: Charles E. Tuttle.

Stevens, John. 1995. *Three Budô Masters*. New York: Kodansha International.

Tegner, Bruce. 1973. *Complete Book of Judo*. New York: Bantam Books.

Westbrook, Adele, and Oscar Ratti. 1973. *Secrets of the Samurai: The Martial Arts of Feudal Japan*. Rutland, VT: Charles E. Tuttle.

K

Kajukenbo

A pragmatic American martial art that was developed in Honolulu, Hawaii, between 1947 and 1949. The name of the art is an acronym from the names of the martial systems that served as its basis. KA refers to Korean karate (Tang Soo Do), KEN refers to Okinawan kenpô, JU refers to Japanese Kôdôkan Jûdô and Kodenkan Jûjutsu, and BO refers to Chinese boxing and European boxing. The Kajukenbo system of self-defense is an eclectic blend. The roots or various martial arts (including the ones cited above and others such as Filipino escrima) ground the trunk of the Kajukenbo family tree, but as the martial art continues to evolve, its heart remains kenpô.

Within the traditions of Kajukenbo the creators of the art are known as "the original Black Belt Society." They were Peter Y. Y. Choo, Joseph Holck, Frank F. Ordonez, Adriano D. Emperado, and George "Clarence" Chang. These men quit their day jobs and met secretly in abandoned buildings to develop the ultimate self-defense system over a two-year period. They aspired to combine their deep knowledge of Eastern and Western martial arts into one complete and unique system of self-defense. Afterwards, they tested their system against the reality of barroom brawls and fights on the streets of Honolulu. The traditional history of the system identifies their opponents as huge Samoans and big American sailors stationed on the island.

The components of the art, as catalogued by the acronym Kajukenbo, are the following. From karate were borrowed the high-line kicks and circular hand strikes of the Korean martial arts, techniques that are said to be derived from Northern Shaolin Boxing. These techniques were contributed to the system by Peter Y. Y. Choo, a professional (Western) boxer and a black belt in Tang Soo Dô-Moo Duk Kwan, one of eight major *kwan* (Korean; styles) that formed taekwondo, Korean karate, established in 1955. From jûdô/jûjutsu came the throwing and grappling techniques of the Japanese martial arts. These came to the art of Kajukenbo as the legacy of

Joseph Holck, a black belt in Kôdôkan Jûdô and *Danzan-ryû* (Kodenkan) *Jûjutsu*. Jûdô was created in Japan by Kanô Jigorô in 1882. Danzan-ryû Jûjutsu was founded by H. Seishiro Okazaki, a Japanese immigrant to Hawaii, in 1924. Frank F. Ordonez contributed elements of Sekeino Jûjutsu to the new system; the origin of this style of jûjutsu is obscure. Adriano D. Emperado added kenpô to the Kajukenbo arsenal. Kenpô, commonly translated as "law of the fist" because of its reliance on *atemi* (Japanese; striking techniques), is said to be of Chinese origin. Tradition holds that the twenty-eighth patriarch of Buddhism, Bodhidharma (Daruma in Japanese), brought *Shôrinji Kempô* (Japanese; Shaolin Boxing) from India to China in the early sixth century A.D. Kenpô was introduced to Japan (Okinawa) during the Kamakura period (1192–1333). Emperado had learned kenpô from William K. S. Chow (in the form of *Kara-hô Kenpô*) and James M. Mitose (in the form of *Koshô-ryû Kempô-Jujitsu,* known as "Old Pine Tree Style"). Mitose was the twenty-first consecutive bloodline kenpô master. Adriano left Chow's tutelage in 1946. Adriano's brother Joe and his sister DeChi also studied under Chow and were later to play important roles in the history of Kajukenbo. Adriano Emperado also contributed the European boxing he had learned from his natural father, Johnny "Bulldog" Emperado, and Filipino escrima (i.e., fencing), a martial art of the Philippine archipelago, which he had learned from his stepfather, Alfred Peralta. As has been noted, boxing came to Kajukenbo from a number of sources. Peter Choo was a welterweight champion and Marino Tiwanak—flyweight boxing champion of Hawaii, one of the first students of Kajukenbo, and first recipient of a black belt in the art—obviously brought a strong European boxing component to the art as did Adriano Emperado. The other boxing influence was Chinese boxing, the striking arts popularly labeled kung fu, contributed by George C. Chang.

The tradition of Kajukenbo is based upon Hawaiian culture, where family comes first. In keeping with this value, there is a modern Black Belt Society that meets annually on Father's Day to celebrate Adriano D. Emperado's birthday on June 15. This family reunion allows practitioners of Emperado's Method to gather for seminars, tournament competition, and a ritual luau (Hawaiian festival).

Kajukenbo practitioners wear black kimono as uniforms. The colors used symbolically by the system are black, red, and white. In 1965, a coat of arms was created, with a white clover as the central feature. This symbol refers to the Old Pine Tree Style of kenpô-jûjutsu. Adherents of the Kajukenbo Self-Defense Institute (KSDI) practice Emperado's Method, which is based on kenpô. According to Emperado, the sole purpose of Kajukenbo is self-defense. Nevertheless, Kajukenbo competitors can play exceptionally well in open tournaments against other martial arts styles, due to their ability to adapt themselves to any rules of engagement in the arena. For example, Kajukenbo practitioners compete in sport jûjutsu in their annual tournament, following the increased popularity of grappling arts during the 1990s.

Kajukenbo utilizes a dual rank system, blended from Japanese/Korean and Chinese grading systems. First, there is a belt ranking system proceeding from the lowest rank of white, progressing through purple, brown, black, and finally red. Some schools add an orange belt after the white belt and a green belt after the blue belt. Traditionally, five years are required to progress from white belt to black belt. Black belts are ranked from first through fifth degrees. At sixth through tenth degrees, red belts are worn. The founders hold tenth degree ranking and wear red and gold belts. The second set of categories is based on the Chinese model of ranking by means of kinship titles. The Cantonese term *sifu* (pinyin *shifu;* teacher, literally father) is the title awarded to holders of the fifth degree black belt, but this term traditionally refers to any instructor, regardless of rank, among Chinese systems. *Sigung* (pinyin *shigong;* teacher's teacher, literally grandfather) is the title awarded to the sixth and seventh degree ranks. They usually wear red and white belts in Japanese tradition. In the 1990s, the title of professor was awarded to certain eighth and ninth degrees. Only the five founders retain the title *sijo* (pinyin *shizu*). *Sibak* (pinyin *shibo*) is the title for a student, usually a black belt, who studies directly with a founder. Unlike many Chinese martial arts, Kajukenbo does not use the term for student, *toedai* (pinyin *tudi*), nor does it use the familial term for co-students, *sihing* (pinyin *shixiong*).

During the Korean War (1950–1953), four cofounders, Choo, Ordonez, Holck, and Chang, left Hawaii for military duty, leaving Emperado to teach Kajukenbo with his younger brother Joe and his sister DeChi. In 1965, the Emperado family incorporated as the Kajukenbo Self-Defense Institute (KSDI) in Honolulu. This organization became the vehicle for spreading Kajukenbo to the mainland. Kajukenbo was taught to military men in Hawaii, who afterward spread this uniquely American martial art all over the world.

Although kenpô continues to represent the trunk of the system, Kajukenbo ultimately produced three branches: *Tum Pai, ch'uan'fa,* and *Wun Hop Kuen Do.* Adriano D. Emperado developed Tum Pai in 1959 by adding *taijiquan* (tai chi ch'uan). Incidentally, there is an Emperado "Tai Chi," which is a formal exercise that implements the "alphabet" of self-defense patterns for Kajukenbo. Jon A. Loren now heads up Tum Pai. Emperado also developed ch'uan'fa in 1965. This so-called soft style, because it relies on parries rather than blocks, blended Northern and Southern Shaolin Boxing. Ch'uan'fa (pinyin quanfa) means "Fist Way" in Chinese, and the Japanese word *kenpô* is translated as "fist law." Ch'uan'fa is now headed by Bill Owens. Albert J. Dacascos developed Won Hop Kuen Dô in 1969. This branch was inspired by Bruce Lee's Jeet Kune Do (pinyin Jie quandao), but has "long-fist" (i.e., long-range) techniques. Thus, Won Hop Kuen Dô appears heavily influenced by Northern Shaolin Boxing.

The techniques of Kajukenbo are a blend of many styles, encompassing multiple ranges of combat into a cohesive system. Anyone cross-trained in the styles, methods, and systems that comprise Kajukenbo could recognize root elements of original sources. The high-line long-range kicking comes from Tang Soo Do (pinyin Tang Shou dao). The throwing and grappling techniques come from jûdô and jûjutsu. Kenpô brings to Kajukenbo low-line kicking and hard-style striking. (In hard style, there is an emphasis on meeting force directly with an opposing force for offense and defense.) Shaolin Boxing adds soft-style parries, low kicks, and fluid strikes. Soft style means there is an emphasis on deflecting attacks with indirect counterattacks. European boxing adds "bob-and-weave" defense (lowering the level of the body and swaying) and efficient punching. Filipino escrima adds rhythmic striking and angular footwork that is designed to evade attackers and deliver indirect counterattacks, a principle that is also useful for managing multiple opponents.

Kajukenbo uses deep "horse riding" (i.e., straddle) stances, not only to strengthen the legs, but also to create a stable position from which to deliver pulverizing blows from above to a downed opponent. Another reason for the "horse" stance in Kajukenbo is to save wear and tear on the knees when using follow-up techniques against an opponent who is on the ground. For example, should a downed opponent grab a defender in the horse stance, there is the option to either spring away or drop to the knees in order to pin the opponent. Moreover, no padded floor mats are used in traditional practice, because no mats are available on the street. The horse stance brings one closer to earth, lowering the center of gravity and giving stability to uproot and off-balance attackers.

Trademark techniques of Kajukenbo are the "shadowless" kick, the double grab, the hammer fist, and the cross-cover. The shadowless kick is a low-line attack directed to the legs, groin, or abdomen. The kick is called shadowless because balance is not broken, and telegraphing, or showing preparation for the movement, is minimized. There is also a jump "switching kick" that is deceptive because of foot position replacement while in the air. The "double grab" refers to the cross-hand grab technique, which serves to open the formal movements of the art and, in practice, is designed as an attack and defense combination. The double grab with both hands crossed over hides the secret ripping and tearing movements, using the fingers as claws, which were taken from a Hawaiian self-defense art called *Lua*. The hammer-fist technique uses the bottom of the fist as a striking surface. From combat experience, especially in no-holds-barred street fights, the founders learned that the knuckles could easily be broken by punching. The "chopping" hammer-fist strike saves bare knuckles from destruction while permitting powerful striking against a downed opponent.

The cross-cover refers to the technique developed after Joe Emperado died in a barroom brawl on May 30, 1958. An unidentified assailant stabbed Joe from the rear in the kidney just after he finished defeating an attacker in front of him. Kajukenbo started practicing the way of stepping away from a downed opponent called cross-cover at that time. The cross-cover technique was angular footwork designed specifically to prevent backstabbing. One exits from a single-opponent encounter at an angle, and so pans 180 degrees of vision to take in possible attackers, before crossing over and panning another 180 degrees of vision to assess what threat remains. This allows safe engagement against other opponents.

Describing its use in self-defense may capture the principles of Kajukenbo best. Practice incorporates methods for both single combat and combat against multiple opponents. The objective is to intercept an opponent's attack, such as a punch or kick, then trap the arm or leg with one hand and smash it with the other, causing immediate damage and pain to the attacker. The opponent is then taken down to the ground, usually by sweeping or throwing, where follow-up attacks with striking and locking techniques are used. These are systematic, intended to break joints and damage vital organs. Afterwards, the critical space or "turf" of the downed opponent is exited, usually by passing by the head to avoid getting tripped or grappled to the ground. The exit path facilitates further confrontation against other opponents. Against multiple opponents, the single combat techniques are applied for "overloaded" situational attacks, as for example when partway into a prearranged self-defense sequence another attacker joins the fray. These practice sequences are called *waza* (Japanese; tricks).

Kajukenbo has specialized training methods that are designed to work in reality fighting. For example, the method labeled "ad-libs" refers to thorough pounding and striking of a downed opponent. They are done in freestyle following a takedown. When one is swept or thrown to the ground, the tendency is to curl up into the fetal position. There are "can-opener" techniques designed to break an opponent's covering in order to strike vital areas. Low-line kicks to the spine and kidneys will cause an arched back, exposing liver, heart, and spleen to striking. Strikes to the knees will drop the legs, allowing groin strikes and step-over footwork. Kajukenbo is playing pool in the sense that one shot is designed to set up another until a practitioner can "run the table."

Kajukenbo techniques are battle-tested in actual combat or experiments. For example, Adriano D. Emperado got a job as a janitor in a funeral home to get access to the corpses. He is said to have hung bodies up and practiced joint breaking and striking techniques.

The philosophy of Kajukenbo, like its physical techniques, is derived from a variety of sources. The influences of family and Christianity are evident, as is the desire to maintain a symbolic tie to the Chinese heritage of the art. Practitioners characterize Kajukenbo as a family system. This goes beyond the hierarchy based on the family model, which is described above, to signify that there are powerful loyalties to the founders and among the practitioners, many of whom are related by blood and law. The founders of the art paid homage to their Christian faith in a prayer that was said before each practice session. The "Kajukenbo Prayer" paid homage to the "one true God," asked His blessings for the United States, which was identified as "a nation founded on Christian principles," and sought blessing for practitioners and their martial arts efforts.

Although Kajukenbo is a recent coinage composed of syllables from its parent arts, members of the system have used the rendering of these syllables in Chinese characters both as a means of maintaining ties to this element of their heritage and as a means of expressing the philosophy of the art. Following this translation, in Cantonese *ka* means "long life," *jû* means "happiness," *ken* means "fist," and *bo* means "way." The English translation is given as, "Through this fist way, one gains long life and happiness." A similar rendering of the Kajukenbo philosophy appears in the motto "To train strong, we will remain strong."

Ronald A. Harris

See also Kenpô

References

Barlow, Jeffrey, and Morgan Day. 1993. "Ethnic Strife and the Origins of Kajukenbo." *Journal of Asian Martial Arts* 2: 66–75.

Bishop, John. 1994. "Adriano Emperado: The Force behind Kajukenbo." *IKF Presents,* March, 54–61.

———. 1994. "Lua: Hawaii's Ancient Fighting Art." *IKF Presents,* March, 28–35.

Forbach, Gary. 1984. "Professor Adriano D. Emperado." *Inside Kung Fu* 11, no. 2: 30–36.

Harris, Ronald A. 1990. "Emperado's Black Belt Society." *Inside Kung Fu* 17, no. 4: 68–71. Kajukenbo Self-Defense Institute.

———. 1992. "The Hidden Eskrima of Kajukenbo." *Inside Karate* 30, no. 9: 30–74.

———. 1995. "KSDI Open Tournament, Seminar, and Birthday Luau, Souvenir Program." San Jose, CA: Author.

Kodenkan Yudanshakai. 1999. http://www.danzan.com/HTML/ESSAYS/kdky.html.

Kalarippayattu

Kalarippayattu (Malayalam; *kalari,* place of training; *payattu,* exercise) is a compound term first used in the twentieth century to identify the traditional martial art of Kerala State, southwestern coastal India. Dating from at least the twelfth century in the forms still practiced today, but with roots in both the Tamil and Dhanur Vedic martial traditions, kalarippayattu was practiced throughout the Malayalam-speaking southwestern coastal region of India (Kerala State and contiguous parts of Coorg District, Karnataka), where every village had its own kalari for the training of local fighters under the guidance of the *gurukkal* (honorific, respectful plural of *guru*) or *asan* (teacher). Martial masters also administer a variety of traditional Ayurvedic physical/massage therapies for muscular problems and conditions affecting the "wind humor," and set broken bones. According to oral and written tradition, the warrior-sage Parasurama, who was the founder of Kerala, is also credited with the founding of the first kalari and subsequent lineages of teaching families. Between the twelfth century and the beginning of British rule in 1792, the practice of kalarippayattu was especially associated with subgroups of Hindu Nayars whose duty it was to serve as soldiers and physical therapists at the behest of the village head, district ruler, or local raja, having vowed to serve him to death as part of his retinue. Along with Nayars, some Cattar (or Yatra) Brahmans, one subgroup of the Ilava caste given the special title of chekor, as well as some Christians and Sufi Muslims, learned, taught, and practiced the martial art. Among at least some Nayar and Ilava families, young girls also received preliminary training until the onset of menses. We know from the local "Northern Ballads" that at least a few women students of noted Nayar and Ilava masters continued to practice and achieved a high degree of expertise. Some Ilava practitioners served the special role of fighting duels (*ankam*) to the death to resolve disputes and schisms among higher-caste extended families.

There was an almost constant state of low-grade warfare among local rulers from the twelfth century onward. Warfare erupted for a variety of reasons, from caste differences to pure and simple aggression. One example of interstate warfare that exemplifies the ideal bond between Nayar martial artists and their rulers is the well-documented dispute between the Zamorin of Calicut and the raja of Valluvanadu over which was to serve as convener of the great Mamakam festival held every twelve years. This "great" festival celebrated the descent of the goddess Ganga into the Bharatappuzha River in Tirunavayi, in northern Malabar. Until the thirteenth century, when the dispute probably arose, the ruler of Valluvanadu possessed the right of inaugurating and conducting the festival. The Zamorin set out to usurp this

Satish Kumar (left) and Shri Ajit (right) perform a dagger fight in Bombay, December 27, 1997. The duo are in Bombay to promote Kalarippayattu, the ancient physical, cultural, and martial art of the state of Kerala in southern India. (AP Photo/Sherwin Crasto)

right. After a protracted conflict, the Zamorin wrested power by killing two Vellatri princes. The event created a permanent schism between the kingdoms. At each subsequent festival until its discontinuation in 1766 following the Mysorean invasion, some of the Valluvanadu fighters pledged to death in service to the royal house attended the Mamakam to avenge the honor of the fallen princes by fighting to the death against the Zamorin's massed forces.

So important was kalarippayattu in medieval Kerala that both its heroic demeanor and its practiced techniques were constantly on display, whether in actual combat, in duels, or in forms of cultural performance that included mock combats or displays of martial skills and dances and dance-dramas where the heroic was on display. Kalarippayattu directly influenced the techniques and content of numerous traditional forms of performance such as folk dances; ritual performances such as the *teyyam* of northern Kerala where deified heroes are worshipped; the now internationally known *kathakali* dance-drama, which enacts stories of India's epic heroes based on the *Mahabharata, Ramayana,* and *puranas;* and the Christian dance-drama form, *cavittu natakam,* which used martial techniques for stage combat displaying the prowess of great Christian heroes like St. George and Charlemagne.

A number of today's masters trace their lineage of practice back generations to the era when a special title (*Panikkar* or *Kurup*) was given by the local ruler. K. Sankara Narayana Menon of Chavakkad was trained by his father, Vira Sree Mudavannattil Sankunni Panikkar of Tirur, who in turn was trained by his uncle, Mudavangattil Krishna Panikkar Asan, who learned under his uncle, and so on. As recorded in the family's palm-leaf manuscript, the Mundavannadu family was given the title *Anchaimakaimal* by the Vettattu raja in recognition of its exclusive responsibility for training those who fought on the Raja's behalf and its "responsibility for destroying evil forces" in the region. Similarly, Christian master Thomas T. Tuttothu Gurukkal traces his family tradition back to Thoma Panikkar, who held the rank of commander-in-chief (*commandandi*) for the Christian soldiers serving the Chmpakasserry raja until his fall in 1754.

Kalarippayattu declined under British rule, due to the introduction of firearms and the organization of police, armies, and government institutions along European institutional models, but survived under the tutelage of a few masters in scattered regions of Kerala, especially in the north. During the modern era kalarippayattu was first brought to general public attention during the 1920s in a wave of rediscovery of indigenous arts. In 1958, two years after the founding of a united, Malayalam-speaking Kerala State government, the first modern association, the Kerala Kalarippayat (*sic*) Association, was founded under the leadership of Govindankutty Nayar, with fifteen member kalari, as one of seventeen members of the Kerala States Sports Council. Despite increasing public awareness within the north Malabar region in particular, and in the state capital, kalarippayattu continued to be little known as a practical martial and healing art to the general public in Kerala and in India as late as the 1970s. Since then kalarippayattu has become known throughout Kerala, India, and more recently throughout the world.

Historically there were many different styles and lineages of kalarippayattu, including *Arappukai, Pillatanni, Vatten Tirippu,* and *Dronamballi Sampradayam.* A number of distinctive styles were suppressed or lost, especially during the nineteenth century in the south of Kerala, where a greater effort took place to suppress the authority of the Nayars and to centralize power along European institutional models. Although the Kerala Kalarippayat Association officially recognizes three styles of kalarippayattu according to the rough geographical area where each originated, that is, northern, central, and southern styles, what is called southern-style kalarippayattu today is also known as *varma ati* or *adi murai,* and it is best discussed separately, since its myth of origin and techniques of practice, though clearly related to kalarippayattu, are different enough to warrant separate consideration. The remainder of this entry focuses primarily on northern style, with a brief description of central style.

The traditional practice of kalarippayattu is informed by key principles and assumptions about the body, consciousness, the body-mind relationship, health, and exercise drawn from Kerala's unique versions of yoga practice and philosophy, South Asian medicine (called *Ayurveda* [Sanskrit; science of life]), and religious mythology, practices, and histories. The Malayalam folk expression "The body becomes all eyes" encapsulates the ideal state of the practitioner, whose response to his environment should be like Brahma the thousand-eyed—able to see and respond intuitively, like an animal, to anything. To attain this ideal state of awareness, traditional masters emphasize that one must "possess complete knowledge of the body." This traditionally meant gaining knowledge of three different "bodies of practice": (1) the fluid body of humors and saps, associated with Ayurveda, in which there should be a healthful congruence of the body's humors through vigorous, seasonal exercise; (2) the body composed of bones, muscles, and the vulnerable vital junctures or spots (*marmmam*) of the body; and (3) the subtle, interior body, assumed in the practice of yoga, through which the internal "serpent power" (*kundalini sakti*) is awakened for use in martial practice and in giving healing therapies.

Training toward this ideal began traditionally at the age of 7 in specially constructed kalari, ideally dug out of the ground so that they are pits with a plaited coconut palm roof above. The kalari itself is considered a temple, and in Hindu kalari from seven to twenty-one deities are considered present, and worshipped on a daily basis, at least during the training season. After undergoing a ritual process of initiation into training and paying respects to the gurukkal, the student in the northern style of kalarippayattu begins by oiling the body and practicing a vigorous array of "body preparation" exercises, including poses, kicks, steps, jumps, and leg exercises performed in increasingly complex combinations back and forth across the kalari floor. Most important is mastery of basic poses, named after animals such as the elephant, horse, and lion, comparable to yoga postures (asanas), and steps that join one pose to another. Repetitious practice of these vigorous physical forms is understood to eventually render the external body flexible and "flowing like a river" as students literally "wash the floor of the kalari with their sweat."

In addition to the techniques described above, the central style includes distinctive techniques performed within floor drawings, known as *kalam*, traced with rice powder on the floor of the kalari. Special steps for attack and defense are learned within a five-circle pattern so that the student moves in triangles, or zigzags. In addition, some masters of central style teach *cumattadi*, sequences of "steps and hits" based on particular animal poses and performed in four directions, instilling in the student the ability to respond to attacks from all directions.

Traditionally, preliminary training took place during the cool monsoon period (June-September), and also included undergoing a vigorous full-body massage given with the master's feet as he held onto ropes suspended from the ceiling of the kalari. As with the practice of yoga, special restrictions and observances traditionally circumscribed training, such as not sleeping during the day while in training, refraining from sexual intercourse during the days when one was receiving the intensive massage, not waking at night, and taking milk and ghee (clarified butter) in the diet. From the first day of training students are admonished to participate in the devotional life of the kalari, including paying respects to and ideally internalizing worship of the guardian deity of the kalari, usually a form of a goddess (Bhagavati, Bhadrakali) or Siva and Sakti, the primary god and goddess worshiped in Kerala, in combination.

The exercise, sweating, and oil massage are understood to stimulate all forms of the wind humor to course through the body. Long-term practice enhances the ability to endure fatigue by balancing the three humors, and it enables the practitioner to acquire the characteristic internal and external ease of movement and body fluidity. The accomplished practitioner's movements "flow," thereby clearing up the "channels" (*nadi*) of the internal subtle body.

Only when a student is physically, spiritually, and ethically ready is he supposed to be allowed to take up the first weapon in the training system. If the body and mind have been fully prepared, then the weapon becomes an extension of the body-mind. The student first learns wooden weapons (*kolttari*)—first long staff, later short stick, and then a curved stick known as an *otta*—through which empty-hand combat is taught. After several years of training, combat weapons are introduced, including dagger, spear, mace (*gada*), sword and shield, double-edged sword (*curika*) versus sword, spear versus sword and shield, and flexible sword (*urumi*). In the distant past, bow and arrow was also practiced, but this has been lost in the kalarippayattu tradition. All weapons teach attack and defense of the body's vital spots.

Empty-hand techniques are taught either through otta or through special "empty-hand" techniques (*verumkai*) taught as part of advanced training. For example, C. Mohammed Sherif teaches eighteen basic empty-hand attacks and twelve methods of blocking, which were traditionally part of at least some northern Kerala styles. Eventually, students also should begin to discover applications that are implicit or hidden in the regular daily body exercises. In some forms of empty-hand training, special attention is given to application of techniques to striking or penetrating the vital spots (marmam) of the body—those junctures that are so vulnerable that an attack on them can in some cases lead to instant death. The earliest textual evidence of the concept of the vital spots dates from as early as the Rig Veda (ca. 1200 B.C.), in which the god Indra is recorded as defeating the demon Vrtra by attacking his vital spot with a *vajra* (thunderbolt). By the time that Susruta wrote the classic Sanskrit medical text in the second century A.D., 107 vital spots had been identified as an aid to surgical intervention. Over the years the notion of the vital spots has been central to martial and healing practices, since the master must learn the location of the vital spots to attack them, to provide the emergency procedure of a "counter-application" with his hands when an individual has been injured by having a vital spot penetrated, or to avoid them when giving therapeutic massages.

Martial practice, like meditation, is understood to tame and purify the external body (*sthula-sarira*), as it quiets and balances the body's three humors. Eventually the practitioner should begin to discover the internal/subtle body (*suksma sarira*) most often identified with Kundalini/tantric yoga. For martial practitioners this discovery is essential for embodying power (*sakti*) to be used in combat, or for healing through the massage therapies. Long-term training involves the development of single-point focus (*ekagrata*) and mental power (*manasakti*). A variety of meditation techniques have traditionally been practiced as part of the development of these subtler powers and abilities, so that martial artists could conquer themselves, that is, their fears, anxieties, and doubts, as well as gain access to specific and subtler forms of sakti for application.

These subtler aspects of practice include simple forms of *vratam*—simply sitting in an appropriately quiet place and focusing one's mind on a deity through repetition of the deity's name. A more advanced technique is to sit in the cat pose, facing the guardian deity of the kalari, and repeat the verbal commands for a particular body exercise sequence while maintaining long, deep, sustained breathing. Repetition of such exercises is understood to lead to *dharana*—a more concentrated and "higher" form of one-point concentration. Subtler and secretive practices include becoming accomplished in particular *mantras*. Ubiquitous to Hinduism from as early as the Vedas and to all aspects of kalarippayattu practice from ritual propitiation of the deities, to administering massage, and to weapons practice are repetition of mantras. Usually taking the form of a series of sacred words and/or syllables, which may or may not be translatable, these are considered "instruments of power . . . designed for a particular task, which will achieve a particular end when, and only when, . . . used in a particular manner" (Alper 1989, 6). Kalarippayattu masters in the past had a "tool box" of such mantras, each of which had specific purposes: (1) mantras for worship of a specific deity; (2) personal mantras to develop the character of the student; (3) mantras associated with particular animal poses to gain superior power and actualization of that pose; (4) weapons or combat mantras used for a specific technique to give it additional power; (5) all-purpose mantras to gain access to higher powers of attack or defense; and (6) medical/healing mantras used when preparing a particular medicine or giving a particular treatment. These secrets are given only to the most advanced students, and many masters are loath to teach them today. When they are taught, a student is told never to reveal the mantras since to do so would "spoil the power of the mantras."

Although kalarippayattu has undergone a resurgence of interest during the 1980s and 1990s, its traditional practice can, when compared to more overt streetwise forms of karate and kung fu, seem anachronistic to young people wanting immediate results in order to practice a martial art that looks like what they see at the cinema.

Phillip B. Zarrilli

See also India; Religion and Spiritual Development: India; Varma Ati; Written Texts: India

References

Achutanandan, K. V. 1973, 24. *Vadakkan Pattukal* (Malayalam). Kunnamkulam: A and C Stores.

Alper, Harvey P. 1989. *Mantra.* Albany: SUNY Press.

Ayyar, K. V. Krishna. 1928–32 "The Kerala Mamakam." *Kerala Society Papers* 2, Series 6: 324–330.

Balakrishnan, P. 1995. *Kalarippayattu: The Ancient Martial Art of Kerala.* Trivandrum: C. V. N.

Nayar, Cirakkal T. 1963. *Kalarippayattu* (Malayalam).Calicut: Cannannore Printing Works.

———. 1957. *Marmmadarppanam* (Malayalam). Calicut: P. K. Brothers.

———. Sreedharan. 1983. *Uliccil* (Malayalam). Calicut: Cannannore Printing Works.

Raghavan, M. D. 1932. "A Ballad of Kerala." *The Indian Antiquary* 61. (January): 9–12; (April): 72–77; (June): 112–116; (August): 150–154; (November): 205–211.

———. 1929. "The Kalari and the Angam—Institutions of Ancient Kerala." *Man in India* 9: 134–148.

Rosu, Arion. 1981 "Les marman et les arts martiaux indiens" (The Marmas and the Indian martial arts). *Journal asiatique* 259: 417–451.

Zarrilli, Phillip B. 1986. "From Martial Art to Performance: Kalarippayattu and Performance in Kerala." *Sangeet Natak* 81–82: 5–41; 83: 14–45.

———. 1995. "The Kalarippayattu Martial Master as Healer: Traditional Kerala Massage Therapies." *Journal of Asian Martial Arts* 4, no. 1: 67–83.

———. 1998. *When the Body Becomes All Eyes: Paradigms, Discourses, and Practices of Power in Kalarippayattu, a South Indian Martial Art.* New Delhi: Oxford University Press.

Kali

See Philippines

Karate, Japanese

Combative disciplines are generally reflective of the nature of the society from which they arose. Japanese culture has officially recognized *bujutsu* (martial ways) since A.D. 794, when the Butokuden (Martial Virtues Hall) was established in Kyoto by the emperor Kanmu for the purpose of promoting excellence in the martial arts. The Butokuden eventually became the premier training hall for the Dainippon Butokukai (Great Japan Martial Virtue Association), which was established by the Meiji emperor in 1895 for the preservation of *koryû bujutsu* (classical martial arts). The Dainippon Butokukai was charged with the task of recognizing, solidifying, promoting, and standardizing martial arts in Japan. It was through these processes that *karate-dô* (empty-hand way) became and was recognized as a *ryûha* (school of transmission) in 1933.

Japanese karate originated from a synthesis of civil and military combative disciplines. These disciplines included Okinawan *di* (Japanese *te*, hand), indigenous Japanese martial arts (*bu*), and Chinese *quanfa* (*ch'uan fa*, fist law; in Japanese, *kenpô*). Okinawan di uses striking, throwing, joint locking, and restraining methods similar to various styles of Japanese jûjutsu, and hints at an early sharing of martial knowledge between the cultures. Although *di* means "hand," weapons are also utilized. This sharing of martial culture is evident in the weapons used by di practitioners, which include the sword, spear, and glaive (*naginata*). Japanese jûjutsu was directly influenced by Chinese fighting methods (quanfa), as were the Okinawan fighting styles. The most influential of these arts on the development of Japanese karate was Okinawan di, called *Toudi* (Tang hand) in reference to its Chinese origins.

The Ryûkyû people were first recorded in A.D. 616, when the Yamato (Wo-Yayoi culture) of Kyûshû took thirty Okinawans to the court of Shôtoku Taishi at Nara. Some time later, representatives of the Yamato returned to Hyakuna on the Chinen Peninsula. Among the various cultural innovations that the Yamato brought with them to Okinawa were iron weapons and the martial combative disciplines needed to exploit their use. These combative disciplines probably contained the constituent elements of what eventually evolved into Okinawan di.

During the decentralization of the Heian period (794–1185), minor Japanese houses were displaced and forced to seek refuge in the Ryûkyû Islands. Reintroduction into the Japanese hierarchy was often facilitated by martial proficiency and *heihô* (tactics). The Ryûkyûs acted as a training

Kumite *(free sparring) during karate championships at the Seattle Center Arena, October 23, 1967. (Seattle Post-Intelligencer Collection, Museum of History & Industry)*

ground for these houses to enhance their military and political effectiveness. The combative systems practiced by these houses and their retainers were eagerly absorbed by the Okinawan military chieftains (*anji*), who had their own ambitions for social mobility and conquest.

The second-generation headmaster of *Jigen-ryû Kenjutsu*, Tôgô Bizen-no-Kami Shigekata (1602–1659), was ordered by Lord Shimazu to instruct the inhabitants of Kagoshima (Satsuma) in civil combative disciplines. These traditions were retained in the Jigen-ryû Bô Odori (Staff Dances), which incorporated techniques with the *jô* (stick), *ken* (sword), *rokushaku bô* (six-foot staff), *yari* (spear), *eiku* (oar), *kama* (sickle), *shakuhachi* (flute), and various other utensils. In 1609, the Shiazu clan of Satsuma invaded and conquered the kingdom of Okinawa. The Satsuma invaders enacted and enforced a weapons ban in the subjugated kingdom, which helped foster the practice of di. Some Okinawans were allowed to travel to Satsuma, where they studied the Jigen system.

Kanga Teruya, also known as Sakugawa Toudi, traveled to Satsuma and returned with rokushaku bô kata (forms), which were previously unknown in Okinawa. Matsumura Sôkon "Bushi" (Okinawan, Chikudun Pechin; warrior) (1809–1901) studied Toudi under Sakugawa and the Chinese military attaché, Iwah. Matsumura also traveled to Fujian, where he acquired some knowledge of the Chinese martial arts, and to Satsuma, where he received his *menkyo* (teaching certification) in Jigen-ryû kenjutsu from Ijûin Yashichirô. Matsumura combined Toudi and Jigen-ryû into an eclectic combative style that eventually became known in Okinawa as *Shuri-di* (Shuri hand), so called because it was practiced in and around Shuri.

Matsumura's disciples included Ankô Itosu (Yasutsune) and Ankô Asato. As well as being superb *Karateka* (practitioners) and *sensei* (instructors) in their own right, Itosu and Asato were the primary instructors of Funakoshi Gichin, the single most influential figure in the development of Japanese karate.

In 1917, Funakoshi was invited as a representative of the Okinawa Prefecture to perform karate at the Butokuden in Kyoto. This was the first public demonstration of karate on the Japanese mainland. In March of 1921, Funakoshi demonstrated karate for the Crown Prince Seijô (Hirohito) in the Great Hall at Shuri Castle. In the spring of 1922, the Okinawan Department of Education requested that Funakoshi arrange an exhibition of karate for the Ministry of Education's First National Athletic Exhibition in Tokyo. After the exhibition, Funakoshi was persuaded to remain in Japan and disseminate his knowledge of the art of karate. This resulted in the publication of *Ryûkyû Kenpô: Karate,* in the fall of 1922, and a revision of the work, *Retan Gôshin Karate-jutsu* (Strengthening of Willpower and Self-Defense through Karate Techniques), in 1923.

In 1924, the karate clubs Keiô Gijuku Taiikukai Karatebu, Tokyo Teikoku Daigaku Karatebu, Daiichi Kôtô Gakkô Karatebu, Waseda Daigaku Gakuyûkai Karatebu, Nihon Daigaku Karate Kenkyûkai, Takushoku Daigaku Karatebu, Nihon Daigaku Ikka Karate Kenkyûkai, and Shôin Jôgakkô were established in the Tokyo area. In 1930, the Kansai Daigaku Karatebu, Kansai Daigaku Senmonbu, Ôsaka Kôtô Yakugaku Senmon Gakkô, and Ôsaka Kôtô Igaku Senmon Gakkô were established around Ôsaka.

The All Japan Martial Arts Demonstration was held in Tokyo on May 5, 1930, to celebrate Hirohito's succession to the throne. Shinzato Jinan attended the event as the representative of Okinawan *Naha-di* (Naha hand) master Miyagi Chôjun. In 1932, Miyagi Chôjun was invited to participate in the Sainen Budô Taikai in Tokyo and the Butokusai (Martial Arts Festival) in Kyoto. In 1935, a prospectus was submitted for the Karate Kenkyûkai (Karate Research Club) at Ritsumeikan Daigaku (University), with Miyagi as the honorary master instructor (meiyô shihan).

By 1936, many Okinawan instructors had migrated to Japan and were teaching karate. Among those instructors were Funakoshi Gichin, Mabuni Kenwa, Motobu Chôki, Sawada Masaru, Sakae Sanyû, Yabiku Môden, Miki Nisaburô, Kunishi Yasuhiro, Satô Shinji, Mutsu Mizuhô, Higashionna (Higaonna) Kamesuke, Ôtsuka Shinjun, Taira Shinken, Shiroma Koki, and Uechi Kanbun.

Karate on Okinawa was taught in an informal manner. Students were assigned *tokuigata* (individual forms) at the discretion of the instructor. No ranking system existed, so there were no established criteria for advancement. Students were either *sempai* (senior) or *kohai* (junior). No recognizable uniform (*gi*) was used. Karate was indiscriminately referred to as di, bu (martial arts), or Toudi. This individualism was alien to the Japanese concept of *wa* (harmony). Japanese martial arts were structured around the ryûha system propagated by the Dainippon Butokukai. A ryûha included an historical continuity, methodological transmission, and pedagogical style. Many Okinawan instructors realized that if karate were to be recognized as a true martial art, certain modifications would have to be made in the manner in which it was presented to the Japanese public.

In the early 1920s, Funakoshi Gichin suggested to the karate research group at Keiô University that the kanji character representing "T'ang" be replaced with the character representing "empty" in Dainippon Kenpô Karate-dô (Great Japan Fist Method Empty Hand Way). Funakoshi also stressed the use of *-dô* (way) over *-jutsu* (technique) in an effort to conform to previously established *budô* (martial ways) such as *kyûdô* (archery), kendô, and jûdô. The practice of karate was greatly influenced by that of jûdô, a modified form of jûjutsu created by Kanô Jigorô. Kanô devised a ranking system based on *dan/kyû* grades. Kyû (literally, grade) are lower grades, which begin at tenth kyû and proceed to first kyû. First dan (literally, step or rank) follows first kyû and rankings progress from first dan to tenth dan. The tenth kyû is represented by a white belt, and the first dan is represented by a black belt. Karate adopted the jûdô rankings as well as the jûdôgi. With the recognition of rank within the Japanese karate community came an organized curriculum and a somewhat more objective evaluation of knowledge, skills, and abilities. Miyagi Chôjun was the first Okinawan master to submit the name of his system, *Gôjû-ryû* (hard-soft style) *Karate* (Tang hand) to the Dainippon Butokukai. The Butokukai officially recognized karate-dô (empty-hand way) as a ryûha in 1933.

Once the Japanese people accepted karate, the art began to be influenced by the needs of the people, and various innovations were developed that began to give karate a distinctively Japanese character. From the Shuri-di and Naha-di, which the Okinawans brought to Japan, four major styles of Japanese karate began to emerge. Funakoshi Gichin propagated *Shôtôkan*, Ôtsuka Hioronori created the *Wadô-ryû*, Mabuni Kenwa developed *Shitô-ryû*, and Yamaguchi Gôgen spread Gôjû-ryû.

The brand of Shuri-di that Funakoshi Gichin (1868–1957) taught became known as *Shôtôkan* (Shôtô Hall) *Karate* after Funakoshi's poetic pseudonym, Shôtô (Pine Wave). Realizing that language is culture, Funakoshi Gichin gave the various Shuri-di kata new Japanese names. *Chinto* kata became *Gankaku* (Crane on a Rock), *Jitte* became *Jutte* (Ten Hands), *Kusanku* became *Kankû* (To Look at the Sky), *Naihanchi* became *Tekki* (Horse Riding), *Pinan* became *Heian* (Peaceful Mind), *Patsai* became *Bassai* (To Penetrate a Fortress), *Seisan* became *Hangetsu* (Crescent Moon), *Useishi* became *Gôjûshihô* (Fifty-four Steps), and *Wansu* became *Empi* (Flying Swallow). Funakoshi introduced the *Taikyoku* (Grand Ultimate) kata as beginning forms, and the *Ten no Kata* (Kata of the Universe) as a beginning *kumite* (sparring) form. As the names of these kata imply, however, the principles contained within them are subjects for continual study. Funakoshi Gichin's son, Funakoshi Yoshitaka (Gigô), made modifications in the basic techniques (*kihon*). The side kick (*yoko-geri*), back kick (*ushiro-geri*), and round kick (*mawashi-geri*) were added to the style; the kicking knee was raised; stances became lower; and thrusting with the hips was greatly emphasized. This innovative attitude reflected the views of Funakoshi Gichin, who believed that karate should evolve as human knowledge progressed. In 1949 the Nippon Karate Kyôkai (Japan Karate Association, JKA) was formed. Funakoshi Gichin was honorary chief instructor, Obata Isao was chairman, and Nakayama Masatoshi was the chief instructor. The JKA continues research into the art and science of karate, building upon the philosophy of its founder.

Ôtsuka Hironori (1892–1982) began his martial arts training in Ibaraki, Japan, where he studied *Shindô Yôshin-ryû jûjutsu* under Nakayama Shinzaburô, a style that incorporated various strikes and kicks as well as the conventional jûjutsu *nage-waza* (throws) and *ne-waza* (ground techniques). Ôtsuka received the *menkyo kaiden* (certificate of full proficiency) in the Shindô Yôshin-ryû in 1920, succeeding Nakayama and becoming the fourth headmaster of the ryûha. While attending Waseda University, Ôtsuka studied other forms of jûjutsu and kenpô. Ôtsuka met Funakoshi Gichin in 1922. Impressed by Ôtsuka's dedication to the martial arts and interest in karate, Funakoshi taught Ôtsuka his Shuri-di system. Combining the karate that he learned from Funakoshi and Mabuni Kenwa (of the Shitô-ryû) with various jûjutsu, Toda-ryû, and Yagyû Shinkage-ryû kenjutsu techniques and concepts, Ôtsuka broke away from the Shôtôkan in 1934 and formed a style that would eventually be known as *Wadô* (Way of Peace). Wadô was officially recognized as a ryûha by the Dainippon Butokukai in 1940 under the title Shinshû Wadô jûjutsu. Wadô-ryû uses nine basic kata: Pinan 1–5, Naihanchi, Kusanku, *Seishan* (Seisan), and Chinto. Ôtsuka also developed a series of *yakusoku kumite* (prearranged sparring sets) for further study. In 1972, Ôtsuka Hironori was awarded the title of *meijin* (Excellent Martial Artist of Tenth Dan) in

Left: Practitioners of Japanese karate utilize hard and fast infighting techniques in jiyû-kumite.
Right: Ippon kumite is practiced as a part of the basic curriculum of Japanese karate. (Courtesy of Ron Mottern)

Karate-dô by the Kokusai Budôin (International Martial Arts Federation). Ôtsuka Jirô, Hironori's second son, assumed the leadership of the Wadô-ryû after his father's death.

Mabuni Kenwa (1889–1952) studied Shuri-di under Ankô Itosu (Yasutsune). After studying Shuri-di for some time, Itosu suggested that Mabuni train at the same time with Higashionna (Higaonna) Kanryô in the Naha-di system. Mabuni trained with both Itosu and Higashionna until their deaths in 1915. Mabuni also studied martial arts with Arakaki Seisho and the White Crane instructor Gô Kenki (Okinawan; pinyin Wu Xiangui). In the 1920s, Mabuni traveled to Japan several times, where he participated in public demonstrations of karate. Mabuni taught for a time in Tokyo at the Ryôbukan of Konishi Yasuhiro, a ranking member of the Butokukai, and eventually moved his family to Ôsaka, where he established a dôjô (training hall) in 1929. In 1933, Mabuni's system was registered with the Dainippon Butokukai as Shitô-ryû. Shitô is a contraction of the names of Mabuni's primary karate instructors, Itosu and Higashionna. Rendered into the Chinese *on-yomi*, Itô-Higa is read as Shi-Tô. Mabuni Kenwa structured an official curriculum for the Shitô-ryû that included standardized terminology for all punches, kicks, strikes, blocks, and training exercises. Mabuni organized and classified the kata taught within his style as either *Itosu-ke* (Itosu lineage) or *Higashionna-ke*. The Itosu-ke includes those kata of the general form and type taught within the Shuri system, while the Higashionna-ke includes those of the type taught within the Naha system. Mabuni also recognized twelve drills, which he classified as *kihon* (beginning) kata. Mabuni Kenzo, Mabuni Kenwa's third son, formed the *Seitô* (Pure) *Shitô-ryû* after his father's death and composed the Mabuni-ke from kata developed and modified from the curriculum developed by Mabuni Kenwa. The Mabuni-ke includes *Shinse, Shinpa,* and *Happôsho* from the Higashionna-ke; *Jûroku, Matsukaze, Aoyagi, Myôjô,* and *Shihôkoksôkun* from the Itosu-ke; *Kenki;* and *Kenshu.* The *Aoyagi* (Green Willow) kata was developed by Mabuni and Konishi Yasuhiro, with a contribution by Ueshiba Morihei, the founder of aikidô. The *Shinpa* (Mind Wave) kata was devised in 1925 by Mabuni and Konishi after visiting Uechi Kanbun, the founder of Uechi-ryû, in Wakayama.

Miyagi Chôjun visited Kyoto in 1928 at the invitation of the jûdô club of Kyoto Teikoku Daigaku (Kyoto Imperial University). He performed at the Butokusai in 1933 and again in 1935, assisted by Yogi Jitsuei. Miyagi visited Japan for intermittent periods between 1934 and 1938 and stayed with Yogi, who was a student at Ritsumeikan University. During this period, Yogi introduced Miyagi to Yamaguchi Yoshimi (Gôgen) (1909–1989), who had established a karate club at Ritsumeikan in 1930. After meeting Miyagi, Yamaguchi adopted the Gôjû style. In order to popularize karate, Yamaguchi created a form of *jiyû-kumite* (free sparring). Although many Okinawan Karateka had experimented with free sparring, jiyû-kumite was not used as a part of the basic karate curriculum prior to its introduction by Yamaguchi. With the addition of the competitive aspect fostered through the use of jiyû-kumite, the practice of karate began to attract adherents in Japan. In 1935, Yamaguchi formed the Karate Kenkyûkai at Ritsumeikan University to further propagate the Gôjû-ryû. Miyagi Chôjun was listed in the club's prospectus as *meiyô shihan* (honorary master teacher), with Yamaguchi and Yogi Jitsuei as *shihan-dai* (assistant instructors). In 1940, Yamaguchi formed The East Asia Martial Arts Mission to give demonstrations of karate throughout Japan.

Yamaguchi served as a military attaché in Manchuria during World War II and was captured by the Russians in 1945. He was released in 1947 and returned to Tokyo. Like many Japanese after the war, Yamaguchi was demoralized. At midnight on January 12, 1948, he went to the Tôgô shrine at Harajuku to commit *seppuku* (ritual suicide). While preparing himself to die, Yamaguchi had a mystical experience in which he perceived that he was supposed to live and that his purpose was to renew the spiritual life of the Japanese people through the martial arts. True to this vision, Yamaguchi opened a dôjô in 1948 and went on to establish the All Japan Karate-dô Gôjû-kai in 1950, which was to become one of the largest and most powerful karate organizations in Japan. As his spiritual quest continued, Yamaguchi created the Gôjû-Shintô style, which combined Gôjû karate with Shintô and yoga. Yamaguchi's three sons, Gôsei, Gôshi, and Gôsen, as well as his daughter Gôkyoku, continued the teaching responsibilities of the Gôjû-kai after their father's death.

The Gôjû-kai uses the twelve basic kata of Gôjû (*Gekesai daiichi, Gekesai dain, Sanchin, Tenshô, Saifa, Seiyunchin* or *Seienchin, Seisan, Sanseiru, Shi Sho Chin, Seipa, Kururunfa,* and *Suparunpei*) along with the basic *Taikyoku* (grand ultimate) forms (*Taikyoku jôdan* [upper], *Taikyoku chûdan* [middle], and *Taikyoku gedan* [lower]) created by Funakoshi Gichin. Yamaguchi Gôgen modified Funakoshi's basic Taikyoku kata and created *Taikyoku mawashi-uke* and *Taikyoku kake-uke.*

It is evident from an examination of the major Japanese karate styles that their present state is due to an evolution, rather than a simple transmission, of martial ideas and methodologies. The history of karate in Japan is one of dynamic eclecticism. The "traditional" method is one of adaptation, innovation, and progression.

Ron Mottern

See also Form/Xing/Kata/Pattern Practice; Japanese Martial Arts, Chinese Influences on; Karate, Okinawan; Kenpô

References
Bishop, Mark. 1999. *Okinawan Karate: Teachers, Styles and Secret Techniques.* Boston: Tuttle.
———. 1996. *Zen Kobudô: Mysteries of Okinawan Weaponry and Te.* Rutland, VT: Tuttle.
Castinado, M. 1995. "Gosei Yamaguchi: The Consistent Innovator." *Budô Dôjô,* December, 34–38.
Demura, Fumio. 1971. *Shitô Ryû Karate.* Los Angeles: Ohara.
Egami, Shigeru. 1980. *The Heart of Karate-dô.* New York: Kodansha.
Funakoshi, Gichin. 1981. *Karate-dô kyôhan.* New York: Kodansha.
———. 1982. *Karate-dô: My Way of Life.* New York: Kodansha.
Hebster, R. 1983. "Wadô-ryû's Otsuka: Leader of the Way of Peace." *Black Belt* 21 (June): 40–43.
Higashionna, M. 1996. *The History of Karate: Okinawan Gôjû Ryû.* United States: Dragon Books.
Inter-National Karate Association. http://www.wadoryukarate.com/.
Kim, Richard. 1982. *The Weaponless Warriors: An Informal History of Okinawan Karate.* Burbank, CA: Ohara.
McCarthy, Patrick. 1996. *Bubishi: The Bible of Karate.* Rutland, VT: Tuttle.
———. 1987. *Classical Kata of Okinawan Karate.* Santa Clarita, CA: Ohara.
Noble, Graham. 1998. "Gichin Funakoshi and the Development of Japanese Karate." *Dragon Times* 11: 7–9.

———. 1997. "The Life Story of Karate Master Gogen Yamaguchi." *Dragon Times* 8: 28–31.

Sells, J., and G. McGuinness. 1997. "Seitô Shitô Ryû Karate: The Legacy of Mabuni Kenwa." *Bugeisha* 4: 24–29.

Thomas, M. 1997. "History of Wadô Ryû Karate." http://members.aol.com/mthomas264/wado/wado.htm.

Wadô-Ryû Karate-Do Association. http://www.wado-ryu.org/main/index.asp.

Karate, Okinawan

The development of karate in Okinawa was influenced by civil and martial combative disciplines such as indigenous Okinawan *te* forms and exogenous Japanese and Chinese forms. Significant evolutionary pressures included the Satsuma invasion of Okinawa in A.D. 1609 and sustained cultural cross-pollination with Japan and China (especially Fuzhou, Fujian) throughout Ryûkyû history.

Perhaps the earliest external influences on indigenous Okinawan martial arts were the Japanese martial combative disciplines introduced into the Ryûkyûs by displaced aristocrats during the Heian period (A.D. 794–1185). Seeking refuge from the encroachment of dominant clans on the mainland, minor Japanese houses used the Ryûkyûs as a staging area for retaliatory campaigns. The martial systems brought to the islands by these exiled houses were eagerly absorbed by the Uchinachu (Okinawans).

In 1349 the military chieftain (*aji*) Satto became ruler of the Middle Kingdom of the Ryûkyûs (Chûzan) and entered into a subordinate relationship with China. This relationship continued to be fostered throughout Okinawan history until China's defeat in the Sino-Japanese War (1894–1895).

During the reign of King Shô Shin (1477–1526), an edict was passed that forbade the carrying and stockpiling of weapons in Okinawa. The edict was generally disregarded, and weapons continued to be carried by the islanders of Ôshima and Yaeyama during the reign of King Shô Sei (1527–1555). It was not until the Japanese conquest of Okinawa by the Shimazu clan of Kagoshima (the Satsuma) in 1609 that a weapons ban was strictly enforced. With the capitulation of King Shô Nei and the establishment of Satsuma control, *te* (literally, "hand") began to flourish in Okinawa. That te (in Okinawan, *di*) existed prior to this is suggested in a story concerning the creation of the *hidari gomon* (the triple comma symbol, also called *tomoemon* or *tomoe*).

Jana Ueekata was a counselor to King Shô Nei who refused to submit to Satsuma control. Upon being sent to Kagoshima and sentenced to be boiled alive in a vat of oil, Jana requested that as a warrior of Okinawa he be allowed to practice te before his death. Given into the custody of two Satsuma executioners, Jana was released from his bonds and proceeded to

Sensei Ty Yocham of the Texas Okinawan Gôjû Kai Federation demonstrates bunkai from Seiyunchin Kata of the Gôjû-ryû. (Courtesy of Ron Mottern)

perform various te movements. When he was finished and the two executioners approached him to fulfill the death sentence, Jana grabbed them both and plunged into the vat of boiling oil. The bodies of the three men (in death resembling three linked commas) floated to the top of the vat and began to swirl in a counterclockwise direction.

The significant influence of exogenous Chinese combative disciplines on the development of Okinawan civil combative styles may be observed in the use and evolution of the term *karate*. The use of the term *karate* itself, however, indicates a distinction between the styles. In its original form, *tôte* (Japanese; in Okinawan, *toudi*) karate was written with the Chinese characters, indicating that the art had been significantly influenced by the fighting arts of Tang China. Toudi may be translated as "Tang hand." One of the earliest significant exponents of combative arts in Okinawa was Kanga Teruya, also known as Sakugawa Toudi. That Sakugawa studied Chinese forms is evidenced by the appellation Toudi (Tôte). If he had been known for his skill in indigenous forms, one would surmise that he would have been known as Sakugawa Te.

The kanji character for *tô* (Tang) may be pronounced *kara*, which happens to be the same sound as a different word, *kara*, which means "empty." In the early 1920s, Okinawan master Funakoshi Gichin suggested to the karate research group at Keiô University that the character for "Tang" be replaced with that of "empty" in Dainippon Kenpô Karate-dô. The suggestion was vigorously resisted in Okinawa until 1936, when a meeting of karate exponents, sponsored by Ôta Chôfu of the Ryûkyû Shinpô (Ryûkyû Press), agreed that the character for kara should be written as "empty." The term *karate* was thus elevated to the metaphysical realm by embracing reference not only to unarmed combative applications, but to Buddhist and Daoist concepts of transcendent spirituality as well. In this capacity, kara refers to emptying the mind and releasing the body and spirit from all worldly attachment. The participants at this meeting included Miyagi Chôjun, Motobu Chôki, Hanashiro Chômo, and Kyan Chôtoku. Also present were Yabu Kentsû, Shiroma Shimpan, and Chibana Chôshin.

Chinese in Okinawa

In the twenty-fifth year of the Ming dynasty in China (1392), a group of Chinese arrived in Okinawa from Fuzhou and settled in the Kume village (Kuninda) district of Naha. Referred to as the Thirty-Six Families (the number thirty-six denotes a large rather than a specific number), these families taught a variety of Chinese arts to the Okinawans, including Chinese combative arts.

The settlement at the Kume village and the exchange that it fostered prospered through the years, allowing a steady influx of Chinese combative arts into Okinawan culture. It is reported in the *Ôshima Hikki* (the Ôshima Writings) that in the twelfth year of the Hôreki period (1762) the Chinese kenpô expert Kusanku arrived in Okinawa with a group of his students. Some oral traditions assert that Sakugawa Toudi was a pupil of Kusanku. Other Okinawan students included Sakiyama, Gushi, and Tomoyori, of Naha, who studied *Zhao Lingliu* (*Shôrei-ryû*) for some time with the Chinese military attaché Anson. Matsumura Sôkon of Shuri and Maesato and Kogusuku (Kojô) of Kume (Kuninda) studied Shaolin Boxing with the military attaché Iwah. Shimabukuro of Uemonden and Higa, Senaha, Gushi, Nagahama, Arakaki, Higashionna, and Kuwae, all of Kunenboya, studied Zhao Lingliu with the military attaché Wai Xinxian (Waishinzan). The teacher of Gusukuma (Shiroma), Kanagusuku, Matsumura, Oyadomari, Yamada, Nakazato, Yamazato, and Toguchi, all of Tomari, drifted ashore at Okinawa from Annan (a district of Fuzhou or the old name for Vietnam).

Okinawans Abroad

Although oral history relates that Sakugawa Toudi was a student of either Kusanku or his protégé, Yara Chatan, Sakugawa also studied various fight-

Sensei Ty Yocham demonstrates techniques from a White Crane style, which heavily influenced the development of Okinawan karate. (Courtesy of Ron Mottern)

ing styles in Fuzhou, Beijing, and Satsuma and is considered to be instrumental in the development of the combative arts practiced in and around Shuri, Okinawa. Sakugawa's most famous pupil was Matsumura Sôkon "Bushi" (Okinawan, Chikudun Pechin; warrior), who also studied in Fujian and Satsuma. An expert in Jigen-ryû kenjutsu (a sword style of the Satsuma), Matsumura synthesized the martial principles of Jigen-ryû with those of the Chinese combative arts he had learned to form the basis of Shuri-di (Shuri hand).

Higaonna Kanryô (in Japanese, Higashionna) traveled to Fuzhou around 1867 for the specific purpose of learning Chinese fighting arts in order to avenge the death of his father (Higashionna Kanyo). Kanryô lodged in the Ryûkyûkan (Ryûkû trading center) at the Uchinayaru boarding house until Tanmei Kanpû, the manager of the hostel, introduced him to Xie Zhongxiang (nicknamed Ryû Ryû Ko or Liu Liu Kou) Shifu (*shifu,* or *sensei,* is Japanese for "teacher"; in Okinawan, the word is *shinshi;* in Chinese, *laoshi*).

Xie Zhongxiang was a prominent instructor in the Fuzhou area who had studied martial arts at the Southern Shaolin Temple in Fujian. The style that Xie Zhongxiang taught is believed to be either a derivative of *Kingai-Noon* (pinyin *baihequan;* a form of White Crane) or Shi San Tai Bao. Higashionna Kanryô, however, referred to the style only as *gô no kenpô jû no kenpô* (hard-fist method/soft-fist method).

Higashionna Kanryô stayed in China for fourteen years, eventually becoming the *uchi deshi* (Japanese; live-in disciple) of Xie Zhongxiang. Higashionna learned nine empty-hand kata, various weapons kata, and herbal medicine from Xie Zhongxiang. The kata that formed the basis of Xie Zhongxiang's system, which Higashionna brought back to Okinawa in 1881, were *Sanchin* (Fuzhou, *Sanchen;* Mandarin, *San Zhan*), *Saifa* (*Choy Po; Suipo*), *Seiyunchin* (also romanized as *seienchin; Chak in Chen; Zhi San Zhan*), *Shishochin* (*See Heang Chen; Si Xiang Zhan*), *Sepai* (*So Pak; Shi Ba*), *Kururunfa* (*Kew Liew Tong Po; Jiu Liu Dun Po*), *Seisan* (*Sake Sang; Shi San*), and *Suparinpei* or *Pichurin* (*So Pak Ling Pak; Yi Bai Ling Ba*). These nine kata formed the heart, the core curriculum, of Naha-di (Naha hand).

Uechi Kanbun traveled to Fuzhou in 1897 to avoid conscription in the Japanese army. While in China, Uechi studied various combative styles, including Tiger Boxing, which he learned from the Shaolin-trained Zhou Zihe (Japanese, Shu Shiwa). Uechi eventually open his own *dôjô* (training hall) in China, where he taught an eclectic combination of Tiger, Dragon, and Crane Styles that he referred to as *Pangai-Noon* (pinyin banyingruan; half-hard-half soft). Uechi Kanbun was forced to return to Okinawa in 1907, after one of his students killed a man in a fight. Uechi did not teach Pangai-Noon in Okinawa during this period.

In 1928, Uechi moved his family to Wakayama, Japan. While in Japan, Uechi Kanbun was convinced by Tomoyose Ryûyû to begin teaching his art to other Okinawan expatriates. Uechi returned to Ishima, Okinawa, in 1947 and taught publicly until his death in 1948. The Uechi system is built around three kata: Sanchin, Seisan, and Seiyunchin.

Okinawan Karate

From the eclectic styles disseminated by Matsumura Sôkon (1809–1901) and, later, Higashionna Kanryô (1853–1915) there began to emerge two main schools of karate in Okinawa: Shuri-di and Naha-di, each named for the respective area around which it was propagated. Although *Tomari-di* was originally recognized as a distinct system, the style was later absorbed by Shuri-di, especially as practiced by Itosu Yasutsune. Shuri-di was composed of a variety of forms represented by a core curriculum consisting of Chinto (in Japanese, *Gankaku*), Jion, Jitte (*Jute*), Kusanku (*Kankû*), Naihanchi (*Tekki*), Pinan (*Heian*), Patsai (*Bassai*), Rohai (*Meikyô*), Seisan (*Hangetsu*), Useishi (*Gôjûshihô*), and *Wansu* (*Empi*) kata. The kata *Rohai* and *Wansu* are forms that were incorporated into the Shuri system from Tomari-di. Naha-di consisted of the kata brought back to Okinawa by

Higashionna Kanryô. Apart from subtle differences influenced by the philosophical bent of the instructors who transmitted their individual styles, the major schools may be distinguished by their type of movement. Shuri-di uses natural stances that facilitate a light, quick type of movement. Naha-di uses the Sanchin (Three Battles) stance, which utilizes stepping in a crescent moon pattern and a heavier, slower type of movement. Sanchin, however, is not the only stance used in Naha-di, and practitioners may move both fast and slow, light and quick.

The schools are also differentiated by their kata. Shuri-di forms are a compilation of various individual physical techniques integrated into a complex form. Naha-di kata are composed of various Buddhist mudras (body forms), which function as *kamae* (Japanese; body positionings) within the kata. Sanchin *dachi* (Japanese; stance) places the practitioner in the *vajra* (in Sanskrit, diamond thunderbolt; in Japanese, *kongô*) mudra. Combined with various breathing patterns and mental exercises, these mudra are designed to be a synergistic system to stimulate *ki* (energy) flow throughout the body and bring the adept to spiritual enlightenment. This is one reason that kata *bunkai* (application) may vary between instructors. In Naha-di, the self-defense applications are gleaned from the mudra.

Although informally known as Shuri-di (Shôrin-ryû) and Naha-di (Shôrei-ryû), these styles were still considered to be toudi. The recognition of karate as an Okinawan art form occurred sometime between 1916, when as a representative of Okinawa, Funakoshi Gichin performed karate at the Butokuden ("Martial Virtues Hall") in Kyoto, and 1936, when the Okinawan masters met at the Ryûkyû Shinpô conference and agreed to change the characters from "China hand" to "empty hand." These two events respectively represented exoteric and esoteric recognition of karate as an Okinawan art.

Shuri-di

The development of Shuri-di after the death of Matsumura Sôkon was largely due to the efforts of his disciples Ankô Itosu (Yasutsune), Ankô Asato, Chibana Chôshin, and Kyan Chôtoku. Itosu created the five Pinan forms as standard teaching tools for the popularization of Shuri-di. He also made significant contributions to having karate introduced into the public school system in Okinawa. In 1901, Itosu introduced karate into the physical education program at the Shuri Jinjo Shôgakkô (Elementary School). His continued efforts on behalf of karate eventually led to its being established as a part of the physical education curriculum throughout the Okinawan school system.

Asato and Itosu were the primary instructors of Funakoshi Gichin, who popularized karate on the Japanese mainland and was largely responsible for having karate recognized by the Dainippon Butokukai (Great Japan Martial Virtues Association) in 1933. Funakoshi Gichin practiced a form of Shuri-di that was later to become known as Shôtôkan Karate. Shôtô (Pine Wave) was the poetic pen name used by Funakoshi. Funakoshi trained many influential Karateka, including Egami Shigeru, who assumed the title of chief instructor of the Shôtôkan after Funakoshi's death in 1957; Nakayama Masatoshi, under whose leadership and guidance the Japan Karate Association developed in 1955; and Ôtsuka Hironori, who founded the Wadô-ryû in 1934.

Chibana Chôshin popularized Shuri-di as taught by Itosu on Okinawa and was the first to refer to the art as Shôrin-ryû (Japanese; Kobayashi-ryû). Chibana's student, Nakazato Sugurô, continued the Kobayashi style.

The influence of Kyan Chôtoku may be seen in the Shôrin-ryû karate of Shimabuku (also Shimabukuro) Eizô, who founded the Shobayashi-ryû. Shimabukuro also studied with Miyagi Chôjun, Motobu Chôki, and his elder brother, Shimabukuro Tatsuo, who was also a student of both Kyan Chôtuku and Miyagi Chôjun. Shimabukuro Tatsuo later combined the teachings of Kyan and Miyagi to form the Isshin-ryû. Shimabukuro Eizô preserved the traditional Shuri-di kata, and after Kyan's death he sought out Chibana Chôshin to correct any alterations in the Shobayashi forms. Nagamine Shôshin trained under Kyan and later formed the Matsubayashi-ryû. Nagamine also trained under Motobu Chôki and Arakaki Ankichi, who was Kyan's student and Nagamine's senior.

Sôken Hohan trained in Shuri-di under Matsumura Nabe, the grandson of Matsumura Sôkon, from whom he learned the White Crane form, Hakutsuru (pinyin baihequan). Sôken immigrated to Argentina in 1920, but returned to Okinawa in 1952 and began teaching Matsumura Orthodox Shôrin-ryû. Kise Fusei continues to teach the Matsumua Orthodox style.

Naha-di

Higashionna (Higaonna) Kanryô (1853–1915) was the living embodiment of Naha-di. Naha-di itself was composed of the philosophy and nine kata that Higashionna brought back from Fuzhou and taught at his home in Nishimura. Between 1905 and 1915, Higashionna taught in the Naha Kuritsu Shôgyô Kôtô Gakkô (Naha Commercial High School) at the invitation of the principal, Kabayama Junichi. Training at the high school consisted of warm-up exercises, *hojo undô* (Japanese; supplementary exercises), Sanchin kata, *kakie* (Japanese; pushing hands), and *yakusoku kumite* (Japanese; fixed sparring).

While his group at the high school was taught karate as a form of physical education, Higashionna's private lessons were designed to transmit the combative principles that he had learned from Xie Zhongxiang.

The training was demanding and severe. Higashionna taught only select students who demonstrated good character. Few of these students were able to persist in Higashionna's training. Higashionna taught warm-up exercises, hojo undô, kakie, yakusoku kumite, and *tokuigata* (Japanese; an individual's best kata). Although he learned weapons forms and herbal medicine in China, Higashionna did not teach these as a part of the Naha-di curriculum.

Higashionna influenced many great Karateka, including Miyagi Chôjun, the founder of Gôjû-ryû; Kyôda Jûhatsu, the founder of Tô On-ryû; and Mabuni Kenwa, who combined the teachings of Higashionna and Itosu Yasutsune to form Shitô-ryû. Higashionna passed the nine kata of Naha-di directly to Miyagi Chôjun.

Miyagi Chôjun (1888–1953) was introduced to Higashionna (Higaonna) Kanryô by Arakaki Ryûkô, a Tomari-di instructor who had gained considerable fame for beating the renowned fighter Motobu Chôki. Miyagi began training with Higashionna in 1902 and continued with Higashionna until the latter's death, after which Miyagi was designated as Higashionna's successor. Like all of Higashionna Kanryô's students, Miyagi was first taught the kata Sanchin. As his tokuigata, Miyagi was then assigned Suparumpei. Higashionna would eventually teach Miyagi the complete Shôrei system.

Miyagi's respect and careful attention to Higashionna in his later years were proverbial in Okinawa. Although Miyagi came from a wealthy family and Higashionna was very poor, Miyagi would prepare meals for his master and serve them on a *takaujin* (Japanese; special tray) in a manner befitting only the highest social class. These acts of loyalty and devotion became known on Okinawa as *Magusuku no takaujin* (the Tray of Miyagi).

Miyagi took two trips to China for the purpose of conducting research into the origins of Naha-di. He took his first trip to Fuzhou in 1915 with Nakamoto Eishô and the second sometime between 1920 and 1930 with the Chinese national Wu Xiangui (Gokenki), a White Crane stylist. Miyagi amassed considerable information during his first visit, and he reported that the art taught by Higashionna was developed in 1828. The remainder of Miyagi's information and artifacts were lost in the bombing of Okinawa during World War II. It was also during this visit to China that Miyagi observed the Chinese kata Rokkishu, which he later developed into the kata Tenshô. Miyagi also developed the *junbi undô* (Japanese; warm-up exercises) at this time.

The All Japan Martial Arts Demonstration was performed in Tokyo on May 5, 1930, to celebrate Crown Prince Hirohito's succession to the throne. Miyagi sent his top student, Shinzato Jinan, to represent him. After performing Sanchin and Seisan, Shinzato was asked the name of his style. At this time, the art had no name and was simply referred to as Naha-di. Shinzato returned to Okinawa and reported the incident to Miyagi. After careful consideration, Miyagi named the style Gôjû (hard-soft), using as a reference a passage from the eight *Kenpô Haku* (Poems of the Fists) contained in the *Bubishi: Hô gôjû donto* (The Way is to breathe both hard and soft, a "master text" of Okinawan karate). In 1933, *karate-dô* (empty-hand way) was recognized as a *ryûha* (official martial art) and admitted into the Dainippon Butokukai. It was at that time that Miyagi submitted the name Gôjû-ryû Karate (Toudi, or Tôte) to be registered with the organization. Miyagi, however, never referred to the style as Gôjû, but rather as *bu* (martial arts) or te.

The Karate Kenkyûkai (Karate Research Club) was formed at Ritsumeikan Daigaku (University) in 1935. Miyagi Chôjun was listed as *meiyô shihan* (honorary master teacher), with Yogi Jitsuei and Yamaguchi "Gôgen" Yoshimi as shihan-dai (assistant instructors) in the prospectus for the club, submitted in 1936. Yamaguchi would eventually lead the Gôjû-ryû movement in Japan and form the Gôjû-kai. In his later years, Yamaguchi created the Gôjû-Shintô style.

Realizing a need to foster the spread of karate, Miyagi began to develop forms that could be used both for physical development and to transmit basic karate principles without requiring years of intensive study. Miyagi created the kata *Gekesai dai ichi* and *Gekesai dai ni* in 1940 to achieve this goal. Due to Miyagi's death in 1953, *Gekesai dai san* was unfinished until Toguchi Seikichi completed the form. After Miyagi's death, Yagi Meitoku formed the Meibukan, Miyazato Eiichi formed the Jundôkan, and Toguchi Seikichi formed the Shôreikan.

Miyagi Chôjun never awarded dan ranks. He believed that character was more important than rank, and that classification only led to division. The belt system was adopted in Japan, and later in Okinawa. Miyagi taught Sanchin kata and then assigned tokuigata. The twelve kata of the Gôjû-ryû (Gekesai dai ichi, Gekesai dai ni, Sanchin, Tenshô, Saifa, Seiyunchin, Seisan, Sanseiryû, Shisôchin, Seipai, Kururunfa, and Sûpaarinpei) were passed from Miyagi to Miyagi Anichi. Yagi, Miyazato, Toguchi, Kina, Higa, and the remainder of Miyagi's former students learned the entire repertoire of Gôjû kata from each other. Okinawan Gôjû-ryû Karate Bujutsu, under the leadership of Higashionna Morio, was officially recognized as a *Kobudô* (Ancient Martial Art) by the Nihon Kobudô Kyôkai (Japanese Ancient Martial Arts Association) in 1997.

Ron Mottern

See also Form/Xing/Kata/Pattern Practice; Japanese Martial Arts, Chinese
  Influences on; Kenpô; Kobudô, Okinawan; Okinawa
References
Bishop, Mark. 1999. *Okinawan Karate: Teachers, Styles and Secret
  Techniques.* Boston: Tuttle.

Demura, Fumio. 1971. *Shitô Ryû Karate*. Los Angeles: Ohara.

Egami, Shigeru. 1980. *The Heart of Karate-dô*. New York: Kodansha.

McCarthy, Patrick. 1996. *Bubishi: The Bible of Karate*. Rutland, VT: Tuttle.

Nagamine, S. 1991. *The Essence of Okinawan Karate-dô: Shôrin-ryû*. Rutland, VT: Tuttle.

Nakayama, M. 1981. *Dynamic Karate: Instruction by the Master*. New York: Kodansha.

Toguchi, S. 1982. *Okinawan Gôjû-ryû: The Fundamentals of Shorei-kan Karate*. Burbank, CA: Ohara.

Kata

See Form/Xing/Kata/Pattern Practice

Kendô

Kendô, the Japanese martial art of fencing, is a form of physical culture that developed from combat swordsmanship techniques of Japanese warriors. When these techniques lost practical value, they were still practiced for educational, health, spiritual, and sporting purposes and ultimately developed into modern kendô. There is a plethora of terms for swordsmanship: *tachihaki, tachihiuchi, heihô (hyôhô), kenjutsu,* and gekken among them. But since the mid-1920s, kendô has been used almost exclusively. There is also another modern martial art derived from traditional swordsmanship, *iaidô,* a noncombative form that involves both physical and mental discipline.

Premodern History

Japan's earliest chronicles, from the eighth century A.D., contain many references to use of the sword and other bladed weapons. Indeed, the sword was one of the three sacred treasures that the sun goddess Amaterasu gave to the grandson whom she sent down to rule over the Japanese islands. The techniques of forging swords came from the continent via the Korean peninsula, and the earliest swords of bronze date from the fourth century A.D. These early swords were double-edged broad swords like those common in China, and they were less useful as weapons than as symbols of authority for the powerful. Soon technology improved, and swords became effective weapons. It was not until the rise of the warrior class in the tenth century, however, that the peculiar curved sword commonly associated with the samurai—the *tachi*—came into wide usage. For most of the premodern era, Japanese warriors practiced comprehensive martial techniques, requiring familiarity with several weapons. Even then, the sword was an auxiliary weapon for most samurai, whose reputations were generally established through feats of prowess with the bow and arrow.

In the late Kamakura and Muromachi periods (thirteenth–fifteenth centuries), the techniques of producing superior swords reached the height of development, corresponding to the rise of the warrior class to a position of power. Especially after the two major encounters with the Mongol invading armies of the thirteenth century, warfare began to change in Japan; massed armies with large numbers of foot soldiers began to replace mounted warfare. The introduction of the gun in the mid-sixteenth century revolutionized warfare and heightened the tendency toward massed armies using bladed weapons. During the continuous battles of the so-called Warring States Era (1477–1573), many great swordsmen emerged to codify the techniques of use of the sword into specific schools (*ryûha*) of swordsmanship.

Thus by the late sixteenth century, somewhat later than equestrian skills, archery, and other forms of martial arts, swordsmanship began to be organized, codified, written down in formal fashion, and transmitted from teacher to pupil in the manner of other martial arts. The oldest schools were *Shintô-ryû*, *Kage-ryû*, and *Chûjô-ryû*. Ryûha proliferated to well over 700 during the subsequent Tokugawa period (1600–1867).

An important transition in martial arts, including swordsmanship, occurred in the Tokugawa era, when Japan entered a long period of peace and the demand for battlefield training for warriors declined dramatically. Among the factors affecting the learning, teaching, and practice of swordsmanship were peaceful conditions, rapid urbanization, widespread literacy, and the professionalization of arts such as swordsmanship. Samurai were less warriors than bureaucrats in the service of their lords or the Tokugawa *bakufu* (alone).

The system of comprehensive martial skills broke down, and lance, sword, archery, and other techniques became specialized into separate schools. Professional teachers emerged, passing along the techniques within families of instructors who dispensed certificates of mastery in return for compensation. With the spread of Confucian and Zen Buddhist learning, texts exploring the philosophical implications of techniques (*waza*) and mental awareness (*shin*) proliferated, and swordsmanship became an important ingredient of samurai training and discipline. A number of important texts explicating the techniques and spiritual discipline of swordsmanship were written from the sixteenth to nineteenth centuries, including such well-known works as Yagû Munenori's *Heihô kadensho*, Takuan's *Fudôchi shimmyôroku*, and Miyamoto Musashi's *Gorin no sho*.

Under peaceful conditions, swordsmanship was practiced mainly through the repetition of forms (kata) that often came far removed from battlefield practicality. Sword practice was closed and secretive, and matches between different schools were discouraged if not forbidden. Prac-

Teachers and future teachers of the Hokubei Butokukai, Japan, ca. 1936. In the back row are Yamamoto (1-dan), Nakamura Sensei (6-dan), and Hirano (5-dan). The front row includes Hara (2-dan), Muruyama (4-dan), Fujii Sensi (4-dan), and Imada (2-dan). Although partially blocked, the sign appears to read "dedication meeting." (Courtesy of Joe Svinth)

tice was limited to the constant repetition of kata, whose numbers increased with the proliferation of new schools. The focus on kata came to be criticized as excessive reliance upon empty and beautiful forms, with little combat practicality. It was derided as "flowery swordsmanship."

Criticism of such practices finally resulted in the development of bamboo swords and body protection that allowed warriors to practice striking one another in simulated combat, called *shinai uchikomi keiko*. It marked the arrival of competitive fencing matches. Criticized by purists, this form of early fencing, which first arose in the mid-eighteenth century, became dominant by the end of the Tokugawa period. Training halls were developed in major urban centers as well as the domain schools of most lords. The practice of competitive fencing spread beyond the samurai to townsmen and farmers as well.

There was a noticeable upswing in the popularity of martial arts, especially swordsmanship, in the wake of foreign intrusions into Japanese territory in the mid-nineteenth century. Both local domain academies and the Tokugawa bakufu established martial arts training halls for their warriors. At its Kobusho (Institute for Martial Training), the bakufu appointed only noted fencers from ryûha practicing combat fencing to train its vassals, ignoring its own shôgunal fencing instructors, who were purely focused upon kata training. When the Tokugawa regime was toppled in brief warfare in the mid-nineteenth century, most of the warrior leaders who led the revolt, as well as the major supporters of the regime, had studied swordsmanship by means of training in combat fencing. This experience was to determine the development of modern kendô.

Modern History

The men who overthrew the Tokugawa regime ushered in the Meiji Restoration, a period of rapid modernization. The samurai class was abolished, and along with it, the right to wear swords. Swordsmanship instructors lost their jobs, and interest declined precipitously as Japan sought modern weapons of warfare. Several institutions, however, kept swordsmanship alive and helped its transformation into kendô.

Sakikibara Kenkichi gathered skilled fencers and other martial artists into a performance company (*gekken kaisha*) that appeared around the country, offering competitive matches to curious audiences that helped to maintain interest, employ skilled swordsmen, and spread formerly secret knowledge among a broader populace. After witnessing success with swords and spears in the so-called Seinan War of the late 1870s, the Tokyo Metropolitan Police began to develop training methods in swordsmanship, break down differences between ryûha, establish regularized kata, and promote the popularity of kendô.

In 1895, when the Heian Shrine was built in Kyoto to commemorate the 1100th anniversary of the founding of the city, a martial arts hall (*Butokuden*) was established as well as an organization (the Dainippon Butokukai) to organize and promote training in the martial arts, including swordsmanship. The Butokukai held its first annual tournament in that same year, in a mood of martial fervor that accompanied the outbreak of the Sino-Japanese War, which quickly ended in a victory for Japan. The Butokukai was greatly responsible for the training of teachers, establishment of standards, and the further proliferation of interest in kendô.

The Japanese school system also helped to popularize kendô, although ironically it was slow to add kendô to its curriculum. The Meiji government consistently supported European-style physical education and routinely struck down proposals to allow jûdô and kendô into the curriculum. Nonetheless, kendô flourished as an extracurricular activity, and the government finally relented and allowed it to become a regular part of the physical education curriculum from 1911 on. Thereafter, the All Japan Student Kendô Federation greatly contributed to the spread of kendô. There were also various industrial and other organizations of kendô enthusiasts, and indeed it was even propagated in Japan's colonies, Taiwan, and Korea.

During World War II, kendô, along with all other forms of physical education, became little more than a vehicle to strengthen national defense and nurture the nationalistic spirit of Japanese schoolboys. Consequently, kendô was abolished during the Allied Occupation, along with other martial arts and the Dainippon Butokukai. Yet kendô made a strong comeback after the end of the Occupation, largely by emphasizing the sporting element, purging the remnants of nationalism associated with the imperial Japanese government, and stressing competition for all people: young and old, men and women. It was already reinstated in the school curriculum by 1953, and it was given a great boost in popularity after the 1964 Tokyo Olympics and the rise of interest in national sports. Today there are numerous organizations sponsoring kendô tournaments, organized around schools (both student and teacher groups), gender, geographical region, place of employment, and other factors, all operating under the umbrella of the Zen Nihon Kendô Remmei (All-Japan Kendô Federation).

Kendô has become an international sport. As Japanese martial arts became popular from the 1960s on, organizations like the Japan Foundation dispatched national coaches abroad, helping to raise both the level of awareness of and skill in kendô, especially outside former Japanese colonial territory. In 1965 the first international tournament was held in Taipei; and in 1967, at the hundredth anniversary of the Meiji Restoration, the All-Japan Kendô Federation invited athletes from ten countries to an international tournament. Again in 1970, at the Ôsaka Exposition, another international tournament was held, and the International Kendô Federation (IKF) was formed, with seventeen participating national bodies. IKF currently holds international competitions every three years in different places around the globe.

Ranking and Competition

In late medieval times swordsmanship instruction began to be systematized, so that instructors taught students in graded ranks; but in the modern period the Dainippon Butokukai created a ranking system in 1902 that has remained relatively consistent. Currently there are six *kyû* (literally, grade) ranks for beginners and ten *dan* (literally, rank) degrees for more advanced kendôists, ranked upwards from first degree to tenth. Degrees one through eight are awarded in examination, and the last two degrees are awarded by the respective head of the organization after nomination and appropriate examination. For those above fifth degree, there are three honorary degrees for instructors—*Renshi, Kyôshi,* and *Hanshi*—awarded on the basis not only of demonstrated skill, but also of leadership, ability in judging character, and facilitation of the advancement of kendô.

Training in kendô involves first mastering basic movements, called *waza* (techniques): stances, footwork, cuts, thrusts, feints, and parries. These can then be practiced in basic forms, or kata. Then fencers can engage in freestyle practice (*keiko*). Competitive matches are referred to as *shiai keiko*.

Competition among fencers who have mastered the basic techniques involves fencers in prescribed gear—mask, chest, wrist, and groin/thigh protectors—and holding a bamboo sword, called *shinai*, which differs in length depending upon age. Junior high school fencers use shinai up to 112 centimeters in length and between 375 and 450 grams in weight; high school fencers use up to 115-centimeter shinai weighing between 450 and 500 grams; and adult fencers use shinai that are up to 118 centimeters in length and weigh more than 500 grams. The fencers wear *keikogi* (jackets) and *hakama* (pleated trousers), approximating the dress of Tokugawa samurai.

The fencers meet in rings measuring between 9 and 11 meters on a side, and they compete in matches decided by scoring two of three points. Within the five-minute time limit, the fencer who scores the first two points, or the only point, will be declared the winner. Ties result in a three-minute extension. There are usually a judge and two referees, each of whom uses a red and white flag to designate successful points. Points are scored by striking the opponent with prescribed cuts: cuts to the center of the head or oblique cuts to the temple accompanied by the call *"men!"* (head); cuts to either side of the body with the call of *"dô!"* (chest); and cuts to either wrist with the accompanying call *"kote!"* (wrist). A point can also be won with a thrust to the throat, with the call *"tsuki!"* (thrust). A fencer must deliver thirteen cuts with proper posture and spirit to be awarded a point. Normally, two officials are required to agree in order to award a point.

Kendô is thus largely a competitive sport today, but it retains an association with earlier swordsmanship in its concern for decorum, ritual, character development, and spirit.

G. Cameron Hurst III

See also Form/Xing/Kata/Pattern Practice; Japan; Religion and Spiritual Development: Japan; Swordsmanship, Japanese

References
Craig, Darrell. 2000. *The Heart of Kendô*. Boulder: Shambhala Publications.
Donohue, John J. 2000. *Complete Kendô*. Tokyo: Charles E. Tuttle.
Friday, Karl. 1997. *Legacies of the Sword: The Kashima-Shinryû and Japanese Martial Culture*. Honolulu: University of Hawai'i Press.
Hurst, G. Cameron, III. 1998. *Armed Martial Arts of Japan: Swordsmanship and Archery*. New Haven: Yale University Press.

Ozawa, Hiroshi. 1997. *Kendô: The Definitive Guide.* New York and Tokyo: Kodansha International.

Sasamori, Junzo, and Gordon Warner. 1989. *This Is Kendô: The Art of Japanese Fencing.* Tokyo: Charles E. Tuttle.

Warner, Gordon, and Donn F. Draeger. 1987. *Japanese Swordsmanship: Technique and Practice.* New York and Tokyo: John Weatherhill.

Kenpô

A twentieth-century martial art based on the older kempô tradition of Okinawa and Japan. Kenpô is primarily an empty-hand, fist art. It is translated as "Law of the Fist" or "Fist Law." The modern kenpô systems use a variety of hand strikes known to martial artists as finger thrusts, claws, half fist, full fist (horizontal and vertical), hammer fist, *shuto* (Japanese; edge of the hand "chop"), and ridge hand/reverse hand sword, among others. Kenpôists also may use low-line kicks that are directed below the opponent's waist. The basic five kicks employed are labeled the front snap, the side thrust, the rear thrust, the roundhouse or wheel kick, and the front thrust kick. Some kenpô styles include other kicks such as the flying side kick, inside crescent utilizing the inner edge of the kicking foot, outside crescent with the outer edge of the foot, heel hook, and the spinning back kick. Strikes with the knees, forearms, wrists, and elbows are also found within some kenpô styles. It is quite common to find kenpô styles that are taught in conjunction with jûjutsu techniques, featuring joint locking, throws, takedowns, and submission chokes.

Early History

The exact origins of the art that gave rise to the systems that came to be identified as kenpô are shrouded by myths and legends. There is, however, sufficient circumstantial evidence of a long series of ministerial, cultural, religious, and commercial exchanges between China and Okinawa to support the contention that Chinese boxing had a major impact on the indigenous systems of Okinawa that emerged as karate in the nineteenth century.

The Chinese martial arts that the Okinawans developed into kenpô were collectively known by the Mandarin term *quanfa* (*ch'uan' fa*) or the Cantonese term *ken-fat*. This is romanized as *kenpô* (or, in the works of some authors, kempô) in Japanese, and means "way of the fist," or "fist law." It has been suggested that quanfa was first introduced to the Ryûkyû Islands during the sixth and seventh centuries by visiting Buddhist monks and seafaring traders. These arts were most likely from Fuzhou. In 1392, thirty-six (signifying "many" in the Okinawan worldview rather than a precise number) Chinese families from Fujian province moved to Kumemura,

Japanese men and women practicing Kenpô, ca. 1955. (Hulton Archive)

outside of Naha, Okinawa. It is believed that they brought with them the knowledge of several quanfa systems, which they taught on Okinawa. Two distinct styles of kenpô developed within Okinawa over the course of time: Jû-no-kenpô (soft style) and Gô-no-kenpô (hard style).

Modern Systems of Kenpô

Nippon Kempô and Goshidô Kempô are modern Japanese arts that combine Okinawan kenpô roots with jûjutsu and kendô (modern Japanese fencing). Both arts have blended techniques from the older Japanese arts to form new and effective modern self-defense systems. Blending weapons techniques with empty-hand arts is not a new idea in Japan. As Oscar Ratti and Adele Westbrook note, it is "possible to detect techniques clearly inspired by the use of swords, sticks, parriers and whirling blades" in several Japanese empty-hand arts such as jûjutsu, aikidô, aikijutsu, and kenpô (1973, 344). As Karl Friday demonstrates in his study of the *Kashima-Shin-ryû,* the traditional *ryûha* (Japanese; systems or schools) developed sciences of combat that provided frameworks for both their armed and unarmed disciplines. Other continuities are manifest in the modern karate hand weapons known as the *yawara* stick descendants of the Hindu *vajara.* The vajara, according to Ratti and Westbrook, was held within the fist; it consisted of sharpened prongs at both ends that could be used "to inflict paralyzing damage on the opponent's vital organs in accordance with the techniques and strategic dictates of kenjutsu [martial use of the sword] and tessen-jutsu [martial use of an iron fan]" (324). Later, after World War I, Nakano Michiomi Sô Dôshin founded the *Nippon Shôrinji Kenpô* (NSK) system. The art blends an older form of Shaolin Boxing with jûjutsu and *Daitô-ryû aikijutsu*. The emphasis of NSK is on joint locks and throws that incapacitate the opponent but do not inflict serious bodily injury or death.

Older Okinawan masters maintain a tradition of the Chinese origin of kenpô. One such master is Motobu Chôki, who stated in 1926 that "Ryukyu Kenpô-Karate originally came from China. Sanchin, Go-jushi-ho, Seisan, Seyuchin [kata from various Ryukyu systems at the time of the publication of his book] have been used there for many centuries." Motobu wrote, "I am inclined to believe that this art was taught by Chinese men since there were many contacts made between Ryukyu and China from ancient days" (1926, 17). Despite Motobu's assertion of the historical importance of the traditional kata, however, one of Motubu's earliest Japanese students, Yamada Tatsuô, founded Nippon Kempô Karate, a system that stressed kumite ("sparring") over kata ("forms").

Contemporary Kenpô Karate

The kenpô variants are derivatives of the systems that were first taught in Hawaii by Dr. James M. Mitose and William Kwai Sun Chow, beginning in the late 1930s. Under the leadership of William K. S. Chow, the modern Hawaiian kenpô styles added more circular motions to the art than were taught under the *Koshô-ryû Kempô-Jujitsu* style of Dr. James Mitose. Professor Chow opened his first school in 1949 under the name of Kenpô Karate. This was the first time that the two words had been combined.

The modern era Hawaiian kempô/kenpô styles owe their existence to the Japanese and Okinawan based Koshô-ryû Kempô-Jujitsu system of Dr. James Mitose. The Okinawan connection is through his uncles, Motobu Chôyû and Motobu Chôki.

Dr. James Mitose (Kenpôsai Koshô) was born in pre-statehood Hawaii in 1916. At the age of 4, he was sent to Japan to be educated and trained in the family tradition that would eventually culminate in his being named the twenty-first headmaster of the Koshô-ryû Kempô System. It is most likely that he was educated and trained at a Buddhist temple on Mount Kinai, in a village called Izumi. According to Dr. Mitose, the Koshô-ryû Kempô-Jujitsu style was brought directly from the Shaolin Temple to Japan in the late 1500s by members of his clan. The art was modified by successive family masters until the new Koshô-ryû (Old Pine Tree Style) was developed. According to Thomas Barro Mitose, the current Koshô-ryû

Kempô grand master, the temple where his father studied was administered by the Koshôgi monks, and they combined jûjutsu with Shaolin Boxing to form the martial arts component of a much broader spiritual/philosophical system. Therefore, it is assumed that Dr. Mitose studied the Buddhist religion juxtaposed with his kempô training. It would also seem reasonable that he spent time with both of his uncles, Motobu Chôyû and Motobu Chôki. At least one author, John La Tourrette, believes that Dr. Mitose actually taught Motobu Chôki's "Shôrei Karate Kempô under the system banner of Koshô-ryû Kenpô Juijitsu" (1981, 29).

However, Dr. Mitose taught that Koshô-ryû Kempô was not a variation of Okinawan kenpô, "even though some of the kata of Koshô-ryû resemble, and in a few instances are duplicated in, certain karate styles" (Corcoran and Farkas 1983, 355). There is also a strong similarity between the techniques shown in Motobu Chôki's 1926 publication, *Ryukyu Kempô Karate-jutsu. Kumite* (Okinawan Kempô: Karate-jutsu. Sparring Techniques), and Dr. Mitose's 1953 publication, *What Is Self Defense?* (Kenpô Jui-jitsu). The major difference between the two books seems to be the strong emphasis placed on punching and low-line kicks in Motobu's book, while the Mitose text is very strong on the jujutsu escape defenses, weapon defenses, and techniques that could be applied by women and girls.

Dr. Mitose returned to Hawaii in 1936. In 1942, he organized the Official Self Defense Club and began to train both civilians and servicemen "regardless of their race, color, creed or religion" (Mitose 1953). Between 1942 and 1953, Dr. Mitose promoted six students to *shôdan* (first degree black belt) rank: Nakamura Jirô, Thomas Young, Edward Lowe, Paul Yamaguchi, Arthur Keawe, and William K. S. Chow. William Chow proved to be the most innovative and dynamic of the Mitose students.

It is believed that Chow had studied both boxing and judo before he became a student of Mitose. Some versions of his biography claim that Chow's father taught him kung fu techniques before he met Dr. Mitose, but this remains controversial.

On the other hand, there is no doubt that Chow did train with Dr. Mitose. Also established is the fact that a training partner under Dr. Mitose was Thomas Young, who had extensive knowledge of kung fu. Around 1946, Chow left the Koshô-ryû Kempô group to open his own school. At that time he changed the spelling of *kempô* to *kenpô* and added the term *karate* to his stylistic title. Chow reintroduced some of the circular movements of kung fu, or quanfa (ch'uan' fa), to his version of kenpô, elements that had been removed by the Mitose clan during the development of Koshô-ryû Kempô in Japan.

Over the course of his long teaching career, Professor Chow changed the name of his particular style several times, and the last name change was to *Kara-hô Kenpô*. By substituting the label *kara-hô* for *karate*, he sought to emphasize his own Chinese heritage and acknowledge the Chinese roots of his system. Regardless of the name changes, his roster of black belt students is very impressive. A few of his better-known students are Adriano Emperado, Ralph Castro, Bobby Lowe, John Leone, Paul Pung, Ed Parker, and Sam Kuoha.

Currently, the modern spelling, kenpô, is indicative of a very vibrant, innovative set of martial arts subsystems that are rooted in the Koshô-ryû Kempô Jiujitsu Style of Dr. James Mitose. Professor William Chow's dynamic personality and persistent curiosity breathed new life into the kempô/kenpô arts. He was a major influence on the development of the Kajukenbo System, under Professor Adriano Emperado; the American Kenpô Karate System, founded by the late grand master Ed Parker; and the American Shaolin Kenpô System, headed by Grand Master Ralph Castro.

Beyond that direct and immediate influence, Professor Chow is a figure in the lineage for such diverse kenpô groups as Al and Jim Tracy's Tracy System of Kenpô. The Tracy group claims to have over a thousand club and school affiliates teaching their system of kenpô. In addition they offer a wide selection of training videos, audiotapes, and business-related materials for martial artists. A number of prominent kenpô stylists have trained with the Tracys: Joe Lewis, Jay T. Will, Al Dascascos, Steve "Nasty" Anderson, and Dennis Nackord.

The modern era of kenpô has given rise to a number of groups that have the common denominator of being offshoots of the Hawaiian kenpô roots first established by Dr. Mitose and Professor Chow. The following are just a few of them: CHA-3 (Central Hawaiian Authority #3, the housing project where Grand Master Marino Tiwanak first taught; later referred to by some as the Chinese Hawaiian Association) Kenpô, Hawaiian Kenpô Karate (founded by Grand Master Bill Ryusaki), Worldwide Kenpô Karate Association (Masters Joe Palanzo and Richard "Huk" Planas), United Kenpô Systems (Master Joe Hawkins), The Malone Kenpô Karate Association (Grand Master Ron Malone), the National Chinese Kenpô Association (Steve La Bounty and Gary Swan), John McSweeny's Kenpô Karate Association, and Chinese Kara-hô Kenpô Association headed by Grand Master Sam Kuoha, successor to Professor W. K. S. Chow.

Currently, kenpô is a dynamic martial art. A careful reading of the history of this art indicates that innovation and change are its hallmarks. The art appears to have developed in China and over time was transplanted to Okinawa, Japan, and pre-statehood Hawaii, a martial system as flexible and adaptable as the people who have embraced it.

C. Jerome Barber

See also Kajukenbo; Karate, Japanese; Karate, Okinawan

References
Corcoran, John, and Emil Farkas, ed. 1983. *Martial Arts: Traditions, History, People.* New York: Gallery Books.
Durbin, William. 1997. "Kempô: The Source." *Inside Karate* 18, no. 10 (October): 70–74.
———. 1993. "Rough and Tumble: The Throwing Techniques of Kempô Karate." *Karate Kung Fu Illustrated* 24, no. 6 (December): 50–53.
Friday, Karl, with Seki Humitake. 1997. *Legacies of the Sword: The Kashima-Shinryû and Samurai Martial Culture.* Honolulu: University of Hawai'i Press.
Hallender, Jane. 1992. "James Mitose's Untold Story: Son of the Late Kempô Master Reveals Startling Details about His Father's Crimes." *Black Belt* 30, no. 11 (November): 18–22.
Kirby, George. 1983. *Jujitsu: Basic Techniques of the Gentle Art.* Burbank, CA: Ohara.
La Tourrette, John. 1981. *Secrets of Kenpô Karate.* Boise, ID: Warrior Publications.
Longo, David, and Jose Paman. 1994. "The Japanese Origin of Modern Kempô: Discovered at Last! The Mitose Family Temple." *Inside Karate* 15, no. 1 (January): 16–21.
Mitose, James M. 1953. *What Is Self Defense?* (Kenpô Jiu-jitsu). Sacramento, CA: Kosho-Shôrei Publishing.
Motobu, Chôki. 1926. *Ryukyu Kempô Karate-jutsu. Kumite* (The Okinawan boxing art of karate-jutsu. Sparring techniques). Available as *Okinawa Kempô: Karate-Jutsu on Kumite.* Olathe, KS: Ryukyu Imports.
Noble, Graham. 1985. "Master Choki Motobu: A Real Fighter." *Fighting Arts International.* ca. 1985. The original text appears at http://www.dragon-tsunami.org/Dtimes/Pages/articlec.htm; an updated version appears at http://ejmas.com/jcs/jcsart_noble1_0200.htm.
Persons, Michael. 1982. *Sam Pai Kenpô.* Hollywood, CA: Unique Publications.
Ratti, Oscar, and Adele Westbrook, eds. 1973. *Secrets of the Samurai: The Martial Arts of Feudal Japan.* Rutland, VT: Charles E. Tuttle.
Vandehey, Tim. 1990. "The Tracy Kenpô System: Black Belts to Greenbacks." *Black Belt* 28, no. 1 (January): 32–36.
Wedlake, Lee, Jr. 1993. "Kenpô, Kenpô Everywhere." *Inside Kung-Fu* 20, no. 11 (November): 60–65.

Ki/Qi

Ki is an essential psychobiological force, which may be cultivated by and utilized in the practice of the martial arts. Throughout history, the goals of martial artists have varied between victory in combat and self-cultivation and enlightenment. One of the major theoretical assumptions of the traditional martial arts in China and Japan is an animatistic concept of impersonal power known as *qi* (*ch'i*) in Chinese or *ki* in Japanese. Most often described as a bioelectric life force or psychophysical energy, qi is also commonly referred to as vital breath, subtle energy, and directed intention. Qi is thought to circulate through all living things, and even though it is

often a vague concept, most traditional martial arts prescribe methods of cultivating and directing this subtle energy for higher-level students. The benefits are said to include longevity, good health, power to heal injuries, and power to injure opponents and to break objects.

According to traditional Sino-Japanese medical theory, qi not only permeates the universe, it also flows through the human body along paths or meridians. The flow of qi can be regulated through acupuncture, massage, or mental intent. Indeed, some researchers suggest that qi is both emotional and physiological.

Qi is particularly important in the Daoist-influenced Chinese internal martial arts, taijiquan (tai chi ch'uan), baguazhang (pa kua ch'uan), and xingyiquan (hsing i ch'uan) and in the Japanese arts most affected by aiki-jujitsu. Martial artists learn to concentrate qi in the lower dantian (a spot in the lower abdomen about three inches below the navel) and sometimes use special breathing, relaxation, and visualizations to control and direct the qi throughout their bodies.

Martial arts applications of qi theory vary but basically range from use of *kiai* (Japanese; spirit yell, energy unification), in which the lower abdomen forcefully expels air with a shout such as *"Tô,"* to the development of ESP-like abilities, such as the ability to anticipate an opponent's attack. There are many other paranormal claims made, including the ability to sense danger before it happens, control the weather, and heal with qi.

Meditation using qi energy, such as *qigong* (exercise or effort focused on exercising qi) meditation, appears to have physiological effects on the body and brain. Shih Tzu Kuo notes that the deep relaxation that comes with meditation reduces stress, lowers blood pressure, lowers adrenaline and lactate, and reduces oxygen consumption.

Critics of the qi concept suggest that qi is not a separate force but is simply the correct utilization of breath, mental focus, body weight, timing, and physics. By synchronization of these factors one can achieve a synergistic effect without recourse to such mystical concepts as qi.

Qi is closely associated with breath but appears in several varieties in Daoist lore. *Jing Qi* is a yin (the passive or negative element of the two complementary forces of yin and yang in Chinese cosmology) form of qi closely associated with sexual energy. *Yuan Qi* is the original energy that one inherits with one's body and, according to some Daoists (Taoists), when Yuan Qi is finally dissipated, one dies. *Shen,* or heavenly qi, is associated with spiritual energy. Qi also can be seen as the bridge of energy that connects the physical body/essence to the spiritual body. Cultivation of qi is a vital part of many Asian meditative systems, and these systems have been very influential in the development of traditional martial arts.

Ronald Holt

See also Aikidô; External vs. Internal Chinese Martial Arts; Medicine, Traditional Chinese; Meditation; Religion and Spiritual Development: China; Religion and Spiritual Development: Japan

References

Shih Tzu Kuo. 1994. *Qi Gong Therapy.* Barrytown, NY: Station Hill Press.

Tek, Peter. 1995. "Principles and Practices in Taijiquan." *Journal of Asian Martial Arts* 4, no. 1: 65–72.

Yuasa Yasuo. 1993. *The Body, Self-Cultivation and Ki-Energy.* Trans. by Shigenori Nagatomo and Monte Hull. Albany: State University of New York Press.

Knights

Knight and related words (whose underlying senses are "boy" and thence "male servant") have been used in English since shortly after the Norman Conquest of 1066 as the equivalents of the French *chevalier* and its cognates (e.g., Italian *cavaliere,* Castilian *caballero*). All of these words were derived from the Low Latin *caballarius* (horseman), which had been used since at least A.D. 800 in the empire of the Franks to designate a type of soldier introduced into the Frankish armies ca. 740: a heavy cavalryman, initially protected by a round wooden shield, conical iron helmet, and mail tunic or *brunia,* and armed with a long lance with an iron head and a long, straight, double-edged slashing sword called a *spatha* in Greek and Latin and a **swerdom* in Old Common Germanic. At what point in their history the Frankish caballarii deserve to be called by the modern English name "knight" is a matter of dispute among historians, but down to at least the later tenth century it is better to refer to them as "protoknights," since they still lacked some of the technical military characteristics of the classic knight and all of the social and ideological characteristics of classic knighthood. In most regions where caballarii existed, they did not begin to acquire these additional characteristics until around 1050, and it is only from that time that the term *knight* (whose Old English ancestor was coincidentally first applied to them in 1066) should be applied to them in any context.

The Frankish caballarii or protoknights had been modeled directly on the *klibanarioi* of the Byzantine Empire in southern Italy, who themselves were derived directly from the *cataphracti* of the later Roman armies, and indirectly from the heavy cavalry of the Parthians and ultimately of the Sarmatians of the third century B.C. The early caballarii resembled their Roman and Byzantine precursors in being nothing more than cavalry soldiers who were provided with the best available armor, arms, mounts, equipment, and training, and who fought in units whose principal purpose was to overwhelm and terrify their enemies through a combination of weight, momentum, and virtual invulnerability. The true knights of the period between 1050 and about 1550 continued to function in the same way, using a greatly improved version of the traditional shock tactics made possible by technical improvements in their equipment, and the core definition of the knight always included an ability to fight in this way. Given the nature of warfare in the period, protoknights and their successors were frequently obliged to fight dismounted, and became equally adept in the secondary role of heavy infantry. Nevertheless, although knights eventually adopted additional striking weapons—the mace, battle-ax, war-hammer, dagger, and club—they would continue to rely primarily on the lance and sword, and would never make regular use of projectile weapons like the bow, crossbow, or harquebus. Thus, the essence of knightly warfare remained close combat in full armor, either on horse or on foot.

The knight also remained until the fifteenth century the most valued and privileged form of soldier on the field of battle, though much of the prestige the classic knight enjoyed was derived from the high social status knights had collectively achieved and the intimate relationship that had come to exist between the ideology of knighthood and that of nobility. Unlike the protoknights and their preclassic successors, who were for the most part men of humble birth and standing, the classic knight was always a nobleman and usually a territorial lord, and moreover formed part of a nobility whose greater members, from the emperor down to the most lowly baron, were invariably admitted to the order of knighthood when they reached legal adulthood. Furthermore, the ideology of chivalry, or "knightliness"—created only in the twelfth century—had come to be the dominant ideology of the nobility as a whole, and its code of conduct was universally recognized, if not always followed.

The history of knighthood (a term reserved for the status of knight, per se) is the history first of the perfection of its military character to the level of its classic characteristics, then of its social elevation to the condition of noble dignity and its simultaneous association with the ideology of chivalry, and then of the gradual demilitarization of that dignity to the point where it became purely honorific and served only to convey rank within the nobility. These periods correspond to quite different stages in the history of the status, which for clarity must be designated by different names, and discussed separately as six distinct phases that may be recognized in the history of the status: (1) protoknighthood (ca. 740–1000/ 1100), (2) preclassic knighthood (950/1100–1150/1200), (3) protoclassic knighthood (1150/1200–1250/1300), (4) high classic knighthood (1250/ 1300–1430/50), (5) late classic knighthood, (1430/50–1600/25), and (6) postclassic knighthood (1600/25–present). Each of these phases may be divided into two or three subphases, which may be designated earlier or early, middle, and later or late.

Protoknighthood (ca. 740–ca. 1000/1100)

During the earliest stage in the history of knighthood, the term normally used to designate these warriors in the sources (still exclusively in Latin) was *caballarius*, and the caballarii were still nothing more than elite heavy cavalrymen, with no distinctive social position or professional code. Throughout this phase the social condition of the protoknights remained humble, and the great majority seem to have been free but ignoble and landless dependents of the noble magnates, maintained in their households as military servants. Finally, throughout this phase protoknights remained

A medieval manuscript illumination depicting knights battling. (Archivo Iconografico, S.A./Corbis)

confined geographically to what may be called Great Francia—the Frankish empire and its successor states—and after about 900 were only common in the northern half of one of those states, the Kingdom of West Francia or France.

From ca. 740 to ca. 840, the earliest caballarii were probably raised as part of the expanded and reorganized royal army of the new Arnulfing-Carolingian dynasty under its last mayor and first king, Pepin I. They were maintained first by the king, then by the regional governors, and finally by the greater noble magnates who held no such office, as personal *vassi* (vassals): free clients of a new type invented in the same period, who promised to serve their patron, or seignior, in return for his protection and support. The seignior provided his ordinary vassals not only with food and housing within his palace or villa-complex, but also with the armor, weapons, and horses that were the tools of their trade, and presumably with the training and practice they needed to be effective. Some particularly valued protoknights were eventually supported outside their seignior's household by a *beneficium* (benefice)—a fragment of the seignior's agricultural estate whose produce and peasant labor were assigned to each such protoknight while both the vassal and the seignior lived. Such grants, however, were probably rare on this level of the social hierarchy before the eleventh century, when the benefice began to evolve into the different form of support contemporaries came to call by names derived from the Latinized Frankish word *feus,* "property," including the later Latin *feudum,* the Old French *fee* or *fié,* the Middle French *fief,* and the Middle English *fee.* The fief did not finally assume its classic form until nearly the end of the second phase in the history of knighthood, around 1150.

The second century of the protoknighthood phase, from ca. 840 to ca. 950/1000, saw the rapid rise of the caballarii to the position of being the only effective form of soldier at the disposal of the nobles of Great Francia and the shifting of the great majority from the royal armies to those of the regional and local governors: the dukes, marquises, and counts. The period was marked by the partition of Great Francia among the grandsons and great-grandsons of Charlemagne, by civil wars among the kings of the successor states and their officers the governors, and by the invasion of Great Francia, first by Vikings from the north and then by Magyars from the east. In these wars, the easily mobilized, highly mobile, and economically dependent caballarii come to form the main component of the armies of all of the Frankish leaders. After the final partitions of the empire in 888, they supported the efforts of the regional governors of the four successor states to convert themselves into hereditary princes only nominally dependent on royal authority. Indeed, from 850 to 1250, the strength of most rulers of Latin Christendom depended largely on the number of armored horsemen they had in their service, and in Latin the ordinary word for soldier, *miles,* was increasingly restricted to them.

Preclassic Knighthood (ca. 950/1100–1150/1200)

The second major phase in the history of knighthood was characterized by six developments: the perfecting of the knight's equipment and tactics; a great increase in the number of knights in Great Francia; the exportation of knighthood to most other parts of Latin Christendom; the conversion of the knightage (or body of knights) into an international military corps with distinctive customs (including a rite of initiation), code, and ethos; the conversion of the old ignoble knightage into a social stratum between the nobles and the peasants; and the emergence above that stratum of a new noble knightage that would eventually absorb the upper layers of the old one. These developments—which marked the transition from protoknighthood to classic knighthood—took place in three distinct subphases, whose dates varied significantly from one region to another. Throughout the phase a social gulf still continued to exist between the new noble knights and the ignoble professional knights, most of whom continued to be landless vassals maintained in noble households as servants or even as serfs, and others of whom now served as lordless mercenaries.

From the mid-tenth to the beginning of the twelfth centuries, the political sphere was dominated by the further devolution of political authority in the Romance language–speaking parts of Great Francia from the counts to the new class of castellans, by the vast expansion of Christendom through the conversion of all but two of the remaining pagan and barbarian peoples of Europe both to Christianity and to Christian civilization, and by the first steps in the direction of a policy of offensive warfare against the remaining enemies of Christendom: the Muslims of the south and east. The subphase of preclassic knighthood was characterized in the core regions of Great Francia (northern France and adjacent regions of Germany and Burgundy) by the perfecting of the classic equipment of the knight, a great increase in the number of knights, and the first steps toward the crystallization of the knightage as both an international professional corps and a distinct social category.

The classic profile of the knightly sword appeared ca. 950 with the elongation of the crosspiece on the hilt to either side of the blade—presumably to protect the hand. The main improvement made in knightly armor in this subphase was the replacement of the old round shield of the first phase by a much longer form in the shape of an elongated almond, with the point to the base. This form, apparently first used in Lombard Italy ca. 950, spread to most of France by ca. 1050, presumably because it provided better protection for the exposed left leg of the mounted knight. The other improvements of the subphase affected the equipment of the knight's horse and were probably more important. By 1050, knights generally seem to have adopted not only stirrups—known in Great Francia from ca. 740, but at first little used—but a better saddle (with a high pommel and cantle), a better bridle, and horseshoes for their horses. These, in combination with the new shield (and possibly an improved, longer lance), made possible the classic knightly tactic of charging with couched lance (i.e., with the lance tightly held under the right arm, so that the whole weight of the knight and horse were concentrated in its point). Nevertheless, this tactic seems to have been invented only in the following subphase.

The political developments associated with the rise of the castle-based dominions called castellanies between 990 and 1150 in most of Great Francia led to a rapid increase in the number of knights in the vassalic service of castellans, and the spread of the northern French type throughout the region and beyond it. In some regions, a combination of the degradation of the rights of peasants and a simultaneous increase in the economic and legal standing of the knights led to the emergence of the knightage as a distinct stratum of rural society, between the peasants (whose right to bear arms was restricted and whose access to the courts of supermanorial lords was denied) and their own noble seigniors. The positive development affecting the knights' position was the growth in the number of knights who were provided with support in the form of benefices or protofiefs in the form of manorial land with limited rights over peasant tenants. As a mark of their newly enhanced status, some knights (probably the newly landed ones) began to adopt *miles* (Latin; soldier/knight) as a social title in legal documents.

Nevertheless, the vast majority of knights everywhere remained landless, and continued to be supported either as vassals in lordly households or as mercenaries—an even more demeaning condition. The prestige of the knightage seems to have remained low, and clerics generally seem to have seen them as little better than hired thugs who would not hesitate to murder priests and rape nuns if the occasion presented itself. It is likely that a military code associated with knighthood had begun to emerge: a code demanding that the true knight display at all times the key virtues of courage, prowess (or a perfect command of the martial arts as they pertained to his status), and loyalty to his seignior (for whom he should be prepared to die if necessary). Gradually the code would also impose requirements as to how one should treat fellow knights on the field of battle and would establish rules governing such matters as ransom and the division of spoils. Throughout the preclassic phase, however, observance of this code was probably restricted to the knights who were vassals, as it was represented in Old French and related dialects by the word *vassalage,* in the sense of "vassalic virtue," rather than *chevalerie* (chivalry) in the sense of "knightly virtue."

The classic tactics of the knight were finally introduced and largely perfected in the middle subphase of this period (ca. 1050–ca. 1100), which culminated in the First Crusade and the conquest of Syria-Palestine by an army of knights from all over Latin Europe. This subphase also saw the adoption of the name and status of knight by growing numbers of noblemen in northern France and the conversion of an older rite of manhood into a rite of initiation into knighthood.

The massed charge with couched lance, unknown before 1050 and still not general in 1085 (when the Bayeux "Tapestry" was embroidered), was almost certainly introduced and generalized in this subphase. In addition, a new form of military sport was probably invented to give the caballarii practice in it: the mock battle fought between two very large teams of knights that came to be called the tournament. Both the tactic and the sport were probably in northern France shortly after 1050 and gradually became more accepted throughout the kingdom and neighboring regions (though the tournament was increasingly condemned by the Church authorities as a dangerous and destructive pastime).

Perhaps at least partly because the new tactic required them to practice more frequently in the company of their vassals, noble princes and castellans began in this subphase to equate their own military status of warrior (traditionally represented by words meaning "hero") with the status of caballarius/miles. Between about 1070 and 1140, princes like the duke of Normandy adopted seals for authenticating documents in the manner of the royal chancery, and all of these seals bore an effigy of the owner on horseback in the armor characteristic of a knight. Lesser noblemen in both France and England (who still lacked seals) began instead to assume the title miles/chevaler after their name, in the same fashion as some of their ignoble brethren, and possibly to treat the established rite of *adobement*, or "dubbing"—in which young noblemen had traditionally been vested with the arms and armor of a noble warrior as a rite of initiation into adulthood—as being instead a rite of initiation into knighthood. As a result, by the end of the subphase (around 1100) two distinct types of knighthood had come into existence: the traditional, ignoble, professional type, for whose occupants it was the highest and most important of their statuses; and the new, noble type, for whose occupants it was still only a relatively minor status, overshadowed by those of noble, territorial lord, and seignior. Only the former, however, was generalized even in the more advanced regions of Latin Christendom.

The prestige of knighthood in general finally increased at the end of the subphase when the designation *miles Christi* (soldier/servant of Christ), which had traditionally been used in a metaphorical way to designate monks, was extended to the knights who formed the core of the Christian armies in the First Crusade (1095–1099). This proclamation by Pope Urban II not only converted those who participated into holy warriors, but removed the stigma traditionally attached in Christian doctrine to all soldiers, whose profession required them to perform acts that were inherently sinful, so that they were required to do a major penance whenever they killed, even in a just war. Now that the killing of the enemies of God was to be regarded as a meritorious act, which by implication made all justifiable killing acceptable, all honest knights could thenceforth hold their heads up among Christians. This development, along with others of the same period, encouraged knights to be considerably more pious than they had been, and eventually made both piety and loyalty to the Catholic faith into characteristics of the ideal knight.

The late subphase of this period (1100–1150/1200) saw the full emergence of noble knighthood. Nevertheless, the great majority of knights remained landless and ignoble, and the knightage as a whole was not yet united by a common "chivalrous" ideology or a common set of rites and insignia. Adobement (dubbing), though now universally regarded as an act of initiation into knighthood, remained restricted to the nobility. The classic elements of chivalry did begin to emerge in this subphase, but they remained separate from one another and not formally associated with knighthood as such. The princes of Great Francia and adjacent regions did adopt those hereditary shield designs called (heraldic) arms that later became the chief insignia of noble status. These emblems did not descend to lower substrata of the nobility before the end of the phase and were not associated with knighthood. Thus, there continued to be two distinct knightages in this phase: the old ignoble knightage, some of whose members began to distinguish themselves and take on the characteristics of their noble lords, and the new noble knightage, whose members still regarded their knighthood as only one of their several statuses, and by no means the most important of them.

In the military sphere, this subphase was primarily marked by the generalization of the tactics developed in the previous phase and the simultaneous generalization of the tournament, which seems to have become a sport (comparable to the hunt) that maintained knightly skills between formal wars. In both the tournament and war, most knights now fought much more as members of disciplined units, whose members could charge, wheel, or retreat on command, but this discipline was probably fairly loose by modern standards. The new tactics seem to have proved themselves in the First Crusade, which made the use of knights increasingly attractive to kings and princes outside northern France and its cultural colonies. Nevertheless, it should be emphasized that most warfare in the period consisted of long sieges and combats in terrain ill-suited to cavalry tactics; therefore, knights were obliged to be just as adept at the tactics of heavy infantry as they were at those of heavy cavalry.

Knights became common in Germany and known in the Latin Christian lands to the north and east of it. In these regions, knights remained essentially soldiers, and most of those in Germany were maintained in princely and episcopal households as servants and recruited from among those unfree servants called in Latin *ministeriales,* who were hereditarily attached to those households. In Spain, the militias of the cities organized companies of *caballeros villanos,* or "town knights," whose social status was higher than that of the ministeriales, but far from noble. Elsewhere, professional knights were freemen who lived mainly in rural settings, including in some cases their own manor houses. In fact, the number of enfeoffed (and therefore landed) knights rose steadily in this subphase, and a few of them were given fiefs in the form of a whole manor: a form of agricultural estate whose lordship was formerly held only by nobles. This allowed these knights to see themselves as territorial lords, encouraging them to adopt the fine manners and clothing previously peculiar to nobles.

It seems to have become customary for those whose fathers wished them to be trained as knights to be sent between the ages of 10 and 14 to the court of a lord of higher status, where they spent about seven years as apprentices, studying with a group of youths of roughly their own age. By

1120, the eldest sons of most noblemen of northern France and its colonies destined for a lay career were trained in this way and were dubbed to knighthood between the ages of about 16 (if they were the sons of princes) and 21. The same ceremony was adopted for the initiation of the heirs of the landed ignoble knights. The rite still involved the delivery of knightly equipment, including a horse, but it was now centered on the attachment of the sword belt (to which was attached the classical Latin term *cingulum militiae*, meaning "belt of military status") and of spurs to the heels, and concluded either with an embrace or with a blow with the flat of the officiant's sword blade to the candidate's neck: a blow called in both French and English the *collée*, from *col* (French; neck). This rite could be performed either on the eve of a battle in which the candidates were to fight or in the court of a castellan, prince, or king, where it took on the characteristics of a graduation ceremony. Civil dubbings probably tended to become ever more splendid throughout this phase, but truly elaborate rituals involving vigils and the like are not attested before the next phase. Apparently, dubbings were normally performed on a group of candidates, numbering from three or four to several hundred, who had either trained together or completed their training at roughly the same time. The officiant at dubbings was normally either the seignior of the candidate's father or the lord at whose court the candidate had been trained.

Since only the sons of landed knights were dubbed, a distinction arose among the ignoble knights generally between the landed *milites accincti* (Latin; belted knights) who had received the belt of knighthood and the unlanded *milites gregarii* (Latin; flock knights) who had not. *Miles* finally superseded *caballarius* as the title for the status in Latin, though *eques* (classical Latin; horseman) was occasionally used instead, and the abstract word *militia* came to represent the ideas best represented in English by the term *knighthood*. Vernacular equivalents appeared for the first time around 1100, including the Romance derivatives of *caballarius*, Germanic and Slavic derivatives of the Old Flemish *ridder* (rider), such as Old High German *rîter, ritter,* and Old English *ridder*. After 1066, the peculiarly English *cniht* ("boy," formerly applied to all male servants) was employed.

New titles also began to appear for apprentice knights, including the late Latin scutarius (shield-man) and its vernacular derivatives *scudiero, escudero, escuier,* and squire (which became the standard titles in Italian, Castilian, French, and English). *Armiger* (arms-bearer) became the standard title in Latin; *vaslettus* (little vassal) and its vernacular derivatives (such as *valet*) were preferred in certain regions of France; and *domicellus* (little lord) and its vernacular derivatives *damoisel, donzel,* and the like were preferred in lands of Occitan and Catalan speech. The first three families of titles, however, were also used for servants who assisted noble knights but had no hope of being knighted themselves, and thus these titles remained socially ambiguous until the end of the protoclassic phase. In the dialects of Germany, the usual terms for the assistants of knights were cognates of *knabe* that meant "boy" and "male servant." Those who were training for knighthood, however, came to be distinguished by the titles *edelknabe* and *edelkneht,* meaning "noble youth." In some regions the title *junchêrre* (young lord) came to be preferred, and this ultimately prevailed as the equivalent of the English *squire*, in the sense of "undubbed noble landlord."

Other developments of the late preclassic subphase contributed to the elevation of knighthood. The new concept of the miles Christi promoted in the First Crusade was given an institutional embodiment in the first military religious orders, those of the Poor Knights of Christ of the Temple of Solomon and of the Order of the Hospital of St. John of Jerusalem. In both orders, the dominant class of members came to be restricted to men who were at once knights and monks, thus combining the two forms of "solider of Christ" and creating a new model that would soon be imitated both in other orders and, on a more modest scale, by noble knights generally.

Protoclassic Knighthood (1150/1200–1250/1300)

In the protoclassic phase (1150–1300), the disparate developments of the previous subphase came together, and a new type of knighthood, derived from the preclassic noble type, but absorbing characteristics of the ignoble or professional type, emerged at the end. This development was accompanied and effectively made possible by (1) the social fusion of the preclassic lordly nobility with the upper strata of the preclassic ignoble knightage, which involved the assumption of the attributes of nobility by the richer ignoble (and in Germany servile) knights, just as the nobles had earlier assumed the attributes of knighthood; (2) the identification of the resultant classic nobility with the "order" or "estate" of fighters in the new functional paradigm that gradually came to dominate all social thought; (3) the attachment of the ethos, ideals, and mythologies developed separately by knightly warriors, noble rulers, courtly prelates, courtly poets, and crusader monks during the immediately preceding subphase to the status of knight as the embodiment of the noble identity and function (at once elite warrior, lord, courtier, officer of state, devout Catholic, and crusader), and to chevalerie in the sense of "knightliness" or "chivalry"; and (4) the gradual disappearance of the original ignoble professional knightage, whose landless members—the true heirs of the Frankish caballarii—were replaced by soldiers of comparable function but inferior title and social rank. Chevalerie and its equivalents (including *cnihthad* and *ritterschaft*) finally replaced the words equivalent to vassalage as the names for the qualities and ethos of a noble warrior. As noble landlords, knights were increasingly expected to serve the state not only as warriors, but as officers of the civil administration. In the strictly military sphere, knights were affected by the first stages in a long process whereby their armor (and in consequence their arms) were transformed from the forms largely inherited from the Romans (and borrowed by them from the Germans and Celts) to new and more elaborate forms peculiar to Latin Christendom, and particularly associated with the classic stage of knighthood.

The majority of these developments occurred from 1150 to 1230 in the core regions of Greater Francia, especially in the decades after 1180—which corresponded in France to the reign of Philippe II "Augustus." The principal developments in armor in this period were the extension of mail over the arms, legs, hands, and feet, and the rapid evolution of the old conical helmet with a simple nasal into the cylindrical great helm that covered the whole head and neck. The latter was particularly useful in tournaments, which were finally accepted by the kings and greater princes of this period as useful and, in any case, too popular to ban effectively. They were gradually converted into festivals of chivalry so elaborate that only kings and great princes could afford to hold them. Rules developed to prevent the death of the combatants and the general destruction of the countryside, to make them true sports at which the best knights could win honors for their prowess, and to allow princes to demonstrate their own courage and martial skills, or at least their solidarity with and patronal support of the nobility culture.

The dubbing rite became the only accepted manner of making knights, attaining its classic form by 1225. Its civil form was now commonly preceded by a vigil in a church with the sword laid on an altar, by a ritual bath, and by the donning of a special habit symbolic of purity. The traditional acts were also accompanied on such occasions by priestly blessings, and the whole ritual was frequently performed in the sanctuary of a church, as if it were a form of ordination.

The development of this ritual had repercussions in the world of reality as well as that of high theory. First, the expenses it entailed effectively excluded from knighthood most of the sons of the ignoble, professional knights, who if they wished to follow the profession of arms were thenceforth obliged to serve at the inferior rank of *serviens,* or "sergeant," whose inferior status was designated in Latin by the word *serviens,* "servant," and in French by its derivative *serjeant,* "servant/sergeant." At the same time, the right to undergo the ritual was increasingly restricted to the sons of knights, noble or ignoble. This closed the knightage to upstarts from the rising but socially inferior bourgeoisie (whose members often surpassed the knights in wealth and sought to increase the rank of their sons or grandsons by marrying them to the daughters of knights). It also made the right to train for knighthood hereditary in much the same way that the right to acquire dominions and fiefs had been made hereditary within the nobility—though knighthood itself could not be inherited. Indeed, as the expense of arms and armor increased steadily, knighthood was increasingly restricted to men who had inherited or been granted sufficient amounts of manorial land that they could afford to serve with the equipment, mounts, and military assistants deemed necessary for that increasingly exalted military status. Youths of knightly birth who could not afford these necessities were obliged to postpone dubbing until they had adequate income.

In the meantime, the landed ignoble knights who could afford to do so for themselves and their eldest sons had sought to elevate themselves fully into the nobility—whose poorest members were by this time poorer than the former. From about 1100, ignoble knights who were lords of manors adopted the attitudes and lifestyle of lesser nobles. Central to these were a disdain both for manual labor and trade and for those who gained their living from them; a high respect for distinguished ancestry, wealth, and honor; and a belief that honorableness should be claimed at all times by a conspicuous display of superior taste and wealth in housing, furnishings, clothing, and servants, paid for with sums up to or even beyond the limits of one's income.

From about 1180, landed knights had further assumed, to the extent feasible for them, the formal attributes of the classic lordly nobility—many of which were crystallizing in the same period. Since noble knights had long been in the habit of assuming after dubbing the title "knight" or its local equivalent, the formal assimilation of the landed ignoble knights to the nobility was complete, and "knight" was thereafter treated in social contexts as a grade of the noble hierarchy below that of baron, castellan, or the equivalent. At the same time, most noble and self-ennobling knights adopted (though more slowly and less thoroughly) the ideology and mythology that had come in the same period to be attached to nobility and more particularly to noble knighthood. The romances of the Arthurian cycle—created by the Champenois cleric Chrétien de Troyes between 1165 and 1190 from (1) Robert Wace's pseudohistorical material (including such details as the royal society of the Round Table), (2) the marvels of the Welsh and Breton myths, (3) the form of the classical romance or adventure/love story, and (4) the amorous ideology of *fin' amors* (courtly love) of the Provençal songs—laid out the complex new ideology for noble knights and provided models for knightly behavior in various situations. In addition, the romances of Arthur presented a new quasi-historical mythology whose characters and stories would by 1225 join the legends of the Old Testament; of Greek, Roman, and Germanic antiquity; and of the time of Charlemagne.

Although there was never complete agreement about the full set of attributes of the chivalrous lay knight, the following were highly desirable.

First, of course, were the military virtues of courage, prowess, and loyalty to one's lord (which the knight still needed in his basic capacity as a *pugnator* [Latin; fighter]), and with them the virtues of compassion and fair play toward other knights. The knight was also expected to be a good Catholic Christian, loyal to his faith and Church. In addition, however, as a member of a social estate of noble lords whose rights and duties derived from those of the king as head of the estate, the knight was expected to be an active defender of the faith and Church, and to participate in a crusade if the opportunity arose to do so. Finally, in the same capacity, the knight was expected to carry out on the local level the royal duty of defending the weakest members of society: widows, orphans, unprotected girls, and clerics. Given the social attitudes of the nobility to which all knights belonged, of course, this obligation was only recognized toward the widows, orphans, and unmarried daughters of fellow nobles, and was not extended to any member of the lower orders of society; it was no accident that *damsel* meant "young noblewoman."

As a member of the estate whose principal duties were to rule as well as to fight, the knight was also expected to assist in the administration of government. This duty often required even the landed knight to spend part of the year in his seignior's or prince's court, and made many knights into part-time courtiers. More ambitious knights were required to learn the rules governing proper behavior in this exalted environment, especially in relations with prelates and ladies. The earliest codes of courtliness had been composed by noble prelates resident in the court of the emperor Otto I in the later tenth century, and these seem to have served as models for the later codes governing the behavior of lay nobles in courts of every level of the lordly hierarchy. Their main concerns were with the avoidance of conflict and with pleasing the ruler and his wife with elegance and refinement of speech, behavior, and dress. The chivalric version of the code of courtliness incorporated all of these ideas, but added to them an idea derived from the love songs first composed by the *trobadors* of southern France and Burgundy ca. 1100: the idea that a true knight should have a special devotion to a single noble lady, usually of higher rank than the knight himself, and usually married. Sincere love for such a lady was supposed to inspire the knight to deeds of valor done principally to win her admiration, and possibly a return of the love. In practice, this element of the code seems to have been treated by most knights as a game having nothing to do with the realities of life in a society in which marriages were always arranged and the chastity of both wives and daughters was jealously guarded, but it continued to be played well into the fifteenth century.

The first tournaments in which the entertainments directly imitated events described in Arthurian romances are recorded from the 1220s, by which time the tournament had probably become the principal locus for the new chivalric ideology and mythology. By that time, both the team-fought or melee tournament proper and the mounted duels called jousts that constituted an ever more important alternative to it had also come under the supervision of a new class of specialists called heralds, who had begun as tournament criers and advanced to become experts in the system of armorial or heraldic emblems all knights now set on their shields, flags, and seals.

A more austerely Christian ideal of chivalry (articulated in the later romances of the Arthurian Grail cycle) came to be embodied in the same period in the many new military religious orders. These orders, modeled more or less closely on those of the Templars and Hospitallers of St. John, were founded earlier to carry on the crusade against the enemies of Christ and his Church on every frontier of Latin Christendom, including southern Spain and the Baltic coast. The knights of these orders at first combined only the strictly military ideals of preclassic knighthood with the religious ideals of monasticism, and only in the fourteenth century began to identify with the courtly aspects of lay chivalric culture. On the other hand, those secular knights who were both ignoble and landless generally ignored both the religious and the courtly elements of the new code and adhered at most to the military ideals of the old preclassic vassalic knight.

In the later decades of the thirteenth century, the processes of the earlier subphase were completed and generalized in all parts of Latin Christendom save those on the eastern and northern borders, added since 950. The secular ideals of chivalry were finally set forth in a formal way near the beginning of the subphase in the first vernacular treatises on chivalry, the *Roman des Eles* (French; Romance of the Wings) and the *Livre de Chevalerie* (French; Book of Knighthood), and less formally in the first chivalric biography, the *Vie de Guillaume li Marechal* (French; Life of William the Marshal). What was to be the most influential of all treatises was composed toward the end of the subphase, in 1270: *El libre del orde de cavaleria* (Spanish; Book of the order of knighthood) by the Catalan knight, encyclopedist, and missionary Ramon Llull. A familiarity with the Arthurian legend, and the acceptance of the chivalric ideals presented in the legend and in similar contemporary treatises, also spread gradually among nobles of all ranks after 1225, and by the end of the phase was virtually universal, if only superficially adhered to.

At the beginning of this phase, most knights adopted the fully developed form of great helm that enclosed the whole head, and some form of this helmet was to be characteristic of knightly armor to about 1550. By the same time, knights had come to employ a somewhat smaller version of their traditional shield, with the rounded top cut off to produce the nearly triangular shape of the classic heraldic shield. This shield now bore the knight's personal-lineal arms, and the latter might also be displayed in some fashion on his surcoat, which was now usually brightly colored rather than white. The arms were normally displayed on the knight's lance-flag and on the trappings of his horse, making him a much more splendid figure than ever before. The noble appearance of the knight was eventually topped off by the crest set atop the helm over a protective cloth later called a mantling or lambrequin, but crests were rare outside of Germany before the following phase.

This subphase also saw the first steps in the direction of the replacement of the traditional mail armor with an armor of curved plates. Around the beginning of the phase, continental knights began to wear a poncho-like "coat-of-plates" over their mail hauberk, and knights everywhere began to cover their thighs with quilted tubes and slightly later to protect their knees with small round plates called poleyns. These and other forms of reinforcement, made either of iron or of such materials as whalebone and boiled leather, no doubt contributed to a rise in the cost of knightly equipment, as did the introduction of armor for the horse around 1250.

This splendid new form of knighthood was highly valued by contemporary rulers and nobles, and admission to it came to be generally restricted (by 1250 and 1300) to the descendants of knights. In the same period, all surviving knights came to be accepted as noblemen, and legitimate descent in the male line from knights came in most regions to constitute the effective definition of nobility.

At the same time, the growing cost of the ceremony and the armor required for knighthood discouraged a growing proportion of the sons of knights from assuming knighthood themselves. Thus, by the end of the phase the great majority of lay noblemen remained undubbed for life and set after their names in place of a title equivalent to knight one equivalent to squire, a title indicative of a rank just below knight. The more fortunate among the professional squires of nonknightly birth were simultaneously incorporated into the new noble squirage thus created, which for a century constituted the lowest substratum of the nobility. Many squires continued to serve in the traditional fashion as heavy cavalrymen and seem to have been distinguished from knights in the line of battle primarily by the relative poverty and dearth of their equipment. They thus stood between the knights and the sergeants-at-arms in the military as well as in the social hierarchy.

A formal distinction simultaneously emerged among those nobles who did undertake knighthood: the distinction between a higher grade called knights banneret (in French, *chevalier banneret;* in German, *banerhêrre*), who were rich enough to lead a troop of lesser nobles under their square armorial banner as if they were barons, and a lower grade of simple knights bachelor (in French, *chevalier bachelier*), who were not rich enough to have their own troop and fought under the banner of a banneret. Simple knights bachelor wore the same gold spurs as bannerets, but displayed their personal arms on their lances on a triangular pennon; squires came to be distinguished by silver spurs, and by the display of their arms on a smaller triangular flag called a pennoncelle. By 1300, a distinct chivalric hierarchy of three ranks emerged; a fourth ("gentleman," whose members were of noble birth but too poor to fight in a knightly fashion) was added around 1400. The greatest knights—the kings and princes whom the bannerets themselves served—effectively formed a higher rank of super-bannerets. Although all such men now conferred knighthood on all of their sons in particularly splendid ceremonies, they and their sons rarely used the knightly title themselves before the fifteenth century, when they employed it as members of distinct orders of knights.

High Classic Knighthood (1250/1300–1430/50)

As its name suggests, in the high classic phase of knighthood the status possessed all of its classic characteristics—including restriction to men of noble rank—and remained at the height of its cultural, if not its military, importance. A number of different forms of infantry weapon—the halberd, pike, and longbow—were introduced that proved capable of stopping the massed charge of armored knights, thus challenging their long-established dominance of the battlefield. Neither these weapons, however, nor the potentially more dangerous ones based on the gunpowder introduced into Latin society around 1330 were in wide enough use to be a real threat to knighthood until the next phase, beginning around 1430. High classic knights therefore continued to be thought of as elite mounted warriors, and knights continued throughout the period to fight as such, not only in tournaments or jousts but in battles, and to enjoy a distinctive pay scale in most armies. Finally, until the end of the phase it is likely that the traditional knighting ritual continued to be used on particularly formal occasions.

Knights themselves reacted to the threat of the new offensive weapons that grew steadily in this phase by adopting ever more effective forms of armor. Consequently, the high classic phase saw the complete transformation of the armor required for knighthood from the type in which the body was protected by iron mail and the head alone by a helmet of iron plates, to a harness of fully articulated steel plates covering head and body alike. This transformation, begun around 1225, was completed around 1410. The development of plate armor also required a series of modifications in the knightly sword, which from 950 to 1270 had retained the long, flat blade of its Viking predecessor (Oakeshott Type X), with parallel edges designed primarily for slashing (Oakeshott Types XI–XIII), but between that date and about 1290 was given a blade of an increasingly tapered outline

(Oakeshott Type XIV, 1275–1340) and finally a flattened-diamond section that made it more suitable for piercing mail exposed in the chinks in the plate (Oakeshott Types XV–XVIII, 1290–1500). (Type designations for European swords are based on the system developed by Ewan Oakeshott.) Daggers in the form of miniature swords also came into general use among knights in this period, as did such weapons as the mace, battle-ax, and war-hammer, which could actually damage plate armor.

The sword remained the principal weapon of the knight, however, and this subphase saw the full emergence of the new profession of fencing master, who taught the art of swordsmanship to anyone who could pay his fees. This art remained distinct from the essentially civilian type that emerged in the sixteenth century (along with the light civilian sword called the rapier); the knight could strike any part of his opponent's anatomy, and parried blows with his shield rather than his sword or dagger. When fighting on foot, knights often abandoned their heavy war-shield for a small round type called a buckler, which could be held at arm's length by a central bar across the back.

The old idea of knighthood as a military profession was emphasized in this phase through the foundation of a growing number of knightly associations or societies, comparable to the guilds into which most other professions and trades were organized. Of these the most important were the curial orders, founded from 1325 onward by kings and effectively sovereign dukes throughout Latin Christendom. The phase also saw the steady rise of the parallel profession of the heralds, who became true officers with legal jurisdictions in many countries and were gradually converted into a sort of priesthood for the secular religion of chivalry. The chief herald of each kingdom or quasi-regnal state would eventually be attached to the monarchical order maintained by its ruler, thus cementing the intimate associations that had already grown up among knighthood, chivalry, nobility, and heraldry.

Long before this, heralds had begun the useful practice of compiling lists of the knights present at tournaments or on campaigns, or resident in particular districts, regions, or kingdoms, or even in Latin Christendom generally. Because the names in these lists were accompanied by either descriptions or representations of the knights' armorial bearings, they are called either armorials or rolls of arms. The first known armorial was compiled in England in 1255, but the others date from 1270 or later, and the practice of preparing them was to be characteristic of the high and late classic phases.

These lists and others compiled for military purposes demonstrate that in England the number of knights had dropped by 1270 from perhaps 5,000 to not more than 1,300, of whom perhaps 500 were fit to serve in battle at any one time. The numbers in larger countries such as France and

Germany were probably four or five times as great and never got much higher. The two ranks of knight and fighting squire—collectively known, from the following century at least, as *hommes d'armes* (French; men-at-arms)—were thenceforth to form a small elite at the core of an army in which various infantry arms became increasingly important.

In the early subphase (1270–1330), corresponding to the reigns of Edward I and Edward II in England, of the last "direct" Capetians in France, and of the first Habsburg kings of the Romans in the Holy Roman Empire, the principal developments were the following: (1) the decline in many countries (including England and France) of knight service based upon the traditional feudo-vassalic obligations, and its replacement by a new system of retaining by contract and the payment of a pension and a fixed wage during actual service; (2) the effective end of the Syrian Crusade, the retreat of the Syrian orders, and the eventual suppression of the original order of the Templars (in 1312); (3) the adoption of the first major elements of plate armor; (4) the general adoption in Latin Christendom of the heraldic crest set atop the helm (already generalized in German lands during the previous subphase); and (5) the transformation of the heralds from freelance tournament criers to "officers of arms" employed by kings and princes to oversee all matters related to the proper conduct of tournaments and battles and the identification of nobles.

The next subphase (1330–1380) saw a considerable elaboration of the organization and splendor of royal and princely courts and a major revival in those courts of the classical tournament. It began with the foundation of the first true monarchical order (the Castilian Order of the Band), and ended just before the foundation of the first such order of the second generation (the Neapolitan Order of the Ship, 1381). These orders were modeled directly or indirectly on the fictional societies of the Round Table and the Frank Palace of the Arthurian cycle of romances, and were founded to serve as embodiments of the values of chivalry as well as to promote loyalty to the throne of the founder. The emphasis placed by the princes of this period—especially Alfonso "the Implacable" of Castile, Pere "the Ceremonious" of Aragon, Edward III of England, Jehan "the Good" of France, and Amé "the Green Count" of Savoy—on both tournaments and orders suggests the importance they attributed to knighthood; corps of knights and squires continued throughout this phase to be major elements of all princely armies. Indeed, in some kingdoms (including England) the number of militarily active knights actually rose in the first half of this period. The traditional melee tournament saw its last flowering in most countries in the first half of this subphase. After about 1350, however, such tournaments were held only rarely, their place being taken by the more orderly (and less dangerous) joust.

By 1350, the process of adding ever increasing numbers of plates of ever increasing size to the older mail armor of the knight had reached its practical limits, and thenceforth every part of the body would be covered with some form of metal plate. The plates covering the torso were still covered with cloth, however, and the plates in general continued to be strapped on independently of one another until the end of the century. The traditional great helm was increasingly replaced in this phase by the basinet, a smaller open-faced helmet that was now provided with a hinged visor to protect the face when actually fighting. All of the later forms of knightly helmet were derived from the basinet.

New forms of military organization initiated in the 1270s finally gave rise in the 1360s to a completely new system of emblems, designed to mark the servants, soldiers, and clients of a lord, rather than the members of his lineage. This system (now called paraheraldic, since it was closely associated with heraldry but initially outside the control of the heralds) was centered on the livery color or colors, the livery badge, the motto, and the combined badge and motto now called a "livery device." All were associated primarily with the uniforms distributed by princes and barons as liveries to their household servants, retainers, and allies of various classes (most of whom were knights or squires), but they were also used on the various new forms of triangular military flag (including the standard and guidon) borne by appointed captains rather than (mainly hereditary) bannerets.

By 1380, knights had begun on occasion to incorporate the more important of these new emblems as flankers or supporters to the arms on their shield and helm that indicated what they or their ancestors had achieved. The armorial emblems actually subject to the heralds came at the same time to be subsumed in what are called the laws of arms, enforced by newly formed courts of chivalry, usually headed by constables and marshals (as in modern England), in which heralds acted like court clerks and attorneys. The first serious treatises on all aspects of heraldry and chivalry, including the laws of arms, also appeared in this subphase, the most important of which were Geoffrey de Charny's *Livre de Chevalerie* (French; Book of Chivalry) of 1352 and Honoré Bouvet's *Arbre des Battailles* (French; Tree of Battles) of 1387.

In the half century after 1380, the history of knighthood took its first downward turn, as princes and nobles adjusted to new forms of warfare in which the traditional shock tactics of men-at-arms became increasingly less effective. The defeats at the hands of infantry suffered by the French knights at Crécy in 1346, Poitiers in 1356, Nicopolis in 1396, and Agincourt in 1415, and by the Austrian knights at Sempach in 1386, cast doubt upon the efficacy of the knight as warrior. As a result, few if any true, neo-Arthurian monarchical orders were founded between 1381 and 1430, and most of the existing ones were allowed to decline or disappear through neglect. Instead, many new forms of order and pseudo-order, only superficially resembling the older orders, were founded, both by kings and princes and by nobles of lesser rank.

The traditional tournament was virtually discontinued after 1380 and was replaced by the joust, in which knights fought what were effectively duels. A number of variants of the traditional joust—each designed to provide practice in a different form of knightly combat—emerged in this period, especially in Germany, in which regional societies dedicated to promoting the sport were founded. In France, by contrast, individual knights or small groups of knights began in this subphase to undertake chivalrous enterprises (called *emprinses d'armes*) based on those of the errant knights of the Round Table, and these might involve challenging to a joust all those who passed a certain spot or performing a set of *faits d'armes* (deeds of arms) by a specified day.

For some of the more formalized variants of the joust, the great helm was still employed, though in a modified form now described as "frog-faced." For serious military activities, however, the great helm was abandoned around 1380 in favor of a new type called the great basinet, which was equipped with a movable visor and a separate plate for the chin and neck, or bevor, which remained the dominant form of knightly helmet until the end of the phase. In addition, the classic war-shield was finally abandoned by most knights around 1380, and thereafter shields were employed almost exclusively in jousts. A new form of shield was adopted for this setting around 1380: the concave, cusped, quasi-rectangular type called the targe, which was used into the sixteenth century.

The emergence of the articulated harness of plate around 1410 led to a temporary abandonment of the heraldic surcoat as well as of the heraldic shield, and the heraldic arms of the knight were displayed to the end of the phase mainly on flags and horse trappings (though they continued to monopolize the designs of seals and became increasingly important in funerals and on tombs). The same subphase, however, saw an immense expansion and spread of the use of paraheraldic symbols of all types, especially as livery symbols, but also as marks of military units.

Finally, there is reason to believe that it was during this subphase that the knighting ritual was increasingly reduced from its traditional form, in which the central acts were the attachment of the sword belt and golden spurs of knighthood, to a much simpler one in which the sole act was the delivery by the officiant of the (previously described) collée. This abbreviated form may have been used when knighthood was conferred on the eve of a battle, and it was probably extended to civil settings on a temporary or emergency basis before it was generalized. The collée was commonly accompanied by a short exhortation by the officiant, who said, "I make you knight in the name of God and St. George, to guard loyally faith and justice, to sustain just quarrels loyally with all your power, and to protect the church, widows, and orphans."

Late Classic Knighthood (1430/50–1600/25)

In the years following 1430, knighthood was finally detached from its traditional military role and converted into a mere dignity, whose sole purposes were to honor recipients and to bestow a minimal rank within the hierarchy of the nobility. The clearest signs of this change were the removal of the distinction in the pay scale traditionally maintained between knights and squires, the complete merger of the two ranks in military contexts into the single status of man-at-arms, and the gradual replacement of the knightly status of banneret with the new military office of captain. These changes were accompanied by the completion (by 1500) of the process by which the knighting ritual was reduced to the collée—renamed the accolade—and by a tendency in some countries for the eldest sons of knights to assume that title on attaining adulthood, without benefit of any form of dubbing. This did not happen in the British kingdoms, but it was widespread on the continent.

Nevertheless, throughout this phase all kings and princes, and probably the majority of barons, continued to seek knighthood for at least their eldest son at the age of majority, and other men of noble birth continued to undergo the traditional training and to fight as heavy cavalrymen wearing armor encasing their whole bodies. Rather than surrender the status of knight, indeed, the lesser nobles of some kingdoms began to treat it as a hereditary dignity that could be assumed at majority without any ceremony at all. Furthermore, the joust in its growing variety of forms remained the most important form of noble sport (though many of the type called the *pas d'armes* [French; passage of arms] were little more than allegorical plays), and different types of armor (often with interchangeable pieces) were created for each of its many forms. The armorers of this period—now concentrated in northern Italy (especially Milan) and Germany (especially Augsburg)—continued to produce armors of ever higher technical sophistication and finish, and even developed a series of different forms of helmet derived both from the great basinet (the sallet, barbut, armet, and close-helmet) and from the great helm (the barred and grilled helms) to suit different tastes and purposes. Finally, the code and mythology of chivalry remained powerful forces in many kingdoms to the end of the period. Thus, although their military role was steadily reduced through the rise of newer forms of both infantry and cavalry, the knights of this period retained most of their prestige. Knighthood remained an idealized status central to the contemporary definition of nobility until at least 1550.

From the beginning of this phase around 1430, the principal locus of traditional chivalric knighthood in most kingdoms was the monarchical or comparable princely curial order, and the principal model for all of the later orders was the Golden Fleece, founded by Duke Philippe "the Good" of Burgundy in 1430. The Burgundian dukes of the Valois line founded in 1363 had all been patrons of chivalry, and the enormous wealth and consequent prestige they acquired along with the various principalities of the Netherlands and the Rhineland that they added to their original dominion gave a considerable boost to the chivalric revival that followed the foundation of their elaborate order. The kings of France themselves felt obliged to found new orders of knighthood on the Burgundian model both in 1469 (the Order of St. Michael the Archangel) and again, when membership in that order had been too widely distributed, in 1578 (the Order of the Holy Spirit), and the grand duke of Tuscany founded the last of the religious orders of knighthood, that of St. Stephen, in 1561. Of the older religious orders, however, only that of the Hospital of St. John of Jerusalem (based from 1530 on the island of Malta) carried on the crusading tradition after about 1525. Most of the newer curial orders dissolved around that time as a result of the Reformation in Germany.

The chivalry of the late classic phase was not different in conception from that of the high classic phase, but the glorification of the knight that continued throughout this period (in some courts, at least) was essentially reactionary and had less and less to do with contemporary military reality. Latin princes and nobles of ancient lineages continued to believe that the knight represented the epitome of what a nobleman should be, whatever his lordly rank, and the ideology of chivalry continued to unify the noble estate in many kingdoms until relatively late in the sixteenth century. Older romances of chivalry continued to be printed and reprinted through much of the century, and the greatest Italian poems of that century, Ludovico Ariosto's *Orlando Furioso* of 1516 and Torquato Tasso's *Gerusalemme Liberata* of 1575, were essentially chivalric. The last great chivalric romance to be composed in English was Edmund Spenser's *Faerie Queene* of 1590–1596, dedicated to Elizabeth I. The sixteenth century was thus a sort of Indian summer for both knighthood and chivalry.

Postclassic Knighthood (1600/25–present)

The decline of the general belief in chivalry was first heralded in a major way in Miguel de Cervantes's novel *Don Quixote*, of 1605–1615, though the aging knight of that name is nevertheless portrayed as a noble and sympathetic exemplar of a worthy code that has merely ceased to command general respect. The seventeenth century was nevertheless marked not only by a clear decline in the popularity of romances and other chivalric works, but by a continuous decline in the use of knightly methods of fighting, in the holding of tournaments at which those methods could be practiced and displayed, in the use of body armor, and in the practice of dubbing the eldest sons of barons and princes when they came of age. The last tournaments in Britain were held at the end of the reign of James I around 1625, but in some parts of Germany they continued to about 1715.

By about 1648, when the Thirty Years' War came to an end and the English Civil War was about to begin, knighthood had been detached entirely from its military roots, and had been converted into a purely honorific noble dignity. In most continental kingdoms, this dignity was assumed by the sons of knights at their majority, while in the British Isles it was conferred by the king alone as a form of honor granted in recognition of some special services rendered to him or the state. In the British kingdoms, the traditional status of knight bachelor has continued to be conferred by the simplified rite of dubbing to the present day, but in all continental kingdoms the rite was restricted by about 1600 to those who were admitted to one of the royal orders of knighthood. These orders remained few, small, and elite until 1693, when Louis XIV of France founded the first of the knightly orders designed to reward large numbers of military officers for their services: the Order of St. Louis. The eighteenth century saw the appearance of many more orders of both military and civil merit, and the nineteenth century saw the creation of at least one and often three or more such orders in virtually every country in the world. Today, these orders are the principal bearers of the traditions of knighthood, though it is only in the older monarchical orders like the Garter, the Thistle, and the Golden Fleece that the traditions of chivalry are maintained even in a vestigial form.

D'A. Jonathan D. Boulton

See also Chivalry; Europe; Heralds; Orders of Knighthood, Religious; Orders of Knighthood, Secular; Religion and Spiritual Development: Ancient Mediterranean and Medieval West; Swordsmanship, European Medieval

References

Anglo, Sydney, ed. 1990. *Chivalry in the Renaissance.* Woodbridge, Suffolk, UK: Boydell Press.

Barber, Richard. 1995. *The Knight and Chivalry.* 2d ed. Woodbridge, Suffolk, UK: Boydell Press.

Coss, Peter. 1996. *The Knight in Medieval England, 1000–1400.* Conshohocken, PA: Combined.

Flori, Jean. 1983. 1986. *L'essor de la chevalerie, XIe–XIIe siècles* (The Rise of Chivalry, Eleventh to Twelfth Centuries). Geneva: Droz.

———. *L'idéologie du glaive: préhistoire de la chevalerie* (The Ideology of the Sword: The Prehistory of Chivalry). Geneva: Droz.

Keen, Maurice. 1984. *Chivalry.* New Haven: Yale University Press.

Scaglione, Aldo. 1991. *Knights at Court.* Berkeley: University of California Press.

Kobudô, Okinawan

The term *kobudô* (Japanese, as are all terms that follow unless indicated) translates as "old martial arts." It is generally used, however, to refer to weapons training. Kobudô may be incorporated into an empty-hand curriculum as supplementary instruction or taught as a separate discipline, without cross-training in empty-hand forms. Okinawan *di* (hand) uses empty-hand forms that correspond precisely with the weapons forms used in the system. Weapons may be divided into martial and civil combative categories.

Martial and Civil Classes

There are a number of weapons formally taught in Okinawan kobudô. The term includes the military combative disciplines that utilize the *ôyumi* (longbow); *koyumi* (short bow); *ishi-yumi* (crossbow); *katana* (single-edged curved sword: single- or double-handed); *ryôba katana* (double-edged straight sword); *tantô* or *kogatana* (knife or short sword); *tamanaji* or *yamakatana* (mountain sword: broad-bladed, single-edged sword); *naginata* (Japanese glaive); *bisentô* (Chinese glaive); and *yari* or *hoko* (spear), *hinawajû* (musket), and *kenjû* (flintlock pistol).

Civil combative weapons include the *puku* (hunting spear), *tuja* (fishing trident), *tinbe* (short spear or machete used with shield), *kama* (sickle), *kusarigama* (sickle and chain), *Rokushaku kama* (kama attached to 180 cm [6 *shaku*] staff), *kuwa* (hoe), *sai* (three-pronged truncheon), *manji no sai* (*sai* with swastika-like arrangement of wings), *nunti* (manji no sai attached to 7 shaku [212 cm] staff), *suruchin* (in Japanese, *manrikki*) (weight and chain), *gekiguan* (weight and chain attached to stick), *tekko* (knuckle dusters), *tecchu* (small rod projecting beyond both ends of hand and held on with swivel-type finger ring), *bô* (in Chinese, *kon* or *kun*) (staff, of various lengths), *jô* (stick), *take no bô* (bamboo cane), *gusan jô* (cross-sectioned stick), *tanbô* (short stick), eku or *kai* (oar), *nunchaku* (flail), *sanbon nunchaku* or *sansetsu kun* (three-section flail), *dajô* (rods joined by long length of rope), *uchi bô* (long-handled flail with rods of unequal length), *tonfa* (truncheon with handle affixed at right angle to shaft), *kasa* (umbrella), *ôgi* (fan), *kanzashi* (hairpin), *kiseru* (pipe), and various obscure weapons. The five primary weapons used in conjunction with karate are rokushakubô, sai, tonfa, kama, and nunchaku.

Various Forms

Some of the many kata (forms) that are extant on Okinawa include the bô kata *Sakugawa no kon* (Sakugawa staff, from its creator Sakugawa Toudi) and *Matsumura no kon* (from its creator Bushi Matsumura [*Bushi* here

Sai versus sword. (Courtesy of Ron Mottern)

means "warrior"]). Sakugawa passed his kobudô to his disciple Ginowan Donchi, who perfected the weapons forms given to him by his master. The essence of his art is contained in the *Ginowan no kon*. Other staff kata in Okinawan kobudô include the *Cho Un no kon, Shirotaru no kon, Yonegawa no kon, Chinen Shichanaka no kon, Sesoku no kon, Urasoe no kon, Sueyoshi no kon, Sueishi no kon, Arakaki no kon, Tôyama no kon,* and *Chatan Yara no kon.* Sai kata include *Taira no sai, Tsukenshitahaku no sai, Tawada no sai, Chatan Yara no sai, Hamahiga no sai,* and *Arakaki no sai, Yaka no sai, Kojo no sai,* and *Jigen no sai.* Tonfa kata include the *Hamahiga no tonfa* and *Chatan Yara no tonfa.* Nunchaku is represented by the *Taira no nunchaku.* Different forms exist in different kobudô lineages. The Matayoshi branch of kobudô, for example, may also include *Matayoshi bô, sai, kama, tonfa,* and *nunchaku* kata, as well as kata for sundry other weapons. Taira Shinken mastered a number of weapons and created kata for many of them, including the tekko. An exhaustive listing of the kobudô kata being used in Okinawa would be foolish to attempt and less than useful to produce. Individual artists invariably leave their own distinctive marks on their work. The history of any art is one of dynamic eclecticism and inspired innovation.

Japanese Influence on Okinawan Kobudô

The *kumi* dances of Okinawa are dances performed by two players who simulate sparring with various weapons. These dances may be of Japanese origin. The Nihon Budô Taikei (Martial History of Japan) notes that Satsuma farmers and peasants were taught self-defense by the Jigen-ryû headmaster Tôgô Bizen-no-Kami Shigekata (1602–1659) at the insistence of the Satsuma lord Shimazu Yoshihisa. The transmission of combative techniques was accomplished through the medium of the Jigen-ryû *Bô Odori* (Staff Dance). This dance included two-man sets that simulated combat for jô and katana, rokushaku bô, and yari, and separate techniques for eku, kama, *shakuhachi* (flute), and other implements. Although the original kumi dances of Okinawa may be derived from Japanese prototypes, new dances are periodically created and performed by contemporary kobudô practitioners. The distinguishing factor between kumi dances and weapons kata is that kumi dances are performed for entertainment, with little or no emphasis on the combative *bunkai* (application of techniques) contained in the forms. Movements are judged for aesthetic value, rather than for combat effectiveness.

This is not true of Okinawan *di* (in Japanese, *te*). Okinawan di movements resemble the movements of *onna odori* (ladies' dances), but the bunkai are transmitted with emphasis on combative applications. Okinawa di is composed of various open-hand forms, including *moto-ti* (original hand), *kihon-ti* (basic hand), *tori-ti* (grappling hand), *uragaeshi* (reversal), *ogami-ti* (prayer hand), *koneri-ti* (twist hand), *oshi-ti* (push hand), *kaeshi-ti* (return hand), *nuki-ti* (draw hand), and *nage-ti* (throw hand). The pinnacle of di technique and practice is *Anjikata no Mai no Ti* (Dancing Hand of the Lords). The empty-hand movements exhibit a circularity and flow that correspond to the movements used with di weaponry.

The primary weapons used in Okinawa di are katana, naginata, and yari. These weapons were also the primary martial implements used by Japanese samurai. It is possible that Okinawan di is indirectly derivative of Japanese forms. The Japanese presented the Ming court with katana, naginata, and yari during the fourteenth century. It is possible that the Okinawans were influenced by techniques and weapons from China, which were originally based on Japanese patterns.

It is also possible that the Okinawans received civil combative forms from Ryûkyûan samurai (in Okinawan, *pechin*) traveling to Satsuma after subjugation of the Ryûkyû kingdom by the Satsuma clan in 1609. This possibility is substantiated by the tradition that Okinawan *rokushaku bôjutsu* (staff technique) was unknown in the Ryûkyûs until after Sakugawa "Toudi" (in Japanese, Karate) and Koura Tsuken (1776–1882) returned with them after studying in Satsuma. Matsumura Sôkon "Bushi" (in Okinawan, Chikudun

Peichin; warrior) studied karate in Okinawa from the Chinese master Iwah and from Sakugawa Toudi. Matsumura later served as a security agent for the Okinawan royal house. During this period, he traveled to China and to Satsuma, where he studied the Jigen system and received his *menkyo* (teaching license) from Ijûin Yashichirô. Matsumura returned to Okinawa, where he combined his knowledge of karate with his knowledge of Jigen-ryû to create what would eventually become known as Shuri-di (Shuri Hand). Both Sakugawa and Matsumura transmitted various weapons kata into the Okinawan civil combative disciplines.

Chinese Influence on Okinawan Kobudô

In 1372, the Ming emperor Wu Hong sent an envoy, Zai Yang, to the Okinawan kingdom of Chûzan for the purpose of establishing a tributary alliance

Sensei Ty Yocham of the Texas Okinawan Gôjû Kai Federation sidesteps a downward cut of the sword and delivers a strike with the eku (oar). (Courtesy of Ron Mottern)

with Okinawa. The Chûzan king, Satto, was cognizant of the advantages of being allied with the Ming and welcomed the opportunity of increasing trade with China, especially Fujian. In 1393, the Thirty-Six Families (the number thirty-six denotes a large rather than a specific number), a delegation of Chinese envoys, established a mission at Kume village, in the Kume district of Naha. The settlement at Kume was a point of exchange between the Okinawan and Chinese cultures. It was at Kume that weapons training was introduced by the Thirty-Six Families as part of the combative systems that they brought to Okinawa. The Okinawans absorbed the Chinese fighting arts into their own culture.

In the *Ôshima Hikki* (Ôshima Writings) it is reported that the Chinese *kenpô* (fist method) master Kusanku arrived in Okinawa with a group of his students in 1762. Kusanku exerted a considerable influence on the development of civil combative disciplines in the Ryûkyûs. *Kusanku kata* is one of the highest forms in Shôrin-ryû and Shôtôkan Karate. Kusanku's students included Sakugawa Toudi and Yara Chatan, both of whom made significant contributions to the study and practice of empty-hand forms and kobudô.

Ryûkyû kobudô was also influenced by Okinawans who traveled abroad, learning weapons techniques and then transmitting them through various forms upon returning to Okinawa. Matayoshi Shinkô (1888–1947) studied bô, sai, kama, and eku under Gushikawa no Tigwa in Chatan, Okinawa. He also trained in tonfa and nunchaku under Moshigiwa Ire. Matayoshi then spent a total of thirteen years traveling throughout China. He researched several weapons disciplines in his travels, including *ba-jutsu* (mounted archery technique), *nagenawa-jutsu* (lariat technique), and *shuriken* (throwing spikes) techniques, which he learned from a gang of Manchurian bandits. Matayoshi acquired a knowledge of *nunti, tinbei,* and *suruchin* in Shanghai, as well as learning herbal medicine and a Shaolin Crane Style of boxing known as Kingai-noon (pinyin baihequan). In 1934, Matayoshi studied another Shaolin-based style in Fuzhou.

Matayoshi disseminated his knowledge of kobudô throughout Okinawa and Japan. He demonstrated kobudô in Tokyo in 1915, performing with the karate master Funakoshi Gichin. This was the first performance of Ryûkyûan kobudô on the Japanese mainland. Matayoshi also performed for the crown prince Hirohito at Shuri Castle in 1921. Shinkô's son Shinpô continued the Matayoshi tradition of kobudô until his death in 1997.

Okinawan Kobudô

Taira Shinken (1897–1970) began his study of combative forms in 1922 when he met Funakoshi Gichin in Japan. Taira trained with Funakoshi until 1929, when he expanded his studies to include Ryûkyû kobudô under Yabiku Môden (1882–1945), the leading authority on Okinawan weaponry in Japan.

Taira opened his first dôjô in Ikaho, Gunma Prefecture, in 1932, and was awarded Yabiku's personal *shihan menkyo* (Instructor's Certification) in 1933. In 1934, Taira began studying with Mabuni Kenwa, the founder of Shitô-ryû karate and a respected kobudô practitioner. Returning to Okinawa in 1940, Taira continued to research and teach kobudô. He established the Ryûkyû Kobudô Hozon Shinkô Kai in 1955 for the purpose of consolidating, preserving, and disseminating Ryûkyûan kobudô.

The movement was supported in both Okinawa and Japan by many respected karate and kobudô masters, including (in Japan) Mabuni Kenei (son of Mabuni Kenwa, Seitô Shitô-ryû), Sakagami Ryûshô (Itosu-ha), Kuniba Shiyogo (Motobu-ha), Hatashi Teruo (Hayashi-ha), and Kunishi Yasuhiro (Shindô Jinen-ryû). Supporters in Okinawa included Chibana Chôshin (Shôrin-ryû), Higa Yochoku (Shôrin-ryû), Shimabukuro Eizô (Shobayashi-ryû), Nakazato Sûgûrô (Kobayashi-ryû), Nagamine Shôshin (Matsubayashi-ryû), Sôken Hohan (Matsumura Seitô Shôrin-ryû), Nakamura Shigeru (Shôrin-ryû), Miyahira Katsuya (Naha Shôrin-ryû), Shimabukuro Tatsuo (Isshin-ryû), Higa Seiko (Gôjû-ryû), Yagi Meitoku (Gôjû-ryû), Miyazato Eiichi (Gôjû-ryû), Toguchi Seikichi (Gôjû-ryû), Fukuchi Seiko (Gôjû-ryû),

Chinen Masame (Yamane-ryû), Uechi Kanei (Uechi-ryû), and Kinjo Hiroshi (Shuri-di).

Taira amassed a considerable knowledge of Ryûkyûan forms, as well as creating several of his own kata. Taira created the *Kungo no kun* (Kungo staff) kata, two nunchaku kata, a sansetsukun (three-sectioned staff) kata, the *Maezato no tekko* ("Maezato knuckle duster") kata based on empty-hand forms he learned from Funakoshi, and the *Jigen no manjisai* (sai with wings shaped like a swastika) kata. Perhaps Taira's greatest achievement, apart from the preservation of a unique part of Okinawa's cultural heritage, was his creation of a standardized kobudô curriculum and pedagogy. Taira's senior disciple, Akamine Eisuke, assumed the leadership of the Ryûkyû Kobudô Hozon Shinkô Kai after his teacher's death.

The practice of Okinawan kobudô gained considerable attention and international prestige under the influence of Matayoshi Shinkô and Taira Shinken. Largely due to their efforts of preservation and popularization, the once obscure weapon arts of Okinawa's civil combative traditions have been firmly established as a living Ryûkyûan cultural legacy.

Ron Mottern

See also Form/Xing/Kata/Pattern Practice; Karate, Japanese; Karate, Okinawan; Kenpô; Okinawa

References

Bishop, Mark. 1999. *Okinawan Karate: Teachers, Styles and Secret Techniques.* Boston: Tuttle.

———. 1997. "Okinawan Kobudô Weaponry: Hidden Methods, Ancient Myths." *Bugeisha: Traditional Martial Artist* 4: 46–49.

———. 1996. *Zen Kobudô: Mysteries of Okinawan Weaponry and Te.* Rutland, VT: Tuttle.

Kim, Richard. 1982. *The Weaponless Warriors: An Informal History of Okinawan Karate.* Burbank, CA: Ohara.

Kobudô. 1999. "Kobudô." http://www.bushido-online.com/kobudo/index.htm.

McCarthy, Patrick. 1996. *Bubishi. The Bible of Karate.* Rutland, VT: Tuttle.

———. 1997. "Taira Shinken, 'The Funakoshi Gichin of Kobudô.'" *Bugeisha: Traditional Martial Artist* 3: 21–26.

Sanguinetti, F. 1997. "The Kobudô Legacy of Matayoshi Shinpo." *Bugeisha: Traditional Martial Artist* 4: 19–23.

Korea

Korea is a peninsula situated between China and Japan, and its history has been influenced by both nations. For much of its early history, China was the single most important influence on Korea. Chinese or Korean immigrants settled Japan and eventually, in the nineteenth century, successfully challenged Chinese influence over the region. In the twentieth century, Japan formally annexed Korea and imposed Japanese language and culture

upon the Korean people. Freed by the Allies in 1945, Korea was soon divided by the conflict between Communism and capitalistic democracy. Despite their separation, both Koreas were highly nationalistic and worked to throw off the Japanese influence. These are the chief elements of Korean history necessary to understand the development of Korean martial arts.

The earliest evidence in Korea of systems of unarmed combat date from the Koguryo dynasty (A.D. 3–427). The kingdom of Koguryo actually stretched far north of the current Korean border, into much of modern Chinese Manchuria. Korean folk culture is still very much alive in Manchuria today. A number of Koguryo dynasty tombs in what is now Jilin province of the People's Republic of China are credited by the Koreans as belonging to ancient Korea. These tombs are the Sambo-chong, the Kakjo-chong, and the Muyong-chong. The style depicted in these tombs has been described by martial artists (depending upon the individual artist's style) as *taekwondo, Hapkidô, ssirŭm, t'aek'kyŏn, tangsudô,* or other Korean arts. Most of these claims are exaggerated. The murals show men with goatees, moustaches, and long hair in loincloths. They seem to be wrestling rather than striking, and as such the murals are best used as early antecedents of Korean ssirŭm and Japanese sumô. The claims of Korean nationalists regarding these tombs are also tenuous, since the style depicted in the tombs is very similar to that of other tombs of the Han dynasty (206 B.C.–A.D. 220), including those located deep within Han China itself. In many ways, the Koguryo kingdom was heavily influenced by the Chinese Han dynasty. Koguryo in fact served as the easternmost outpost of the Han dynasty, and remained an important Chinese outpost until A.D. 313.

During the Silla and Koryo dynasties, the largest ssirŭm competitions took place on the holiday of Paekchung or "Day of Servants" (the fifteenth day of the seventh lunar month). The champion was named either *panmugum* (finalist) or *changgun* (general) and was rewarded with an ox as his prize. The *kisaeng* women (who were comparable to the Japanese geisha) sang and danced at the victory ceremony. Today, the largest competitions take place on the Tano Nol or youth festival (on the fifth day of the fifth lunar month). The winner is named *chonha changsa* (strongest man under heaven) and receives cash prizes rather than livestock.

Ancient Korea shows Chinese influence not only on its methods of grappling, but also upon its methods of striking. Chinese advisors not only taught their method of striking to the Koguryo army, but also later to the Silla army, the enemies of Koguryo. The Tang dynasty (A.D. 618–907) helped Silla to defeat Koguryo in 668, which established the Silla dynasty (668–935). It was during the Tang dynasty that Chinese striking arts achieved their greatest fame, thanks to the feats of the monks of the Shaolin Temple. The Koreans called the Chinese striking arts *subak* (striking hand; *Shoubo* in Mandarin), *kwonbop* (fist method; *quanfa* in Mandarin), or simply *tangsu* (Tang hand).

The Silla dynasty also produced a society of young men called the *hwarang* (flowering youth). The hwarang was intended to develop young leaders for the Silla kingdom, and it was predated by a similar but unsuccessful experiment with a group of young women known as the *wonhwa*. These hwarang played songs and music, and roamed over mountains and remote places seeking amusement. They lived according to a code of behavior set forth by the Buddhist monk Wongwang in his *Sesok Ogye* (Five Common Precepts), written about A.D. 602. The code called for loyalty to one's king, obedience to one's parents, honorable conduct toward one's friends, never retreating in battle, and only killing for a sensible reason. The most famous hwarang was General Kim Yushin (595–673), a master of the double-edged sword. Because of Kim and other heroes, hwarang became known as the "shining knights of the Silla dynasty," and are still regarded as heroes by modern Koreans.

More important than the military traditions that Korea adopted from China was the influence of the Confucian tradition. Koreans embraced Confucianism so completely that Korea was in many ways more Confucian than was China itself. The only martial art that Confucius praised was archery, so it is not surprising that Korean archers are still famous for their skill. Martial arts in general were frowned upon, since Confucianism prized scholars more than warriors. Korean practice of the martial arts revived briefly during the Japanese invasions led by Toyotomi Hideyoshi (1536–1598) in 1592 and 1597, but once the Japanese were driven off, the practice of these arts again declined due to lack of attention at the royal court.

The Koreans continued to emulate Chinese military technique until the nineteenth century. The Korean military used the Chinese work *Jixiao Xinshu* (New Book for Effective Discipline) as their standard manual until the 1790s. Yi Dok-mu then produced his *Mu Yei Do Bo Tong Ji* (Illustrated Manual of Martial Arts), a Korean manual that drew from classical Chinese sources. The *Mu Yei Do Bo Tong Ji* included methods of unarmed combat called *kwon-bop* and distinguished between the External School of the Sorim Temple (Shaolin Temple) and the Internal School of Chang Songkae (Zhang Sanfeng in Mandarin), the legendary founder of Chinese internal styles (*taijiquan*).

By the 1890s, there seemed to be only three native martial arts of any great importance. Ssirŭm was still popular, as was archery, and there was also the street art of t'aek'kyŏn, which seems to have appeared around the 1790s. In its modern form, t'aek'kyŏn is an art emphasizing circular kicking, leg sweeps, and leg trapping followed by a throw. T'aek'kyŏn was discouraged among the intelligentsia, as it was associated with thugs and criminals.

In the late nineteenth century, Japanese influence gradually supplanted Chinese in Korea. In 1894, pro-Japanese members of the Korean cabinet invited the Japanese army to enter Korea and put down a revolt. The Japanese put down the revolt but then refused to leave, which led to the Sino-Japanese War of 1894. China came to the aid of Korea, one of its tributary states, but was defeated. The Japanese retained their grip on Korea. Japanese agents murdered Queen Min in 1896, and King Kojong fled the palace and was sheltered in the Russian legation for nearly a year. Russian influence in Korea was ended by the Russo-Japanese War (1904–1905), at which point the United States tacitly recognized Japanese control of Korea with the Taft-Katsura Memorandum (1905). The Japanese forced the Korean king to abdicate in 1907. A Korean assassinated Prince Hirobumi Ito of Japan in 1909, but in 1910 Japan officially annexed Korea.

Japan was determined to turn Korea into a Japanese colony. The Japanese established segregated Korean and Japanese public schools, with the Koreans receiving an inferior education. Thousands of Koreans were killed after making a Declaration of Independence in 1919, believing that American commitment to self-government would bring the United States to their side. It did not. Japanese control tightened over the years. The Japa-

Junior high school students compete in a taekwondo tournament in Seoul, Korea, 1986. (Michael S. Yamashita/Corbis)

nese language was taught in the schools rather than Korean, and many Koreans raised in that era never learned to read the Korean language. During World War II, the Japanese took over half a million Koreans to Japan as laborers, primarily in mining and in heavy industry, where American bombing was taking its toll. Sixty thousand of these forced laborers died in Japan during the war. Back home, the Japanese army forced Korean women to serve as "comfort women" (prostitutes) for the soldiers. The Japanese were in absolute control of Korea from 1910 to 1945.

Korean youth were forcibly indoctrinated with Japanese culture, including the Japanese martial arts. Jûdô (in Korean, *yudô)* was introduced through the Seoul YMCA in 1909. Both jûdô and kendô (*kumdô)* were taught in the Japanese-controlled schools. Ssirŭm competition continued in Korea until the Japanese attack on Pearl Harbor, but was then outlawed. T'aek'kyŏn was outlawed for most of the occupation, although Song Dok-ki (1893–1987) and others continued to train in secret.

After the war, Korean martial arts consisted largely of Japanese styles, including yudô, *yusul* (jûjutsu), kumdô, kwonbop (kenpô), and tangsudô, or *kongsudô (karate-dô).* Koreans who had served in the Japanese army or who had trained with the Japanese police retained a great deal of control in the country, often serving the same role that they had before the Japanese withdrawal. Moreover, Korean students who had studied in Japanese universities often returned with knowledge of karate. Korea was devastated by war, by the occupation, and by its postwar division into Soviet and American spheres of influence.

The nation, of necessity, retained a military economy, fuelled by the conflict between North Korea and South Korea. The Korean military supported the martial arts not only as a method of unarmed combat, but also as a means of building morale. General Choi Hong-Hi in particular supported the development of a Korean form of karate, which he named taekwondo in 1955.

Korean martial arts were also supported by the Korean Yudô College (now Yong In University), founded in 1953. In 1957 it expanded to a four-year institution, and in 1958 it graduated its first yudô instructors. These professionally trained instructors were responsible for much of the later commercial success of Korean martial arts around the world.

Various *kwan* (schools) of karate were opened in Korea after 1945. These called their art either kongsudô (empty-hand way), tangsudô (Chinese hands way), or kwonbop (fist method, kenpô in Japanese). Early leaders included Lee Won-Kuk, Ro Pyong-Chik, Choi Hong-Hi, Chun Sang-Sup, Yun Pyung-In, and Hwang Ki. Most of these schools taught Japanese forms up through the 1960s.

A few Koreans stayed in Japan to teach, including Yung Geka, Cho Hyung-Ju, and Choi Yong-I. Choi Yong-I became the most famous of these, and he is best known by his Japanese name, Masutatsu Oyama. Oyama was perhaps the most famous Japanese *Karateka* (karate practitioner) of the twentieth century. He founded Kyokushinkai Karate, sometimes known as Oyama Karate, and became famous for fighting bulls with his bare hands.

After the Chinese Revolution of 1949, many Chinese fled to Korea. The best known of these instructors taught Praying Mantis kung fu, *changquan* (long fist), and *baguazhang*. They tended to teach only Chinese students until the 1960s. Eventually, changquan became the most popular of these systems.

Hapkidô developed in the 1950s and 1960s from Japanese jûjutsu. Choi Yong-Shul (1904–1986) trained in *Daitô-ryû Aikijutsu* in Japan before 1945. Following the war, Choi returned to Korea and taught a system composed of joint locking, striking, and throwing techniques to various students in Taegu City. Choi used a variety of names for his art, including Yusul (yielding art), *Yukwonsul* ("soft fist art"), *Kidô* ("energy way"), and finally *Hapkidô* (coordinated energy way). Choi taught at a school run by Suh Bok-Sup, an experienced practitioner of yudô. Among his first young students were Ji Han-Jae and Kim Mu Hyun (also spelled Kim Moo Woong). Suh, Kim, and Ji all eventually moved to Seoul.

Ji Han-Jae was greatly responsible for the spread of Hapkidô, both through his own efforts and through the students whom he introduced to the art, including Han Bong-Soo, Choi Seo-Oh, Myung Kwang-Shik, and Myung Jae-nam. Choi Seo-Oh brought Hapkidô to the United States in 1964, and Bong-Soo Han popularized the art by providing the choreography for the Billy Jack movies in the 1970s. Myung Kwang-Shik founded the World Hapkidô Federation and introduced the use of forms into Hapkidô. Myung Jae-nam linked his style of Hapkidô with Japanese aikidô and formed the International Hapkidô Federation in 1983. Ji also supported the spread of Hapkidô in his role as bodyguard for President Park. Ji used his influence to have the Korean Presidential Security Forces train in Hapkidô beginning in 1962, a practice they maintained through the 1990s. Ji also convinced the Dae Woo company to hire Hapkidô black belts as security consultants. Ji himself formed the Korea Hapkidô Association.

After the beginning of the Korean War, the Republic of Korea (ROK) became ever more nationalistic. There was increasing pressure to develop a Korean form of karate, rather than continue to practice in the Japanese way. A series of national associations formed and disbanded as the Koreans argued over the shape of the new national art. The Korea Kongsudô Association was founded in 1951, followed by the Korean Tangsudô Association in 1953. These eventually merged to form the Subakdo Association in 1959. The Subakdô Association was opposed by the Korea Taekwondo Association (KTA), also founded in 1959. Hwang Ki was the head of the Subakdô Association, while General Choi Hong-Hi was the head of the KTA. General Choi had the most political power and the KTA quickly grew in power.

General Choi's efforts ran into difficulties following the 1961 military coup d'état in the ROK. The coup ousted the Second Republic and placed General Park Chung Hee in control of Korea. President Park quickly moved to remove his political rivals from power. He appointed General Choi, who had supported the coup, as ambassador to Malaysia in 1962, and for three years General Choi was removed from Korean politics. While he was gone, the KTA changed its name to the Korea Taesudo Association. The KTA also became an affiliate of the Korean Amateur Sports Association (KASA) in 1962 and a member of the Korean Athletic Association in 1964. Many black belts joined the KTA after the government began to support the establishment of national standards. Hwang Ki of the Subakdo Association was the most obvious opponent of growing KTA consolidation, and the KTA often harassed Hwang and his supporters.

During his time in Malaysia, General Choi developed a new set of purely Korean forms to replace the Japanese forms still taught in taekwondo. Upon his return to Korea in 1965, he again took control of the

KTA and changed the name back to the Korea Taekwondo Association. In 1966, KASA began the development of a training center for international competition, hoping to emulate the success of the Tokyo Olympics of 1964. General Choi founded the International Taekwondo Federation (ITF) in 1966 with an eye to supporting the spread of taekwondo around the world.

Taekwondo continued to gain in importance in Korea in the 1970s. Construction of the Kukkiwon, the Seoul headquarters of taekwondo, began on November 19, 1971, and the building was inaugurated on November 30, 1972. On February 14, 1972, taekwondo became a part of the official curriculum of Korea's primary schools. It entered the middle school curricula on August 31 and on December 5, the National High School and Middle School Taekwondo Federation was established, followed by the National Collegiate Taekwondo Federation on December 28, 1972.

In 1971, due to increasing tension with President Park, General Choi began to make secret plans to leave Korea and move the ITF to Canada. The KTA did not want the headquarters of taekwondo to move outside of the ROK and severed ties with the ITF, forming a new international organization, the World Taekwondo Federation (WTF). Ironically, both General Choi and his old rival Hwang Ki left the Republic of Korea in 1974. Choi went to Canada to spread taekwondo, while Hwang went to the United States where he continued to teach tangsudô.

The WTF was officially founded during the first World Taekwondo Championships held at the Kukkiwon in 1973. The WTF continued to support international competition in taekwondo. In 1988, taekwondo became a demonstration sport at the Seoul Olympics, and in 2000, taekwondo became an official Olympic sport.

Choi Hong-Hi began teaching taekwondo in North Korea in the 1980s, and the ROK National Intelligence Service has therefore declared that the ITF "is nothing but an unauthorized organization" and that "it is a private organization operated under Northern support rather than a genuine sports organization and has been utilized as a means of expanding Northern influence overseas." The dispute between the ITF and WTF remains unresolved.

Dakin R. Burdick

See also Korean Martial Arts, Chinese Influences on; Swordsmanship, Korean/Hankuk Haedong Kumdô; T'aek'kyŏn; Taekwondo
References
Burdick, Dakin. 1997. "People and Events of Taekwondo's Formative Years." *Journal of Asian Martial Arts* 6, no. 1: 30–49.
Choi Hong Hi. 1965. *Taekwon-Do: The Art of Self-Defence.* Seoul: Daeha Publication Company.
———. 1993. *Taekwon-Do: The Korean Art of Self-Defence.* Mississauga, Ontario: International Taekwon-Do Federation. 15 vol.

Choi Hong Hi, and He-Young Kimm. 2000. "General Choi Hong Hi: A Tae kwon-Do History Lesson." *Taekwondo Times* 20, no. 1: 44–58.

Frankovich, Robert. 1995. *Tradition and Practice of Tae Kwon Do Song Moo Kwan (Including History, Techniques and Poomse)*. Minneapolis, MN: Robert Frankovich.

Henning, Stanley E. 1981. "The Chinese Martial Arts in Historical Perspective." *Military Affairs* 45 (December): 173–178.

Hwang Kee. 1995. *The History of Moo Duk Kwan*. Springfield, NJ: U.S. Soo Bahk Do Moo Duk Kwan Federation, Inc.

———. 1978. *Tang Soo Dô (Soo Bahk Dô)*. Seoul: Sung Moon Sa.

Son Duk Sung, and Robert J. Clark. 1983. *Black Belt Korean Karate*. Englewood Cliffs, NJ: Prentice-Hall.

Young, Robert. 1993. "The History and Development of Tae Kyon." *Journal of Asian Martial Arts* 2, no. 2: 44–69.

———. 1991. *Korean Martial Arts Resource Newsletter*. 4 issues.

Korean Martial Arts, Chinese Influences on

The earliest archaeological evidence of Korean martial arts practices can be seen in a tomb in northeast China, an area under the Koguryo Kingdom (37 B.C.–A.D. 668), but colonized and under Chinese military control between 108 B.C. and A.D. 313. The wall murals at this site include one scene that depicts wrestling (*juedi* in Chinese and *kakjo* in Korean), and another with two men rushing at each other, which has been interpreted by some as depicting boxing (*shoubo* in Chinese and *subak* in Korean). Whether or not the latter scene actually depicts boxing as opposed to wrestling remains a matter of conjecture. In any case, the Chinese and other peoples bordering China all appear to have practiced wrestling.

The *Former Han History* (completed in A.D. 83), covering the period 206 B.C.–A.D. 24, reveals that, during this time, Chinese martial arts had already developed to a relatively high degree of sophistication, with a clear distinction made between wrestling and boxing practices. Although there are no adequate Korean references to the martial arts prior to the *Koryo History* (completed in 1451, and covering the period 918–1392), its citations provide evidence that the Koreans maintained a strict distinction between wrestling and boxing in the military, similar to the Chinese pattern, which they may have emulated as far back as the Koguryo period. This practice was continued at least into the fifteenth century, as confirmed in the *Veritable Records of the Yi Dynasty*.

During the end of the eighteenth century, King Jongjo displayed an interest in military affairs and commissioned a book on martial skills, which was completed by Yi Dok-Mu in 1790 under the title *Encyclopedia of Illustrated Martial Arts Manuals*. Yi Dok-Mu's *Encyclopedia* offers a fairly comprehensive view of traditional Korean and Chinese martial arts practices up to that time. It draws on research from numerous Chinese sources, including Ming general Qi Jiguang's (1528–1587) *New Book of Effective Discipline* (ca. 1561), together with contemporary Korean practices, and includes illustrated routines, on foot and from horseback, for broadsword (a cross between cutlass and saber), flail, and a variety of poled weapons such as spear, trident, crescent halberd, and others. The chapter on boxing (*quanfa* in Chinese, *kwonbop* in Korean, *kenpô* in Japanese) is taken primarily from General Qi Jiguang's manual. Some Korean sources refer to this chapter as illustrating subak practice. It is possible that a combination of Chinese boxing and seizing techniques similar to those shown in Qi's manual influenced *t'aek'kyŏn,* a nineteenth-century Korean sport described as employing "flying foot" and grappling techniques.

Although the references to traditional Korean martial arts are scattered and there are large gaps in information for some periods, it is still possible to piece together a broad outline, which generally reflects Chinese influence. The Koreans appear to have modeled their military martial arts system on that prevailing as early as the Chinese Han period (206 B.C.–A.D. 220) and to have retained the term *subak,* originally associated with that period, through the fifteenth century, long after the Chinese terminology had changed. The term for wrestling changed from *kakjo* to *kakryuk* (*jueli* in Chinese and *ssirŭm* in colloquial Korean) during the Yi period.

Modern Korean *taekwondo* appears to be based mainly on Japanese karate, which was, itself, based primarily on Chinese boxing modified in Okinawa and introduced to the Japanese martial arts community in the 1920s.

Stanley E. Henning

See also Hapkidô; Korea; T'aek'kyŏn; Taekwondo
References
Burdick, Dakin. 1997. "People & Events in Taekwondo's Formative Years." *Journal of Asian Martial Arts* 6, no. 1: 30–49.
Capener, Steven D. 1995. "Problems in the Identity and Philosophy of T'aegwondo and Their Historical Causes." *Korea Journal* (Winter): 80–94.
Chonui Samguk Sagi (Complete Translation of the History of the Three Kingdoms). 1963. Edited by Shin Sa-Guk, translated by Kim Chong-Kwon. Seoul: Sonjin Munhwasa, 8.
Henning, Stanley E. 2000. "Traditional Korean Martial Arts." *Journal of Asian Martial Arts* 9, no. 1: 8–15.
Il Yon. 1995. *Samguk Yusa* (Memorabilia of the Three Kingdoms). 2d ed. Translated by Kim Pong-Du. Seoul: Gyumunsa.
Kim, Un-Yong. 1978. *Taekwondo.* Seoul: Korean Overseas Information Service.
Ministry of Foreign Affairs, Republic of Korea. 1956. *Korean Arts.* Vol. 1, *Painting and Sculpture.* Seoul, 194–195.
Mizuno Masakuni. 1972. *Kokuri Heikiga Kofun to Kikajin* (Koguryo Ancient Tomb Wall Murals and Naturalized Persons). Tokyo: Yuzan Kaku.

No Sa-Sin. 1481 (Tangi Year 4291). *Sinchong Dongguk Yeji Songnam*
(New Expanded Dongguk Gazetteer). Seoul: Dongguk Munhaksa.

No Sun-Song. 1974. *Hanguk Cheyuksa Yongu* (Korean Physical Culture
History Research). Seoul: Munsonsa.

Yasiya Munhaksa. 1972. *Koryo Sa* (Koryo History). Seoul: Yasiya Munhaksa.

Yi Dok-Mu. 1970 [1790]. *Muye Dobo Tongji* (Encyclopedia of Illustrated
Martial Arts Manuals). Seoul: Hakmungak.

Yi Hyon-Gun. 1955. Tangi Year 4287. *Hwarangdô Yongu*. Seoul:
Munhwasa, 15.

Yi Sok-Ho. 1991. *Chosŏn Sesigi* (Korean Annual Customs). Seoul:
Dongmunson, 99, 225.

Yijo Sillok. (Veritable Records of the Yi Dynasty). 1953. Tokyo.

Yijo Sillok Pullyujip (Classified Index of the Veritable Records of the Yi
Dynasty). 1961. Seoul: Gwahakwon.

Koryû Bugei, Japanese

The *koryû bugei* are the classical styles or systems through which the samurai acquired their military skills, as well as many of their key values and convictions. They are distinguished from the better-known and more widely practiced modern cognate arts of Japan, such as kendô and jûdô, by their origins, organizational structures, and senses of purpose.

To be classified as a koryû, a school must be able to trace its origins to at least the early nineteenth century. Most are in fact considerably older than this, and the traditional histories of some profess roots in the twelfth, tenth, or even the seventh century—although scholars generally view such claims as hyperbole.

Military training in Japan dates back to before the dawn of recorded history, and organized drill can be documented by the early eighth century, but the solidification of martial art into systems, or *ryûha*, was a development of the mid to late medieval period, a part of a broad trend toward the systemization of knowledge and teaching in various pursuits. In the late fourteenth and fifteenth centuries, virtuosos of poetry, the tea ceremony, flower arranging, music, Nô drama, and the like began to think of their approaches to their arts as packages of information that could be transmitted to students in organized patterns, and began to certify their students' mastery of the teachings by issuing written documents. Thus, samurai began to seek out warriors with reputations as expert fighters and appeal to them for instruction, even as such masters of combat began to codify their knowledge and experience and to methodize its study. During the Tokugawa period (1600–1868), bugei training became increasingly formalized and businesslike, with adepts opening commercial training halls and instructing students for fees, turning the teaching of martial art into a full-time profession.

The opening to the West and rapid modernization of Japan in the late nineteenth century brought dramatic changes to the role and status of the koryû by virtually ending perceptions of practical military value in the arts of sword, spear, bow, glaive, and grappling. Participation in the classical bugei flagged rapidly as the new Meiji government closed many urban martial art academies and encouraged instead the development of a new military system based on European models. When public and government interest in traditional martial arts began to revive, from the 1890s onward, it was directed not to the koryû, but to new, synthesized forms of fencing and grappling promulgated as means of physical and moral education for the general public. By the 1930s, the study of these modern cognate arts had become compulsory in Japanese middle schools, where the emphasis was on developing aggression, speed, and a self-sacrificing "martial spirit" appropriate to the imperial armed forces. Consequently, the martial arts became closely identified with militarism, "feudalism," and the war effort, resulting, under the postwar Allied Occupation, in a ban on most forms of bugei training that lasted until 1952, when the Ministry of Education permitted the reintroduction of fencing to high schools, provided that it be taught as physical education and not as a martial art.

A great many koryû died out during the Meiji transformation or the upheavals of the postwar era. Nevertheless, many survived and several dozen thrive today. A few are even practiced overseas.

While modern enthusiasts tend to view the koryû as corporate entities existing across time, this perception is anachronistic. Until the very end of the medieval period, most ryûha had no institutional structure at all, and those that did derived it from familial or territorially based relationships between teachers and students. Medieval bugei masters often traveled about, instructing students as and where they found them. Some students followed their teachers from place to place; others trained under them for short periods while the teacher was in the area. In either case, during this era a ryûha had little practical existence beyond the man who taught it.

Bugei ryûha can often be clearly identified only in retrospect. Teacher-student relationships can be traced backward through time to establish the continuity of lineages, but few martial art adepts prior to modern times belonged exclusively to a single lineage, and few had only a single successor. Unlike many schools of tea ceremony, flower arranging, calligraphy, and other traditional Japanese arts, in the premodern era most bugei ryûha did not develop articulated organizational structures whereby senior disciples were licensed to open branch schools that remained under the authority of the ryûha headmaster. Instead, martial art teachers tended to practice total transmission, in which all students certified as having mastered the school's arts were given complete possession of them—effectively graduated from the school with full rights to propagate or modify what they had been taught as they saw fit. Such students normally left their masters to open their own schools, teaching on their own authority; instructors retained no residual control over former students or students of students. It was common practice for such graduates to blend what they had learned with personal insights and/or with techniques and ideas gleaned from other teachers. Often, the former students changed the name of the style, in effect founding new ryûha in each generation. Consequently, lines of descent from famous warriors tend to fork and branch again and again, over time giving rise to many hundreds of ryûha.

During the Tokugawa period, the procedures surrounding martial art instruction and the master-disciple bond became much more formal and cabalistic, and the koryû assumed the shapes they have retained into modern times. One of the first steps toward institutionalization of martial art koryû was the issuing of diplomas and licenses to students. This practice began in the sixteenth century with certificates given to acknowledge "graduation" from an instructor's tutelage. The vocabulary used on and for these certificates varied from teacher to teacher, but the most common term for this level of achievement was *menkyo-kaiden*. *Kaiden*, which means "complete transmission," indicated that the student had learned all that the teacher had to offer. *Menkyo* means "license" or "permission," and signified authorization to use the name of the teacher's style in dealings with persons outside the school—such as in duels or when seeking employment.

Medieval bugei instructors seldom formally differentiated students by level prior to graduation; there was little need for such distinctions, inasmuch as the period of tutelage was usually brief—sometimes only a few months. But during the Tokugawa period, as instruction became more professionalized and more commercialized, apprenticeships became longer. Thus, more elaborate systems of intermediate ranks were introduced, providing students with tangible measures of their progress.

Today, a few koryû have adopted the standardized *dan-kyû* system of ranks and grades introduced by jûdô pioneer Kanô Jigorô in the late nineteenth century and embraced by most modern cognate martial arts. Prior to Kanô's innovation, however, each ryûha maintained its own system of ranks and its own terminology for them, and most koryû continue to use these systems today. This situation makes it difficult to compare the levels of students from different ryûha, inasmuch as even terms used in common sometimes represent completely different levels of achievement from school to school. Similarly, there is no simple formula for calculating equivalencies between koryû ranks and those of the dan-kyû system, which many koryû view as being based on fundamentally different premises from those of their own systems. Ranks within the koryû tend to certify not skills mastered or status achieved so much as initiation into new and deeper levels of training. Promotion in "rank," therefore, signifies the granting of permission for the student to move on to the next level of training. The principal criteria for promotion are aptitude (including, but not limited to, skills and knowledge mastered) and moral fitness to be allowed to share in the teachings of the school at a higher and deeper level, and to be trusted with more of its secrets.

Koryû, in fact, tend to be far smaller, more closed, and more private organizations than those associated with the modern cognate martial arts. The membership of most numbers in the dozens or less. Many are, or were until a generation or two ago, restricted family traditions. Most are taught in only a single location, under the direct supervision of the headmaster and/or instructors (*shihan*) operating under him or her.

Traditionally, koryû teachers have been extremely careful about admitting students to instruction and have usually demanded long commitments and considerable control over students' behavior during their terms of apprenticeship. Many still follow elaborate procedures for screening new students, requiring letters of recommendation and even investigations into the backgrounds of applicants. Those who pass such screenings are initiated into their ryûha as though into a brotherhood or secret society. Some koryû hold entrance ceremonies ranging from the very simple to the very ornate. Most collect initiation gifts and fees. And nearly all require students to sign written pledges, or kishômon, in which they promise to abide by the school's rules and keep its secrets. In the past—and sometimes even today—these pledges were often sealed with the students' own blood, pressed onto the paper next to their signatures or ciphers.

What most definitively distinguishes koryû bugei from modern cognate martial arts, however, is not the age or the organizational structure of the schools, but the holistic and cabalistic manner in which they view the educational process. The essence of the koryû bugei experience is one of socialization to the ryûha, the complete subordination of the individual to the system—a course that promises that those who stay with it long enough will emerge, paradoxically, with a more fully developed sense of individualism. This idea derives from basic Confucian principles of education that predate their application to bugei training in Japan by centuries. The process centers on wholehearted devotion to the mastery of detail.

The koryû bugei are extraordinarily complex arts. At their most fundamental levels as methodologies of combat and war, they are largely collections of particulars, expressed in dozens of individual techniques and strategies, described in a profoundly unsystematized, sometimes opaque, and often overlapping argot of terms. Much of this apparent chaos is intentional, for—at least until modern times—martial art schools, as competitive organizations training warriors for deadly combat, deliberately sought to keep outsiders from grasping what they taught.

And yet each ryûha does have an essence, a conceptual core around which the details of the school's arts revolve. This core becomes increasingly perceptible to initiates as they advance in their studies, particularly as they turn their attentions beyond the initiatory functions of the bugei as arts of war to their deeper purpose as arts of peace and self-realization. To adepts who have entered this realm, each one of their school's terms and concepts reveals multiple levels of meaning—mechanical, psychological, moral, and so forth—understood not as sequential steps, but as interpenetrating spheres of activity. As the koryû conceptualize it, the value and the benefits imparted by the practice of the bugei lie in the combination of all the various elements involved. Koryû see this combination as having a special meaning and existence over and above the sum of the parts. Thus koryû bugei is a means to broad personal development that exists only in whole form: Studying a koryû necessarily involves a willingness to embrace the whole package in a particularly defined way.

The arcane nature of the arts themselves, the lack of competitions and other sportive applications, the cabalistic atmosphere surrounding admission and the educational process, and the length and seriousness of the commitments expected from initiates limit the appeal of classical martial art for modern audiences in, as well as outside of, Japan. Moreover, the aversion of most headmasters to licensing branch instructors and academies severely restricts opportunities for training for those who might otherwise be attracted. Thus koryû bugei are, and will likely continue to be, a rather small part of the Japanese martial art world. Nonetheless, the koryû are, historically and conceptually, the core of this world, and remain a vital—and quintessential—part of it today.

Karl Friday

See also Budô, Bujutsu, and Bugei; Form/Xing/Kata/Pattern Practice; Japan; Samurai; Swordsmanship, Japanese

References

Draeger, Donn F. 1973. *The Martial Arts and Ways of Japan*. Vol. 1, *Classical Bujutsu*. New York: Weatherhill.

———. 1973. *The Martial Arts and Ways of Japan*. Vol. 2, *Classical Budô*. New York: Weatherhill.

Friday, Karl. 1997. *Legacies of the Sword: The Kashima-Shinryû and Samurai Martial Culture*. Honolulu: University of Hawai'i Press.

Hurst, G. Cameron, III. 1998. *The Armed Martial Arts of Japan: Swordsmanship and Archery*. New Haven: Yale University Press.

Skoss, Diane, ed. 1995. *Koryû Bujutsu: Classical Warrior Traditions of Japan*. Berkeley Heights, NJ: Koryû Books.

———. 1998. *Sword and Spirit: Classical Warrior Traditions of Japan*. Berkeley Heights, NJ: Koryû Books.

Krav Maga

Krav maga (Hebrew; contact combat) is an Israeli martial art that was developed in the 1940s for use by the Israeli military and intelligence services. The creator of the system was Imi Lichtenfeld, an immigrant to Israel from Bratislava, Slovak (formerly Czechoslovakia). Today it is the official fighting art of the Israeli Defense Forces (IDF) and has gained popularity worldwide as an effective and devastating fighting method. It is a fighting art exclusively; sport variants do not exist. Krav maga has earned high marks from police forces and elite military units worldwide as a practical martial art that is easy to learn. Although a fairly recently developed martial art, its growth has been impressive and shows no sign of abating.

Imi Lichtenfeld was born in Budapest in the Austro-Hungarian Empire in 1910. The family later moved to Bratislava. His father, Samuel, had been a circus performer and taught Imi wrestling, physical fitness, and various martial art techniques he had learned from his years of travels. Samuel Lichtenfeld was also a chief inspector and self-defense instructor for the Bratislava police department. Imi developed into an athlete and won several wrestling, boxing, and gymnastics competitions throughout his youth.

In the 1930s, the political situation for Jews in Czechoslovakia began to turn grim. Germany had become a Nazi state characterized by rabid anti-Semitism as its ideological base. This anti-Semitism exploded onto the streets of Bratislava. Nazi sympathizers created gangs and political parties who began to harass and physically assault Jews on the streets. Imi often found himself in the middle of fights, and because of his background, gave self-defense lessons to fellow Jews.

Lichtenfeld soon found that there was a vast difference between the sport combat systems he had studied and actual street fighting. The Nazi and fascist gang members had no qualms about using knives and rocks as weapons or attacking the vital points of the human body, none of which was allowed in sporting events. Fortunately, Lichtenfeld was quick to adapt his knowledge to the new realities in order to defend himself successfully. These experiences, however, fixed in his mind the necessity of developing an actual combat system as opposed to relying for defense on sport fighting constrained by rules.

Imi left Bratislava and immigrated to Palestine (later Israel) in 1942. Palestine was at that time assigned by the League of Nations as a mandate to Great Britain. Immigration by Jews to Palestine was severely restricted, despite the Nazi death camps that were being used to kill European Jews. In addition, Jewish residents of Palestine were under attacks constantly from the Arabs in the region. To combat these attacks, the Jewish residents had formed the Hagana, the forerunner of the IDF. The Hagana's purpose was to bring as many Jews as possible through the British blockade and to fight back Arab assaults.

Lichtenfeld joined the Hagana soon after his arrival and became a self-defense instructor for Hagana soldiers and special operations units. Weapons were scarce at this time for Jews, so hand-to-hand combat was a vital necessity. From his arrival until 1948, Lichtenfeld constantly worked on the theories and curriculum of what he eventually labeled krav maga. He developed his system according to three criteria: It had to be effective, it had to be simple enough to be learned by anyone with any type of body shape and size, and it had to be learned quickly.

In 1947, Israel was declared an independent nation by the United Nations, a decision that quickly led to war between Israel and its surrounding Arab neighbors. Despite overwhelming odds, the Israelis won the conflict and established the independent State of Israel as a homeland for Jews.

World War II had left devastating psychological and physical scars on Jews. The Nazis had killed six million, one-third of the total number of Jews worldwide. Many of the survivors fled to Israel. The "lesson" of the Holocaust, as the destruction of European Jews came to be known, imprinted on Israelis the realization that the survival of Israel would depend on Jews alone. Even after the victory of 1948, Israel would have to remain in a state of high alert because of the hostility of its Arab neighbors. This readiness is reflected in the intensely combative nature of krav maga.

By the time the IDF was fully organized, Lichtenfeld had prepared the curriculum of krav maga. All Israeli soldiers were given basic training in the system. Israeli special operatives received advanced training. Often Israeli Mossad (Secret Service) agents were sent into regions where carrying a weapon was not practical. Krav maga was the only "weapon" that these operatives could use. In 1961, several of the Mossad agents who captured the infamous Nazi leader Adolph Eichmann in Argentina were krav maga experts.

Krav maga is, therefore, one of the most modern martial arts, and it is also one of the few that was developed directly for battlefield and urban combat. The constant state of warfare and terrorist attacks that have become a part of Israeli life have meant that any system of self-defense would have to be effective and realistic. Due to these extreme circumstances, Lichtenfeld had, in effect, a laboratory for the development of the art. Soldiers and practitioners in combat conditions who were forced to use the art for self-defense could report back to Lichtenfeld which techniques were effective. Lichtenfeld consequently modified techniques based on these actual experiences. As a result, krav maga is a proven warfare combat system.

Although the system was originally intended for the military, by the early 1960s Lichtenfeld was teaching krav maga to civilians. Because of in-

Krav Maga practitioners are taught to deal with attacks quickly and effectively, as the series of photographs on this and the following pages shows. (Courtesy of Gene Tausk)

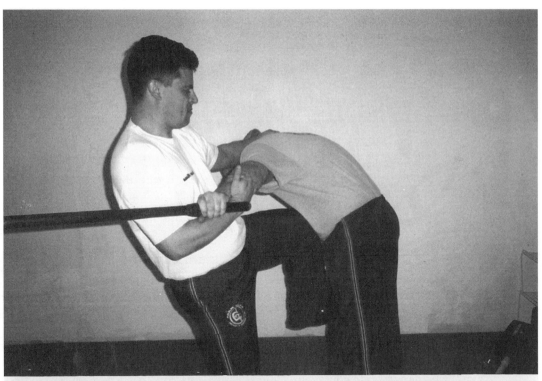

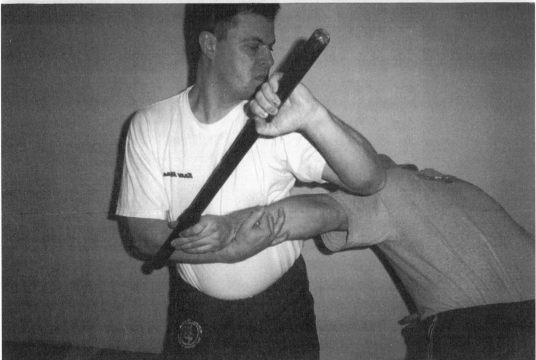

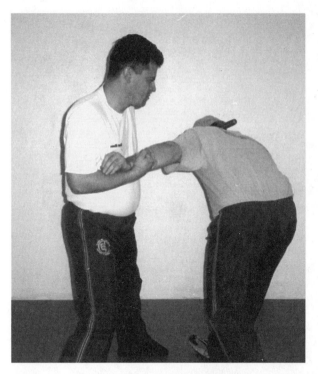

terest from the general public, after retiring from the IDF, Lichtenfeld began to modify the art for civilian use. In 1978, the International Krav Maga Federation was founded to teach the art worldwide. Its headquarters are located in Netanya, Israel. Branches of the main school can be found all over Israel, and at the present time the art is being taught worldwide. It is most popular in Israel, Finland, Sweden, Brazil, the United States, and France. Although Imi Lichtenfeld died in 1998, the success and popularity of krav maga continues.

Krav maga is divided into two main systems. The first, Self-Defense Krav Maga, is a standardized basic course of self-defense that can be learned in as little as twenty hours' time. It teaches students how to defend themselves effectively against the most common attacks. Practitioners also learn to strike the weak points of the human body, to use basic holds and throws, and to recognize the danger signs of an attack.

The second system, Combat Krav Maga, is a combat martial art. It is mastered over a period of time, like other martial arts, and practitioners are graded according to a belt system. Belts begin with white (beginner) and proceed to black for advanced students. Combat Krav Maga practitioners are taught all phases of combat, including kicks, punches, throws and takedowns, grappling techniques, and weapons use.

Krav maga differs from most Asian martial arts in three respects. First, there are no kata or forms that practitioners must learn. Kata (Japanese; form, forms) are prearranged patterns of movement that teach practitioners the correct way to move and punch, block, kick, or execute a throw. Krav maga techniques are designed to be instinctive rather than learned. Second, krav maga has no ritual or ceremony attached to it. In Asian martial arts, a fighting match usually opens with a bow. By contrast, krav maga practitioners are expected to move directly into combat, with the assumption that the opponent is trying to kill the practitioner; no opening ceremonies are expected or practiced. Third, krav maga immediately attempts to psychologically prepare the practitioner for fighting. This training is intended to develop the fight-or-flight response that is innate in humans into either correctly fighting or seizing an opportunity to escape. Often, when a combat situation is initiated, an untrained individual will be powerless for a few seconds while the psyche attempts to adjust to the situation. These few seconds can be enough to give an opponent time to kill or injure. Krav maga practitioners are taught to overcome this initial hesitation with action, whether it is action to fight or to escape.

The krav maga curriculum begins with learning to be aware of possible danger situations. Practitioners also are taught that it is important to be able to size up a situation before entering into peril. This part of the training reflects Lichtenfeld's initial experiences with fascist gangs in Europe and also addresses the contemporary situation in Israel, where sudden terrorist attacks are a constant threat. At this beginning stage, students are also taught the basics of human anatomy (specifically weak points of the human body), how to fall from various positions and land safely, how to make a fist and punch, and the basics of boxing.

As students progress, they are taught advanced boxing techniques and other empty-hand strikes, kicking techniques, and defenses against punches and kicks. Students are then taught how to break free of choke holds, neck locks, and holds against the legs, waist, and chest. Later, students are introduced to higher-level concepts of fighting, including more kicks, throws, and takedowns (attempts to destabilize the balance of an opponent and force him to the ground). At the highest levels of training, students are taught to recognize the threats that involve being attacked with a knife, gun, or even a submachine gun, and disarming techniques against these weapons. Krav maga practitioners are also expected to continue development of their sense of danger awareness.

At higher levels, students also can learn techniques that can aid in various professions. For example, there are techniques that are designed for police and other law enforcement officers, to help these professionals in subduing opponents without seriously injuring the opponent. Advanced techniques also exist for bodyguards and special operations soldiers.

Krav maga techniques are designed to be simple and direct. There are no high kicks used in the art; kicks are directed at waist level or below. Knee strikes, especially against the groin and inner thigh area, are especially used. Practitioners also use kicks against the legs, similar to those used in *Muay Thai* (Thai kickboxing), to unbalance an opponent. Punches are based on boxing moves and are intended for vital points or to place the mass of the body behind a blow to gain punching power. Open-hand techniques to the eyes, ears, throat, and solar plexus are used. Elbow techniques are used extensively. These techniques require little strength but have devastating results; an elbow strike to the face or floating ribs can easily disable an opponent.

Throwing techniques are not of the type usually seen in jûdô or *sambo* (a modern Russian martial art); they have more in common with freestyle wrestling takedowns. The purpose is not to gain points, as in a sporting match, but to get the attacker in a weak position as quickly as possible. Practitioners are taught to restrain attackers through arm bars, which attempt to hyperextend the elbow joint unless the attacker submits, or by twisting the wrist joint until the attacker is in pain. At advanced levels, choke holds, which attempt to cut off the supply of air or blood to the brain, are taught. Choke holds are powerful techniques that enable a smaller person to endanger a larger one.

Krav maga is also unique in that students are taught to take advantage of material objects that may be at hand for aiding in a self-defense situation. One of the theories behind krav maga is that ordinary objects can be turned into weapons, if only for a few seconds, to provide a critical advantage to the person being attacked. Women who carry purses are taught to initially throw them at an attacker to off-balance him and provide a few additional seconds to escape or attack. Objects such as ordinary writing pens can be turned into weapons, and practitioners are taught how to use them as such.

In addition to the martial benefits of studying krav maga, students are introduced to an effective form of exercise. A krav maga workout exercises the body in every way, from intense stretching to aerobic and anaerobic conditioning. Even though the art can be studied by people of all ages, the serious participant will become more physically fit through the intense training that the art demands.

Krav maga is a martial art that is intended to be self-defense in its purest form. The art is not intended to change the individual to conform to the system, which is expected in many traditional Asian martial systems. Rather, the art conforms to the unique personality and body structure of the practitioner. Every human is physically different, and krav maga teachers realize this. The primary goal of practitioners is to become aware of how to defend themselves. This involves learning how to best use the situation to the advantage of the practitioner in accordance with the unique abilities of each individual. Krav maga is also expected to instill in its practitioners a sense of confidence, calmness, and mental readiness to respond to danger situations. The only criterion for inclusion in the art is usefulness to one's survival. Practitioners take the tools they are given through the art and adapt them to their own needs.

The effectiveness of the art can be seen in the growth of the demand for instructors. Krav maga is now the official martial art of many police departments and special operations units in the United States. In an ironic twist, it is also the martial art of choice for many special military units and antiterrorist teams in European countries, including France, Finland, Sweden, and Germany. The reasons cited for the popularity are the effectiveness of the art and the ease with which it can be learned by practitioners.

Krav maga has been called the "first unarmed combat system of the twentieth century." This is meant to convey the fact that it developed in this century with the understanding and awareness of modern combat. Firearms are the weapons of choice for twentieth-century warriors, and terrorism and sudden violence often define the battlefield of this century. Imi Lichtenfeld took this situation into account when he developed the art, and the current instructors use this understanding as the basis for further refinements of the system. Just as karate was developed for self-defense when weapons were banned for use by civilians on the island of Okinawa, and certain forms of jūjutsu were developed as auxiliary weapons when a Japanese warrior lost his weapons in battle, krav maga was developed as a way for modern warriors to defend themselves against the unpredictable nature of modern combat. It is not intended to reflect a cultural background or a way of life, but simply to be studied as a system of effective self-defense. In this respect, krav maga is also one of the most universally applicable martial systems. Although a recent arrival on the martial arts stage, krav maga has become a very popular style. As the demand rises for soldiers to fight in unconventional contexts, as well as for civilians to be able to cope with dangerous situations, the demand for krav maga will likely rise as well.

Gene Tausk

References

"Krav Maga: A New Twist on Street Fighting." 1998. *Let's Live,* November, 68.

Lichtenfeld, Imi, and Eyal Yanilov. 1998. *Krav Maga: Self Defense and Fighting Tactics.* Tel Aviv: Dekel.

Kung Fu/Gung Fu/Gongfu

Kung fu (often romanized as *gung fu* or *gongfu*) is a Cantonese phrase meaning, depending on context and the connotations an interpreter applies to the term, "hard work," "human effort," "exertion," or "skill"; especially in the context of the martial arts, *gong* carries the meaning of "inner power." In contemporary Western usage, *kung fu* has been used as a generic term for Chinese martial arts ranging from what have been labeled the "soft" or "internal" arts of *taijiquan* (tai chi ch'uan), *baguazhang* (*pa kua ch'uan*), and *xingyiquan* (*hsing i ch'uan*) to the so-called hard or external arts of Northern and Southern Shaolin. The term *kung fu* has been associated particularly with those martial systems that tradition claims are descended from the Shaolin Temple arts. In addition, the label *kung fu* tends to be more strongly associated, outside China at least, with the forms of Chinese martial arts that are presumed to emphasize striking over grappling techniques. According to some sources, the term originated as an admonition to practice diligently and was associated, in Hong Kong and Taiwan, with *wugong* (fighting skill).

David Carradine practicing the art of kung fu on a studio lot in Hollywood. (Hulton Archive)

The use and spread of the term *kung fu* have been attributed to the popularity of Hong Kong motion picture and television star Bruce Lee and the television series of the early 1970s, *Kung Fu,* starring David Carradine. *Kung fu* as a generic term for Chinese martial arts appeared at least three years before Lee's initial appearance on U.S. television in 1966, as the character "Kato" in *The Green Hornet* series, after the term was used by Ed Parker in his *Secrets of Chinese Karate.* In this volume, Parker gave what he called Chinese Karate the name *kung fu,* or *chuan* (pinyin *quan*; fist) *shu* (art). This latter phrase, despite a similarity of sound in its English rendering, is unrelated to the term *kung fu* and more closely connected with the term *quanfa* (*ch'uan' fa*), "fist way," which is fighting with the bare hand or empty hand. Another term for the Chinese martial arts, *Chinese boxing,* likely derives from translation of the term *quanfa.*

In the 1920s, the term adopted by the KMT (Kuomintang; pinyin Guomindang, or GMD), the National People's Party, for Chinese martial arts was *guoshu* (national art). With the establishment of the People's Republic of China in the 1950s, the Mandarin term *wushu* (war art/technique/method) was adopted for the fighting arts of China and has gained

Two young women demonstrate Chinese boxing (popularly known as kung fu) in a public square in San Francisco, February 9, 1979. (Hulton-Deutsch Collection/Corbis)

general acceptance, particularly in academic circles. Nevertheless, *kung fu* continues to be used in Hong Kong and other areas outside mainland China, as well as internationally in the popular media.

Thomas A. Green

See also Animal and Imitative Systems in Chinese Martial Arts; Boxing, Chinese; Boxing, Chinese Shaolin Styles

References

Amos, Daniel M. 1997. "A Hong Kong Southern Praying Mantis Cult." *Journal of the Asian Martial Arts* 6: 31–61.

Draeger, Donn, and Robert Smith. 1981. *Comprehensive Asian Fighting Arts.* Tokyo: Kodansha International.

Parker, Ed. 1963. *Secrets of Chinese Karate.* Englewood Cliffs, NJ: Prentice-Hall.

Reid, Howard, and Michael Croucher. 1983. *The Way of the Warrior.* Woodstock, NY: Overlook Press.

Smith, Robert. 1974. *Chinese Boxing: Masters and Methods.* Tokyo: Kodansha International.

Kwoon

See Training Area

Masters of Defence

European fighting experts from the Middle Ages and Renaissance who taught the use of contemporary weapons of military combat and civilian street-fighting skills along with unarmed defense methods were known as Masters of Defence. A multitude of martial art styles were practiced from the Greek peninsula to Spain, the British Isles, Germany, Scandinavia, Russia, the Baltics, and Turkey. Recognizing that armed fighting and unarmed fighting were only different facets of personal combat, Masters of Defence taught an integrated art. The manuals that many of these masters compiled describe sophisticated techniques for the use of swords, shields, spears, staffs, and daggers, as well as discussing unarmed skills.

In 1617, Sir Joseph Swetnam wrote, "Then he is not worthy to be called a Master of Defence, which cannot defend himself at all weapons . . . and therefore greatly wronged are they which will call such a one a Fencer, for the difference between a Master of Defence and a Fencer, is as much as between a Musician and a Fiddler, or betwixt a Merchant and a Peddler" (Swetnam 1617). In 1599, English master George Silver wrote, "A swordsman should not be so interested in the destruction of his opponent that he disregards his own defence. A Master of Defence is he who can take to the field and know that he shall not come to any harm" (Silver 1599). Moreover, martial artists of the period recognized the differences between true masters and mere theatrical performers or commercial stunt fighters, whom the Germans called *leichmeistere* (dance-masters) and *klopffechter* (clown-fighters).

From the 1200s through the 1600s, Masters of Defence produced over a hundred detailed, often well-illustrated, technical manuals on their fighting methods. These manuscripts, produced by hand in the 1300s and 1400s or printed and published in the 1500s and 1600s, are invaluable resources on all but lost Western martial arts. These works, produced by professionals who fought and killed in battles and duels, present a portrait of European fighting skills that were systematic and highly dynamic. These experts developed and taught a craft that had been learned through life-

and-death encounters and cultivated over generations in contexts ranging from brutal medieval battlefields to Renaissance civilian street fights. During the period from the mid-1300s to the early 1500s, the Germans and Italians were particularly industrious in teaching fighting arts as well as in producing books on their techniques.

Skilled martial experts were never unfamiliar in the West. The Greeks were known to have their professional *hoplomashi* (weapon instructors), and among the Romans, senior veteran soldiers trained their juniors in the handling of weapons for combat. The later Roman gladiator schools too had their *lanistae* (fight coaches). The Germanic tribes as well as the Celts and Vikings were known to have their most skillful veterans placed in charge of teaching youth the ways of war. The Vikings recognized a number of specific war skills preserved by special teachers. Much later, by an order of the Spanish royal court, special categories of fencing masters, *Tenientes Examinadores de la destreza de las armes* (roughly, "individual's weapon ability examining lieutenants"), were organized in 1478. King Alfonso el Sabio (the Wise) of Castille himself wrote a textbook on warfare in 1260, and in the 1400s Duarte, king of Portugal, produced a manual on fighting skills.

Not until the Middle Ages in Europe, however, did true experts in the martial arts begin to teach in ways we would associate with martial mastery. Throughout the medieval period, because of the obligations of the feudal system, training in arms was a requirement for both the nobility and the common folk who were pressed into military service. It is reasonable to assume that much of the martial knowledge the common warriors learned was individually passed down from person to person within households, clans, or families. These were not skills just for use in the local village or remote forest paths, but were intended for the battlefield complexities encountered with whole armies at war.

Yet more formal mechanisms existed as well, since, despite being poorly armed, the common folk always had need to protect themselves and, if called upon, to defend the kingdom from invasion. Of course, training for war and tournament was an everyday fact of life for knights. For the chivalric warrior class there was always the ideal of the preudome (man of prowess) skilled in military arts. Prowess in arms was itself one of the fundamental tenets of chivalry.

German and English histories indicate clearly that professional masters and teachers of swordsmanship and weaponry existed at least from the late twelfth or early thirteenth century. In France in the 1200s, there are references to royal privileges granted to a group of Paris masters. By the late Middle Ages, there were sword masters and fighting experts both teaching and fighting for pay, yet they themselves were typically commoners. Many of the instructors of various fencing guilds, especially in Italy

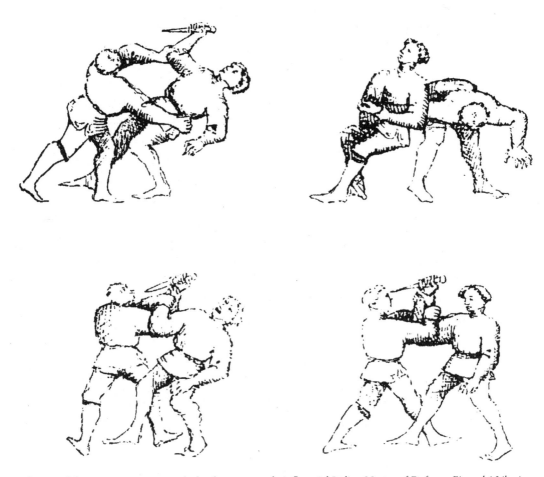

Defense and disarming moves as taught by the enormously influential Italian Master of Defence, Fiore dei Liberi. This illustration appeared in his Flos Duellatorium *(Flower of Battle), first published in 1410. (Courtesy of John Clements)*

and Germany, tutored the nobility in fighting. In Germany, there were long-lived *Fechtschulen* (fighting schools), a collection of guilds run by common citizens and soldiers. There were fighting guilds such as the Marxbrüder (Brotherhood of St. Mark), Luxbrueder (Company of St. Luke), and Federfechter, which specialized in many weapons, including two-handed swords and later rapiers. The English too had schools of defence that survived well into the Renaissance. They continued for some time, however, to teach the older medieval swords and weaponry. Also, there were clandestine teachers of arms and even traveling professional fighters who, for money, would act as stand-ins during trial by combat. In 1286, Edward II ordered fencing schools teaching *Eskirmer au Buckler* (Buckler Fighting) banned from the city of London—ostensibly to "control villainy" and "prevent criminal mischief" said to be associated with such activities. In 1310, one Master Roger, *Le Skirmisour* (The Fighter), was even charged with and found guilty of running a fencing school in London.

"Masters of fencing" are mentioned in Italy in the 1300s as offering advice and exercises for fighting. In the 1400s, there were well-established fencing academies in Milan, Venice, and Verona, and later Bologna; even earlier, a master swordsman by the name of Goffredo taught the youth of Civildale in 1259. There are also references in Italy during the 1400s to the "trial for status" of a master of *Ars Palistrinae* (Martial Arts). The Bolognese school in Italy existed since the early 1200s under instructors in the 1300s such as Master Rosolino, Master Francesco, and Master Nerio. In the 1400s, Master Filippo di Bartolomeo Dardi, an astrologer, mathematician, and professor at Bologna University, also kept a school there. An Italian fencing master from the late 1600s also stated that a "Corporation of Fencing Masters," headquartered in Madrid, existed in Spain from the Middle Ages. There are numerous references to *Esgrimidors* (fencing masters) in Portuguese civil documents from the late 1400s.

The people of the Germanic states were the most prolific writers among the European martial artists. German sword masters are first mentioned as early as 1259; Hans Liechtenauer (or Johannes Lichtenawer) is considered the grand *Fechtmeister* (fighting master) of the German schools of fighting and swordplay. A whole series of fencing manuals, or *Fechterbuecher* (fight books), are based on his work. One of the earliest was compiled in 1389 by Hanko Doebringer, a priest who at one time appears to have studied fighting under Liechtenauer. As was common practice at the time, it is written in rhymed verse. In order to conceal his teachings, he also utilized highly cryptic phrasing. Liechtenauer himself appears to have studied under several earlier unknown masters such as Lamprecht from Bohemia, Virgily from Krakow, and Liegnitzer in Silesia. His influential teachings, reflecting fighting methods developed over a century earlier, cover a variety of weapons from sword and shield to staff, plus a range of unarmed fighting techniques.

Other major German masters include Joerg Wilhalm, whose text of 1523 survives, as well as Hans Lebkommer, who in 1530 put his methods on paper in *Der Alten Fechter an fengliche Kunst* (The Original Art of the Ancient Fencers) and *Fechtmeister Kal* (Fight Master). Lebkommer's fechtbuch is actually the compilation of Christian Egenolph, and as with many of the others, it includes materials from earlier works such as those by Andre Pauerfeindts of 1516, and the student of Liechtenauer, Fechtmeister Sigmund Ringeck, of ca. 1440. Ringeck's material includes the use of the sword, the scimitar-like falchion, and other weapons. As with many later German masters, Ringeck interpreted Hans Liechtenauer's earlier verses and added them to his own method.

Hans Talhoffer is a more widely known major Master of Defence from the Middle Ages. His fechtbuch from 1443 was reprinted many times during the 1400s but now only exists in various editions from the sixteenth and seventeenth centuries. Talhoffer, likely a student of Liechtenauer, reveals an array of great-sword and two-handed sword techniques, sword and buckler moves, dagger fighting, seizures and disarms, grappling techniques, and the Austrian wrestling of Otto the Jew. His work also describes methods of fighting against pole-arms. Like the works of many other fechtmeisters, Talhoffer's manual includes fighting with swords both while unarmored and in full plate armor. Talhoffer also covers material relating to dueling, and, like other masters, he was concerned with the secrecy of his art.

There are more than a dozen other significant German masters whose works on fighting still survive. Many of their methods suggest influence from one another. Among the most notable are Paulus Kal, Master Peter von Danzig, Johannes Leckuechner, Peter Falkner, H. von Speyer, and Gregor Erhart.

In Italy, a particularly significant figure was the Italian Fiore dei Liberi, leading master of the Bolognese school of fighting, whose work remains a primary source for practice of the medieval Italian long-sword. Originally taught by German masters, dei Liberi studied swordsmanship for some fifty years. His illustrated text on fighting skills, the *Flos Duellatorum* (Latin; Flower of Battle) was first published in 1410. This pragmatic work was devoted primarily to the use of the long-sword and great-sword and offered a contrast to exclusively German systems. He covered assorted sword and staff weapons, dagger fighting, fighting in heavy armor, and mounted combat, as well as unarmed techniques. Dei Liberi's work influenced Italian masters, particularly during the later Renaissance.

Another important medieval Italian master was Fillipo Vadi of Padua. Little is known about Vadi except from his treatise on fighting, *De Arte Gladiatoria Dimicandi* (About the Gladiatorial Art of Fighting), written between 1480 and 1487. He was a master from the town of Pisa who served noblemen. His treatise is in two parts: One consists of text and the other mainly of illustrations. Vadi taught that fencing is a "science," not an art. His teaching offered a glimpse of the ethics of a master at the time and espoused the view that a master only needed to teach noblemen, since they have the role of protecting the weak. Like dei Liberi's, Vadi's text displays knowledge of a wide range of armed and unarmed fighting skills. The postures and guards he uses often have the same names as the guards of Fiore dei Liberi, but interestingly the positions and their names are not always identical to dei Liberi's. Obviously, many guard names circulated among various schools and masters with modifications in name and/or position.

From the fourteenth through the fifteenth centuries, medieval warfare underwent significant changes. The process of change intensified in the 1500s. The massed use of longbow and crossbow, the development of articulated plate armor, and the invention of weapons associated with fighting both in it and against it profoundly changed individual combat. Moreover, social and technological forces severely affected the conditions under which combat took place. As a result, throughout the Renaissance, Masters of Defence began to more systematically study and analyze fighting in an effort to raise the art of combat to a higher degree of sophistication and effectiveness. Crucial changes came about with the convergence of, among other factors, the discarding of heavy armor (primarily due to the advent of firearms), the reduced role of the individual warrior on the battlefield, and the rise of an armed urban middle class.

In this environment, Renaissance Masters of Defence began to teach fencing and fighting both publicly and privately. Specialized civilian fighting guilds and Schools of Defence began to thrive. Masters such as Joachim Meyer, Jeronimo de Carranza, Henry de Sainct Didier, D. L. P. de Narvaez, Salvator Fabris, Joachim Koppen, Francesco Alfieri, Jacob Sutor, and others became highly regarded experts. They approached their craft seriously, earnestly, and scientifically. Martial arts masters, who traveled and tutored widely, arose both from the gentry and the lower classes. Italian and Spanish instructors of the new rapier ultimately became the most admired. The intellectual climate of the Renaissance influenced their profession, in that geometry, mathematics, and philosophy played major roles in their styles.

The history of European arms and armor is one of established continuity marked by sudden developments of forced innovation. Renaissance sword blades were generally lighter than medieval ones, and the thrust was used to a far greater extent during the Renaissance. The fundamentals that early Renaissance masters built upon were not entirely of their own invention, however. They called upon a long-established foundation from medieval fighting methods. Like much of the progress in Renaissance learning and scientific advance, their art was based on principles that had been established for centuries.

The Bolognese master Achille Marozzo, one of the most significant masters of his day, was one of the first to focus on the use of the thrust over the cut. He produced two manuals on fence, *Opera Nova* (1536) and *Il Duello* (1550). His countryman, Camillo Agrippa, was another to focus on the thrust over the cut, and in 1553 produced one of the earliest rapier manuals, "His Treatise on the Science of Arms with a Philosophical Dialogue," which received wide acclaim after being translated into English. These masters, among others of their day, revealed methods that reflected the transition by early Renaissance martial artists to civilian cut-and-thrust swordsmanship and the emerging emphasis on urban self-defense.

By the late 1500s the vicious new slender civilian thrusting sword, the rapier, became the favored dueling weapon. In 1595 Master Vincentio Saviolo wrote "His Practice in Two Books," one of the first true rapier manuals, an influential treatise at the time, which retains its popularity. Saviolo was instrumental in bringing the art to England when he settled in London to teach his method. A fellow Italian master, Giacomo Di Grassi, had another major rapier manual, translated into English, under the title *His True Arte of Defence*, in 1594. Also, Salvator Fabris was a master from Bologna who in the late 1500s traveled in Germany, France, and Spain and synthesized the best of many other teachers. Their methods reflect important changes in the blades, techniques, and attitudes of Western Masters of Defence. Because firearms had rendered the traditional individual weapons of war less relevant on the battlefield, the focus of masters was now less on weapons of war and unarmed skills than on personal civilian dueling. Masters now became far less concerned with running schools for common warrior skills than with teaching the upper classes the newly popular art of defense. Of these later masters, Ridolfo Capo Ferro, author of *Gran Simulacro* (Great Representation/Description) of 1610, is considered the undisputed Italian grand master of the rapier and the father of modern fencing. He taught a linear style of fence and emphasized the superiority of the thrust over the cut in order to utilize the rapier's advantage of quick, deceptive reach.

Other notable Renaissance masters and their works include Vigianni's *Lo Schermo* (The Shield) of 1575, the Milanese master Lovino's *Traite d'Escrime* (Fencing Treatise) of 1580, Jacob Sutor's 1612 *Neues Kunstliches Fechtbuch* (New Artistic Fencing Book), and Nicoletto Giganti's 1606 *Scola overo Teatro* (School or Theater). There was also Sir William Hope, a military veteran who taught and between 1691 and 1714 wrote numerous books, including *The Scots Fencing-Master* (1687) and *The Complete Fencing-Master* (1692). Other contemporary works treat the use of the slender thrusting small-sword, sabers, cutlasses, spadroons, and assorted cavalry blades.

Germany produced important Renaissance masters, also. Paulus Mair, an official from the city of Augsburg, compiled three large manuals covering a great variety of swords and weaponry. Fechtmeister Joachim Meyer wrote his own teachings down in 1570, as did Jacob Sutor, who described his methods in 1612. In general, the Germans resisted adopting the rapier in favor of their traditional weaponry.

The English fighting guilds, like the German ones, resisted for some time the encroaching civilian system of the Hispano-Italian rapier in favor of their traditional militarily focused methods. During the 1500s, The Corporation of Maisters of the Noble Science of Defence, or the "London Company of Maisters," was an organized guild offering instruction in the traditional English forms of self-defense. Training was offered in the use of swords, staffs, pole-arms, and other weapons. It also included wrestling, pugilism, and grappling and disarming techniques. In keeping with the Renaissance spirit of the times, the English Masters of Defence rigorously studied their craft and openly plied their trade. Concentrated around London, the English guilds essentially followed in the centuries-old practices of the traditional medieval master-at-arms, but adapted these to the changed times.

Each public school or "Company" had special rules, regulations, and codes that were strictly upheld. No student could fight with another student or harm a master. No master could challenge another. No master could open a school within seven miles of another or without prior permission from an "Ancient Maister" (senior faculty). No student was to raise his weapon in anger or be a drunkard, a criminal, or a traitor. As well, no one could reveal the secret teachings of the school. Most of the rules were designed to preserve the school's status, prestige, and economic monopoly on the trade. Similar conditions existed in later eighteenth-century small-sword salons and among contemporary sport fencing halls.

The English fighting guilds, following the precedent of academic colleges of the age, developed a four-tiered hierarchy: scholar, free-scholar, provost, and master. Only four Ancient Maisters were allowed at any one school. New students were recruited, paid a tuition, and apprenticed. Fines and penalties were levied for violations of regulations and custom. Unlike his continental peers of the age, the essentially "blue-collar" English master-at-arms had to earn his title through rigorous public trial of his skill. The schools of defence held public tests of their students called Playing the Prize. When the time came to test their skill and advance to the next grade, students fought a series of test bouts with blunt weapons (usually with long-sword, backsword, staff, and sword and buckler) against a number of senior students.

Generally, the profession of private instructor of arms was denigrated in England, and early fencing schools acquired unsavory reputations as hangouts for ruffians and rogues. Nonetheless, prize playing was popular with the common folk. Although Henry VIII granted a charter to an English school of fencing in 1540, the guild's monopoly was not entirely official. By the end of the 1600s, Prize Playing declined, and the guilds faded or became mere sporting salons.

However, indigenous English fighting systems are described in various English manuals, such as the *Pallas Armata* (Latin; Pallas Athena Armed) of 1639, and those by gentleman masters such as Joseph Swetnam. Swetnam taught the use of the new rapier and dagger, along with the traditional English staff, backsword, long-sword, and short-sword. His teachings were presented in a fashion that allowed either military man or civilian gentleman to heed his advice. There is also the well-known grand master of the English tradition, George Silver (*Paradoxes of Defence,* 1598, and *Brief Instructions,* 1599). Silver and his brother, Toby, like many Masters of Defence of the time, also taught wrestling, grappling, disarms, dagger fighting, and the use of two-handed swords, staffs, and pole-arms. Silver taught four "governors," or key principles: judgment, distance, time, and place. He argued that the new methods of defense were inferior to the existing English art.

The Renaissance masters systematized the study of fighting skills, particularly swordsmanship, into sophisticated, versatile, and highly effective martial arts, which culminated in the development of the ultimate street-fighting and dueling weapon, the quick and deadly thrusting rapier. The innovations in Renaissance fighting methods did not happen in a vacuum; they resulted from the needs of urban encounters and private quarrels as opposed to strict battlefield conditions.

Moreover, links between the brutal, practical fighting methods of the Middle Ages and the more sophisticated, elegant Renaissance fencing systems are evident. The English, for example, followed some of their old fighting traditions well into the 1800s, as did the Germans and Spanish. They did not discard or ignore, but rather used, adapted, and, in some cases, refined methods that had persisted for centuries. Differences in the two periods lie in the overall attitude toward the study of the craft and the specific techniques developed (e.g., civilian dueling and self-defense as opposed to war, tournament, and trial by combat). Although there was considerable innovation in the European martial arts of the Renaissance, there should be no doubt that such innovations were built upon the legacy of the medieval arts.

The various Masters of Defence were not always clear or complete in their ideas. Moreover, masters sometimes contradict one another. Overall, however, their works describe well-reasoned, effective fighting arts built upon the legacy of arms and armor and skills of their ancestors.

European warrior skills were for the most part the indigenous fighting arts of a wide range of heterogeneous peoples and not specifically limited to a warrior class. The familiar principles of timing, distance, technique, and perception, defined in various ways, have been identified and stressed by experts in countless martial arts and were clearly recognized by Western Masters of Defence. Yet there is more to the European martial arts than sheer technique. Although there is an unmistakable pragmatism concerned with sheer effectiveness, this is always balanced by a strong and clear humanistic philosophy and respect for law and one's fellow man—the very qualities so often associated with the modern idealized practice of Asian martial arts.

While it is easy today to find hundreds of books on the techniques of Asian fighting arts, it remains far more difficult to obtain similar information regarding the European traditions. Even though practitioners of historical Western arts cannot rely on traditional oral transmission from one practitioner to another, detailed technical manuals have been preserved. In the classic Western approach to learning, modern practitioners can examine methods of the Masters of Defence from their own words and pictures.

The old schools of the Noble Science, as the martial art of fencing became known, relied on time-honored lessons of battlefield and street duel, but due to historical and social forces (e.g., introduction of firearms and industrialization) the traditional teachings of European masters fell out of common use. With each generation, fewer students arrived, and the old experts died off. As a fighting tradition in Europe, the Renaissance martial arts that had descended from those of medieval warriors became virtually extinct, and no direct lineage back to historical teachings or traditional instructors exists. Later centuries in Europe saw only limited and narrow application of swords and traditional arms, which survived to become martial sports. What survives today of the older teachings in the modern poised sport of fencing is only a shadow, which bears little resemblance to its Renaissance street-fighting predecessor and is far removed from its martial origins in the early Middle Ages. Although, unlike many Asian arts, no true schools survive, many enthusiasts are hard at work reconstructing European martial traditions. Through the efforts of modern practitioners studying the works of the masters and training with replica weapons, the heritage of the Masters of Defence is slowly being recovered.

John Clements

See also Chivalry; Europe; Knights; Swordsmanship, European Medieval; Swordsmanship, European Renaissance; Wrestling and Grappling: Europe

References

Anglo, Sydney. 1988. "How to Kill a Man at Your Ease: Chivalry in the Renaissance." *Antiquaries Journal* 67: 1–4.

———. 1989. "How to Win at Tournaments: The Techniques of Chivalric Combat." *Antiquaries Journal* 68: 248–264.

Aylward, J. D. 1956. *The English Master of Arms, from the Twelfth to the Twentieth Centuries*. London: Routledge and Kegan Paul.

Castle, Egerton. 1969. *Schools and Masters of Fence: From the Middle Ages to the Eighteenth Century*. 1885. Reprint, London: Arms and Armour Press.

Chronik alter Kampfkünst: Zeichnungen und Texte aus Schriften alter Meister, entsanden 1443–1674. 1997. Berlin: Weinmann.

Clements, John. 1998. *Medieval Swordsmanship: Illustrated Techniques and Methods*. Boulder, CO: Paladin Press.

———. 1997. *Renaissance Swordsmanship: The Illustrated Use of Rapiers and Cut and Thrust Swords*. Boulder, CO: Paladin Press.

di Grassi, Giacomo. 1594. *His True Arte of Defence*. London: I. G. Gentleman.

Galas, S. Matthew. 1997. "Kindred Spirits: The Art of Sword in Germany and Japan." *Journal of Asian Martial Arts* 6, no. 3: 20–47.

Hutton, Alfred. 1892. *Old Swordplay: The System of Fence in Vogue during the XVIth, XVIIth, and XVIIIth Centuries, with Lessons Arranged from the Works of Various Ancient Masters*. London: H. Grevel.

———. 1980. *The Sword and the Centuries: or, Old Sword Days and Old Sword Ways.* 1901. Reprint, Rutland, VT: Charles E. Tuttle.

Meyer, Joachim. 1570. *Grundliche Beschreibung der Freyaen, Ritterlichen und Adelichen Kunst des Fechten.* Strasbourg.

Rapisardi, Giovanni. 1998 [1410]. *Fiore de' Liberi Flos Duellatorum: In armis, sine armis, equester et pedester.* Padua, Italy: Gladitoria.

Silver, George. 1599. *Paradoxes of Defence.* London: Edward Blount.

Swetnam, Joseph. 1617. *The Schoole of the Noble and Worthy Science of Defence.* London.

Turner, Craig, and Tony Soper. 1990. *Methods and Practice of Elizabethan Swordplay.* Carbondale: Southern Illinois University Press.

Medicine, Traditional Chinese

Editorial note: Bracketed number codes in this entry refer to the list of ideograms that follows.

Most scholars agree that the origin of Chinese civilization occurred in the Yellow River Valley of central China over 5,000 years ago. Stone antecedents to modern metal acupuncture needles have been dated to as much as 20,000 years old. In modern times, vestiges of Chinese culture persist throughout and beyond China. As is natural for all living things, these have mutated and adapted to foreign environments.

Through cross-cultural comparison it is apparent that current Chinese culture retains a remarkable number of features from ancient times. Chinese culture has always maintained both a strong conservative function and a powerful evolutionary drive. This conservative function is responsible for the durability of ancient cultural traditions, and the innate cultural drive for progress has transformed these traditions into useful contemporary tools.

Two Chinese disciplines that have received the attention of the non-Chinese world as well as the renewed attention of modern China are traditional Chinese medicine and martial arts. In the popular view—as demonstrated in film, literature, and even the advertisements of martial arts schools—martial arts and medicine are linked together. In fact, there is a profound convergence of medicine and martial arts in traditional Chinese culture. Both share a common cultural and philosophical foundation. Both are elite traditions. And both contribute to the common social goal of maintaining and restoring the health of the culture.

Medicine

Medicine, or more generally healing, is a feature of all societies. The healing arts are society's intermediary between Nature and human beings. The way that a society views Nature will determine how it attempts to achieve health and balance. The most ancient records of Chinese medicine reveal that the fundamental Chinese worldview remains intact after five millennia. This worldview is the force that has shaped the development of Chinese medicine.

Chinese medicine, like much of Chinese culture, is based upon the science of Daoism. Daoism (Taoism) is the cosmological basis of Chinese medicine. It is scientific in that it is based on observation, states regularities, and is both explanatory and predictive. Daoism provides functional descriptions of the relationships among phenomena. It recognizes the underlying compositional unity of all things (*wan wu* [1]), which have qualities and functions differentiated on a continuum, much as colors are differentiated on a spectrum. There is no absolute differentiation between "this" and "that." These notions are defined on the basis of both sensed qualities and function. This view provides for a mutual, organic association among all entities, even among those that are in opposition.

In both theory and application, the most important term in Daoism is *qi* [2]. Qi is both that which "glues" and that which is "glued." Qi simultaneously fulfills the dual roles of constituting and directing the stuff (or essence) of the universe. All manifestations of qi are described relative to their unique admixture of the basic contrasting pair: yin [3] and yang [4]. This pair is unitary. One could not exist without the other. The central theme of Daoism and thus Chinese medicine and the martial arts is that all things are conditions for the existence of all other things. Therefore, there is no ultimate creation or destruction, only change. In Chinese, this is described as change-transformation without impoverishment [5].

The *Yijing* (*I Ching*), or Book of Changes, states, "Unceasing life, call it 'change'" [6]. Life is a constant process of transformation, of which creation and extinction are secondary manifestations. Whereas these categories are value neutral—neither creation nor extinction is viewed as inherently good or evil—this process has a natural progression. It is this progressive order that is the focus of the Chinese physician's attention. The physician views the normal state of a system as one in which transition is simultaneously unimpeded and well regulated. Disease is identified in a system that does not meet these conditions, resulting in either systemic or regional surpluses or deficits of qi. Simply stated, order (*zheng* [7]) is "good." Disorder (*luan* [8]) is "bad."

The practice of Chinese medicine has two interrelated aspects. The first is diagnosis. *Zhenduan* (diagnosis [9]) is the accurate perception of reality: recognition of the actual admixture of yin and yang. The second aspect, therapy (*yi zhi* [10], literally, "to heal, to put into order"), is the response to that diagnosis. Therapy is the manipulation of yin and yang. The goal of this manipulation is to restore the life-promoting balance between these two vital forces. Both excess and deficiency result in a tendency toward extinction, which in turn is the cusp of creation.

The doctor must decide if a situation deserves restoration. This in-

Preparation of traditional herbal medicine. A man in a Hong Kong apothecary uses a large chopper to slice up root herbs, ca. 1950. The bottles on the shelves behind him contain the herbs in powdered form. (Hulton Archive)

volves a moral determination of goodness versus evil, or between health and disease. Therefore, all medical decisions are ultimately moral decisions. The physician decides if the situation is worthy or unworthy of restoration. He might decide to not act and allow natural forces to bring the situation to its conclusion. Alternatively, he might decide to actively promote a conclusion of the abnormal state, thereby promoting the creation of a new state.

Thus, action (*you wei* [11]) and nonaction (*wu wei* [12]) are the basic tools of the physician. Action has two types of applications: enhancement (*bu* [13]) and depletion (*xie* [14]). If an organ system is weak, it can be enhanced by various means. If an organ system is too strong, and its strength saps the resources of its neighbors and injures the system, the physician depletes it. Of course, enhancement and depletion are also relative terms, since an organ that is overly strong relative to its neighbors can also be controlled by strengthening its neighbors. Thus the manipulation of yin and yang can be complex and subtle.

It is important to describe the native understanding of medicine as a concept. Confucius described the spectrum of possibilities inherent in the physician-patient relationship when he said, "Only [one who embodies] humanness has the ability to both love and detest a person" [15] (Sec. 4.3).

In other words, a patient's presentation may require a physician's response to occur anywhere along a continuum from total acceptance to total rejection. The function of the physician is to reject disorder and to affirm order. His response is dictated by the needs of the patient, not his personal preferences, which are rigorously suppressed through self-cultivation. Thus, it is stated in a medical primer, the *Dao de Jing (Tao-te Ching):*

The sage has no constant heart.
His heart is simply the heart of the people. [16] (Chap. 49)

The Tang dynasty physician Sun Simiao [17] wrote that there are three levels of physicians: high, middle, and low: "In ancient times, of those well-versed in the practice of medicine, the High Doctor cured society, the Median Doctor cured the man, the Low Doctor cured illness. Or one could say, the High Doctor looks at color, the Median Doctor listens to sound, the Low Doctor feels the pulse. Yet another way of expressing this would be to say, the High Doctor cures illnesses not yet begun (does not allow problems to arise), the Median Doctor cures those disorders which may develop into illnesses, the Low Doctor cures extant illnesses" [18] (Sun).

Martial Arts

What features make Chinese martial arts uniquely Chinese? There are ancient references to primitive predynastic martial activities. However, these do not reveal any uniquely Chinese characteristics. The principle of unity and the orderly progression of yin and yang, which are the central features of Chinese culture, are present in the earliest literary artifacts. But the development of these principles into a distinctly Chinese civilization occurred over thousands of years. The features that distinguish Chinese martial arts from the fighting traditions of other civilizations are most apparent in the millennia following the Zhou dynasty (1122–255 B.C.).

The key feature identifying Chinese martial arts is the use of *dao* [19] as the central reference. As the influence of Chinese culture spread across Asia, the philosophy of Daoism was integrated into other cultures, such as those of Japan and Korea. These cultures adapted features of Daoist philosophy to their needs. Yet the invention of a generalized philosophy based on the principle of the dao and the generalized application of this principle, its associated worldview, and common linguistic references are uniquely Chinese.

The main issue facing all martial artists is when to use a lethal skill. A skilled fighter who randomly applies his skill soon becomes an enemy of all people and is marked for destruction. This negates the goal of *self*-defense. Thus, a martial artist must have some measure of what constitutes a threat against his being, or his extended being, as embodied by his family or social unit. This measure depends on the moral judgment of what is "right" or "wrong."

The moral compass of Chinese culture is the dao. It identifies the orderly transition of life. That which impedes the orderly transition of life is defined as "evil" (*nie* [20]). That which promotes this orderly transition is "good" (*shan* [21]). The Chinese martial artist is culturally authorized to apply his lethal skill against evil and to apply his life-enhancing skills in support of that which is good.

Since ancient times, China has been a huge and inconsistently governed territory. Remote states, cities, villages, and individuals have not universally received the benefits of the rule of law. Furthermore, this rule has frequently been imperfect. Thus, there has been an enduring need for self-defense. As indigenous self-defense skills entrained the potent Daoist philosophy, they evolved into characteristically Chinese martial art forms.

The durability of these forms is the result of transmission through a closed system. The same parafamilial, teaching father–following son, *shifu-tu'er* [22] relationship that was used to transmit medical knowledge also was used to guarantee the continuity of the martial discipline. Yet, martial skills required by organized groups differ from those needed for individual combat. Thus, there were parallel means of teaching the requisite skills, such as boxing schools and military training. But none of these matched the durability of the parafamilial tradition.

Although Chinese martial arts training involves both life-enhancing and life-destroying skills, it is considered to be an essentially destructive skill. Therefore, throughout Chinese civilization, the military arm of government, *wu* [23], has been subservient to the civil arm, *wen* [24]. The underlying rationale is that, ideally, the civil (or high medical) aspect of government establishes conditions that render the military aspect unnecessary. Confucius referred to this ideal in his essay on *Da Tong*. However, Chinese rulers were not naive about the realities of the human condition, and martial training was a persistent feature throughout all governments.

As in medicine, it is apparent that the application of martial skills can occur at many levels. The pre–Qin dynasty general Sunzi (Sun Wu, probably fourth century B.C.) wrote, in *The Art of War,* that the highest strategy is "to bend the enemy without battle" [25] (Chap. 3). A middle strategy would be "a decisive victory a thousand leagues away" [26] ("Designs," Chap. 1). A low strategy would be victory on the home front or victorious fisticuffs.

The Daoist principle that unites medicine and martial arts is the intent (*yi* [27]) of life. All things have a drive to exist. This drive is not only present in the individual, but over time, through succeeding generations. Mengzi stated that, of the three major offenses against the family, the worst was "no posterity" [28] (Book 4, Chap. 26), no succeeding generations. Therefore, in Chinese culture, existence is understood to encompass both the individual and the familial line.

Thus, martial artists defend not only themselves as individuals but also their generational units, their families, and the social units that sustain their families, as well as the cultural environment that nourishes these social units. Martial artists function as an element of the social body's immune system. Their unique role is to eliminate violent threats to the health of the social system at whatever sphere of influence they operate.

Physicians are also responsible for the health of the society. Applying their knowledge of nature, they promote those features that are healthy and discourage those things that are unhealthy. The physician and the martial artist share a common social purpose. Since they both recognize the directive of the *dao,* they operate in tandem to create the conditions for health. Physicians affirm order. Martial artists use their unique skills to exorcise disorder. Yet, because martial operations are considered to be essentially destructive and depleting, they are ideally subservient to the direction of medicine.

In return for this service to medicine, the physician contributed to the development of the martial artist. In traditional Chinese medicine, there was an entire discipline of military medicine, *jun yi* [29]. As in modern times, military physicians traveled with their army and were versed in battlefield care as well as means of dealing with sanitation and nutritional problems. Furthermore, the most evolved features of Chinese martial arts are based on the utilization of Chinese medical physiology. These include nutrition, strength and endurance training, and breathing techniques.

Since martial arts training and applications are inherently dangerous, typically one of the earliest secrets passed to a disciple is the use of medicines for training injuries. These medicines, formulated by physicians, were passed down through the generations. Over the years, many martial artists have frequented markets, selling these preparations and performing simple therapies. This practice also contributed to the popular connection between medicine and martial arts. But these medicine salesmen and bonesetters were never mistaken for physicians. Nor did they represent themselves as such.

Disease, dissension, and strife are universal human conditions. Prehistoric artifacts reveal that combat is contemporaneous with the human species. The drive for preservation of self, family, and social community is very powerful. It is the basis for all martial methods. Just as healing traditions are common to all civilizations, so too combat traditions are found in all cultures.

There is a profound association between medicine and martial arts within Chinese civilization. Both disciplines are born of a common premise: the need to sustain the life and health of the individual, the social unit, and the culture. Each represents a relative aspect of this life-sustaining function. Medicine is relatively life-enhancing. Martial arts are relatively life-destroying. The convergence of these two techniques offers therapeutic options along the continuum of human existence.

Anthony Schmieg, M.D.

See also Boxing, Chinese; Ki/Qi; Religion and Spiritual Development: China

References
Confucius. *Analects of Confucius* [30]. Translated by Anthony Schmieg.
Dao De Jing [31]. Translated by Anthony Schmieg.
Griffith, Samuel B. 1963. *Sun Tzu: The Art of War.* New York: Oxford University Press.
Holbrook, Bruce. 1981. *The Stone Monkey: An Alternative, Chinese-Scientific, Reality.* New York: William Morrow.
———. 1974. "World-View Revisited through Ethnographic Semantic Analysis: The 'Kinship'- and 'Color'-Focal World-View of Traditional Chinese Physicians." In *Cross-Cultural Context.* New Haven: Yale University Press.
Legge, James. 1885. *The Li Ki.* Vols. 27 and 28, *The Sacred Books of the East.* Oxford: Clarendon Press.
Lewis, Mark Edward. 1990. *Sanctioned Violence in Early China.* New York: SUNY Press.
Mengzi. Numerous translations. Book 4 [32].
Needham, Joseph. 1954. *Science and Civilization in China.* Vol. 2. New York: Cambridge University Press.
Porkert, Manfred. 1974. *The Theoretical Foundations of Chinese Medicine: Systems of Correspondence.* Cambridge: MIT Press.
Sun Si-miao. 1975. *Prescriptions Worth a Thousand in Gold* [33]. Translated by Tony Schmieg. Taibei: Di Qiu Chu Ban She [34].
Sunzi. *The Art of War.* Chap. 3 [35].
"Designs of the State." 1970. In *Wuzi* [36]. From Sun-Wu Bing Fa [37]. Taibei: Ji Wen Shu Zhu.

List of Ideograms

1	*wan wu*	萬物
2	*qi*	氣
3	*yin*	陰

4	*yang*	陽
5	change-transformation	變化無窮
6	unceasing life	生生謂之易
7	*zheng*	正
8	*luan*	亂
9	*zhenduan*	診斷
10	*yi zhi*	醫治
11	*you wei*	有為
12	*wu wei*	無為
13	*bu*	補
14	*xie*	瀉
15	Only one who embodies humanness…	唯仁者，能愛人能惡人
16	The sage has no constant heart…	聖人無常心，以百姓心為心
17	Sun Si-miao	孫思邈
18	In ancient times…	古之善為醫者，上醫醫國。下醫醫病。又曰，上醫聽聲。中醫察色。下醫診脈。又曰，上醫醫未中醫醫。中醫醫欲病之病。下醫醫已病之病。
19	dao	道
20	*nie*	孽
21	*shan*	善
22	*shifu-tu'er*	師父-徒兒
23	*wu*	武
24	*wen*	文
25	bend the enemy without battle	不戰而屈人之兵善之善者
26	a decisive victory a thousand leagues away	決戰千理
27	*yi*	意
28	no posterity	無後為大
29	*jun yi*	軍醫
30	*Analects of Confucius*	論語

31	Dao De Jing	道德經
32	Mengzi	孟子離婁章二十六
33	*Prescriptions Worth a Thousand in Gold*	千金藥方
34	*Di Qiu Chu Ban She*	地球出版社
35	Sunzi. *The Art of War.* Chap. 3	孫子兵法，謀攻第三
36	*Wuzi*	吳子圖國篇
37	Sun-Wu Bing Fa	孫吳兵法

Meditation

Meditation is the general term for various techniques and practices designed to induce an altered state of consciousness, develop concentration and wisdom, and relieve stress and induce relaxation. On the simplest levels it is utilized to calm, cleanse, and relax the mind and body and to increase concentration and mental focus. On higher levels, it is practiced to produce a radical transformation of the character. Meditation is really mind/body training that is learned through discipline and practice. Meditation systems such as Zen and Daoist (Taoist) qigong may stimulate the autoimmune system, change brain waves from beta to alpha or theta, and lower heart and respiratory rate while increasing respiratory volume and decreasing muscular tension.

Dimitri Kostynick defines the martial arts as "practices of combat outside of organized warfare, utilized for self-actualization, augmented with noncombative practices and formulae from the materia medica" (1989). In this view, the martial arts are a nexus between the techniques of combat and psychophysical self-cultivation. The Asian martial arts grew up intertwined with Daoism (Taoism), Shintô, Buddhism, and other magico-religious traditions that emphasize meditation as a means of gaining some form of enlightenment. It is no surprise that the traditional martial arts include meditation as either an integral part of or an adjunct to training. The classic martial arts have a long history in Japan, China, and elsewhere of using meditative practices as instruments of "spiritual forging." Asian martial arts share a basically similar animatistic theory of energy (*ki* in Japanese; *qi* [*chi*] in Chinese) that is present in human beings and all living creatures. Ki is commonly taken to mean "vital breath," bioelectric life energy, "spirit," and "directed intention." Japanese aikidô and Chinese taijiquan (tai chi ch'uan) and qigong are based on the ki notion. Although ki is a rather vague concept, most traditional martial arts prescribe methods of cultivating and directing this subtle energy. Meditation, relaxation, visualization, and movement sets (or kata) are used to generate, store, and utilize ki. In general, the serious use of ki energy has been

A sculpture of Buddha in seated meditation at Borobudur Temple in Indonesia, built in the ninth century. (Charles & Josette Lenars/Corbis)

the realm of the most advanced masters of the martial arts.

Meditative states can be induced through various postures incorporating breathing, movement, chanting, stress, and visualization. Deep abdominal breathing is a fundamental practice in many martial arts. Slow, smooth, deep, long abdominal breathing increases the volume of blood flow, calms the mind, and brings more oxygen into the body.

In China, Daoist meditation often plays an important role in the internal arts of taijiquan, baguazhang (pa kua ch'uan), and xingyiquan (hsing i ch'uan). Daoist meditation begins with an emphasis on breath control and posture and moves on to visualizations and direction of energy throughout the body. Three major kinds of energy are cultivated: qi (vital life energy), *qing* (sexual energy), and *shen* (spiritual energy). By calming the mind and eliminating our normal internal mental dialogue, meditation restores access to what the Daoists call original mind: a state of mind that is spontaneous and rejuvenating, more intuitive than the conscious mind. Daoist meditation allows access to the natural potential for fluid and appropriate responses to the situation at hand.

Buddhism gives two major approaches to meditation: concentration, or mindfulness, meditation; and insight meditation.

The most basic approach to mindfulness is awareness of breathing to the extent that breathing occupies one's full attention. Once concentration is developed, this power is then used in insight meditation to gain wisdom through observing the mind.

In Japan, the early martial arts (ca. A.D. 800–1200) were influenced by Daoism, Shintô, and Mikkyo (or esoteric) Buddhism. Shingon and Tendai are the two major schools of Mikkyo. Esoteric Buddhism utilizes visualizations, mudras, mandalas, and mantras to harmonize body, mind, and speech.

Zen arrived in Japan from China around A.D. 1200 and was often used by the samurai as an adjunct to their martial training. The Zen approach to any task is single-minded concentration. *Mushin (munen musô)* is a state of mind that is cultivated in Zen and the Zen-influenced arts. In mushin, the mind is open to everything but not distracted by delusive thoughts—they come and go but the mind does not dwell upon them. The mind in a state of mushin is often likened to a mirror—reflecting everything. This is important in true combat, because if a warrior centers only on one opponent, another will cut him down. Mushin, in the West, is often mistaken for impersonal, amoral, automatic reactions. Speed is not necessarily spontaneity, and, in real combat, timing is more important than speed. Conditioned reflexes and fluid awareness are not the same. *Fudoshin* (which follows from the cultivation of mushin) means "immovable heart" or "spirit," which means that one understands what an opponent is going to do before the attack. When attacked, one is never surprised, the mind and nerves are calm, and what is appropriate to the situation is done. Even the feeling "This is the enemy" means that the mind is moving. "Empty mind" gives rise to *fudochi* (immovable wisdom).

Today in the United States, the majority of books, articles, and advertisements dealing with the martial arts at least pay lip service to the idea that some kind of "self-control" or "mental discipline" is a by-product of the training. Often Yellow Pages ads list meditation and spiritual growth as some of the benefits of training in a particular discipline. In fact, however, the majority of martial artists practice sport karate and spend little or no time in meditation. In many classes, meditation is defined as a few short seconds at the beginning of a class to relax and get the mind ready for the physical workout to follow. Most martial arts teachers do not have any formal meditative training. However, they often retain the short period of "meditation" because that was the way their teachers did it, or perhaps for marketing purposes, to lend a vague flavor of Eastern culture and mystery. Practicing the modern sport martial arts is no guarantee either of being able to fight effectively without rules or of spiritual accomplishment.

Ronald L. Holt

See also Baguazhang (Pa Kua Ch'uan); Ki/Qi; Medicine, Traditional Chinese; Religion and Spiritual Development: China; Religion and Spiritual Development: India; Religion and Spiritual Development: Japan; Taijiquan (Tai Chi Ch'uan); Written Texts: China; Written Texts: India; Written Texts: Japan; Xingyiquan (Hsing I Ch'uan)

References
Austin, James H. 1998. *Zen and the Brain*. Cambridge: MIT Press.
Friday, Karl, with Seki Humitake. 1997. *Legacies of the Sword: The Kashima-Shinryû and Samurai Martial Culture*. Honolulu: University of Hawai'i Press.
Kauz, Herman. 1992. *A Path to Liberation: A Spiritual and Philosophical Approach to the Martial Arts*. Woodstock: Overlook Press.
Keenan, John P. 1989. "Spontaneity in Western Martial Arts: A Yogacara Critique of MuShin." *Japanese Journal of Religious Studies* 16: 285–298.

Maliszewski, Michael. 1996. *Spiritual Dimensions of the Martial Arts.* Rutland, VT: Charles E. Tuttle.

Sato, Hiroaki, ed. 1985. *The Sword and the Mind.* Woodstock: Overlook Press.

Sayama, Mike. 1986. *Samadhi: Self-Development in Zen, Swordsmanship, and Psychotherapy.* Albany: SUNY Press.

Yasuo, Yuasa. 1993. *The Body, Self-Cultivation and Ki-Energy.* Albany: SUNY Press.

Middle East

The Middle East consists of Egypt and the Arab nations to the east of Israel, Turkey, and Iran; and of the North African countries of Algeria, Morocco, Tunisia, Libya, and the Sudan. Although the following comments are limited to these nations, the boundaries of the Middle East may be extended into other nations such as Pakistan, Afghanistan, and Cyprus as well. The rise of Islam and the domination of much of the area by the Arab Muslims beginning in the seventh century A.D. bound together the various groups of the region under the banner of Islam. Later, the Ottoman Empire in the thirteenth century further expanded and confirmed the Muslim character of the region under militant Islamic leadership.

Ancient Egypt during the Middle Kingdom (2040–1785 B.C.) offers the earliest convincing evidence of systematic martial arts development, not only in the Middle East, but in recorded history. Painted on the walls of the tombs of Beni Hassan are pairs engaged in grappling maneuvers (some of which are as sophisticated as any used in modern Olympic competition), boxing (including the use of protective equipment such as a forerunner of modern protective headgear), kicking, and stickfighting. The stickfighting techniques have been preserved into the present as *tahteeb* (a martial art system using sticks and swords). The system continues to be practiced in the religious schools of the Ikhwaan-al-Muslimeen (Muslim Brotherhood). The Bedouin continued until the modern era to utilize a staff in a combat art called *naboud*. Practice is reported to involve spinning, dancelike forms with the weapon. Similar whirling dances are associated with other martial practice in the region, as well as with the mystical sect of Islam called Sufism. In addition, the Egyptians developed two-handed spears that could be wielded as lances, shields, and specialized weapons such as the *khopesh*, a sword that could be used to disarm opponents.

At about the same time, the oldest surviving work of literature, the Mesopotamian epic of *Gilgamesh,* portrayed the semidivine protagonist as a wrestler. In this work, Gilgamesh employed his grappling skills to subdue the wild man, Enkidu, who then swore allegiance and became his ally in fu-

An Indian copy done in Persian style from an Islamic book depicts Rustan, a seventh-century Persian general, slaying White Deity. (Angelo Hornak/ Corbis)

ture battles. The central character is reputed to be based on an historical Sumerian king (ca. 2850 B.C.); therefore, it is interesting that Enkidu specifically accedes to Gilgamesh's right to rule. Thus, although the epic offers no detailed description of grappling in the second millennium B.C., it may reflect a principle of "war by champions" that prevailed in the area around this time.

Somewhat later (ca. 1000 B.C.), Semitic tribes could exercise the option of substituting single combat between champions in the place of massed battles. The most famous of these is likely to be the battle between David representing the Hebrews and Goliath of the Philistines, as described in the Bible (1 Samuel). Even closer to the Gilgamesh archetype is the story of Muhammad's wrestling match with the skeptical sheikh, Rukana ibn 'Abdu Yazid, as a demonstration of the power of his revelations from God. The Prophet succeeded in his opponent's conversion after scoring his second fall.

As previously noted, after the initial Arab Muslim conquests of the Middle East, the Ottoman Turks extended the boundaries of the Islamic world and consolidated to a large degree the identity of the Middle East, at least into the twentieth century. The *ghazis* were a prime force behind the Ottoman expansion. The Ghazi Brotherhoods are of particular relevance to martial history. Members of the Ghazi Brotherhood were roughly comparable to the European knights who were their contemporaries. They were bound by a code of virtue within a democratic organization, and in contrast to the European knight, whose worth eventually became bound to ancestry and rank, the brother was judged on the merits of his own character (e.g., valor, piety) rather than by his wealth or lineage. Brothers were most often followers of Sufism, the mystical sect of Islam that gave rise to the dervishes, whose whirling dances were mentioned above. This dervish influence may have been pervasive in the Ottoman training regimen, given the fact that vigorous dancing even extended to the military training of Janissaries (Christians who either had rejected their faith or had been branded as holding heretical beliefs, who served in the Turkish army) from the fourteenth century, continuing until their dissolution in the nineteenth century. To return to the ghazis, however, they were sworn to the militant expansion of Islam. With the spread of the faith came the dissemination of Turkish martial traditions. Among the most lasting of these traditions has been wrestling.

Turkey is a nation with a long history of wrestling excellence. Turkish tribes originated in Asia, probably somewhere between the Ural Mountains, the Caucasus, and the Caspian Sea. To the east were the Mongols; Turkish contact was primarily with the Huns and the Tatars. Apparently, however, they brought with them many wrestling techniques in their mi-

Alireza Dabir of Iran waves his country's flag after winning the gold medal for freestyle wrestling at the Sydney Olympics, October 1, 2000. (Reuters NewMedia Inc./Corbis)

grations westward, possibly influenced by *shuaijiao* (*shuai-chiao*) and other sources of Chinese and Mongolian wrestling. Turkey was overrun by the Persians in the sixth century B.C., remained under Persian domination until the invasion of Alexander (334 B.C.), and was a part of the Roman Empire (through the Byzantine period) until the eleventh-century invasions of the Seljuk Turks. Even today, in the former "Turkish" republics of the former Soviet Union, such as Azerbaijan, Kazakhstan, and Uzbekistan, local wrestling traditions influenced by both classical European and Asian styles survive among the local populations and nomads. History provides various glimpses of Turkish wrestling, and gymnasiums for wrestlers (*tekke*) began to appear by the fifteenth century.

Today, Turkish wrestling, known as *Yagli-Gures,* is one of the nation's most popular sports, and there is evidence that this is a form related to Persian/Iranian *koshti.* Similarities abound. Wrestlers wear trousers only; they otherwise are naked and do not wear shoes. Turkish wrestling is unique in that the competitors, known as *pehlivans,* oil themselves down completely before a match. Note that the name *pehlivan* resembles the term for traditional Iranian wrestlers (*pahlavani*). The foregoing characteristics argue for a strong link between this system and Iranian systems, as do many of the techniques.

The oil obviously makes it much more difficult to grab an opponent, and competitors must rely on a great deal of skill to throw or take down a wrestler. Grabbing and holding onto the pants, known as a *kispet,* is allowed in Yagli. Both holds and throws are allowed in the sport; the match continues until one concedes defeat or a referee stops the match to ensure a wrestler's safety. The lack of a time limit can make for grueling competitions. In 1969, a national championship match lasted for fourteen and a half hours. The Turkish wrestling techniques are essentially those of modern freestyle. For example, techniques include the *sarma,* known in contemporary wrestling as a "grapevine" hold. The sport is now growing on the European continent, started by Turks who migrated from Turkey, but now including participants from other nationalities as well.

Iranian (formerly Persian) wrestling is a second major grappling tradition of the Middle East. Known for much of its history as Persia, Iran is an ancient nation, with civilizations in this region extending as far back as 2000 B.C. Certainly by the seventh century B.C., Persian civilization had reached one of the many high points of its power and was building itself into an empire that covered much of the Middle East and North Africa. Iranians themselves incorporated wrestling techniques into their warrior skills, and there are accounts of Greek wrestlers and *pankration* experts challenging these wrestlers as the two cultures met, and ultimately clashed with, each other. Martial arts academies developed as well, known as *Varzesh-e-Pahlavani.* From these sources, Iran developed its own unique system of wrestling, *koshti.* Koshti apparently had both combat and sport aspects, and koshti exponents were trained to use the system as an unarmed battlefield art when necessary. With the Islamic invasions of the seventh and eighth centuries A.D., and with Islamic discouragement of practices that were considered pagan, koshti apparently fell into unpopularity.

Iranian wrestling systems apparently employed all the aspects of Greek wrestling. Although the systems seemed to lack any emphasis on striking, koshti exponents used throws, takedowns, and trips, as well as arm and leg locks and choke holds. Practitioners were expected to be able to disarm weaponed opponents when necessary as well. It is likely that in sport competitions, many of the more dangerous holds were not allowed. Practitioners would compete in trousers, naked from the waist up. In many respects, koshti, in all of its variants, may be compared to many Western systems of wrestling and to jûjutsu from Japan.

Centuries later, however, the Iranian Shah Ismail "the Great," after making himself shah, made the Shiite Twelver sect of Islam (believers in the twelve descendants of their spiritual leader Ali, Muhammad's son-in-law) the state religion in Azerbaijan and Iran. He was noted for the persecution of Sunnism and the suppression of non-Safawid Sufism. As a consequence, the Safawid Brotherhood (a Sufi brotherhood whose sheiks claimed descent from Muhammad's son-in-law, Ali) maintained considerable military and political power. This fact may have led to Ismail's patronage of martial arts.

He was noted for his promotion of the *Zour Khaneh*, or *Zur Khane* (House of Strength). A contemporary description (written in 1962) notes that there was in the center of the mosquelike building an octagonal pit, 15 feet in diameter, lined in blue tile, but filled with earth. Beyond the pit lay weight-lifting apparatus, and on the wall hung a portrait of Ali. Training featured preliminary rhythmic calisthenics, followed immediately by whirling dances accompanied by bells, drums, gongs, and passages sung from the *Shahnama* (the great Persian epic the *Book of Kings*). This form of training bears clear connections to Sufi practices that incorporate both song and whirling dances into worship—as well as suggesting analogies to a vast cross-cultural range of martial dances/exercises. In addition to the more contemporary apparatus, traditional devices (dating back at least to Ismail's reign) are used in the Zour Khaneh. These exercise tools are essentially oversized weapons (for example, the *kadabeh*, an iron bow with a chain bowstring) that are brandished during the training dances. In addition to these conditioning exercises, the trainees at the Zour Khaneh practice koshti.

In the middle of the twentieth century, as Iran sought to enter the modern world, traditional Iranian arts such as koshti were replaced by modern wrestling systems such as the Olympic types of Greco-Roman and freestyle. With the Islamic Revolution in 1979, whose adherents view all pre-Islamic practices as pagan, any current prospects for development of koshti are not bright. Iranians have excelled at modern wrestling competitions, however, reflecting the long and distinguished history of wrestling that exists in this nation.

Finally, the Middle East has produced at least one contemporary combat system, as well: krav maga. Krav maga (Hebrew; contact combat) is an Israeli martial art that was developed in the 1940s for use by the Israeli military and intelligence services. The creator of the system was Imi Lichtenfeld, an immigrant to Israel from Bratislava, Slovak (formerly Czechoslovakia). Today it is the official fighting art of the Israeli Defense Forces (IDF) and has gained popularity worldwide as an effective and devastating fighting method. It is a fighting art exclusively; sport variants do not exist. Krav maga techniques are designed to be simple and direct. High kicks are used sparingly in the art; kicks are directed at waist level or below. Knee strikes, especially against the groin and inner thigh area, are especially used. Practitioners also use kicks against the legs, similar to those used in Muay Thai (Thai kickboxing), to unbalance an opponent. Punches are based on boxing moves and are intended for vital points or to place the mass of the body behind a blow to gain punching power. Open-hand techniques to the eyes, ears, throat, and solar plexus are used. Elbow techniques are used extensively.

These techniques require little strength but have devastating results; an elbow strike to the face or floating ribs can easily disable an opponent. Throwing techniques are not the type usually seen in jûdô or *sambo;* they have more in common with freestyle wrestling takedowns. Krav maga has been called the "first unarmed combat system of the twentieth century." This is meant to convey the fact that it developed in the twentieth century with the understanding and awareness of modern combat. Firearms were the weapons of choice for twentieth-century warriors, as they are for those of the twenty-first century, and terrorism and sudden violence often define the battlefield in the modern world.

The martial arts systems of the Middle East are a unique chapter in the fighting skills of the world. This area is the cradle of civilization, so it is no great surprise that many of the first fighting arts were practiced here as well. Since many trade routes existed through these regions, it is also not surprising that the techniques and styles from various civilizations can be seen. In this respect, perhaps the fighting arts of the Middle East are among the most eclectic in the world.

Gene Tausk

See also Africa and African America; Krav Maga; Pankration; Stickfighting, Non-Asian; Wrestling and Grappling: China; Wrestling and Grappling: Europe

References
Gardiner, E. Norman. 1930. *Athletics of the Ancient World.* Oxford: Clarendon Press.
Gluck, Jay. 1962. *Zen Combat.* New York: Ballantine.
Hitti, Philip Khoury. 1970. *History of the Arabs: From the Earliest Times to the Present.* New York: St. Martin's.
Lichtenfeld, Imi, and Eyal Yanilov. 1998. *Krav Maga: Self Defense and Fighting Tactics.* Tel Aviv: Dekel.
Nicolle, David, and Angus McBride. 1982. *The Armies of Islam, 7th–11th Centuries.* London: Osprey Publishing.
———. 1983. *Armies of the Ottoman Turks, 1300–1774.* London: Osprey Publishing.
Poliakoff, Michael B. 1987. *Combat Sports in the Ancient World: Competition, Violence and Culture.* New Haven: Yale University Press.
Svinth, Joseph R. 2000. "Kronos: A Chronological History of the Martial Arts and Combative Sports." http://www.ejmas.com/kronos.

Mongolia

"The three manly games" of Mongolia are horse racing, archery, and wrestling. It is important to understand that all three of the heavenly games, as they are also called, are tied closely to the pastoral nomadic traditions of the Central Asian steppe. Today, these disciplines are still held in reverence, but for the most part have been codified into martial sport, with much of the military application no longer practiced or obvious.

The culmination of the sporting year in Mongolia falls during the second week of July. The festival, known as *Naadam,* lasts one week, during which all three sports reach their annual competitive pinnacle.

Mongolian folk wrestling as a sport dates well back into antiquity and holds a position of unrivaled cultural importance. Today Mongolian wrestling is generally held outdoors on grass, with no time limits and no weight classes. Wrestling tournaments are held during most holidays.

The objective is to get the opponent to touch any part of his back, elbow, or knee to the ground. Each match is supervised by two men who act as both referees and "corner men." These men determine the winners and prompt the individual wrestlers to action when necessary. These individuals are arbitrarily appointed to each wrestler prior to each match. They also direct the action away from the spectators and other matches in progress. There is also a panel of judges who are solely spectators and not actively involved with the matches. They serve as the final word in disputes about takedowns and handle the logistics of the tournament.

Each wrestler has a rank, which is determined by the number of rounds successively won in each Naadam festival. (A round for an individual is made up of one match, with the winner moving to the next round and the loser being eliminated from the tournament. The winner then waits for the remainder of the matches to finish before the next round commences.) Rank can only be attained during the Naadam festival, and therefore it is not uncommon for a wrestler to wrestle his whole career without rank, though he may be successful in other tournaments throughout the year. The ranks (in order from lowest to highest) are unranked, bird, elephant, lion, and titan. The privilege of rank is that the highest-ranked wrestlers choose their opponents in each round. In addition, after each match, the lower-ranked wrestler passes under the right arm of the senior, win or lose.

Mongolian wrestling matches begin with each wrestler exhibiting a ritual dance of a great bird in flight. At the end of a match the victorious wrestler again engages in a more elaborate version of the dance. There are two popular opinions as to the type of bird being imitated. Some say the bird in question is a great falcon, while others say it is an imitation of the Garuda bird from Buddhist mythology. If the dance is done correctly, it is intended to exhibit the wrestler's power and technique, and also serves to loosen the muscles prior to the match. In Inner Mongolia the dance is one of an eagle running before it flies. While performing the dance, the wrestler is supposed to mentally focus on *Tengri* (sky) and *gazar* (earth)—sky, or heaven, for skill and blessing and earth for stability and strength.

The attire of each wrestler is the point of most divergence between the

Two Inner Mongo-lian wrestlers await the match. (Cour-tesy of Almaz Khan)

Mongolian and Inner Mongolian versions of this wrestling style. The Mongolians wear a traditional Mongolian cap (which is removed by the referees prior to each match), traditional Mongolian boots, and briefs and a short tight-fitting top, both made out of heavy cloth and silk, though today rip-stop nylon often replaces the silk. The top has long sleeves and comes midway down the back. The front of the top is cut away, exposing the chest. A rope is attached to both sides of the top and is tied around the stomach. This keeps the top on the wrestler and is used as a grip point for the opponent.

Inner Mongolians wear a heavy leather top with metal studs, which is short-sleeved and exposes much less of the chest. In addition they wear long, baggy pants and a more ornate boot. They do not use the cap at all, but do have the addition of a necklace, called a *jangga,* for wrestlers of rank.

Legend says that the increased exposure of the chest and the switch to briefs in Mongolia were the result of the success of a female wrestler disguised as a man several hundred years ago.

In addition to the difference in dress, Inner Mongolian wrestling has several traditions and rules different from those practiced in Mongolia. The Inner Mongolian wrestler cannot grab an opponent's leg with his hands. In addition, any part of the body above the knee touching the ground signals a loss. Another major feature change is that in certain tournaments a circle is used as a ring boundary and a time limit is employed.

In both versions of the wrestling form, a variety of throws, trips, and lifts are employed to topple the opponent. In both versions, strangles and striking are illegal. The absence of groundwork in Mongolian wrestling is grounded (so to speak) in history. The Mongol military was entirely composed of cavalry units (except in the case of conscripts); therefore a soldier on the ground would likely be trampled by horses or killed by his opponent with a weapon. Though no longer explicitly practiced, wrestling on horseback was also a tradition that was found in Mongolia.

Two Outer Mongolian wrestlers in the middle of a tournament. (Courtesy of Aaron Fields)

Archery is a skill for which the Mongols of antiquity were famous. The Mongol empire at its zenith owed its success to the bow and the hoof. The image of Mongol soldiers astride their mounts raining waves of arrows down upon their enemies is recorded in many histories throughout the Eurasian continent.

No account of Mongolian archery is complete without first examining the construction of the bow (*num*). The steppe bow, which shares some design features with the Turkish bow and is sometimes called the Chinese bow, was the primary weapon of the nomad. The steppe bow is what is today called a recurve or a reflex bow. This means that both ends of the bow curve back forward away from the archer. This feature greatly increases the power of the bow. The bow is made from composite materials of different types of wood, bone, and sinew, and is held together by a protein-based glue. The handle is made from lacquered birch bark.

According to bow makers, each material adds specific qualities to the bows: "wood for range, horn for speed, sinew for penetration, glue for union, silk bindings for firmness, lacquer for guard against frost and dew." By the Han period, the nomads of Central Asia were employing bows of this design. The extremes in temperature found on the steppe would quickly warp other styles of bows, especially single-material bows.

The steppe bow was short, about 4 feet long, and had an extreme range of up to 500 yards in battle. The mounted archer could get off between six and twelve shots per minute. In antiquity the pulls of the bows often exceeded 100 pounds, sometimes in the range of 110–120 pounds pull. One of the advantages of a recurve bow is that after the initial pull, the bow "works with the archer" and is easier to hold at full draw.

The manner in which the bow is drawn (or in this case pushed) is also unique, in that the bow is primarily pushed away from the string rather than the string being solely pulled away from the bow. This feature has a twofold purpose. Not only is the bow stronger and often more flexible than the string, but it is an advantage, biomechanically, to push rather than pull.

The "Mongolian grip" used on the string is also unique. This grip can be identified by how the thumb hooks the string and is placed between the middle and forefinger. Traditionally, the archer wore a metal, bone, or antler ring on the thumb. Once the Chinese adopted this style of bow, the thumb ring was also sometimes made out of jade in China. The ring had a square stud on the palm side of the ring, which helped the archer in getting and maintaining his/her grip on the bowstring. In addition, the thumb ring helped the archer maintain control over the string, which, when the bow is completely drawn, is at an acute angle.

Arrowheads were constructed primarily out of bone and horn. Even today in sporting archery, bone arrowheads with squared-off tips are the standard. Modern arrows today are approximately 75 centimeters in length. Most modern bows have pulls in the 50–70 pounds pull range.

In times past, archery was practiced both afoot and mounted. Today mounted archery is rarely practiced. Though there still exist several styles of archery within Mongolia, there has been a gradual shift toward a standardized version for competitive reasons.

During archery competitions, contestants fire from afoot at targets that are traditionally made from sheep gut and are individually approximately 8 centimeters by 8 centimeters. The distance from archer to target is between 35 meters and 75 meters, depending upon the style of archery.

Archers shoot twenty arrows at two separate target constructions. One construction is a wall of stacked targets approximately 50 centimeters high and 4 meters long. The second target is a square made up of thirty individual targets. Scorers relate how the archer is faring via style-specific singing. There is some divergence in targets, bows, and ranges depending upon the style of archery in question.

Traditionally, the central feature of Mongolian society was the horse. The horse was used in every facet of steppe life. Herding, hunting, and war all took place on horseback. This lifestyle allowed the nomads to constantly perfect the major skills that gave them the military success that carried them across the world. Nomads learned to ride as soon as they could walk. Children were often placed on sheep to practice riding when they were still too small for horseback.

Horse racing in Mongolia is over natural terrain tracks that range in distance from 15 to 35 kilometers. The riders are children usually between 5 and 12 years of age. Today most races include the use of saddles, but sometimes riders, as they commonly did in the past, use modified saddles or no saddle at all.

Horse breeders pay close attention to and place equal emphasis on both mare and sire when making breeding decisions. Horses are not usually raced until about 2 years of age. As for the winners, both horse and rider are celebrated equally. Prizes are given for the first few finishers. Ceremonial songs are sung for the victorious horses. An interesting side note is that the last-place finisher also receives a ceremonial song of encouragement and promise for a strong showing next year.

Clearly, the traditional martial arts of Mongolia grew directly out of the methods of economic production dictated by life on the steppe. In essence, a Mongol was in constant preparation for war, as the horse and bow were tools of daily survival as well as war. Today we find the remnants of these methods in competitive archery and horse racing. Wrestling also is a traditional Mongolian pastime, which continues today in popularity and has widespread participation. Overall, Mongolian martial arts have become national sports as the combative uses have decreased over time. Nevertheless, today the passion among the people for their sports is still strong, and their sports elicit memories of the traditional lifestyle, which is still held in high regard.

Aaron Fields

See also China; Wrestling and Grappling: China

References

Beck, Salim. 1926. *The Mongolian Horse.* Tienstien: Société Française de Librairic ct d'Edition, 1926.

Erdene, G. 1992. *Bairldax Or* (Wrestling Masterfully). Ulaanbaator, Mongolia.

Grousset, Rene. 1970. *The Empire of the Steppes.* Camden, NJ: Rutgers University Press.

Jagchid, Sechin, and Paul Hyer. 1979. *Mongolia's Culture and Society.* Folkestone, UK: Westview.

Keirman, Frank, and John K. Fairbank. 1974. *Chinese Ways in Warfare.* Cambridge: Harvard University Press.

Munkhtsetseg. 1999. "Mongolian National Archery." *Instinctive Archer* (Spring). Available online at http://www.atarn.org/mongolian/mn_nat_arch/mn_nat_arch.htm.

Needham, Joseph. 1994. *Science and Civilization in China.* Cambridge: Cambridge University Press.

Schafer, Edward. 1964. *The Golden Peaches of Samarkand.* Berkeley: University of California Press.

Sinor, Denis. 1990. *The Cambridge History of Early Inner Asia.* Cambridge: Cambridge University Press.

Smith, John. 1984. "Mongol Campaign Rations: Milk, Marmots, and Blood?" *Journal of Turkish Studies* 8: 223–229.

Vernam, Glen. 1972. *Man on Horseback.* New York: Harper and Row.

Muay Thai

Muay Thai (Thai Boxing) is a style of kickboxing that comes from Thailand (land of the free), formerly known as Siam. Thai Boxing is one of several Siamese (Thai) martial arts, such as *Krabi-krabong, Lerdrit, Chuparsp, Thaiplum, Kemier,* and *Thaiyuth.* Krabi-krabong is sword and staff fighting using prearranged sets. Lerdrit (pronounced lerd-lit) is an empty-hand battlefield art. Chuparsp (weaponry) includes the pike, knife, stick, sword, shield, and flexible weapons. Thaiplum (grappling) emphasizes pressure point and blood vessel strikes. Kemier is a ninjutsu-like stealth and survival art taught only to head monks at temples. Thaiyuth ("Thai skills") includes Muay Thai, Krabi-krabong, and close-quarter combat techniques. Known as "the science of eight weapons," Muay Thai is a striking art for ring fighting that uses the fists, elbows, knees, and feet.

Muay Thai has developed over several centuries in Southeast Asia. Precise information on the origin of Muay Thai remains unavailable, partly because the Burmese purportedly burned all Siamese records in A.D. 1767. According to one story, in A.D. 1560 the Siamese "black" prince Naresuen fought the Burmese crown prince and defeated him in single combat with Muay Thai. This martial display persuaded Burmese king Bayinnaung not to attack Thailand. Others trace the origins of Muay Thai to a contest held in 1774. In the Burmese city of Rangoon (after the ancient Thai capital of Ayuthya fell in 1767), Lord Mangra the Burmese king called for a seven-day Buddhist festival. A Thai Boxer named Nai Khanom Tom defeated more than nine Burmese fighters one after another before Lord Mangra, thereby earning his admiration.

In modern Thailand, matches are held every day in Bangkok at the Lumphini Stadium and the Ratchadamnoen Stadium. Fights last five rounds of three minutes each with two-minute rest periods in between. There is a center referee who issues a ten count for knockdowns. Three knockdowns in a single round can end the match. Two judges score the fight on points, unless there is a knockout or the referee stops the contest, in which case the match ends.

Fighters enter the ring wearing robes. Trainers wear vests. In bouts, the fighters wear trunks, hand wraps, gloves, mouthpieces, and groin protectors. Elastic and cotton anklets are optional equipment. In contemporary bouts, the international boxing gloves that are used for European box-

Combatants in a Muay Thai match in Bangkok, Thailand. (Earl & Nazima Kowall/Corbis)

ing are standard protection. Under traditional rules, boxers bound their hands with cotton cloth, dipped them in glue, and sprinkled them with ground glass. Glue and glass were abandoned earlier, but cotton bindings, rather than gloves, were used until 1929.

Blows with fists, elbows, and knees and kicks are all delivered with tremendous force in the ring. The Muay Thai strikes, especially the trademark low-line roundhouse, or hook, kicks, are extremely powerful. During the opening round of a match, players may trade low roundhouse kicks to each other's legs to prove who is the better-conditioned fighter. Kicks to the legs are debilitating, limiting a fighter's mobility. Spectators then start their betting after the first round. Contemporary Muay Thai has been accused of having a seedy side because betting is said to dehumanize the martial spirit of the fighters. Some promoters, in fact, consider their fighters to be subhuman and call them animals.

Fight music (*si muay*) is an essential and inspiring part of every match. Songs (*sarama*) are played by a four-piece orchestra consisting of a Javanese clarinet (*pi Java*), drums (*klong kaek, kong*), and cymbals (*shing*). It is believed that the music of wind instruments is particularly inspiring to the fighters. Dance music accompanies the practice of other Thai martial arts, also.

As it does not use the ranking systems of popular Japanese and Korean martial arts, with Muay Thai it is said that "the belt is in the ring"

(Praditbatuga 2000). A fighter demonstrates level of expertise through combat. Like other Asian martial arts, Muay Thai has a spiritual side that is rooted in Buddhism. For example, there is a ceremony called "paying homage to the teacher." This ceremony includes a prefight ritual dance (*ram muay, wai kruh*) in which the fighter hexes his enemy with magic. Also, fighters wear magical charms, such as the *mongkon* (headband) and *praciat* (armband), before and during the bout. In the mid- to late 1960s, after the 1964 Olympics, Muay Thai gained popularity in Japan. *Karatekas* (Japanese; practitioners of karate) blended techniques into an international kickboxing style. Japanese fighters, however, have not adhered to the traditions and rituals associated with the art as practiced in Thailand. The techniques, however, still work without the rituals. The practice of Muay Thai has spread throughout Europe and to the Western Hemisphere as well.

Muay Thai practitioners train in professional boxing camps, such as the Lanna Boxing Camp (*Kiat Busaba*) in Chiang Mai. Trainers hold practice every day and fighters compete at least monthly. Boxers by tradition carry the name of their camp into the ring. A boxer's training regimen includes stretching; calisthenics; weight lifting; rope skipping; running; swimming; shadowboxing; equipment drills with focus mitts, kicking pads, and heavy bags; and sparring. Many strikes are not permitted during sparring in order to ensure the fighters' safety by limiting potential injury. Training sessions may last for about two hours, but are held throughout each day. Therapeutic massage with boxing liniment is included in the training regimen. Diet is key; proper nutrition is essential for stamina.

Training routines may vary, but generally stretching and limbering exercises are included in the ritual dance (ram muay or wai kruh). The hissing sound of exhaling air is heard during movements as fighters practice their breath control. They target vital points when learning striking techniques. A special type of heavy bag, called a "banana bag," which is longer and heavier than a punching bag, is used for kicking. Other training equipment includes a speed bag of the type used by boxers, bag gloves, double-end bag, jump rope, timer, focus mitts, kicking pads, sparring gloves, headgear, and medicine ball. Fighters condition their shins to withstand the impact of their opponents' kicks by striking them with sticks or by kicking banana trees. To improve their focus and control, fighters practice kicking at a lemon hanging from a rope or string.

There is only one stance, or posture, in Muay Thai. For a right-handed fighter, the left leg leads and the right leg follows. Hands are held high. Closed and gloved fists protect the head with the elbows held inward, arms protecting the body. The fighter's body is turned slightly sideways, with the head held slightly forward. The shuffle step is used to move forward and backward. The fighter's front foot moves first going forward, while the rear foot moves first going backward. In moving sideways or laterally, the fighter's left foot moves first when going to the left, and the right foot moves first when going to the right.

Punching includes the basic five moves used in Western boxing: jab, cross, hook (*mat tong*), uppercut (*mat aat*), and overhead. Another type of punch is the swing, which is a long-range hook. *Savate* uses a similar punch, because of a similar need to close the gap from kicking range. A difference between Muay Thai and international boxing can be seen in the way Muay Thai boxers hold up their guard. Because the Thai boxer must counter kicks, knees, and elbows with punches, the guard position tends to keep the hands farther away from the body.

Elbows are delivered in many ways: horizontally, downward, upward, spinning, and driving. The horizontal elbow whips the point of the elbow across the target, usually the side of the head, like a hook. The downward elbow technique first raises the point backward and then drops it downward, using the body weight while moving forward with the hand held low. A variation on the downward elbow technique is done with jumping, in which the elbow point is dropped down from above with the hand held high. Upward elbows are usually delivered like the uppercut punching techniques. Spinning elbows are horizontal elbows with body turns. Driving elbows come straight in like the boxing jab.

Knee attacks are dangerous techniques in Muay Thai and are often fatal. The knee strikes are delivered in three basic ways: straight, round, and jumping. Usually either the straight knee or the round knee is used. The straight knee is used to close distance in close-quarter fighting, while the round knee is delivered from the clinch, usually for an attack to the ribs and kidneys. The jumping knee may be used against an opponent trapped in a corner. This is a flamboyant technique employed to impress the audience.

Kicking techniques include, in order of preference, the roundhouse kick, front kick, and spinning kick. The round kick is directed at low, middle, and high targets. The low kicks are full-force and committed. They differ in execution from other martial arts like Boxe Française Savate or Kyukushinkai Karate. There is a front kick, which is usually used as a "stop hit" or pushing-away technique to halt the opponent's forward progress. The spin kick is a reverse whipping kick. This technique is seldom used in ring fighting. Similar to the high round kick, the spinning kick is prudently saved for the bout's final blow. There is no side kick in the traditional Muay Thai repertoire, but Japanese kickboxers who have converted from karate use this technique effectively.

Muay Thai camps may differ in the strategies they emphasize. For example, the method emphasized in the Prapaisilp-Kitipitayangkul Camp in St. Louis, Missouri, by *Arjan* (Teacher) Supat Prapaisilp and *Kruh* (Trainer)

Ron Smith emphasizes kicking an opponent's legs. These techniques are called cut kicks, because by using them you can cut out the legs from under the opponent. Cut kicks are sweeping, low-line leg attacks or round kicks with the shins against either the inside or outside thighs of an opponent. These kicks can be countered by using footwork to evade the attacks, by lifting the leg out of harm's way, or by toughening the legs to permit them to resist the blows of the other fighter. The use of this array of kicks to the legs helps Muay Thai techniques negate most of what other striking arts (e.g., taekwondo, European boxing, and karate) offer to the combative martial artist.

Moreover, Muay Thai competitors have demonstrated success using Western rules as well. For example, Khaosai Wanghompu (who fought professionally as "Galaxy" Khaosai) was the longest-reigning World Boxing Association (WBA) bantamweight champion in history, with a record of fifty wins and one loss and nineteen title defenses. He was elected to the Boxing Hall of Fame in 1999. In addition, when his twin brother, Khaokor, later won the WBA bantamweight title, they became the first twin brothers to ever win World Boxing titles. In 1995, Saman Sorjaturong won the WBA and International Boxing Federation (IBF) flyweight titles, and with his brother Chana's subsequent win they became the second twin Muay Thai–trained fighters to win international titles in Western boxing. Finally, top-ranked no-holds-barred (NHB) fighters, especially Brazilian Marco Ruas, in the final years of the twentieth century utilized a blend of Muay Thai and Brazilian jiu-jitsu (and other grappling systems) to achieve success in mixed martial arts competitions.

Ronald Harris

See also Southeast Asia

References

Draeger, Donn F., and Robert W. Smith. 1981. *Comprehensive Asian Fighting Arts*. New York: Kodansha.

Kraitus, Panya, and Pitisuk Kraitus. 1988. *Muay Thai: The Most Distinguished Art of Fighting*. Bangkok: Asia Books.

Lanna Muay Thai Boxing Camp. 2000. http://lannamuaythai.com.

Praditbatuga, Pop. 2000. *Muay Thai: The Belt Is in the Ring*. http://www.themartialartsschool.iwarp.com/thai.htm.

Rebac, Zoran. 1987. *Thai Boxing Dynamite: The Explosive Art of Muay Thai*. Boulder, CO: Paladin Press.

Ninjutsu

Ninjutsu is the Japanese martial art of espionage, called in English the "techniques of stealth" or the "arts of invisibility." Practitioners were trained to sneak into enemy territory to learn and report on troops, arms, provisions, and fortifications. The techniques developed further to include active attempts to alter the course of battles, such as arson, assassination, intercepting and/or destroying arms and supplies, and the like. Practitioners were commonly known as *ninja*, but there were numerous alternative terms: *shinobi* (spy), *onmitsu* (secret agent), *rappa* (wild wave), *suppa* (transparent wave), *toppa* (attacking wave), *kasa* (grass), *monomi* (seer of things), and *nokizaru* (monkey under the eaves).

Although earlier Japanese chronicles suggest ninjalike activities, ninjutsu developed primarily during the Sengoku period (late fifteenth to sixteenth centuries) when warfare was endemic. Ninjutsu became organized into schools (*ryûha*) and its techniques systematized. According to Fujita Seiko, there were seventy-one different ryûha, but the three most well known were the Iga-ryû, Kôga-ryû, and Kishû-ryû, others being derivative of these.

In Tokugawa times (1600–1867), during two centuries of peace, ninjutsu lost most of its practical value, although some ninja were employed by the Tokugawa *bakufu* for surveillance and police purposes. The practice of ninjutsu was transformed into one form of martial arts. Due to the secrecy associated with their activities, ninja were often perceived as mysterious and elusive. During the Tokugawa period, after they had virtually passed from the scene, ninja were being portrayed as supermen in drama, art, and literature. Their reputed ability to disappear at will, or leap over walls, or sneak undetected into a castle captured the imagination of people.

That image remains strong today. Ninja were already popular in the era before World War II, in fiction and in the films of such directors as Makino Shôzô. Then, during the 1960s, the Daiei Series of *Shinobi no mono* (Ninja; Band of Assassins) films, starring Ichikawa Raizô, ignited a ninja boom that spread widely overseas as part of a larger international fascination with martial arts. Consequently, ninjutsu has been incorporated widely into action novels and films set in locations worldwide and has even lost its Japanese character, as American kids and even cartoon character turtles have been cast as ninja. The ninja has become a thoroughly romanticized and orientalized figure in contemporary global culture.

Early History of Ninjutsu

Ninjutsu ryûha texts maintain legends about its origins, but scholars consider them to be highly inaccurate. It seems probable that techniques of spying and scouting, gathering information for purposes of waging war, were introduced in the seventh and eighth centuries—most likely in organized form through the Chinese military classic by Sunzi (ca. 300–237 B.C.), *The Art of War*. Prince Shôtoku is said to have been the first to employ someone as a shinobi in the defeat of the Mononobe in 587. Others suggest that *yamabushi* (mountain ascetics) who were practitioners of *shugendô*—a syncretic form of Shintô-Buddhist belief focusing on the worship of mountains—may be the progenitors of later ninjutsu. In general, early accounts of ninja activities are unsubstantiated.

As the scale of battles increased and war bands became better organized in medieval times, the need for spies and unconventional tactics became critical. In the early fourteenth century, for example, Kusunoki Masashige is said to have relied on ninjalike activities. He reputedly employed Iga ninja to steal into Kyoto to discern the military situation. Moreover, in defense of his fortress, Masashige placed lifelike dolls on the battlements to make his troops appear more numerous. His skills in guerilla warfare led later schools of ninjutsu to claim connection with Masashige.

After the Ônin War (1467–1477) and the spread of warfare throughout Japan, various daimyo (regional warlords) began to employ ninja as spies on a regular basis to assist them in expanding their domains. Although ninjutsu ultimately spread from the capital region to central and eastern Japan, local village samurai families in Iga and Kôga (plains areas surrounded by mountains on the border of Iga and Ômi provinces) primarily developed the techniques. By the late fifteenth century there were reputedly fifty-three Kôga and two Iga ninja houses, the leading families being the Hattori and two of that house's offshoots, the Fujibayashi and Momochi.

Among the daimyo who employed ninja for their skills in espionage were Takeda Shingen, Uesugi Kenshin, and Hôjô Ujiyasu. In the Battle of Magari in Ômi province in 1487, Rokaku Takayori sent ninja into the camp of the besieging Ashikaga bakufu army, where they set fire to the headquarters and forced the withdrawal of Ashikaga troops. It was through such deeds that the reputation of ninja spread among the daimyo

of Japan. With the destruction of the Iga and Kôga territories by Oda Nobunaga in 1581, many of the local warriors fled to daimyo in eastern Japan, thus further spreading the knowledge of ninjutsu.

The daimyo most closely connected with the use of ninja was Tokugawa Ieyasu, first shôgun of the Tokugawa bakufu established in 1603. The connection dated back two generations, to the time when his grandfather, Matsudaira Kiyoyasu, employed several hundred Iga ninja under Hattori Hanzô Yasunaga. When Akechi Mitsuhide's troops assassinated Oda

Nobunaga in Kyoto in 1582, Ieyasu avoided attack himself and escaped from Sakai back to his home territory of Mikawa with the assistance of Hattori Hanzô Masanari and a group of ninja. When he became shôgun, Ieyasu called Hanzô to Edo, and employed him to lead Iga and Kôga ninja to spy on potential enemies of the bakufu. Ninja assisted the Tokugawa at the major engagements of Sekigahara, the sieges of Ôsaka Castle, and the Shimabara Rebellion. Later, Iga and Kôga ninja were incorporated formally into police and surveillance organizations of the regime.

Texts and Sources

Information about ninjutsu can be gleaned from a number of extant scrolls and other texts from the Tokugawa period. Fujita Seiko identified thirty-one texts transmitting ninjutsu teachings. One of the first was the *Ninpiden* (Legends of Ninja Secrets), a collection of documents and techniques compiled by Hattori Kiyonobu in 1655. The most important extant text is the *Bansen shûkai* (Ten Thousand Rivers Flow into the Sea) of Fujibayashi Yasutake, who completed it in 1675, after twelve years of work. Another important text is the *Shôninki* (Record of True Ninjutsu) of Fujibayashi Masatake (1681).

Ninjutsu texts appeared somewhat later than those describing the techniques of other martial arts, breaking with a past tradition of secret oral transmission from master to disciple. Martial arts ryûha sprang up throughout Japan, heads of houses possessing knowledge became professional instructors, and samurai were attracted to various schools to learn martial arts as part of the bakufu's emphasis upon the cultivation of Confucian culture, which stresses a balance between martial and civil arts. Scrolls recounting the history of the school, with appropriate connection with various gods and historical figures, and presenting the techniques of the tradition, became an important part of the teaching and ritual components of the various schools, including ninjutsu.

Techniques and Weapons

Since ninja were first and foremost spies, completing one's missions and returning to report were of the essence. Ninjutsu can thus be seen as the art of escape, and techniques were designed to ensure survival. "In ninjutsu there are both overt and covert techniques. The former refer to techniques utilized when one does not disguise his appearance and uses strategy and ingenuity to penetrate enemy territory, while the latter refers to stealing into the enemy camp using techniques of concealment, so as not to be seen by others" (*Bansen shûkai* 1982, 481). Ninja were taught how to disguise themselves to pass unnoticed and were trained in multiple forms of fleeing, based on knowledge of animal behavior. Night provided an excellent cover for ninja actions. For night work, ninja wore black clothing and a hood to avoid detection; but in the daylight, they normally wore brown clothing with reversible gray on the inside, which blended in with natural surroundings. Naturally, they were often in disguise, as an itinerant priest, a merchant, or the like.

Ninjutsu taught familiarity with natural elements as a means of concealing one's presence: using the shade of trees or rocks to hide; carrying out operations at night; employing the confusion created by storms, fog, or fires to sneak into a castle or house. Festivals, brawls, and other occasions where crowds gathered could be utilized for similar purposes.

Ninja might pass a guard post by posing as comrades, calling out false commands, or shouting "Fire." Familiarity with the details of the enemy territory, including knowledge of the local dialect, was also considered invaluable. Naturally, not all contingencies could be covered, so above all, ninja were expected to be inventive and not be limited by their training. "Since secret techniques for necessary penetration (of the enemy's camp) are but temporary and expedient forms of deception, you need not always follow old ninja techniques. Neither need you discard them" (*Bansen shûkai* 1982, 481)

Ninja developed a bewildering variety of tools to assist them in accomplishing their missions, including the "six utensils" normally carried by ninja: sedge hat, rope, slate pencil, medicine, *tenugui* (a form of small towel), and *tsuketake* (for lighting fires). For longer missions, a ninja would carry drink and dried food. For certain tasks, there were specialized tools of various kinds, divided in the *Bansen shûkai* into climbing tools, water utensils (various means of crossing ponds and moats, or hiding in them), opening tools for entering residences, and fire and explosive devices—smoke bombs, fire arrows, and gunpowder for rifles and cannon. The *Bansen shûkai* warns ninja not to be overloaded with equipment, but to discern what is necessary for the mission and take only those tools. "Thus a successful ninja is one who uses but one tool for multiple tasks" (*Bansen shûkai* 1982, 535).

In order to carry out missions of spying, assassination, and ambush, and even in order to fight in regular battle or defend himself against attack, the ninja had to be well trained in martial skills and at the height of physical and mental discipline. This required mastery of most of the major weapons systems and martial skills of the day: sword, lance, bow and arrow (ninja, however, used short bows), grappling, staff, gunnery, and horsemanship. There were other weapons more likely to be employed by ninja than by other warriors, such as throwing missiles (*shuriken*), which ranged from simple short knives to three-, four-, six- or even eight-pointed "stars." Ninja practiced swimming, running to cover long distances without fatigue, breath control, and various ways of walking to avoid sound and, thus, detection. They also had to be skilled at climbing, employing various tools to assist them, such as rope ladders and metal claws that attached to the hands. Working often at night, they trained to increase their ability to see in the dark and hear especially well.

Ninjutsu scholars note forms of chanting, magic spells, incantations, and mudras (hand gestures) in order to focus one's mental power and receive divine protection. These techniques presumably derived from similar esoteric Buddhist practices of *yamabushi* (mountain warriors), *shugendô* practitioners whose purpose was to attain Buddhahood through such ascetic discipline. Though secondary sources often stress these magical aspects of ninjutsu, major texts are silent regarding them.

Yet clearly, severe spiritual training was necessary to accomplish difficult missions. Thus, the first two sections of *Bansen shûkai* stress spiritual or mental preparation. "A correct mind [*seishin*] is the source of all things and all actions. Now, since ninjutsu involves using ingenuity and stratagems to climb over fences and walls, or to use [various ninja tools] to break in, it is quite like the techniques of thieves. If someone not revering the Way of Heaven should acquire [ninjutsu] skills and carry out evil acts, then my writing this book would be tantamount to revealing the techniques of robbery. Thus I place greatest importance on a correct mind" (*Bansen shûkai* 1982, 438).

Yasutake devotes two sections to developing a correct mind. Rather than providing prescriptions for spiritual training such as techniques of meditation or the use of mudras, he instead quotes from classical Chinese texts espousing that the ninja practice Confucian virtues of loyalty, benevolence, justice, and truth. Yasutake considers the most essential ingredient of the correct mind for a ninja to be the ability to rise above concerns for life and death, which he notes is as hard for a man to comprehend as it is for a bird to speak. He explains the workings of the universe in terms of the interaction of yin and yang and the five elements, in order for students to understand that life and death are intimately related and thus death is natural: "Life is man's yang, and death is his yin," as he puts it (*Bansen shûkai* 1982, 459).

The practice of ninjutsu has been revived since World War II and taught openly in several places in Japan. It has also been exported abroad, with the result that there are centers of training in so-called ninjutsu in many places throughout the world. Several years ago, on a Japanese *What's My Line*, a young American stumped the panel, who could not discern that his occupation was ninja. As the martial arts have become internationalized, cross-fertilization has taken place, with the result that schools teaching ninjutsu often incorporate standard techniques from karate, kung fu, and other martial arts into their repertoire. Ninjutsu continues to fascinate audiences worldwide, and modern warfare still allows considerable room for employment of commando forces, so the fascination with mastery of ninja skills of espionage provides a welcome marketing device for teachers. Yet there are no ninja today, only practitioners of some of the techniques and students of the tradition. Achievement of some rank within a school teaching ninjutsu cannot make one a ninja, any more than learning techniques with the sword can qualify one as a samurai.

G. Cameron Hurst III

See also Japan; Meditation
References
Bansen shûkai (Ten Thousand Rivers Converge into the Sea). 1982. In *Nihon Budô Taikei* (Compendium of Japanese Martial Arts). Vol. 5. Kyoto: Dôbôsha. 422–535.
Fujita Seiko. 1936. *Ninjutsu Hiroku* (Secret Records of Ninjutsu). Tokyo: Chiyoda Shôin.
Hatsumi, Masaaki. 1988. *The Essence of Ninjutsu: The Nine Traditions.* Lincolnwood, IN: NTC Publications.
———. 1981. *Ninjutsu: History and Tradition.* Burbank, CA: Unique Publications.
Hayes, Steven. 1988. *Ninja: Spirit of the Shadow Warrior.* Burbank, CA: Ohara Publications.
Okuse Heishichirô. 1982. "Ninjutsu." In *Nihon budô taikei* (Compendium of Japanese Martial Arts). Vol. 5. Kyoto: Dobosha.
———. 1959. *Ninjutsu hiden* (Secret Teachings of Ninjutsu). Tokyo: Heibonsha.
———. 1963. *Ninjutsu: Sono rekishi to ninja* (Ninjutsu: Its History and Ninja). Tokyo: Jimbutsu Ôraisha.
———. 1964. *Ninpô: Sono hiden to jitsurei* (Ninja Methods: Secret Teachings and Examples). Tokyo: Jimbutsu Ôraisha.
Turnbull, Stephen. 1991. *Ninja: The True Story of Japan's Secret Warrior Cult.* London: Firebird Books.
Watanabe Ichirô. 1984. "Iga-ryû." In *Encyclopedia Nipponica 2001.* Tokyo: Shôgakukan.
———. 1984. "Ninjutsu." In *Encyclopedia Nipponica 2001.* Tokyo: Shôgakukan.
Yamaguchi Masashi. 1963. *Ninja no seikatsu* (Lives of Ninja). Tokyo: Yûzankaku.

Okinawa

Okinawa means a "rope in the offing" (Japanese), and is the general name given to a chain of approximately 140 islands and reefs, situated south of Japan and north of Taiwan in the East China Sea. The islands are divided into three separate geographical regions, known as the Northern, Central, and Southern Ryûkyûs. Okinawa itself is the largest island in the chain and is located in the Central Ryûkyû region. The Southern Ryûkyûs are separated from the Central and Northern Ryûkyûs by a large expanse of open sea. Miyako Island, at the northernmost part of the southern region, is some 282 kilometers away from Okinawa Island, in the central region.

This oceanic divide and the Black Current, which runs from below the Philippines in the south and sweeps northward past Japan, effectively separated the Ryûkyûs into two cultural units, one formed by the northern and central regions and the other formed by the islands in the south. The Sakishima Islands in the south are believed to have been inhabited as early as 6000 B.C., but their culture appears to have been uninfluenced by their northern neighbors for roughly 7,000 years. Japanese and Chinese artifacts from the region date only to A.D. 1000. Habitation of the Northern and Central Ryûkyûs occurred some 30,000 years ago and was undertaken by the *Yamashita dôkutsujin* (Yamashita cavemen), who crossed the land bridges that then existed between the Ryûkyûs and Japan.

The Okinawan Shell Mound Era lasted from 2000 B.C. to A.D. 616, when the Yamato (Wa people of the Yayoi culture) of Kyûshû, the southernmost island of Japan, sent thirty Ryûkyû islanders to the court at Nara (Japan), ostensibly to learn about the advanced culture of Prince Shôtoku Taishi. The Yayoi culture had been acquainted with the use of iron and bronze tools and weapons since their social formation, about 300 B.C. And while there does exist some evidence that the Northern Ryûkyû islanders of Yakushima had knowledge of martial weaponry in A.D. 608, when some 1,000 were captured and enslaved by Sui Chinese explorers seeking the

Land of Happy Immortals, the Central Ryûkyûs remained effectively de-militarized until expansion by the Yamato after 616.

Shortly after 616, the Kami jidai (Age of the Gods) was established in the Central Ryûkyûs with the arrival of a group of Yamato on Seifa Utaki on the Chinen Peninsula. The exact nature of the Yamato mission is un-known, but it is obvious that they had planned an extended occupation. The Yamato from Nara brought with them a rice-based agricultural sys-tem, as well as iron implements to both farm and defend themselves. Folk history declares that it was on Seifa Utaki that the first rice was planted in the Ryûkyûs by the *kami* (gods) Shinerikyo and Amamikyo, who had de-scended from Heaven. That Heaven was probably Nara is evidenced in the Yamato chronicles by Shôtoku Taishi's appellation as Tennô (Ruler of Heaven). Amamikyo was impregnated by a divine wind and gave birth to two boys and a girl, who defined the Ryûkyûan social hierarchy into rulers (first son), priestesses (daughter), and farmers (second son), and began the Kami jidai. The sister or daughter of the king at Shuri, on Okinawa, served as the chief *noro* priestess (the chief priestess was called "kikoe-ôgimi") for the royal family until Shô Tai's abdication to the Japanese in 1879. To-gether with the divine gifts of iron tools and weapons came the quasi–Zen Buddhist teachings promulgated by the pious Shôtoku during his reign. Both the weapons and the religiosity influence Ryûkyûan martial arts to this day. And it is most probable that the martial art known as *te* was brought to Okinawa at this time.

Although *te* literally means "hand," the art has always been inti-mately associated with the use of weapons, so much so that the advanced empty-hand forms precisely correspond to applications with weapons. The primary weapons of te are the sword (*katana*), spear (*yari*), and halberd (*naginata*), which were also the principal weapons of the Japanese *bushi* (warrior). Te footwork and *taijutsu* (techniques for maneuvering the body) also suggest a Japanese origin of the art.

The belief that the Ryûkyûan martial arts were divinely influenced and intimately associated with royalty, itself of divine origin and establish-ment, is evidenced in the oral history of the art of te. The first mention of te occurs after the Satsuma invasion and subjugation of Okinawa in 1609. The Satsuma domain was based in Kagoshima, that is, Satsuma. They launched their invasion and subsequent conquest of the Ryûkyûs from their home in southern Kyûshû. King Shô Nei sent Jana Ueekata (Japanese; counselor) to negotiate the occupation treaty with the Japanese. Appalled by the terms set forth in the document and the general treatment of the Okinawans, Jana refused to ratify the agreement and was subsequently ex-iled to Kagoshima, home of the Satsuma, where he was sentenced to be boiled alive in oil. On the day of his execution, Jana requested that as a

Sensei Ty Yocham of the Texas Okinawan Gôjû Kai Federation deflects an upward cut of the sword with the eku (boat oar). (Courtesy of Ron Mottern)

bushi of the Ryûkyûs, he be allowed to practice te before his death. His request was granted, and he was released from his bonds, whereupon Jana performed a series of te exercises. When he had completed his forms, two executioners approached him to fulfill the death sentence, but before they could bind him, Jana grabbed the guards and plunged into the vat of boiling oil. The bodies of the men floated to the top of the vat and, resembling three linked commas, began to swirl in a counterclockwise direction. The linked comma symbol is known as the *hidari gomon* (outside karate systems, this symbol is commonly labeled *tomoemon* or *tomoe*), and it was adopted as the crest of the Ryûkyû royal family out of admiration for Jana Ueekata's act of loyalty to the king and devotion to Okinawa.

The close relationship between Ryûkyû royalty and the art of te is also evidenced in the position of the Motobu Udun government as te instructors of the royal court. The Motobu Udun lineage traces its roots to Prince Shô Koshin, sixth son to King Shô Shitsu, who ruled under the Satsuma from 1648 until 1668. Eleven successive generations of the Motobu Udun inherited the art of te and passed that knowledge on to the Ryûkyû royal line. Motobu Chôyû, who died in 1926, was the last in the Motobu Udun line and te instructor of the Marquis Shô Ten. It is also interesting to note that the epitome of te is contained in the Anji Kata no Me (Dance

Form of the Lords), thus furthering the association between the nobility (*anji*) and te.

The consideration that the divine progenitors of Ryûkyûan genesis myths were probably Japanese missionaries who came from the court of Shôtoku Taishi at Nara about A.D. 616, together with the association between te and successive generations of Ryûkyûan royalty and the fact that the principal weaponry of te was also the principal weaponry of the Japanese bushi, lends support to the idea that te itself is of Japanese origin.

The Japanese arts also influenced the development of karate on Okinawa. Karate should not be confused with te. The original name for karate was *Toudi*, or *Tôte* (Tang hand), denoting its roots in the Chinese martial arts. The name was later changed to *karate*, meaning "empty hand." Kanga Teruya, also known as Sakugawa Toudi (Tang Hand), studied combative forms in Satsuma, which he combined with forms he learned in Fuzhou and Beijing. Sakugawa's student, Matsumura Sôkon (1809–1901), traveled to Fuzhou and also to Kagoshima, where he studied the art of *Jigen-ryû Kenjutsu,* the sword style of the Satsuma samurai. On his return to Okinawa, Matsumura combined this knowledge of Jigen-ryû with the Chinese-based systems he learned in Fuzhou and Okinawa to form the basis of Shuri-di (*see* Karate, Okinawan).

Chinese martial arts (*wuyi*) entered Ryûkyû culture through interaction with Chinese immigrants who settled in Okinawa, and through Okinawans who traveled abroad. The Thirty-Six Families who settled at Kume Village in Kuninda, Naha, in 1392 undoubtedly brought combative disciplines with them. And in 1762, the Chinese *kenpô* expert, Kusanku, arrived in Okinawa with several of his students and began to disseminate his art.

Fuzhou, in the province of Fujian, was a major trading port between Okinawa and China. Fuzhou was also the home of many renowned Chinese martial artists, several of whom were reported to have studied at the famed Southern Shaolin Temple, and many young *Uchinachu* (Japanese; Okinawans) traveled to Fuzhou to study the martial arts. Sakugawa Toudi and Matsumura Sôkon studied in Fuzhou. Higashionna (Higaonna) Kanryô (1853–1915) studied *go no kenpô jû no kenpô* (hard-fist method/soft-fist method) in Fuzhou with the Chinese master Xie Zhongxiang, as did Nakaima Norisato. Higashionna returned to Okinawa and laid the foundation for Naha-di and, subsequently, the Gôjû-ryû (*see* Karate, Okinawan). Nakaima founded the Ryûei-ryû. Uechi Kanbun (1877–1948) also studied in Fuzhou. He learned the art of Pangai-Noon (also PanYing Jen, banyingruan, or Pan Ying Gut), which later became known in Okinawa as Uechi-ryû, from Zhou Zihe (Japanese, Shu Shi Wa). The Kojô family was one of the original Thirty-Six Families who came from Fuzhou and settled in the Kume village. The family continues to be a prominent martial arts source in Okinawa. The family operated its own dôjô in Fuzhou, where many young Uchinachu trained while in China. Until the 1970s, the Kojô family retained their close association with mainland China.

In 1936, Miyagi Chôjun, the founder of the Gôjû-ryû, presented an outline of karate in which he observed that the age of secrecy in karate had ended, and he predicted the internationalization of the art. The effects of World War II saw Miyagi proved correct. Okinawa underwent a change from the age of Japan to the age of America. And with this change came many changes for the martial arts community, both in Okinawa and Japan. Allied servicemen began to train in and disseminate karate throughout Europe, America, and the world. With a ready market, many unqualified, and some simply bogus, instructors began to teach various "styles" of karate to an eager public. The effects of these charlatans are still felt throughout the martial arts community. The traditional Okinawan concept of the *genkoki* (village training hall), where the deepest secrets of the art were studied and passed on solely for the continuation of the system, was virtually abandoned and lost. And although the postwar commercialization greatly contributed to this effect, the trend began with the public teaching of karate. Well-meaning instructors who felt that karate had much to offer the public attempted to disseminate karate for the benefit of the masses, rather than for the perpetuation of the classical system that was the cause from which those benefits sprang. Many new styles came into existence that utilized the forms of the old styles but were devoid of the spirit that made them worthwhile treasures. Rather than act in a synergistic system, mental and spiritual training took a backseat to the physical perpetuation of empty technique. In some cases, Okinawan karate kata were usurped by other styles, which claimed the forms originated with them. The advent of presenting kata and training methods on videotape, and more recently the Internet, has further diluted the essence of the art but has furthered the spread of karate's popularity.

Ron Mottern

See also Karate, Okinawan; Kobudô, Okinawan
References

Bishop, Mark. 1999. *Okinawan Karate: Teachers, Styles and Secret Techniques.* 2d ed. Boston: Tuttle.
———. 1996. *Zen Kobudô: Mysteries of Okinawan Weaponry and Te.* Rutland, VT: Tuttle.
Higashionna, Morio. 1996. *The History of Karate: Gôjû Ryû.* Dragon.
Kerr, George. 1960. *Okinawa: The History of an Island People.* Rutland, VT: Tuttle.
McCarthy, Patrick. 1995. *The Bible of Karate: Bubishi.* Rutland, VT: Tuttle.
Sandoval, Anthony. n.d. "The Traditional Genko Ki (Village Hall) Dojo." Unpublished paper.

Orders of Knighthood, Religious

Despite many legends indicating a greater antiquity, the first religious orders of knighthood (or military religious orders) were created in the aftermath of the First Crusade, which culminated in the Latin Christian conquest of Jerusalem and the whole Levantine coast in 1099. The earliest orders, indeed, were all founded and based in the city of Jerusalem itself, which became the capital of the new kingdom of that name.

The first body of men to which the term *military religious order* may justly be applied was formed around 1120 of a small group of lay knights led by Hugues de Payens, a nobleman from Champagne in France who was apparently related both to the ruler of that principality and to the future St. Bernard, abbot of Clairvaux. Hugues and his followers took the usual monastic vows of poverty, chastity, and obedience, but with the permission of the patriarch of Jerusalem, undertook the unusual task of defending the pilgrims then flocking to the newly reconquered Holy City. The king of Jerusalem, Baudouin II, gave the monk-knights a residence in his own palace, the former al-Aksa Mosque, and as the Crusaders mistook this building for the Temple of Solomon, they soon came to be known as the "Knights of the Temple" or "Templars." By 1129 they had taken on the additional duty of contributing to the defense of the Holy Land itself and lacked only a distinctive rule to make them a true military religious order.

There is no reason to suppose (as some historians have since 1818) that the first Christian order of knighthood was inspired by the similar Islamic institution of the *ribat,* but an understanding of its origins does require an examination of the contemporary state both of knighthood and of monasticism. As knights, the Templars belonged to an international category of professional warriors whose profession had traditionally suffered in the context of Christian society by the absolute moral prohibition of homicide imposed by the leaders of the Church. This prohibition had been effectively mitigated in the context of just wars since at least the eighth century, however, and had just been modified still further by the terms of the papal proclamation of the crusade in 1095: a proclamation that implicitly made homicide not only licit but actually praiseworthy if committed by a man bound by the vows and living the quasi-religious life of a crusader, in the context of a consecrated war against the enemies of Christ and his Church. This new doctrine, expounded and elaborated by various authorities in the first decades of the twelfth century, who were seeking to give knighthood in general a moral dimension it had previously lacked, allowed knightly crusaders to claim for themselves in a literal sense the old title *miles Christi* (Latin; soldier of Christ), long claimed in a purely metaphorical sense by the monks. Coincidentally, knightly status had also just begun to be seen by members of the old lordly nobility as the contemporary em-

A meeting of a branch of the Knights Templar with the grand master seated in the center. The order, founded in 1118, was originally formed to protect pilgrims on their journey to the Holy Land. (Hulton Archive)

bodiment of their own traditional military ideal, and therefore to be conferred by a special ritual called *adobement* (French; dubbing) on the eldest sons of nobles when they attained their majority. The prestige of knighthood was thus on the rise in both clerical and noble circles, and this would lead before the end of the century to the formulation of a complex new code of behavior for the nobility as a whole associated with knighthood and actually called "knightliness" or "chivalry." Nevertheless, in 1120 knights in general were still much less highly regarded than monks and clerics, and the small body of knights founded in Jerusalem to defend pilgrims initially lacked both the organization and the legitimacy conferred on contemporary monastic and clerical bodies by their constitutions, or "rules" of life.

The number and variety of monastic and quasi-monastic rules grew steadily in the early twelfth century, however, as different groups of men and women sought different ways to lead an ideal Christian life and founded new religious "orders," whose houses followed the same rule and increasingly submitted to a single central government as well. The most influential of the new orders of the latter type throughout the twelfth century was certainly that based in the Abbey of Cîteaux in northern Burgundy (founded in 1098), and in its four eldest daughter houses of La Ferté (1113), Pontigny (1114), Clairvaux (1115), and Morimond (1115). The Cistercians (as their members are called) were militant Benedictine monks who restored serious manual labor and apostolic simplicity to the monastic life, and introduced for the first time the incorporation of "lay brothers," who were not required to take full monastic vows, but nevertheless lived within the monastery and carried out many useful tasks for the salvation of their souls. Not surprisingly, the Cistercian rule and ethos—and possibly even their plain white habit—served as models for many of the military orders.

Among the other rules established in this period, the one that had the most influence on those of the military orders was the semimonastic rule actually written about 1100, but attributed to St. Augustine of Hippo, designed to provide a holy and communal life suitable for people who (unlike monks and nuns) had to perform some function in the secular world. It was adopted independently in the same period by numerous bodies of previously secular priests attached to collegiate churches such as cathedrals (who came to be known as "Augustinian Canons" or simply "Canons Regular"), and also by the attendants of many "hospitals," which were not merely institutions for the sick, but hostels for pilgrims and other travelers. Some hospitallers (as their attendants were called) were also priests, but the majority were either clerics in minor orders or simple laymen, so the Augustinian Rule, like that of the Cistercians, was capable of organizing people of different conditions in the same community.

Given the prestige of monastic status and monastic rules in the twelfth century, it was almost inevitable that the body of knights who undertook to protect the pilgrims to Jerusalem in 1118 should seek a form of monastic rule tailored to their own peculiar religious function. Given the fact that their leader was a Champenois nobleman, it follows that he should seek this rule from the nobly born Bernard, abbot of Clairvaux in Champagne, who was in any case the effective leader of the Cistercians from 1115 to his death in 1153 and the most influential spiritual leader in Latin Christendom in the second quarter of the twelfth century. Bernard probably helped to compose the new rule the knights received from the Council of Troyes in 1129 (a rule that bore a general resemblance to that of his own order). He certainly wrote for them the tract "In Praise of the New Knighthood" (*De laude novae militiae*), which justified the foundation of a religious order dedicated to military activities that only a short time earlier would have been unthinkable for monks. The new order took the formal name the "Order of the Poor Knights of Christ of the Temple of Solomon," or the "Knights of Christ" for short, but its members continued to be called Templars. The idea of a religious order made up largely of men who were at once monks and knights immediately struck a chord in the hearts of many contemporaries, from the pope on down. The new order was soon showered with privileges and properties scattered all over Latin Europe, making it one of the largest and most widespread religious orders (and one of the richest international corporations) of its time. It was also given a number of key fortresses in the lands of the crusader states of the Levant and soon became, with its rival the Order of the Hospital, a key element of the defensive system of those states as a whole.

The Order of the Hospital of St. John of Jerusalem grew to be a military order in a completely different way. It began as a body of hospitallers under the Augustinian Rule, attached to a hospital in Jerusalem founded by merchants from Amalfi in Italy at some time after 1060. This hospital had initially been placed under the patronage of St. John the Almoner, patron saint of hospitallers, and subordinated to two Benedictine abbeys, one for men and one for women, founded at the same time. Its services impressed the crusaders who conquered Jerusalem in the First Crusade, and it was erected into a separate (though still very minor) order in 1103, and soon rededicated to the much greater saint, John the Baptist. Under the government of its first master, the Blessed Gerard (who died in 1120), other privileges and donations quickly followed, and the young order developed along the same general lines as that of the Temple after 1130, with properties and minor houses scattered throughout Latin Christendom. The order's first nobly born master, Raymond du Puy, composed the earliest rule of the order, probably between 1145 and 1153. The rule incorporated not only the primitive unwritten customs of the order, but certain elements of both the Augustinian and (to a lesser extent) Benedictine Rules and certain elements in common with (but not necessarily borrowed from) the Rule of the Temple. Nevertheless, this rule made no mention of the knights who in the meantime had certainly come to form, with the lay hospitallers and their priestly chaplains, one of the distinct classes into which the membership of the order was divided.

How the Order of the Hospital came to include knights has indeed remained something of a mystery. Recent arguments, however, contend, on the basis of the small amount of evidence that has survived, that the order began to take in knights as brethren almost immediately after the election of Raymond du Puy to the mastership in 1123, that their admission was probably the result of a desire on the part of Raymond to recruit from the same pool as the Templars (not yet organized as an order), and that these knights from the start carried out military duties similar to those undertaken by the Templars. Certainly the order had been given major castles to defend by the time the statutes were written (Bethgibelin in 1136; Krak de Chevaliers, Bochee, Lacu, and Felicium in 1144), and soon rivaled the Templars in the number and importance of their military possessions in the Holy Land. Nevertheless, in contrast to that of their rivals of the Temple, the role of the knights in the Order of the Hospital was for a long time contrary to the statutes and actively opposed by the higher authorities of the Church, and they did not achieve a position of numerical preponderance within the order until after the conquest of Jerusalem by Saladin in 1187. Furthermore, they were not formally distinguished from the other lay brethren until the adoption in 1204 through 1206 (under the mastership of Prince Afonso de Portugal) of the Statutes of Margat, which gave the newly recognized class of brother knights the dominant place in the order's government. Thus, while the Order of the Hospital of St. John may have been the first monastic order to include a body of professed knights, it did not become a primarily military order until about the time of the Third Crusade and did not become an officially military order until between 1204 and 1206—almost a century after it became an independent order.

By 1150 at the latest, it is clear that both the Temple and the Hospital of St. John were important international orders and that they included significant numbers of men (at first mainly knights) dedicated to an essentially military way of life. Also, these men were full members of the respective orders, bound by the same vows of poverty, chastity, and obedience to their superiors as their nonmilitary brethren and members of other orders following a monastic or "religious" life. In addition, they were either wholly (in the case of the former) or partly (in the case of the latter) dedicated to the war against the enemies of Christ and his Church in the Holy Land. They thus presented two distinct models for other men with similar ideals who wished to contribute to the crusade, either in the Holy Land itself or on other frontiers of Christendom where Muslims or pagans could be seen either as threatening Christians or as occupying lands that could be subjected to Christian rule and evangelization.

Four additional military orders were actually founded in the Holy Land before the end of the century, to incorporate groups of knights who for one reason or another did not fit comfortably in any of the established orders. The rather obscure Order of the Hospital of St. Lazarus of Jerusalem had its origins in a hospital for lepers, served by Augustinian Canons. It is first mentioned in 1142, and it probably acquired its first knights—all of whom were themselves infected with leprosy—from the two older orders. It may, therefore, have played some part in the Second Crusade (organized by Bernard of Clairvaux himself, and fought from 1146 to 1148), but the first references to its participation in warfare date from the 1240s, so it may not have been militarized much before that.

The other two orders were apparently established (or rather converted into military orders) to serve different linguistic communities—the first three orders being dominated by Francophones—and were both based in the city of Acre, to which the king of Jerusalem had been forced to withdraw after the (permanent) loss of Jerusalem to Saladin in 1187. That of the Teutonic Knights of the Hospital of St. Mary was founded as a hospital for German pilgrims by German crusaders during the Third Crusade in 1191, and was militarized by about 1198, while that of the Hospital of St. Thomas of Acre was founded as a hospital for English pilgrims by English crusaders about 1191 and was militarized only in 1227 or 1228. Despite their origins (and continuing minor vocation) as hospitallers, the Teutonic Knights adopted a rule based quite closely on that of the Templars.

By the time the Third Crusade had begun in 1188, however, several military orders had already been founded to support the Iberian Reconquista (the irredentist war against the Moors of southern Iberia that had been in progress since shortly after the original conquest in 711–718 and had been declared to be a crusade by Pope Eugenius III in 1147). The Order of Calatrava was founded by the Cistercian Abbot of Fitero in 1158, just to the south of the Castilian frontier, and quickly acquired lands and houses in southern Castile and Aragon. A second order was founded ca. 1166 at Evora in Portugal under the name the Order of St. Benedict of Evora, but it was soon affiliated with Calatrava, became its Portuguese branch, and after moving its seat to Avis called itself the Order of Avis. The Order of St. Julian of Pereiro was similarly founded as an independent order in Leon by 1176, but it affiliated with Calatrava, became its Leonese branch, and took new names from its successive seats at Trujillo (in 1188) and Alcántara (in 1218). All three of these orders remained affiliated with the Cistercian Order and were treated as direct or indirect dependencies of the Cistercian Abbey of Morimond. The Order of St. James (or Santiago) of Compostela in Galicia, by contrast, was created by the archbishop of that pilgrimage city in 1170 by imposing a semimonastic rule on the older military confraternity called the Fratres de Caceres, based far to the south. Its knights were actually permitted to marry. Its Portuguese branch, called the Order of São Thiago or Sant' Iago, became independent in 1290.

The three branches of the Cistercian Order of Alcántara and the two branches of the peculiar Order of Santiago were the most important indigenous orders in Iberia, but several other orders were founded in the later twelfth and thirteenth centuries that ultimately proved less successful. The Order of Mountjoy (in Spanish, Montegaudio) was established in Leon ca. 1173 by Rodrigo, former count of Sarria and a former knight of Santiago who wanted a stricter way of life; it started with another name, but after it had been given some properties in the crusader states, it took that of the hill from which pilgrims first saw Jerusalem. It does not seem to have taken part in the Levantine crusade, however, and after several further changes of seat and name (including those of Trafac and Monfragüe) and several partial amalgamations with other orders (including the Temple), what remained of the order was suppressed in 1221, and its members and possessions annexed to Calatrava. The Order of St. George of Alfama (San Jorge de Alfama) was founded by King Pere II of Aragon in 1201, probably to provide a safer alternative to the Templars, who were already too strong in his kingdom, and it survived for several centuries as a purely Aragonese order. A tenth order—the Order of Our Lady of Mercy (Nuestra Señora de Merced)—was added in 1233, but its members, called Mercedarians, were more concerned with ransoming captives than with fighting the Moors, and it was definitively demilitarized in 1317. An eleventh, St. Mary of Spain (Santa María de España), was founded by Alfonso X of Castile after 1253, but it had a short life, as it was annexed to Santiago to compensate the latter for a terrible defeat it suffered in 1280.

As both the Temple and the Hospital of St. John had extensive holdings in Iberia, that peninsula was thenceforth to have the highest concentration of military orders of any region in Latin Christendom. All of these orders played an active role in the reconquest of Spain from the Moors, and so successful were they that by 1253 the only remaining Moorish state in Iberia was the diminutive Emirate (or later Kingdom) of Granada in the mountains of the far south, which survived with essentially the same boundaries down to 1492. The role of the orders for the next century or so was therefore reduced largely to defending the Christian realms against counteroffensives from the Moors of North Africa.

In the years between the Third and Fourth Crusades to the Holy Land (1192–1204), a third front in the ongoing crusade had been opened on the frontier between the Christian Germans and the still pagan Balts—the Prussians, Lithuanians, and Latvians—and their neighbors the Finnic Estonians, stretched out along the shores of the Baltic Sea. The crusade against the Balts was first undertaken in the far north by the new German order officially called the Knighthood of Christ of Livonia, but more commonly known as the Order of the Brethren of the Sword. A missionary German bishop founded this order for that purpose in 1202. By 1230 it had succeeded in conquering most of what was called Livonia, corresponding to what is now southern Estonia and most of Latvia. In or shortly before 1228 (when it received its papal confirmation), a Polish bishop founded the Order of Dobrzyn on the same model to conquer the pagan Prussians at the western end of the region, but this order had a much more limited success. In the meantime, however, Duke Konrad of Mazovia had offered to the Teutonic Order the district of Culmerland if they sent a force to fight the Prussians, and the emperor Frederick II had in 1226 confirmed this offer and promised to make the high master of the Teutonic Knights, Hermann von Salza, and his successors princes of the empire in respect of any lands their order might conquer in Prussia. The Teutonic Order was still based in Acre, but it had already been given a territory to defend in eastern Hungary in 1211 and had just been expelled from that kingdom in 1225 for creating a state within a state. The dispossessed knights began almost immediately to take possession of their newly granted lands, and in 1235 and 1237 they respectively absorbed the weaker Order of Dobrzyn and amalgamated with the more powerful Order of the Swordbrethren.

In 1240 the Teutonic Order moved its seat from Acre to Prussia, most of which it conquered by 1283. The knights quickly made themselves the collective lords of this peculiar order-state, which by 1309—when they established their headquarters in the great Castle of Marienburg—was slightly larger than England and included all of the lands now incorporated in northern Poland (centered on Danzig, Polish Gdansk), Russian Kaliningrad (the Königsberg of the knights), Lithuania, Latvia, and Estonia. The high master, under the purely theoretical suzerainty of the pope, ruled all of these lands (divided between Prussia and Livonia). Although its reason for existence ceased to be in 1386, when the last pagan grand prince of Lithuania, Jogaila, married the heiress to the crown of Poland and converted to Catholic Christianity, the order-state survived intact into the 1460s, when the ruler of Poland-Lithuania seized control of both eastern and western Prussia and divided the domain into two parts. What remained of Prussia became a fief of the Polish crown, and it passed out of the order's control in 1525, when the reigning high master, Albrecht von Hohenzollern, decided to become a Protestant and rule it as a duke. Livonia continued under the control of the (newly independent) Brethren of the Sword until 1561, when their high master decided to do the same and became a Polish vassal as duke of Courland.

Long before these developments in the far north, the original crusade against the Muslims in the Holy Land had suffered a series of setbacks. It finally failed entirely in 1291, when the remaining Christian strongholds, centered on the cities of Acre and Tripoli, were retaken by the Mamluk sultan of Egypt, the successor of Saladin. This forced the military orders that had remained there to fall back to Cyprus, regroup, and decide what to do next—under considerable pressure from such men as the indefatigable preacher Ramon Llull and a whole succession of popes to amalgamate in a single great order. This idea was fiercely resisted, however, and all but the Templars withdrew from Cyprus as soon as they could find somewhere else to settle. The Knights of St. Thomas moved their headquarters to England, and the Lazarites to France, while the Hospitallers of St. John merely moved slightly westward in 1310 to the island of Rhodes. There they soon established an order-state, comparable in nature (if not in extent) to that of the Teutonic Knights, and continued an active war against the Muslims by sea. They were commonly called the Knights of Rhodes from 1310 to 1527, when they finally lost that island and its dependencies to the Ottoman sultan. In 1530 they were granted Malta in its place, and as the Knights of Malta carried on the original crusade until Napoleon Bonaparte finally dispossessed them in 1798.

The two orders that had retired to Europe, by contrast, ceased to play any active role in the crusade, and the Temple, after some years of interfering in the politics of Cyprus, was officially suppressed by a papal decree of 1312, responding to charges from King Philippe IV of France that the knights had engaged in impious and blasphemous activities. Philippe had in fact had these charges fabricated because he feared the presence in his kingdom of a powerful military order without a clear external goal and coveted their estates and income. In fact the pope gave their estates throughout Latin Christendom to the Hospitallers, who still needed (and deserved) their income. The decision to suppress the Templars had, however, been received coldly in both Portugal and Aragon, where a fear of attack from Muslim North Africa remained quite serious down to about 1350. In each of those kingdoms, therefore, the local province of the Temple was erected by the king into an independent order: the Order of the Knights of Christ in the former (established in 1317), and the Order of Our Lady of Montesa in the latter (founded in 1319).

All of the surviving Iberian orders continued to exist for some centuries after 1319, and all played an active part in the defense of the peninsula led by Alfonso XI of Castile from 1325 to his death in 1350. So successful was this campaign, however, that the orders thenceforth had few opportunities to fight the Moors and devoted most of their energies to their traditional pastime of quarreling both within and among themselves and interfering in secular politics. In the later fourteenth century their members, like the members of most other religious orders, became increasingly worldly in outlook and behavior, and the monastic discipline under which they were supposed to live rested ever more lightly on their shoulders. This led the Iberian kings to seek new ways to control the orders based in their domains. Before the conquest of Granada in 1492, the principal device the kings employed for this purpose was securing the election of one of their sons or brothers as master, but once the Reconquest had been completed they controlled the orders by annexing the masterships to their own crowns: at first in fact, and finally, through a papal bull of 1523, in law. Since all of the Iberian kingdoms except Portugal had been joined in a personal union since 1416, this meant that the indigenous orders were thenceforth annexed either to the crown of Spain (Calatrava, Alcántara, Santiago, Alfama, Montesa) or to that of Portugal (Avis, Christ, São Thiago).

A few other military orders were founded at much later dates, especially to fight the new crusade that had to be mounted against the Ottoman Turks in the Balkans from 1359. The most important, of these at least, was the Knightly Order of St. George, founded by the emperor Frederick III in 1469 and maintained at least to the death of his son the emperor Maximilian in 1519. Perhaps the most peculiar was the Order of St. Maurice, founded in 1434 by Amé VIII, duke of Savoy, and maintained until his election as antipope under the name Felix V in 1439, for it was made up of knights who lived in the fashion of Carthusian hermits rather than as crusaders. It was "revived" by Duke Emmanuel Philibert in 1572 in order to serve as a basis for the annexation of the long-useless Order of St. Lazarus to the throne of Savoy. The French branch of the latter order resisted the papal act of consolidation, but it was eventually annexed in 1608 to the new French Order of Our Lady of Mount Carmel, similarly founded for the purpose in the previous year. Various minor orders had already been annexed to the Order of the Hospital, which for a time in the sixteenth century was the only order still actively engaged in the crusade, but a new Order of St. Stephen was founded in 1561 by the first grand duke of Tuscany, Cosimo de' Medici, to carry on a similar form of naval warfare in the western Mediterranean. Orders based in countries that accepted the Reformation, including the English Order of St. Thomas, were simply suppressed.

The religious orders of knighthood all differed from one another in a variety of minor ways, and were all jealous of their identity, ethos, and traditions. Nevertheless, most of them had a great deal in common. All but the smallest and least successful were organized as multihouse monastic orders on the general model of the Cistercians, and all but the two Iberian Orders of St. James had fully monastic rules that were based, directly or indirectly, upon either the Rule of St. Benedict or the so-called Rule of St. Augustine. Over the years, the original rule of most of the orders came to be supplemented by a growing number of statutes and customs, both written and unwritten, and by the later thirteenth century the statutes, broadly conceived, were hundreds of very specific ordinances, regulating almost every aspect of their organization, communal life, and corporate activities.

Like many other comparable bodies in the period, the military orders also came to have several distinct classes of membership, often as well as one or more classes of people merely associated with the order. By 1200 the dominant class in every order had come to be made up of "brother knights," who were already drawn largely from the noble order and the landed upper stratum of the knightly order of society, and after 1250 were drawn entirely from the new knightly nobility that had resulted from the fusion of those social categories. The number of brother knights varied widely from order to order, and fluctuated wildly, depending on casualties, within those that bore the brunt of battles, but the greater orders, such as the Templars, Hospitallers, and Teutonic Knights, normally included several hundred professed knights, and the lesser orders like St. Lazarus and St. Thomas probably never included more than a few dozen. In addition to the brother knights, most orders included a second class of military brethren, called "brother sergeants" by the Templars and their imitators and "brother sergeants-at-arms" by the Hospitallers and their imitators. They were drawn from the families of landless knights (before ca. 1250) and mere freemen, and served in much the same manner as the knights.

All orders also included a certain (relatively small) number of men in holy orders called "brother chaplains," who performed the numerous services deemed necessary for the spiritual health of the order and its members, and a larger class of servants of humble birth (called "brothers-of-work" by the Templars and "brother sergeants-of-office" by the Hospitallers), who performed all of the other necessary tasks at the order's various houses, including the hospitals that several orders always maintained. The brethren of this class were often heavily supplemented with men merely hired for the purpose, but the members of the other classes were made up entirely of "professed" brethren, who took solemn vows and lived in community under the strict monastic rule of their order, either in the convent or in one of the numerous daughter houses that served either as military outposts or as sources of revenue and recruitment.

A number of orders, including both the Templars and Hospitallers, also maintained associated lay confraternities, whose members (*confratres,* or "fellow-brethren") were admitted to all of the order's spiritual privileges in return for certain donations (whence the later title "donats") and vows of protection. The confratres who were also knights might even join in the campaigns of the order for a season or two, and in the later fourteenth century the Teutonic Knights in particular made a practice of inviting knights from all over Latin Christendom to join them during their annual campaigning season. Many of these knights—like the one in Chaucer's *Canterbury Tales* who had participated in all the important battles fought by the order against the heathen—probably became confratres of the order.

Like those of monastic orders generally, the professed brethren of most military orders were distinguished from the beginning by a peculiar habit (mode of dress) suggestive of their religious status. The nature of the habit evolved gradually over time. By the end of the thirteenth century the more formal version normally included a long mantle opening down the front like a clerical cope, and as most monks wore nothing like it, the mantle became and has since remained the most distinctive mark of membership in a military order. In some orders, indeed (and possibly in all), new members were solemnly invested with the mantle during the induction ceremonies into the order. The mantles and habits of most orders were made of undyed or white wool, like the habits of the Cistercians, but the Hospitallers of St. John wore a habit and mantle of black, like many Augustinian orders of canons, and a military surcoat of red.

The mantle was normally charged on the left breast with the cross that distinguished all crusaders, but these crosses tended to be made of cloth of a more or less distinctive color (e.g., red among the Templars) and of an increasingly distinctive shape. The classic shapes were not generally achieved before the later fourteenth or even the fifteenth century, however, and the eight-pointed crosses of the Hospitallers of St. John were rarely rectilinear before their transfer from Rhodes to Malta in 1530. The rectilinear "Maltese" version of their white cross was soon adopted by the Knights of St. Lazarus (in green) and the Knights of St. Stephen (in red), and after 1693 became the normal form for the cross assigned to newer orders of lay knights, but nothing like it was used by any other order before 1530, and its common modern assignment to the Templars is without foundation. In fact, the red cross of the Templars seems to have been either quite plain, like that of their Portuguese continuators the Knights of Christ, or slightly splayed at the ends, like the black cross of their northern brethren the Teutonic Knights, later adopted (with its white field included as edging) as the cross of the German armed forces.

As was usual in monastic orders, the supreme government of every military order was vested in a single chief officer, but that officer was not called by the usual title of *abbas* (Latin; abbot), but by the distinctive (and often military) title of *magister* (master), modified in the Temple and Teutonic Order (and in the late fifteenth century in that of the Hospital) by the adjective *magnus* (grand) (represented in German by *hoch* [high]). The master, or grand master, was elected for life from among the brother knights of the order by a complex process that varied from one order to another, but increasingly tended to involve only those knights who held some administrative office in the order. Once elected, the master was charged with the general administration of the order, which usually included the appointment and supervision of all subordinate officials; the reception of candidates for admission as brothers, or confratres; the maintenance of discipline among the members of the various classes; and the oversight of the order's finances. He also led the forces of the order on campaign, and both convoked and presided over the meetings of the order's officers, normally referred to as *Capitula Generalia* (Chapters General). In the early days of most orders, the master lived in community with the ordinary knights of the order, but as the orders became richer and their houses more and more dispersed, their masters (like bishops generally and the abbots of many orders) tended to live apart and to adopt a lifestyle similar to that of the great barons or secular princes with whom they spent much of their time.

In the day-to-day business of the order, the master governed with the assistance of the great officers of the order, who resided with him in the order's convent and were charged with the oversight of the various administrative departments into which the central government was divided. These departments and their heads represented a mixture of those found in all religious houses and those maintained by secular kings and princes. In the Order of the Hospital of St. John, for example—the most widespread and best documented of the orders—the officers in question included the prior of St. John and the "conventual bailiffs." At first these were only five in number, but in 1301 it was decided that each bailiff should be given, in addition to his duties in the convent, the government of one of the seven *langues* (tongues) into which the regional administration of the order had just been organized. This required raising the admiral and the *turcopolier* (the officer who commanded the auxiliary forces) to the rank of bailiff and produced the following set of officers (in descending order of precedence): the grand commander (finances, tongue of Provence), the marshal (military matters, tongue of Auvergne), the hospitaller (medical services, tongue of France), the drapier or (from 1539) conservator (clothing and material supplies, tongue of Aragon), the admiral (navy, tongue of Italy), and the turcopolier (auxiliary forces, tongue of England). To these were added in 1428 the office of grand bailiff (fortifications, tongue of Germany) and in 1462 that of chancellor (chancery, foreign affairs, tongue of Castile and Portugal).

The master carried out the ordinary business of most orders with the assistance of the great officers' equivalent to the conventual bailiffs of St. John and their staffs. At regular intervals, however (about once a year in the great orders of the Levant, and at the three great feasts of Easter, Pentecost, and Christmas in the Spanish Order of Calatrava), the master was obliged to convene a meeting of the full Chapter General, which in addition to the order's great officers normally included many of the administrators of the order's outlying possessions. The normal purpose of such meetings was to consider the general situation of the order, to debate any major changes in policy or strategy, to hear and judge accusations of dereliction of duty and deviation from the Rule made against any of its members, and to assign punishments to those found guilty. The members of most orders were also obliged to submit any disputes that had arisen among themselves to the binding arbitration of the Chapter General.

Regional and local administration varied in detail from order to order, but once again the Hospital of St. John may reasonably serve as an example, especially if contrasted to the usages of the Temple. The seven or eight tongues of the hospital, governed by the conventual bailiffs (only four of whom were required to be in residence at the convent at any one time), had as their immediate dependencies from one to seven regional priories, or in some places grand priories, including two or more priories; the government of these was entrusted to appointive officers called priors and grand priors respectively. In exceptional cases units of this level bore the title "castellany" or "(grand) bailiwick," and their governors were called "castellan" or "(grand) bailiff." The tongue of Aragon, for example, included the priories of Aragon, Navarre, and Catalonia, while that of Germany included the priories of Germany, Bohemia, and Hungary and the grand bailiwick of Brandenburg. The Templars, by contrast (whose chief officer bore the title grand master), preferred to call their regional governors masters rather than priors.

These regional units, in their turn, consisted of about a dozen to about sixty local units, called "commanderies" in the Hospital and "preceptories" in the Temple, governed by commanders or preceptors. These units had originally been much smaller and more numerous, but were generally consolidated to the point where they were roughly the size of a manor, and could justify having a brother knight assigned to their administration. The majority of Hospital commanderies came in fact to be reserved to knights, but a few were reserved to brother chaplains and brother sergeants.

As most of the higher administrative positions in the order were also restricted to members of the order's knightly class, there came to be in effect five distinct grades of brother knight under the master: those of (1) ordinary brother knight, (2) commander, (3) prior (or castellan or bailiff), (4) grand prior, and (5) conventual bailiff. The conventual bailiffs came to be distinguished symbolically by a larger than normal version of the order's cross, and thus they came to be known—at first informally but eventually in a formal way—as "bailiffs of the grand cross" or simply "grand crosses." All of these grades, of course, reflected real differences of authority within the order, and though honorable, were never merely honorific. Within the grade of (ordinary) brother knight, however, a purely honorific distinction began to emerge in the fourteenth century between those whose noble ancestry was sufficient to qualify them for membership according to the current rules of their own langue, so that they could be described as "knights of justice," and those who required some sort of dispensation or act of grace to be admitted under those rules, who formed the inferior category of "knights of grace." Other orders developed similar hierarchies or grades and a similar obsession with the purity and antiquity of their members' nobility.

Finally, most orders possessed a large number of buildings, including those of the principal convent, of other lesser convents, and of the seats of provincial and local administrators. Although the oldest orders were at first based in buildings within the city walls of Jerusalem or Acre, these orders later emulated all of the other orders in setting their principal convent within the walls of a major castle. Most of the provincial convents were similarly housed, and indeed all of the castles manned by the orders had to function as convents for the professed brethren assigned to their defense. The seats of priories and comparable regional units were also housed for the most part in castles belonging to the order, but the commanderies—which might have only one professed brother—were typically housed in smaller and less fortified establishments resembling those of a manor house. Within the castles that served as their convents, at least, the brethren usually provided themselves with the set of buildings associated with the monastic life: a church, in which the daily office was maintained by the clerical brethren and any others available; a kitchen, refectory, and dormitory for eating and sleeping; a chapter house for meetings; stables for their horses; various outbuildings for storing equipment, grain, wine, and other things necessary to their lives and activities; and buildings for housing and feeding auxiliaries. The master and conventual officers in the seat and the priors in their seats usually maintained separate housing for themselves and honored guests that bore more resemblance to the dwellings of princes than to those of monks.

The military missions of the religious order varied significantly both from theater to theater and from period to period. In the Levant, their task was mainly defensive, except during a more general crusade, and this was also true in Iberia after 1250 and in the Baltic after 1309. Between 1158 and 1250, however, the Iberian orders' primary task was retaking lost Christian territory, whereas between 1202 and 1309, the Baltic orders were mainly involved in conquering the lands of pagan peoples whom they were perfectly prepared to slaughter if they did not convert. The very different physical and climatic environments of the three theaters also necessitated different strategies and tactics, so it is difficult to generalize about these matters.

In the leading orders, the brother knights and brother sergeants-at-arms constituted the principal fighting force, and although the former were provided with better equipment and more horses than the latter, both groups were trained to fight primarily as heavy cavalry or (when the occasion required it) heavy infantry. In this they resembled the knights and squires of secular companies, but there is no evidence that nobly born recruits to any order had to postpone dubbing to knighthood beyond their attainment of the age of majority, as was increasingly true in the secular world. The religious knights did not differ from their secular equivalents in arms, armor, or tactics, but the hosts of the military orders were much larger and better disciplined than those led by any secular prince or baron, and had more esprit de corps. Indeed, in the Levant the Muslims looked upon them as their most dedicated and therefore dangerous enemies, and Saladin systematically killed any of them who fell into his hands. Their dis-

cipline was enforced by written regulations, by the formal vow of obedience they took on joining, by the harsh punishments meted out to those
who deviated, and by their custom of living, exercising, and fighting as part
of a stable community. The number of fighting brethren maintained by
each order varied considerably, but at their height in the thirteenth century
each of the three great orders in the Levant could field about three hundred, of whom about a third were knights. Nine hundred might not seem
like a very high number, but it was half again as great as that of the whole
feudal levy of the kingdom. When one bears in mind the fact that other
types of fighting men always supplemented the warrior brethren more or
less closely tied to the order, it becomes clear that the orders were vitally
important for the defense of the Holy Land.

The nature of the supplementary forces also varied. In some orders,
the brother sergeants-of-office could be called upon to take up arms in
emergencies, but they were not expected to fight very well and were not
under the same discipline. Most of the major orders also permitted knights,
squires, and probably sergeants to join them for a season or a year, and to
live under their rule without taking vows of permanent membership. The
Teutonic Order had a theoretical right to command all those who joined
the ongoing Baltic crusade, and the leading orders also acquired numerous
estates held for them by vassals whom they could compel to serve the order without acquiring any formal association with it. Finally, most orders
relied to some extent on mercenaries, some of whom presumably served in
capacities other than heavy cavalry. In the Levant they were commonly referred to as *turcopoles,* but what precisely that term implied militarily is
unclear. The principal military duties of the orders consisted of manning
castles and using them as bases for both defensive and offensive operations
against enemies, serving in the field either on their own or as major units
in a royal or princely host, and later (from 1299) maintaining and fighting
from fleets of galleys dedicated to protecting Christian shipping and harry-
ing the Muslims whenever and in whatever ways were feasible.

The more or less sharp decline in the fortunes of all of the orders other
than the Hospital after 1291, and even more after 1350, was due to a number of distinct factors. Of these the most important were the success or failure of their original enterprise, a destructive rivalry among the orders, and
the decline of the monastic ideals they represented in the eyes of the population at large. Certainly the problem was not initially an inherent defect in
their nature or organization, for on all three frontiers of Latin Christendom
the orders had demonstrated again and again the value of a disciplined
body of carefully trained knights who trained and practiced their skills as
a unit, were maintained in constant readiness, and fought under the familiar and unquestioned authority of a single commander who could require

their service whenever he needed it and for as long as he needed it, without considerations of remuneration. In all of these respects, the military orders compared very favorably to the motley bodies of often recalcitrant, ill-trained, and unruly vassals (all of whom had first to be summoned and then to be paid) who made up a large part of the forces available to most contemporary princes before the middle of the fifteenth century.

Either complete success or total failure had reduced most of the orders to the condition of uselessness by the end of the fourteenth century, however, and it was inevitable that kings would begin to look upon them as sources of income and favors to noble clients rather than as military aid. The decline in the value nobles placed on monastic ideals further led to a drastic decline in monastic discipline among the brother knights of most orders and a widespread abandonment of the communal life that was finally recognized by changes in the rules. The complete reorganization of national armies effected in the fifteenth and sixteenth centuries removed even the potential utility of most of the surviving orders as military units, and all but the two naval orders were quickly reduced to a condition not essentially different from that of the secular monarchical orders many princes had founded since 1325.

D'A. Jonathan D. Boulton

See also Chivalry; Europe; Knights; Orders of Knighthood, Secular; Religion and Spiritual Development: Ancient Mediterranean and Medieval West

References

Barber, Malcolm. 1994. *The New Knighthood: A History of the Order of the Temple.* Cambridge: Cambridge University Press.

Forey, Alan. 1992. *The Military Orders from the Twelfth to the Early Fourteenth Centuries.* Toronto: University of Toronto Press.

Riley-Smith, Jonathan. 1967. *The Knights of St John in Jerusalem and Cyprus, 1050–1310.* London and New York: St. Martin's.

———, ed. 1991. *The Atlas of the Crusades.* New York: Oxford University Press.

Sire, H. J. A. 1994. *The Knights of Malta.* New Haven: Yale University Press.

Orders of Knighthood, Secular

Order (of knighthood) has been loosely applied since the later fourteenth century to all forms of military, knightly, or more generally noble body bearing some resemblance (often of the most superficial kind) to the military religious orders, or religious orders of knighthood, founded from about 1130 onward to serve as the corps d'elite of the armies of the various regional crusades. The latter were made up of men who were bound by the religious or monastic vows of poverty, chastity, and obedience. Although they normally included men from all three of the orders of society (clerics, lay nobles, and simples), by the end of the twelfth century they were all dominated by that class of their lay members who were also knights and who by about 1250 (when knighthood was restricted to men of knightly or noble birth) were nobles as well. Secular bodies of soldiers similarly dominated by knights were founded at about the same time as the earliest religious orders, but seem to have been unknown outside Spain and northern Italy before about 1325, and flourished primarily between that date and about 1525.

Although all such bodies are now commonly called "orders," most did not use that title, and many were not even bodies corporate. Therefore, the more accurate name is "secular military associations." Most were effectively restricted to laymen, and were thus "lay military associations," but others included a dependent class of secular priests as well. All such bodies may also be sorted into nonnoble, seminoble, and strictly noble types, according to the dominant class of lay members, and each of these into various subtypes. The term *order* is reserved for certain of the more elaborate noble subtypes, by which the title was actually used. The qualification "of knighthood" is reserved for the small minority that actually restricted their principal class of membership to dubbed knights.

Unlike the religious orders on which they were partly modeled, the secular associations were extremely diverse because they drew upon a variety of models other than the religious or monastic order of knighthood both for their forms and attributes and for their goals and activities. The most important of these additional models were the fictional orders or military brotherhoods of both the Arthurian and (later) the Greek tradition (especially the companies of the Round Table, the Grail-Keepers, the Frank Palace, and the Argonauts); the professional guild or confraternity; the military brotherhood formed to share the prizes and losses of war; the military and political league established with growing frequency by the princes and barons of many regions of France, Germany, and Italy to counter political pressures felt by their members and promote collective advancement; and finally the bodies of retainers or clients who were increasingly maintained by kings and princes from the later fourteenth century onward to secure the loyalty and service of the more prominent members of their own nobility and of the lesser princes and barons of their region. Most of these emerged only during the course of the thirteenth and fourteenth centuries, and therefore could not have influenced the earliest form of the religious orders.

Any particular association might include the characteristics of two or more of these six models, but there was actually no single characteristic or set of characteristics that can be attributed to all of them. Given this diversity, it is impossible to generalize about the secular associations in any

A medieval woodcut depicting King Arthur and his valiant Knights of the Round Table, who served as a model for secular orders. (Bettmann/Corbis)

meaningful way without sorting them into types sharing at least limited sets of characteristics. This can most readily be done on the basis of a series of dichotomies that ran in different directions through their ranks.

One of the most important distinctions is between the associations that were endowed with statutes and a corporate organization, which can be called societies, and those that lacked them, called groups. Simple groups, whose members usually wore some sort of common badge, and in some cases undertook a vow of loyalty either to a prince or to one another, did not act together in a corporate way. A few of them—including those that represented true orders that had ceased to function (e.g., the Castilian Order of the Band after 1350 and the Breton Order of the Ermine after 1399)—were regarded as highly honorable, and referred to by the title "order," but these must be distinguished from true orders (which were all societies) by the term *pseudo-order*. The pseudo-orders fell into three classes: ceremonial pseudo-orders, whose members were knighted in a special ceremony (principally the Knights of the Bath of England and those of St. Mark of Venice); peregrine pseudo-orders, whose members were knighted at a place of pilgrimage (principally the Knights of the Holy Sepulchre, of St. Catherine of Mount Sinai, and of the Golden Spur of the Lateran Palace); and cliental pseudo-orders, whose members were bound by ties of clientship to the prince who admitted them (notably the Order of the Broom-Pod of Charles VI of France and the Order of the Porcupine of his brother Duke Louis of Orléans and his heirs).

All other secular military and noble associations—the great majority—were true societies endowed with some sort of corporate constitution. The earliest known were founded in the twelfth century, before knighthood had come to be bound to nobility, and probably took the constitutional form of the lay devotional confraternity. Certainly that was the most common form taken by the later societies whose statutes are known to us, but not all such societies took a fully or even a partly confraternal form. As the non-confraternal societies conformed to no single alternative model, all military and noble societies may usefully be classified as either confraternal or non-confraternal in their organization.

Not surprisingly, perhaps, confraternities—still numerous in some parts of the Catholic world—were in effect lay equivalents to religious orders, and included among them the various "third orders" attached to the greater religious orders of the age, including the Hospitallers of St. John. Confraternities (usually bearing a title equivalent to the Latin *societas* [society, company] or *fraternitas* [fraternity, brotherhood]) were so common throughout Latin Christendom from the late twelfth to the eighteenth centuries that it is thought that by the late fourteenth century almost every adult belonged to at least one. Societies of this sort were used to organize people of all ranks and orders of society to carry out any of a variety of social functions, from providing insurance for funerals, supporting widows and orphans, and ransoming of captives to regulating the standards of a craft, profession, or trade. The most important of them were the merchant guilds that from the twelfth to the eighteenth centuries dominated both the economic and the political life of the majority of towns in much of Latin Christendom. However, the category included thousands of lesser guilds, including many made up of archers, crossbowmen, and other types of soldiers attached to a particular city or princely household.

Despite their varied purposes, however, such societies shared a common set of seven basic characteristics. These included a set of written statutes formally adopted by the founding members and modified from time to time by some process of amendment; dedication to a patron saint associated with the principal activity of the society or the place in which it was based; the establishment of a chapel dedicated to the saint and staffed with one or more priests paid to say masses for the benefit of the members, living and dead; and the holding of an annual general meeting (commonly called the "chapter general") at or near that chapel, beginning or centered on the feast day of the patron saint and normally including a solemn mass and banquet in his or her honor, and often a vespers and memorial mass for deceased members. In addition, during the course of the meeting there was often a session devoted to the praise and criticism of the behavior of members relative to the goals and standards of the society. The statutes of such societies normally imposed a number of obligations on their members, most of which were related to the particular purpose of the society, but some of which were fraternal in nature, requiring mutual support or aid. Finally, the statutes of confraternities of all kinds normally entrusted the running of the society to one or more officers, who in the great majority of cases were subject to annual election by the members of the dominant class. The confraternal societies of knights and nobles, like those of ignoble soldiers of various types, seem generally to have adhered quite closely to this general model, though the most important subclasses modified the usual provisions for governance in a number of ways.

Confraternal societies were normally intended to be perpetual associations, but this was not true of a number of the non-confraternal military societies founded at this time. Military and noble societies may therefore be divided into perpetual and temporary subclasses. The former subclass included almost all of the fully confraternal societies and most of the non-confraternal ones founded to perform comparable political and military functions. The temporary subclass, by contrast, was made up of societies that were founded either to cement alliances among a number of lords or princes during some sort of political crisis or military campaign, or to serve as the vehicle for the collective achievement of some chivalrous enterprise.

The former set of temporary bodies (which had either an open-ended or fixed time limit, usually of between one and twenty years) were "fraternal societies," as they were based on the institution of fraternity or brotherhood-in-arms. By the fourteenth century, brotherhoods of two or more members were commonly created among knights and men-at-arms by vows of mutual support throughout a campaign and of the equal partition of the spoils (and possibly the losses) of war. The fraternal military societies were essentially institutionalized networks of this sort that borrowed various features from contemporary confraternities to give them a corporate character. They seem to have originated in the Holy Roman Empire around 1350, and to have flourished in the kingdoms of Burgundy, Germany, and France between that time and about 1430. In the Francophone kingdoms, the best known are the Company of the Black Swan, founded in 1350 by Count Amé VI of Savoy, two other princes, and eleven knights; the Corps and Order of the Young Male Falcon, founded between 1377 and 1385 by the viscount of Thouars and seventeen minor barons in Poitou; the Order of the Golden Apple, founded in 1394 by fourteen knights and squires in Auvergne; and the Alliance and Company of the Hound, founded in 1416 for a period of five years by forty-four knights and squires of the Barrois. In Germany, where they were particularly numerous, the earliest known is the Company of the Pale Horse of the Lower Rhineland (1349). Its successors included the Company of the Star of Brunswick (1372), the Company of the Old Love (ca. 1375–ca. 1378) in Hesse, the Company with the Lion (1379) in Wetterau and Swabia generally, the Company of the Fool (1381) in Cleves, and the Company of the Sickle (1391) in southern Saxony and Franconia. Most of these were founded for precise periods of two to twelve years, though the last was to endure for as long as its founding members still lived. Like societies with a fully confraternal form of constitution, they were intended to serve as military-political leagues promoting the interests of their members and had no higher goals.

The latter set of temporary bodies (which usually had a fixed limit for their existence of between one and five years) should be called votal societies, as they were based on a vow (*votum* in Latin) undertaken by their members to achieve a set of feats of arms comparable to those of the knights of the Arthurian romances. Contemporaries commonly knew them by a name meaning "enterprise" (*emprinse, impresa*) and transmitted that name both to profoundly different types of knightly societies and to the badge or figural sign that represented the undertaking. Such societies appeared around 1390 (when new forms of tactics were emerging that required practice of the type actually provided by these societies) and seem to have flourished only for a few decades after that date, primarily in France. Their number included the Enterprise of the White Lady with Green Shield, undertaken in 1399 for a period of five years by the heroic marshal of France, Jehan le Meingre de Boucicaut, and twelve other knights; the Enterprise of the Prisoner's Iron, undertaken in 1415 for two years by Jehan, duke of Bourbon, and sixteen other knights; and the Enterprise of the Dragon, undertaken at about the same time, probably by Jehan de Grailly, count of Foix, and "a certain number of ladies, damsels, knights, and squires."

The line of cleavage separating the perpetual and the limited-term societies within the non-confraternal category coincided with another line that ran across both the confraternal and non-confraternal categories: that between societies that were endowed with a democratic or oligarchic constitution (the normal types in confraternities) and those that were endowed with constitutions of a monarchical nature, which attached the presidential office on a permanent and hereditary basis to the throne or, in one case, the dynasty of the founder. These latter usually gave the president a leading, if not dominant, role in their activities. Monarchical societies were invariably founded by a king or an effectively sovereign prince and were intended above all to promote and reward loyalty to him. They were therefore instruments of the state, rather than mere private societies of nobles or soldiers like all of the others. The first known society of this type (the Castilian Order of the Band) was founded only in 1330, but most of the more important societies founded after that date were of the same type, so it is useful to sort all military and noble societies into monarchical and non-monarchical categories. In practice, the great majority of monarchical orders were also confraternal in nature, but at least two were not, and the two non-confraternal monarchical societies (the Castilian Order of the Band and the Hungarian Company of the Dragon) constituted the balance of the category of non-confraternal societies, after the temporary fraternal and votal types.

All of the remaining societies were therefore both confraternal and perpetual, and many of them were also monarchical. Societies that were not monarchical fell into two general categories: those founded by a prince but not annexed to his throne and those not founded by a prince. The former societies may be termed princely noble confraternities. Though not actually governed by their prince, they were always closely associated with his court or dynasty, and may be placed in a broader category of courtly or curial bodies. This category also includes all of the monarchical societies and most of the noble groups as well. Thus, the dichotomy curial/noncurial cuts across most of the other categories established.

The curial societies labeled princely noble confraternities were either sportive or political in their goals and activities. The former were dedicated largely to organizing tournaments, and they differed from the noncurial societies founded for the same ends only in enjoying princely patronage. The political curial societies (including the political princely confraternities and all of the monarchical societies), by contrast, were the only lay bodies that even approached the religious orders of knighthood in the extent of their endowment and organization and the high level of their goals. The generic designation "order" is restricted to them.

The only confraternal noble societies that did not fit into any of these classes were what may be called the normal noble confraternities, which were not in any way associated with a royal or princely court. Like their princely, curial analogues, these also fell into sportive and political-military subtypes, which were designed to fulfill many of the same purposes, but served the interests of regional nobilities rather than those of kings and princes. The middle of the fourteenth century to the second half of the fifteenth seems to have been their heyday. In Germany, the sportive subtypes took it upon themselves to promote the fellow feeling and exclusiveness of members of the old knightly nobility by insisting upon ever more stringent genealogical and practical qualifications for membership and by promoting the ideal of tournament-worthiness as the best indicator of noble status. They were also associated with the steadily growing variety of forms of combat that were included in tournaments in the fifteenth century and persisted well into the sixteenth. Those of the political-military type differed only in the details of their constitutions from the fraternal and curial societies founded to serve the same ends. Among the most important were the Company of the Buckle, founded in Franconia ca. 1392, and the Company of St. George's Shield, founded in Swabia in 1406. All served to organize and bind together members of the middle to lower nobility of an extensive region, most of whom were probably already related to one another by blood or marriage, and therefore had similar sets of rivals and enemies.

There were also many nonnoble military confraternities, typically made up of ignoble soldiers of some particular type, such as crossbowmen, archers, halberdiers, or bombardiers. The soldiers in these confraternities were always professionals, and the confraternities were for them what the guilds were for members of other trades and professions—including the armorers, who made armor and weapons forged of metal; the bowyers, who made bows; and the fletchers, who made arrows. At the end of the period under consideration, two strictly military but seminoble confraternities, the Confraternity of St. George (1493) and the Distinguished and Laudable Company of St. George (1503), were founded by the emperor Frederick III and his son the emperor Maximilian I as lay auxiliaries to a new religious order established by the former to defend Latin Europe from the Turks: the Knightly Order of St. George (1469).

In fact, by the later fourteenth century, confraternities dedicated to appropriate patron saints probably united the members of virtually every group associated with warfare. The guilds of knights and soldiers, normally organized on a local basis, were usually dedicated to a saint who had been a soldier and could be seen as a knight; the most important were St. George of Lydda, St. Maurice of the Theban Legion, and St. Michael the archangel, captain of the hosts of Heaven. Guilds of bowyers and fletchers, by contrast, were commonly dedicated to St. Sebastian, who had been martyred by being shot through with arrows.

A handful of societies did not fit into any of the categories just described, being in effect hybrids of the older religious order with the lay confraternity of knights. These may be described as semireligious orders of knighthood, since they were made up of a body of monks and a body of knights who, though living in community with the monks, remained laymen and were even permitted to marry. There seem to be only two examples of this type: the Castilian Order of Santiago, founded in 1170 on the general model of the Order of the Temple, and the Bavarian Company of the Cloister of Ettal, founded by the emperor Ludwig IV in the 1330s and apparently dissolved shortly after his death in 1347. The latter, however, probably served as an inspiration for the more conventional princely-confraternal order of the Grail-Templars.

The curial orders were the most important military and noble societies restricted to laymen in the history of Latin Christendom, the only ones to survive the Reformation, and the only ones to exist in any numbers today.

The first society of the curial class as a whole to be founded was a princely confraternal order, the Hungarian Society of St. George, established in 1325 by King Károly I. It was given most of the features typical of the contemporary confraternity and lacked only a formal presidential office to make it a true monarchical order as well. As it was the first order designed to bind lay knights or nobles to a royal or princely patron and put chivalry into the service of the state, it cannot be surprising that the Society of St. George was endowed with a number of features peculiar to it, in addition to the lack of a monarchical presidency. Several other orders of this type were founded by or under the influence of princes, the most notable of which were the Order of St. Catherine in the Dauphiny of Viennois (1330/40), the Company of St. George of the Grail-Templars in the Duchy of Austria (1337), the Order of the Hound in the Duchy of Bar (1422), the Company of Our Lady (of the Swan) in the Electoral Marquisate of Brandenburg (in its earliest form, 1440), and the Order of the Crescent in the Duchy of Anjou (1448). The last, in particular, differed from the existing monarchical orders outside Germany exclusively in lacking a monarchical presidency.

Although they too were confraternities, the earliest true monarchical orders drew their inspiration from the religious orders of knights and the lay orders depicted in the Arthurian cycle of romances. Indeed, only because the form of the religious order was inappropriate for their purposes and the fictional orders lacked any clearly described statutes, the founders of the earliest orders adopted the confraternal structures familiar to them from their own time and easily adaptable to their purposes. In fact, the inventor of the fully realized monarchical order, Alfonso XI of Castile and Leon, took from the confraternal model little more than the idea of an annual meeting, and his Order of the Band, proclaimed in 1330, was essentially a wholly lay equivalent of the military religious orders in which his kingdom abounded.

Edward III of England, who founded the second such order, may well have intended to follow Alfonso's example in his initial plan to revive the Round Table Company announced in 1344 on the return of his cousin Henry "of Grosmont," count of Lancaster, from a long sojourn at the

Castilian court. Before he could complete that project, however, he was distracted by the need to prosecute his claim to the French throne in the campaign that ended with the triumph of English arms at Crécy and Calais. In the meantime, he had almost certainly learned of the plans of his rival, Jehan, duke of Normandy (son of King Philippe VI), to found what was meant to be a confraternity of two hundred knights dedicated to the Blessed Virgin and St. George. The latter project, possibly modeled on the princely confraternal Order of St. Catherine recently founded in the Dauphiny of Viennois, served as the principal model for all of the later foundations. On his return to England, Edward founded, in place of the new Round Table that was to have been established there with three hundred knights, a more modest confraternity of twenty-six knights supporting twenty-six priests and (in theory) twenty-six poor veteran knights, dedicated to St. George alone—the traditional patron of English arms. Although its formal name, the Order of St. George, was taken in the traditional confraternal fashion from that of its patron saint, its secondary name, the Order, Society, or Company of the Garter, was taken from its badge, which probably represented the belt of knighthood and was probably inspired by the badge of the Order of the Band. Two years later Jehan of Normandy, having succeeded his father as King Jehan II of France, finally established his own projected confraternity. This took essentially the same form as its English rival, but was dedicated to the Blessed Virgin alone under the new title Our Lady of the Noble House. Like the Castilian and English orders, however, its name in ordinary usage, the Company of the Star, was taken from its badge. In the following year, Loysi (or Lodovico), king consort of peninsular Sicily or Naples, founded another order even more closely modeled on that of his French cousin, the Company (or Order) of the Holy Spirit of Right Desire, commonly called from its badge the Order of the Knot.

Thus, by 1352 the full confraternal model had become the norm for monarchical orders, although the identification of the order with its badge rather than its patron or its seat prevailed. By the same date, the monarchical order itself had become an adjunct of the courts of the leading monarchs of Latin Christendom, though it remained exceptional among royal courts in general, and unknown in Germanophone lands. The practice of maintaining such an order was adopted in the royal court of Cyprus in 1359 (when Pierre I made the Order of the Sword he had founded earlier a royal order) and in that of the Aragonese domain at some time between 1370 and 1380 (when Pere "the Ceremonious" founded the rather obscure but apparently deviant Enterprise of St. George).

In the meantime, however, the practice had spread to the court of several princes of less than regal rank. Amé VI de Savoie, count of Savoy and duke of Chablais and Aosta in 1364, founded the Order of the Collar, under the patronage of the Blessed Virgin Mary. By the end of the year 1381, when the Order of the Ship (dedicated to the Holy Trinity) was founded by King Carlo III in Naples to replace the defunct Company of the Knot, five more princes had founded orders that were probably monarchical: Duke Louis II of Bourbon, the Order of the Golden Shield (1367); Duke Louis I of Anjou, the Order of the True Cross (1365/75); Enguerrand VII of Coucy, count of Soissons and titular duke of Austria, the Order of the Crown (1379); Duke Albrecht III "with the Tress" of Austria, the Order of the Tress around 1380; and (probably) Duke Wilhelm I of Austria, the Order of the Salamander around 1380.

Of the fourteen orders founded by 1381, however, the great majority were maintained for less than two decades, and only two or three of them were still maintained in their original condition by 1410: the Garter and the Collar and possibly the Salamander (which may have lasted to 1463). Furthermore, between 1381 and 1430, the foundation of fully realized neo-Arthurian orders ceased completely, and only two orders that were certainly monarchical are known to have been founded: the Order of the Jar of the Salutation or of the Stole and Jar in 1403 by Ferran, duke of Peñafiel and future king of Aragon and Sicily (from 1412), and the Company of the Dragon in 1408 by Sigismund or Zsigmond von Luxemburg, king of Hungary and future king of Germany (1416) and Bohemia (1419) and Roman emperor (1453). The former remained a vestigial society down to 1458, when it was given new statutes by King Alfons "the Magnanimous" and lasted to 1516. The latter was at first no more than a military-political league, but was converted into a monarchical order for Sigismund's several kingdoms under new statutes of 1433 and seems to have survived in that condition to 1490.

A second wave of foundations of true monarchical orders of knighthood seems to have been set off by the creation and lavish endowment of the Order of the Golden Fleece by Philippe "the Good," duke of Burgundy, in 1430. Its statutes were based primarily on those of the Garter, but borrowed freely from those of the two other monarchical and knightly orders still surviving at the time of its foundation: those of the Collar and of the Stole and Jar. The foundation of a truly grand order by a prince of ducal rank whose lands lay mainly within the Holy Roman Empire seems to have encouraged other imperial princes to create monarchical orders of their own.

What appears to have been a monarchical order had been founded in virtually every imperial principality of the rank of duchy or electorate by 1468. Nevertheless, these orders bore only a general resemblance to the Order of the Golden Fleece. None of them was limited to knights, and only four of them (the orders of the Eagle, the Towel, St. George and St.

William, and St. George of the Pelican) were even limited to men. The remainder were open noble societies admitting women as well as men, more concerned with the promotion of Catholic piety and loyalty than of chivalry among their members. Although most were provided with at least a chapel, none was given a hall—presumably because only two of them (St. George of the Pelican and St. Hubert) held annual meetings on their patronal feast (or at any other time), and neither seems to have provided a banquet on that occasion. Like their predecessors of the fourteenth century, most of the German orders were maintained for only one or two generations; only one survived the first outburst of the Reformation in Germany between 1517 and 1525, and the last of them—a branch of the Brandenburgish Order—dissolved in 1539.

In the meantime, two more kings had founded orders that were probably (in the first case) or certainly (in the second case) of the monarchical type: Christian I von Oldenburg, king of Denmark, Norway, and Sweden, seems to have established the Confraternity of the Virgin Mary (or Order of the Elephant) at his Swedish coronation in 1457, but it seems to have been modeled on the German orders and was little more than an ordinary confraternity of nobles attached to the Danish court. By contrast, when King Ferrante of peninsular Sicily founded the Order of the Ermine (dedicated to the archangel St. Michael) as the third such order in his kingdom in 1465, he took the Garter and the Golden Fleece as his models, while King Louis XI of France lifted most of the statutes of the Order of St. Michael, which he founded in 1469, directly from those of the Order of the Golden Fleece. Of these three, only the last survived past 1523, and thus joined the English Order of the Garter, the Savoyard Order of the Collar (renamed the *Ordre de l'Annonciade* [Annunciated One] after its patroness the Virgin Mary in 1518), and the Burgundian Order of the Golden Fleece as one of the four early monarchical orders destined to survive into the modern era. By 1520, reforms in the Order of the Collar in 1518 and in the Order of the Garter itself in 1519 had given all four orders similar constitutions based on those of the Garter and the Golden Fleece.

The founders of the monarchical orders drew upon all of the institutional models used by the founders of lay military associations generally, but drew most heavily on the confraternity, the religious order, the contractual retinue, and the fictional company. Inevitably, the characteristics of each of these types had to be modified to combine them effectively. Among the characteristics of the confraternity that underwent some modification in the monarchical orders of this period were the maintenance of a chapel and a chantry priest and the maintenance of some sort of hall to serve as the headquarters, meeting place, and banqueting room for the members on feast days. Most confraternities could afford nothing more than a small side-chapel or chantry in the local parish church and a single priest to offi-ciate there on their behalf, and merely rented a hall for their annual festiv-ities. The greater guilds, by contrast, and especially those of the merchants, often established a major chapel in a major church marked with memori-als to their presidents and other leading members, and built their own hall on a grand scale, often facing on the principal square of their town or city. The religious orders of knighthood provided themselves with similar facil-ities at their convent or seat on an even grander scale. The Arthurian tra-dition, for its part, placed a great emphasis on knightly fellowships gather-ing in a hall of the royal palace at a great round table, around which were set the names and heraldic arms of their current members.

The founders of the monarchical orders drew upon these three tradi-tions with varying degrees of emphasis, but the great majority outside Ger-many declared their intention to establish for their order at least one major church and at least one major hall with attendant buildings, both to be set close together in a rural palace belonging to the founder and situated within about a day's ride of the capital city of his principal dominion. In addition, they declared that they would staff the principal church of the order with a whole college of priests, commonly equal in number to the knights, whose professional lives were to be devoted entirely to the service of the lay mem-bers of the order, living and dead. Thus, the requirements of the confrater-nal form were to be realized in the buildings and clerical membership of the monarchical orders on a grandiose scale not otherwise approached or even imagined except in the religious orders. Furthermore, most founders of monarchical orders declared that at least the shield of arms, and often the crested helmet and banner of the current companions, would be set up in their functional or their standard iconic form, either in the hall (in the fash-ion of the Arthurian knights) or, more commonly (following the example of the Order of the Garter), over their stalls in the chapel choir, where the com-panions were assigned seats in the collegiate churches.

In effect, the companions of most orders were treated as lay canons, and in a number of orders (including all four of those that survived) they were paired with clerical canons attached to the order who might sit in the stalls of the choir just below their own. During the religious services that formed an important part of their annual convocation, the companions sat in their stalls wearing their mantles and presented an appearance not very different from that of the monk-knights of the religious orders during one of the regular services in which they were bound to participate. Either dur-ing their lifetime or after their death, the companions also were required to make an heraldic memorial to themselves to set in their stall, rather the way the leading members of the greater confraternities set their names or arms on the walls or in the windows of the humbler chapels attached to their societies. One order—that of the Ship—actually promised to provide full-scale tombs for all of its companions.

The direct influence of the religious orders on the monarchical orders was more diffuse. Although by 1312, when the Order of the Temple was suppressed, the crusading movement had seen its best days, the Teutonic Knights still campaigned annually against the heathen Lithuanians, and the Knights of the Hospital of St. John still carried on an active war against the Muslims from their new base in Rhodes. In addition, many princes and nobles continued to dream of reconquering the Holy Land or driving the Turks back into inner Asia. This dream was reflected in the statutes of a number of the monarchical orders of the period. For example, the Order of the Sword, founded by Pierre I of Cyprus in 1359, had been intended to secure a force from Europe to retake the lost kingdoms of Jerusalem and Armenia, while Pierre's erstwhile chancellor, Philippe de Mézières, attempted to create a new form of order to accomplish the same end, the Order of the Passion of Our Lord. It was modeled more directly on the surviving religious orders, but was to be made up of laymen and led jointly by the kings of England and France. Among the other fourteenth-century foundations, the Orders of the Star of France, of the Knot and the Ship of peninsular Sicily, and of St. George of Aragon all included statutes that paid lip service to the crusading ideal. Although the Crusade of Nicopolis (which ended in disaster in 1396) was the last major campaign of its type actually launched, the goal of leading a crusade died slowly. Among the fifteenth-century orders, those of the Dragon of Hungary, the Golden Fleece of the Burgundian domain, the Ermine of Sicily, and St. Michael of France were all endowed with statutes concerned with crusading activities, though none of them can be taken too seriously. None of the orders other than the Sword was ever involved in anything like a real crusade against the enemies of Christendom.

More important borrowings from the religious orders of knighthood in the period before 1520 included the formal title "order" increasingly adopted by the monarchical orders and universal by the end of the period, the assignment of the title "brother knight" to those otherwise known as "companions" in most orders, and the assignment to the members of many of the orders of a mantle opening down the front like a cope and charged on the left breast with a badge. The mantle had been a distinctive mark of knightly status in a military order since the twelfth century, and its eventual adoption by all of the orders that survived to 1520 was the clearest sign that the founders or sovereigns of these orders identified with the traditions of the crusading orders before 1578.

Before the latter date, however, the founder of only one monarchical order (that of St. George of Aragon) chose to emulate both the form and the material of the badges worn by the religious knights: a cross of a distinctive color and increasingly distinctive shape made of textile and applied as a plaque to the left breast of the mantle, and later to the surcoat as well. Two other orders dedicated to St. George (the Hungarian confraternal Order of St. George and the Order of the Garter) used a textile shield of the arms of their patron as a badge, though in neither case the primary one.

The other founders all adopted badges of markedly different forms and materials. Some of these badges resembled the badges common among pilgrims, confraternities, and bodies of retainers in taking the form of a jewel worn as a brooch or suspended from a simple chain about the neck, while others took the more distinctive form of a band or belt worn wrapped around some part of the body, including the neck (the Collar). Still others resembled the badge of the Collar in being worn around the neck but took the very distinct form of a linked collar with or without a pendant jewel in the fashion of most of the pseudo-orders from the 1390s. The type of insignia that ultimately prevailed was the collar made up of links in the form of distinct badges or symbols and having a pendant jewel that was either the principal badge of the order or a symbol or effigy of the order's patron saint, or both. The latter type of insignia was finally combined with the eight-pointed cross of the Order of St. John in the badge of the Holy Spirit of France in 1578, and that served as the model for all badges from 1693.

The most important models for the monarchical orders after the devotional confraternities, however, were the fictional companies of knights described in the Arthurian cycle of romances: principally the Round Table Company of King Arthur himself; the Company of the Frank Palace (*Franc Palais*) of his pre-Christian ancestor, Perceforest; and the company of knights established by Joseph of Arimathea to guard the Holy Grail. To these were later added (by the Valois dukes of Burgundy) the mythical company of the Argonauts who accompanied Jason on his quest for the Golden Fleece of Colchis, and (by Louis XI of France) the company of loyal angels who fought with the Archangel Michael to drive Lucifer and his rebel angels from Heaven.

Of these, the company of the Round Table was surely the most important, especially as the two other Arthurian companies were merely literary doublets of it. Indeed, like Charlemagne himself and Godefroi de Bouillon, hero of the First Crusade and baron of the Holy Sepulchre, only Arthur was regarded throughout the fourteenth and fifteenth centuries as one of the three Christian members of that glorious company of preeminent heroes referred to as the Nine Worthies (*Neuf Preux* in French). Although only Edward III of England (who claimed to be Arthur's heir, and identified his castle of Windsor with the legendary Camelot) explicitly evoked the Round Table when he proclaimed his intention of establishing a knightly order in 1344, there can be little doubt that the king from whom he certainly borrowed the idea (Alfonso XI of Castile) thought of his Order of the Band as a neo-Arthurian society that would convert him into a new Arthur surrounded by the best knights in the world. As all of the later orders were inspired either directly or indirectly by the Order of the Garter that Edward actually founded and all included Arthurian elements of one sort or another, the whole set of monarchical orders can be described as neo-Arthurian in character. In the orders most thoroughly modeled on the Band and the Garter (i.e., most of those outside Germany and Scandinavia), this meant not only that the members of the order were expected to practice the highest ideals of chivalry, but that the order itself was presented as an embodiment of those ideals. This made both patronage of and membership in such orders highly honorable, for just as it identified the prince-president with Arthur as a patron of chivalry, so it identified the companions of the order with the knights of the Round Table as paragons of chivalry.

The extent to which the founders of monarchical orders borrowed the other distinctive characteristics of the Round Table Society reported in the romances varied considerably. Alfonso of Castile was unique in requiring the knights of his order to challenge anyone they found wearing what looked like the band of the order to armed combat and to send back to the royal court any who acquitted themselves well in such a conflict. Alfonso was also more explicit than any later founder in insisting that the knights of his order live up to the highest standards of *curialitas* (Latin; courtliness) or *courtoisie* (French; source of English *courtesy*) and abjure the vices common to noblemen. Most later founders promoted the courtliness ideally associated by 1330 with knightliness in the same ways they promoted the military virtues of prowess, courage, and loyalty: by asking not only for annual reports of the sort that Arthurian knights commonly delivered on returning to the royal court after accomplishing some quest, but annual sessions of mutual criticism of the sort more common in professional confraternities. In three orders, however (the Company of the Star, the Company of the Knot, and its successor the Order of the Ship), the statutes actually provided a further reward for meritorious conduct in the form of a seat at a special table of honor (resembling the Round Table) at the annual banquet, and the last two of those added a series of honorific alterations to the badge of the order that in effect replaced the sorts of promotion in formal rank practiced in most modern multigrade orders of merit.

Another aspect of the fictional model that was borrowed by the great majority of the founders of monarchical orders was a fixed number of knights. Religious orders and confraternities sought to have as many members as possible. An unlimited (or at least large) number was also indicated by two of the main objects of many founders: to bind the leaders of the nobility of their domain to themselves and their dynasty and to establish unity, harmony, and peace among them. Nevertheless, the essential characteristic of the fictional societies of the Round Table and Frank Palace was selectivity, and this implied a limitation. The limits suggested in the romances were actually fairly high—between 50 and 300 knights. A number of founders initially sought to achieve similar or larger memberships.

These figures proved impossible to achieve, and while we have no precise numbers for most orders, it is unlikely that the number of companions in any order ever surpassed 100 before the middle of the sixteenth century. Aside from the difficulty of finding several hundred knights worthy both of the honor and of the trust involved in admission to such an order, providing chapels and halls large enough for meetings would have been difficult. No doubt recognizing these problems, most founders chose to set much lower limits on the size of the membership in each of the order's classes. Edward III of England once again led the way by setting the limit at 26, the number that could sit in the uppermost stalls of the choir of his chapel in Windsor Castle. Thereafter, the number of companions in most later orders (beginning with the Order of the Collar of Savoy in 1364) would be closely comparable to this: between a low of 15 (the Collar of Savoy) and a high of 36 (St. Michael of France).

Although most orders were made up largely of knights politically subject to their president, like the fictional orders on which they were partly modeled, virtually all included a number of distinguished foreign knights. In theory, all of the companions in the more thoroughly neo-Arthurian orders were chosen primarily or exclusively on the basis of the knightly qualities, and differences in lordly rank among them were either ignored or made the basis of differential burdens in the matter of paying for purgatorial masses. In practice, however, the desire to use the order as an instrument to secure the loyalty and reward the services of barons and princes gave rise to a marked tendency to prefer knights of high lordly rank. By the end of the period the majority of the companions of the greater orders (the Garter and the Golden Fleece) were men of high birth and lordly rank, including a number of foreign princes and even kings. The membership of the latter in the orders was largely passive, but it served to increase considerably the prestige of the order, to the point where foreign kings felt honored by "election" to the order. (The statutes of most orders set forth a process by which the existing companions were to elect new members when places became vacant by death, resignation, or expulsion; in practice, the prince-president of every order was usually able to secure the election of anyone he wished.)

As these developments suggest, in addition to being the institutional embodiments of the ideals of chivalry within their prince-president's dominion or domain, the monarchical orders and indeed the curial orders more generally were also the embodiments of the ideals of nobility within the same territories. To serve both ideals, many founders or later presidents of such societies attached to them the office of the chief herald of their lands: a role still played by Garter, Principal King of Arms of the English, to this day. In principle these ideals always included distinguished military service, and if the surviving orders have never admitted the most decorated soldiers from the ranks, they have usually included the most distinguished generals and admirals of their presidents' lands, along with the most distinguished prime ministers, princes, and peers.

D'A. Jonathan D. Boulton

See also Chivalry; Europe; Knights; Orders of Knighthood, Religious

References

Barber, Richard. 1994. *The Knight and Chivalry.* 3d ed. Woodbridge, Suffolk, UK: The Boydell Press.

Boulton, D'Arcy Jonathan Dacre. 2000. *The Knights of the Crown: The Monarchical Orders of Knighthood in Later Medieval Europe, 1325–1520.* 2d ed. Woodbridge, Suffolk, UK: The Boydell Press.

Keen, Maurice. 1984. *Chivalry.* New Haven: Yale University Press.

Kruse, Holger, Werner Paravicini, and Andreas Ranft, eds. 1991. *Ritterorden und Adelsgesellschaften im Spätmittelalterlichen Deutschland.* Frankfurt: Peter Lang.

Ranft, Andreas. 1994. *Adelsgesellschaften: Gruppenbildung und Genossenschaft im Spätmittelalterlichen Reich.* Sigmaringen: J. Thorbecke.

P

Pa Kua Ch'uan

See Baguazhang (Pa Kua Ch'uan)

Pacific Islands

The South Pacific islands (Hawaii, Samoa, New Zealand, Guam, and Tahiti) were inhabited, before the arrival of Europeans and the decimation of much of the native population, by peoples who were united by a common group of languages, the Polynesian languages. Examples of these languages include Hawaiian, Samoan, Maori, and Tahitian. The technology level of the Pacific islanders was not advanced, never progressing beyond late Paleolithic technology. The islanders did not have the use of metals or metalsmithing techniques. As a result, when one discusses martial arts among these peoples, unarmed combat techniques and fighting with wooden weapons become paramount, and there did exist several unique weapons native only to these islands.

The peoples of the Pacific islands were the world's first long-distance navigators. Beginning from their homes in Asia, these peoples spread, by outrigger canoe, to islands throughout the South Pacific, including Easter Island (Rapa Nui), the most remote place on earth. By the 1500s, these islands were completely colonized by the Polynesians. Although navigation and commerce broke down between these islands for reasons that are still unknown, the very act of reaching these farthest outposts of land indicates the bravery of these peoples, which, to no great surprise, was often reflected in their fighting arts.

The oral traditions of these islands tell of a long history of warriors accomplished in martial arts. The reasons for the necessity to know how to fight are many, but it can be surmised that given the scarce resources and population pressures of a limited physical area, such as these islands, the competition for these resources must have been fierce. It is therefore not surprising that different tribes or clans of peoples would have had to know how to fight well to survive during times when population pressures would have led to brutal warfare. These oral histories probably reflect the fighting skills of those exceptional warriors who were able to prevail in such a climate.

An example of the scarce resources and demand for warriors is documented through the colonization of Easter Island and the eventual ruin of the society established there. After the island was colonized by Polynesians, the inhabitants channeled their energies into building great representations of their gods after warfare became too destructive. Unfortunately, the sublimated behavior of building these figures used up most of the natural resources of the island. The islanders entered a new phase of their existence when it was apparent that no new figures could be constructed. They developed a ritual event. Once a year a contest was held to see who could swim the shark-infested seas to one of the smaller islands and return with a bird's egg. The winner then helped select the chief. Even this eventually placed a strain on the resources of the island, and by the time Easter Island was "discovered" by the Europeans, the Rapa Nui culture was once again on the road to intra-island warfare due to population pressures and lack of technology. Warriors in this culture were revered as individuals who could help a group survive during these bloody times. Unfortunately, little is known about the actual fighting arts of the Pacific islanders. The colonization of the islands by the Europeans was marked by events that not only decimated the populations of these islands, but in so doing destroyed their cultures. So complete was this destruction that today, long after the European colonization of the Hawaiian islands, fewer than 10 percent of native Hawaiians can speak their own language.

The Europeans who contacted and later settled these islands also brought with them diseases, such as smallpox, for which the native populations had no immunity. Just as destructive to the natives, the invaders also brought with them a zeal to convert the "heathens" to the "correct" paths of Western religious traditions. These factors, combined with the awe many native peoples felt for the overwhelming technical superiority of the Europeans, led to the loss of many native art forms. Without a doubt, martial art traditions must be included in this list.

The native arsenal relied heavily on the wood and stone that were found on the islands. Most Pacific islands were young in terms of geological age (Hawaii still contains more active volcanoes than any other American state), so a wide variety of stones were readily available for use in the construction of knives, daggers, and spear points. The variety of hard woods available on the islands also led to the creation of superior fighting staves and sticks. It is not surprising, therefore, that the use of the knife, spear, and staff weapons became critical for the armed martial arts of these islands.

A late-nineteenth-century engraving by J.W. Warren of a bare-knuckle boxing match between Hapae islanders. (Hulton-Deutsch Collection/Corbis)

Two staff weapons deserve special mention due to their uniqueness and lethality. The Maori, the aboriginal peoples of New Zealand, developed a special type of massive war club. With a length of about 1.5 meters and a weight of approximately 5 kilograms, this curved, two-handed club was powerful enough to shatter the largest bones in a human body. Maori warriors were able to close against the British invaders and use the weapon to good effect. Another type of club, used by the Samoans, was the *tewha-tewha*, a long stick (1.5 meters) with a wooden haft at its end. This axlike device was also a fierce weapon in a premetal technology.

Even in this Neolithic world, an extensive range of unique weapons was developed for self-defense by these ingenious peoples. For example, lacking metal to construct swords, the Pacific islanders nevertheless developed the *tebutje*. These "swords" were made from long clubs inlaid with shark's teeth. The teeth constituted excellent cutting edges against an opponent. The fighting arts for these weapons have since become extinct, but this leaves intriguing room to speculate on how they were used and how effective the tebutje was in combat.

The combat systems of Polynesia were centered on these and similar weapons. They also included a great deal of hand-to-hand combat. What few oral histories remain from these islands tell of warriors trained in striking with both the hands and feet and in wrestling, and possessing an impressive knowledge of human anatomy. The struggles and warfare between the islanders would have necessitated such a development in martial arts.

Perhaps the most well-documented martial arts from these islands are from Hawaii. They were among the last to be settled by the European colonizers, and to a great extent, the Hawaiians were able to keep their independence until 1893, longer than most other South Sea island nations. The islands themselves were united only in the early 1800s by King Kamehameha I. Until this time, warfare between the Hawaiians was common, which led to the development and practice of both armed and unarmed combat. Unfortunately, once again because of the destruction of native Hawaiian culture, even descriptions of these martial arts are scarce.

One of the best-known examples of Hawaiian martial arts is the unarmed combat art of *Lua,* which is close to extinction today. The word translates as "the art of bone-breaking." It might be compared to the art of *koppo* in traditional Japanese martial arts. Due to the lack of written historical records among the Hawaiians, a preliterate people, there is no accurate way of dating just how long this fighting system existed.

Lua was a hand-to-hand system of combat that emphasized the use of a knowledge of anatomy to strike the weak points of the human body. Expert practitioners were expected to have the ability to injure or even kill an opponent with such strikes. The techniques that were practiced included the arts of dislocating the fingers and toes, striking to nerve cavities, and hitting and kicking muscles in such a way as to inflict paralysis. Lua was intended as a self-defense art; in its purest form it was not to be considered a sport. Demonstrations of Lua to the general public were forbidden, as it was an art for warriors only.

Among the arts encompassed by Lua were the specific art of bone-breaking, also known as *hakihaki,* kicking (*peku*), wrestling (*hakoko*), and combat with the bare hands (*kui*). Hawaiian warriors were expected to become proficient in all aspects of the art. In addition to these martial skills,

Lua practitioners were taught the art of massage (*lomilomi*) and a Hawaiian game of strategy known as *konane*. In this respect, it can be surmised that the education of a Hawaiian warrior was similar in many ways to the education of Japanese *bushi* (warriors) and European knights, who were expected to master both the martial arts of self-defense and the civilian arts of refinement.

Lua systems included a form of ritualized combat that is common in other martial arts as well. Ritualized combat, known as kata in Japanese systems and *hyung* in Korean systems, consists of forms of prearranged movement that teach the practitioner how to punch, kick, throw, and move effectively. These forms existed in European combat systems as well; the Greeks used to practice a type of war dance to train their warriors for combat. These forms are practiced individually or in groups, and the practitioner uses them to develop, among other skills, timing, balance, and technique. The Hawaiian version of this was called the hula. Although this word today conjures up a Hawaiian dance for tourists, evidence indicates that the word also has the older meaning of "war dance." Indeed, tourists to Hawaii can see Lua movements demonstrated in hula dances during the shows displayed for travelers.

The importance of the hula was critical for developing Lua skills. Warriors were expected to practice the hula daily, not only as a form of exercise but also for developing individual and group martial abilities. There existed both single hula and hula for multiple persons, where groups of warriors would practice the same movements together. This helped to create groups of warriors who could fight together, even if they did not always use the same movements simultaneously.

The practice of Lua was not always confined to the battlefield. There are some accounts that suggest that Lua practitioners would sometimes test their skills on unwary travelers who attended a celebration unaware of the danger that faced them. When the visitor was completely relaxed by the surroundings, the Lua practitioners would strike.

Using their knowledge of human anatomy, the Lua practitioners would dislocate joints and break the bones of the victim. This was done to test the practitioner's knowledge of his skills, apparently in the belief that these arts had to be put to an actual test to demonstrate the practitioner's ability. Some victims were resuscitated and allowed to go, but others were left to die after the Lua practitioner was through. On the Hawaiian islands, as on many of the other Pacific islands, the ability to protect oneself was held in high regard, and the need to perfect this ability was paramount, sometimes even more important than the lives of strangers.

In addition to the unarmed combat systems listed above, Hawaiians were taught weapons skills. Weapons that were available to the native

Hawaiians included one-handed spears (*ihe*), a dagger made from wood (*pahoa*), a short club (*newa*), a two-handed club (*la-au-palau*), the sling (*maa*), and a cord that was used for strangulation (*kaane*). Lua could therefore be considered a complete martial arts system, covering both weaponry and unarmed combat.

There also existed sportive forms of Hawaiian martial arts that were presented before crowds of onlookers, unlike Lua. Hawaiian-style boxing, known as *mokomoko* (from the verb *moko,* "to fight with the fists"), was practiced and demonstrated during religious festivals. From descriptions of the art, mokomoko was apparently a form of bare-fist fighting where the closed fist was used as the exclusive offensive weapon. This Hawaiian boxing differed profoundly from Western styles.

From accounts given by eyewitnesses, the participants were not allowed to block their opponents' punches with anything other than their own closed fist. This type of deflection is not used in Western or Asian martial arts. In addition, mokomoko combatants would evade their opponents' blows by either retreating or moving the body out of the way. All blows were aimed for the face, and the person who was the first to fall to the ground was the loser. It was a contest that was designed to test the abilities of the contestants to persevere despite extreme consequences.

It is also important to note that these boxing matches occurred during the season of Makahiki, the Hawaiian New Year. The Hawaiian pantheon contained a multitude of deities, and during this time of the year the god Makahiki was worshipped. Therefore, these Hawaiian sporting events may be considered analogous to other combinations of ritual with sport, such as the Olympic games of the ancient Greeks, who organized those games to honor Zeus, the father of the gods who dwelt on Mount Olympus.

Reports of the outcome of mokomoko contests state that the combat was brutal and the competitors could expect no mercy. Those who did fall to the ground after being defeated were screamed at by the spectators, shouting the phrase, "Eat chicken shit!" Western observers noted that even the winners of matches would have bloody and broken noses, bruises around the eye sockets, and bloody lips. It was not uncommon for teeth to be lost. Participants who excelled in the sport would probably have hands that had become callused and hardened from the repeated blows they inflicted and had inflicted on them. The danger of developing arthritis in the hands, of course, also proportionally increased.

Hawaiians practiced other types of martial disciplines as well. An example is the art of wrestling, hakoko, mentioned earlier. The exact parameters of this wrestling style, or styles, are unknown. From the few remaining descriptions of the art, it seems to have been a sportive as well as combative form of wresting. For the sport variant, the opponent would signal defeat and the match would end. Since this form of wrestling was also displayed during the Makahiki ceremonies, it is also a form of sacred wrestling (wrestling for religious purposes). In any case, the descriptions of the art also state that injuries were common, just as in boxing. Competitors expected danger.

Other martial disciplines that apparently were practiced by the ancient Hawaiians included the art of arrow cutting. This art, known as *yadomajutsu* in Japan, was a series of techniques that taught the practitioner to deflect arrows, spears, and javelins that were targeted at his person. Skilled practitioners of this art could face multiple projectiles and have the ability to dodge and deflect them without injury.

One of the best practitioners of this art was the greatest king in Hawaiian history: King Kamehameha I. As indicated earlier, this individual was responsible for the unification of the islands, which occurred just prior to European colonization. Hawaiian oral legends tell of Kamehameha dodging twelve spears thrown simultaneously at him. Even if this is an exaggeration, it signifies the importance of this skill in Hawaiian warrior society.

The survival of Polynesian martial arts following the arrival of Europeans was, as noted, very difficult. Firearms took away a great deal of the necessity for hand-to-hand combat, and disease and cultural genocide took its toll. There presently exist some modern forms of Polynesian unarmed combat, most notably the system of *lima-lama,* which is translated as "hands of wisdom." The direct origin of this art is unknown. Most, if not all, of the weapons systems that marked Polynesian armed combat have disappeared.

Polynesian martial arts encompassed the arts of self-defense, but were used for sport and religious purposes also. In this respect, they formed a complete martial arts system that was practiced by peoples over a large area of the globe. The lack of metal did not hamper the development of these arts. Rather, the arts grew around the materials that were available. In this respect, like many martial arts, the Polynesian arts were representative of a particular time and culture, which allowed them to flourish and develop.

The martial arts of the South Pacific islanders have, unfortunately, been lost to history. A shadow of them can still be seen in the traditional dances performed for tourists, but these only reflect dimly what was once a proud and unique history. The rediscovery of various forms of martial arts is currently under way; therefore, the possibilities of a rebirth of Polynesian arts cannot be discounted. In this respect, perhaps the future of Polynesian martial arts will be brighter than their recent past.

Gene Tausk

See also Boxing, European; Form/Xing/Kata/Pattern Practice; Jûdô;
Wrestling and Grappling: Europe; Wrestling and Grappling: Japan

References

Balent, Matthew. 1993. *The Compendium of Weapons, Armour and Castles*. Taylor, MI: Palladium Books.

Corcoran, John, and Emil Farkas. 1983. *Martial Arts: Traditions, History, People*. New York: Gallery Books.

Draeger, Donn F. 1976. "Classical Hawaiian Martial Culture." Unpublished manuscript. Honolulu: East-West Center and the Bishop Museum.

Judd, Henry. *The Hawaiian Language and Hawaiian-English Dictionary*. Australia: Hawaiian Service.

Stewart, C. S. 1970. *Journal of a Residence in the Sandwich Islands during the Years 1823, 1824, and 1825*. Reproduced by the University of Hawai'i Press for the Friends of the Library of Hawaii. Honolulu: University of Hawai'i Press.

Pankration

Pankration (Greek; all powers), a Greek martial art utilizing both striking and grappling, was created almost 3,000 years ago. It was practiced primarily as a sport, but found applications in combat, both on the battlefield and for self-defense. Pankration was designed to be the ultimate test of a person's physical, intellectual, and spiritual capabilities. Pankration is one of the oldest confirmed martial arts practiced by human beings. The art had an extensive influence on Western martial arts, and possibly on Asian arts as well.

Pankration was an all-out form of fighting. The competitors were allowed to do anything except biting and eye-gouging. The Spartans, however, allowed even these techniques in their local athletic festivals. Punches and open-hand strikes with the hands, kicks, all types of throws and takedowns, joint locks and choke holds—all of these techniques were legal in a pankration bout. The goal of the pankration match was to get the opponent to signal defeat. Failing this, it was expected that one opponent would be knocked out or choked to unconsciousness.

The origin of pankration is the subject of speculation. The Egyptians developed high-level fighting arts, as evidenced by pictures of these fighting techniques displayed in the tombs of Beni-Hassan (Middle Kingdom period). One theory suggests that Egyptian traders brought these techniques to the Greeks, who eventually adopted them for their own use. Another theory speculates that pankration developed out of primitive, instinctual fighting for survival and eventually was systematized as a martial art. The Greeks themselves believed that the hero Theseus, who used pankration to defeat the Minotaur in the labyrinth, had created the art. The historical record, however, begins after approximately 1000 B.C. when the Greek city-states established athletic festivals whose events included pankration.

In 648 B.C., at the Thirty-third Olympic Games, pankration was accepted as an official sport. It quickly became one of the most popular events, so much so that pankration was later added to the boys' Olympic Games. Practitioners of the art (pankrationists) received the highest honors and accolades from adoring crowds. Winners of the pankration became instant celebrities and were assured of income for the rest of their lives. Those few who won repeatedly at the games achieved legendary fame in the sports-obsessed Greek world and were sometimes even worshipped as semidivine beings.

Pankration enjoyed continued popularity throughout the Greek city-states. Plato, Aristotle, and Socrates all enjoyed the art. Plato, in fact, was a practitioner, but warned that this style of fighting did not teach its practitioners to "keep to their feet," possibly a reference to the fact that most pankration matches were decided by grappling on the ground. Alexander the Great, a Hellenized Macedonian, was also a pankration expert. Alexander took many pankrationists with him when he set out to conquer the globe, including Dioxipus of Rhodes, one of the most formidable pankrationists in history. In addition, many of his troops were trained in the art. It has been argued that, during Alexander's Indian campaign, pankration techniques were disseminated to the population of southern Asia. If this is the case, then these techniques might have influenced Asian martial arts. This theory remains a source of debate among scholars of fighting arts.

Pankration matches began with the two competitors stepping into the arena or onto a platform. There were no rings or barriers. Falling off the platform meant that the match would resume again; running away from the combat area was a sign of cowardice, which resulted in a loss. A referee armed with a switch supervised the match. If he observed an illegal maneuver, he employed the switch to break the competitors apart. In addition, it is speculated that the referee would employ the switch if the action between competitors lagged.

There were no weight classes in the art; it is not surprising, therefore, that pankration became the domain of heavyweight contenders who could use their superior size to their advantage. Competitors fought naked without any body or hand protection. Pankration matches had no time limit. The only way to end a match was to signal surrender by raising a hand or by being rendered unconscious through a choke hold or blow. The matches sometimes ended in death. With joint locks also allowed in competition, disfigurement and loss of limbs were also dangers.

Pankration had two basic forms: *kato* (literally, down) pankration and *ano* (up) pankration. Ano pankration was a less severe form of the art, in which the pankrationists had to remain standing. Ano pankration was essentially a form of kickboxing, in which blows from both the hands and feet were permitted. All types of hand strikes were permitted, not just those with the closed fist, and a pankrationist was allowed to hold his opponent and hit him with the other hand. Strikes to the groin and elbow and knee strikes were also permitted. When one competitor fell to the ground, the match ended. Ano pankration was usually restricted to training or to preliminary bouts before a kato pankration match.

Kato pankration was the all-out form of fighting that has come to be associated with pankration. Practitioners began the match standing, but as the fight progressed, falling to the ground and grappling techniques were used. The fight was not over until surrender, knockout, or death. It has been suggested that the great majority of kato pankration matches ended up being decided on the ground through grappling techniques. All the techniques from ano pankration were legal in kato pankration.

Pankration techniques were numerous and varied. Techniques were divided into four basic categories: arm techniques, leg techniques, throws and takedowns, and grappling. Arm techniques included all types of punches with the hands and elbows. Boxing techniques, the jab, cross, uppercut, and hook, were most likely the primary weapons. Elbow strikes were also used, which meant that hook punches were probably a secondary weapon when the elbow could not be employed. Open-hand strikes were also permitted; there is artwork on surviving Greek vases dating from 500 B.C. that clearly demonstrates chopping blows.

Leg techniques were kicks and knee strikes. At close range, a pankrationist grabbed his opponent and attempted to apply knee strikes in rapid succession in much the same way as a modern Thai boxer. It is unlikely that high kicks were used; most of the artwork demonstrates pankrationists employing rising kicks to the stomach, striking with the ball of the foot. Pankrationists also likely employed powerful kicks against the legs of opponents in attempts to either sweep the feet or strike the upper portion of the leg with enough force to cause the limb to collapse. Once again, a modern application of this technique is found in Thai boxing. When an opponent was doubled over or on the floor, pankrationists would then likely attempt kicks to the head. Because of pankration's extensive use of kicks, pankration is one of the first documented complete fighting systems used by humans.

Throws and takedowns were numerous and varied. Pankrationists were free to employ the takedowns that are commonly seen in modern wrestling systems, in which practitioners attempt to seize one or both of the opponent's legs and unbalance the opponent. However, pankrationists also employed throws that are seen in modern jûdô or jûjutsu, in which the practitioner attempts to either throw the opponent over the shoulder or hip to the ground or sweep the leg out from under the opponent by use of the feet.

Holds used in pankration were those designed to force an opponent to submit. For this reason, the most popular holds employed were choke holds and joint locks. Choke holds are attempts to cut off either the blood supply or the air supply, or both, from the torso to the head. This is achieved usually by blocking the windpipe or the carotid artery and vagus nerve.

Joint locks attempt to hyperextend a joint of the body beyond its normal range of motion. Thus, a successfully applied joint lock can break an arm, leg, wrist, or ankle. The elbow lock was probably the most popular. Interestingly, leg holds were also used, which gives an indication of the many techniques that were available to the pankrationists. Leg holds have traditionally not been popular in most wrestling systems around the world, but because of the very nature of pankration combat, this skill was an essential one for pankrationists to master. This gives an indication of the versatility and demands of this art.

One of the unique aspects of the art was the fact that pankrationists were able to employ unusual holds against the fingers or toes of opponents, even breaking them when necessary. There were even standing grappling holds that were employed by pankrationists, in which one practitioner would literally climb on top of another, while the opponent was still standing, and attempt to get the opponent into a choke hold or use body mass to force him to the ground. These unusual techniques are rarely found in other combat systems.

The Greeks were very familiar with human anatomy. Surviving statues and artwork clearly demonstrate the attention to detail of the artists and the realism of the figures. It is likely that this knowledge was applied to pankration. Knowledge of human anatomy, especially the weak points of the body, was essential for pankrationists of any level to survive in competition.

It is likely that there were different schools, or academies, of pankration located throughout the Greek world. These schools are believed to have specialized in certain techniques. Although pankrationists were expected to master all four aspects of pankration fighting, certain schools emphasized one aspect of fighting over others. The instructors for these academies were likely to be former pankration champions who retired into teaching. Those instructors who were former Olympians were highly sought out and were well paid for their instruction.

Training in pankration was accomplished through innovative techniques, some of which were not replicated for thousands of years. Pankrationists trained in special gymnasiums known as *korykeions*. Students learned striking techniques by hitting bags stuffed with sand suspended from the ceiling. Kicking techniques were practiced by striking heavier bags suspended about 2 feet off the floor. These were intended to make the student hit correctly, as striking improperly would be painful. These striking bags were known as *korykos*.

Students were taught wrestling techniques in sequence, that is, to master each move in a progressive order. Ultimately, students could learn the combinations of different techniques. Wrestling techniques were divided into separate categories. Thus, a pankrationist might first learn how to throw and take down the opponent in such a way that a hold could be applied. Later, ground-fighting techniques as a separate category would be introduced. Finally, all aspects of wrestling were practiced in conjunction.

When these basics were learned, the students combined both striking and wrestling in kato pankration matches. Schools held competitions to determine which students would have the honor of being sent to the games. Once again, with the enormous pressures for victory, only the best would have an opportunity to compete.

The Greek pankration schools employed masseuses to help the athletes recover from matches. It is likely that doctors also were employed, as well as dietitians and different types of coaches. In a way, the pankration schools would have been much like the gladiator schools of the Roman Empire, where a mini-industry of professions shared their experiences and expertise to help students learn how to win in their chosen art.

Competition among the city-states during the Olympic and other games was fierce. Competitors represented not only themselves, but also their particular city during a festival, and winning brought glory not only to the individual, but also to the city. Likewise, a losing competitor reflected poorly on his city. For these reasons, among others, athletes in these competitions were highly motivated to win, sometimes at all costs. Pankrationists often risked death or mutilation rather than acknowledge defeat, in order to avoid shaming their city by a poor performance. This helped to make pankration an event in which fatalities could be expected.

Pankration was thought useful by the ancient Greeks for two main reasons. First, it taught the practitioners about the art of war. Warfare was a constant threat in the Greek world (ca. 700 to 146 B.C.), and males were expected to be able to fight against external threats. Second, and more important, pankration helped its practitioners to develop *arete* (excellence). Greek males were expected to display this quality in all areas of their lives, and especially in combat. The possibility of dying in combat to protect a person's city or friends was very real. A person who displayed arete would have no hesitation in making a personal sacrifice to protect his friends or city.

Although pankration was expected to develop arete in its practitioners, the Greek world's obsession with sports led to much cheating and game fixing in various events. It is almost certain that this kind of behavior affected pankration as well. Although practitioners were expected to swear to compete fairly and honestly, the enormous pressure for victory would have led to instances of cheating. Authors from the period, such as Xenophanes, regularly decried the loss of pure athletic competition and the evils of professionalism in the local and Olympic games, indicating the magnitude of the problem.

It is unknown if pankration was taught exclusively as a sport or also taught as a means of self-defense in and of itself. Pankration experts obviously were sought out as bodyguards and instructors, just as was the case with retired gladiators during the Roman Empire. Evidence suggests that the emphasis would most likely have been on sport development. Roman sources sometimes did mention, however, the effectiveness of "Greek boxing" as a method of self-defense; whether they were talking about pankration or Greek boxing proper is unknown. However, by the time of the Greek incorporation into the Roman Empire, the emphasis would have been on learning proper striking techniques so that the lethal cestus (a spiked metal glove) could be employed. This alone might indicate a loss of interest in grappling techniques for self-defense, suggesting that boxing proper was probably employed.

The Romans conquered much of Greece in 146 B.C. The athletic skill and combat spirit displayed by pankrationists were less appreciated by the Romans than the slaughter of the gladiatorial games in the Colosseum. Pankration was relegated to secondary status. Therefore, pankration gradually began to disappear from the mainstream of Greek and Roman life. With the fall of the Western Roman Empire, pankration continued to be practiced within the Eastern (Byzantine) Empire, but never achieved the same level of popularity as it had among the ancient Greeks.

The Olympic Games were banned in the fourth century A.D. as pagan rituals, and pankration was relegated to local athletic festivals. Soon, the chaotic circumstances following the fall of the Western Roman Empire, the constant struggle for survival by the Byzantine Empire against external threats, and the prohibition by the Church of any form of paganism discouraged the practice and transmission of the art. By the tenth century, pankration had, for all practical purposes, died out under the impact of social events of the times. Medieval Christianity suppressed events associated with the pagan world as well as prohibiting the study of the human body, critical for unarmed fighting systems. In addition, the nature of warfare in the Middle Ages, specifically the development of vastly superior armor and the counterdevelopment of innovative weapon systems to counteract the defensive abilities of armor, placed a much greater emphasis on weapons training. With the decline and eventual extinction of pankration, the Western world lost its preeminent unarmed martial art. Historical conditions in Europe did not allow for a revival.

With the explosion of popularity of martial arts in the 1960s and 1970s in America and Europe, pankration began a rebirth. Modern systems of pankration have been developed and are gaining popularity. In addition, the development and spectacular popularity of no-holds-barred fighting, also known as "ultimate fighting," has created a demand for fighters remarkably similar to the pankrationists of antiquity. Ultimate fighters are allowed to punch, kick, and grapple, and many contests are decided through a choke hold or joint lock. The vast number of techniques and the innovative manner in which they are used resemble in many ways Greek pankration. Modern differences, such as the use of protective equipment and uniforms (notably jûdô or jûjutsu uniforms), are often the only distinctions between ultimate fighting and ancient pankration.

Although pankration can be considered a "lost" martial art, it survives into the present day through re-creation. Just how much modern no-holds-barred events resemble the ancient art can never be established, but the spirit of total fighting with minimal rules certainly brings the ideals of pankration into the contemporary world.

Pankration is one of the pivotal events in the history of combat systems. It was developed to teach males the art of war and to develop an individual's virtue and bravery. It led to the development of innovative and creative fighting methods that profoundly influenced the ancient world. Indeed, that individuals such as Plato, Aristotle, and Socrates were familiar with the art is a signal of the importance of this combat system in the Greek world. The contributions of the ancient Greeks to human society were incalculably important. Pankration is yet another example of the outstanding gifts the Greeks bestowed on the world. Although lost to history, ancient pankration was one of the critical steps in martial arts development and stands as an important milestone in the history of combat systems.

Gene P. Tausk

See also Europe; Gladiators; Performing Arts; Wrestling and Grappling: Europe

References

Arvanitis, Jim. 1979. *Mu Tau: The Modern Greek Karate.* New York: Todd and Honeywell.

Corcoran, John, and Emil Farkas. 1983. *Martial Arts: Traditions, History, People.* New York: Gallery Books.

Gardiner, E. Norman. 1910. *Athletics of the Ancient World.* Oxford: Oxford University Press.

———. 1930. *Greek Athletic Sports and Festivals.* Oxford: Oxford University Press.

Hines, Nick. 1997. "Pankration: The Granddaddy of No Holds Barred Fighting." *Black Belt* 35, no. 11: 80.

Poliakoff, Michael. 1995. *Combat Sports in the Ancient World: Competition, Violence, and Culture.* New Haven: Yale University Press.

Pattern Practice

See Form/Xing/Kata/Pattern Practice

Pentjak Silat

See Silat

Performing Arts

Combat systems and specific martial arts techniques have had a profound and lasting impact on the development of cultural performances throughout human history. From decentralized tribal cultures to politically centralized states, specific techniques of the hunt or fight have been transformed into cultural performances, enacted either by warriors themselves or by performers who have incorporated or modified such techniques to fit a culturally specific, yet evolving, aesthetic and performance style. The specific forms of cultural performance centered on martial systems may be best thought of as stretching along a continuum from actual to virtual combat.

Classical Greece offers one example of the wide range of combat or martially related cultural performances along this continuum. Actual combat in ancient Greece was common, but in addition there were other important forms of cultural performance in which the use of fighting techniques was central—the game-contests, and preparations or training for warfare. Both were characteristically violent.

Sociologist Norbert Elias has ably illustrated that unlike today's rather tame modern versions of the original Olympic Games, the early Greek game-contests were regarded "as an exercise for war and war as an exercise for these contests" (1972, 100). Further toward the virtual end of the continuum, many of the same martial techniques served as the basis for two important forms of performance—the *Pyrrhic* and *Anapale*. These two forms illustrate the symbiotic relationship that has always existed between martial training, dance, and performance. The Pyrrhic was part of the training of boys in Sparta from the age of 5. Similar to the dramatic contests, where the chorus was trained at the expense of the *choregus* (citizen-patron) and performed as part of the festival of Dionysus, Phyrric competitions were held at the Panathenaea Festival. Plato was ready to include the Pyrrhic in his ideal state and provided a vivid description of this martially based performance, which mimetically transformed actual offensive and defensive maneuvers into a graceful and athletic dance. For Plato the Pyrrhic imitated the modes of avoiding blows and missiles, "by dropping or giving way or springing aside, or rising up or falling down; also the opposite postures which are those of action as, for example, the imitation of archery and the hurling of javelins, and of all sorts of blows. And, when

An opera singer in full costume waves two swords during a Beijing Opera performance of The Monkey King *at the Dzung He Theater in Beijing, 1981. (Dean Conger/Corbis)*

the imitation is of brave bodies and souls, the action is direct and muscular, giving for the most part a straight movement of the limbs of the body" (*Laws* 7.815A). While the Pyrrhic was in essence a performance that also served as a preparation for armed combat, the Anapale, practiced at the *gymnopaedia* (literally, naked boy; a sports festival) in Sparta, was a dance performed by naked young boys "moving gracefully to the music of flute and lyre, [which] displayed posture, and movements used in wrestling and boxing" (Lawler 1964, 108).

Whether on the battlefield, the game field, or in the dancing place in mimetically transformed versions, both armed and unarmed martial techniques were a highly visible and important part of classical Greek culture and social life. Each specific display or cultural performance context embodied a shared "display ethos" founded on commonly held assumptions regarding important attributes of the heroic warriors who practiced such techniques and who were prepared to die in battle. Elias discusses how both game-contests and fighting in classical Greece "centered on the ostentatious display of the warrior virtues which gained for a man the highest praise and honor among other members of his own group and for his group. It was glorious to vanquish enemies or opponents but it was hardly less glorious to be vanquished" (Lawler 1964, 100).

The heroic display ethos of a culture or subculture is that collective set of behaviors, expected actions, and principles or codes of conduct that ideally guide and are displayed by a hero, and are the subject of many traditional ballads or epics where seemingly superhuman heroes display bravery, courage, and valor in the face of death. As Elias points out, for the Greeks, Hector was as glorious in defeat as his conqueror, Achilles, since he too fought as one must to be a hero, with all one's "might until one was maimed, wounded, or killed and could fight no longer. . . . What was inglorious and shameful was to surrender victory without a sufficient show of bravery and endurance" (1972, 100). The game-contests and dances provided opportunities for the performative display of the heroic ethos that was a legacy of the Homeric epics.

The heroic display ethos of a culture, the oral and/or written mythologies and histories of martial exploits, and the specific martial techniques per se collectively constitute a network of three symbiotically interrelated phenomena, which combine to constitute a variety of genres of cultural performance ranging from aesthetic, virtual displays choreographed in highly stylized dance or dramatic forms (such as the Anapale), to game-contests or mock combats arranged as part of a public festival (such as the original Olympic contests), to duels or combats (the later gladiatorial combats/contests of the Roman Empire), to external warfare itself. Public displays of power or arms, socially and legally sanctioned arenas where tests of strength or duels occur, and mock combats or exhibitions of martial skills have always served as discrete and important types of cultural performance in which martial techniques have played an important role. Through such public performances a particular (sub)culture's warrior-hero ethos itself is displayed to a wide public through use of actual techniques.

In the West there are many examples of historically significant heroic literatures that embody a particular period's display ethos; however, few examples of performance forms exist in the modern West that are based on martial forms or that embody the heroic or display ethos of a former era. The forms that do exist in the West are often examples of what Schechner has called "restored behavior," today's Renaissance Fairs, for example, which employ actors dressed in period costumes reconstructing jousting matches in which knights stage mock combats for the hands of fair ladies of court, or stage combat techniques historically reconstructing the precise use of historically accurate weaponry as part of a staged drama.

Unlike the West, in Asia and other parts of the world we find many cases of living martial traditions whose techniques have formed the core of many cultural performances that display the culture's heroic ethos as well as bring to life its mythic, epic, or historical heroic literatures. Such performances include ritual and folk, as well as "classical," genres. Indeed, it can be impossible to distinguish in some cases where a martial art ends and a performing art begins, as with the *randai* and *silek* of the Minangkabau of Sumatra, or Brazilian *capoeira*. In both these cases, so integral have the martial art and performance elements become to each other that training takes place through performance, and performance through the martial arts training.

In many other cases martial arts techniques have been subsumed within, and gradually transformed into, virtuosic training and/or performance systems. One of the most obvious historical connections is that between the traditional Chinese theater (Beijing Opera), which evolved its *wu-kung* (literally, martial effort) techniques employing both hand-to-hand fighting and manipulation of halberds, lances, and swords. Seen today in the spectacular acrobatic feats and mass stylized combat displays of the Beijing stage, the process of transformation through which wu-kung stage combat and choreography developed is as yet unexplored and undocumented, if not lost in the maze of individual schools of Chinese martial traditions.

Similarly, the popular Kabuki theater of Japan developed its *Tachi-mawari* or stylized fight-scene techniques associated with portrayal of samurai. In Kabuki the *tateshi* (fight specialist) was the acting company's stage-fight specialist, responsible for combining various acrobatic moves, *mie* poses used for highly emotional dramatic effect, and specific fighting techniques brought from the martial arts into Kabuki's exciting, fast-paced battle scenes. Even the more reserved and restrained Nô drama of Japan, the predecessor of Kabuki, was influenced by the martial arts and ways. For example, the *Kita Noh* tradition (one of the five main schools of acting) was born from the samurai class. Some of today's contemporary Kita school actors compare the concentration and mental state of the Nô performer to those of the martial artist. In some plays, such as the demon play, *Funa Benkei,* the staging of the demon's attack is taken from the use of sword and halberd (*naginata*).

A third example of the close relationship between martial arts and performance is that found in India. As early as the writing of the encyclopedia of dramaturgy, *Natyasastra* (between 200 B.C. and A.D. 200), the link between martial techniques, performer training, and stage combat had been made. The performer is enjoined to prepared himself for the stage by taking "exercise on the floor as well as high up in the air, and should have beforehand one's body massaged with the [sesame] oil or with barley gruel. The floor is the proper place [literally, "mother"] for exercise. Hence one should resort to the floor, and stretching oneself over it one should take exercise" (Ghosh 1956). The neophyte receives instructions to follow dietary restrictions as part of the training. The text also records the types of movement to be used for onstage "release of weapons" and use of sword

A Cossack soldier performs a dance with knives for Russian General Alexander Komaroff. A group of musicians provide accompaniment for the dancer, 1885. (Corbis)

and shield, as well as other weapons in the stage combat arsenal used to enact scenes drawn from India's great epics, the *Mahabharata* and *Ramayana.* The early Indian connection between martial and performing arts is witnessed in the legacy of extant martial and performance genres today throughout the subcontinent, from Orissa's now refined dance genre, *Seraikella chhau,* which originated in martial exercises before it became a masked-dance/drama, to the *kathakali* dance-drama of Kerala, whose entire training, massage system, and stage combat are derived directly from its martial precursor, *kalarippayattu.*

In addition to the symbiotic relationship between traditional Asian martial and performing arts, over the past twenty years contemporary performers both in Asia and the West have begun to make use of martial arts in training performers and as part of the development of a contemporary movement vocabulary. Among contemporary Western theater practitioners and actor trainers, A. C. Scott, Herbert Blau, and Rachel Rosenthal were some of the pioneers during the 1960s, all making use of taijiquan (tai chi ch'uan)—Scott in training performers at the Asian/Experimental Theatre Program at the University of Wisconsin–Madison, Blau and Rosenthal in training members of their performance ensembles. Following their examples in using taijiquan, but also making use of the Indian martial art kalarippayattu, as well as yoga, in the 1970s Phillip Zarrilli began to develop a now internationally known system of training performers using the principles of techniques of Asian martial and meditation arts as a foundation for the psychophysiological process of the performer (see Zarrilli 1993, 1995).

One example of the actual use of a martial art in contemporary theater performance is that of Yoshi and Company. In the 1970s Yoshi Oida, an internationally known actor with Peter Brook's company in Paris, created a complete performance piece, *Ame-Tsuchi,* based on kendô. Yoshi used the rituals of combat and full contact exchanges as a theatrical vehicle for transmission of the symbolic meaning behind the Japanese origin myth that served as the text for the performance.

Of the many examples from Asia per se, during the 1980s in India a number of dancers, choreographers, and theater directors began to make use of martial arts in training their companies or for choreography. Among some of the most important have been theater directors Kavalam Narayana Panikkar of Kerala, who used kalarippayattu in training his company, Sopanam, and Rattan Theyyam in Manipur, who made use of thang-ta. Among Indian choreographers, Chandralekha of Madras and Daksha Seth of Thiruvananthapuram have both drawn extensively on kalarippayattu in training their companies and creating their contemporary choreographies.

Phillip Zarrilli

See also Africa and African America; Capoeira; Form/Xing/Kata/Pattern Practice; Japan; Kalarippayattu; Mongolia; Thang-Ta

References
Elias, Norbert. 1972. "The Genesis of Sport as a Sociological Problem." In *Sport: Readings from a Sociological Perspective.* Edited by Eric Dunning. Toronto: University of Toronto.
Ghosh, M. 1956. *Natyasastra.* Vol. 1. Calcutta: Manisha Granthalaya.
Lawler, Lillian B. 1964. *The Dance in Ancient Greece.* Seattle: University of Washington Press.
Schechner, Richard. 1983. *Performative Circumstances from Avante Garde to Ramlila.* Calcutta: Seagull Books.
Zarrilli, Phillip B., ed. 1995. *Acting (Re)Considered.* London: Routledge Press.
———. 1993. *Asian Martial Arts in Actor Training.* Madison, WI: Center for South Asia.

Philippines

The title *Filipino martial arts* (FMA) refers to several styles, methods, and systems of self-defense that include armed and unarmed combat. Mostly, FMA are just "Filipino fencing," because they include personal armed combative techniques that emphasize weaponry skills over skills in empty hands. Unarmed combat is practiced in FMA, but is traditionally studied after weaponry training. This training sequence sets FMA apart from other martial arts, especially Asian, that initiate with empty hands.

Filipino armed combat is known variously as *arnis, eskrima* (fencing; Spanish, escrima), and *kali. Arnis* derives from the Spanish word *arnes,* meaning "armor." Arnis, or "harness," no doubt also refers to the battle harness worn by Filipino soldiers under Spanish command. *Arnis-de-mano,* or "harness of hand," denotes the deft hand movements made by Filipino grooms working for Spanish officers. Lightning-quick hand movements were alleged to be native martial arts techniques in disguise. Forbidden by the Spanish to practice indigenous martial arts, defiant Filipinos purportedly retained their fighting skills in secret by hiding them inside dance forms called *Santikan, Sayaw,* and *Moro-Moro.* An alternative thesis proposes that FMA is classical fencing that evolved with incipient nationalism. Hence, FMA is the modern expression of fencing evolution.

Other etymologies have been suggested for the names of the various Filipino arts. The Spanish term *esgrima* (skirmish) has entered the Pilipino language. Kali, according to some accounts, might be named after the Hindu goddess of destruction. Internationally recognized FMA master Dan Inosanto contends that Kali is the conjunction of the first syllables of two words from the Philippine Visayan language—*kamot,* meaning "hand," and *lihok,* meaning "motion." Thus, *Kali* means "hand motion." An examination of the Pilipino language indicates otherwise. In the Hiligaynon dialect of the Western Visayas, the term *kali* means "to dig," as with a shovel (*pala*). A shovel is a spade and the word for sword is *espada.* Kali probably derives from the Visayan word *kalis,* meaning "sword," which was written in a shipboard chronicle of Magellan's voyage in A.D. 1534.

Unarmed combat is *mano-mano* (Spanish; hand-to-hand), but is also *kuntao* and *silat.* To describe the plethora of FMA styles, methods, and systems is arduous; some—Doce Pares, Lacoste, Modern Arnis, and Pekiti Tirsia—are publicized through seminars and are associated with particular instructors such as Ciriaco C. Canete, Dan Inosanto, Remy A. Presas, and Leo T. Gaje Jr., who spread the FMA in Australia, Canada, Germany, Great Britain, and the United States.

Geographically situated at the crossroads of Southeast Asia, the Philippines are located near the equator above Borneo and below Taiwan. With a population estimated at 60 million, the Philippines are larger in area than Great Britain, but smaller than Japan. Those unfamiliar with the 7,107 islands and three major regions of the Philippine Archipelago, Luzon (north), Visayas (central), and Mindanao (south), may be confused by the eighty-seven different dialects of Pilipino (Tagalong), the national language. English is the language of business and education, and Spanish is spoken to a lesser extent.

Foreign languages are remnants of immigration to and colonization of the Philippine islands, which influenced native Filipino martial arts. It is of-

ten said that Filipinos have Malay ancestry, Chinese culture, Spanish religion, and American education. Mestizos are racially mixed Filipinos with Chinese, Spanish, and American bloodlines. The varied cultural milieu facilitated the blending of FMA. Filipino martial arts are a blend of at least Indonesian, Malaysian, Chinese, Spanish, American, and Japanese origins.

Filipino martial culture has both tradition and history. The tradition is oral and the history is written. The culture was alternately destroyed and created by foreign colonization. Martial fiestas offer keys to understanding Filipino martial culture. For example, the mythical meeting of the ten *datus* (chiefs) of Borneo with the *Negritos* of Panay is celebrated annually at the Ati-Atihan in Kalibo, Aklan. Similarly, the defeat of Captain Ferdinand Magellan by Datu Lapu-Lapu of Mactan Island is celebrated at the Sinulog in Cebu. This is in conjunction with the Santo Niño Fiesta, which marks the introduction of the Catholic faith to the Philippines.

Theory posits that in a prehistoric period, aboriginal Negritos (Aetas), a pygmy race, crossed over a land bridge from mainland Asia to become the first settlers of the Philippine islands. Next, waves of immigrants from the area called Malaysia colonized the islands, around 200 B.C. Anthropological evidence shows that the prehistoric people of Southeast Asia all belonged to a single population. They were later divided into cultural groups (i.e., Filipinos, Malaysians, and Indonesians) in accordance with territorial boundaries established by their European (i.e., Spanish, British, and Dutch) colonizers.

In the ninth century A.D., trade relations began with China. Colonies were established in the Philippines during the Song dynasty (A.D. 960–1127). Kuntao, an FMA with empty-hand movements similar to taijiquan, has been traced to Kuntung province. Chinese rivalry with the Hindus and Javanese continued into the Ming period (A.D. 1402–1424). Ancient civilizations—the Sri Vishayan and Majapahit—are prominent in Filipino history. Hindu influence includes the Tantra: a form of yoga that includes sexual magic and celebrates the feminine force. Tantric influence could explain the prominent role of women in Filipino society. *Visaya* means "slave" to the Moros, Muslims who dominate the southern region of the Philippine Archipelago, and refers to people of the central region whom the Moros frequently captured or killed. The Majapahit Empire was formed in Java around the twelfth century in the area of modern Indonesia. This ancient Islamic empire included Burma, Indonesia, Thailand, Malaysia, Cambodia, Madagascar, and the Philippines. The martial arts from these countries, such as Muay Thai, bersilat, and pentjak silat, have techniques, such as silat, that are similar to FMA.

Islam came to Mindanao in the south around A.D. 1380, spreading to the Visayas and Luzon. These Muslim Malays ventured north from Borneo (Kalimantan) led by the ten datus (chieftains), the most important of whom was Datu Puti. Datu Puti, "the Great White Chief," traveled from Borneo to Panay, from Panay to Luzon, and from Luzon back to Borneo, after helping the datus to settle other islands. In A.D. 1433, Datu Kalantiyaw, third chief of Panay and descendent of Datu Sumakwel from Borneo, issued or codified civil and social orders called the Kalantiyaw for guiding his people. Although its authenticity is questionable, the eighteen commandments of the Kalantiyaw code may be one of the few written records surviving from pre-Spanish times.

Western history of the Philippines begins with Captain Ferdinand Magellan landing on the island of Cebu in the central Visayas on April 15, 1521. The conquistador was circumnavigating the globe and claiming lands for the Spanish Crown. The name *Philippines* comes from the Spanish version of "Philip's Pines," the name Magellan gave the islands as he claimed them for King Philip II. In the Battle of Mactan, near Cebu, Captain Magellan was killed while retreating in the surf from an attack by native forces led by Datu Lapu-Lapu. The Spanish colonial period brought Catholic religion to the Philippine islands and helped to unify them into a single nation. Independence from Spain was declared on June 12, 1898. The Filipino revolution for independence was led by secret societies, such as the Katipunan. Most Katipunan members were Freemasons following pre-Spanish traditions and were known to practice both Filipino Martial Arts and Spanish swordsmanship. After the Spanish-American War, the United States got Puerto Rico and the Philippines as booty.

The U.S. forces fought a guerilla war against the Moros in Mindanao to claim the islands. Fierce resistance from local Muslim tribes caused the United States military to recall the .38 caliber revolver and issue .45 caliber revolvers to increase stopping power. Moros tied tourniquets on their limbs to prevent blood loss and charged into the American trenches. The nickname "leatherneck" refers to the United States Marines' wearing leather gorgets around their necks to stop the Moros from cutting their throats.

Japanese imperial armed forces invaded the Philippines and occupied the islands from 1942 to 1945. An ideological battle was fought for the soul of the Filipino people, who were reminded by the Japanese that despite their history under Spain and America, they were oriental, not occidental. The Japanese encountered fierce guerilla resistance in the islands from Filipino nationalists and their American allies. Following General Douglas MacArthur's historic return landing in Leyte, the Philippines headed for self-determination. There is an indelible mark on the Filipino psyche from the Japanese occupation during World War II. Some of the two-handed stickfighting styles, such as *Dos Manos* in Doce Pares Eskrima, were developed to encounter Japanese swords. After the American commonwealth ended in 1946, the Philippines developed like other former Spanish colonies as an agricultural society.

Nowadays, Filipino martial arts include many types of skills, but not all styles include the entire range of them. Inosanto classifies Filipino skills into twelve categories: (1) single stick, sword, or ax; (2) double stick, sword, or ax; (3) single stick, sword, or ax and dagger or shield; (4) double knife; (5) single knife and empty hands; (6) empty hands; (7) short stick; (8) flexible weapons; (9) throwing weapons; (10) projectile weapons like archery and blowgun; (11) distance weapons like spear and staff; and (12) double-handed long stick or healing arts.

The single stick (*solo baston, garote, olisi*) category includes the ax and sword—when used singly. A single cane refers to a wooden weapon about 1 inch in diameter and ranging from 22 to 44 inches in length. Sticks are used to practice and are often made of rattan for safety. Rattan is a noduled porous climbing palm tree with a tough skin. Some FMA techniques are executed with either sticks or swords, but most techniques are oriented to sticks, rather than blades. Practitioners seldom play with either blunted or sharpened edged weapons, with the exception of aluminum sword blanks and steel training knives.

A misconception on the part of some practitioners is that rattan is a suitable wood for self-defense applications. However, rattan sticks are merely used for safe practice; they lack the density needed for combat. Oral tradition holds that Datu Lapu-Lapu killed Captain Magellan with a rattan stick in single combat! This is absurd. Hardwood weapons made of *bahi* (palm) or *kamagong* (ebony) are favored in fighting.

The *vara* was a Spanish unit of measurement about 31 to 33 inches in length. The vara was also a wooden implement used for wrapping bolts of cloth and so would be convenient to wield, say, in a marketplace. Thus, the vara is plausibly the fighting stick length used by escrimadores during the Spanish period. The vara is the length of weapon used by the Original Doce Pares system.

The stick is held in either the long-range (*largo*) or close-range (*corto*) grip. In the long-range grip, the hand is pursed with the hand held as if wielding a screwdriver, while in the close-range grip the hand is clenched with the hand held as if wielding a hammer. These two grips provide reach and strength, respectively. A variation on the close-range grip is the reverse grip (an "ice-pick" grip), which is used for infighting. This grip, however, is more likely to be used in knife fighting, being impractical for swords.

Stick length varies according to personal style and with practitioner morphology. An example illustrates both category one and category twelve (single long stick) of the Inosanto weapons typology. The late Angel Cabales, of *Serrada* (closed; Spanish, *cerrada*) *Eskrima,* who was 4 feet 11 inches tall and weighed 100 pounds, used a 22-inch stick to close with his opponents. In contrast, Romeo C. Mamar Sr. of *Tapado,* who is about 5 feet, 7 inches tall and weighs 160 pounds, likes a 44-inch stick to strike his opponents from a long distance. A stylistic difference is that while the Serrada practitioner uses one hand to strike, the Tapado practitioner uses two hands to wield the primary weapon.

Also in the first category are the ax (*wasay*), club (*batuta*), and sword (*kalis*), when such weapons are used by themselves. Filipino swords come in many shapes and sizes, especially down south in Moroland. Moro weapons include the kris, *barong*, and *kampilan*. Krises have three or more (odd-numbered) flaming waves in the blade (labeled the flamberge blade type) and their double edge is designed for thrusting. The Filipino kris is larger, wider, and heavier than the Indonesian kris. The barong is a shorter, leaf-shaped, single-edged sword for chopping and thrusting, without a hilt. The kampilan is a longer chopping sword with a blunted point, which may be swung with one, but usually two, hands. Visayan swords include the *talibong* and *ginonting*. The talibong is hilted with a crossguard and is single edged, made by stock removal along one side of the blade. Unlike the forged swords characteristic of Mindanao, stock removal is used to shape bar stock steel to fashion weapons in the central and northern regions. The ginonting has a blunted point with no crossguard and is more like a utility knife. Farming tools, such as the bolo or machete, are prevalent.

The second category is double stick (*doble baston, sinawali*) and refers to two canes or swords of equal length. The philosophy that prevails in this category of weapons is that "two swords are better than one, when you know how to use them both in conjunction." *Sawali* means "to weave," while sinawali refers to the striking patterns that are made by two coordinated weapons. Thus, the label sinawali is more specific than doble baston in general, because of patterns employed.

Category three is called sword and dagger (*espada y daga*). Techniques in this category recognize the natural hand dominance in human physiology. If an opponent is holding one weapon, then it will probably be held in the dominant hand. If an enemy is holding two weapons, then either the lighter or the smaller weapon will be held in the submissive hand, and the heavier or longer weapon will be held in the dominant hand. This is not true for the sword and shield, but the principle of warding with the awkward or submissive hand still holds.

The shield (Pilipino; *kalasag*) is used in combination with either the sword or the spear (see category eleven). The principle remains the same as with appropriate-handed weapons wielded. Fighters wore armor during the time of Magellan, but armor is seldom used for contemporary FMA practice. Beginning with the Spanish colonial period, European martial arts, notably the Spanish (De La Destreza) geometric theory of fencing, was blended with native fighting. For example, the concept of angular attack influenced Filipino karate. Filipino espada y daga might have evolved from Spanish sword-and-dagger techniques, not the rapier and dagger. The European fencing schools include the French, Italian, Spanish, and German. *Rikarte Eskrima* has attack and counterattack methods for each European fencing school. Since General Ricarte campaigned in the Filipino revolution against Spain, these foreign methods may be a result of the revolutionary experience. Moreover, some FMA styles have European roots. Mariano Navarro founded the Black Eagle Eskrima Club of Cebu in the Visayas. Navarro's Portuguese father taught swordsmanship. An *arnisidor* (practitioner of arnis) from Bacolod, Federico Serfino Jr., was the national fencing champion, representing the Philippines in the 1964 Olympic Games. Serfino learned arnis from his father, but learned about European fencing at the Indonesian embassy in Manila.

The fourth, or double knife, category is a progression from double stick and stick and dagger, because the theory of their usage is the same for gripping two weapons. The way in which the knives are held, gripped in the hands with palms facing down, is connected with *suntukin,* the Filipino boxing style. There are two basic ways to hold the knife: with the point upward in a hammer grip and with the point downward in an ice-pick grip. The "up and down" knife grips are known as *dusak* and *pakal* in the Visayan language. An important principle in knife fighting is "equalization." The student is taught to carry two or more knives in case an attacker has a bigger knife. For example, Pekiti Tirsia practitioners carry three knives at all times. In double knife fighting, there is a dominant and a recessive side of the body that come into play. One strategy is to hold a single-bladed slashing weapon in the dominant hand and hold a double-bladed thrusting weapon in the submissive hand. The dominant hand leads the body into combat, while the submissive hand destroys the enemy after the closure.

Category five is single knife utilizing empty hands, but this category also includes dagger versus dagger (daga y daga). Important principles taught in this category are the following. A single-edged knife is better for cutting than a double-edged knife, because the wider blade cleaves flesh. A double-edged dagger has the advantage of penetration, because the knife is usually more narrow and pointed. Still, the slimmer dagger makes it more susceptible to breakage than the wider-bellied knife. Different styles favor various knife shapes and grips. In *Lapu-Lapu,* the practitioners preferred to use ordinary tools as weapons, like the *songut,* or sickle (for cutting sugar cane), and the *bita,* used for making shoes. Both knives can be found on streets and in alleys.

In category five, certain FMA evolved into long-knife or bolo styles from sword techniques. Thus, Philippine Army general Faustino Ablin originally developed his *Derobio Eskrima* for cavalry sabers. After this FMA went to Hawaii with the late Braulio Pedoy, saber techniques were practiced with stick, knife, and bolo. An emphasis was placed on locking and disarming for close-quarter combat, but such techniques were not suitable while mounted.

While the sixth category, empty hands, is certainly not undeveloped, battlefield commanders considered training in hand-to-hand combat less pragmatic than weapons training. It is notable that the experiences of Filipino guerrilla fighters in World War II infused realism into the modern Filipino martial arts. The late Felimon "Momoy" Canete of Doce Pares Eskrima devised many-bladed striking techniques based on his experiences in jungle patrols fighting against Japanese soldiers. For him, the stick represented a blade. The unarmed methods of Filipino combat (mano-mano) include kicking (*sikaran* or *sipa*), boxing (*suntukin*), trapping (*gapos*), grappling (*buno, dumog*), and disarming (*disarma*). Sikaran is similar to *taekwondo* (Korean), with emphasis on high-line kicking. Sipa is a children's kicking game like hacky-sack (a game in which a small footbag is kicked between players without being allowed to touch the ground). Dan Inosanto calls kicking *pananjakman. Suntukin* is "to box." Inosanto calls punching *Panantukan.* Trapping (gapos) refers to immobilization or hacking, but may include strikes such as thrusting and palming. Grappling includes sweeps, throws, and locks. Locking the joints is called *tranka* or *kunsi.* Pinching, biting, gouging, and tearing are elements of close-range combat. Native grappling methods are called *buno* in Luzon and *dumog* in the Visayas. Traditionally, local disputes were settled and justice dispensed through trial by ordeal. *Bultong* was a "trial by ordeal" FMA in which adversaries wrestled until the victor proved the other party guilty. The Filipino term *agaw* means "disarming," but the Spanish term is *disarma.* Disarma refers to using weapons and/or empty hands to neutralize armed opponents by taking away weapons. For example, the Lapu-Lapu Arnis Affecianados practiced a unique method of disarming by using reverse principles. They used reverse psychology like *jûdô* (Japanese) in which they pushed when the attacker pulled.

The short stick in category seven is a pocket weapon, such as a roll of coins, that can be held in the hand and used for striking. This category includes closed knives like the *balisong.* The balisong, or butterfly knife, is a three-piece, gravity-operated (not automatic) folding knife. The *kubotan* (hand-sized cylinder with a key ring attached) is a similar Japanese weapon.

The flexible weapons (*ligas armas*) in category eight include the flail (*panlugas, tayak tobok*), whip (*latiko, kaburata*), chain (*cadena*), and stingray tail (*ikog-pagi*). Like the Okinawan/Japanese *nunchaku*, the flail is a farm tool (rice thresher). Flails are portable, concealable, and quick to strike their targets, but difficult to control. Rikarte Eskrima prefers short whips, approximately 6 feet long. Panandata Arnis uses a 52- or 60-inch horsewhip. Filemon Canete made 12-foot-long rope whips by hand and wove spells into them. This is considered to be Christian white magic. Although it stings and is useful for punishing restrained persons, the whip is not adequate for combat. Heavier and more flexible than the whip, the chain (la cadena) requires the right timing for adequate striking. The stingray tail is usually about a yard long or more. After sun drying, the stingray tail gets hard and leathery and has sharp spiky edges that tear. The stingray tail is considered suitable for crowd control.

The projectile weapons (inihagis ng armas) in category nine cover slingshot (tirador), throwing knives (kutsilyong panghagis), darts (palasong), blowgun (buguhan), archery (pana), and firearms (putok). The Filipino martial arts do have prescribed ways to use these weapons. For example, in Doce Pares Eskrima, single-edged knives are thrown by the blade, while double-edged knives are thrown by the handle.

Category ten includes not only the bow and arrow, but also firearms for modern times. Archery is the martial art of the Negritos, but those reclusive tribes stay in the mountains. In cities, firearms are more suitable, especially in civil wars. The restrictive Philippine laws on gun ownership can be circumvented by ingenuity. Hence, revolvers are handmade by "blacksmiths" to chamber 5.56 mm NATO bullets that Filipino soldiers carry in M16 Armalites. Ammunition is not available for pistols and revolvers (except .38 caliber), so soldiers are bribed with cigarettes for carbine bullets.

The distance weapons (agwat armas) in category eleven include spear (bangkaw) and staff (tungkod, sibat) fighting techniques. Bangkaw means the pointed mast of an outrigger boat (bangka). The masts of the longboats are used as spears after landing. In the pre-Spanish period, Malay villages called barangays were settled by longboat people.

In category twelve, Dos Manos (Spanish; two hands) refers to two-handed stick and sword methods. Tapado is a long-stick fighting method using a 44-inch stick. In San Miguel Eskrima, a 50-inch stick simulates samurai swords or Spanish sabers. Also, two-handed techniques can be executed with a panabas (also lantip or tabas), which is a farm tool with a short blade and a long handle for cutting sugarcane. The kampilan is a single-edged long sword from Mindanao that is suitable for Dos Manos moves. Single-edged Kampilans differ from the medieval European longswords (the hand-and-a-half Bastard swords), which are double-edged.

Not many styles, methods, or systems cover these twelve categories. Some have only a few, and others focus on alternative techniques, emphasizing other skills. For example, the skill category can instead include healing arts and metaphysics. Healing arts and metaphysics are a "higher understanding" of the Filipino martial traditions. Healing arts are linked to the FMA, but are not integrated with training methods as they are in the Chinese martial arts. The former include massage or chiropractic (hilot, kiropraktika), herbalism, and faith healing. Hence, Rosita M. Lim is a curer (*seruhana, arbolaryo*) and chiropractor (*manughilot*), but not an FMA practitioner. She uses massage, exorcism, and incense to heal people, but her skill is "gingering." Gingering uses prayers to transfer evil spirits into a ginger root, which is discarded with the trapped spiritual essence. The metaphysics (*lubos*) include *anting-anting* (amulet, charm), *kalaki, orasyon* (prayers), and *palabras* (words). In the metaphysics associated with Filipino martial arts in the Philippines, overt Catholic religiosity is layered onto a substratum of *Huna* magic. Huna (secret) is a Polynesian practice, says Max Freedom Long (1965). Kalaki, meaning "abilities," is associated with practitioners of the native martial arts. Eskrimadores are known as mystics, faith healers, and sorcerers, using mesmerism and visualization (*larawan*). Thus, the potent anting-anting can be made from the kneecaps of deceased persons. Grave robbers dig up such "treasures," which then are made into a belt or necklace. Warriors prepare themselves for victory or death before combat using orasyon, with palabras (spells) and incantations worked against sworn enemies.

Otherwise, most Filipinos are resigned to fate, which is tempered only by Providence. The fatalistic attitude of Filipinos comes from their God concept. You will often hear the phrase "Bahala Na" (leave it to God). Resignation to fate or determinism is deeply ingrained in Filipino martial culture. Westerners remark with frustration when encountering Bahala Na, but it helps people survive in a difficult world. Filipino fatalism shows its most negative side when people "run amok," killing everyone in their path in a frenzy of rage, called jurimentado. This extreme reaction is understood by a society in which repressed feelings are harbored daily.

Certain concepts are central to all Filipino martial arts. The striking concept, spatial concept, and sectoring concept are a few. The strikes are angles of attack; space is the geometry of the fight zone, and sectoring is division of the problem set into a finite solution. The geometric theory of angles of attack was probably derived from Spanish fencing. *Abisidario* refers to the *abekada*, or ABCs, of learning how to fight. Usually, there are twelve basic attacking techniques and striking angles with five (i.e., *cinco teros*) in common among all FMA. Included are slashes, thrusts, and butts. Slashes are strikes with the side of a stick or with the edge of a blade. Thrusts use the pointed tip, while butts use the blunted end. Weapons and empty hands are used alone or in combination, depending on the range. There are three ranges: largo (long), *media* (medium), and corto (short). Media is often ignored; few fighters stay in the hot spot. Slashes are delivered from long range (*layaw*), while butts are delivered from close range (*dikit*). Besides the alphabeto (the ABCs of fighting), there is numerado.

Practitioners can reach the counter-for-counter stage of training after they develop basic (alphabet) techniques, using numerado—to play by the numbers. To play by numbers means to work counters and recounters against attacks in an ordered sequence of play. Few exceed this stage, because they lack a safe way to spar. Techniques that seem combat valid in training drills are invalidated with full contact. To prepare for full contact, fluid movement is developed in flow drills. The art is not played well without flowing. The Hiligaynon dialect has a word for the opposite of flow; players may be described as *pugoso*—meaning "pushing too hard, too stiff, not relaxed, or unnatural." Fluid movements are found in those fighters in the higher levels of training.

The FMA ranking structure has students, fighters, and teachers (i.e., instructors, masters, and grand masters). Traditional Filipino society was divided into nobles, freemen, and serfs. Nobles wore red, while the lower classes wore black or blue clothing. The color worn by students is blue (*asul*), associating them with the lower classes. Fighters can wear black (*itim*) and teachers wear red (*pula*). Novices are called *likas,* or natural, because they have no preconceptions. The intermediate students are called *likha,* or creation, because they have learned fundamentals. The advanced students are called *lakas,* or strength, because their skills are well developed. A fighter is an expert student on the way to becoming a teacher. Some teachers have never fought, not even in contests or among friends, and lack the quintessential stage of martial development. The name for a teacher in Filipino is *guro,* from *guru* (Sanskrit; teacher).

An instructor may be either an apprentice, assistant, junior, or senior instructor. Master instructors may be called Maestro in Spanish nomenclature. Some groups use Datu (chieftain), while others use *Lakan* (lord) to refer to an FMA master. The grand master is simply the grandfather of the school. Traditionally, one must reach age 50 to be acclaimed as a grand master. Founders of Filipino martial arts are rare.

The purpose of contests in the Filipino martial arts is to simulate the conditions of actual combat in order to learn to overcome the fear of loss. The learning process is facilitated through contests in the arena rather than an actual life-or-death experience. Combat is usually risky, and learning experiences can end prematurely. Dueling, particularly the death match, is FMA tradition, but was outlawed in 1982. Before this time, however, champions often fought many duels: Romeo ("Nono") Mamar of Bago City was undefeated after one hundred duels from 1960 to 1982. With cash betting as an incentive to public spectacle, duels were often bloody affairs; at their worst, human cockfights. Organized competitions have been held in the Philippines since 1949. Sanctioning organizations, such as the National Arnis Association of the Philippines (NARAPHIL) and World Eskrima, Kali Arnis Federation (WEKAF), sponsor national and international stickfighting events, and do not permit the bloody spectacles of the past.

Besides reasons of civilian self-defense and cultural preservation, Filipino martial arts are used for police and military training, especially for defending against edged weapons. Because FMA are a blend of moves, other martial artists can readily adopt them. For instance, the FMA now provide a vehicle for expressing the late Bruce Lee's Jeet Kune Do (JKD), as Lee's system contains the JKD concepts. Eskrima is the "secret recipe" for angling and fluidity in Kajukenbo. Likewise, FMA can be expected to absorb what is useful from other martial arts that its practitioners encounter.

Ronald A. Harris

See also Silat; Southeast Asia

References

Agoncillo, Teodoro A. 1990. *History of the Filipino People.* 8th ed. Quezon City, RP: Garotech Publishing.

Andres, Tomas D., and Pilar B. Ilada-Andres. 1987. *Understanding the Filipino.* Quezon City, RP: New Day Publishers.

Cabiero, J. C., and Gary Vatcher. 1996. *The Pure Art of Cabales Serrada Escrima.* Fresno, CA: CSE Productions.

Clements, John C. 1998. *Medieval Swordsmanship.* Boulder, CO: Paladin Press.

Draeger, Donn F., and Robert W. Smith. 1969. *Asian Fighting Arts.* Palo Alto, CA: Kodansha International Ltd.

Giron, Leo M. 1991. *Memories Ride the Ebb of Tide.* Stockton, CA: Bahala Na Publications.

Harris, Ronald A. 1991. "Arnis: Classic vs. Modern." *Inside Kung Fu,* May: 74–79.

———. 1990. "Ask the Experts (FMK)." *Inside Karate,* April, 64–67.

———. 1992. "The Hidden Eskrima of Kajukenbo." *Inside Karate,* September, 30–74.

———. 1993. "OHIDO—Playing by the Numbers." *Inside Karate,* October, 72–100.

———. 1989. "The 'Secret' Art of Tapado." *Inside Kung Fu,* May, 46–49.

———. 1990. "The Truth behind Lapu Lapu Kali." *Inside Kung Fu,* August, 64–68.

Inosanto, Dan. 1980a. *The Filipino Martial Arts.* Los Angeles, CA: Know Now Publishing Company.

———. 1980b. *Jeet Kune Do: The Art and Philosophy of Bruce Lee.* Los Angeles, CA: Know Now Publishing Company.

Jocano, F. Landa. 1975. *Questions and Challenges in Philippine Prehistory.* Quezon City: University of the Philippines Press.

Long, Max Freedom. 1965. *The Huna Code in Religions.* Marina Del Rey, CA: DeVorss Publications.

Marinas, Amante P. 1994. "The Philippine Latiko." *IKF Presents.* Burbank, CA: Unique Publications, Inc.

Pigafetta, Antonio. 1969. *Magellan's Voyage.* Translated by R. A. Skelton. New Haven, CT: Yale University Press.

Segura, Manuel F. 1975. *Tabunan: The Untold Exploits of the Famed Cebu Guerillas in World War II.* Cebu City, RP: MF Segura Publications.

Political Conflict and the Martial Arts

In social conflict, martial arts emerge not only as direct confrontations, but particularly in politically stratified situations (e.g., in colonial contexts) oppressed groups commonly employ martial arts to confront oppressors symbolically. In such cases martial arts have been utilized to support sociopolitical action pursued by subordinated groups. Such strategies draw on both indigenous combative traditions and newly synthesized systems as focal points for resistance. Examples of the former are provided by the Chinese Boxer Rebellion (1900), the fugitive slave resistance of the Brazilian *macambos* (nineteenth century), Okinawan opposition to Japanese Satsuma domination (seventeenth–nineteenth centuries), and Indonesian resistance to Dutch colonization (eighteenth–twentieth centuries). The latter strategy emerges in modern taekwondo and Vovinam-Viet Vo Dao.

The martial traditions in the first category share common elements: indigenous origins that promote ethnic pride, a belief in the superiority of their techniques to competing systems (particularly those of the dominant group), notions of elitism within an oppressed ethnic group, the belief in the ability to magically generate power that confers invulnerability and invincibility, and a body of oral tradition that substantiates claims as to origins and efficacy. The catalyst for their symbolic deployment in cultural conflict comes with the perception of a politically dominated status.

Responses to sociocultural disorganization that culminate in movements to regenerate traumatized populations and synthesize new worldviews have been labeled by Anthony F. C. Wallace as cultural revitalization movements. The revitalization response may be triggered by various forms of stress; however, in the cases considered here the stress is political (e.g., military invasion, economic hegemony). While such movements are, essentially, politically motivated, their trappings are most often spiritual/religious. Frantz Fanon notes that when a people want to regain a sense of self-worth they return to ancient religions and creation myths in order to validate cultural or political resistance. Martial arts practitioners often claim that their esoteric martial traditions have their origins in the remote legendary, or even mythic, past. This feature of martial arts lends itself to revitalization strategies. Finding solutions for current pressures in terms of past events provides a point of cohesion for oppressed people.

Moreover, in the majority of cases of cultural revitalization (whether they seek a return to a past "golden age" or a new world order) there is the implementation of a special ethnic or religious identity (often as a means of directly confronting stereotypes imposed by dominant groups) for purposes of unification. These ethnic and religious identities engender feelings of elitism among the subordinated group and create a debased image of the dom-

A painting of a burning station and derailed train on the Manchurian railway, with Chinese Nationalists celebrating their action during the Boxer Rebellion, ca. 1900. (Hulton Archive)

inant group, thus establishing the basis (and justification) for ethnic warfare. In the martial traditions under consideration, it is common for practitioners to argue for the superiority of their tradition over systems maintained among oppressors.

Colonial situations provide a vast array of case studies on the role of martial arts in revitalization. The reasons for the correspondence between colonialism and revitalization are obvious. There is a dominant-dominated relationship between two groups who differ in terms of culture, ethnic identification, and political loyalties. In addition, there are feelings of relative deprivation on the part of the dominated group and a conviction that a prevailing religious, social, or political system has failed them. Thus, an alternative that can confront the current dilemma must emerge to prevent collapse of the dominated culture.

Despite the spiritual orientation of many of these movements, there remains a potential for conflict with the dominant group. For example, the Ghost Dance movement that swept the western United States from 1888 to 1890 as espoused by the Paiute messiah Wovoka—despite prophecies foretelling the eradication of the whites—was pacifistic in orientation. Wovoka urged his followers to cooperate and enter into no conflicts with whites. As the religion spread from the Basin Cultures of Nevada to the Northern Plains Cultures, the rhetoric became increasingly militant, and the power that would bring about renewal was increasingly drawn upon for protection in warfare through the creation of "Ghost Dance Shirts" that would turn aside knives and bullets in battle. These "Ghost Shirts" were based on a traditional Plains model, the war shirt, which, like the ghost shirt, was painted with magical symbols designed to protect the wearer.

Anthropologist James C. Scott's observations regarding magic in millenarian movements are illuminating. He considers a belief in invulnerability engendered by magical means to be a standard feature of most millenarian movements. In the case of millenarian movements, both the oppressors and the power that supports their regime are to be negated by supernatural intervention. In one form or another, many indigenous martial arts claim to invest practitioners with supernormal powers, including resistance to injury or even invulnerability. Therefore, in certain cases not only is there a general divine mantle of protection created through the use of ritual practice or talismans, but also the resistance incorporates indigenous esoteric martial systems into its arsenal. Unlike the doctrines accompanying the movement that may be new revelations, esoteric militarism turns a traditional fighting art—with all its traditional powers—to new goals.

Perhaps the most widely known example of the use of esoteric martial arts in resisting political domination is found in the Boxer Rebellion. Rising during the Chinese Qing monarchy, the Boxers responded to attempts to colonize China from without and to modernize the nation from within at the close of the nineteenth century. In about 1898, members of a secret society of martial artists called Yi He Tuan (Righteous Harmonious Fist) arose against modernization and foreign influence. The Yi He Tuan (or I Ho) Boxers claimed that their rites rendered them impervious to bullets. With the invulnerability promised by their esoteric tradition and the blessings of Empress Dowager Ci Xi, they began a campaign of terrorism by attacking Christian missionaries, destroying symbols of foreign influence (e.g., telegraph lines), and ultimately storming the Legation Quarter in Beijing in June of 1900. Susan Naquin, in her analysis of the White Lotus sects of nineteenth-century China, reports similar claims of invulnerability to various weapons in these and related sects that combined esotericism with boxing.

Similarly, during the Dutch colonial period in Indonesia, esoteric indigenous martial traditions played a role. According to contemporary sources, in Java the secrets of the system of Southeast Asian combat called *pentjak* or *pencak silat* have been guarded largely because of the role played by groups of silat adepts in the fight for independence from the Dutch in the wake of World War II. At least some of these secrets entail the ways of developing *tenaga dalam,* a form of mystical energy utilized in various styles of silat. Like the power of the Ghost Shirt and that engendered by the Boxers' exercises, tenaga dalam is said to turn aside bullets. According to some sources, the origins of silat should be traced to the variety of Islamic mysticism called Sufism. Clearly, the extraordinary powers be-

A photo of the Ghost Dance of the Arapaho Indians, who believed the ritual would make them invincible, ca. 1900. (Corbis)

lieved to follow in the wake of Sufi enlightenment would prove an asset to the practice of silat. Although the connections between pentjak silat and Sufism are based primarily on oral traditions at this point, the esoteric martial system appears to have originated in a milieu that saw the rise of a religious tradition that had as at least one of its goals the generation of mystical power. Especially in the light of other esoteric martial traditions, the subsequent incorporation of magical elements of silat into the final struggle against Dutch colonialism (1945–1949) was predictable. Moreover, the fact that some Javanese claim the Dutch were ousted because of the magical superiority of silat over European technological warfare suggests that the martial tradition as a whole, as distinct from any individual technical aspects of it, bolstered ethnic and national pride. Accordingly, we see not merely a connection to a colonial rebellion, but to incipient Indonesian nationalism as well.

From neighboring Malaysia, James Scott reports compelling evidence of a bond between millenarianism and esoteric martial traditions when the eruption of Malaysian urban race riots in 1969 brought attention to the Red Sash Society (Pertubohan Selendang Merah), whose membership included not only politicians and religious figures but silat masters as well. The ties between ethnicity, nationalism, religion, and martial esotericism are clear in the Red Sash Society's dedication to defending the race and religion and its relationship to UMNO (United Malay Nationalists' Organization) politicians. Similarly, ten years later, the 30,000-member organization Nasrul Haq (NH) was singled out not only for its suspect political connections, but because of claims that members of NH posed a threat to the prevailing social order not only by teaching silat and allowing female participation, but also by practicing magical chants and engaging in trances. Both practices suggest a connection to martial esotericism. For Malaysia as a whole, the record demonstrates the reappearance of millennial and ecstatic Islamic cults during virtually every episode of historical crisis. It is likely that research would reveal crucial ways in which religion, silat, and nationalism are intertwined in these movements.

Okinawan martial arts oral tradition depicts similar ethnic and cultural struggles, supported in similar ways by the esoteric indigenous art of *di,* or *te* (hand). Like all folk histories, these narratives are sometimes at odds with the written record. Nevertheless, the historical traditions of te trace its development as an underground art to the conquest of the Ryûkyû Islands by the Shimazu clan of Satsuma in southern Japan (Kyûshû Island) in 1609. At this time, the private possession of weapons, banned by Okinawan king Sho Shin's edict of the late fifteenth century, came to be more stringently enforced by the Shimazu, as did prohibitions on the practice of the arts of war. Oral tradition maintains that Ryûkyûans (Okinawans) continued to practice martial arts at odd hours and in secret locations to avoid detection, and that for over three hundred years te was practiced secretly and transmitted orally or by means of privately transcribed "secret texts." After the Satsuma conquest and until the Meiji Restoration (1868), Okinawans were systematically oppressed. Oral narratives among practitioners of te consistently embody the theme of turning adversity to strength via martial esotericism, a theme that is consistent with the situations described above. In addition, these traditions maintain that the practice of te leads to the development of *ki* (Japanese) or *qi* (Chinese; *chi*)—a form of intrinsic energy said to ward off blows and increase the practitioner's strength to supernormal levels. Te, according to oral tradition, was used against the Japanese in a guerilla fashion reminiscent of the strategies described for Indonesia.

Brazilian *capoeira* constitutes a final example of a connection between esoteric martial arts, a dominated group, and ethnic conflict. In attempting to determine the origins of the martial art, J. Lowell Lewis cites a range of oral traditions tying the development of capoeira to the African Brazilian slave population; some commentators, in fact, posit an African origin for the fighting techniques and some of the terminology employed. The early record (pre-1920) is sketchy and heavily dependent on folk history, but the relevance of capoeira to the current issue is obvious. Oral tradition connects capoeira with the fugitive slave "kingdom" of Palmares in the region of Pernambuco, Brazil. The successful resistance movement by the Palmareans was attributed to the skills of "King" Zumbi, reputedly a capoeira master. Even as the art exists in the twentieth century among the urban underclasses, there is a strong identification with the slave experience—even down to the typical attire of some modern *capoeiristas,* which is said to be patterned on the dress of slaves during the colonial period. The esotericism noted for the other arts emerges in the dedication of some capoeiristas to specific *orixás* (divinities) of the African Brazilian syncretic religion Candomble who aid and even possess the fighter from time to time. A contemporary master, Mestre Nô, speaks of a mystic leap he takes, describing it as an attitude similar to the "no-mind" state of Asian Zen-based martial traditions. A further, linguistic, connection is provided by the synonym for capoeirista, *mandigueiro* (sorcerer). Not surprisingly, capoeira tradition claims that invulnerability, labeled *corpo fechado* (closed body), may be ritually attained by practitioners. The practice of the art continues to have nationalistic significance and especially, in the style called Capoeira Angola, serves as a source of ethnic pride and a link to African heritage. Lewis notes the power of this martial art as a means of both real and symbolic empowerment for economic and political underclasses.

Martial arts connect to political conflict in a less mystical but equally crucial way as well. In colonial situations in twentieth-century Asia, martial arts have been utilized by threatened cultures, not only according to the Indonesian and Malaysian patterns discussed above, but as vehicles for modern nationalism. The cases of Korean taekwondo and Vietnamese Vovinam-Viet Vo Dao are representative.

Taekwondo is a Korean martial art synthesized in the latter half of the twentieth century from native styles (primarily t'aek'kyŏn and subak, which had survived a Japanese occupation of almost fifty years) and elements of both Chinese and Japanese combat arts. In 1945, the end of Japanese occupation served as the catalyst for Korean nationalism, which was signaled in part by the opening of the Chung Do Kwan ("School," from the Chinese *guan*) for instruction in Korean martial arts. The formation of the Korean Armed Forces (1945) and the ensuing Korean Conflict (1950) further fueled the fires of nationalism and, not incidentally, provided the rationale for the study of martial skills. While no existing kwan (or kwon) had attained dominance, t'aek'kyŏn was introduced into some military training programs as early as 1946. In 1952, a half-hour martial arts demonstration attended by South Korean president Syngmann Rhee led to the official recognition of the Korean arts by means of Rhee's order for all Korean troops to be trained in these arts. Although t'aek'kyŏn was formally introduced into Korean military training by the end of the war (1953), the unification of various kwan into what eventually became modern taekwondo did not occur until 1955. Tradition maintains that the name *taekwondo* was agreed upon because of its resemblance to the more traditional art of t'aek'kyŏn, which makes the nationalistic qualities of the art obvious.

Vovinam (later renamed Viet Vo Dao) is a Vietnamese martial arts system founded by Nguyen Loc (1912–1960) in the late 1930s. The system was developed with both the practical intent of providing, after a short period of study, an efficient means of self-defense, and establishing a focus for national identity for the Vietnamese people. Founder Nguyen saw martial arts as a vehicle for freeing Vietnam, under French rule from 1859 to 1954, from outside domination. Thus, the traditional history maintains that at the age of 26 he added elements of Chinese and Japanese systems to his knowledge of indigenous Vietnamese arts to create an early version of Vovinam by at least 1938. Therefore, Vovinam, like taekwondo, is a modern eclectic system created, at least in part, as a nationalistic response to political conflict. At this time, the impulse to overthrow foreign domination gained impetus across Vietnam. In 1940, Nguyen and his disciples were invited to Hanoi to demonstrate Vovinam publicly, which led to an invitation to teach the art at Hanoi Ecole Normal (Hanoi University of Education). Slogans such as "Vietnamese practice Vietnamese martial arts" and "Not a Vovinam disciple, not a Vietnamese patriot" attest to the fact that the system succeeded in promoting nationalism. In 1940 and 1941, in this nationalistic climate and on the heels of a Japanese invasion, Communist-led revolts erupted in the south as Tay tribesmen rebelled in the north. At the end of this period, Ho Chi Minh founded the nationalistic Vietminh to oppose both Japanese and French colonialism. At this time, Vovinam training focused on endurance, speed, and strength with a course of study designed to last about three months; the system also maintained a political orientation beyond simple physical improvement. Therefore, the art was suppressed by both the French and the Japanese. By the time an agreement was signed by France and the Vietminh that provided for the temporary partition of Vietnam at about the 17th parallel, with North Vietnam under control of the Communist Vietminh and South Vietnam under Nationalist control (1954), Nguyen Loc had immigrated to South Vietnam, opening a Vovinam school in Saigon and others subsequently. Following the fall of Saigon, teachers immigrated to Europe and the Americas. Vovinam currently exists as Vovinam-Viet Vo Dao, a contemporary martial art without overt political focus.

Whether deployed as magic used to esoterically defeat an enemy or utilized as a focus for nationalism, the symbolic functions of the martial arts in political conflict seem to be a cross-cultural strategy. This facet of combatives deserves further study.

Thomas A. Green

See also Africa and African America; Capoeira; China; Folklore in the Martial Arts; Korea; Okinawa; Silat; Southeast Asia; Taekwondo; Vovinam Viet Vo Dao; Yongchun (Wing Chun)

References

Almeida, Bira. 1986. *Capoeira, a Brazilian Art Form: History, Philosophy, and Practice.* 2d ed. Berkeley: North Atlantic Books.

Bishop, Mark. 1996. *Zen Kobudô: Mysteries of Okinawan Weaponry and Te.* Rutland, VT: Charles E. Tuttle.

Green, Thomas A. 1976. "Folk History and Cultural Reorganization: A Tigua Example." *Journal of American Folklore* 89: 310–318.

———. 1997. "Historical Narrative in the Martial Arts: A Case Study." In *Usable Pasts: Traditions and Group Identities in North America.* Edited by Tad Tuleja. Logan: Utah State University Press.

Hobsbawm, Eric, and Terence Ranger, eds. 1985. *The Invention of Tradition.* Cambridge: Cambridge University Press.

Hudson, Charles. 1966. "Folk History and Ethnohistory." *Ethnohistory* 13: 52–57.

Kim, Richard. 1974. *Weaponless Warriors: An Informal History of Okinawan Karate.* Burbank, CA: Ohara.

Lewis, J. Lowell. 1992. *Ring of Liberation: Deceptive Discourse in Brazilian Capoeira.* Chicago: University of Chicago Press.

McCarthy, Patrick, ed. and trans. 1995. *Bubishi: The Bible of Karate.* Rutland, VT: Tuttle.

Naquin, Susan. 1976. *Millenarian Rebellion in China: The Eight Trigrams Uprising of 1813.* New Haven: Yale University Press.

Park, Yeon-Hee, Yean-Hwan Park, and Joe Gerrard. 1989. *Taekwondo.* New York: Facts on File.

Scott, James C. 1985. *Weapons of the Weak: Everyday Forms of Peasant Resistance.* New Haven: Yale University Press.

Vansina, Jan. 1985. *Oral Tradition as History.* Madison: University of Wisconsin Press.

Wallace, Anthony F. C. 1956. "Revitalization Movements." *American Anthropologist* 58: 264–281.

Qi
See Ki/Qi